IET PROFESSIONAL APPLICATIONS OF COMPUTING SERIES 22

Many-Core Computing

Other volumes in this series:

Many-Core Computing

Hardware and software

Edited by
Bashir M. Al-Hashimi and Geoff V. Merrett

The Institution of Engineering and Technology

Published by The Institution of Engineering and Technology, London, United Kingdom

The Institution of Engineering and Technology is registered as a Charity in England & Wales (no. 211014) and Scotland (no. SC038698).

The Institution of Engineering and Technology
Michael Faraday House
Six Hills Way, Stevenage
Herts, SG1 2AY, United Kingdom

www.theiet.org

British Library Cataloguing in Publication Data
A catalogue record for this product is available from the British Library

ISBN 978-1-78561-582-5 (hardback)
ISBN 978-1-78561-583-2 (PDF)

Typeset in India by MPS Limited
Printed in the UK by CPI Group (UK) Ltd, Croydon

Contents

Preface

Computing systems have a tremendous positive impact on everyday life, from the Internet to mobile devices. However, they are facing a once-in-a-generation technical challenge, as the relentless half-century increase in processor speed for improving performance has come to an end. As a result, computing systems have switched from a focus on performance-centric serial computation to energy-efficient parallel computation. This switch is driven by the higher energy efficiency of using multiple slower processor cores instead of a single high-speed one. As the number of parallel cores increases, we continue to transition from the traditional single- and multicore computing to many-core computing. The ability of these systems to compute, communicate, and respond to the real-world will transform how we work, do business, shop, travel, and care for ourselves, continuing to transform our daily lives and shaping the next phase of a digital society for the twenty first century.

There has been considerable interest worldwide in developing methods, tools, architectures, and applications to support the many-core computing paradigm. The field of many-core computing is broad and expanding, and at present, the technical literature about the overall state-of-the-art in many core computing is dispersed across a wide spectrum of journals, special issues and conference and workshops proceedings, different research communities and a limited number of research books focusing on specific areas.

The aim of this edited book is to provide a timely and coherent account, in a single volume, of recent advances in some of the key many-core computing research areas. To achieve this, we invited 22 leading international research groups from academia and industry to contribute to this book. Contributions include an up-to-date survey of the research literature, highlighting key achievements and future trends. To facilitate the understanding of the numerous research topics covered in the book, chapters present background information covering the basic principles and include an extensive up-to-date list of references. To enhance readability, the book's 22 chapters are grouped into four sections, with each section examining a particular theme of many-core computing: (I) programming models, OS and applications; (II) runtime management; (III) modelling, verification and testing; and (IV) architectures and systems.

Realising the full potential of many-core computing requires highly parallelised application software which can utilise the available hardware. This is a non-trivial task, and is considered in Part I of the book. Effective programming models are needed to annotate software for parallel execution (Chapter 1) and for execution on heterogeneous and reconfigurable hardware (Chapter 2). Furthermore, significant developments are needed to enable operating systems to effectively utilise many-core platforms (Chapter 3), and in virtualisation to decouple the application programmer from underlying hardware resources and their runtime allocation (Chapter 4). Part I concludes by considering software tools and performance benchmarks for many-core systems (Chapter 5), and performance challenges of deep learning applications (Chapter 6).

Many-core platforms typically bring with them a significant increase in resource complexity, potentially providing wide array of different homogeneous and heterogeneous cores. The design space for managing these resources explodes, and new approaches to the runtime management are needed (Part II). This includes management of power/energy (Chapters 7–8), thermal (Chapter 9) and GPGPU packet throughput (Chapter 10). Chapter 11 considers the future of power-driven computing systems, where continuous runtime adaptation is required to meet instantaneous power budgets and constraints.

The complexity of many-core systems renders their effective modelling increasingly important, alongside the verification and self-test of their operation. Part III contains five chapters further exploring this, covering the modelling of many-core architectures (Chapter 12), power modelling approaches enabling the decomposition of consumption across a many-core platform (Chapter 13), and the modelling and automated code generation of runtime management algorithms (Chapter 14). Part III then continues by exploring errors sources and dependability management approaches for FPGA-based reconfigurable many-core platforms (Chapter 15) followed by a review of the approaches to self-test the many-core systems (Chapter 16).

The final section of the book, Part IV, considers the systems and architectures which provide the foundation of many-core computing (Chapter 17). This is followed by architectural technologies to enable the efficient interconnect required by future massively distributed systems, including silicon photonics (Chapter 18) and 3D-integration (Chapter 19), and approaches to enable the runtime tunability of power, energy and performance metrics through cross-layer approximate computing (Chapter 20). Part IV concludes by considering many-core architectures and systems for big data computing (Chapter 21), and SpiNNaker: a million-core computing system inspired by biology in order to reconsider the way in which computing is performed and systems are engineered (Chapter 22).

Book audience

It is the intention of this book to contain a diverse coverage of research topics in multi- and many-core computing systems, targeting the challenges and current state-of-the-art across the system stack, in both hardware and software. Each theme is discussed in depth, and therefore the book will appeal to broader readership. Multi- and many-core computing is a popular postgraduate research topic, appearing as part of the syllabus for both undergraduate and postgraduate electronics, computer engineering, and computer science courses at many universities, and we hope that this book will complement the research and teaching that is taking place in this area. Also, the book should serve as a valuable reference for industrial designers and managers who are interested in various aspects of multi- and many-core system design.

Acknowledgements

First and foremost, we are indebted to all of the contributing authors of this book; their dedication and technical expertise ultimately dictate its quality. We would like to acknowledge the financial support from the Engineering and Physical Sciences Research Council (EPSRC), UK, to our research activities in multi- and many-core computing through the PRiME Programme Grant (www.prime-project.org), which has helped to develop our understanding and knowledge of this exciting area. Finally, we would like to thank Kath Kerr for her continued assistance in managing the process of editing the book (and the unenviable job of chasing authors), and Olivia Wilkins (Assistant Editor) at the IET for their assistance during this project.

Bashir M. Al-Hashimi and Geoff V. Merrett
Southampton, UK
October 2018

Part I

Programming models, OS and applications

Chapter 1
HPC with many core processors

*Xavier Martorell[1], Jorge Bellon[2], Victor Lopez[3],
Vicenç Beltran[3], Sergi Mateo[3], Xavier Teruel[3],
Eduard Ayguade[1], and Jesus Labarta[1]*

The current trends in building clusters and supercomputers are to use medium-to-big symmetric multi-processors (SMP) nodes connected through a high-speed network. Applications need to accommodate to these execution environments using distributed and shared memory programming, and thus become hybrid. Hybrid applications are written with two or more programming models, usually message passing interface (MPI) [1,2] for the distributed environment and OpenMP [3,4] for the shared memory support.

The goal of this chapter is to show how the two programming models can be made interoperable and ease the work of the programmer. Thus, instead of asking the programmers to code optimizations targeting performance, it is possible to rely on the good interoperability between the programming models to achieve high performance. For example, instead of using non-blocking message passing and double buffering to achieve computation–communication overlap, our approach provides this feature by taskifying communications using OpenMP tasks [5,6].

In this context, we use OmpSs [7] as the shared-memory programming model. At the Barcelona Supercomputing Center (BSC), we develop OmpSs as the prototyping infrastructure to test new OpenMP extensions, with the goal to facilitate shared memory and hybrid programming. OmpSs is a directive-based programming model that enables the execution of sequential programs in parallel, with a data-flow approach. With OmpSs, the programmer specifies portions of code that can potentially run in parallel, also named *tasks*, and the data which is going to be read (*in*) and/or written (*out*) inside this (*task*). We name as *data directionality hints* this additional information provided to the compiler. Tasks and data directionality hints are used by our source-to-source Mercurium compiler to transform the original program by off-loading the tasks inside functions and invoking them asynchronously. Then the runtime takes into account when the data becomes available to schedule the tasks.

[1]Computer Science Department, Barcelona Supercomputing Center, and Computer Architecture Department, Universitat Politècnica de Catalunya, Spain
[2]Cray, Inc., United States
[3]Computer Science Department, Barcelona Supercomputing Center, Spain

Tasks data directionality hints were incorporated on the OpenMP standard in its 4.0 version of the specification, in 2013.

OmpSs is built using two main components: the Mercurium compiler, used to transform the application code according to the directives annotations, and the Nanos++ runtime system, which offers the application programming interface (API) to the compiler for managing tasks, and it is in charge of their execution.

1.1   MPI+OmpSs interoperability

Hybrid applications use two or more parallel programming models altogether with the goal of achieving better performance. Usually, such composition comes from the mixture of message passing and shared memory programming models, like MPI and OmpSs. For example, the programmer may decide to run one or more MPI processes per node, and fill the remaining cores in each node with OmpSs parallelism. Depending on the structure of the application and its computation/communication pattern, the performance of the application may vary.

Unfortunately, even though hybrid applications are common in high performance computing (HPC), they typically use one or another model depending on the phase of the algorithm. For example, an MPI+OmpSs application may use OmpSs for the computation intensive parts of the application, and MPI for the communication phases. This programming style enforces an intra-node barrier across all threads executing the parallelism of the application. And most of the times, the communication phase also implies a barrier among all communicating processes. This happens, for instance, when the MPI communication is a collective call. As a result, with this approach, the MPI and threaded parts do not overlap. Applications may be implemented with non-blocking MPI calls and double buffering to achieve computation/communication overlap, thus increasing their programming complexity.

An alternative technique for programming these applications is to use tasks that call MPI communication primitives. The goal with this option is also to allow the overlap of tasks implementing computation on a set of data, with tasks sending and/or receiving independent data. As it may be difficult for the programmer to know if tasks are really parallel between each other, we propose the use of the OmpSs/OpenMP task dependences and let the runtime system decide if those computations and communications can proceed in parallel or not. If not, the runtime executes the tasks in the correct order. In addition, the runtime has the freedom to execute in an out-of-order way tasks that are independent and perform communications.

The implications of this approach are 2-fold. On one hand, the increase of flexibility on the selection of the tasks to be executed also increases the potential to obtain a benefit in application performance.

On the other hand, this approach also impacts on programming:

- There is the need to correctly specify the data directionality hints for the communication tasks. If the correct execution of the application depends on the order on which the MPI calls are executed, the tasks implementing communications need to be annotated with *inout* hints, in order to be serialized. In this case, the

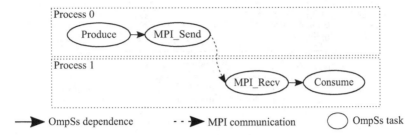

Figure 1.1   MPI point-to-point messages as inter-process extension of OmpSs data dependences

communications will follow the original order. Instead, we recommend to use MPI tags to enforce the proper message matching at the MPI level and let the tasks—and the communications—to proceed in parallel.

- When using blocking MPI calls, tasks executing these blocking primitives may block if the message has not yet been received by the node. In this situation, the block functionality is implemented at the operating system level, and the thread executing the task is stopped. As a result, the core resource is lost for this application, and its parallelism is reduced, even if there are other tasks ready to be executed. In some cases, the reduction in the amount of resources available may end up in a deadlock. A solution to this situation is to virtualize the communications in such a way that the runtime ensures that the cores freed due to blocking communications get other tasks ready to be executed from the task pool. With this option, the programmer does not need to worry about losing the cores or the possibilities of deadlock. In this work, we describe the details of the implementation of this technique.

- When using task priorities in an OmpSs program, the application may end up having the *priority inversion* problem. In this case, higher priority tasks are not able to be executed as soon as they are created due to other lower priority tasks being in execution, and taking still some time before finishing. If the high priority tasks are communication tasks, this may also delay the execution of the counterparts in other nodes. The solution is to annotate such communication tasks at the application level, and reserve a specific thread to execute them, so that their execution is not delayed.

Thus, the recommended approach is to place MPI blocking communication routines inside tasks annotated with the correspondent data dependences (i.e., producing and/or consuming the message buffer). This allows programs to synchronize task execution beyond the process level, as seen in Figure 1.1, since a task will not finish until the communication is completed.

1.2   The interposition library

A portable and convenient solution for the programmers consists of developing an intermediate library wrapping all common MPI communication services in order to

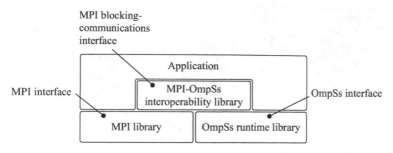

Figure 1.2   *The new library provides alternate implementations for MPI blocking communication routines, and it leaves other MPI and OmpSs operations in their original implementation*

```
int MPI_Send( const void *buf, int count, MPI_Datatype datatype,
              int dest, int tag, MPI_Comm comm )
{
    int err, flag;
    MPI_Request req;
    err = MPI_Isend( buf, count, datatype, dest, tag, comm, &req );
    err = MPI_Test( &req, &flag, MPI_STATUS_IGNORE );
    if( flag == 0 ) {
        // - Save the request
        // - Stop task execution (explained in section 1.3)
    }
    return err;
}
```

Listing 1.1   *MPI_Send transformation using MPI profiling interface*

automatically perform the proposed technique. The MPI interposition library is in charge of transforming all blocking MPI communication primitives onto their equivalent MPI non-blocking counterparts. It also registers the communication *requests* and blocks the current context (i.e., task) executing this code, it yields the thread to any other *ready-to-run* task and finally, it checks periodically the *on-the-fly* requests in order to wake-up the tasks waiting for them to complete.

Therefore, the library provides an alternative implementation for MPI point-to-point and collective blocking routines (Figure 1.2). The implementation is based on using the MPI profiling interface in such a way that the interoperability library can intercept these blocking routine calls made by applications. Once a blocking communication routine has been called, we start the communication using its respective non-blocking version and immediately check whether or not the communication is completed. In case it is not, the task execution is stopped, and the runtime system takes care of the blocked task, as explained in Section 1.3. Listing 1.1 shows the typical schema of the interposition functions, using the MPI_Send primitive as example.

Applications that already make use of MPI non-blocking routines can also be supported. Non-blocking routines such as MPI_Isend or MPI_Test need not to

```
int MPI_Waitall( int count, MPI_Request array_of_requests[],
                  MPI_Status array_of_statuses[] )
{
  int err, flag;
  err = MPI_Testall( count, array_of_requests,
                     &flag, array_of_statuses );
  if( flag == 0 ) {
    // - Save all pending requests
    // - Stop task execution (explained in section 1.3)
  }
  return err;
}
```

Listing 1.2 MPI_Waitall transformation using MPI profiling interface

be intercepted because they do not produce any means of synchronization. However, it is very common to use MPI_Wait family of functions with non-blocking communications. These functions are indeed blocking, and they are also intercepted and replaced with their corresponding non-blocking MPI_Test version; in a similar way it is done with blocking communications (see Listing 1.2).

Applications may exhibit bursts of short communications with little or no blocking time. In this situation, they may get better response time if the task execution is not blocked. Such tasks can be marked by the programmer to disable the task block by using the MPI_Pcontrol interface. A new flag has been added to this interface to implement this feature.

1.3   Implementation of the MPI+OmpSs interoperability

In order to fulfill the previous library requirements, the following features are needed in the OmpSs Nanos++ runtime library:

1. A synchronization mechanism that allows blocking indefinitely and releasing the execution of a task.
2. A polling mechanism that performs periodic calls to one or multiple arbitrary functions.

These mechanisms will allow the runtime to periodically check the completion state of all pending communications. In the case that one or multiple of these communications are completed, it will be possible to resume the execution of the tasks that were waiting for them.

At this point, one may think of using the existing taskyield feature to force a task-scheduling point and allow other tasks to execute. But this is a nonoptimal solution, as even though it allows the execution of other tasks, the yielding task remains ready (eligible for execution by any thread) after the task switch. If the execution cannot make progress (some requests are still pending), it might cause additional unnecessary task switches: a thread resumes the task, checks the completion status and performs a task switch again.

It is possible to produce a much more efficient implementation, if part of the mechanism that control changes between ready and blocked task states is exposed through an API. We call this mechanism *task condition variables*, because their functionality and interface (proposed in Listing 1.3), resembles to the condition variables implemented in the POSIX threads library.

It is important to understand that blocking a task execution does not cause the underlying thread to block: a task does not make any further progress but the thread is allowed to start or resume other tasks that are ready to be executed. This means that programs such as the example shown in Listing 1.4 can even be run with a single thread, without causing a deadlock.

Handling of the pending MPI requests needs a mechanism to perform a periodic check of a specific condition. In this case, the check consists of querying the completion state of all pending requests on which tasks are waiting for.

```
// An opaque condition variable object.
typedef void* nanos_wait_cond_t;

// Creates a new condition variable.
void nanos_create_wait_condition( nanos_wait_cond_t* cond );

// Blocks current task on the condition variable.
void nanos_block_current_task( nanos_wait_cond_t* cond );

// Wakes a task waiting on a condition variable.
void nanos_signal_wait_condition( nanos_wait_cond_t* cond );
```

Listing 1.3   OmpSs task condition variable interface

```
int value = 0;
nanos_wait_cond_t cond;
nanos_create_wait_condition(&cond);

#pragma omp task shared(value, cond) label(waiter)
{  // Wait until value is equal to 1
   while( value != 1 )
      nanos_block_current_task(&cond);
}

#pragma omp task shared(value, cond) label(signaler)
{  // Make waiter task ready again
   value = 1;
   nanos_signal_wait_condition(&cond);
}
```

Listing 1.4   Task condition variables allow explicit synchronization without blocking the execution resources

We have included a generic mechanism in out Nanos++ library to invoke polling services at idle time. The interface of this mechanism is shown in Listing 1.5. This way, the OmpSs runtime library registers the function and arguments that will be invoked every time a thread enters the idle state.

Thus, when a thread is idle, the OmpSs runtime library will call the service function with the argument that we initially specified when registering the service. Service function arguments are defined as opaque pointer types, which give enough flexibility to pass any type of parameters (see Listing 1.6). In addition, service functions can be

```
// Function that will be periodically called.
typedef int (*nanos_polling_function_t)(void *service_data);

/* Registers a function and an opaque parameter that must be
 * periodically called.
 * Using the same function with different parameters is allowed.
 * The function is never called again if it returns a
 * logical 'true' (1).
 */
void nanos_register_polling_service( const char *service_name,
        nanos_polling_function_t service_function,
        void *service_data );

// Unregisters a function and parameter combination.
void nanos_unregister_polling_service( const char *service_name,
        nanos_polling_function_t service_function,
        void *service_data );
```

Listing 1.5   OmpSs polling interface

```
// Function that will be periodically called.
int myfunc( int * args ) {
    if( *args == 0 ) {
        printf("The condition is now satisfied!\n");
    return 0;
}

int args_1 = 1, args_2 = 2;

int main() {
    nanos_register_polling_service( "Polling test",
        myfunc, &args_1 );

    nanos_register_polling_service( "Polling test",
        myfunc, &args_2 );

    // ...
    args_2 = 0;
    // ...
    return 0;
}
```

Listing 1.6   Using polling interface to register multiple polling services

unregistered at will. When the service is invoked, normally the function will return a 0 to the idle thread calling it. In case the function returns 1, the thread will proceed to unregister the function, so it will not be called again. Later on, the user of the polling service may decide to register the function back.

1.4   Solving priority inversion

In order to avoid the *priority inversion* problem, we design a new scheduling policy for the Nanos++ runtime library. The new scheduler specializes one worker thread (called the *communication thread*), which focuses on the execution of the so named *communication tasks*. It is a thread dedicated to the execution of the tasks annotated with the clause `comm_thread`.

Listing 1.7 shows the creation of a communication task which executes a MPI receive service. The reserved thread can only execute this type of tasks, being idle when none of these tasks are available. In addition, we implemented a new scheduling policy with a local priority queue, which will contain all communication tasks ready to be executed.

Although the new scheduler policy may lead to having the communication thread idle during the phases in which there are no MPI operations to execute, it highly improves the response time of these operations. The overall execution time improvement will depend on the application characteristics. In some cases, it will improve due communication tasks being on the critical path; in some other cases, it will get worse due thread idleness.

```
int main() {

  // ...

  #pragma omp task out(buffer) comm_thread
  MPI_Recv( buffer, SIZE, MPI_INT, source, MPI_COMM_WORLD );

  #pragma omp task in(buffer)
  // using buffer here

  // ...

  return 0;
}
```

Listing 1.7   OmpSs extension to annotate a communication task: the `comm_thread` *clause*

1.5   Putting it all together

Now that the extensions to OmpSs programming model are available, task execution can stop whenever it reaches a blocking communication routine. Figure 1.3 shows how the procedure looks like for the particular case of `MPI_Send`.

Moreover, the polling mechanism is used to periodically check for the completion status of the pending communications. A polling function is registered by the time MPI is initialized (during `MPI_Init` or `MPI_Init_thread`) and unregistered before it is finalized (`MPI_Finalize`). Whenever MPI informs that some communications are completed, the polling function will be responsible of resuming the tasks waiting for them (Figure 1.4).

There are some details that must be taken into consideration:

- Some tasks may wait for more than one MPI request object simultaneously. For example, using `MPI_Waitall`, which waits for multiple requests at once.
- Some tasks may not be eligible for blocking, due to the usage of `MPI_Pcontrol` function.

Therefore, the library stores additional information related to how each task waits:

- A task condition variable that allows blocking/resuming a task.
- A counter of the remaining operations before the task can be resumed.
- A flag indicating if the task can become blocked (set to false through `MPI_Pcontrol`).

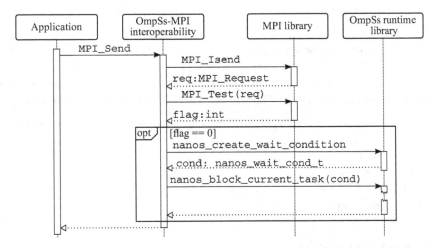

Figure 1.3   OmpSs-MPI interoperability library intercepts `MPI_Send` call from the application and blocks the task, since the operation is not completed, as pointed by `MPI_Test` output argument `flag`

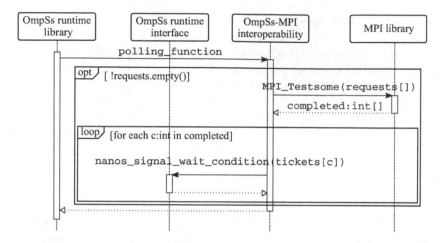

Figure 1.4   Polling function iterates over completed requests and wakes up those tasks without unfinished requests

- A flag indicating whether the task is waiting or not.
- A pointer to the status argument passed by the user in calls such as MPI_Recv. If necessary, output status is copied from the result of MPI_Testsome to the array of statuses that the user has specified.

Whenever MPI informs that a communication request is completed, we decrease its corresponding task counter. When the counter reaches zero, the library signals the task condition variable, returning the waiting task to a ready state.

1.6   Machine characteristics

The evaluation of these techniques has been done in the BSC Nord3 computer. This machine has 84 compute nodes. The characteristics of each node are as follows:

- 2× Intel SandyBridge-EP E5-2670 CPUs, 8 cores each, 20 MB data cache, at 2.6 GHz.
- 8× 16 GB DDR3-1600 DIMMs, for a total of 128 GB per node, separated in 2 NUMA nodes.
- Mellanox Infiniband FDR10 network.
- SuSe Linux distribution 11 SP3.

1.7   Evaluation of NTChem

NTChem is a high-performance software package for the molecular electronic structure calculation developed by RIKEN [8].

NTChem-mini includes a subset of NTChem known as NTChem/RI-MP2 that includes the efficient scheme to account for the electron correlations based on the resolution of identity second-order Møller–Plesset perturbation (RI-MP2) method that enables the computation of the large molecular systems such as nano-molecules and biological molecules [9].

1.7.1 Application analysis

The public NTChem-mini version is an MPI + OpenMP hybrid parallel algorithm, which also relies on the BLAS library implementation. The analysis and performance results of the original version have been performed using Intel MPI (IMPI) and the Math Kernel Library (MKL) parallel library. Figure 1.5 shows the parallel efficiency of NTChem-mini, which is the speedup divided by the number of CPUs, for this version executed with MKL 15.0.2 and IMPI 5.1.3 on Nord3 (see Section 1.6). Given the architecture of Nord3, 2^4 total CPUs corresponds to a full compute node, and 2^9 to 32 nodes of 16 CPUs each.

Another observation of the performance analysis is that enabling the OpenMP threading model only improves the execution time in a few scenarios, mainly on the higher values of MPI ranks. The worst series is the execution of 16 threads per process, where the execution is constantly paying the NUMA cost.

These executions have also been analyzed with Paraver [10] to find the causes of the performance loss. The useful duration configuration shows the duration of each computational chunk in a timeline. Basically, it shows which phases belong

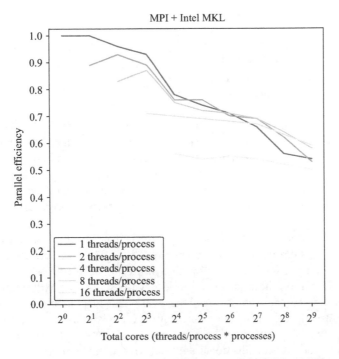

Figure 1.5   NTChem Parallel efficiency with IMPI + MKL

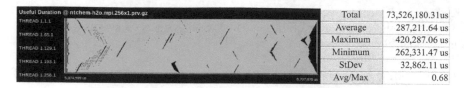

Figure 1.6   NTChem useful duration

to computational code, and which ones belong to I/O communication. All this data can be categorized into a histogram to extract some information. This is shown in Figure 1.6, where Paraver reports the average and maximum of the accumulated times of useful duration of each thread, which directly corresponds to the difference of the load imbalance ratio. Thus, this execution has a load imbalance ratio of 32%.

The NTChem algorithm follows a structure of multiple inner loops inside the main loop. The innermost loop performs a DGEMM operation and an MPI collective reduction over the local result of each rank. The second most inner loop performs an `MPI_Isend` and an `MPI_Irecv` operation in a ring-like fashion needed for subsequent DGEMMs operations.

The DGEMM operation is computed by the MKL parallel library, the reduction is computed in parallel using OpenMP pragmas, and the communication is done in serial by the MPI runtime.

1.7.2   Parallelization approach

The goal is to reduce the load imbalance produced by the MPI communications. In order to do so, the DGEMM and the reduction operations are taskified as well as the MPI send and receive communications. These tasks will be annotated with input and output dependences to properly overlap both phases and keep the correctness of the program.

Also, the MPI interoperability library developed for OmpSs is used to switch MPI tasks out of context when the MPI call is waiting for the incoming message. This is useful to suspend tasks that cannot continue doing useful computations until this MPI call returns. By switching the task out of context, the runtime can schedule another ready task into the just liberated CPU and advance useful work. The OmpSs runtime itself will periodically check if the pending MPI message has been already processed to resume the suspended task.

One of the issues when taskifying MPI calls is that the out-of-order execution of tasks may cause a deadlock between communications. The original code implements the ring-like communication using non-blocking versions of MPI Send and Receive. We want to transform these calls into blocking calls so that the MPI interoperability library can intercept them and suspend these tasks but separate blocking calls would cause a dead-lock if the MPI interoperability mechanism is not used. To solve this issue, these two MPI calls have been merged into an `MPI_Sendrecv` primitive. This way the code is still functional and lock-free when running without the MPI interoperability library.

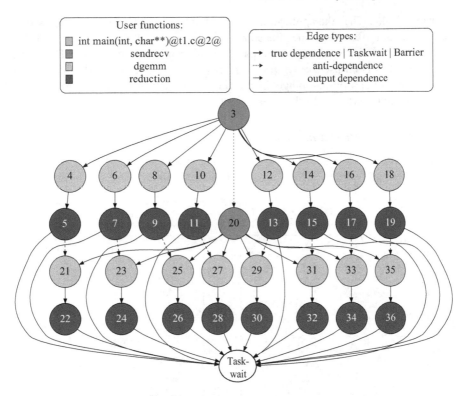

Figure 1.7   NTChem simplified task-dependency graph

After merging the MPI calls and annotating all dependences in the code, a simplified task-dependency graph is shown in Figure 1.7. The graph shows how the MPI_Sendrecv tasks release an output dependence that enables multiple DGEMM tasks to become ready. It is important to keep as many tasks in the ready queue as possible because it increases the potential parallelism and by consequence, the maximum efficiency of each worker thread. For this particular issue, sendrecv tasks have been annotated with the priority clause. This clause hints the runtime to execute those tasks as soon as they become ready for execution.

Another useful tweak used in the code parallelization is the use of the INOUT clause with a sentinel to ensure the serialization of certain tasks. In particular, several sendrecv tasks could potentially be executed in parallel, but it is much more important that any of them finishes as soon as possible in order to improve the parallelism of the DGEMM tasks. For this reason, these tasks are better executed serialized between them, so each rank is only doing at most one MPI_Sendrecv operation at a time. As an added benefit, the overhead in the communication layer is reduced.

The last modification performed to improve the parallelization is to increase an internal variable of the application, NUM_STREAMS. This variable is used to specify an additional dimension on some application buffers. This variable is used in the original code when the application is compiled for GPU devices. The increase on the number of buffers facilitates the communication–computation overlap in GPUs, by avoiding anti-dependences in the parallelization of some functions. This same mechanism has been used in OmpSs to increase the number of ready tasks. After several tests, an appropriate range for the variable is between 1 and 2 multiplied by the number of threads per MPI process.

1.7.3   Performance analysis

Figure 1.8 shows the scalability test for executions running with MPI+OmpSs, and executions running with MPI+OmpSs and the MPI interoperability library. Each

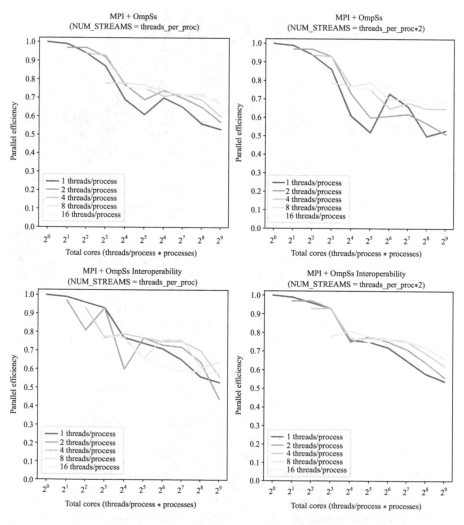

Figure 1.8   NTChem parallel efficiency plots for MPI+OmpSs (top row) and MPI+OmpSs + MPI interoperability (bottom row)

one of the versions have been tested with NUM_STREAMS being equal to 1 or 2 multiplied by the number of threads.

In these experiments, the MPI+OmpSs version obtains better performance with fewer extra dimensions in the auxiliary buffers. Having more memory in the buffers means that the dependency graph has less anti-dependences, thus more tasks in the ready queue. If the performance does not increase, it is because this version does not benefit of this situation since the runtime cannot switch tasks out of context to pick another ready task.

The version of MPI+OmpSs with MPI interoperability performs better with an increased number of auxiliary buffers for the opposite reason. The MPI interoperability library is continuously intercepting MPI calls and invoking the runtime to suspend the task. Having a larger pool of buffers allows to keep the reception of messages active, increasing the communication throughput, and achieving a better overlap of communication and computation. In this situation, the performance obtained is also more stable than the versions using a smaller pool of buffer or no interoperability.

1.8   Evaluation with Linpack

1.8.1   Application analysis

The original High Performance Linpack (HPL) benchmark is a pure MPI program. The execution flow of the main application is single threaded, and it relies on the BLAS library implementation in order to execute in parallel or sequentially. Programmers may decide which version to execute by linking the benchmark against the parallel or sequential version of the BLAS library, respectively.

In the implementation of the parallel version of BLAS, each time a routine is called, the library splits the work among all the available threads (i.e. fork). Afterwards, when the routine completes (and before the library service returns) all threads are joined again. This multi-threading model is known as fork/join.

The execution of the application following this fork/join model produces spikes of CPU load, which grows during parallel regions and drops during synchronization and sequential parts of the application, as seen in Figure 1.9(a). Note that for a small problem size, such as the execution shown in the figure, CPU load does not exceed 80% in average at any point of the execution. Furthermore, the parallelism decreases toward the end of the execution in line with the size of the trailing matrix being computed.

When solving bigger problems (by increasing the matrix size), the amount of work performed by each linear algebra operation also increases, reducing the impact of the synchronization and sequential parts of the application. As an additional observation, by increasing the matrix size, we also increase the relative weight of the matrix multiplication kernel (i.e., the dgemm() function) compared with the total execution time. Figure 1.9(b) shows the percentage of time taken by the dgemm() function out of the total execution time as the matrix size increases. The reason behind this behavior is that dgemm() complexity is cubic: $O(n^3)$ (e.g., doubling the input sizes increases the execution time 8-fold).

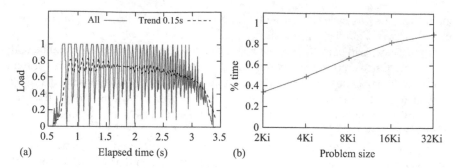

Figure 1.9   *Linpack profile based on BLAS parallel execution. (a) Average CPU
load (N = 8K, 4 processes, 8 threads). (b) DGEMM execution time
(4 processes, 1 thread)*

In light of the above observations, when Linpack is used to benchmark a new system's performance, typical configurations use as much memory in each compute node as possible increasing the total execution time.

Improving the efficiency on smaller problem sizes will allow us to reach asymptotic maximum performance earlier, reducing the required execution time for the whole benchmark. Therefore, instead of exploiting thread-level parallelism inside the BLAS library, we aim to develop a task-based parallel implementation based on the version that we have just analyzed.

1.8.2   Parallelization approach

The goal of the task-based hybrid HPL is to accelerate the computations that are either on the critical path or close to it. From now on, thread-level parallelism (based on OmpSs) is provided in the host application, so multithreaded BLAS is not used anymore.

The same matrix partitioning (blocks of *NB* columns) is used, assigning a block to each OmpSs task. Since trailing matrix updates of consecutive iterations of the algorithm may overlap, tasks are synchronized using data dependences. The runtime will compute a dependence graph similar to the one shown in Figure 1.10.

OmpSs offers the possibility of using task priorities as a scheduler hint. Higher priority tasks usually spend less time waiting on the ready queues and they are executed before lower priority ones. The closer a task is to the critical path, the higher priority it has.

It must be noted that some parts of the algorithm exchange messages with other MPI processes (e.g., pivoting during factorization and update). We leverage OmpSs-MPI interoperability library functionality to overlap communication of these tasks with the execution of others.

To ensure point-to-point message correctness, concurrent point-to-point communications that share the same communicator use unique tag values. These values are generated with the following equation, where *code(op)* is a unique identifier for each

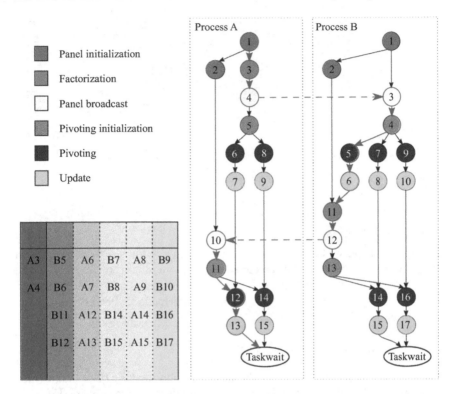

Figure 1.10 Simplified task dependence diagram for two consecutive iterations using two MPI processes (P = 1 and Q = 2)

operation (e.g., factorization, update, etc.) and *j* is the block index in the local trailing submatrix of each process:

$$Tag(op,j) = code(op) + j \tag{1.1}$$

For example, messages in tasks *A6* and *A8* are tagged with the values *Tag(pivoting, 0)* and *Tag(pivoting, 1)*.

The look-ahead methodology is the recommended way to proceed with the OmpSs programming model. The main task creates enough tasks in order to (1) create parallelism and (2) allow exploring future needs and take better scheduler decisions (e.g., executing chains of producers and consumers tasks, increasing data affinity or advancing the execution of high priority tasks as much as possible). As the runtime computes the dependences among all instantiated tasks according with the produced and consumed data, the algorithm correctness is guaranteed.

In some cases, the resulting synchronization is the result of using auxiliary data structures which prevent concurrency on operations that potentially may run in parallel. From the point of view of the synchronization, it is only necessary to ensure that the communications and auxiliary data structures used by HPL are not used by operations of different iterations simultaneously. This is solved by the use of a multiple

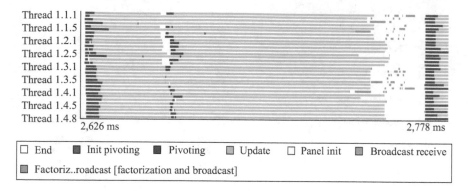

Figure 1.11   Task execution diagram for a single iteration

buffering technique: we allocate several copies of these structures and assign them to iterations in a cyclic way. All the communicators are duplicated as well. Consequently, there is no risk of collision between messages of consecutive iterations (e.g., $A6$ and $A12$): their message envelopes will never match due to the usage of different communicators.

1.8.3   Performance analysis

Figure 1.11 shows that, despite the look-ahead technique and the prioritization tasks in the critical path, their execution is postponed until the end of the update. This limits the amount of parallelism, which makes most of the threads to wait until the end of the iteration.

OmpSs-MPI interoperability is conceived to take advantage of the wasted time that threads spend on blocking communication routines. This is specially useful when delaying their completion slightly does not affect the overall performance of the application. However, if communication tasks are located at the critical path, priority inversion is possible: coarse grain low priority tasks can take their place. In this case, high priority tasks will not be able to go back to execution until a task switching points is reached.

In order to avoid priority inversion, we design a new scheduling policy for the OmpSs runtime library. The new scheduler specializes one worker thread, which focuses on execution of high priority tasks. We call it *communications thread*, as we will devote it to execute most of the tasks with communications, including the factorization. In addition, we improve the response time of `factorization` tasks by disabling OmpSs-MPI interoperability features (with `MPI_Pcontrol`) during the communication burst and by increasing the parallelism on the column updates they depend on (we call it `urgent_dgemm`, whose computation is split in multiple row blocks).

Figure 1.12 shows the results executing the benchmark with all these optimizations. Even though it looks like the communication thread generates inefficiencies (there are gaps in the execution diagram where it remains idle), it helps to keep all the

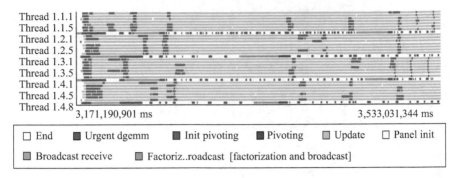

Figure 1.12 *Task execution diagram including two iterations. Factorizations and high priority tasks are processed by the communications thread (the eighth thread of each process)*

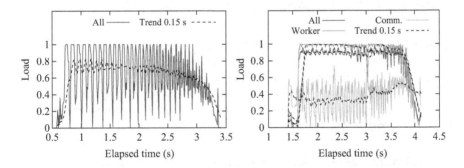

Figure 1.13 *CPU load comparison between original version (using multithreaded BLAS) and communications thread (using four processes with eight threads). The average load increases from 80% to 90%, even though one of the threads has a lower amount of work*

other threads busy performing the updates and avoids the priority inversion scenario that happened before. Figure 1.13 shows how the overall CPU load reaches a stable 90% during the central part of the algorithm. Note how the amount of parallelism drops toward the end of the execution. This effect is caused by the reduced amount of work that update tasks perform, as the trailing submatrix size decreases with time.

In order to improve the efficiency of the application during the last group of iterations, we repartition the problem *on-the-fly* (data distribution at MPI level does not change), which consists on reducing the block size to half its original value. Consequently, the factorization is divided in two steps (the two diagonal submatrices of the original block). OmpSs allows us to do this without much effort: first we detail the memory region accessed by each task based on the current column and the block size, then we create the necessary additional tasks to finish the problem. Since the loop that generates all the tasks already iterates using columns and block size, we

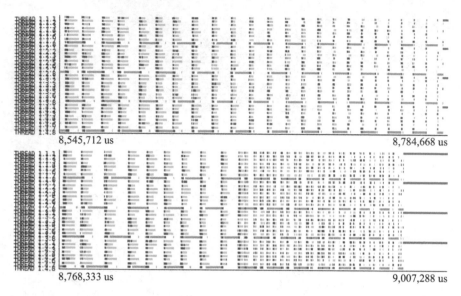

8,545,712 us   8,784,668 us

8,768,333 us   9,007,288 us

Figure 1.14   Execution diagram of the last 24 iterations of a 16K problem size. The
amount of work performed by update *tasks gets reduced, so*
factorization times become more important (top diagram). We
repartition the problem dividing the block size by half, which reduces
the factorization times by four (bottom figure), hereby improving
slightly the last part of the application

only need to change the block size at the proper place and the program will readapt
itself automatically (see bottom diagram of Figure 1.14).

Figure 1.15 compares the benchmark results of the original version with our task-
based implementation. Top-left plot shows the results obtained using 4 MPI processes
and 2 threads per process, for a total of 8 cores. The performance obtained with OmpSs
in this case, with two threads per process, is low because the communications thread
does not execute any update tasks, other than the urgent matrix products used to
accelerate the critical path. When we increase the amount of threads per process (top-
right plot, $P = 2$, $Q = 2$, with four threads per process), the performance gets closer
to the original version.

When further increasing the number of threads per node (8 and 16, in the bottom—
left and right—plots of Figure 1.15), the OmpSs version gets better performance, and
it improves over the original version in the larger experiments with 16 threads per
node (problem sizes of 16,384 and 32,768).

We expected that the performance gap between the original and task-based
versions would be larger for the problem sizes we have studied. Unfortunately,
the benchmark results show that it is actually not that big, despite the differences
in synchronization. We have found that one of the reasons behind this is dgemm
kernel's throughput, which is 25% lower on average when running our task-based
implementation (see Figure 1.16).

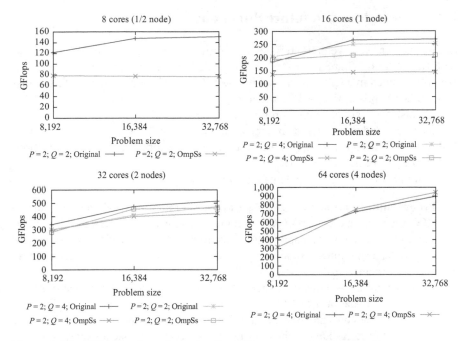

Figure 1.15   HPL benchmark results for different core counts. OmpSs implementation suffers at low core counts, where nearly half of the resources are taken by communication threads. On the other hand, its efficiency increases when the number of cores per process is higher

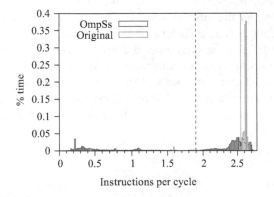

Figure 1.16   dgemm throughput comparison between original and task-based implementations

1.9   Conclusions and future directions

In this chapter, we have presented the use of multicore processors in HPC systems, with the MPI and OmpSs programming models. In this environment, applications are programmed in a hybrid way, that is, use MPI to cope with data transfers across nodes, and OmpSs or OpenMP to support the shared memory parallelism.

By taskifying applications, OmpSs allows to remove the synchronization barriers that usually introduce work or communication imbalance. This fact, and the improved MPI+OmpSs interoperability, is the source of better performance on the applications under study: NTChem and Linpack.

A number of key open problems are still challenging:

- **Programming support tools.** Easy of programming is a challenge for current HPC systems. The execution environments become too complex to fully understand their behavior. The application-development cycle needs to be supported by parallel programming supporting tools providing guidance [11] and execution and performance analysis [10].
- **Load balancing.** Another challenge is to run efficiently several applications sharing the same nodes in an SMP cluster. This is of special importance, as SMP nodes grow to 32, 64 cores and beyond. In this regard, applications can take advantage of time-sharing resources when not used. There are approaches integrating the workload management, with the application execution, to allow applications to expand or shrink dynamically on the use of cores [12]. Also, the dynamic load balancing approach uses transparent detection of idle resources in applications to redistribute cores across MPI processes [13].
- **Resiliency.** Due to the increasing size of the HPC computing environments, resiliency is getting higher interest than in previous years. New resiliency techniques are being developed for task-based systems [14]. They propose a fault-tolerant design for the runtime system, allowing to detect and solve errors in application data. Solutions include re-execution and checkpointing for coarse-grain tasks. For fine granularity tasks, the input data is augmented with additional information to allow error corrections, if necessary. Resiliency is also improved for MPI off-loading environments [15]. This work implements fault tolerance for MPI off-load applications, in coordination with the workload manager. The proposed implementation shows low runtime overhead and efficient recovery for coarse-grain tasks.

Acknowledgments

This work is partially supported by the European Union H2020 program through the Mont-Blanc 3 project (grant H2020 RIA 671697) and HiPEAC (grant agreements 687698 and 779656), by the Spanish Government through Programa Severo Ochoa (SEV-2015-0493), by the Spanish Ministerio de Economía y Competitividad under contract Computación de Altas Prestaciones VII (TIN2015-65316-P), and the

Departament d'Innovació, Universitats i Empresa de la Generalitat de Catalunya, under project MPEXPAR: Models de Programació i Entorns d'Execució Paral·lels (2014-SGR-1051).

References

[1]   Snir M, Otto S, Huss-Lederman S, Walker D, and Dongarra J. MPI: The Complete Reference. Cambridge, MA: MIT Press, 1996.

[2]   MPI Forum; 2017. [Online; accessed 18-Nov-2017]. http://mpi-forum.org.

[3]   Dagum L, Menon R. OpenMP: an industry standard API for shared-memory programming. IEEE Computational Science & Engineering. 1998;5(1):46–55.

[4]   OpenMP 4.5 Specification; 2015. [Online; accessed 18-Nov-2017]. http://www.openmp.org/wp-content/uploads/openmp-4.5.pdf.

[5]   Marjanović V, Labarta J, Ayguadé E, *et al.* Overlapping Communication and Computation by Using a Hybrid MPI/SMPSs Approach. In: Proceedings of the 24th ACM International Conference on Supercomputing. ICS'10. New York, NY, USA: ACM; 2010. p. 5–16. Available from: http://doi.acm.org.recursos.biblioteca.upc.edu/10.1145/1810085.1810091.

[6]   Brömmel D, Gibbon P, Garcia M, *et al.* Experience with the MPI/STARSS Programming Model on a Large Production Code. In: Parallel Computing: Accelerating Computational Science and Engineering (CSE), Proceedings of the International Conference on Parallel Computing, ParCo 2013, 10-13 September 2013, Garching (near Munich), Germany; 2013. p. 357–366. Available from: https://doi.org/10.3233/978-1-61499-381-0-357.

[7]   Duran A, Ayguadé E, Badia RM, *et al.* OmpSs: a proposal for programming heterogeneous multi-core architectures. Parallel Processing Letters. 2011;21(02):173–193.

[8]   Nakajima T, Katouda M, Kamiya M, *et al.* NTChem: A high-performance software package for quantum molecular simulation. International Journal of Quantum Chemistry. 2014;115:349–359. Available from: http://dx.doi.org/10.1002/qua.24860.

[9]   NTChem-mini: GitHub Repository. (2014) [Last accessed Nov 2017] https://github.com/fiber-miniapp/ntchem-mini.

[10] Pillet V, Labarta J, Cortes T, *et al.* PARAVER: A Tool to Visualize and Analyze Parallel Code. In: Nixon P, editor. Proceedings of WoTUG-18: Transputer and Occam Developments; 1995. p. 17–31.

[11] Arenaz M, Hernandez O, Pleiter D. The Technological Roadmap of Parallware and Its Alignment with the OpenPO WER Ecosystem. In: Kunkel JM, Yokota R, Taufer M, *et al.*, editors. High Performance Computing. Cham: Springer International Publishing; 2017. p. 237–253.

[12] Iserte S, Mayo R, Quintana-Ortí ES, *et al.* Efficient Scalable Computing through Flexible Applications and Adaptive Workloads. In: 2017 46th International Conference on Parallel Processing Workshops (ICPPW); 2017. p. 180–189.

[13]   Garcia-Gasulla M, Houzeaux G, Ferrer R, *et al.* MPI+X: task-based parallelization and dynamic load balance of finite element assembly. Clinical Orthopaedics and Related Research. 2018;abs/1805.03949. Available from: http://arxiv.org/abs/1805.03949.

[14]   Cao C, Hérault T, Bosilca G, *et al.* Design for a Soft Error Resilient Dynamic Task-Based Runtime. In: 2015 IEEE International Parallel and Distributed Processing Symposium. 2015;p. 765–774.

[15]   Peña AJ, Beltran V, Clauss C, *et al.* Supporting Automatic Recovery in Offloaded Distributed Programming Models Through MPI-3 Techniques. In: Proceedings of the International Conference on Supercomputing. ICS'17. New York, NY, USA: ACM; 2017. p. 22:1–22:10. Available from: http://doi.acm.org.recursos.biblioteca.upc.edu/10.1145/3079079.3079093.

Chapter 2

From irregular heterogeneous software to reconfigurable hardware

John Wickerson[1] and George A. Constantinides[1]

The performance benefits associated with shrinking transistors are tapering off, so to meet society's ever-increasing demand for computation, computing systems are increasingly turning to parallelism and heterogeneity.

A heterogeneous system is the one that incorporates more than one kind of computing device. Such a system can offer better performance per Watt than a homogeneous one if the applications it runs are programmed to take advantage of the different strengths of the different devices in the system. A typical heterogeneous setup involves a master processor (the 'host' CPU) offloading some easily parallelised computations to a graphics processing unit (GPU) or to a custom accelerator implemented on a field-programmable gate array (FPGA). This arrangement can benefit performance because it exploits the massively parallel natures of GPU and FPGA architectures.

Heterogeneous systems are increasingly tightly coupled, so as to decrease the communication overhead between their component devices. For instance, IBM's Coherent Accelerator Processor Interface technology gives its POWER processors a direct and high-speed connection to accelerator devices [1], and Intel's Xeon/FPGA hybrid is forthcoming [2]. Modern fabrication technology even allows multiple computing devices to fit onto a single integrated circuit; examples of these 'systems-on-chip' (SoCs) include Xilinx's Zynq [3] and Intel's Cyclone V [4].

So that a programmer need not learn a different language for each device in a heterogeneous system, standards such as CUDA, HSA, and OpenCL have emerged. Each of these standards defines a computing model to which all devices conform, and thereby allows applications to be portable between different heterogeneous systems. The dominant vendor-agnostic standard for heterogeneous programming, and the one on which this chapter focuses, is OpenCL.

There are many examples of substantial performance improvements obtained by porting traditional CPU applications to OpenCL and executing them on heterogeneous systems, in domains ranging from computational fluid dynamics [5] to gene sequencing [6]. Many of OpenCL's success stories are on *regular* applications: those

---

[1]Department of Electrical and Electronic Engineering, Imperial College London, UK

that step through array-based data structures in predictable patterns. Because it is often straightforward to partition regular computation into equally sized, independent work items, these applications are well suited to devices that offer a large number of parallel computing elements operating in lock step. Conversely, in this chapter, we focus on OpenCL's support for the broader class of *irregular* applications. Such applications may rely on more advanced data structures such as trees and linked lists. They may be harder to break down into work items of equal magnitude and hence require work items to synchronise with one another more frequently.

This inter-work-item synchronisation is traditionally managed via mutual exclusion locks and, in OpenCL specifically, *barriers*. (A barrier is a point in a program that no work item is allowed to pass until all work items have reached it.) Unfortunately, barriers and locks can cause applications to suffer from problems like barrier divergence [7] and deadlock, and when used in irregular applications, it can unnecessarily inhibit the amount of parallelism achieved. Better performance can sometimes be obtained by rewriting applications to avoid the need for locks and barriers, and to rely on *atomic operations* to manage synchronisation instead. (Atomic operations are operations that are guaranteed to be performed indivisibly—without interference from any operations being executed simultaneously by other work items. They include memory loads and stores, as well as compound operations such as fetch-and-add and compare-and-swap.) In this chapter, we focus on irregular applications that use atomic operations to perform synchronisation.

OpenCL applications can target a range of computing devices, including CPUs, GPUs, FPGAs and digital signal processors; this chapter focuses on its support for FPGAs.

2.1 Outline

We begin by describing OpenCL and its programming model (Section 2.2).

Section 2.3 uses a K-means clustering application [8] to measure the performance impact of employing OpenCL's atomic operations for inter-work-item synchronisation. We demonstrate that although the atomic operations themselves are expensive, they bring an overall performance improvement by enabling work items to share their workloads.

We then show how the performance of the K-means clustering application can be improved (and the programming effort greatly reduced) by giving the FPGA direct access to the host CPU's memory, via OpenCL's *shared virtual memory (SVM)* feature (Section 2.4).

Section 2.5 describes the mechanisms provided by recent versions of OpenCL that allow a programmer to manage how expensive each atomic operation in a program needs to be. These include the *consistency mode*, which controls the extent to which an atomic operation can be reordered with other instructions, and the *memory scope*, which controls which work items are synchronised.

Finally, in Section 2.6, we discuss how these less expensive atomic operations can be mapped to FPGAs by adjusting the algorithm that schedules software instructions to hardware clock cycles. We demonstrate, using a data structure from the Linux kernel as a case study, that using cheaper atomic operations to synchronise work items has the potential to yield a substantial performance improvement.

2.2 Background

2.2.1 OpenCL's hierarchical programming model

OpenCL models a heterogeneous system as a *host processor* (typically a CPU) together with one or more *devices*, such as GPUs and FPGAs. An OpenCL application begins its execution on the host, but certain functions, which the programmer labels as *kernels*, can be offloaded to the devices for accelerated execution.

Each device is modelled as a collection of *compute units*, and each compute unit is further divided into *processing elements*. Each processing element executes one *work item* at a time. Work items are gathered into *work groups*; all the work items in the same work group are executed on processing elements in the same compute unit. Work groups in turn are gathered into *NDRanges* (*N*-dimensional ranges) that execute on a single device.

Just as OpenCL's work items are organised hierarchically, so is its memory. A single region of *global memory* is accessible to all devices in the system. Each work group has its own region of *local memory* for sharing data between its work items, and each work item has its own region of *private memory*.

Table 2.1 summarises OpenCL's execution and memory hierarchies, and how they correspond to each other.

2.2.2 Executing OpenCL kernels

An OpenCL programmer can accelerate a function by labelling it as a kernel and instructing the host processor to offload its execution to a device. When this happens, all of the work items execute the same kernel function. In order to identify different work items, the code of the kernel is parameterised by a work-item identifier. The control flow that a work item takes, and the data that it accesses, thereby depend on that work-item's identifier.

Table 2.1   OpenCL's hierarchical model of computation

SW execution hierarchy			HW execution hierarchy			Memory hierarchy
–			system			global memory
NDRange	is executed on a		device	has its own		–
Work group			compute unit			local memory
Work item			processing element			private memory

```
1  kernel void vec_mult(global float *x, global float *y,
2                       global float *out)
3  {
4    int wiid = get_global_id(0); // obtain work-item identifier
5    out[wiid] = x[wiid] * y[wiid];
6  }
```

Figure 2.1   An OpenCL kernel for multiplying two vectors pointwise

Example 2.1. *Consider the OpenCL kernel in Figure 2.1, which can be used to calculate the pointwise product of two N-dimensional vectors. The elements of these vectors are stored in the arrays* x *and* y, *respectively; the resultant vector is written to the array* out. *Each work item that executes this kernel is responsible for producing a single element of the output vector. Which element is accessed by a work item is determined by the work item's identifier, which is stored into the variable* wiid. *The host launches N work items to run this kernel, numbered with identifiers that range from 0 to N − 1.*

2.2.3   Work-item synchronisation

The work items that execute the kernel in Figure 2.1 do so completely independently. However, many workloads are not amenable to such straightforward parallelisation, so OpenCL provides two mechanisms that allow work items to synchronise with one another during computation: barriers and atomic operations.

Barriers.   Work items are generally allowed to execute the instructions of a kernel at different rates, except barrier instructions: no work item may proceed beyond a barrier until all the work items in the work group have reached it. Barriers are useful because any data produced by a work item before a barrier can be consumed after the barrier by any other work item in the work group. Nonetheless, they do not support inter-work-group synchronisation, and pausing *all* work items in a work group may be unnecessarily coarse grained for some applications.

Atomic operations.   These operations are guaranteed to be performed in their entirety without interference from other work items. They include simple operations such as loads and stores, and compound operations such as fetch-and-add and compare-and-swap. The use of atomic operations instead of coarse-grained constructions like locks and barriers can lead to better performance, because it can avoid work items being unnecessarily blocked from making progress. It is, however, notoriously tricky to write lock-free programs correctly.

2.3   The performance implications of mapping atomic operations to reconfigurable hardware

In the realm of conventional processors, such as CPUs and GPUs, atomic operations have been shown empirically to be the most efficient method for synchronising work items [9]. In this section, we investigate the performance of atomic operations in the context of the other major class of computing device that OpenCL supports: FPGAs. This section builds upon a paper written by the authors in collaboration with Ramanathan and Winterstein [10].

Atomic operations are inherently expensive; indeed, Intel explicitly warns against their use in programs, asserting that they 'might decrease kernel performance or require a large amount of hardware to implement' [11, p. 24]. However, we show in this section that introducing atomic operations into an OpenCL application can yield an overall performance *improvement*, because the atomic operations give work items the opportunity to synchronise with each other, and thereby rebalance their workloads at runtime.

The application we use as a case study in this section is K-means clustering [8]. The task is to take as input a set of N points in space, and output a set of K 'centroid' points, which must be positioned so as to minimise the sum of the squared distances between each input point and its nearest centroid. Figure 2.2 illustrates the case when $K = 3$ using a sample input with $N = 8$.

In a heuristic algorithm for K-means clustering due to Kanungo *et al.* [12], all of the input points are stored in a binary tree that is obtained by recursively bisecting the space. The algorithm works by first placing the centroids randomly and then iteratively refining their positions until a local minimum is reached. Each of these iterations involves traversing the tree of points to find each point's nearest centroid.

Winterstein *et al.* [13] have presented an implementation of this algorithm that is optimised for FPGAs. The key to their implementation is to exploit the inherent parallelism of the FPGA hardware by performing each tree traversal in parallel. The parallelisation is obtained by partitioning the tree into four subtrees, each rooted at one of the four grandchildren of the main tree's root, and then traversing each subtree independently. With this technique, Winterstein *et al.* obtain a roughly 4-fold speedup over a sequential version, at the cost of a 3-fold increase in hardware resource utilisation [13, Fig. 5].

Nonetheless, Winterstein *et al.*'s technique is limited because the division of the workload between parallel processing elements is insensitive to the shape of the tree.

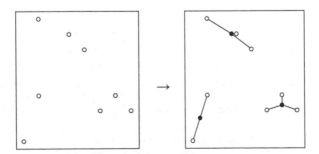

Figure 2.2   An example of K-means clustering, in which eight input points (white) are clustered using three centroids (black)

If the binary tree is not balanced, the workload will not be parallelised evenly, leading to some processing elements being underutilised.

Accordingly, Ramanathan *et al.* [10] have presented an alternative FPGA implementation of this algorithm in which the workload is redistributed at runtime among the available processing elements, via a system of *work stealing* [14]. Each work item maintains a queue of tree nodes it has yet to process; if any work-item's queue becomes empty, the work item steals from another work item's queue. This strategy ensures that no work item becomes idle while other work items still have unfinished work.

The introduction of work stealing requires the work items to synchronise with each other during the computation; they can no longer proceed in isolation as in Winterstein *et al.*'s implementation. This synchronisation is implemented using atomic operations. Specifically, whenever a tree node is taken from a work item's queue, an `atomic_cmpxchg` operation ('atomic compare and exchange') is used to update the queue's pointer. The use of an atomic operation here ensures that if two work items attempt to take the same tree node from the same queue, only one will succeed in doing so.

The effect of introducing work stealing is summarised in Figure 2.3. The figure shows how changing the number of work items affects both the kernel's execution time and the size of the circuit, with and without work stealing. On the left-hand part of the graph, the 'no stealing' implementation offers better performance per block RAM, because when the number of work items is small, there is little to be gained by having them steal work from each other. However, when the number of work items increases, the overhead incurred by the work-stealing mechanism is dominated by the advantages it brings in terms of load balancing. At maximum resource utilisation

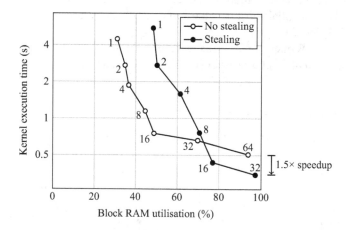

Figure 2.3   How the introduction of work-stealing affects kernel execution time and block RAM utilisation [10]. Each data point is labelled with the number of work-items deployed. At maximum resource utilisation, the work-stealing implementation is 1.5× faster.

(which happens at 32 work items with work stealing, and 64 work items otherwise), the work-stealing implementation is $1.5\times$ faster than Winterstein *et al.*'s implementation.

A conclusion that can be drawn from this case study is that although atomic operations are inherently expensive, they are nonetheless useful for allowing work items to synchronise with each other and thereby balance their workloads at runtime. As such, they can yield an overall improvement in an application's performance.

2.4 Shared virtual memory

SVM has been a feature of OpenCL since version 2.0. It provides the illusion of a single memory address space accessible to the host and all devices. This contrasts with the situation in OpenCL 1.x, where a host and a device can only communicate by explicitly copying data from the host's memory to the device's memory before launching a kernel.

In this section, which extends a paper written by the second author in collaboration with Winterstein [15], we describe how OpenCL's SVM feature can be provided in CPU/FPGA systems, and the performance benefits of doing so.

2.4.1 Why SVM?

A consequence of explicitly copying data structures from one memory to another is that addresses are not preserved. This is not a problem for simple array-based data but inhibits the use of pointer-based data structures, such as linked lists that have each node store the address of the next node. With SVM, pointer-based data structures can be shared seamlessly between the host and the devices: the only data that must still be transferred explicitly is the address of the data structure. This greatly eases the burden of heterogeneous programming. It can also lead to significant speedups, because it is no longer necessary for the host to transfer the entirety of a large data structure to a device before invoking a kernel; instead, the device can fetch the data it needs on-the-fly. Moreover, assuming appropriate synchronisation mechanisms are in place, hosts and devices can modify data structures in SVM simultaneously, which can lead to even higher degrees of parallelism during computations.

2.4.2 Implementing SVM for CPU/FPGA systems

Providing SVM in a heterogeneous CPU/FPGA system requires three pieces of functionality to be implemented.

Translating virtual addresses to physical addresses. CPUs typically use virtual addresses, which means that a pointer into the host's address space must be translated into a physical address before it can be dereferenced. The mapping from virtual addresses to physical addresses is maintained in the CPU's *page table*. So that the pointers used in data structures on the host remain meaningful when they are transferred to the FPGA, the FPGA must perform the same virtual-to-physical address translation before each of its SVM accesses.

This functionality can be enabled by allowing the FPGA direct access to the page table in the host's memory. On the ARM-based SoC targeted by Winterstein *et al.*, for instance, this connection can be established through ARM's *accelerator coherence port*.

Loading from and storing to SVM. The actual data transfer to/from the host's memory is orchestrated by a module implemented on the FPGA. For each SVM access by the kernel, this module makes three accesses to the host's memory: two to perform the virtual-to-physical address translation in the (two-level) page table, and one to carry out the desired load or store. Winterstein *et al.*'s implementation seeks to coalesce accesses to consecutive addresses into single bursts, which can be more efficient than a sequence individual accesses. It also implements a *translation lookaside buffer* that caches recently retrieved entries from the page table.

Atomically accessing host memory. OpenCL's SVM feature not only allows a device to access the host's memory but also allows it to access the host's memory simultaneously with the host itself. This allows threads on the host and work items on the devices to process the same data structures in a truly concurrent manner.

In order to coordinate simultaneous access to the same memory addresses, the host and the devices participate in a locking protocol. A single lock variable is maintained on the FPGA; if the host or a device wishes to perform a memory access, it must first acquire this lock.

2.4.3   Evaluation

Figure 2.4 shows how the introduction of SVM affects the performance of our running example, *K*-means clustering. The two bars show the time taken for the host to build the tree of input points, for that data to be transferred to the FPGA, and for the clustering kernel to be executed. The left bar is for a non-SVM implementation, in which the original pointer-based tree structure proposed by Kanungo *et al.* [12] has been rewritten to use indices into an array. Note that a substantial amount of time is required to transfer the entire tree into the FPGA. The right bar gives the timing breakdown for a variant that uses SVM. Although the kernel now takes longer to

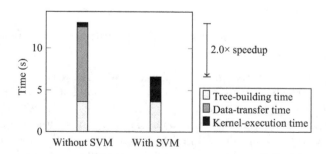

Figure 2.4   The effect of SVM on the overall execution time of K-means clustering

execute, because the data required by the kernel must now be loaded into the FPGA on-the-fly from the host's memory, the elimination of the bulk-data-transfer phase means that SVM brings an overall $2.0\times$ speedup, as well as a significant reduction in programming effort.

2.5 Weakly consistent atomic operations

In Section 2.3, we demonstrated that atomic operations can usefully be deployed in OpenCL applications, despite being expensive themselves. Not all atomic operations are equally expensive, however. Recent versions of C, C++, and OpenCL have all defined a range of atomic operations, some of which sacrifice the guarantees they provide to programmers in exchange for better performance.

The aim of this section, which draws on a paper written by the first author in collaboration with Batty and Donaldson [16], is to explain how the various kinds of atomic operation work in OpenCL and also to explain some of the pitfalls associated with using them. The next section will investigate how these atomic operations can be mapped to reconfigurable hardware, both correctly and as efficiently as possible.

In their default mode, OpenCL's atomic operations are guaranteed:

- to execute atomically, that is to execute either completely or not at all, and without interference from any concurrently running work items;
- to take effect in the order in which they are written within a work item by the programmer; and
- to ensure that all work items have a consistent view of any memory locations they share.

These guarantees are expensive for implementations of the OpenCL language to meet, and some of them are not always necessary in order for an application to function correctly. For instance, the second guarantee prevents a compiler from reordering the instructions in a program, which may inhibit certain optimisations. For another instance, the third guarantee may be over-restrictive because an application may only rely on *some* work items being synchronised, rather than *all* of them.

Accordingly, all atomic operations in OpenCL (from version 2.0 onwards) expose two parameters that can be controlled by the programmer: a *consistency mode*[1] and a *memory scope*. Exactly how these parameters affect the allowed behaviours of any given kernel is defined by OpenCL's *memory consistency model* [17, §3.3.4].

2.5.1 *OpenCL's memory consistency model*

The behaviour of an OpenCL kernel is determined via a two-stage process. First, the text of the kernel is mapped to a set of *candidate executions*. An execution is a mathematical graph whose vertices represent runtime memory-related events (i.e. reads and writes) and whose edges represent various relationships between those

---

[1] OpenCL refers to this parameter as the 'memory order'.

```
1    kernel void mp(global int *msg, global atomic_int *rdy,
2                   global int *out)
3    {
4      int wiid = get_global_id(0); //obtain work-item identifier
5      if (wiid == 0) { //Work-item 0 produces message
6        *msg = 42;
7        atomic_store(rdy,1);
8      } else { //Work-item 1 attempts to consume message
9        int r0 = atomic_load(rdy);
10       *out = (r0 == 1) ? *msg:1;
11     }
12   }
```

Figure 2.5   A simple OpenCL kernel demonstrating the use of atomic operations to pass a message from one work item to another

events. The executions produced by this first stage are only 'candidates' because they are generated using a simplistic over-approximation of how shared memory works: each event that reads from a shared memory location x is permitted to observe *any* event that writes to x, including those from the distant past and even the future. In the second stage of the process, the rules of OpenCL's memory consistency model are applied to each candidate execution in turn, and those that are deemed inconsistent are rejected. Of the consistent executions that remain,

- if any contains a *data race* then the entire kernel is meaningless, and its behaviour is completely unconstrained;
- otherwise, the kernel is allowed to behave according to any of the consistent executions.

We now demonstrate this approach, using a worked example.

Example 2.2. *Figure 2.5 shows a simple OpenCL kernel that is designed to be executed by two work items, work item 0 and work item 1. When work item 0 executes this kernel, it writes the message '42' to the location* msg *and then sets the ready flag at location* rdy *using an atomic store. When work item 1 executes this kernel, it reads the ready flag using an atomic load, and if it has been set, it copies the message into the output location* out.

2.5.1.1   Executions

Events in executions take the form R x v, which means 'read value v from location x', or W x v, which means 'write value v to location x'. (The full model also includes read-modify-write events and fence events.) We tag atomic events with the subscript 'SC', which stands for 'sequentially consistent', the default consistency mode for atomic operations – other consistency modes will be introduced in the next subsection. Events are linked by 'program order' (*po*) arrows that show how the instructions that correspond to these events are ordered in the kernel, and by 'reads from' (*rf*) arrows that show which write event each read event observes. A read event with no incoming *rf* arrow is assumed to observe the initial value, zero.

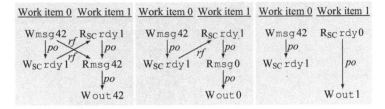

Figure 2.6   The three candidate executions of the OpenCL kernel in Figure 2.5. Left: the consumer observes the ready flag and then receives the message. Middle: the consumer observes the ready flag but then fails to receive the message. Right: the consumer does not observe the ready flag

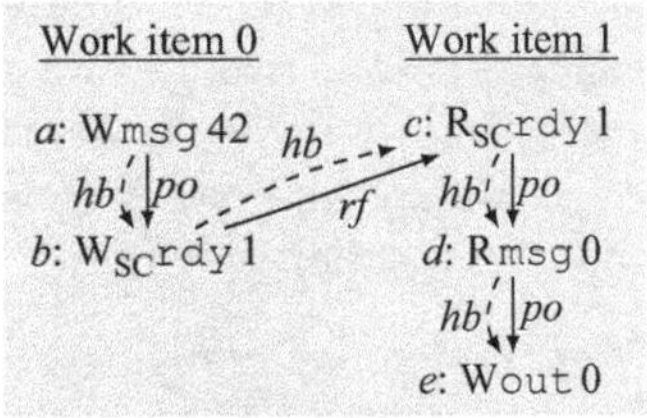

Figure 2.7   The middle execution from Figure 2.6 with the 'happens before' arrows added. This execution is deemed inconsistent

Example 2.3. *Figure 2.6 shows three executions: the candidate executions of the kernel in Figure 2.5. They range over the three possible ways that the two loads of the global locations by work item 1 can behave. The left execution shows both* rdy *and* msg *being loaded with their new values; the middle execution has work item 1 observing the new value of* rdy *but the initial value of* msg; *and in the right execution, work item 1 observes the initial value of* rdy, *in which case* msg *is not loaded.*

2.5.1.2   Consistent executions

When an atomic read observes an atomic write in another work item, we say that the write 'happens before' the read. This 'happens before' relation also includes the program order within each work item. One of the rules of the OpenCL memory consistency model is that every read must observe the most recent write to that location according to 'happens before'.

Example 2.4. *Figure 2.7 adds arrows that show how 'happens before' is derived for the middle execution in Figure 2.6. The execution is deemed inconsistent because the read event d observes the (implicit) event that initialises* msg *to zero, despite the existence of the write event a that happens before d more recently than the initialisation event. (Initialisation events are assumed to happen before all other events.)*

Work item 0	Work item 1
a: Wmsg 42	c: R$_{SC}$rdy0
$hb'_t \downarrow po$	$hb'_t \downarrow po$
b: W$_{SC}$rdy1	d: Rmsg0
	$hb'_t \downarrow po$
	e: Wout1

Figure 2.8   A candidate execution of the kernel obtained from Figure 2.5 by changing line 10 to `*out = *msg;`. *The execution is consistent but racy*

2.5.1.3   Data races

The consistent candidate executions of a kernel are its allowed executions, unless any of the consistent candidates exhibits a data race. To define a data race in OpenCL, we rely once more on the 'happens before' relation. We say that there is a data race between two events in different work items if they are not both atomic, they are unrelated by 'happens before', and they conflict. Two events conflict if they access the same location and at least one is a write.

Example 2.5. *The left and right executions in Figure 2.6, which are the consistent candidate executions of the kernel in Figure 2.5, are both free from data races. Therefore, the allowed executions of this kernel are those two consistent candidates.*

However, suppose the kernel were changed so that it reads the message even if it sees that the ready flag has not yet been set (i.e. line 10 becomes `*out = *msg`). *In this case, additional candidate executions would emerge, including the one shown in Figure 2.8. This candidate execution does not violate any rules of the OpenCL memory consistency model, so is deemed consistent. Nevertheless, because there is no chain of 'happens before' arrows between the two non-atomic accesses to* msg, *a and d, it is deemed a racy execution. This means that the modified kernel is meaningless.*

2.5.2   Consistency modes

Each atomic operation in an OpenCL kernel can be tagged with a consistency mode. The four consistency modes for load and store operations are:

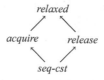

The *release* mode only applies to stores and the *acquire* mode only applies to loads. The default consistency mode is *seq-cst*. (There also exists an *acq-rel* mode for read-modify-write operations, which we do not cover here.) The arrows depict the relative strength of the modes: $m_1 \rightarrow m_2$ means that mode m_1 is 'stronger' than m_2, in the sense that replacing an m_2-atomic with an m_1-atomic can never give rise to additional kernel behaviours.

2.5.2.1 The *acquire* and *release* consistency modes

In the previous subsection, we defined the 'happens before' relation as being induced when an atomic read observes an atomic write. Now that we have different kinds of atomic operation, we can be more precise: 'happens before' is only induced when the read is an *acquire* or stronger and the write is at least a *release*. Therefore, the two accesses to the `rdy` location in the kernel in Figure 2.5 can be safely downgraded to `atomic_store_explicit(rdy, 1, memory_order_release)` and `atomic_load_explicit(rdy, memory_order_acquire)`, respectively, without affecting the kernel's behaviour.

2.5.2.2 The *seq-cst* consistency mode

Not all *seq-cst* operations can be replaced with their acquire/release counterparts, however. Consider the kernel in Figure 2.9, which is based on Dekker's mutual exclusion algorithm [18] and is designed to be invoked by two work items, work item 0 and work item 1. A work item set its element of the `try` array to register an attempt to enter the critical section, and then checks that the other element of `try` has *not* been set before actually entering. The correctness of the algorithm relies on the impossibility of both work items observing that the other work item has not set its `try` element – that is on the execution depicted in Figure 2.10 not being allowed.

We have seen that *acquire* and *release* operations only induce 'happens before' arrows when the *acquire* reads from the *release*. The execution in Figure 2.10 has no

```
1  kernel void dekker(global atomic_int *try, global int *out)
2  {
3    int wiid = get_global_id(0);  // obtain work-item identifier
4    atomic_store(&try[wiid], 1);  // try to enter critical section
5    if (atomic_load(&try[1-wiid]) ==0)   // has other work-item tried?
6      *out = wiid + 1;  // critical section
7  }
```

Figure 2.9   An OpenCL kernel for two work items that uses (a simplified version of) Dekker's mutual exclusion algorithm to protect access to the non-atomic location out

Work item 0	Work item 1
a: W_{SC}try[0]1	d: W_{SC}try[1]1
$\downarrow$po	$\downarrow$po
b: R_{SC}try[1]0	e: R_{SC}try[0]0
$\downarrow$po	$\downarrow$po
c: Wout1	f: Wout2

Figure 2.10   A candidate execution of the kernel in Figure 2.9

```
1  kernel void relaxed_example(global atomic_int *started)
2  {
3    atomic_store_explicit(started, 1, memory_order_relaxed);
4    /*
5     * rest of kernel
6     */
7  }
```

*Figure 2.11   An OpenCL kernel in which all work items begin by writing the same
value to the same location*

'*rf*' arrows, however, so *acquire* and *release* atomics are insufficient. Nevertheless,
the OpenCL memory consistency model has another rule that applies only to *seq-cst*
operations. It states that there must exist a total order over all of the *seq-cst* events in
an execution, consistent with program order, such that every *seq-cst* read observes the
most recent write in this total order. In the execution in Figure 2.10, any total ordering
of the four *seq-cst* events {a, b, d, e} that is consistent with *po* will necessarily order
a before e or d before b. Yet if a is ordered before e, then the execution is inconsistent
because e is not observing the most recent write to try[0] in the total order, and if d
is ordered before b, then the execution is still inconsistent because b is not observing
the most recent write to try[1].

2.5.2.3   The *relaxed* consistency mode

Finally, we turn to the *relaxed* consistency mode. Operations that use this mode are
still atomic, so they cannot cause data races, but unlike *acquire* or *release* operations,
they do not induce the 'happens before' relation, and unlike *seq-cst* operations, they
are not assumed to be totally ordered. A kernel that illustrates a situation where *relaxed*
atomic operations suffice is given in Figure 2.11. The started location is written
simultaneously by multiple work items, so the stores must be atomic in order to avoid
data races, but no further guarantees are required because the location is not relied
upon for synchronising work items.

2.5.3   Memory scopes

Each atomic operation in an OpenCL kernel can be tagged not only with a consistency
mode, as described in the previous subsection, but also with a *memory scope*. The
three memory scopes are

- *work group*,
- *device*, and
- *all devices*.

An operation at *work-group* scope provides consistency guarantees only among
work items in the same work group as the work item performing the operation; *device*-
scope operations guarantee consistency within the current device; and *all-devices*
operations guarantee consistency across all devices.

Memory scopes can be useful in situations where a memory location is only accessed by work items within one part of the OpenCL execution hierarchy. For instance, suppose x is an atomic location in global memory and is hence visible to all work items (cf. Table 2.1). If it is the case that the only work items accessing x are all in the same work group, all the accesses to x can safely be performed using *work-group* scope. Doing so may bring a performance benefit when the kernel is executed on a device where global memory is cached within each compute unit, because the updates to x need not propagate beyond these caches.

Memory scopes interact in some interesting ways with the rest of the OpenCL memory-consistency model. For instance, in Section 2.5.1, we defined two conflicting events to have a data race if they are not both atomic, are not in the same work item, and are unordered by 'happens before'. In the presence of memory scopes, those events also have a data race if they do not have 'inclusive scopes'. The events have inclusive scopes if they both have at least *work-group* scope and are in the same work group, or they both have at least *device* scope and are in the same device, or they both have *all-devices* scope. The definition of 'happens before' is similarly affected: in the presence of memory scopes, 'happens before' arrows are induced when an *acquire* read observes a *release* write only if those two events have inclusive scopes.

Orr *et al.* [19,20] give a practical demonstration of OpenCL's memory scopes in action, by using them to construct a work-stealing system in which each work group maintains a task queue, and work items steal work from other work groups should their own queue become empty. The key idea is that when a work item pushes/pops work to/from its local queue, it can use *work-group* scope, but when it steals work from a different work group's queue, it falls back to the more expensive *device* scope.

2.5.4 Further reading

Gaster *et al.* [21] and Batty *et al.* [16] both study the details of the OpenCL memory consistency model, focusing on memory scopes. In particular, Gaster *et al.* question whether two events with *different* memory scopes can or should ever be deemed to have inclusive scopes, and Batty *et al.* question whether a *seq-cst* event that is limited to *work-group* scope is still expected to take part in the total order over all *seq-cst* events in the execution.

2.6   Mapping weakly consistent atomic operations to reconfigurable hardware

Atomic operations with a variety of consistency modes are supported by compilers for multiprocessor architectures such as ×86, Power, and ARM [22]. Yet OpenCL does not only support conventional processors – it can also target reconfigurable hardware devices (FPGAs), via a *high-level synthesis* tool. Existing tools for mapping C or OpenCL applications to FPGAs either do not support atomic operations at all (such as Xilinx SDAccel [23]), or only support *seq-cst* operations (e.g. Intel FPGA SDK for OpenCL [24]).

The aim of this section, which builds upon a paper written by the authors in collaboration with Ramanathan and Fleming [25], is to explain how high-level synthesis can be extended so that it becomes sensitive to the consistency mode of atomic operations.

We focus on the scheduling phase of the high-level synthesis process. This is the phase in which software instructions are allocated to hardware clock cycles. A key objective of the scheduler in a high-level synthesis tool is to exploit instruction-level parallelism; that is to schedule multiple software instructions for simultaneous execution on parallel hardware units whenever the data and control dependencies in the program permit this. Towards this objective, the tool constructs a set of constraints between instructions and then seeks the shortest possible resource-constrained schedule that respects all of these constraints.

We apply these ideas to the open-source LegUp tool from the University of Toronto. LegUp's input is a C program rather than an OpenCL kernel, but since OpenCL's atomic operations are inherited from C, the ideas discussed in this section are applicable to both languages equally.

2.6.1   Scheduling constraints

Our strategy for implementing atomic operations is to start with ordinary, non-atomic operations and then to add just enough scheduling constraints within a thread to ensure that the atomic operations guarantee the behaviours described in Section 2.5.2. In the absence of the complicated caching hierarchies that appear in conventional multiprocessors, this approach based merely on scheduling is sufficient to implement atomic operations correctly.

The constraints essentially enforce that atomic operations that access the same location cannot be reordered, that *acquire* loads cannot move up, that *release* stores cannot move down, and that *seq-cst* operations can move neither up nor down. More precisely, we constrain instruction A to be scheduled before instruction B if A precedes B in program order and either:

Constraint 1 A and B are atomic operations that access the same location,
Constraint 2 A is an *acquire* load and B is any load or store,
Constraint 3 B is a *release* store and A is any load or store,
Constraint 4 A is a *seq-cst* operation and B is any load or store, or
Constraint 5 B is a *seq-cst* operation and A is any load or store.

The following example illustrates these constraints in action.

Example 2.6. *Figure 2.12 shows valid schedules for work item 0 and work item 1 executing the OpenCL kernel in Figure 2.5. In both schedules, each column represents one hardware clock cycle, the rows are labelled with the corresponding line numbers in Figure 2.5, and the shaded cells indicate how the basic operations (written in a pseudo-LLVM style) are mapped to clock cycles. It is a feature of LegUp's memory architecture that* **load** *operations require two clock cycles while* **store** *operations require only one.*

In the absence of our additional constraints, LegUp's scheduler would schedule the two **store** *operations in work item 0 to the same clock cycle, since they access*

Cycle:	1	2
6	store 42,msg	
7		store 1,rdy

Cycle:	1	2	3	4	5	6
9	r0=load rdy					
10			r1=load msg			
10					r2=(r0==1)?r1:1	
10						store r2,out

Figure 2.12   Valid schedules for work item 0 (top) and work item 1 (bottom) executing the OpenCL kernel in Figure 2.5

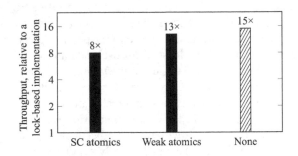

Figure 2.13   The effect of three variants of the scheduling constraints on the throughput of a lock-free circular queue

different locations. However, since the second operation is a release, *our* **Constraint 3** *requires that it is scheduled after the first. Similarly,* **Constraint 2** *ensures that work item 1's two* **load** *operations – the first of which is an* acquire *– are executed in strict sequence. Together, these constraints ensure that message-passing violations can never occur, that is the kernel can only exhibit behaviours that are allowed by the OpenCL memory-consistency model.*

2.6.2   Evaluation

Atomic operations with *relaxed* mode give rise to fewer scheduling constraints than *acquire* and *release* operations, which in turn involve fewer constraints than *seq-cst* operations. To evaluate the extent to which fewer scheduling constraints give rise to shorter schedules and higher performance hardware, we used LegUp to generate hardware from a software application based on a single-producer–single-consumer lock-free circular queue – a widely used data structure that appears in the Linux kernel [26]. The application uses these queues to pass messages among three work items.

Figure 2.13 shows how the scheduling constraints affect the rate at which messages are passed between work items. The throughput is relative to a naïve implementation of atomic operations, in which every individual operation is protected by a single global lock. Treating every atomic operation as if it uses *seq-cst* mode yields an $8\times$ performance improvement over the lock-based baseline. Relaxing the constraints for *acquire*, *release*, and *relaxed* operations yields a $13\times$ performance improvement over the baseline. This is quite close to the $15\times$ performance improvement that can be obtained by ignoring the new scheduling constraints altogether and just treating atomic operations as non-atomic, though such an implementation would be unsound and could generate incorrect hardware.

2.7   Conclusion and future directions

We are at a time of rapid changes, both to programming languages and models and to computer architecture. In this chapter, we have aimed to highlight both aspects together with their interaction. We have identified OpenCL as an example of the style of programming that is becoming particularly popular given the rise of heterogeneous computing. One of the least well-developed areas in this setting, both theoretically and practically, is the efficient implementation of multithreaded algorithms that communicate through some form of synchronisation, and so we have focused our discussion on this point, in particular on the use of atomic operations, and support for SVM. The rise of FPGA-based computation provides particular opportunities for efficient implementation; we have described how high-level programming constructs for synchronisation can be automatically synthesised into low-level specialised accelerator hardware, through adaptations to standard high-level synthesis flows and infrastructure for SVM support. We believe there is much promise in encouraging the programming languages community and the computer architecture community to develop such approaches in lock step, given the results we present.

There are numerous directions for future research in this area. For instance, in Section 2.6, we described how a high-level synthesis tool can be made to exploit the consistency mode of each atomic operation appearing in the input program simply by adapting the scheduling constraints (so that, for instance, *seq-cst* atomics are scheduled in strict program order but *relaxed* atomics are allowed to overlap with each other). Although consistency-sensitive scheduling has been shown to improve the performance of the generated hardware significantly, scheduling is but one phase of the overall high-level synthesis flow. FPGAs offer enormous flexibility in how an application can be implemented, so an implementation of atomic operations that can exploit more of this freedom has the potential to yield far larger performance improvements than the one based on adjusting scheduling rules alone. For instance, a high-level synthesis tool could build an application-specific cache hierarchy on the FPGA using a framework such as LEAP [27], and automatically configure these caches so that their coherence guarantees are sensitive to the consistency modes of the atomic operations that access them [28].

Another future direction involves exploiting the observation that high-level synthesis tools, unlike ordinary compilers, are typically presented with the *entire* source code of a program in one go. Hence, there are numerous opportunities to use a whole-program analysis to inform the high-level synthesis process, with the aim of generating higher quality hardware. Our recent work with Ramanathan has already used whole-program analysis to justify a more aggressive scheduler [29]; other potential uses include determining memory sharing patterns between threads to justify the removal of unnecessary circuitry.

Both of the aforementioned research directions involve increasingly complex implementations; as such, the issue of *correctness* grows ever more important. In our work to date, we have addressed this issue by using the Alloy model checker [30] to verify (up to a bound) that our implementations conform to the programming language specifications [25,29,31]. However, while bounded verification is an effective bug-finding technique, it does not give complete assurance of correctness. As such, there is an opportunity for future research to investigate how to formally prove, using an interactive theorem prover such as Coq or Isabelle, that a given high-level synthesis tool will always generate correct hardware. Some progress has been made on this front by Braibant and Chlipala [32], who have built a Bluespec compiler that outputs not only Verilog but a Coq proof that the Verilog corresponds to the Bluespec input; challenges remain to lift the input to an ordinary software language like C or OpenCL. Meanwhile, Ellis [33] has formalised a high-level synthesis process within Isabelle, but the result is difficult to apply in practice because the synthesis process is idealised for the purpose of formalisation. Nonetheless, if these challenges can be overcome, the prize is substantial, because the safety net that formal verification provides can give designers the confidence to build ambitious and aggressively optimising high-level synthesis tools – tools that will ultimately produce the high-performance, low-power hardware that is needed to meet society's ever-increasing demand for computation.

Acknowledgements

The authors wish to acknowledge the work of Nadesh Ramanathan and Felix Winterstein, upon which several sections of this chapter build, as well as financial support from the EPSRC (EP/P010040/1, EP/K034448/1, EP/I020357/1), the Royal Academy of Engineering, Imagination Technologies, and an Imperial College Research Fellowship.

References

[1] IBM Corp. Coherent Accelerator Processor Interface (CAPI); 2014. Online. Available from: https://developer.ibm.com/linuxonpower/capi/.

[2] Prickett Morgan T. Intel Gears up for FPGA Push; 2017. Online. Available from: https://www.nextplatform.com/2017/10/02/intel-gears-fpga-push/.

[3] Xilinx, Inc. Zynq-7000 SoC; 2018. Online. Available from: https://www.xilinx.com/products/silicon-devices/soc/zynq-7000.html.

[4] Intel Corp. Cyclone V SoCs; 2018. Online. Available from: https://www.altera.com/products/soc/portfolio/cyclone-v-soc/overview.html.

[5]   Bednarz T, Domanski L, Taylor JA. Computational Fluid Dynamics using OpenCL – A Practical Introduction. In: Int. Congress on Modelling and Simulation; 2011. p. 608–612.

[6]   Razmyslovich D, Marcus G, Gipp M, *et al.* Implementation of Smith-Waterman Algorithm in OpenCL for GPUs. In: Int. Workshop on High Performance Computational Systems Biology; 2010. p. 48–56.

[7]   Betts A, Chong N, Donaldson AF, *et al.* The design and implementation of a verification technique for GPU kernels. ACM Transactions on Programming Languages and Systems (TOPLAS). 2015;37(3):10:1–10:49.

[8]   MacQueen J. Some Methods for Classification and Analysis of Multivariate Observations. In: Proc. 5th Berkeley Symp. on Mathematical Statistics and Probability. University of California Press; 1967. p. 281–297.

[9]   Gramoli V. More Than You Ever Wanted to Know about Synchronization: Synchrobench, Measuring the Impact of the Synchronization on Concurrent Algorithms. In: ACM Symp. on Principles and Practice of Parallel Programming (PPoPP); 2015. p. 1–10.

[10]   Ramanathan N, Wickerson J, Winterstein F, *et al.* A Case for Work Stealing on FPGAs with OpenCL Atomics. In: ACM/SIGDA Int. Symp. on Field-Programmable Gate Arrays (FPGA); 2016. p. 48–53.

[11]   Intel. Intel FPGA SDK for OpenCL – Best Practices Guide; 2017. UG-OCL003. Available from: http://bit.ly/2xLAgxh.

[12]   Kanungo T, Mount D, Netanyahu N, *et al.* An efficient k-means clustering algorithm: Analysis and implementation. IEEE Transactions on Pattern Analysis and Machine Intelligence. 2002;24(7):881–892.

[13]   Winterstein F, Bayliss S, Constantinides GA. FPGA-based K-means Clustering Using Tree-based Data Structures. In: Field Programmable Logic and Applications (FPL); 2013. p. 1–6.

[14]   Arora NS, Blumofe RD, Plaxton CG. Thread Scheduling for Multiprogrammed Multiprocessors. In: ACM Symp. on Parallelism in Algorithms and Architectures (SPAA); 1998. p. 119–129.

[15]   Winterstein F, Constantinides GA. Pass a Pointer: Exploring Shared Virtual Memory Abstractions in OpenCL Tools for FPGAs. In: Int. Conf. on Field-Programmable Technology (FPT); 2017. p. 104–111. To appear.

[16]   Batty M, Donaldson AF, Wickerson J. Overhauling SC Atomics in C11 and OpenCL. In: ACM Symp. on Principles of Programming Languages (POPL); 2016. p. 634–648.

[17]   Khronos Group. The OpenCL Specification. Version 2.2; 2017.

[18]   Dijkstra EW. Cooperating Sequential Processes (1965). In: Brinch Hansen P, editor. The Origin of Concurrent Programming. New York: Springer-Verlag; 2002. p. 65–138.

[19]   Orr MS, Che S, Yilmazer A, *et al.* Synchronization Using Remote-Scope Promotion. In: Int. Conf. on Architectural Support for Programming Languages and Operating Systems (ASPLOS); 2015. p. 73–86.

[20]   Wickerson J, Batty M, Beckmann BM, *et al.* Remote-Scope Promotion: Clarified, Rectified, and Verified. In: ACM Int. Conf. on Object-Oriented

Programming, Systems, Languages, and Applications (OOPSLA); 2015. p. 731–747.

[21]   Gaster BR, Hower DR, Howes L. HRF-Relaxed: Adapting HRF to the complexities of industrial heterogeneous memory models. ACM Transactions on Architecture and Code Optimization. 2015;12(7), p. 7:1–7:26.

[22]   Sewell P. C/C++11 Mappings to Processors; 2018. Online. Available from: https://www.cl.cam.ac.uk/~pes20/cpp/cpp0xmappings.html.

[23]   Inc. Xilinx. SDAccel Environment User Guide (UG1023 v2017.1). Xilinx, Inc.; 2017.

[24]   Intel. Intel FPGA SDK for OpenCL – Programming Guide; 2017. UG-OCL002. Available from: http://bit.ly/2blgksq.

[25]   Ramanathan N, Fleming ST, Wickerson J, *et al.* Hardware Synthesis of Weakly Consistent C Concurrency. In: ACM/SIGDA Int. Symp. on Field-Programmable Gate Arrays (FPGA); 2017. p. 169–178.

[26]   Blechmann T. Lock-free Single-Producer/Single-Consumer Ringbuffer; 2013. Boost C++ Libraries. Available from: http://www.boost.org/doc/libs/1_59_0/boost/lockfree/spsc_queue.hpp.

[27]   Fleming K, Yang HJ, Adler M, *et al.* The LEAP FPGA Operating System. In: Field Programmable Logic and Applications (FPL); 2014. p. 1–8.

[28]   Winterstein F, Fleming K, Yang HJ, *et al.* Custom-Sized Caches in Application-Specific Memory Hierarchies. In: Int. Conf. on Field-Programmable Technology (FPT); 2015. p. 144–151.

[29]   Ramanathan N, Constantinides GA, Wickerson J. Concurrency-Aware Thread Scheduling for High-Level Synthesis. In: IEEE Int. Symp. on Field-Programmable Custom Computing Machines (FCCM); 2018. p. 101–108.

[30]   Jackson D. Software Abstractions – Logic, Language, and Analysis. Revised edition ed. Cambridge, MA: MIT Press; 2012.

[31]   Wickerson J, Batty M, Sorensen T, *et al.* Automatically Comparing Memory Consistency Models. In: ACM Symp. on Principles of Programming Languages (POPL); 2017. p. 190–204.

[32]   Braibant T, Chlipala A. Formal Verification of Hardware Synthesis. In: Int. Conf. on Computer Aided Verification (CAV); 2013. p. 213–228.

[33]   Ellis M. Correct synthesis and integration of compiler-generated function units [PhD thesis]. Newcastle University; 2008.

Chapter 3

Operating systems for many-core systems

Hendrik Borghorst[1] and Olaf Spinczyk[2]

The ongoing trend toward many-core computer systems and adequate new programming models has spawned numerous new activities in the domain of operating system (OS) research during recent years. This chapter will address the challenges and opportunities for OS developers in this new field and give an overview of state-of-the-art research.

3.1 Introduction

This section will introduce the reader to the spectrum of contemporary many-core CPU architectures, application programming models for many-core systems, and give a brief overview of the resulting challenges for OS developers.

3.1.1 Many-core architectures

While Gordon Moore's "law" [1], which originally predicted in 1965 that the number of on-chip components would double every year for a decade, held for an even longer period, technological advances now seem to have reached a serious barrier. Going below structure sizes of 10 nm comes at high costs, growing leakage currents, reliability issues, and first of all, cooling problems [2]. To reduce leakage currents, deal with cooling problems, and to save energy in general, it is desirable to minimize the supply voltage. However, this conflicts with ever-increasing clock speeds. Therefore, during the last decade, improvements in the compute power of CPUs have mainly been achieved by increasing the number of processing cores instead of clock speed.

Table 3.1 gives an overview of widely known contemporary processors and their main architectural characteristics. The upper part of the table presents general purpose CPUs, while in the lower part special accelerators are listed, which are normally used in combination with one or more general purpose CPUs. In the following, we will use the terms *homogeneous* and *heterogeneous system architecture* to distinguish between these two classes of systems.

While today's notebook and desktop CPUs are equipped with 2 to 16 CPU cores, the presented high-end architectures feature up to 260 cores in general purpose CPUs

[1]Department of Computer Science, TU Dortmund, Germany
[2]Institute of Computer Science, Osnabrück University, Germany

Table 3.1   Characteristics of contemporary multi- and many-core processors

Name	ISA	#Cores	#Threads	Interconnect
Intel Xeon Scalable	x86_64	28	56	UPI
Sparc M7	Sparc V9	32	256	On-chip network
AMD Epyc	x86_64	32	64	Infinity fabric
Qualcomm Centriq 2400	AArch64	48	48	Multi ring
Cavium ThunderX2	AArch64	54	54	CCPI
Mellanox Tile-Gx 72	Proprietary (VLIW)	72	72	iMesh
Sunway SW26010	Proprietary (RISC)	260	260	NoC/Mesh
NVidia Volta	Proprietary	40 SMs	5,120[a]	NV-Link
AMD GCN	GCN	64 CUs	4,096[b]	Crossbar/Infinity Fabric[c]
Intel Xeon Phi KNL	x86_64	72	288	Mesh (36 tiles)
Kalray MPPA2-256	Proprietary (VLIW)	288	288	NoC
PEZY-SC2	Proprietary (RISC)	2,048	16,384	–

[a] 128 SP-ALUs (CUDA-Cores) per SM.
[b] "16-lane ALU" per SIMD-VU, 4 SIMD-VU per CU = 4,096.
[c] For GCN5 and newer GPUs.

and many more in special purpose processors such as graphics processing units (GPUs). Each CPU core might be *multi-threaded* or *single-threaded*. For example, each Sparc M7 core can run up to eight threads of control simultaneously. Multi-threading is beneficial, as the functional units of the processor can be utilized better than with a single thread. However, it is virtually impossible to calculate the execution speed of a thread running on a multi-threaded CPU core, as concurrent threads might slow it down significantly.

Most of the presented processors have caches that are shared between multiple CPU cores. This supports very fast memory-based communication between these cores and reduces average memory access latencies. However, the number of cores that can share a traditional monolithic cache is technically limited [3]. Therefore, most modern many-core processors use a distributed last-level cache architecture. For example, on the Intel Xeon Platinum, all 28 cores share a distributed L3 cache. Main memory is typically addressed via one or more memory controllers that are integrated on the processor chip. An on-chip network connects the cores with each other, the memory controllers, and optionally an interface that links the processor with others on the mainboard. While multicore CPUs used to have point-to-point connections or a ring structure for on-chip communication between cores, the trend for many-core CPUs goes toward more flexible meshes where core, memory controllers, and I/O components are organized in a grid. Independently of the network topology, all cores of the presented processors can access the shared memory space. However, access latencies might differ. A cache coherence protocol on the on-chip network is used to make sure that all cores have a consistent view on the state of the memories. This is called a *cache-coherent non-uniform memory access* (ccNUMA).

Larger systems that are build out of more than one physical processor can also have a shared (and cache coherent) memory space. An eight-socket Intel Xeon

Platinum system could have, for instance, 224 cache coherent cores. While most architectures do not support cache coherence over mainboard boundaries (*distributed memory architectures*) and provide only message passing services, some systems support a shared memory of virtually arbitrary size [4]. Yet, the world's most powerful supercomputers, e.g., the Chinese Sunway TaihuLight system with more than 1,000,000 CPU cores, has a *hybrid architecture* with shared-memory nodes that are connected via a 5-level hierarchical PCIe-based network [5].

In the remainder of this chapter, we will focus solely on shared-memory and hybrid many-core systems. Large-scale distributed memory architectures have been used in the domain of high-performance computing (HPC) for decades and are covered by other literature [6].

3.1.2 Many-core programming models

Parallel computing resources can either be used by a vast number of independent applications or by parallel applications that are aimed to exploit the hardware parallelism to solve a problem faster.

At a first glance, it does not seem to be necessary to execute independent applications on a many-core system. However, running a few powerful servers instead of myriads of dedicated small machines is much more economical, as hardware utilization can be optimized. Virtualization technology [7] is often used to manage such systems, which not only supports live migration and high availability but also guarantees strong isolation between workloads of different users. Virtualization technology thus became the basis of cloud computing [7].

Parallel programs are designed according to a parallel programming model. Such models are abstract. They hide the details of the real hardware and the underlying OS from the programmer. However, a good match of programming model and execution platform helps to achieve high performance. A programming model can be either control-flow-oriented or data-flow-oriented. Figure 3.1

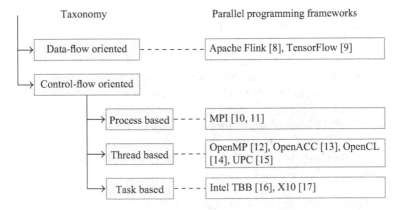

Figure 3.1   State-of-the-art frameworks for parallel programming

gives an overview on different state-of-the-art parallel programming frameworks and their underlying programming model. Data-flow programs are described as a graph of nodes with multiple input and output edges, which implement calculations on data streams. The nodes can be mapped naturally on the compute nodes of distributed memory machines or be run on cores with shared memory. Control-flow-oriented programs are not that flexible. For example, process-based parallel programming frameworks such as MPI assume a separate address space for each program instance, which means that the capability to share data between nodes is not used. The thread-based approaches, on the other hand, assume a shared memory, and cannot be used in a distributed memory environment. A popular new model is task-based parallel programming, which organizes work in short-lived asynchronously executed control flow entities. Creation and synchronization of these tasks is more efficient and therefore more scalable than the equivalent operations with threads.

3.1.3   Operating system challenges

OSs for many-core systems with shared memory or for hybrid system architectures are presented with the following new challenges:

Synchronization bottlenecks: Early Linux kernels have shown that the OS can become a bottleneck on multicore computers. To avoid this problem, different OS structures and internal synchronization mechanisms had to be explored.

Memory architectures: NUMA architectures with many cores and complex cache hierarchies add another level of complexity to the resource management within an OS and also offer opportunities for optimization. For instance, threads and their data should ideally be placed close to each other.

Core partitioning: The availability of a vast number of cores raises the question how to assign processor cores to software functions, such as OS components and application threads. The possibilities range between classic single-OS architectures and treating the many-core system as an on-chip compute cluster with arbitrary OSs on each node.

Heterogeneous computing: GPUs and other accelerators add unconventional cores to the systems. To maximize performance and to guarantee fair resource multiplexing, these cores should be under OS control behind an easy-to-use API.

Energy management: Balancing the power consumption on a many-core chip is a crucial new requirement, which is necessary to avoid overheating and thus throttling of the CPU.

Reliability: With billions of transistors and many CPU cores on a huge die, the probability of a failure is increasing. A modern many-core OS must be able to handle hardware faults and keep the system up and running for as long as possible.

In the remainder of this chapter, we will address these challenges in more detail and describe proposed solutions from the OS research community.

3.2 Kernel-state synchronization bottleneck

From a user's point of view, an increased number of CPU cores should lead to a proportional improvement in application performance. However, this "scalability" is restricted by the proportion of execution time that cannot benefit from the parallel computing resources. Unfortunately, this happens, for instance, when application processes enter a traditional monolithic OS kernel—such as Linux—and try to access shared kernel state. In this situation, proper synchronization must be enforced to avoid race conditions.

Early versions of Linux synchronized their whole kernel state with only one multiprocessor lock. This design was simple and correct but led to bad scalability even on systems with only four CPU cores if the applications frequently used OS services [18], because concurrency within the kernel was restricted to only one core. Over the years, more fine-grained locking for individual kernel data structures was introduced. This allowed cores to execute more kernel code in parallel and reduced the average waiting times when acquiring a lock. However, fine-grained locking also comes at a cost: for one OS service many locks have to be acquired—even in situations where there is no other core trying to access the same data structure.

The most basic kernel-level synchronization abstraction for multicore systems is the *spinlock*. Simple spinlocks are just shared Boolean variables that are atomically set to *true* when the lock is acquired and returned to *false* upon release. If a spinlock is already taken, one has to wait actively in a loop until it becomes *false* and try again. An issue of using this method is that it creates substantial load on the memory system. A study by Boyd-Wickizer *et al.* showed that Linux spinlocks could affect the system performance to such an extent that the overall performance degraded with an increasing number of processors [19]. A superior alternative are so-called scalable locks that try to reduce the access rate on shared lock objects [20]. One example is the *MCS lock* [20], which uses a queue for threads that are waiting for an acquisition of the lock. If an *MCS lock* is requested, a per-thread lock object is atomically added to the end of the queue. The object is a thread-local variable. Therefore, the load on the memory system is reduced. An enhanced version of the *MCS lock* is the Hierarchical CLH Queue lock that takes NUMA systems into account by reducing the internode communication through node-local and global lists. It could be demonstrated that this leads to considerable performance gains in Linux [19].

An alternative to the aforementioned synchronization techniques are *lock-free* synchronization mechanisms. These are ingenious algorithms for accessing data structures concurrently without risking damage [21]. They are solely based on atomic memory operations and do not rely on locks. Therefore, better scalability on many-core systems can be achieved. A disadvantage of lock-free synchronization is that the algorithms tend to be complex and hard to understand. This can result in erroneous confidence and, thus, data corruption unless they are carefully verified. Lock-free synchronization is typically used only for non-complex data structures such as linked lists for which a formal verification is feasible. The synthesis OS [22] was pioneering the integration of lock-free synchronization and, thereby, reduced the synchronization overhead and increased concurrency. It only required that the hardware provides a one and double word atomic compare-and-swap instruction.

Modern multiprocessor synchronization mechanisms typically combine lock-free algorithms with classic spinlocking. *Read-copy-update (RCU) locks*, for instance, are able to update locked data without affecting ongoing readers by changing only a copy, which is reintegrated later. Only concurrent writes require a spinlock [23]. An extension of the *RCU locks* are the *read-log-update (RLU) locks* allowing multiple concurrent readers and writers [24]. The algorithm works by keeping per thread object logs of manipulations. *RLU locks* scale better than *RCU locks* on systems with more than eight processor cores. However, RLU is quite complex and has an overhead in cases with low contention. A study done by David *et al.* revealed that there is no locking method that fits all use cases. Different hardware properties such as the distribution of memory controllers, interconnects of the processor cores, hierarchy of the cache system and even the distribution of shared cache memory cells have a strong impact on the performance of a lock [25].

3.3   Non-uniform memory access

Many-core systems often provide a shared memory based on a ccNUMA architecture. In order to utilize the full potential of the hardware platform, a many-core OS must be aware of the topology and typical memory-access latencies [26]. Based on that information, the placement of processes and data must be optimized at runtime. The cache coherence protocols, which make sure that a memory modification by one core does not get unnoticed by the others, significantly contribute to the traffic on the on-chip interconnect and, thus, has a negative impact on the performance. It has been shown that software in general and especially the OS can influence this traffic [27].

Traditionally, the focus of NUMA-aware OS optimizations was set on avoiding transfer delays caused by memory distance. However, modern systems have quite fast interconnects, and recent work in this area shows that the congestion due to con-currently accessed shared resources, such as memory controllers or the interconnect itself, has a bigger impact on the system performance [28]. For example, multi-threaded applications, which make multiple cores access a shared memory region, can cause heavy traffic on the respective parts of the interconnect and the memory controller. It turned out that for this kind of application, interleaved memory pages provide better performance, because the traffic on the interconnect is more balanced and the bandwidth of more memory controllers can be used. Four page allocation methods were proposed: the most intuitive one is *page colocation* where the memory page resides on the NUMA node running the accessing thread. This allocation tech-nique will only work efficiently for unshared data. Another allocation technique is *page interleaving* that evenly distributes pages across the NUMA nodes accessing the data. This works well for shared data applications as bottlenecks are prevented. Fur-thermore, *page replication* allows to replicate pages to the NUMA nodes accessing them. This method can result in huge performance increases if done right, e.g., read-only data shared across an application, but it can also result in a huge performance regression, because this method is a coherence protocol on the software-level [28]. The last proposed technique is *thread clustering* that does not move the data across the NUMA nodes but tries to cluster threads to the data. An evaluation of the algorithms in a Linux-based prototype shows that a reduction of interconnect traffic can result in a performance increase by a factor of 3.6 for best case scenarios and not more than 4 percent performance regression for worst case scenarios [28].

3.4   Core partitioning and management

The availability of many cores directly leads to the question of how they should be assigned to software functions, namely, OS instances, OS components and application tasks.

3.4.1   Single OS approaches

Besides optimizing existing OSs, new systems for the many-core era are getting designed. *Corey* OS [29] was one of the first. In contrast to many existing OSs, *Corey* follows the essential design principle to avoid sharing of kernel data between cores wherever possible. For this purpose and to avoid disturbance of applications by "OS noise," *Corey* does not support time multiplexing. This means that application threads and OS functions are executed on dedicated cores. In consequence, applications have to adapt dynamically to the number of available cores. To minimize the amount of shared data, each core can have its own lightweight network protocol stack using a physical or virtualized NIC. If application threads require sharing of data, explicit permission by the OS must be granted.

The *Factored OS (fos)* [30] shares some of the ideas of *Corey* by also not including time multiplexing. On the conceptual level, applications and OS services are isolated *Servers* that only communicate via a message passing interface. This hardware-independent interface could be realized with shared memory as well as an on-chip network interface. Requests to *Servers* are inherently serialized in message queues. Therefore, *Servers* can be implemented without additional synchronization mechanisms.

This concept is similar to distributed computing, a concept that has also been applied in the *Barrelfish* OS [31], which has been designed for future heterogeneous and many-core processors. The key idea of the OS is that many-core processors resemble distributed computers and all communication should be explicit via messages, and no shared OS state should exist to prevent contention on shared data and locks. Instead, each core runs its own OS instance with a replicated, hardware-independent state. This approach is called *Multikernel* [31]. Keeping the replicated state consistent causes some overhead, but the authors claim that this is outweighed by performance improvements during normal operation.

The OSs *Akaros* and *Tessellation* are designed to improve efficiency of many-core systems [32,33]. One of the key ideas is that applications should get more control over the resources they are using. Therefore, applications are gang-scheduled in the so-called *many-core processes* (MCP), called *Cells* in *Tessellation OS*, that consist of multiple hardware threads. A two-level scheduling allows applications to schedule their threads within an *MCP* or *cell*. This gives applications better control over their parallelism as they can continue doing work while waiting for I/O operations or other asynchronous system services to complete.

3.4.2 Multiple OS approaches

An alternative to single OS approaches is to run multiple independent OSs on one system. This can result in less interference on shared resources and better utilization of processor cores.

For most hardware platforms, running multiple OSs at the same time can be easily achieved by using virtualization [7]. However, virtual machines can suffer from bad scalability in the same way as applications on ccNUMA processors if they are not placed correctly in NUMA regions. For example, studies have shown that performance of virtual machines can degrade over time due to a complex two-level memory management (hypervisor and virtualized OS) [34,35] and resulting bad page locality across NUMA nodes. Hypervisors usually hide NUMA details from the guest system prohibiting the OS to optimize memory allocation for the underlying NUMA hierarchy. This can lead to a performance degradation of 82 percent. This could be mitigated by exposing NUMA details to the VM. Even better results are achieved if VMs do not span multiple NUMA nodes [34].

One framework that tries to avoid bad memory placement is *Virtualization Technologies for Application-Specific Operating Systems* (VT-ASOS) that utilizes the Xen project [36] to partition many-core processors [37]. The framework allows application developers to request specific properties, such as physical processor cores or some guaranteed memory. The requests are handed down to the virtual machine monitor (VMM). Furthermore, the framework allows the application to specify its preferred scheduling strategy. With this knowledge, the VMM is able to optimize the memory placement in NUMA regions or to reduce cache competition of VMs [38].

SHIMOS (Single Hardware with Independent Multiple Operating Systems) is a mechanism to run multiple OS without virtualization [39]. The advantage of this solution, in contrast to virtualization, is the independence of the hardware architecture. Therefore, this method could be applied to almost any many-core architecture. The guest system needs modification though to be able to run side-by-side with other OS instances. In contrast to virtualization, processor cores are not shared between virtual machines but are dedicated to one OS instance resulting in better performance, especially for I/O-intensive tasks. The performance of the SHIMOS system is competitive with that of a native Linux execution [39].

A lightweight virtualization solution called *OSV* is an alternative to *SHIMOS*. It executes one OS per NUMA node with very little code modification to the guest system [40]. Each VM runs on one NUMA node with physical core and memory access and only very little resource sharing, e.g., interrupt management. Device drivers are running in a privileged OS instance that provides access to devices via "standard distribution protocols," e.g., the network file system for storage [41]. Communication of virtual machines is done via virtual Ethernet devices for communication with the outside world and virtual sockets for communication between virtual machines.

Both, SHIMOS and OSV, rely on the trustworthiness of the guest OSs. For example, processor and memory isolation is done in OSV by manipulating the BIOS tables, which are used by the guest system during startup. A malware-infected guest kernel could easily break the isolation.

3.5   Integration of heterogeneous computing resources

It is still unclear whether future many-core systems will have a homogeneous or a heterogeneous system architecture. Mixing general purpose CPU cores with smaller or more specialized cores can have a positive effect on energy efficiency and performance. A strong indicator for a trend toward heterogeneous many-core systems is the structure of the Sunway SW26010 processor, which has been used to build today's fastest and extremely energy efficient super computer (see Table 3.1). Each of its four "core groups" consists of one general purpose core and 64 so-called computing processing elements (CPEs) [5]. A CPE is a powerful 64-bit RISC core. However, it does not even provide a user-mode/supervisor-mode separation, which means that it is intended for heavy computations, but not for executing a full OS.

For platforms like the SW26010, it would make sense to run a *light-weight kernel* (LWK) on each CPE and a full-weight kernel (FWK) on the general purpose core, because "number-crunching" application tasks on CPEs typically do not require complex system services—OS-overhead could be reduced.

One of the first OSs that has provided an LWK *and* an FWK was *FusedOS* [42]. The idea behind FusedOS is to integrate power-efficient cores (PECs) and single-thread-optimized-cores within one runtime environment. For the FWK FusedOS used the Linux kernel. Their LWK is the CNK OS [43], which is especially designed for HPC applications with very little noise and jitter. FusedOS allows computational intense applications to run on the PECs without a shared memory interface but with very high performance. When system services are needed, the LWK relays the request to the FWK. Although being designed for HPC applications, the idea behind FusedOS could be used for other heterogeneous systems, such as CPU/GPGPU combinations, as well.

Based on the same idea, Shimosawa *et al.* developed a generalized interface for heterogeneous kernels [44]. In their terminology, a "master kernel" is the OS that takes control over the startup of the device and that manages global resources. "Slave kernels" are small kernels that are started by the master kernel on demand. The communication between kernels is done over a message passing interface. In their implementation for the Xeon Phi platform, the authors used a modified Linux kernel as master and the minimal McKernel [45] for slaves. This software architecture provides the full range of complex system services and an overhead-free execution of compute-intensive tasks without the typical temporal "noise" that a fully fledged OS can cause.

The common management of heterogeneous computing resources is more difficult if they require using different programming models. GPUs, for instance, are processors that are designed to execute code in a highly parallel SIMD manner. They are usually programmed via user-space frameworks such as OpenCL [46] or CUDA [47]. Sequential application code running on the host CPU executes parallel parts on the GPU.

A disadvantage of this software architecture is that the OS does not have full control over GPU resources. One negative consequence is, for instance, that the OS cannot guarantee that the scheduling of GPU resources does not conflict with the CPU scheduling strategy. Furthermore, the OS cannot use the GPU for its own compute-intensive tasks. To address the first problem, researchers are looking into a common model of computation that can be used for CPUs as well as for GPUs and that allows the OS to make optimized scheduling decisions. Rossbach *et al.* came up with *PTasks* [48]. Each PTask is a node in a data-flow graph that can either be scheduled on the GPU or the CPU in a fine-grained manner. *Gdev* [49] addresses the second problem: the authors argue that an OS could substantially benefit from using a GPU and demonstrate this with a prototypical implementation of an encrypted filesystem within an OS. Using GPU acceleration they achieved a speedup of $2\times$.

3.6   Reliability challenges

The trend toward many-core chips led to huge dies and extreme structural densities ("nanoscale technology"). At the same time—in order to keep heat production under control—the supply voltage must be kept at a minimum. In combination, this increases the probability of *transient hardware faults*, such as bit flips induced by cosmic particle strikes [50]. Furthermore, the active chip regions are exposed to high thermal stress, which is known to lead to aging effects, which means earlier *permanent hardware faults*.

It is possible to tackle the reliability challenge purely on the hardware level. For instance, RAM can be equipped with the widely used SEC-DED ECC or the more expensive and energy-hungry chipkill ECC [51]. Many-core CPUs could have spare cores that would replace cores with a permanent failure [52] when necessary. However, based on real measurements on two supercomputers, Sridharan *et al.* predict that this will not be sufficient to keep overall system error rates at the same level [53]. Therefore, researchers are now looking into *software-implemented hardware fault tolerance* (SIHFT) measures, which are more flexible and thus possibly more economic. OS mechanisms that tackle the reliability challenge will never be able to guarantee failure-free operation, but certain measures are able to reduce the failure probability significantly. In the following sections, we will have a deeper look into recently proposed SIHFT mechanisms for many-core OSs to handle both transient and permanent hardware faults.

3.6.1 OS measures against transient faults

Transient faults can have very different effects: they alter the system's state, lead to invalid results of machine instructions, trigger traps or spurious interrupts, or even crash the system. Not all of these affects can be detected and corrected on the software level. Nevertheless, software-based mechanisms have the potential to improve reliability significantly.

The Romain extension of the L4 μ-kernel OS [54] provides a transparent mechanism for N-modular redundancy for user-level applications. The replica are distributed on process-level across available CPU cores. By monitoring all process interactions, such as system calls, IPC and events signaled by the OS, Romain can detect behavioral deviations with a voter and copy the state of a correct replica over the wrong one to correct the error. With this approach, a many-core OS can trade the available compute power for reliability, especially for mission-critical applications, in a transparent manner.

This could be combined with the approach by Li *et al.* [55] who recently proposed a mathematical model and algorithms for calculating optimized process-to-core mappings. This model takes into account that different CPU cores typically have individual error rates due to manufacturing variations and environmental conditions.

Most research papers on dependability assume that the underlying OS kernel works correctly—including the ones mentioned so far. However, the goal should be to minimize this "reliable computing base" [56]. Pioneer work toward reliable OS kernels was conducted already in 2003 with Nooks OS [57], which is a mechanism for reliably extending an OS kernel. Nooks extensions are isolated and interact with the kernel only via a dedicated API. Invalid interactions are detected. In this case, a user-mode recovery agent decides on how to recover from the fault. As an example, the authors have isolated Linux device drivers, which can be restarted in case of a misbehavior.

The C^3 system [58] comes even closer to the goal of detecting and recovering from kernel-level faults. This is achieved by using a component-based OS kernel instead of a monolithic kernel such as Linux. Components, for example, the scheduler and the memory manager, only interact via well-defined interfaces. These interactions are tracked by C^3 including the current component state so that it can be restored in the case of an error. Drawbacks of the approach are that it assumes "the fault will be detected immediately," that is, there are no silent data corruptions, and that the recovery functionality itself is reliable. The OSIRIS OS [59] has a similar approach in the sense that it can recover from faults in fine-grained OS "compartments". It has a lightweight checkpointing mechanism and achieves a very good ratio between resource consumption and reliability improvements by recovering only in cases where it can be conservatively inferred that performing local recovery will not lead to global state inconsistencies. Borchert *et al.* have shown how lightweight error detection and recovery mechanisms can be implemented on the OS level efficiently with aspect-oriented programming language extensions [60].

3.6.2   OS measures against permanent faults

Permanent failure of CPU cores often does not come completely unexpected. In many cases, it is a consequence of an aging process, which is caused by thermal stress in very active chip regions. The OS can mitigate this effect and, thus, extend the lifetime of the CPU cores by reliability-aware task-to-core mapping.

Haghbayan *et al.* therefore argue that *a paradigm shift from the conventional performance-centric runtime resource management to performance-reliability co-management is inevitable in many-core systems* [61]. They propose a software architecture with two layers: Layer 1 is responsible for long-term monitoring of each core for estimating its aging status. Layer 2 performs a short-term mapping of runnable tasks to cores and thereby balances between workload performance and the system's reliability in order to meet the required lifetime target.

For long-running threads or processes, the approach by Haghbayan would have to be extended by a mechanism for dynamic migration. Rauchfuss *et al.* achieved this goal with their prototypical tiled many-core architecture, which supports hardware virtualization. Here each node runs a VMM, which is able to halt, migrate and resume any virtual machine running on top [62].

3.7   Energy management

Every processor has a so-called thermal design power (TDP). It is an upper bound for the power flowing into the processor and needed by manufacturers to dimension the power supply system and the cooling infrastructure. Therefore, typical objectives of OS-level power management are to cap the power (at TDP) and to make sure that a certain processor temperature is not exceeded. Besides this, *balancing* power—and thus the temperature—on a many-core chip has certain advantages: it reduces aging of cores by minimizing thermal stress (see also Section 3.6) and avoids situations in which single cores have to be throttled, because their individual temperature exceeds an upper limit. Furthermore, energy consumption should be minimized in general. This is possible, for instance, if it is known for a particular application that a certain performance loss is acceptable.

3.7.1   Hardware mechanisms

There are various power-management mechanisms available on modern processors that can be controlled by the system software:

Clock gating (CG) and power gating (PG): These are two techniques for halting and shutting down an on-chip component. CG has the advantage over PG that the component retains its state while it is halted and, thus, can be restarted quickly. However, even in a halted component, there are leakage currents. This can be avoided with PG. Typically these techniques are controlled via "sleep modes," which halt or shut down more or less components on the chip.

Dynamic voltage and frequency scaling (DVFS): As the voltage has a quadratic influence on the power consumption, a combination of voltage and frequency scaling can save energy if a computation does not need to run at full speed or would be slowed down by other effects, such as many cache misses, anyway.

Boost: Heating up a processor takes some time. Therefore, some processors support short intervals of high power consumption (higher than TDP). Intel and AMD, for instance, call this feature Turbo Boost and Turbo CORE, respectively.

Temperature monitoring: Processors that support DVFS typically also have one or more integrated temperature sensors. This gives the hardware the ability to throttle cores in critical situations and a software interface allows the OS to implement a power-management strategy based on the aforementioned mechanisms.

Many-core processors also have these features. In a visionary paper from 2007, Shekhar Borkar from Intel proposed that each core of a 1,000-core processor should be capable of individual voltage and frequency scaling [63]. However, in order to simplify the design, he proposed that only three frequencies (0, f/2 and f) and two voltage levels ($V_{CC}/2$, V_{CC}) should be supported. With this number of cores, it would still allow for a very fine-grained power management. Later, Intel presented its Single Chip Cloud Computer (SCC) with 48 cores on a single die [64], which probably reflects future power management hardware more adequate: On the SCC, there is an on-chip mesh network that connects 24 tiles with 2 cores each. Every tile is a "frequency domain." This means that there are 24 "islands" with potentially different clock speeds on the chip, but the two cores on a tile always run at the same speed. It can be scaled in 16 steps between 100 MHz and 1.6 GHz. Voltage scaling is implemented with course-grained "voltage domains" of 8 cores each. External voltage regulators allow for dynamic V_{CC} scaling from 1.3 to 0 V in 6.25 mV steps. Even though each core has a separate temperature sensor, the OS-level power management cannot control each core individually but has to take the additional constraints imposed by voltage and frequency domains into account. Nevertheless, power management in many-core systems is complex due to a large solution space. Typically, the hardware monitors and enforces safety limits, but the OS is responsible for power saving, dealing with task privileges, and performance optimization by avoiding throttling. In order to be effective, these OS mechanisms need full control over power-management hardware. Therefore, approaches that put power management into the hands of applications, such as [65], are rare.

3.7.2 OS-level power management

One of the early pioneer works on balancing the power consumption between cores on a multicore or many-core processor was presented by Merkel *et al.* [66]. The authors used on-chip performance counters, e.g., the number of cache misses or page faults, to estimate energy profiles for each running process. The Linux scheduler was extended in a way that "hot tasks" are migrated to "cold cores" and vice versa. Thereby, the power consumption is distributed more evenly over the cores. Measurements showed that throttling was avoided in some situations. This led to performance gains, especially with mixed workloads of hot and cold tasks.

Haghbayan *et al.* [67] took a slightly different approach to the problem of dynamically mapping application tasks to cores: their primary design goals was to avoid violation of the TDP constraint. Second, they wanted to make sure that even with fine-grained DVFS, real-time and soft real-time tasks will finish in time. The authors have realized that dynamic power management leads to the development of a control loop. If not designed properly, this could have negative effects such as oscillations in the system. Therefore, they implemented a *Proportional Integral Derivative* (PID) controller for actuator manipulation. Its output can be intuitively interpreted as the urgency to change the system's state. With the PID controller, this value is always well balanced—the system does not overreact.

As an extension to Haghbayan's work, Martins *et al.* [68] have recently presented a control-loop-based approach that handles groups of cores in a distributed manner and thus improves scalability. Furthermore, they provided an excellent overview of related works in this domain.

3.7.3   Reducing the algorithmic complexity

The more cores a system has, the more difficult it becomes to make a coordinated power management decision quickly. This could at some point become a bottleneck. Therefore, several research groups have addressed dynamic task-to-core mapping strategies and ways to find optimized power-management settings from the algorithmic perspective. While most dynamic placement algorithms solve the problem in polynomial time, e.g. [69], some achieve linear or even sublinear time complexity.

Liu *et al.* start from a queuing model and derive two fast algorithms that jointly operate CPU and memory DVFS [70]. Both algorithms have linear time complexity in the number of cores.[1] In their simplified system model, the authors assume N cores issuing requests to K memory banks (after a cache miss). To return the fetched data access to a common bus is needed. After that, a core is calculating for some "think time" z_i, using the cache for a time c_i and the cycle restarts. While N and K are fixed system parameters, z_i and c_i are determined at runtime with the help of performance counters. Global average queue lengths for accessing the memory banks and the bus are assumed. Based on this strongly simplified model, the necessary equations for calculating optimal DVFS performance scaling factors can be solved easily. Despite the simplifications, the authors show that the approach is effective and that their model is accurate enough.

A novel way to approach the performance problem of task-mapping algorithms was proposed by Fattah *et al.* with their Smart Hill Climbing (SHiC) [71]. Instead of trying to calculate the optimal solution, they propose a heuristic based on stochastic hill climbing, which achieves a remarkably low time complexity of $O(\sqrt{N})$.

3.8   Conclusions and future directions

More many-core processors are becoming commercially available. The hardware development goes on very fast as evidenced by the presentation of a 1,000-core processor in mid-2016 [72]. This growing availability combined with many open

---

[1] $O(N \cdot \log M)$ and $O(N \cdot M)$, where N is number of cores and M the number of memory DVFS frequency levels (constant).

research questions inspires a lot of activity in the OS research community. In this chapter, we have presented a survey on recent work.

Many new ideas have already been explored. For example, one particular challenge is the *state synchronization bottleneck*. It is caused by heavy lock contention when OS threads running on different cores are synchronized to avoid race conditions [18,19]. Novel OS architectures such as the multikernel approach implement a replication of the OS state and therefore shift the problem to a controllable replication [31]. A different approach is to depend on *lock-free* synchronization mechanisms, which avoids the problem by construction [21]. The high complexity of lock-free synchronization spawned hybrid approaches that combine both traditional lock based and more modern lock-free techniques [23,24].

Core partitioning is another key challenge. The abundance of cores leads to the difficult question on how to assign them to software components. Basically two approaches exist. The more traditional solution is the *single OS* approach where all cores are managed by one OS. Special designs tailored for many-core processors have been proposed, e.g., Corey [29], fos [30], Barrelfish [31], Akaros [32] and Tessellation [33]. Alternatively, *multi OS* architectures run multiple OS instances on different cores. This could, for example, be achieved by leveraging virtualization techniques [36,40]. In many usage scenarios, such as cloud computing on many-core systems, this is beneficial, as unnecessary resource sharing is avoided.

There are also unexplored areas left. For example, efforts have been made to optimize the placement of application and OS activities on processor cores with detailed knowledge of the complex memory and interconnect structures of modern ccNUMA and NUCA architectures [3,26–28]. This is inherently difficult and requires runtime adaption mechanisms if the many-core OS has limited knowledge about the application's future behavior, which is the case for the traditional thread-based programming model. Therefore, looking into a combination of optimized activity placement with other *programming models* seems worthwhile.

Furthermore, *heterogeneous system architectures* are becoming more prevalent [5]. OS support for such systems, however, is still rudimentary, but work on the integration of heterogeneous computing resources has been done [42,44]. Improving the situation would require an effort not only on the OS layer but would also affect the programming model, development tools and language runtimes.

Reliability is another area of research that will become more relevant in the next years, as the trend toward many-core systems has just begun. The same holds for *energy management*. Here, more work can be expected on the management of heterogeneous architectures. Besides this, the underlying models have to become more realistic. For instance, they should consider voltage and frequency domains of arbitrary granularity.

References

[1]   Moore G. Cramming More Components onto Integrated Circuits. Electronics Magazine. 1965;38(8):114.

[2]   Iwai H. CMOS Scaling for Sub-90 nm to Sub-10 nm. In: 17th International Conference on VLSI Design. Proceedings; 2004. p. 30–35.

[3]   Huh J, Kim C, Shafi H, *et al.* A NUCA Substrate for Flexible CMP Cache Sharing. IEEE Transactions on Parallel and Distributed Systems. 2007;18(8):1028–1040.

[4]   Hewlett Packard Enterprise. HPE Superdome Flex Server Architecture and RAS; 2017. Available from: https://www.hpe.com/h20195/v2/getpdf. aspx/a00036491enw.pdf?ver=1.0.

[5]   Dongarra J. Report on the Sunway TaihuLight System. University of Tennessee, Oak Ridge National Laboratory; 2016.

[6]   Nitzberg B, Lo V. Distributed Shared Memory: A Survey of Issues and Algorithms. Computer. 1991;24(8):52–60.

[7]   Smith JE, Nair R. Virtual Machines: Versatile Platforms for Systems and Processes. ProQuest Ebook Central. Morgan Kaufmann Publishers; 2005.

[8]   Carbone P, Katsifodimos A, Ewen S, *et al.* Apache Flink: Stream and Batch Processing in a Single Engine. IEEE Data Engineering Bulletin. 2015;38:28–38.

[9]   Abadi M, Barham P, Chen J, *et al.* TensorFlow: A System for Large-scale Machine Learning. In: Proceedings of the 12th USENIX Conference on Operating Systems Design and Implementation. OSDI'16. Berkeley, CA, USA: USENIX Association; 2016. p. 265–283.

[10]   Snir M, Otto S, Huss-Lederman S, *et al.* MPI-The Complete Reference, Volume 1: The MPI Core. 2nd ed. Cambridge, MA, USA: MIT Press; 1998.

[11]   Gropp W, Lusk E, Doss N, *et al.* A High-Performance, Portable Implementation of the MPI Message Passing Interface Standard. Parallel Computing. 1996;22(6):789–828.

[12]   Dagum L, Menon R. OpenMP: An Industry Standard API for Shared-Memory Programming. IEEE Computational Science and Engineering. 1998;5(1):46–55.

[13]   OpenACC-Standard org. The OpenACC Application Programming Interface, Version 2.6; 2017. Available from: https://www.openacc.org/sites/ default/files/inline-files/OpenACC.2.6.final.pdf.

[14]   Khronos Group. The OpenCL Specification, Version 2.0; 2015. Available from: https://www.khronos.org/registry/cl/specs/opencl-2.0.pdf.

[15]   UPC Consortium. UPC Language Specifications, Version 1.3. Lawrence Berkeley National Lab Tech Report LBNL-6623E; 2013. Available from: http://upc-lang.org.

[16]   Reinders J. Intel Threading Building Blocks. 1st ed. Sebastopol, CA, USA: O'Reilly & Associates, Inc.; 2007.

[17]   Charles P, Grothoff C, Saraswat V, *et al.* X10: An Object-Oriented Approach to Non-uniform Cluster Computing. In: Proceedings of the 20th Annual ACM SIGPLAN Conference on Object-Oriented Programming, Systems, Languages, and Applications. OOPSLA'05. New York, NY, USA: ACM; 2005. p. 519–538.

[18]   Bryant R, Hawkes J. Linux Scalability for Large NUMA Systems. In: Proceedings of the Linux Symposium; 2003. p. 76.

[19] Boyd-Wickizer S, Kaashoek MF, Morris R, *et al.* Non-scalable locks are dangerous. In: Proceedings of the Linux Symposium; 2012. p. 119–130.

[20] Mellor-Crummey JM, Scott ML. Algorithms for Scalable Synchronization on Shared-Memory Multiprocessors. ACM Transactions on Computer Systems. 1991;9(1):21–65.

[21] Herlihy M, Shavit N. The Art of Multiprocessor Programming. Morgan Kaufmann; 2011.

[22] Massalin H, Pu C. A Lock-Free Multiprocessor OS Kernel. ACM SIGOPS Operating Systems Review. 1992;26(2):108.

[23] McKenney PE, Slingwine JD. Read-copy Update: Using Execution History to Solve Concurrency Problems. In: Parallel and Distributed Computing and Systems; 1998. p. 509–518.

[24] Matveev A, Shavit N, Felber P, *et al.* Read-log-update: A Lightweight Synchronization Mechanism for Concurrent Programming. In: Proceedings of the 25th Symposium on Operating Systems Principles. SOSP'15. New York, NY, USA: ACM; 2015. p. 168–183.

[25] David T, Guerraoui R, Trigonakis V. Everything You Always Wanted to Know About Synchronization but Were Afraid to Ask. In: Proceedings of the Twenty-Fourth ACM Symposium on Operating Systems Principles. SOSP'13. New York, NY, USA: ACM; 2013. p. 33–48.

[26] Brecht T. On the Importance of Parallel Application Placement in NUMA Multiprocessors. In: Symposium on Experiences with Distributed and Multiprocessor Systems (SEDMS IV); 1993. p. 1–18.

[27] Caheny P, Casas M, Moretó M, *et al.* Reducing Cache Coherence Traffic with Hierarchical Directory Cache and NUMA-Aware Runtime Scheduling. In: 2016 International Conference on Parallel Architecture and Compilation Techniques (PACT); 2016. p. 275–286.

[28] Dashti M, Fedorova A, Funston J, *et al.* Traffic Management: A Holistic Approach to Memory Placement on NUMA Systems. In: Proceedings of the Eighteenth International Conference on Architectural Support for Programming Languages and Operating Systems. ASPLOS'13. New York, NY, USA: ACM; 2013. p. 381–394.

[29] Boyd-Wickizer S, Chen H, Chen R, *et al.* Corey: An Operating System for Many Cores. In: OSDI. vol. 8; 2008. p. 43–57.

[30] Wentzlaff D, Agarwal A. Factored Operating Systems (Fos): The Case for a Scalable Operating System for Multicores. SIGOPS Operating Systems Review. 2009;43(2):76–85.

[31] Baumann A, Barham P, Dagand PE, *et al.* The Multikernel: A New OS Architecture for Scalable Multicore Systems. In: Proceedings of the ACM SIGOPS 22nd Symposium on Operating Systems Principles. SOSP'09. New York, NY, USA: ACM; 2009. p. 29–44.

[32] Rhoden B, Klues K, Zhu D, *et al.* Improving Per-node Efficiency in the Datacenter with New OS Abstractions. In: Proceedings of the 2Nd ACM Symposium on Cloud Computing. SOCC'11. New York, NY, USA: ACM; 2011. p. 25:1–25:8.

[33]   Colmenares JA, Eads G, Hofmeyr S, *et al.* Tessellation: Refactoring the OS Around Explicit Resource Containers with Continuous Adaptation. In: Proceedings of the 50th Annual Design Automation Conference. DAC'13. New York, NY, USA: ACM; 2013. p. 76:1–76:10.

[34]   Ibrahim KZ, Hofmeyr S, Iancu C. Characterizing the Performance of Parallel Applications on Multi-socket Virtual Machines. In: 2011 11th IEEE/ACM International Symposium on Cluster, Cloud and Grid Computing; 2011. p. 1–12.

[35]   Ibrahim KZ, Hofmeyr S, Iancu C. The Case for Partitioning Virtual Machines on Multicore Architectures. IEEE Transactions on Parallel and Distributed Systems. 2014;25(10):2683–2696.

[36]   Barham P, Dragovic B, Fraser K, *et al.* Xen and the Art of Virtualization. In: Proceedings of the Nineteenth ACM Symposium on Operating Systems Principles. SOSP'03. New York, NY, USA: ACM; 2003. p. 164–177.

[37]   Back G, Nikolopoulos DS. Application-Specific System Customization on Many-Core Platforms: The VT-ASOS Framework Position Paper; 2007.

[38]   Nikolopoulos DS, Back G, Tripathi J, *et al.* VT-ASOS: Holistic System Software Customization for Many Cores. In: 2008 IEEE International Symposium on Parallel and Distributed Processing; 2008. p. 1–5.

[39]   Shimosawa T, Matsuba H, Ishikawa Y. Logical Partitioning without Architectural Supports. In: 2008 32nd Annual IEEE International Computer Software and Applications Conference; 2008. p. 355–364.

[40]   Dai Y, Qi Y, Ren J, *et al.* A Lightweight VMM on Many Core for High Performance Computing. In: Proceedings of the 9th ACM SIGPLAN/SIGOPS International Conference on Virtual Execution Environments. VEE'13. New York, NY, USA: ACM; 2013. p. 111–120.

[41]   Nowicki B. NFS: Network File System Protocol Specification; 1989.

[42]   Park Y, Hensbergen EV, Hillenbrand M, *et al.* FusedOS: Fusing LWK Performance with FWK Functionality in a Heterogeneous Environment. In: 2012 IEEE 24th International Symposium on Computer Architecture and High Performance Computing; 2012. p. 211–218.

[43]   Giampapa M, Gooding T, Inglett T, *et al.* Experiences with a Lightweight Supercomputer Kernel: Lessons Learned from Blue Gene's CNK. In: 2010 ACM/IEEE International Conference for High Performance Computing, Networking, Storage and Analysis; 2010. p. 1–10.

[44]   Shimosawa T, Gerofi B, Takagi M, *et al.* Interface for Heterogeneous Kernels: A Framework to Enable Hybrid OS Designs Targeting High Performance Computing on Manycore Architectures. In: 2014 21st International Conference on High Performance Computing (HiPC); 2014. p. 1–10.

[45]   Soma Y, Gerofi B, Ishikawa Y. Revisiting Virtual Memory for High Performance Computing on Manycore Architectures: A Hybrid Segmentation Kernel Approach. In: Proceedings of the 4th International Workshop on Runtime and Operating Systems for Supercomputers. ROSS'14. New York, NY, USA: ACM; 2014. p. 3:1–3:8.

[46]   Stone JE, Gohara D, Shi G. OpenCL: A Parallel Programming Standard for Heterogeneous Computing Systems. Computing in Science & Engineering. 2010;12(3):66–73.

[47]   Nickolls J, Buck I, Garland M, *et al.* Scalable Parallel Programming with CUDA. Queue – GPU Computing. 2008;6(2):40–53.

[48]   Rossbach CJ, Currey J, Silberstein M, *et al.* PTask: Operating System Abstractions to Manage GPUs as Compute Devices. In: Proceedings of the Twenty-Third ACM Symposium on Operating Systems Principles. SOSP'11. New York, NY, USA: ACM; 2011. p. 233–248.

[49]   Kato S, McThrow M, Maltzahn C, *et al.* Gdev: First-Class GPU Resource Management in the Operating System. In: Presented as Part of the 2012 USENIX Annual Technical Conference (USENIX ATC 12). Boston, MA: USENIX; 2012. p. 401–412.

[50]   Baumann R. Soft Errors in Advanced Computer Systems. IEEE Design & Test. 2005;22(3):258–266.

[51]   Dell TJ. A White Paper on the Benefits of Chipkill-Correct ECC for PC Server Main Memory. IBM Whitepaper; 1997.

[52]   Huang L, Xu Q. On Modeling the Lifetime Reliability of Homogeneous Manycore Systems. In: 2008 14th IEEE Pacific Rim International Symposium on Dependable Computing; 2008. p. 87–94.

[53]   Sridharan V, DeBardeleben N, Blanchard S, *et al.* Memory Errors in Modern Systems: The Good, The Bad, and The Ugly. In: Proceedings of the Twentieth International Conference on Architectural Support for Programming Languages and Operating Systems. ASPLOS'15. New York, NY, USA: ACM; 2015. p. 297–310.

[54]   Döbel B, Härtig H, Engel M. Operating System Support for Redundant Multithreading. In: Proceedings of the Tenth ACM International Conference on Embedded Software. EMSOFT'12. New York, NY, USA: ACM; 2012. p. 83–92.

[55]   Li HT, Chou CY, Hsieh YT, *et al.* Variation-Aware Reliable Many-Core System Design by Exploiting Inherent Core Redundancy. IEEE Transactions on Very Large Scale Integration (VLSI) Systems. 2017;25(10): 2803–2816.

[56]   Engel M, Döbel B. The Reliable Computing Base – A Paradigm for Software-based Reliability. In: Goltz U, Magnor MA, Appelrath HJ, *et al.*, editors. GI-Jahrestagung. vol. 208 of LNI. Bonn: Gesellschaft für Informatik e.V.; 2012. p. 480–493.

[57]   Swift MM, Bershad BN, Levy HM. Improving the Reliability of Commodity Operating Systems. In: Proceedings of the Nineteenth ACM Symposium on Operating Systems Principles. SOSP'03. New York, NY, USA: ACM; 2003. p. 207–222.

[58]   Song J, Wittrock J, Parmer G. Predictable, Efficient System-Level Fault Tolerance in C^3. In: 2013 IEEE 34th Real-Time Systems Symposium; 2013. p. 21–32.

[59]   Bhat K, Vogt D, van der Kouwe E, *et al.* OSIRIS: Efficient and Consistent Recovery of Compartmentalized Operating Systems. In: 2016 46th Annual IEEE/IFIP International Conference on Dependable Systems and Networks (DSN); 2016. p. 25–36.

[60]   Borchert C, Schirmeier H, Spinczyk O. Generative Software-based Memory Error Detection and Correction for Operating System Data Structures.

In: Proceedings of the 43rd IEEE/IFIP International Conference on Dependable Systems and Networks (DSN'13). Piscataway, NJ, USA: IEEE Press; 2013. p. 1–12.

[61]   Haghbayan MH, Miele A, Rahmani AM, *et al.* Performance/Reliability-Aware Resource Management for Many-Cores in Dark Silicon Era. IEEE Transactions on Computers. 2017;66(9):1599–1612.

[62]   Rauchfuss H, Wild T, Herkersdorf A. Enhanced Reliability in Tiled Manycore Architectures through Transparent Task Relocation. In: ARCS 2012; 2012. p. 1–6.

[63]   Borkar S. Thousand Core Chips: A Technology Perspective. In: Proceedings of the 44th Annual Design Automation Conference. DAC'07. New York, NY, USA: ACM; 2007. p. 746–749.

[64]   Howard J, Dighe S, Hoskote Y, *et al.* A 48-Core IA-32 Message-Passing Processor with DVFS in 45 nm CMOS. In: 2010 IEEE International Solid-State Circuits Conference – (ISSCC); 2010. p. 108–109.

[65]   Bortolotti D, Tinti S, Altoé P, *et al.* User-Space APIs for Dynamic Power Management in Many-Core ARMv8 Computing Nodes. In: 2016 International Conference on High Performance Computing Simulation (HPCS); 2016. p. 675–681.

[66]   Merkel A, Bellosa F. Balancing Power Consumption in Multiprocessor Systems. In: Proceedings of the 1st ACM SIGOPS/EuroSys European Conference on Computer Systems 2006. EuroSys'06. New York, NY, USA: ACM; 2006. p. 403–414.

[67]   Haghbayan MH, Rahmani AM, Weldezion AY, *et al.* Dark Silicon Aware Power Management for Manycore Systems Under Dynamic Workloads. In: 2014 IEEE 32nd International Conference on Computer Design (ICCD); 2014. p. 509–512.

[68]   Martins ALM, Sant'Ana AC, Moraes FG. Runtime Energy Management for Many-Core Systems. In: 2016 IEEE International Conference on Electronics, Circuits and Systems (ICECS); 2016. p. 380–383.

[69]   Pagani S, Khdr H, Munawar W, *et al.* TSP: Thermal Safe Power – Efficient Power Budgeting for Many-Core Systems in Dark Silicon. In: 2014 International Conference on Hardware/Software Codesign and System Synthesis (CODES+ISSS); 2014. p. 1–10.

[70]   Liu Y, Cox G, Deng Q, *et al.* Fast Power and Energy Management for Future Many-Core Systems. ACM Transactions on Modeling and Performance Evaluation of Computing Systems. 2017;2(3):17:1–17:31.

[71]   Fattah M, Daneshtalab M, Liljeberg P, *et al.* Smart Hill Climbing for Agile Dynamic Mapping in Many-core Systems. In: Proceedings of the 50th Annual Design Automation Conference. DAC'13. New York, NY, USA: ACM; 2013. p. 39:1–39:6.

[72]   Bohnenstiehl B, Stillmaker A, Pimentel J, *et al.* A 5.8 pJ/Op 115 Billion Ops/Sec, to 1.78 Trillion Ops/Sec 32nm 1000-Processor Array. In: 2016 IEEE Symposium on VLSI Circuits (VLSI-Circuits); 2016. p. 1–2.

Chapter 4

Decoupling the programming model from resource management in throughput processors

Nandita Vijaykumar[1], Kevin Hsieh[1], Gennady Pekhimenko[2], Samira Khan[3], Ashish Shrestha[1], Saugata Ghose[1], Adwait Jog[4], Phillip B. Gibbons[5], and Onur Mutlu[1,6]

This chapter introduces a new resource virtualization framework, *Zorua*, that *decouples* the graphics processing unit (GPU) programming model from the management of key on-chip resources in hardware to enhance programming ease, portability, and performance. The application resource specification—a static specification of several parameters such as the number of threads and the scratchpad memory usage per thread block—forms a critical component of the existing GPU programming models. This specification determines the parallelism, and, hence, performance of the application during execution because the corresponding on-chip hardware resources are allocated and managed purely based on this specification. This *tight coupling* between the software-provided resource specification and resource management in hardware leads to significant challenges in programming ease, portability, and performance, as we demonstrate in this chapter using real data obtained on state-of-the-art GPU systems.

Our goal in this work is to reduce the dependence of performance on the software-provided static resource specification to simultaneously alleviate the above challenges. To this end, we introduce Zorua, a new resource virtualization framework, that *decouples* the programmer-specified resource usage of a GPU application from the actual allocation in the on-chip hardware resources. Zorua enables this decoupling by *virtualizing* each resource transparently to the programmer.

The virtualization provided by Zorua builds on two key concepts—*dynamic allocation* of the on-chip resources and their *oversubscription* using a swap space in memory. Zorua provides a holistic GPU resource virtualization strategy designed to (i) adaptively *control the extent* of oversubscription and (ii) *coordinate* the dynamic management of multiple on-chip resources to maximize the effectiveness of virtualization.

[1] Electrical and Computer Engineering Department, Carnegie Mellon University, USA
[2] Computer Science Department, University of Toronto, Canada
[3] Computer Science Department, University of Virginia, USA
[4] Computer Science Department, College of William and Mary, USA
[5] Computer Science Department, Carnegie Mellon University, USA
[6] Information Technology and Electrical Engineering department, ETH Zürich, Switzerland

We demonstrate that by providing the illusion of more resources than physically available via controlled and coordinated virtualization, Zorua offers several important benefits: (i) **Programming ease.** It eases the burden on the programmer to provide code that is tuned to efficiently utilize the physically available on-chip resources. (ii) **Portability.** It alleviates the necessity of retuning an application's resource usage when porting the application across GPU generations. (iii) **Performance.** By dynamically allocating resources and carefully oversubscribing them when necessary, Zorua improves or retains the performance of applications that are already highly tuned to best utilize the resources. The holistic virtualization provided by Zorua has many other potential uses, e.g., fine-grained resource sharing among multiple kernels, low-latency preemption of GPU programs, and support for dynamic parallelism, which we describe in this chapter.

4.1   Introduction

Modern GPUs have evolved into powerful programmable machines over the last decade, offering high performance and energy efficiency for many classes of applications by concurrently executing thousands of threads. In order to execute, each thread requires several major on-chip resources: (i) registers, (ii) scratchpad memory (if used in the program), and (iii) a thread slot in the thread scheduler that keeps all the bookkeeping information required for execution.

Today, these hardware resources are *statically* allocated to threads based on several parameters—the number of threads per thread block, register usage per thread, and scratchpad usage per block. We refer to these static application parameters as the *resource specification* of the application. This resource specification forms a critical component of modern GPU programming models (e.g., CUDA [1], OpenCL [2]). The static allocation over a fixed set of hardware resources based on the software-specified resource specification creates a *tight coupling* between the program (and the programming model) and the physical hardware resources. As a result of this tight coupling, for each application, there are only a few optimized resource specifications that maximize resource utilization. Picking a suboptimal specification leads to under-utilization of resources and hence, very often, performance degradation. This leads to three key difficulties related to obtaining good performance on modern GPUs: programming ease, portability, and resource inefficiency (performance).

Programming ease. First, the burden falls upon the programmer to optimize the resource specification. For a naive programmer, this is a very challenging task [3–9]. This is because, in addition to selecting a specification suited to an algorithm, the programmer needs to be aware of the details of the GPU architecture to fit the specification to the underlying hardware resources. This *tuning* is easy to get wrong because there are *many* highly suboptimal performance points in the specification space, and even a minor deviation from an optimized specification can lead to a drastic drop in performance due to lost parallelism. We refer to such drops as *performance cliffs*. We analyze the effect of suboptimal specifications on real systems for 20 workloads (Section 4.3.1) and experimentally demonstrate that changing resource specifications can produce as much as a $5\times$ difference in performance due to the change in parallelism. Even a minimal change in the specification (and hence, the resulting allocation) of one resource can result in a significant performance cliff, degrading performance by as much as 50% (Section 4.3.1).

Portability. Second, different GPUs have varying quantities of each of the resources. Hence, an optimized specification on one GPU may be highly suboptimal on another. In order to determine the extent of this portability problem, we run 20 applications on three generations of NVIDIA GPUs: Fermi, Kepler, and Maxwell (Section 4.3.2). An example result demonstrates that highly tuned code for Maxwell or Kepler loses as much as 69% of its performance on Fermi. This lack of *portability* necessitates that the programmer *retune* the resource specification of the application for *every* new GPU generation. This problem is especially significant in virtualized environments, such as cloud or cluster computing, where the same program may run on a wide range of GPU architectures, depending on data center composition and hardware availability.

Performance. Third, for the programmer who chooses to employ software optimization tools (e.g., autotuners) or manually tailor the program to fit the hardware, performance is still constrained by the *fixed, static* resource specification. It is well known [10–16] that the on-chip resource requirements of a GPU application vary throughout execution. Since the program (even after auto-tuning) has to *statically* specify its *worst-case* resource requirements, severe *dynamic underutilization* of several GPU resources [10–14,17] ensues, leading to suboptimal performance (Section 4.3.3).

Our goal. To address these three challenges at the same time, we propose to *decouple* an application's resource specification from the available hardware resources by *virtualizing* all three major resources in a holistic manner. This virtualization provides the illusion of *more* resources to the GPU programmer and software than physically available and enables the runtime system and the hardware to *dynamically* manage multiple physical resources in a manner that is transparent to the programmer, thereby alleviating dynamic underutilization.

Virtualization is a concept that has been applied to the management of hardware resources in many contexts (e.g., [18–25]), providing various benefits. We believe that applying the general principle of virtualization to the management of *multiple* on-chip resources in GPUs offers the opportunity to alleviate several important challenges in modern GPU programming, which are described above. However, at the same time, effectively adding a new level of indirection to the management of multiple latency-critical GPU resources introduces several new challenges (see Section 4.4.1). This necessitates the design of a new mechanism to effectively address the new challenges and enable the benefits of virtualization. In this work, we introduce a new framework, *Zorua*,[1] to decouple the programmer-specified resource specification of an application from its physical on-chip hardware resource allocation by effectively virtualizing the multiple on-chip resources in GPUs.

---

[1] Named after a Pokémon [26] with the power of illusion, able to take different shapes to adapt to different circumstances (not unlike our proposed framework).

Key concepts. The virtualization strategy used by Zorua is built upon two key concepts. First, to mitigate performance cliffs when we do not have enough physical resources, we *oversubscribe* resources by a small amount at runtime, by leveraging their dynamic underutilization and maintaining a swap space (in main memory) for the extra resources required. Second, Zorua improves utilization by determining the runtime resource requirements of an application. It then allocates and deallocates resources dynamically, managing them (i) *independently* of each other to maximize their utilization and (ii) in a *coordinated* manner, to enable efficient execution of each thread with all its required resources available.

Challenges in virtualization. Unfortunately, oversubscription means that latency-critical resources, such as registers and scratchpad, may be swapped to memory at the time of access, resulting in high overheads in performance and energy. This leads to two critical challenges in designing a framework to enable virtualization. The first challenge is to effectively determine the *extent* of virtualization, i.e., by how much each resource appears to be larger than its physical amount, such that we can minimize oversubscription while still reaping its benefits. This is difficult as the resource requirements continually vary during runtime. The second challenge is to minimize accesses to the swap space. This requires *coordination* in the virtualized management of *multiple resources*, so that enough of each resource is available on-chip when needed.

Zorua . In order to address these challenges, Zorua employs a hardware-software codesign that comprises three components: (i) **the compiler** annotates the program to specify the resource needs of *each phase* of the application; (ii) **a runtime system**, which we refer to as the coordinator, uses the compiler annotations to dynamically manage the virtualization of the different on-chip resources; and (iii) **the hardware** employs mapping tables to locate a virtual resource in the physically available resources or in the swap space in main memory. The coordinator plays the key role of scheduling threads *only when* the expected gain in thread-level parallelism outweighs the cost of transferring oversubscribed resources from the swap space in memory and coordinates the oversubscription and allocation of multiple on-chip resources.

Key results. We evaluate Zorua with many resource specifications for eight applications across three GPU architectures (Section 4.7). Our experimental results show that Zorua (i) reduces the range in performance for different resource specifications by 50% on average (up to 69%), by alleviating performance cliffs, and hence eases the burden on the programmer to provide optimized resource specifications, (ii) improves performance for code with optimized specification by 13% on average (up to 28%), and (iii) enhances portability by reducing the maximum porting performance loss by 55% on average (up to 73%) for three different GPU architectures. We conclude that decoupling the resource specification and resource management via virtualization significantly eases programmer burden, by alleviating the need to provide optimized specifications and enhancing portability, while still improving or retaining performance for programs that already have optimized specifications.

Other uses. We believe that Zorua offers the opportunity to address several other key challenges in GPUs today, for example: (i) By providing a new level of indirection, Zorua provides a natural way to enable dynamic and fine-grained control over resource partitioning among *multiple GPU kernels and applications*. (ii) Zorua can be utilized for *low-latency preemption* of GPU applications, by leveraging the ability to swap in/out resources from/to memory in a transparent manner. (iii) Zorua provides a simple mechanism to provide dynamic resources to support other programming paradigms, such as nested parallelism, helper threads, and even system-level tasks. (iv) The dynamic resource management scheme in Zorua improves the energy efficiency and scalability of expensive on-chip resources (Section 4.8).

The main **contributions** of this work are as follows:

- This is the first work that takes a holistic approach to decoupling a GPU application's resource specification from its physical on-chip resource allocation via the use of virtualization. We develop a comprehensive virtualization framework that provides *controlled* and *coordinated* virtualization of *multiple* on-chip GPU resources to maximize the efficacy of virtualization.
- We show how to enable efficient oversubscription of multiple GPU resources with dynamic fine-grained allocation of resources and swapping mechanisms into/out of main memory. We provide a hardware–software cooperative framework that (i) controls the extent of oversubscription to make an effective trade-off between higher thread-level parallelism due to virtualization versus the latency and capacity overheads of swap space usage and (ii) coordinates the virtualization for multiple on-chip resources, transparently to the programmer.
- We demonstrate that by providing the illusion of having more resources than physically available, Zorua (i) reduces programmer burden, providing competitive performance for even suboptimal resource specifications, by reducing performance variation across different specifications and by alleviating performance cliffs; (ii) reduces performance loss when the program with its resource specification tuned for one GPU platform is ported to a different platform; and (iii) retains or enhances performance for highly tuned code by improving resource utilization, via dynamic management of resources.

4.2 Background

The GPU architecture. A GPU consists of multiple simple cores, also called *streaming multiprocessors* (SMs) in NVIDIA terminology or *compute units* (CUs) in AMD terminology. Each core contains a large register file, programmer-managed shared memory, and an L1 data cache. Each GPU core time multiplexes the execution of thousands of threads to hide long latencies due to memory accesses and ALU operations. The cores and memory controllers are connected via a crossbar and every memory controller is associated with a slice of a shared L2 cache. Every cycle, a set of threads, referred to as a *warp*, is executed in lockstep. If any warp is stalled on a long-latency operation, the scheduler swaps in a different warp for execution. Figure 4.1 depicts our baseline architecture with 15 SMs and 6 memory controllers. For more details on the internals of modern GPU architectures, we refer the reader to [27–30].

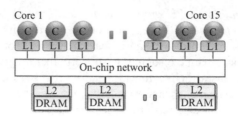

Figure 4.1   Baseline GPU architecture. © 2016. Reproduced, with permission, from Reference [14]

The programming model—exploiting parallelism in GPUs. Programming models like CUDA or OpenCL allow programmers to define and invoke parallel functions, called kernels, on a GPU. Each kernel consists of a number of threads that execute in parallel on the GPU cores.

Applications running on GPUs require some on-chip resources for execution. Each thread, among the hundreds or thousands executing concurrently, requires (i) registers, (ii) scratchpad memory (if used in the application), and (iii) a warp-slot which includes the necessary book-keeping for execution—a slot in the thread scheduler, PC, and the SIMT stack (used to track control divergence within a warp). Programming languages like CUDA and OpenCL also provide the ability to synchronize execution of threads as well as exchange data with each other. These languages provide the abstraction of a *thread block* or *cooperative thread array*, respectively— which are a group of threads that can synchronize using barriers or fences, and share data with each other using scratchpad memory. This form of thread synchronization requires that *all* the threads within the same thread block make progress in order for *any* thread to complete execution. As a result, the on-chip resource partitioning as well as the launch for execution at any SM is done at the granularity of a thread block.

The GPU architecture itself is well provisioned with these on-chip resources to support the concurrent execution of a large number of threads, and these resources can be flexibly partitioned across the application threads according to the application requirements. This flexible partitioning implies that the amount of parallelism that the GPU can support at any time depends on the per-thread block resource requirement.

The programming models, hence, also require specification of several key parameters that decide the utilization of these resources. These include (i) the number of thread blocks in the kernel compute grid, (ii) the number of threads within the thread block (which dictates the number of warp slots required per thread block), (iii) the number of registers per thread, and (iv) the scratchpad usage per thread block. These parameters are typically decided by the programmer and/or compiler. Programmers who aim to optimize code for high efficiency hand-optimize these parameters or use software tools such as autotuners [3,31–35] and optimizing compilers [36–41] to find optimized parameter specifications.

4.3 Motivation

The amount of parallelism that the GPU can provide for any application depends on the utilization of on-chip resources by threads within the application. As a result, suboptimal usage of these resources may lead to loss in the parallelism that can be achieved during program execution. This loss in parallelism often leads to significant degradation in performance, as GPUs primarily use fine-grained multi-threading [42,43] to hide the long latencies during execution.

The granularity of synchronization—i.e., the number of threads in a thread block—and the amount of scratchpad memory used per thread block are determined by the programmer while adapting any algorithm or application for execution on a GPU. This choice involves a complex trade-off between minimizing data movement, by using *larger* scratchpad memory sizes, and reducing the inefficiency of synchronizing a large number of threads, by using *smaller* scratchpad memory and thread block sizes. A similar trade-off exists when determining the number of registers used by the application. Using *fewer* registers minimizes hardware register usage and enables higher parallelism during execution, whereas using *more* registers avoids expensive accesses to memory. The resulting application parameters—the number of registers, the amount of scratchpad memory, and the number of threads per thread block—dictate the on-chip resource requirement and, hence, determine the parallelism that can be obtained for that application on any GPU.

In this section, we study the performance implications of different choices of resource specifications for GPU applications to demonstrate the key issues we aim to alleviate.

4.3.1 Performance variation and cliffs

To understand the impact of resource specifications and the resulting utilization of physical resources on GPU performance, we conduct an experiment on a Maxwell GPU system (GTX 745) with 20 GPGPU workloads from the CUDA SDK [44], Rodinia [45], GPGPU-Sim benchmarks [46], Lonestar [47], Parboil [48], and US DoE application suites [49]. We use the NVIDIA profiling tool (NVProf) [44] to determine the execution time of each application kernel. We sweep the three parameters of the specification—number of threads in a thread block, register usage per thread, and scratchpad memory usage per thread block—for each workload and measure their impact on execution time.

Figure 4.2 shows a summary of variation in performance (higher is better), normalized to the slowest specification for each application, across all evaluated specification points for each application in a Tukey box plot [50]. The boxes in the box plot represent the range between the first quartile (25%) and the third quartile (75%). The whiskers extending from the boxes represent the maximum and minimum points of the distribution, or 1.5× the length of the box, whichever is smaller. Any points that lie more than 1.5× the box length beyond the box are considered to be outliers [50] and are plotted as individual points. The line in the middle of the box represents the median, while the "X" represents the average.

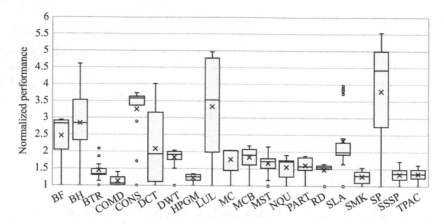

Figure 4.2　*Performance variation across specifications. © 2016. Reproduced, with permission, from Reference [51]*

We can see that there is significant variation in performance across different specification points (as much as $5.51\times$ in *SP*), proving the importance of optimized resource specifications. In some applications (e.g., *BTR, SLA*), few points perform well, and these points are significantly better than others, suggesting that it would be challenging for a programmer to locate these high performing specifications and obtain the best performance. Many workloads (e.g., *BH, DCT, MST*) also have higher concentrations of specifications with suboptimal performance in comparison to the best performing point, implying that, without effort, it is likely that the programmer will end up with a resource specification that leads to low performance.

There are several sources for this performance variation. One important source is the loss in thread-level parallelism as a result of a suboptimal resource specification. Suboptimal specifications that are *not* tailored to fit the available physical resources lead to the underutilization of resources. This causes a drop in the number of threads that can be executed concurrently, as there are insufficient resources to support their execution. Hence, better and more balanced utilization of resources enables higher thread-level parallelism. Often, this loss in parallelism from resource underutilization manifests itself in what we refer to as a *performance cliff*, where a small deviation from an optimized specification can lead to significantly worse performance, i.e., there is very high variation in performance between two specification points that are nearby. To demonstrate the existence and analyze the behavior of performance cliffs, we examine two representative workloads more closely.

Figure 4.3(a) shows (i) how the application execution time changes and (ii) how the corresponding number of registers, statically used, changes when the number of threads per thread block increases from 32 to 1,024 threads, for *minimum spanning tree (MST)* [47]. We make two observations.

First, let us focus on the execution time between 480 and 1,024 threads per block. As we go from 480 to 640 threads per block, execution time gradually decreases. Within this window, the GPU can support two thread blocks running concurrently for

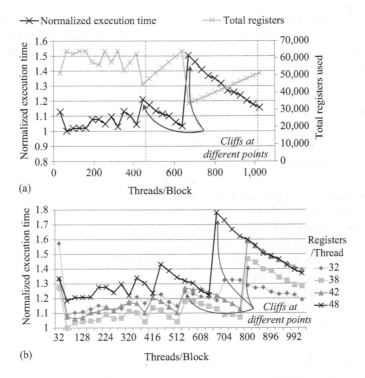

*Figure 4.3   Performance cliffs in minimum spanning tree (MST): (a) threads/block
sweep and (b) threads/block and registers/thread sweep. © 2016.
Reproduced, with permission, from Reference [51]*

MST. The execution time falls because the increase in the number of threads per block improves the overall throughput (the number of thread blocks running concurrently remains constant at two, but each thread block does more work in parallel by having more threads per block). However, the corresponding total number of registers used by the blocks also increases. At 640 threads per block, we reach the point where the total number of available registers is not large enough to support two blocks. As a result, the number of blocks executing in parallel drops from two to one, resulting in a significant increase (50%) in execution time, i.e., the *performance cliff*.[2] We see many of these cliffs earlier in the graph as well, albeit not as drastic as the one at 640 threads per block.

Second, Figure 4.3(a) shows the existence of performance cliffs when we vary *just one* system parameter—the number of threads per block. To make things more difficult for the programmer, other parameters (i.e., registers per thread or scratchpad memory per thread block) also need to be decided at the same time. Figure 4.3(b)

---

[2]Prior work [52] has studied performing resource allocation at the finer warp granularity, as opposed to the coarser granularity of a thread block. As we discuss in Section 4.9 and demonstrate in Section 4.7, this does *not* solve the problem of performance cliffs.

demonstrates that performance cliffs also exist when the *number of registers per thread* is varied from 32 to 48.[3] As this figure shows, the performance cliffs now occur at *different points* for *different registers/thread curves*, which make optimizing resource specification, so as to avoid these cliffs, much harder for the programmer.

Barnes–Hut (BH) is another application that exhibits very significant performance cliffs depending on the number of threads per block and registers per thread. Figure 4.4 plots the variation in performance with the number of threads per block when *BH* is compiled for a range of register sizes (between 24 and 48 registers per thread). We make two observations from the figure. First, similar to *MST*, we observe a significant variation in performance that manifests itself in the form of performance cliffs. Second, we observe that the points at which the performance cliffs occur change greatly depending on the number of registers assigned to each thread during compilation.

We conclude that performance cliffs are pervasive across GPU programs and occur due to fundamental limitations of existing GPU hardware resource managers, where resource management is static, coarse-grained, and tightly coupled to the application resource specification. Avoiding performance cliffs by determining more optimal resource specifications is a challenging task, because the occurrence of these cliffs depends on several factors, including the application characteristics, input data, and the underlying hardware resources.

4.3.2   Portability

As shown in Section 4.3.1, tuning GPU applications to achieve good performance on a given GPU is already a challenging task. To make things worse, even after this tuning is done by the programmer for one particular GPU architecture, it has to be *redone* for every new GPU generation (due to changes in the available physical resources

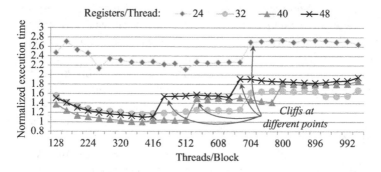

Figure 4.4   *Performance cliffs in Barnes–Hut (BH). © 2016. Reproduced, with permission, from Reference [51]*

---

[3]We note that the register usage reported by the compiler may vary from the actual runtime register usage [44], hence slightly altering the points at which cliffs occur.

across generations) to ensure that good performance is retained. We demonstrate this *portability problem* by running sweeps of the three parameters of the resource specification on various workloads, on three real GPU generations: Fermi (GTX 480), Kepler (GTX 760), and Maxwell (GTX 745).

Figure 4.5 shows how the optimized performance points change between different GPU generations for two representative applications (*MST* and *DCT*). For every generation, results are normalized to the lowest execution time for that particular generation. As we can see in Figure 4.5(a), the best performing points for different generations occur at *different* specifications because the application behavior changes

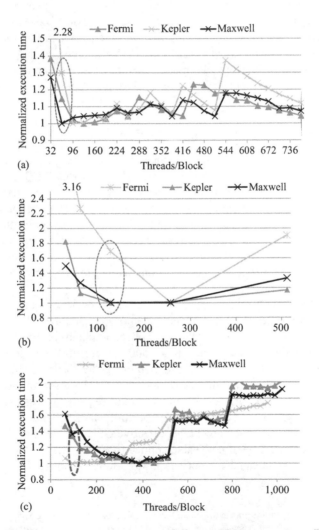

Figure 4.5   Performance variation across different GPU generations (Fermi, Kepler, and Maxwell) for (a) MST, (b) DCT, and (c) BH. © 2016. Adapted, with permission, from Reference [51]

with the variation in hardware resources. For *MST*, the *Maxwell* architecture performs best at 64 threads per block. However, the same specification point is not efficient for either of the other generations (*Fermi* and *Kepler*), producing 15% and 30% lower performance, respectively, compared to the best specification for each generation. For *DCT* (shown in Figure 4.5(b)), both *Kepler* and *Maxwell* perform best at 128 threads per block, but using the same specification for *Fermi* would lead to a 69% performance loss. Similarly, for *BH* (Figure 4.5(c)), the optimal point for *Fermi* architecture is at 96 threads per block. However, using the same configuration for the two later GPU architectures—*Kepler* and *Maxwell*—could lead to very suboptimal performance results. Using the same configuration results in as much as a 34% performance loss on *Kepler* and a 36% performance loss on *Maxwell*.

We conclude that the tight coupling between the programming model and the underlying resource management in hardware imposes a significant challenge in performance portability. To avoid suboptimal performance, an application has to be *retuned* by the programmer to find an optimized resource specification for *each* GPU generation.

4.3.3   Dynamic resource underutilization

Even when a GPU application is *perfectly* tuned for a particular GPU architecture, the on-chip resources are typically not fully utilized [5,10–13,15,53–57]. For example, it is well known that while the compiler conservatively allocates registers to hold the *maximum number* of live values throughout the execution, the number of live values at any given time is well below the maximum for large portions of application execution time. To determine the magnitude of this *dynamic underutilization*,[4] we conduct an experiment where we measure the dynamic usage (per epoch) of both scratchpad memory and registers for different applications with *optimized* specifications in our workload pool.

We vary the length of epochs from 500 to 4,000 cycles. Figure 4.6 shows the results of this experiment for (i) scratchpad memory (Figure 4.6(a)) and (ii) on-chip registers (Figure 4.6(b)). We make two major observations from these figures.

First, for relatively small epochs (e.g., 500 cycles), the average utilization of resources is very low (12% for scratchpad memory and 37% for registers). Even for the largest epoch size that we analyze (4,000 cycles), the utilization of scratchpad memory is still less than 50%, and the utilization of registers is less than 70%. This observation clearly suggests that there is an opportunity for a better dynamic allocation of these resources that could allow higher effective GPU parallelism.

Second, there are several noticeable applications, e.g., *cutcp*, *hw*, *tpacf*, where utilization of the scratchpad memory is always lower than 15%. This dramatic

---

[4] Underutilization of registers occurs in two major forms—*static*, where registers are unallocated throughout execution [13,52–58], and *dynamic*, where utilization of the registers drops during runtime as a result of early completion of warps [52], short register lifetimes [10–12] and long-latency operations [10,11]. We do not tackle underutilization from long-latency operations (such as memory accesses) in this paper and leave the exploration of alleviating this type of underutilization to future work.

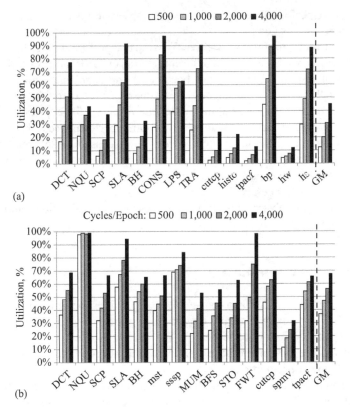

Figure 4.6   *Dynamic resource utilization for different length epochs:*
(a) scratchpad memory and (b) registers

underutilization due to static resource allocation can lead to significant loss in potential performance benefits for these applications.

In summary, we conclude that existing static on-chip resource allocation in GPUs can lead to significant resource underutilization that can lead to suboptimal performance and energy waste.

4.3.4   Our goal

As we see above, the tight coupling between the resource specification and hardware resource allocation, and the resulting heavy dependence of performance on the resource specification, creates a number of challenges. In this work, our goal is to alleviate these challenges by providing a mechanism that can (i) ease the burden on the programmer by ensuring reasonable performance, *regardless of the resource specification*, by successfully avoiding performance cliffs, while retaining performance for code with optimized specification; (ii) enhance portability by minimizing the variation in performance for optimized specifications across different GPU generations; and (iii) maximize dynamic resource utilization even in highly optimized code to further improve performance. We make two key observations from our above studies to help us achieve this goal.

Observation 1: *Bottleneck resources.* We find that performance cliffs occur when the amount of any resource required by an application exceeds the physically available amount of that resource. This resource becomes a *bottleneck* and limits the amount of parallelism that the GPU can support. If it were possible to provide the application with a *small additional amount* of the bottleneck resource, the application can see a significant increase in parallelism and thus avoid the performance cliff.

Observation 2: *Underutilized resources.* As discussed in Section 4.3.3, there is significant underutilization of resources at runtime. These underutilized resources could be employed to support more parallelism at runtime, and thereby alleviate the aforementioned challenges.

We use these two observations to drive our resource virtualization solution, which we describe next.

4.4   Zorua: our approach

In this work, we design Zorua, a framework that provides the illusion of more GPU resources than physically available by decoupling the resource specification from its allocation in the hardware resources. We introduce a new level of indirection by virtualizing the on-chip resources to allow the hardware to manage resources transparently to the programmer.

The virtualization provided by Zorua builds upon two *key concepts* to leverage the aforementioned observations. First, when there are insufficient physical resources, we aim to provide the illusion of the required amount by *oversubscribing* the required resource. We perform this oversubscription by leveraging the dynamic underutilization as much as possible, or by spilling to a swap space in memory. This oversubscription essentially enables the illusion of more resources than what is available (physically and statically) and supports the concurrent execution of more threads. Performance cliffs are mitigated by providing enough additional resources to avoid drastic drops in parallelism. Second, to enable efficient oversubscription by leveraging underutilization, we dynamically allocate and deallocate physical resources depending on the requirements of the application during execution. We manage the virtualization of each resource *independently* of other resources to maximize its runtime utilization.

Figure 4.7 depicts the high-level overview of the virtualization provided by Zorua. The *virtual space* refers to the *illusion* of the quantity of available resources. The *physical space* refers to the *actual* hardware resources (specific to the GPU architecture), and the *swap space* refers to the resources that do not fit in the physical space and hence are *spilled* to other physical locations. For the register file and scratchpad memory, the swap space is mapped to global memory space in the memory hierarchy. For threads, only those that are mapped to the physical space are available for scheduling and execution at any given time. If a thread is mapped to the swap space, its state (i.e., the PC and the SIMT stack) is saved in memory. Resources in the virtual space can

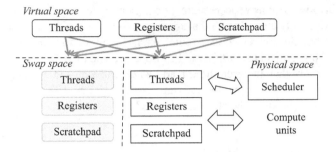

Figure 4.7   *High-level overview of Zorua. © 2016. Reproduced, with permission, from Reference [51]*

be freely remapped between the physical and swap spaces to maintain the illusion of the virtual space resources.

In the baseline architecture, the thread-level parallelism that can be supported, and hence the throughput obtained from the GPU, depends on the quantity of *physical resources*. With the virtualization enabled by Zorua, the parallelism that can be supported now depends on the quantity of *virtual resources* (and how their mapping into the physical and swap spaces is managed). Hence, the size of the virtual space for each resource plays the key role of determining the parallelism that can be exploited. Increasing the virtual space size enables higher parallelism, but leads to higher swap space usage. It is critical to minimize accesses to the swap space to avoid the latency overhead and capacity/bandwidth contention associated with accessing the memory hierarchy.

In light of this, there are two key challenges that need to be addressed to effectively virtualize on-chip resources in GPUs. We now discuss these challenges and provide an overview of how we address them.

4.4.1   Challenges in virtualization

Challenge 1: *Controlling the extent of oversubscription.* A key challenge is to determine the *extent* of oversubscription or the size of the virtual space for each resource. As discussed above, increasing the size of the virtual space enables more parallelism. Unfortunately, it could also result in more spilling of resources to the swap space. Finding the trade-off between more parallelism and less overhead is challenging, because the dynamic resource requirements of each thread tend to significantly fluctuate throughout execution. As a result, the size of the virtual space for each resource needs to be *continuously* tuned to allow the virtualization to adapt to the runtime requirements of the program.

Challenge 2: *Control and coordination of multiple resources.* Another critical challenge is to efficiently map the continuously varying virtual resource space to the physical and swap spaces. This is important for two reasons. First, it is critical to minimize accesses to the swap space. Accessing the swap space for the register file or scratchpad involves expensive accesses to global memory, due to the added latency and contention. Also, only those threads that are mapped to the physical space are available to the warp scheduler for selection. Second, each thread requires multiple resources for execution. It is critical to *coordinate* the allocation and mapping of these different resources to ensure that an executing thread has *all* the required resources allocated to it, while minimizing accesses to the swap space. Thus, an effective virtualization framework must coordinate the allocation of *multiple* on-chip resources.

4.4.2   Key ideas of our design

To solve these challenges, Zorua employs two key ideas. First, we leverage the software (the compiler) to provide annotations with information regarding the resource requirements of each *phase* of the application. This information enables the framework to make intelligent dynamic decisions, with respect to both the size of the virtual space and the allocation/deallocation of resources (Section 4.4.2.1).

Second, we use an adaptive runtime system to control the allocation of resources in the virtual space and their mapping to the physical/swap spaces. This allows us to (i) dynamically alter the size of the virtual space to change the extent of oversubscription and (ii) continuously coordinate the allocation of multiple on-chip resources and the mapping between their virtual and physical/swap spaces, depending on the varying runtime requirements of each thread (Section 4.4.2.2).

4.4.2.1   Leveraging software annotations of phase characteristics

We observe that the runtime variation in resource requirements (Section 4.3.3) typically occurs at the granularity of *phases* of a few tens of instructions. This variation occurs because different parts of kernels perform different operations that require different resources. For example, loops that primarily load/store data from/to scratchpad memory tend to be less register heavy. Sections of code that perform specific computations (e.g., matrix transformation, graph manipulation) can either be register heavy or primarily operate out of scratchpad. Often, scratchpad memory is used for only short intervals [15], e.g., when data exchange between threads is required, such as for a reduction operation.

Figure 4.8 depicts a few example phases from the *NQU* (*N-Queens Solver*) [59] kernel. *NQU* is a scratchpad-heavy application, but it does not use the scratchpad at all during the initial computation phase. During its second phase, it performs its primary computation out of the scratchpad, using as much as 4,224B. During its last phase, the scratchpad is used only for reducing results, which requires only 384B. There is also significant variation in the maximum number of live registers in the different phases.

Another example of phase variation from the *DCT* (*discrete Fourier transform*) kernel is depicted in Figure 4.9. *DCT* is both register-intensive and scratchpad-intensive. The scratchpad memory usage does not vary in this kernel. However, the register usage significantly varies—the register usage increases by $2\times$ in the second and third phase in comparison with the first and fourth phase.

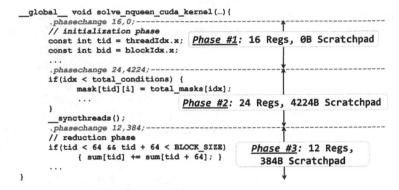

Figure 4.8   *Example phases from NQU. © 2016. Reproduced, with permission, from Reference [51]*

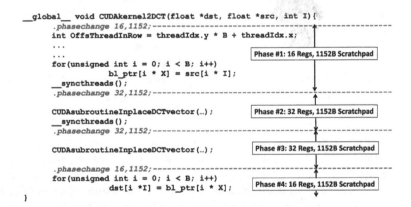

Figure 4.9   *Example phases from DCT*

In order to capture both the resource requirements as well as their variation over time, we partition the program into a number of *phases*. A phase is a sequence of instructions with sufficiently different resource requirements than adjacent phases. Barrier or fence operations also indicate a change in requirements for a different reason—threads that are waiting at a barrier do not immediately require the thread slot that they are holding. We interpret barriers and fences as phase boundaries since they potentially alter the utilization of their thread slots. The compiler inserts special instructions called *phase specifiers* to mark the start of a new phase. Each phase specifier contains information regarding the resource requirements of the next phase. Section 4.5.7 provides more detail on the semantics of phases and phase specifiers.

A phase forms the basic unit for resource allocation and deallocation, as well as for making oversubscription decisions. It offers a finer granularity than an *entire thread* to make such decisions. The phase specifiers provide information on the *future resource usage* of the thread at a phase boundary. This enables (i) preemptively controlling the extent of oversubscription at runtime and (ii) dynamically allocating and deallocating resources at phase boundaries to maximize utilization of the physical resources.

4.4.2.2 Control with an adaptive runtime system

Phase specifiers provide information to make oversubscription and allocation/ deallocation decisions. However, we still need a way to make decisions on the extent of oversubscription and appropriately allocate resources at runtime. To this end, we use an adaptive runtime system, which we refer to as the *coordinator*. Figure 4.10 presents an overview of the coordinator.

The virtual space enables the illusion of a larger amount of each of the resources than what is physically available, to adapt to different application requirements. This illusion enables higher thread-level parallelism than what can be achieved with solely the fixed, physically available resources, by allowing more threads to execute concurrently. The size of the virtual space at a given time determines this parallelism, and those threads that are effectively executed in parallel are referred to as *active threads*. All active threads have thread slots allocated to them in the virtual space (and hence can be executed), but some of them may not be mapped to the physical space at a given time. As discussed previously, the resource requirements of each application continuously change during execution. To adapt to these runtime changes, the coordinator leverages information from the phase specifiers to make decisions on oversubscription. The coordinator makes these decisions at every phase boundary and thereby controls the size of the virtual space for each resource (see Section 4.5.2).

To enforce the determined extent of oversubscription, the coordinator allocates all the required resources (in the virtual space) for only a *subset* of threads from the active threads. Only these dynamically selected threads, referred to as *schedulable threads*, are available to the warp scheduler and CUs for execution. The coordinator, hence, dynamically partitions the active threads into *schedulable threads* and the *pending threads*. Each thread is swapped between *schedulable* and *pending* states, depending on the availability of resources in the virtual space. Selecting only a subset

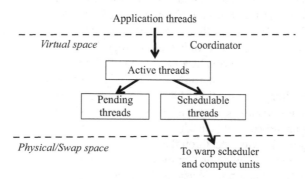

Figure 4.10   *Overview of the coordinator. © 2016. Reproduced, with permission, from Reference [51]*

of threads to execute at any time ensures that the determined size of the virtual space is not exceeded for any resource and helps coordinate the allocation and mapping of multiple on-chip resources to minimize expensive data transfers between the physical and swap spaces (discussed in Section 4.5).

4.4.3   Overview of Zorua

In summary, to effectively address the challenges in virtualization by leveraging the above ideas in design, Zorua employs a software—hardware codesign that comprises three components: (i) **The compiler** annotates the program by adding special instructions (*phase specifiers*) to partition it into *phases* and to specify the resource needs of each phase of the application. (ii) **The coordinator**, a hardware-based adaptive runtime system, uses the compiler annotations to dynamically allocate/deallocate resources for each thread at phase boundaries. The coordinator plays the key role of continuously controlling the extent of the oversubscription (and hence the size of the virtual space) at each phase boundary. (iii) **Hardware virtualization support** includes a mapping table for each resource to locate each virtual resource in either the physical space or the swap space in main memory, and the machinery to swap resources between the physical and swap spaces.

4.5   Zorua: detailed mechanism

We now detail the operation and implementation of the various components of the Zorua framework.

4.5.1   Key components in hardware

Zorua has two key hardware components: (i) the *coordinator* that contains queues to buffer the *pending threads* and control logic to make oversubscription and resource management decisions and (ii) *resource mapping tables* to map each of the resources to their corresponding physical or swap spaces.

Figure 4.11 presents an overview of the hardware components that are added to each SM. The coordinator interfaces with the thread block scheduler (❶) to schedule new blocks onto an SM. It also interfaces with the warp schedulers by providing a list of *schedulable warps* (❷).[5] The resource mapping tables are accessible by the coordinator and the CUs. We present a detailed walkthrough of the operation of Zorua and then discuss its individual components in more detail.

4.5.2   Detailed walkthrough

The coordinator is called into action by three events: (i) a new thread block is scheduled at the SM for execution, (ii) a warp undergoes a phase change, or (iii) a warp or a thread block reaches the end of execution. Between these events, the coordinator performs

---

[5]We use an additional bit in each warp slots to indicate to the scheduler whether the warp is schedulable.

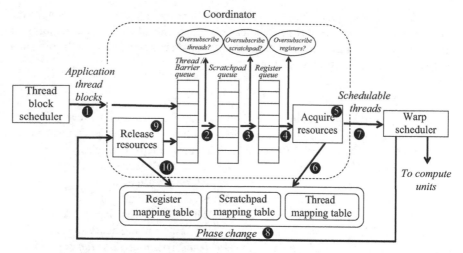

Figure 4.11   *Overview of Zorua in hardware. © 2016. Reproduced, with permission, from Reference [51]*

no action and execution proceeds as usual. We now walk through the sequence of actions performed by the coordinator for each type of event.

Thread block: execution start. When a thread block is scheduled onto an SM for execution (❶), the coordinator first buffers it. The primary decision that the coordinator makes is to determine whether or not to make each thread available to the scheduler for execution. The granularity at which the coordinator makes decisions is that of a warp, as threads are scheduled for execution at the granularity of a warp (hence we use *thread slot* and *warp slot* interchangeably). Each warp requires three resources: a thread slot, registers, and potentially scratchpad. The amount of resources required is determined by the phase specifier (Section 4.5.7) at the start of execution, which is placed by the compiler into the code. The coordinator must supply each warp with *all* its required resources in either the physical or swap space before presenting it to the warp scheduler for execution.

To ensure that each warp is furnished with its resources and to coordinate potential oversubscription for each resource, the coordinator has three queues—*thread/barrier, scratchpad, and register queues*. The three queues together essentially house the *pending threads*. Each warp must traverse each queue (❷ ❸ ❹), as described next, before becoming eligible to be scheduled for execution. The coordinator allows a warp to traverse a queue when (i) it has enough of the corresponding resource available in the physical space or (ii) it has insufficient resources in the physical space, but has decided to oversubscribe and allocate the resource in the swap space. The total size of the resource allocated in the physical and swap spaces cannot exceed the determined virtual space size. The coordinator determines the availability of resources in the physical space using the mapping tables (see Section 4.5.5). If there is an insufficient amount of a resource in the physical space, the coordinator needs to decide whether or not to increase the virtual space size for that particular resource by oversubscribing and using swap space. We describe the decision algorithm in Section 4.5.4. If the warp cannot traverse *all* queues, it is left waiting in the first (*thread/barrier*) queue until the next coordinator event. Once a warp has traversed *all* the queues, the coordinator acquires all the resources required for the warp's execution (❺). The corresponding mapping tables for each resource is updated (❻) to assign resources to the warp, as described in Section 4.5.5.

Warp: phase change. At each phase change (❽), the warp is removed from the list of schedulable warps and is returned to the coordinator to acquire/release its resources. Based on the information in its phase specifier, the coordinator releases the resources that are no longer live and hence are no longer required (❾). The coordinator updates the mapping tables to free these resources (❿). The warp is then placed into a specific queue, depending on which live resources it retained from the previous phase and which new resources it requires. The warp then attempts to traverse the remaining queues (❷ ❸ ❹), as described above. A warp that undergoes a phase change as a result of a barrier instruction is queued in the *thread/barrier queue* (❷) until all warps in the same thread block reach the barrier.

Thread block/warp: execution end. When a warp completes execution, it is returned to the coordinator to release any resources it is holding. Scratchpad is released only when the entire thread block completes execution. When the coordinator has free warp slots for a new thread block, it requests the thread block scheduler (❶) for a new block.

Every coordinator event. At any event, the coordinator attempts to find resources for warps waiting at the queues, to enable them to execute. Each warp in each queue (starting from the *register queue*) is checked for the availability of the required resources. If the coordinator is able to allocate resources in the physical or swap space without exceeding the determined size of virtual space, the warp is allowed to traverse the queue.

4.5.3   Benefits of our design

Decoupling the warp scheduler and mapping tables from the coordinator. Decoupling the warp scheduler from the coordinator enables Zorua to use any scheduling algorithm over the schedulable warps to enhance performance. One case when this is useful is when increasing parallelism degrades performance by increasing cache miss rate or causing memory contention [60–62]. Our decoupled design allows this challenge to be addressed independently from the coordinator using more intelligent scheduling algorithms [27,30,61,62] and cache management schemes [27,63–65]. Furthermore, decoupling the mapping tables from the coordinator allows easy integration of any implementation of the mapping tables that may improve efficiency for each resource.

Coordinating oversubscription for multiple resources. The queues help ensure that a warp is allocated *all* resources in the virtual space before execution. They (i) ensure an ordering in resource allocation to avoid deadlocks and (ii) enforce priorities between resources. In our evaluated approach, we use the following order of priorities: threads, scratchpad, and registers. We prioritize scratchpad over registers, as scratchpad is shared by all warps in a block and hence has a higher value by enabling more warps to execute. We prioritize threads over scratchpad, as it is wasteful to allow warps stalled at a barrier to acquire other resources—other warps that are still progressing toward the barrier may be starved of the resource they need. Furthermore, managing each resource independently allows different oversubscription policies for each resource and enables fine-grained control over the size of the virtual space for that resource.

Flexible oversubscription. Zorua's design can flexibly enable/disable swap space usage, as the dynamic fine-grained management of resources is independent of the swap space. Hence, in cases where the application is well-tuned to utilize the available resources, swap space usage can be disabled or minimized, and Zorua can still improve performance by reducing dynamic underutilization of resources. Furthermore, different oversubscription algorithms can be flexibly employed to manage the size of the virtual space for each resource (independently or cooperatively). These algorithms can be designed for different purposes, e.g., minimizing swap space usage, improving fairness in a multikernel setting, reducing energy. In Section 4.5.4, we describe an example algorithm to improve performance by making a good trade-off between improving parallelism and reducing swap space usage.

Avoiding deadlocks. A resource allocation deadlock could happen if resources are distributed among too many threads, such that *no* single thread is able to obtain enough necessary resources for execution. Allocating resources using *multiple* ordered queues helps avoid deadlocks in resource allocation in three ways. First, new resources are allocated to a warp only once the warp has traversed *all* of the queues. This ensures that resources are not wastefully allocated to warps that will be stalled anyway. Second, a warp is allocated resources based on how many resources it already has, i.e., how many queues it has already traversed. Warps that already hold multiple live resources are prioritized in allocating new resources over warps that do *not* hold any resources. Finally, if there are insufficient resources to maintain a minimal level of parallelism (e.g., 20% of SM occupancy in our evaluation), the coordinator handles this rare case by simply oversubscribing resources to ensure that there is no deadlock in allocation.

Managing more resources. Our design also allows flexibly adding more resources to be managed by the virtualization framework, for example, thread block slots. Virtualizing a new resource with Zorua simply requires adding a new queue to the coordinator and a new mapping table to manage the virtual to physical mapping.

4.5.4 Oversubscription decisions

Leveraging phase specifiers. Zorua leverages the information provided by phase specifiers (Section 4.5.7) to make oversubscription decisions for each phase. For each resource, the coordinator checks whether allocating the requested quantity according to the phase specifier would cause the total swap space to exceed an *oversubscription threshold*, or *o_thresh*. This threshold essentially dynamically sets the size of the virtual space for each resource. The coordinator allows oversubscription for each resource only within its threshold. *o_thresh* is dynamically determined to adapt to the characteristics of the workload and to ensure good performance by achieving a good trade-off between the overhead of oversubscription and the benefits gained from parallelism.

Determining the o_thresh. In order to make the above trade-off, we use two architectural statistics: (i) idle time at the cores, c_idle, as an indicator for potential performance benefits from parallelism and (ii) memory idle time (the idle cycles when all threads are stalled waiting for data from memory or the memory pipeline), c_mem, as an indicator of a saturated memory subsystem that is unlikely to benefit from more parallelism.[6] We use Algorithm 1 to determine *o_thresh* at runtime. Every *epoch*, the change in c_mem is compared with the change in c_idle. If the increase in c_mem is greater, this indicates an increase in pressure on the memory subsystem, suggesting both lesser benefit from parallelism and higher overhead from oversubscription. In this case, we reduce *o_thresh*. On the other hand, if the increase in c_idle is higher, this is indicative of more idleness in the pipelines, and higher potential performance from parallelism and oversubscription. We increase *o_thresh* in this case, to allow more oversubscription and enable more parallelism. Table 4.1 describes the variables used in Algorithm 1.

Algorithm 1: Determining the oversubscription threshold

1: *o_thresh = o_default*   ▷ Initialize threshold
2: **for** *each epoch* **do**
3:      *c_idle_delta = (c_idle − c_idle_prev)*   ▷ Determine the change in c_idle and c_mem from the previous epoch
4:      *c_mem_delta = (c_mem − c_mem_prev)*
5:      **if** *(c_idle_delta − c_mem_delta) > c_delta_thresh* **then**   ▷ Indicates more idleness and potential for benefits from parallelism
6:          *o_thresh + = o_thresh_step*
7:      **end if**
8:      **if** *(c_mem_delta − c_idle_delta) > c_delta_thresh* **then**   ▷ Traffic in memory is likely to outweigh any parallelism benefit
9:          *o_thresh − = o_thresh_step*
10:     **end if**
11: **end for**

4.5.5 *Virtualizing on-chip resources*

A resource can be in either the physical space, in which case it is mapped to the physical on-chip resource, or the swap space, in which case it can be found in the memory hierarchy. Thus, a resource is effectively virtualized, and we need to track the mapping between the virtual and physical/swap spaces. We use a *mapping table* for each resource to determine (i) whether the resource is in the physical or swap space and (ii) the location of the resource within the physical on-chip hardware.

---

[6]This is similar to the approach taken by prior work [60] to estimate the performance benefits of increasing parallelism.

Table 4.1   *Variables for oversubscription*

Variable	Description
o_thresh	Oversubscription threshold (dynamically determined)
o_default	Initial value for *o_thresh* (experimentally determined to be 10% of total physical resource)
c_idle	Core cycles when no threads are issued to the core (but the pipeline is not stalled) [60]
c_mem	Core cycles when all warps are waiting for data from memory or stalled at the memory pipeline
*_prev	The above statistics for the previous epoch
c_delta_thresh	Threshold to produce change in *o_thresh* (experimentally determined to be 16)
o_thresh_step	Increment/Decrement to *o_thresh*, experimentally determined to be 4% of the total physical resource
epoch	Interval in core cycles to change *o_thresh* (experimentally determined to be 2,048)

The CUs access these mapping tables before accessing the real resources. An access to a resource that is mapped to the swap space is converted to a global memory access that is addressed by the logical resource ID and warp/block ID (and a base register for the swap space of the resource). In addition to the mapping tables, we use two registers per resource to track the amount of the resource that is (i) free to be used in physical space and (ii) mapped in swap space. These two counters enable the coordinator to make oversubscription decisions (Section 4.5.4). We now go into more detail on virtualized resources in Zorua.[7]

4.5.5.1   Virtualizing registers and scratchpad memory

In order to minimize the overhead of large mapping tables, we map registers and scratchpad at the granularity of a *set*. The size of a set is configurable by the architect—we use 4*$warp\_size$[8] for the register mapping table, and 1KB for scratchpad. Figure 4.12 depicts the tables for the registers and scratchpad. The register mapping table is indexed by the warp ID and the logical register set number (*logical_register_number / register_set_size*). The scratchpad mapping table is indexed by the block ID and the logical scratchpad set number (*logical_scratchpad_address / scratchpad_set_size*). Each entry in the mapping table contains the physical address of the register/scratchpad content in the physical register file or scratchpad. The valid bit indicates whether the logical entry is mapped to the physical space or the swap space. With 64 logical warps and 16 logical thread blocks (see Section 4.6.1), the register mapping table takes 1.125 kB ($64 \times 16 \times 9$ bits, or 0.87% of the register

---

[7]Our implementation of a virtualized resource aims to minimize complexity. This implementation is largely orthogonal to the framework itself, and one can envision other implementations (e.g., [12,15,16]) for different resources.

[8]We track registers at the granularity of a warp.

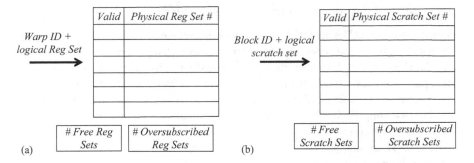

Figure 4.12   Mapping tables: (a) register mapping table and (b) scratchpad mapping table

file) and the scratchpad mapping table takes 672 B ($16 \times 48 \times 7$ bits, or 1.3% of the scratchpad).

4.5.5.2   Virtualizing thread slots

Each SM is provisioned with a fixed number of *warp slots*, which determine the number of warps that are considered for execution every cycle by the warp scheduler. In order to oversubscribe warp slots, we need to save the state of each warp in memory before remapping the physical slot to another warp. This state includes the book-keeping required for execution, i.e., the warp's PC (program counter) and the SIMT stack, which holds divergence information for each executing warp. The thread slot mapping table records whether each warp is mapped to a physical slot or swap space. The table is indexed by the logical warp ID and stores the address of the physical warp slot that contains the warp. In our baseline design with 64 logical warps, this mapping table takes 56 B (64×7 bits).

4.5.6   Handling resource spills

If the coordinator has oversubscribed any resource, it is possible that the resource can be found either (i) on-chip (in the physical space) or (ii) in the swap space in the memory hierarchy. As described above, the location of any virtual resource is determined by the mapping table for each resource. If the resource is found on-chip, the mapping table provides the physical location in the register file and scratchpad memory. If the resource is in the swap space, the access to that resource is converted to a global memory load that is addressed either by the (i) thread block ID and logical register/scratchpad set, in the case of registers or scratchpad memory or (ii) logical warp ID, in the case of warp slots. The oversubscribed resource is typically found in the L1/L2 cache but in the worst case could be in memory. When the coordinator chooses to oversubscribe any resource beyond what is available on-chip, the least frequently accessed resource set is spilled to the memory hierarchy using a simple store operation.

4.5.7 Supporting phases and phase specifiers

Identifying phases. The compiler partitions each application into phases based on the liveness of registers and scratchpad memory. To avoid changing phases too often, the compiler uses thresholds to determine phase boundaries. In our evaluation, we define a new phase boundary when there is (i) a 25% change in the number of live registers or live scratchpad content and (ii) a minimum of ten instructions since the last phase boundary. To simplify hardware design, the compiler draws phase boundaries only where there is no control divergence.[9]

Once the compiler partitions the application into phases, it inserts instructions—*phase specifiers*—to specify the beginning of each new phase and convey information to the framework on the number of registers and scratchpad memory required for each phase. As described in Section 4.4.2.1, a barrier or a fence instruction also implies a phase change, but the compiler does not insert a phase specifier for it as the resource requirement does not change.

Phase specifiers. The phase specifier instruction contains fields to specify (i) the number of live registers and (ii) the amount of scratchpad memory in bytes, both for the next phase. Figure 4.13 describes the fields in the phase specifier instruction. The instruction decoder sends this information to the coordinator along with the phase change event. The coordinator keeps this information in the corresponding warp slot.

4.5.8 Role of the compiler and programmer

The compiler plays an important role, annotating the code with phase specifiers to convey information to the coordinator regarding the resource requirements of each phase. The compiler, however, does *not* alter the size of each thread block or the scratchpad memory usage of the program. The resource specification provided by the programmer (either manually or via autotuners) is retained to guarantee correctness. For registers, the compiler follows the default policy or uses directives as specified by the user. One could envision more powerful, efficient resource allocation with a programming model that does *not* require *any* resource specification and/or compiler policies/autotuners that are *cognizant* of the virtualized resources.

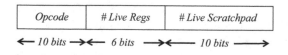

Figure 4.13   Phase specifier

---

[9]The phase boundaries for the applications in our pool easily fit this restriction, but the framework can be extended to support control divergence if needed.

4.5.9   Implications to the programming model and software optimization

Zorua offers several new opportunities and implications in enhancing the programming model and software optimizations (via libraries, autotuners, optimizing compilers, etc.) which we briefly describe below. We leave these ideas for exploration in future work.

4.5.9.1   Flexible programming models for GPUs and heterogeneous systems

State-of-the-art high-level programming languages and models still assume a fixed amount of on-chip resources and hence, with the help of the compiler or the runtime system, are required to find *static* resource specifications to fit the application to the desired GPU. Zorua, by itself, also still requires the programmer to specify resource specifications to ensure correctness—albeit they are not required to be highly optimized for a given architecture. However, by providing a flexible but dynamically controlled view of the on-chip hardware resources, Zorua changes the abstraction of the on-chip resources that is offered to the programmer and software. This offers the opportunity to rethink resource management in GPUs from the ground up. One could envision more powerful resource allocation and better programmability with programming models that do *not* require static resource specification, leaving the compiler/runtime system and the underlying virtualized framework to completely handle *all* forms of on-chip resource allocation, unconstrained by the fixed physical resources in a specific GPU, entirely at runtime. This is especially significant in future systems that are likely to support a wide range of compute engines and accelerators, making it important to be able to write high-level code that can be partitioned easily, efficiently, and at a fine granularity across any accelerator, *without* statically tuning any code segment to run efficiently on the GPU.

4.5.9.2   Virtualization-aware compilation and auto-tuning

Zorua changes the contract between the hardware and software to provide a more powerful resource abstraction (in the software) that is *flexible and dynamic*, by pushing some more functionality into the hardware, which can more easily react to the runtime resource requirements of the running program. We can reimagine compilers and autotuners to be more intelligent, leveraging this new abstraction and, hence the virtualization, to deliver more efficient and high-performing code optimizations that are *not* possible with the fixed and static abstractions of today. They could, for example, *leverage* the oversubscription and dynamic management that Zorua provides to tune the code to more aggressively use resources that are underutilized at runtime. As we demonstrate in this work, static optimizations are limited by the fixed view of the resources that is available to the program today. Compilation frameworks that are cognizant of the *dynamic* allocation/deallocation of resources provided by Zorua could make more efficient use of the available resources.

4.5.9.3   Reduced optimization space

Programs written for applications in machine learning, computer graphics, computer vision, etc., typically follow the *stream* programming paradigm, where the code is decomposed into many *stages* in an *execution pipeline.* Each stage processes only a part of the input data in a pipelined fashion to make better use of the caches. A key challenge in writing complex pipelined code is finding *execution schedules* (i.e., how the work should be partitioned across stages) and optimizations that perform best for *each* pipeline stage from a prohibitively large space of potential solutions. This requires complex tuning algorithms or profiling runs that are both computationally intensive and time-consuming. The search for optimized specifications has to be done when there is a change in input data or in the underlying architecture. By pushing some of the resource management functionality to the hardware, Zorua reduces this search space for optimized specifications by making it less sensitive to the wide space of resource specifications.

4.6   Methodology

4.6.1   System modeling and configuration

We model the Zorua framework with GPGPU-Sim 3.2.2 [46]. Table 4.2 summarizes the major parameters. Except for the portability results, all results are obtained using the Fermi configuration. We use GPUWattch [66] to model the GPU power consumption. We faithfully model the overheads of the Zorua framework, including an additional 2-cycle penalty for accessing each mapping table, and the overhead of memory accesses for swap space accesses (modeled as a part of the memory system). We model the energy overhead of mapping table accesses as SRAM accesses in GPUWattch.

4.6.2   Evaluated applications and metrics

We evaluate a number of applications from the Lonestar suite [47], GPGPU-Sim benchmarks [46], and CUDA SDK [44], whose resource specifications (the number of registers, the amount of scratchpad memory, and/or the number of threads per

Table 4.2   Major parameters of the simulated systems

System overview	15 SMs, 32 threads/warp, 6 memory channels
Shader Core Config	1.4 GHz, GTO scheduler [62], 2 schedulers per SM
Warps/SM	Fermi: 48; Kepler/Maxwell: 64
Registers	Fermi: 32,768; Kepler/Maxwell: 65,536
Scratchpad	Fermi/Kepler: 48 kB; Maxwell: 64 kB
On-chip cache	L1: 32 kB, 4 ways; L2: 768 kB, 16 ways
Interconnect	1 crossbar/direction (15 SMs, 6 MCs), 1.4 GHz
Memory model	177.4 GB/s BW, 6 memory controllers (MCs), FR-FCFS scheduling, 16 banks/MC

Table 4.3   Summary of evaluated applications

Name (abbreviation)	(R: register, S: scratchpad, T: thread block) Range
Barnes–Hut (BH) [47]	R: 28–44 × T: 128–1,024
Discrete cosine transform (DCT) [44]	R: 20–40 × T: 64–512
Minimum spanning tree (MST) [47]	R: 28–44 × T: 256–1,024
Reduction (RD) [44]	R: 16–24 × T: 64–1,024
N-queens solver (NQU) [46,59]	S: 10,496–47,232 (T: 64–288)
Scan large array (SLA) [44]	R: 24–36 × T: 128–1,024
Scalar product (SP) [44]	S: 2,048–8,192 × T: 128–512
Single-source shortest path (SSSP) [47]	R: 16–36 × T: 256–1,024

thread block) are parameterizable. Table 4.3 shows the applications and the evaluated parameter ranges. For each application, we make sure the amount of work done is the same for all specifications. The performance metric we use is the execution time of the GPU kernels in the evaluated applications.

4.7   Evaluation

We evaluate the effectiveness of Zorua by studying three different mechanisms: (i) *Baseline*, the baseline GPU that schedules kernels and manages resources at the thread block level; (ii) *WLM* (warp level management), a state-of-the-art mechanism for GPUs to schedule kernels and manage registers at the warp level [52]; and (iii) *Zorua*. For our evaluations, we run each application on 8–65 (36 on average) different resource specifications (the ranges are in Table 4.3).

4.7.1   Effect on performance variation and cliffs

We first examine how Zorua alleviates the high variation in performance by reducing the impact of resource specifications on resource utilization. Figure 4.14 presents a Tukey box plot [50] (see Section 4.3 for a description of the presented box plot), illustrating the performance distribution (higher is better) for each application (for all different application resource specifications we evaluated), normalized to the slowest Baseline operating point *for that application*. We make two major observations.

First, we find that Zorua significantly reduces the *performance range* across all evaluated resource specifications. Averaged across all of our applications, the worst resource specification for Baseline achieves 96.6% lower performance than the best performing resource specification. For WLM [52], this performance range reduces only slightly, to 88.3%. With Zorua, the performance range drops significantly, to 48.2%. We see drops in the performance range for *all* applications except *SSSP*. With *SSSP*, the range is already small to begin with (23.8% in Baseline), and Zorua

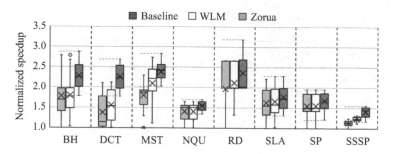

Figure 4.14   *Normalized performance distribution. © 2016. Reproduced, with permission, from Reference [51]*

exploits the dynamic underutilization, which improves performance but also adds a small amount of variation.

Second, while Zorua reduces the performance range, it also preserves or improves performance of the best performing points. As we examine in more detail in Section 4.7.2, the reduction in performance range occurs as a result of improved performance mainly at the lower end of the distribution.

To gain insight into how Zorua reduces the performance range and improves performance for the worst performing points, we analyze how it reduces performance cliffs. With Zorua, we ideally want to *eliminate* the cliffs we observed in Section 4.3.1. We study the trade-off between resource specification and execution time for three representative applications: *DCT* (Figure 4.15(a)), *MST* (Figure 4.15(b)), and *NQU* (Figure 4.15(c)). For all three figures, we normalize execution time to the *best* execution time under Baseline. Two observations are in order.

First, Zorua successfully mitigates the performance cliffs that occur in Baseline. For example, *DCT* and *MST* are both sensitive to the thread block size, as shown in Figures 4.15(a) and 4.15(b), respectively. We have circled the locations at which cliffs exist in Baseline. Unlike Baseline, Zorua maintains more steady execution times across the number of threads per block, employing oversubscription to overcome the loss in parallelism due to insufficient on-chip resources. We see similar results across all of our applications.

Second, we observe that while WLM [52] can reduce some of the cliffs by mitigating the impact of large block sizes, many cliffs still exist under WLM (e.g., *NQU* in Figure 4.15(c)). This cliff in *NQU* occurs as a result of insufficient scratchpad memory, which cannot be handled by WLM. Similarly, the cliffs for *MST* (Figure 4.15(b)) also persist with WLM because *MST* has a lot of barrier operations, and the additional warps scheduled by WLM ultimately stall, waiting for other warps within the same block to acquire resources. We find that, with oversubscription, Zorua is able to smooth out those cliffs that WLM is unable to eliminate.

Overall, we conclude that Zorua (i) reduces the performance variation across resource specification points, so that performance depends less on the specification provided by the programmer and (ii) can alleviate the performance cliffs experienced by GPU applications.

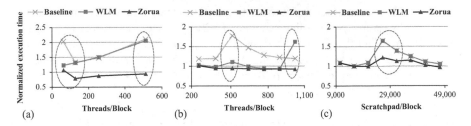

*Figure 4.15   Effect on performance cliffs: (a) DCT, (b) MST, and (c) NQU. © 2016.
Reproduced, with permission, from Reference [51]*

4.7.2   Effect on performance

As Figure 4.14 shows, Zorua either retains or improves the best performing point for each application, compared to the Baseline. Zorua improves the best performing point for each application by 12.8% on average, and by as much as 27.8% (for *DCT*). This improvement comes from the improved parallelism obtained by exploiting the dynamic underutilization of resources, which exists *even for optimized specifications*. Applications such as *SP* and *SLA* have little dynamic underutilization and hence do not show any performance improvement. *NQU does* have significant dynamic underutilization, but Zorua does not improve the best performing point as the overhead of oversubscription outweighs the benefit, and Zorua dynamically chooses not to oversubscribe. We conclude that even for many specifications that are optimized to fit the hardware resources, Zorua is able to further improve performance.

We also note that, in addition to reducing performance variation and improving performance for optimized points, Zorua improves performance by 25.2% on average for all resource specifications across all evaluated applications.

4.7.3   Effect on portability

As described in Section 4.3.2, performance cliffs often behave differently across different GPU architectures and can significantly shift the best performing resource specification point. We study how Zorua can ease the burden of performance tuning if an application has been already tuned for one GPU model, and is later ported to another GPU. To understand this, we define a new metric, *porting performance loss*, that quantifies the performance impact of porting an application without retuning it. To calculate this, we first normalize the execution time of each specification point to the execution time of the best performing specification point. We then pick a source GPU architecture (i.e., the architecture that the GPU was tuned for) and a target GPU architecture (i.e., the architecture that the code will run on), and find the point-to-point drop in performance for all points whose performance on the source GPU comes within 5% of the performance at the best performing specification point.[10]

---

[10]We include any point within 5% of the best performance as there are often multiple points close to the best point, and the programmer may choose any of them.

Figure 4.16 shows the *maximum* porting performance loss for each application, across any two pairings of our three simulated GPU architectures (Fermi, Kepler, and Maxwell). We find that Zorua greatly reduces the maximum porting performance loss that occurs under both Baseline and WLM for all but one of our applications. On average, the maximum porting performance loss is 52.7% for Baseline, 51.0% for WLM, and only 23.9% for Zorua.

Notably, Zorua delivers significant improvements in portability for applications that previously suffered greatly when ported to another GPU, such as *DCT* and *MST*. For both of these applications, the performance variation differs so much between GPU architectures that, despite tuning the application on the source GPU to be within 5% of the best achievable performance, their performance on the target GPU is often more than twice as slow as the best achievable performance on the target platform. Zorua significantly lowers this porting performance loss down to 28.1% for *DCT* and 36.1% for *MST*. We also observe that for *BH*, Zorua actually increases the porting performance loss slightly with respect to the Baseline. This is because for Baseline, there are only two points that perform within the 5% margin for our metric, whereas with Zorua, we have five points that fall in that range. Despite this, the increase in porting performance loss for *BH* is low, deviating only 7.0% from the best performance.

To take a closer look into the portability benefits of Zorua, we run experiments to obtain the performance sensitivity curves for each application using different GPU architectures. Figures 4.17 and 4.18 depict the execution time curves while sweeping a single resource specification for *NQU* and *DCT* for the three evaluated GPU architectures—Fermi, Kepler, and Maxwell. We make two major observations from the figures.

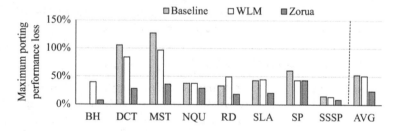

Figure 4.16   Maximum porting performance loss. © 2016. Reproduced, with permission, from Reference [51]

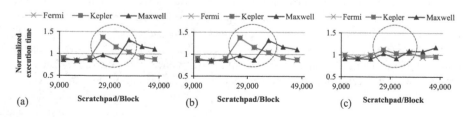

Figure 4.17   Impact on portability (NQU): (a) baseline, (b) WLM and, (c) protean

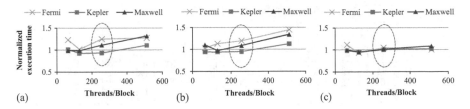

Figure 4.18 Impact on portability (DCT): (a) baseline, (b) WLM and, (c) protean

First, Zorua significantly alleviates the presence of performance cliffs and reduces the performance variation across *all* three evaluated architectures, thereby reducing the impact of both resource specification and underlying architecture on the resulting performance curve. In comparison, WLM is unable to make a significant impact on the performance variations and the cliffs remain for all the evaluated architectures.

Second, by reducing the performance variation across all three GPU generations, Zorua significantly reduces the *porting performance loss*, i.e., the loss in performance when code optimized for one GPU generation is run on another (as highlighted within the figures).

We conclude that Zorua enhances portability of applications by reducing the impact of a change in the hardware resources for a given resource specification. For applications that have already been tuned on one platform, Zorua significantly lowers the penalty of not retuning for another platform, allowing programmers to save development time.

4.7.4 A deeper look: benefits and overheads

To take a deeper look into how Zorua is able to provide the above benefits, in Figure 4.19, we show the number of *schedulable warps* (i.e., warps that are available to be scheduled by the warp scheduler at any given time excluding warps waiting at a barrier), averaged across all of specification points. On an average, Zorua increases the number of schedulable warps by 32.8%, significantly more than WLM (8.1%), which is constrained by the fixed amount of available resources. We conclude that by oversubscribing and dynamically managing resources, Zorua is able to improve thread-level parallelism and, hence, performance.

We also find that the overheads due to resource swapping and contention do not significantly impact the performance of Zorua. Figure 4.20 depicts resource hit rates for each application, i.e., the fraction of all resource accesses that were found on-chip as opposed to making a potentially expensive off-chip access. The oversubscription mechanism (directed by the coordinator) is able to keep resource hit rates very high, with an average hit rate of 98.9% for the register file and 99.6% for scratchpad memory.

Figure 4.21 shows the average reduction in total system energy consumption of WLM and Zorua over Baseline for each application (averaged across the individual energy consumption over Baseline for each evaluated specification point). We observe

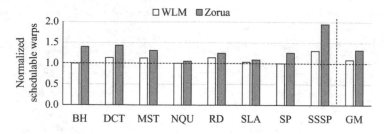

Figure 4.19   Effect on schedulable warps. © 2016. Reproduced, with permission, from Reference [51]

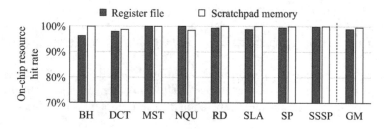

Figure 4.20   Virtual resource hit rate in Zorua

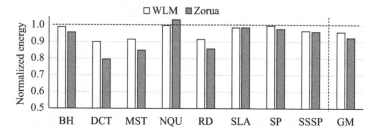

Figure 4.21   Effect on energy consumption. © 2016. Reproduced, with permission, from Reference [51]

that Zorua reduces the total energy consumption across all of our applications, except for *NQU* (which has a small increase of 3%). Overall, Zorua provides a mean energy reduction of 7.6%, up to 20.5% for *DCT*.[11] We conclude that Zorua is an energy-efficient virtualization framework for GPUs.

We estimate the die area overhead of Zorua with CACTI 6.5 [67], using the same 40-nm process node as the GTX 480, which our system closely models. We include all the overheads from the coordinator and the resource mapping tables (Section 4.5).

---

[11]We note that the energy consumption can be reduced further by appropriately optimizing the oversubscription algorithm. We leave this exploration to future work.

The total area overhead is 0.735 mm² for all 15 SMs, which is only 0.134% of the die area of the GTX 480.

4.8 Other applications

By providing the illusion of more resources than physically available, Zorua provides the opportunity to help address other important challenges in GPU computing today. We discuss several such opportunities in this section.

4.8.1 Resource sharing in multi-kernel or multi-programmed environments

Executing multiple kernels or applications within the same SM can improve resource utilization and efficiency [5,53,54,68–72]. Hence, providing support to enable fine-grained sharing and partitioning of resources is critical for future GPU systems. This is especially true in environments where multiple different applications may be consolidated on the same GPU, e.g., in clouds or clusters. By providing a flexible view of each of the resources, Zorua provides a natural way to enable dynamic and fine-grained control over resource partitioning and allocation among multiple kernels. Specifically, Zorua provides several key benefits for enabling better performance and efficiency in multi-kernel/multi-program environments. First, selecting the optimal resource specification for an application is challenging in virtualized environments (e.g., clouds), as it is unclear which other applications may be running alongside it. Zorua can improve efficiency in resource utilization *irrespective* of the application specifications and of other kernels that may be executing on the same SM. Second, Zorua manages the different resources independently and at a fine granularity, using a dynamic runtime system (the coordinator). This enables the maximization of resource utilization, while providing the ability to control the partitioning of resources at runtime to provide quality-of-service (QoS), fairness, etc., by leveraging the coordinator. Third, Zorua enables oversubscription of the different resources. This obviates the need to alter the application specifications [5,72] in order to ensure there are sufficient resources to co-schedule kernels on the same SM and, hence, enables concurrent kernel execution transparently to the programmer.

4.8.2 Preemptive multitasking

A key challenge in enabling true multiprogramming in GPUs is enabling rapid preemption of kernels [71,73,74]. Context switching on GPUs incurs a very high latency and overhead, as a result of the large amount of register file and scratchpad state that needs to be saved before a new kernel can be executed. Saving state at a very coarse granularity (e.g., the entire SM state) leads to very high preemption latencies. Prior work proposes context minimization [73,75] or context switching at the granularity of a thread block [71] to improve response time during preemption. Zorua enables fine-grained management and oversubscription of on-chip resources. It can be naturally extended to enable quick preemption of a task via intelligent management of the swap space and the mapping tables (complementary to approaches taken by prior work [73,75]).

4.8.3   Support for other parallel programming paradigms

The fixed static resource allocation for each thread in modern GPU architectures requires statically dictating the resource usage for the program throughout its execution. Other forms of parallel execution that are *dynamic* (e.g., Cilk [76], staged execution [77–79]) require more flexible allocation of resources at runtime and are hence more challenging to enable. Examples of this include *nested parallelism* [80], where a kernel can dynamically spawn new kernels or thread blocks, and *helper threads* [13] to utilize idle resource at runtime to perform different optimizations or background tasks in parallel. Zorua makes it easy to enable these paradigms by providing on-demand dynamic allocation of resources. Irrespective of whether threads in the programming model are created statically or dynamically, Zorua allows allocation of the required resources on the fly to support the execution of these threads. The resources are simply deallocated when they are no longer required. Zorua also enables *heterogeneous* allocation of resources—i.e., allocating different amounts of resources to different threads. The current resource allocation model, in line with a GPU's SIMT architecture, treats all threads the same and allocates the same amount of resources. Zorua makes it easier to support execution paradigms where each concurrently running thread executes different code at the same time, hence requiring different resources. This includes helper threads, multiprogrammed execution, nested parallelism, etc. Hence, with Zorua, applications are no longer limited by a GPU's fixed SIMT model which only supports a fixed, statically determined number of homogeneous threads as a result of the resource management mechanisms that exist today.

4.8.4   Energy efficiency and scalability

To support massive parallelism, on-chip resources are a precious and critical resource. However, these resources *cannot* grow arbitrarily large as GPUs continue to be area-limited and on-chip memory tends to be extremely power hungry and area intensive [11,12,16,57,58,81]. Furthermore, complex thread schedulers that can select a thread for execution from an increasingly large thread pool are required in order to support an arbitrarily large number of warp slots. Zorua enables using smaller register files, scratchpad memory, and less complex or fewer thread schedulers to save power and area while still retaining or improving parallelism.

4.8.5   Error tolerance and reliability

The indirection offered by Zorua, along with the dynamic management of resources, could also enable better reliability and simpler solutions toward error tolerance in the on-chip resources. The virtualization framework trivially allows remapping resources with hard or soft faults such that no virtual resource is mapped to a faulty physical resource. Unlike in the baseline case, faulty resources would not impact the number of the resources seen by the thread scheduler while scheduling threads for execution. A few unavailable faulty registers, warp slots, etc. could significantly reduce the number of the threads that are scheduled concurrently (i.e., the runtime parallelism).

4.8.6 Support for system-level tasks on GPUs

As GPUs become increasingly general purpose, a key requirement is better integration with the CPU operating system and with complex distributed software systems such as those employed for large-scale distributed machine learning [82,83] or graph processing [84,85]. If GPUs are architected to be first-class compute engines, rather than the slave devices they are today, they can be programmed and utilized in the same manner as a modern CPU. This integration requires the GPU execution model to support system-level tasks like interrupts, exceptions and more generally provide support for access to distributed file systems, disk I/O, or network communication. Support for these tasks and execution models require dynamic provisioning of resources for execution of system-level code. Zorua provides a building block to enable this.

4.8.7 Applicability to general resource management in accelerators

Zorua uses a program *phase* as the granularity for managing resources. This allows handling resources across phases *dynamically*, while leveraging *static* information regarding resource requirements from the software by inserting annotations at phase boundaries. Future work could potentially investigate the applicability of the same approach to manage resources and parallelism in *other* accelerators (e.g., processing-in-memory accelerators [84,86–104] or direct-memory access engines [105–107]) that require efficient dynamic management of large amounts of particular critical resources.

4.9   Related work

To our knowledge, this is the first work to propose a holistic framework to decouple a GPU application's resource specification from its physical on-chip resource allocation by virtualizing multiple on-chip resources. This enables the illusion of more resources than what physically exists to the programmer, while the hardware resources are managed at runtime by employing a swap space (in main memory), transparently to the programmer. We design a new hardware/software cooperative framework to effectively virtualize multiple on-chip GPU resources in a controlled and coordinated manner, thus enabling many benefits of virtualization in GPUs.

We briefly discuss prior work related to different aspects of our proposal: (i) virtualization of resources, (ii) improving programming ease and portability, and (iii) more efficient management of on-chip resources.

Virtualization of resources. *Virtualization* [20–23] is a concept designed to provide the illusion, to the software and programmer, of more resources than what truly exists in physical hardware. It has been applied to the management of hardware resources in many different contexts [18–25], with virtual memory [21,23,108] being one of the oldest forms of virtualization that is commonly used in high-performance processors today. Abstraction of hardware resources and use of a level of indirection in their management leads to many benefits, including improved utilization, programmability, portability, isolation, protection, sharing, and oversubscription.

In this work, we apply the general principle of virtualization to the management of multiple on-chip resources in modern GPUs. Virtualization of on-chip resources offers the opportunity to alleviate many different challenges in modern GPUs. However, in this context, effectively adding a level of indirection introduces new challenges, necessitating the design of a new virtualization strategy. There are two key challenges. First, we need to dynamically determine the *extent* of the virtualization to reach an effective trade-off between improved parallelism due to oversubscription and the latency/capacity overheads of swap space usage. Second, we need to coordinate the virtualization of *multiple* latency-critical on-chip resources. To our knowledge, this is the first work to propose a holistic software–hardware cooperative approach to virtualizing multiple on-chip resources in a controlled and coordinated manner that addresses these challenges, enabling the different benefits provided by virtualization in modern GPUs.

Prior works propose to virtualize a specific on-chip resource for specific benefits, mostly in the CPU context. For example, in CPUs, the concept of virtualized registers was first used in the IBM 360 [18] and DEC PDP-10 [19] architectures to allow logical registers to be mapped to either fast yet expensive physical registers, or slow and cheap memory. More recent works [24,109,110], propose to virtualize registers to increase the effective register file size to much larger register counts. This increases the number of thread contexts that can be supported in a multi-threaded processor [24] or reduces register spills and fills [109,110]. Other works propose to virtualize on-chip resources in CPUs (e.g., [111–115]). In GPUs, Jeon et al. [12] propose to virtualize the register file by dynamically allocating and deallocating physical registers to enable more parallelism with smaller, more power-efficient physical register files. Concurrent to this work, Yoon *et al.* [16] propose an approach to virtualize thread slots to increase thread-level parallelism. These works propose specific virtualization mechanisms for a single resource for specific benefits. None of these works provide a cohesive virtualization mechanism for *multiple* on-chip GPU resources in a controlled and coordinated manner, which forms a key contribution of our MICRO 2016 work.

Enhancing programming ease and portability. There is a large body of work that aims to improve programmability and portability of modern GPU applications using software tools, such as autotuners [3,31–35], optimizing compilers [36–41], and high-level programming languages and runtimes [116–119]. These tools tackle a multitude of optimization challenges and have been demonstrated to be very effective in generating high-performance portable code. They can also be used to tune the resource specification. However, there are several shortcomings in these approaches. First, these tools often require profiling runs [3,34–36,40,41] on the GPU to determine the best performing resource specifications. These runs have to be repeated for each new input set and GPU generation. Second, software-based approaches still require significant programmer effort to write code in a manner that can be exploited by these approaches to optimize the resource specifications. Third, selecting the best performing resource specifications statically using software tools is a challenging task in virtualized environments (e.g., cloud computing, data centers), where it is unclear which kernels may be run together on the same SM or where it is not known, apriori, which GPU generation the application may execute on. Finally, software tools assume a fixed amount of available resources. This leads to runtime underutilization due to static allocation of resources, which cannot be addressed by these tools.

In contrast, the programmability and portability benefits provided by Zorua require no programmer effort in optimizing resource specifications. Furthermore, these autotuners and compilers can be used in conjunction with Zorua to further improve performance.

Efficient resource management. Prior works aim to improve parallelism by increasing resource utilization using hardware-based [12,15,27,30,52,55,68, 106,120–124], software-based [5,15,69,125–128], and hardware–software cooperative [13,53,54,57,77,79,129] approaches. Among these works, the closest to ours are [12,16] (discussed earlier), [15], and [52]. These approaches propose efficient techniques to dynamically manage a single resource and can be used along with Zorua to improve resource efficiency further. Yang *et al.* [15] aim to maximize utilization of the scratchpad with software techniques and by dynamically allocating/deallocating scratchpad memory. Xiang *et al.* [52] propose to improve resource utilization by scheduling threads at the finer granularity of a warp rather than a thread block. This approach can help alleviate performance cliffs, but not in the presence of synchronization or scratchpad memory, nor does it address the dynamic underutilization within a thread during runtime. We quantitatively compare to this approach in Section 4.7 and demonstrate Zorua's benefits over it.

Other works leverage resource underutilization to improve energy efficiency [10–12,58,81] or perform other useful work [13,56]. These works are complementary to Zorua.

4.10 Conclusion and future directions

We propose Zorua, a new framework that decouples the application resource specification from the allocation in the physical hardware resources (i.e., registers, scratchpad memory, and thread slots) in GPUs. Zorua encompasses a holistic virtualization strategy to effectively virtualize multiple latency-critical on-chip resources in a controlled and coordinated manner. We demonstrate that by providing the illusion of more resources than physically available, via dynamic management of resources and the judicious use of a swap space in main memory, Zorua enhances (i) *programming ease* (by reducing the performance penalty of suboptimal resource specification), (ii) *portability* (by reducing the impact of different hardware configurations), and (iii) *performance* for code with an optimized resource specification (by leveraging dynamic underutilization of resources). We conclude that Zorua is an effective, holistic virtualization framework for GPUs.

We believe that the indirection provided by Zorua's virtualization mechanism makes it a generic framework that can address other challenges in modern GPUs.

For example, Zorua can enable fine-grained resource sharing and partitioning among multiple kernels/applications, as well as low-latency preemption of GPU programs. Section 4.8 details many other applications of the Zorua framework. We hope that future work explores these promising directions, building on the insights and the framework developed in this paper.

Acknowledgments

We thank the reviewers and our shepherd for their valuable suggestions. We thank the members of the SAFARI group for their feedback and the stimulating research environment they provide. Special thanks to Vivek Seshadri, Kathryn McKinley, Steve Keckler, Evgeny Bolotin, and Mike O'Connor for their feedback during various stages of this project. We acknowledge the support of our industrial partners: Facebook, Google, IBM, Intel, Microsoft, NVIDIA, Qualcomm, Samsung, and VMware. This research was partially supported by NSF (grant no. 1409723), the Intel Science and Technology Center for Cloud Computing, and the Semiconductor Research Corporation.

References

[1]   NVIDIA CUDA Programming Guide, 2011.

[2]   Advanced Micro Devices, Inc. AMD Accelerated Parallel Processing OpenCL Programming Guide, 2011.

[3]   Andrew Davidson and John Owens. Toward Techniques for Auto-Tuning GPU Algorithms. In *Applied Parallel and Scientific Computing*, pages 110–119. Springer, 2010.

[4]   Jiří Matela, Martin Šrom, and Petr Holub. Low GPU Occupancy Approach to Fast Arithmetic Coding in jpeg2000. In *Mathematical and Engineering Methods in Computer Science*, pages 136–145. Springer, 2011.

[5]   Sreepathi Pai, Matthew J. Thazhuthaveetil, and R. Govindarajan. Improving GPGPU Concurrency With Elastic Kernels. In *ASPLOS*, 2013.

[6]   Shane Ryoo, Christopher I. Rodrigues, Sara S. Baghsorkhi, Sam S. Stone, David B. Kirk, and Wen-mei W. Hwu. Optimization principles and application performance evaluation of a multithreaded GPU using CUDA. In *Proceedings of the 13th ACM SIGPLAN Symposium on Principles and Practice of Parallel Programming*, PPoPP'08, 2008.

[7]   Shane Ryoo, Christopher I. Rodrigues, Sam S. Stone, *et al.* Program Optimization Space Pruning for a Multithreaded GPU. In *CGO*, 2008.

[8]   Shane Ryoo, Christopher I. Rodrigues, Sam S. Stone, *et al.* Program optimization carving for GPU computing. *J. Parallel Distrib. Comput.*, 68(10):1389–1401, 2008.

[9]   John A. Stratton, Christopher Rodrigues, I-Jui Sung, *et al.* Algorithm and data optimization techniques for scaling to massively threaded systems. *Computer*, 45(8):26–32, IEEE 2012.

[10]   Mark Gebhart, Daniel R. Johnson, David Tarjan, *et al.* A Hierarchical Thread Scheduler and Register File for Energy-Efficient Throughput Processors. 2012.

[11]   Mark Gebhart, Stephen W. Keckler, and William J. Dally. A Compile-Time Managed Multi-Level Register File Hierarchy. In *MICRO*, 2011.

[12]   Hyeran Jeon, Gokul Subramanian Ravi, Nam Sung Kim, and Murali Annavaram. GPU register file virtualization. In *MICRO*, 2015.

[13]   Nandita Vijaykumar, Gennady Pekhimenko, Adwait Jog, *et al.* A Case for Core-Assisted Bottleneck Acceleration in GPUs: Enabling Flexible Data Compression With Assist Warps. In *ISCA*, 2015.

[14]   Nandita Vijaykumar, Gennady Pekhimenko, Adwait Jog, *et al.* A Framework for Accelerating Bottlenecks in GPU Execution with Assist Warps. *Advances in GPU Research and Practices, Elsevier*, 2016.

[15]   Yi Yang, Ping Xiang, Mike Mantor, Norm Rubin, and Huiyang Zhou. Shared Memory Multiplexing: A Novel Way to Improve GPGPU Throughput. In *PACT*, 2012.

[16]   Myung Kuk Yoon, Keunsoo Kim, Sangpil Lee, Won Woo Ro, and Murali Annavaram. Virtual Thread: Maximizing Thread-Level Parallelism beyond GPU Scheduling Limit. In *ISCA*, 2016.

[17]   Onur Kayiran, Adwait Jog, Ashutosh Pattnaik, *et al.* μC-States: Fine-Grained GPU Datapath Power Management. In *PACT*, 17–30, IEEE 2016.

[18]   Gene M. Amdahl, Gerrit A. Blaauw, and Frederick P. Brooks. Architecture of the IBM System/360. In *IBM JRD*, 1964.

[19]   Gordon Bell, Kotok Alan, Thomas N. Hastings, and Richard Hill. The Evolution of the DEC System 10. In *CACM*, 1978.

[20]   Robert J. Creasy. The Origin of the VM/370 Time-sharing System. In *IBM JRD*, 1981.

[21]   Peter J. Denning. Virtual memory. *ACM Comput. Surv.*, 2(3):153–189, 1970.

[22]   Peter H. Gum. System/370 Extended Architecture: Facilities for Virtual Machines. In *IBM JRD*, 1983.

[23]   Bruce Jacob and Trevor Mudge. Virtual memory in contemporary microprocessors. *IEEE Micro*, 18(4):60–75, 1998.

[24]   David W. Oehmke, Nathan L. Binkert, Trevor Mudge, and Steven K. Reinhardt. How to Fake 1000 Registers. In *MICRO*, 2005.

[25]   Carl A. Waldspurger. Memory Resource Management in VMware ESX Server. In *OSDI*, 2002.

[26]   Nintendo/Creatures Inc./GAME FREAK inc. Pokémon. http://www.pokemon.com/us/.

[27]   Rachata Ausavarungnirun, Saugata Ghose, Onur Kayiran, *et al.* Exploiting Inter-Warp Heterogeneity to Improve GPGPU Performance. In *PACT*, 2015.

[28]   John L. Hennessey and David A. Patterson. *Computer Architecture, A Quantitaive Approach*. Morgan Kaufmann, 2010.

[29]   David B. Kirk and Wen-Mei Hwu. *Programming Massively Parallel Processors: A Hands-on Approach*. Morgan Kaufmann, 2010.

[30]   Veynu Narasiman, Michael Shebanow, Chang Joo Lee, Rustam Miftakhutdinov, Onur Mutlu, and Yale N. Patt. Improving GPU Performance

via Large Warps and Two-level Warp Scheduling. *Proceedings of the 44th Annual IEEE/ACM International Symposium on Microarchitecture*, pages 308–317, 2011.

[31]   Yuri Dotsenko, Sara S. Baghsorkhi, Brandon Lloyd, and Naga K. Govindaraju. Auto-Tuning of Fast Fourier Transform on Graphics Processors. In *ACM SIGPLAN Notices*, 46(8):257–266, 2011.

[32]   Malik Khan, Protonu Basu, Gabe Rudy, Mary Hall, Chun Chen, and Jacqueline Chame. A script-based autotuning compiler system to generate high-performance cuda code. *ACM Trans. Archit. Code Optim.*, 9(4):31, 2013.

[33]   Katsuto Sato, Hiroyuki Takizawa, Kazuhiko Komatsu, and Hiroaki Kobayashi. *Software Automatic Tuning: From Concepts to State-of-the-Art Results*, chapter Automatic Tuning of CUDA Execution Parameters for Stencil Processing. 2010.

[34]   Christoph A. Schaefer, Victor Pankratius, and Walter F. Tichy. Atune-il: An Instrumentation Language for Auto-Tuning Parallel Applications. In *Euro-Par*. 2009.

[35]   Kyle Spafford, Jeremy Meredith, and Jeffrey Vetter. Maestro: Data Orchestration and Tuning for OpenCL devices. In *Euro-Par*. 2010.

[36]   Guoyang Chen, Bo Wu, Dong Li, and Xipeng Shen. Porple: An Extensible Optimizer for Portable Data Placement on GPU. In *MICRO*, 2014.

[37]   Amir H. Hormati, Mehrzad Samadi, Mark Woh, Trevor Mudge, and Scott Mahlke. Sponge: Portable Stream Programming on Graphics Engines. In *ASPLOS*, March 2011.

[38]   Juan Carlos Juega, José Ignacio Gómez, Christian Tenllado, and Francky Catthoor. Adaptive Mapping and Parameter Selection Scheme to Improve Automatic Code Generation for GPUs. In *Proceedings of Annual IEEE/ACM International Symposium on Code Generation and Optimization*, pages 251, CGO'14, 2014.

[39]   Yixun Liu, Eddy Z. Zhang, and Xipeng Shen. A Cross-Input Adaptive Framework for GPU Program Optimizations. In *IPDPS*, 2009.

[40]   Yi Yang, Ping Xiang, Jingfei Kong, Mike Mantor, and Huiyang Zhou. A unified optimizing compiler framework for different GPGPU architectures. *ACM Trans. Archit. Code Optim.*, 9(2):9, 2012.

[41]   Yi Yang, Ping Xiang, Jingfei Kong, and Huiyang Zhou. A GPGPU Compiler for Memory Optimization and Parallelism Management. In *PLDI*, 2010.

[42]   Burton J. Smith. A Pipelined, Shared Resource MIMD Computer. In *ICPP*, 1978.

[43]   James E. Thornton. Parallel Operation in the Control Data 6600. In *AFIPS FJCC*, 1964.

[44]   NVIDIA. CUDA C/C++ SDK Code Samples, 2011.

[45]   Shuai Che, Michael Boyer, Jiayuan Meng, *et al.* Rodinia: A Benchmark Suite for Heterogeneous Computing. In *IISWC*, 2009.

[46]   Ali Bakhoda, George L. Yuan, Wilson W. L. Fung, Henry Wong, and Tor M. Aamodt. Analyzing CUDA Workloads Using a Detailed GPU Simulator. In *IEEE International Symposium on Performance Analysis of Systems and Software (ISPASS 2009)*, pages 163–174, April 2009.

[47]   Martin Burtscher, Rupesh Nasre, and Keshav Pingali. A quantitative study of irregular programs on GPUs. In *IISWC*, 2012.

[48]   John A. Stratton, Christopher Rodrigues, I-Jui Sung, *et al.* Parboil: A Revised Benchmark Suite for Scientific and Commercial Throughput Computing. Technical Report IMPACT-12-01, University of Illinois, at Urbana-Champaign, March 2012.

[49]   Oreste Villa, Daniel R. Johnson, Mike O'Connor, *et al.* Scaling the Power Wall: A Path to Exascale, pages 830–841, 2014.

[50]   Robert McGill, John W. Tukey, and Wayne A. Larsen. Variations of box plots. *Am. Stat.*, 32(1):12–16, 1978.

[51]   Nandita Vijaykumar, Kevin Hsieh, Gennady Pekhimenko, *et al.* Zorua: A Holistic Approach to Resource Virtualization in GPUs. In *MICRO*, 2016.

[52]   Ping Xiang, Yi Yang, and Huiyang Zhou. Warp-Level Divergence in GPUs: Characterization, Impact, and Mitigation. In *HPCA*, 2014.

[53]   Rachata Ausavarungnirun, Joshua Landgraf, Vance Miller, *et al.* Mosaic: A GPU Memory Manager with Application-Transparent Support for Multiple Page Sizes. *MICRO*, 2017.

[54]   Rachata Ausavarungnirun, Vance Miller, Joshua Landgraf, *et al.* MASK: Redesigning the GPU Memory Hierarchy to Support Multi-Application Concurrency. In *ASPLOS*, 2018.

[55]   Mark Gebhart, Stephen W. Keckler, Brucek Khailany, Ronny Krashinsky, and William J. Dally. Unifying Primary Cache, Scratch, and Register File Memories in a Throughput Processor. In *MICRO*, 2012.

[56]   Nagesh B. Lakshminarayana and Hyesoon Kim. Spare Register Aware Prefetching for Graph Algorithms on GPUs. In *High Performance Computer Architecture (HPCA), 2014 IEEE 20th International Symposium on*, pages 614–625. IEEE, 2014.

[57]   Mohammad Sadrosadati, Amirhossein Mirhosseini, Seyed Borna Ehsani, *et al.* LTRF: Enabling High-Capacity Register Files for GPUs via Hardware/ Software Cooperative Register Prefetching. In *ASPLOS*, 2018.

[58]   Mark Gebhart, Daniel R. Johnson, David Tarjan, *et al.* Energy-Efficient Mechanisms for Managing Thread Context in Throughput Processors. 2011.

[59]   Ping-Che Chen. N-Queens Solver. 2008.

[60]   Onur Kayiran, Adwait Jog, Mahmut T. Kandemir, and Chita R. Das. Neither More Nor Less: Optimizing Thread-level Parallelism for GPGPUs. In *PACT*, 2013.

[61]   Onur Kayiran, Nachiappan Chidambaram Nachiappan, Adwait Jog, *et al.* Managing GPU Concurrency in Heterogeneous Architectures. In *MICRO*, 2014.

[62]   Timothy G. Rogers, Mike O'Connor, and Tor M. Aamodt. Cache-Conscious Wavefront Scheduling. In *MICRO*, 2012.

[63]   Chao Li, Shuaiwen Leon Song, Hongwen Dai, Albert Sidelnik, Siva Kumar Sastry Hari, and Huiyang Zhou. Locality-Driven Dynamic GPU Cache Bypassing. 2015.

[64]   Dong Li, Minsoo Rhu, Daniel R. Johnson, *et al.* Priority-Based Cache Allocation in Throughput Processors. In *HPCA*, pages 89–100, 2015.

[65]   Xiaolong Xie, Yun Liang, Yu Wang, Guangyu Sun, and Tao Wang. Coordinated Static and Dynamic Cache Bypassing for GPUs. In *HPCA*, 2015.

[66]   Jingwen Leng, Tayler Hetherington, Ahmed ElTantawy, *et al.* GPUWattch: enabling energy optimizations in GPGPUs. *SIGARCH Comput. Archit. News*, 41(3):487–498, 2013.

[67]   Steven J. E. Wilton and Norman P. Jouppi. CACTI: An enhanced cache access and cycle time model. *IEEE J. Solid-State Circ.*, 31(5):677–688, 1996.

[68]   Rachata Ausavarungnirun, Kevin Kai-Wei Chang, Lavanya Subramanian, Gabriel H. Loh, and Onur Mutlu. Staged Memory Scheduling: Achieving High Performance and Scalability in Heterogeneous Systems. In *ISCA*, 2012.

[69]   Chris Gregg, Jonathan Dorn, Kim Hazelwood, and Kevin Skadron. Fine-Grained Resource Sharing for Concurrent GPGPU Kernels. In *HotPar*, 2012.

[70]   Adwait Jog, Evgeny Bolotin, Zvika Guz, *et al.* Application-aware Memory System for Fair and Efficient Execution of Concurrent GPGPU Applications. In *GPGPU*, 2014.

[71]   Zhenning Wang, Jun Yang, Rami Melhem, Bruce Childers, Youtao Zhang, and Minyi Guo. Simultaneous Multikernel GPU: Multi-Tasking Throughput Processors via Fine-Grained Sharing. In *HPCA*, 2016.

[72]   Jianlong Zhong and Bingsheng He. Kernelet: High-Throughput GPU Kernel Executions With Dynamic Slicing and Scheduling. In *TPDS*, 2014.

[73]   Jason Jong Kyu Park, Yongjun Park, and Scott Mahlke. Chimera: Collaborative Preemption for Multitasking on a Shared GPU. *SIGARCH Comput. Archit. News*, 50(4):593–606, 2015.

[74]   Ivan Tanasic, Isaac Gelado, Javier Cabezas, Alex Ramirez, Nacho Navarro, and Mateo Valero. Enabling Preemptive Multiprogramming on GPUs. In *ISCA*, 2014.

[75]   Jaikrishnan Menon, Marc De Kruijf, and Karthikeyan Sankaralingam. iGPU: Exception support and speculative execution on GPUs. *SIGARCH Comput. Archit. News*, 40(3):72–83, 2012.

[76]   Robert D. Blumofe, Christopher F. Joerg, Bradley C. Kuszmaul, Charles E. Leiserson, Keith H. Randall, and Yuli Zhou. Cilk: An Efficient Multithreaded Runtime System. In *ASPLOS*, 1995.

[77]   José A. Joao, M. Aater Suleman, Onur Mutlu, and Yale N. Patt. Bottleneck Identification and Scheduling in Multithreaded Applications. In *ASPLOS*, 2012.

[78]   José A. Joao, M. Aater Suleman, Onur Mutlu, and Yale N. Patt. Utility-based Acceleration of Multithreaded Applications on Asymmetric CMPs. In *ISCA*, 2013.

[79]   M. Aater Suleman, Onur Mutlu, José A. Joao, Khubaib, and Yale N. Patt, Data Marshaling for Multi-core Architectures. In *ISCA*, 2010.

[80]   HyoukJoong Lee, Kevin J. Brown, Arvind K. Sujeeth, Tiark Rompf, and Kunle Olukotun. Locality-Aware Mapping of Nested Parallel Patterns on GPUs. In *MICRO*.

[81]   Mohammad Abdel-Majeed and Murali Annavaram. Warped Register File: A Power Efficient Register File for GPGPUs. In *Proceedings of the 2013 IEEE*

19th International Symposium on High Performance Computer Architecture (HPCA), HPCA'13, pages 412–423, Washington, DC, USA, 2013. IEEE Computer Society.

[82] Martín Abadi, Paul Barham, Jianmin Chen, *et al.* TensorFlow: A System for Large-Scale Machine Learning. In *OSDI*, 2016.

[83] Kevin Hsieh, Aaron Harlap, Nandita Vijaykumar, *et al.* Gaia: Geo-Distributed Machine Learning Approaching LAN Speeds. In *NSDI*, 2016.

[84] Junwhan Ahn, Sungpack Hong, Sungjoo Yoo, Onur Mutlu, and Kiyoung Choi. A Scalable Processing-in-Memory Accelerator for Parallel Graph Processing. In *ISCA*, 2015.

[85] Yucheng Low, Danny Bickson, Joseph Gonzalez, Carlos Guestrin, Aapo Kyrola, and Joseph M. Hellerstein. Distributed GraphLab: A Framework for Machine Learning and Data Mining in the Cloud. In *Proc. VLDB Endow.*, April 2012.

[86] Junwhan Ahn, Sungjoo Yoo, Onur Mutlu, and Kiyoung Choi. PIM-Enabled Instructions: A Low-Overhead, Locality-Aware Processing-in-Memory Architecture. In *ISCA*, 2015.

[87] Berkin Akin, Franz Franchetti, and James C. Hoe. Data Reorganization in Memory Using 3D-Stacked DRAM. In *ISCA*, 2015.

[88] Amirali Boroumand, Saugata Ghose, Youngsok Kim, *et al.* Google Workloads for Consumer Devices: Mitigating Data Movement Bottlenecks. In *ASPLOS*, 2018.

[89] Saugata Ghose, Kevin Hsieh, Amirali Boroumand, Rachata Ausavarungnirun, and Onur Mutlu. Enabling the Adoption of Processing-in-Memory: Challenges, Mechanisms, Future Research Directions. arxiv:1802.00320 [cs.AR], 2018.

[90] Qi Guo, Nikolaos Alachiotis, Berkin Akin, *et al.* 3D-Stacked Memory-Side Acceleration: Accelerator and System Design. In *WoNDP*, 2014.

[91] Kevin Hsieh, Eiman Ebrahimi, Gwangsun Kim, *et al.* Transparent Offloading and Mapping (TOM): Enabling Programmer-Transparent Near-Data Processing in GPU Systems. In *ISCA*, 2016.

[92] Kevin Hsieh, Samira Khan, Nandita Vijaykumar, *et al.* Accelerating Pointer Chasing in 3D-Stacked Memory: Challenges, Mechanisms, Evaluation. In *ICCD*, 2016.

[93] Jeremie S. Kim, Damla Senol Cali, Hongyi Xin, *et al.* LazyPIM: An Efficient Cache Coherence Mechanism for Processing-in-Memory. In *CAL*, 2016.

[94] Jeremie S. Kim, Damla Senol Cali, Hongyi Xin, *et al.* GRIM-filter: fast seed location filtering in DNA read mapping using processing-in-memory technologies. *BMC Genomics*, 19(2):89, 2018.

[95] Peter M. Kogge. EXECUBE—A New Architecture for Scaleable MPPs. In *ICPP*, 1994.

[96] Zhiyu Liu, Irina Calciu, Maurice Herlihy, and Onur Mutlu. Concurrent Data Structures for Near-Memory Computing. In *SPAA*, 2017.

[97] David Patterson, Thomas Anderson, Neal Cardwell, *et al.* TOP-PIM: Throughput-oriented Programmable Processing in Memory. In *HPDC*, 2014.

[98]   David Patterson, Thomas Anderson, Neal Cardwell, *et al*. A Case for Intelligent RAM. *IEEE Micro*, 17(2):34–44, 1997.

[99]   Ashutosh Pattnaik, Xulong Tang, Adwait Jog, *et al*. Scheduling Techniques for GPU Architectures with Processing-in-Memory Capabilities. In *PACT*, 2016.

[100]   Vivek Seshadri and Onur Mutlu. Simple Operations in Memory to Reduce Data Movement. In *Advances in Computers, Volume 106*. Academic Press, 2017.

[101]   Vivek Seshadri, Kevin Hsieh, Amirali Boroum, *et al*. Fast Bulk Bitwise AND and OR in DRAM. In *CAL*, 2015.

[102]   Vivek Seshadri, Donghyuk Lee, Thomas Mullins, *et al*. Ambit: In-memory Accelerator for Bulk Bitwise Operations Using Commodity DRAM Technology. In *MICRO*, 2017.

[103]   David Elliot Shaw. The NON-VON database machine: a brief overview. *IEEE Database Eng. Bull.*, 961–963, 1981.

[104]   Harold S. Stone. A Logic-in-Memory Computer. In *IEEE TC*, 1970.

[105]   Kevin K. Chang, Prashant J. Nair, Donghyuk Lee, Saugata Ghose, Moinuddin K. Qureshi, and Onur Mutlu. Low-Cost Inter-Linked Subarrays (LISA): Enabling Fast Inter-Subarray Data Movement in DRAM. In *HPCA*, 2016.

[106]   Donghyuk Lee, Lavanya Subramanian, Rachata Ausavarungnirun, Jongmoo Choi, and Onur Mutlu. Decoupled Direct Memory Access: Isolating CPU and IO Traffic by Leveraging a Dual-Data-Port DRAM. In *PACT*, 2015.

[107]   Vivek Seshadri, Yoongu Kim, Chris Fallin, *et al*. RowClone: Fast and Energy-Efficient In-DRAM Bulk Data Copy and Initialization. In *MICRO*, 2013.

[108]   A. Bensoussan, Charles T. Clingen, and Robert C. Daley. The Multics Virtual Memory. In *SOSP*, 1969.

[109]   Jun Yan and Wei Zhang. Virtual Registers: Reducing Register Pressure Without Enlarging the Register File. In *HIPEAC*, 2007.

[110]   Jun Yan and Wei Zhang. Exploiting Virtual Registers to Reduce Pressure on Real Registers. In *TACO*, 2008.

[111]   Edward Brekelbaum, Jeff Rupley, Chris Wilkerson, and Bryan Black. Hierarchical Scheduling Windows. In *MICRO*, 2002.

[112]   Henry Cook, Krste Asanovic, and David A. Patterson. Virtual Local Stores: Enabling Software-Managed Memory Hierarchies in Mainstream Computing Environments. In *EECS Department, University of California, Berkeley, Tech. Rep. UCB/EECS-2009-131*, 2009.

[113]   Mattan Erez, Brian P. Towles, and William J. Dally. Spills, Fills, and Kills – An Architecture for Reducing Register-Memory Traffic. Technical Report TR-23, Stanford Univ., Concurrent VLSI Architecture Group, 2000.

[114]   Antonio María González Colás, José González González, and Mateo Valero Cortés. Virtual-Physical Registers. In *HPCA*, 1998.

[115]   Javier Zalamea, Josep Llosa, Eduard Ayguadé, and Mateo Valero. Two-level Hierarchical Register File Organization for VLIW Processors. In *MICRO*, 2000.

[116] Romain Dolbeau, Stéphane Bihan, and François Bodin. HMPP: A Hybrid Multi-Core Parallel Programming Environment. In *GPGPU 2007*, 2007.

[117] Tianyi David Han and Tarek S. Abdelrahman. hiCUDA: High-level GPGPU programming. *IEEE Trans. Parallel Distrib. Syst.*, 22(1):78–90, 2011.

[118] Jonathan Ragan-Kelley, Connelly Barnes, Andrew Adams, Sylvain Paris, Frédo Durand, and Saman Amarasinghe. Halide: A Language and Compiler for Optimizing Parallelism, Locality, and Recomputation in Image Processing Pipelines. In *PLDI*, 2013.

[119] Sain-Zee Ueng, Melvin Lathara, Sara S. Baghsorkhi, and Wen-mei W. Hwu. *Languages and Compilers for Parallel Computing: 21th International Workshop, LCPC 2008, Edmonton, Canada, July 31–August 2, 2008, Revised Selected Papers*, chapter CUDA-Lite: Reducing GPU Programming Complexity. 2008.

[120] Adwait Jog, Onur Kayiran, Asit K. Mishra, *et al.* Orchestrated Scheduling and Prefetching for GPGPUs. In *ISCA*, 2013.

[121] Adwait Jog, Onur Kayiran, Nachiappan C. Nachiappan, *et al.* OWL: Cooperative Thread Array Aware Scheduling Techniques for Improving GPGPU Performance. In *ASPLOS*, 2013.

[122] Minseok Lee, Seokwoo Song, Joosik Moon, *et al.* Improving GPGPU Resource Utilization Through Alternative Thread Block Scheduling. In *High Performance Computer Architecture (HPCA), 2014 IEEE 20th International Symposium on*, 2014.

[123] Gennady Pekhimenko, Evgeny Bolotin, Mike O'Connor, Onur Mutlu, Todd C. Mowry, and Stephen W Keckler. Toggle-Aware Compression for GPUs. In *HPCA*, 2016.

[124] David Tarjan and Kevin Skadron. On demand register allocation and deallocation for a multithreaded processor, 2011. US Patent 20110161616.

[125] Ari B. Hayes and Eddy Z. Zhang. Unified On-Chip Memory Allocation for SIMT Architecture. In *Proceedings of the 28th ACM International Conference on Supercomputing*, ICS'14, 2014.

[126] Rakesh Komuravelli, Matthew D. Sinclair, Johnathan Alsop, *et al.* Stash: Have Your Scratchpad and Cache It Too. In *ISCA*, 2015.

[127] Chao Li, Yi Yang, Zhen Lin, and Huiyang Zhou. Automatic Data Placement Into GPU On-Chip Memory Resources. In *Code Generation and Optimization (CGO), 2015 IEEE/ACM International Symposium on*, 2015.

[128] Xiaolong Xie, Yun Liang, Xiuhong Li, *et al.* Enabling Coordinated Register Allocation and Thread-Level Parallelism Optimization for GPUs. In *Proceedings of the 48th International Symposium on Microarchitecture*, pages 293–302, New York, NY, USA, 2015. ACM, ACM.

[129] M. Aater Suleman, Onur Mutlu, Moinuddin K. Qureshi, and Yale N. Patt. Accelerating Critical Section Execution with Asymmetric Multi-core Architectures. In *ASPLOS*, 2009.

Chapter 5

Tools and workloads for many-core computing

Amit Kumar Singh[1], Piotr Dziurzanski[2], Geoff V. Merrett[3], and Bashir M. Al-Hashimi[3]

Proper tools and workloads are required to evaluate any computing systems. This enables designers to fulfill the desired properties expected by the end-users. It can be observed that multi/many-core chips are omnipresent from small-to-large-scale systems, such as mobile phones and data centers. The reliance on multi/many-core chips is increasing as they provide high-processing capability to meet the increasing performance requirements of complex applications in various application domains. The high-processing capability is achieved by employing parallel processing on the cores where the application needs to be partitioned into a number of tasks or threads and they need to be efficiently allocated onto different cores. The applications considered for evaluations represent *workloads* and toolchains required to facilitate the whole evaluation are referred to as *tools*. Figure 5.1 provides a three-layer view of a typical computing system, where the top layer contains applications and thus represents workloads. The tools facilitate realization of different actions (e.g., thread-to-core mapping and voltage/frequency control, which are governed by OS scheduler and power governor, respectively) and their effect on different performance monitoring counters leading to a change in the performance metrics (e.g., energy consumption and execution time) concerned by the end-users.

The design of multi/many-core chips has been the focus of several chip manufactures. The examples of some industrial chips include Samsung Exynos 5422 System-on-Chip (SoC) [1] that contains 4 ARM Cortex-A15 cores, 4 ARM Cortex-A7 cores and a six-core ARM Mali T628 MP6 GPU, Intel's Teraflop 80-core processor [2] and Xeon Phi 64-core processor [3], 16 and 64 core Epiphany processors [4], Tilera's TILE-Gx family 100-core processor [5], AMD's Opteron 16-core processor [6], Kalray's MPPA® 256-core processor [7] and recently developed KiloCore 1000-core chip [8] by IBM and UCDavis. Even world's fastest supercomputers such as Tianhe-2 (MilkyWay-2) and Titan use many-cores, and the total number of cores in Tianhe-2 is around 3 millions. The large number of cores within a chip is usually connected by an on-chip interconnection network [9,10], whereas bus-based or

[1] School of Computer Science and Electronic Engineering, University of Essex, UK
[2] Department of Computer Science, University of York, UK
[3] School of Electronics and Computer Science, University of Southampton, UK

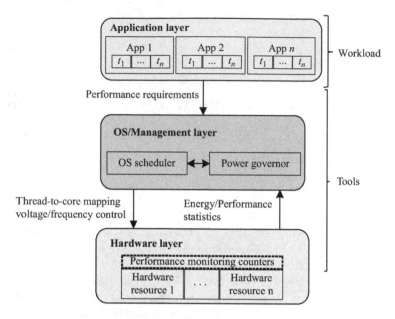

Figure 5.1   Three-layer view of a computing system [11]

point-to-point interconnections are used when the number of cores is small. The hardware in bottom-layer of Figure 5.1 can represent any of these chips.

These chips power systems of different scales to meet the respective user requirements. For small-scale systems such as mobile phones and desktops, usually a single chip is used, whereas multiple chips are used for large-scale systems such as data centers. Figure 5.2 classifies these systems into single-chip and multi-chip systems, where the hardware layer contains one and multiple chips, respectively. Examples of single and multiple chip multicore systems are embedded systems (including mobile phones) and data centers, respectively. In embedded systems, typically a single chip containing small number of cores is used, e.g., Samsung Exynos 5422 SoC [1], which powers popular Samsung Galaxy series of mobile phones [11]. In a desktop computer, a chip having higher numbers of cores, e.g., Intel's Xeon Phi 64-core processor [3] and AMD's Opteron 16-core processor [6], is used [12]. An HPC data center connects a set of nodes (servers) [13], where each node contains a set of cores within a chip and the cores communicate via an interconnection network and the nodes communicate via a high-speed network, e.g., InfiniBand. When the number of cores within a chip is relatively smaller, it is referred to as a multicore chip and the cores are usually interconnected by a shared bus or point-to-point links. However, the chip is referred to as a many-core chip when the number of cores is relatively higher and they are usually connected by a network-on-chip. Further, some of these systems might incorporate cores of different types to achieve efficiency over only one types of cores [14].

As shown earlier, since many-core systems can employ a single or multiple chips, it is important to identify appropriate tools and workloads to evaluate them. In this chapter, the tools for these systems are reviewed from three

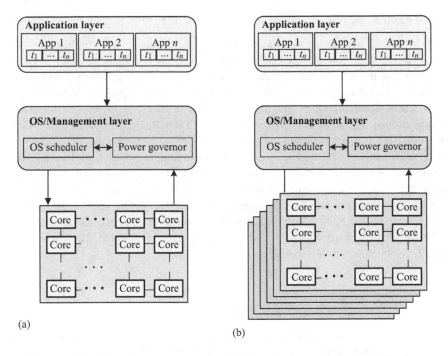

Figure 5.2   Many-core systems with: (a) single chip and (b) multiple chips

categories: (i) toolchains or scripts generated by designers to map and schedule application codes, e.g., C/C++ codes, on real hardware platforms, e.g., Samsung Exynos 5422 SoC [1]; (ii) simulation tools, to evaluate systems by simulating the descriptions of applications and architectures at a high level, e.g., task graphs [15] and synchronous data flow graphs [16] and (iii) commercial tools or software development environments to program the real hardwares to run application(s), e.g., Xilinx's Software Development Kit (SDK) to program many-core systems available or created in a field-programmable gate array (FPGA) chip [17].

This chapter is organized around the descriptions/discussions of tools and workloads for these systems as follows. Section 5.1 provides overview of identified tools and workloads for systems using single chips. The same has been covered in Section 5.2 for systems using multiple chips. Section 5.3 provides a discussion about the tools and benchmarks covered in Sections 5.1 and 5.2. Section 5.4 concludes the chapter.

5.1   Single-chip multi/many-core systems

In this section, the typical tools used for design and analysis of single-chip many-core systems are investigated. Then, the characteristic workloads of these systems are discussed.

5.1.1 Tools

Table 5.1 lists various tools employed to evaluate single-chip multi/many-core systems. The first few entries list developed tools for the Epiphany microprocessor, probably the most widely supported many-core architecture. Despite the recent problems related to the public release of the 1,024-core Epiphany-V version, its predecessor Epiphany-III is still publicly available as a coprocessor in the Parallella Board [4]. The Epiphany SDK [18] and CO-PRocessing THReads (COPRTHR) OpenCL SDK [19] are officially supported. The former is composed of Eclipse IDE, GCC, GDB, an Epiphany driver, loader and runtime library. The toolchain includes a functional simulator for a single core. The COPRTHR SDK provides libraries and tools facilitating programming low-power many-core RISC coprocessors. It offers a portable application programming interface (API) for targeting accelerators with an message passing interface (MPI) programming model for parallel code development. An integrated many-core coprocessor debugging tool is included. An open-source OpenCL implementation is available.

Table 5.1 Tools for single-chip multi/many-core systems

Category	Reference	Comments/Remarks
Toolchains/ Scripts	Epiphany SDK [18]	For Epiphany
	COPRTHR SDK [19]	For Epiphany
	ARL OpenSHMEM [20]	For Epiphany
	ePython [21]	For Epiphany
	OMPi OpenMP compiler [22]	Ported for Epiphany
	Epiphany BSP [23]	For Epiphany
	SMYLE OpenCL [24]	Framework for OpenCL
	Adrenaline [25]	Framework for OpenVX
	GSNoC [26]	Frameworks for 3D NoC design perspectives
Simulation	HORNET [27]	Applicable to many-cores of various scales
	FOLCS [28]	Applicable to many-cores of various scales
	BookSim2 [29]	Applicable to many-cores of various scales
	Gem5+GPU [30]	Applicable to many-cores of various scales
	VIPPE [31]	Parallel native simulation
	SMVM-NoC [32]	NoC simulator based on OMNeT++
	OVPSim [33]	Fast simulation of virtual platforms
Commercial tools	Multicore Development Environment [34]	For TILE-Gx72 and TILE-Gx36
	MPPA DEVELOPER [35]	For Kalray MPPA2®-256
	AccessCore® SDK [35]	For Kalray MPPA2-256
	eMCOS IDE [36]	Profiler, trace analyzer for eMCOS
	Sourcery CodeBench [37,38]	Complete development environment
	AbsInt aiT [39]	WCET static analyzer
	Open Virtual Platforms (OVP) [33]	For creating software virtual platforms

The US Army Research Laboratory (ARL) has developed the ARL OpenSHMEM for Epiphany, which is a standardized interface to enable portable applications for partitioned global address space architectures. Its high-performance execution while approaching hardware theoretical networking limits is demonstrated in [20]. ePython is a Python-based parallel programming environment for Epiphany and similar many-core coprocessors [21]. It offers the capability of off-loading specific Python functions (kernels) from an existing Python code to a many-core coprocessor. Despite OpenMP was intended for shared memory multiprocessing programming and thus is more suitable for symmetric multiprocessing (SMP) architectures than for the cores with local memories, there exists its implementation for Epiphany [22]. A bulk synchronous parallel (BSP) programming environment developed by Coduin is also available [23]. The programs following the BSP model are composed of so-called supersteps performing local computations and non-blocking communication, finished with a barrier synchronization. Some popular Google technologies such as MapReduce and Pregel are based on this model.

The processors developed by Tilera, including TILE64, TILEPro64, TILEPro36, TILE-Gx72, TILE-Gx36, TILE-Gx16 and TILE-Gx9 are also suitable for many-core embedded systems. After the acquisition of EZchip in February 2016, TILE-Gx72 and TILE-Gx36 are offered by Mellanox Technologies. This company offers the toolset named Multicore Development Environment™ (MDE) [34]. In this environment, cross-compilation is performed using a typical C/C++ GNU compiler. An Eclipse IDE facilitates many-core application debugging and profiling. A complete system simulator and hardware development platform is also available.

Kalray offers MPPA2-256 (Bostan) many-core processors with 288 cores, optimized for networking and storage applications [35]. The EMB boards from the same company provide a complete environment to develop compute-intensive embedded systems. This processor is programmed using MPPA DEVELOPER and AccessCore SDK. Kalray's SDK is based on Eclipse and offers a set of simulation, profiling, debugging and system trace tools. Three programming styles are allowed: a low-level DSP style, POSIX-level CPU Style and graphic processing unit (GPU) style based on OpenCL.

On Kalray MPPA, eMCOS [36] and ERIKA Enterprise [40] operating systems can be installed. The eMCOS IDE Plug-in development tools shipped with the former OS consist of eMCOS-specific system analysis tools and utility software for building, debugging and system analysis. They include Real-time Profiler for run-time analysis of each core, thread and function, Message Profiler for the analysis of the message communication behaviors from the OS to the driver, middleware and application and Trace Analyzer for tracing the system events. Kalray cores are also targeted by Absint aiT static analysis tool for determining the worst case execution time of a given taskset [39].

Despite the existence of the OpenCL SDK for Epiphany or Kalray mentioned above, OpenCL is rather rarely used in embedded many-core systems in general. The reasons for this fact, as explained in [24], are the large runtime overhead for creation and mapping of threads at runtime. Similarly, memory buffers and command queues required for an OpenCL program execution are created at runtime.

In that paper, SMYLE OpenCL, a framework for OpenCL dedicated to embedded many-cores, is proposed. This framework reduces the runtime overhead by creating the threads and objects statically, as demonstrated on a five-core SMYLEref architecture implemented on an FPGA prototype board.

OpenVX is an open standard for cross-platform acceleration of computer vision applications specified at a higher level of abstraction than OpenCL. In OpenVX, a computer vision application is specified as a connected graph of vision nodes executing a chain of operations. In [25], an open framework for OpenVX named Adrenaline is presented. It targets an embedded SoC platform with a general-purpose host processor coupled with a many-core accelerator, such as STM STHORM, KALRAY MMPA or Adapteva Epiphany.

Embedded Sourcery™ CodeBench from Mentor® is a commercial set of embedded C/C++ development tools [37]. It includes an Eclipse-based IDE with a performance-optimized compiler based on GCC and optimized runtime libraries for selected embedded cores. An advanced software insight allows the developers to identify and correct functional, timing and performance bottlenecks. The attached multicore debugger facilitates simultaneous debug of multiple operating systems or applications running on different cores. The applications can be simulated using the QEMU hypervisor. This toolset has been used for embedded many-core systems in, e.g., [38].

A set of simulation tools, used for embedded many-cores, can be also applied to larger systems. The examples of such tools are HORNET [27], FOLCS [28], Book-Sim2 [29] and GEM5 (with a GPU extension) [30]. However, there exist a couple of simulators that are dedicated solely to the small-scale many-core systems. One of them is VIPPE [31] that offers a parallel host-compiled simulation methodology, which make an efficient use of multicore host platforms. Some simulators are applicable only to embedded NoCs, such as SMVM-NoC, an OMNeT++ based Network-on-Chip simulator for embedded systems [32]. In this simulator, such parameters as network size, buffer size and clock frequency are customizable. To reduce the communication cost in NoCs, 3D chip technologies are emerging. Similarly, the necessary tools have been developed recently. One of them is Generic Scalable Networks-on-Chip (GSNoC) [26], which is a comprehensive design platform. It handles the 3D NoCs design at the application, architecture and circuit design levels. The platform is equipped with an application generator, design framework and a cycle accurate system simulator.

OVPsim [33] is one of the most mature embedded many-core simulators. This tool is a component of Open Virtual Platforms (OVP). OVP offers APIs allowing the users to model processors, peripherals and platforms to create software virtual platforms. Such platforms can be fast simulated with the OVPsim simulator, as the instruction accurate simulation can achieve up to 1,000 MIPS. Numerous example platform models including up to 24 processors are provided. These platforms benefit from the attached peripheral models, such as Ethernet or USB. Finally, several processor models can be used, including such families as OpenCores, ARM, Synopsys ARC, MIPS, PowerPC, Altera, Xilinx and Renesas. These OVP models are provided with interface wrappers for C, C++, SystemC and OSCI SystemC TLM2.0 environments.

OVP is free for noncommercial usage and thus can boast with a huge community and numerous related research projects. For example, an accurate energy estimation for embedded many-core systems has been added to OVPSim in [38].

5.1.2 Workloads

Table 5.2 lists various workloads/benchmarks used to evaluate single-chip multi/many-core systems. Among them are both industry-standard benchmark suites and the sets developed in academia.

Industry-standard benchmarks for embedded systems are licensed by the industry alliance named EEMBC. This organization offers benchmark sets for various mobile devices, networking, IoT, digital media, automotive, etc. Three of their suites are labeled as multicore and can be also applicable to many-core architectures. The first of them, AutoBench 2.0, is dedicated to automotive processors. MultiBench, the second multicore processor suite, includes more than 100 data processing and computationally intensive workloads for evaluating an impact of parallelization and scalability of multi- and many-core processors. Some workloads realize typical networking tasks (e.g., reassembling TCP/IP packets or compressing H.264 video streams), image processing (e.g., image rotations or color model conversions) or cryptographic functions (e.g., MD5 checksum calculation). These workloads are especially suitable for identifying memory bottlenecks and measure the efficiency of parallel task

Table 5.2　Benchmarks for single-chip multi/many-core systems

Category	Reference	Comments/Remarks
Benchmark sets	Autobench 2.0 [41]	Commercially licensed
	MultiBench [42]	Commercially licensed
	SPLASH-2 [43]	HPC workloads mainly
	PARSEC [44]	Modern problems, not HPC
	E3S [45]	For high-level synthesis
	MiBench [46]	Wide range of embedded apps
	SD-VBS [47]	Vision domain apps
	Rodinia [48]	For heterogeneous platforms
	StreamIt [49]	Streaming apps
Popular workloads	Sobel [25,50–52]	Edge detector filter
	MMUL [53–57]	Matrix multiplication
	QSORT [53]	Parallel versions from [58]
	NCC [50,55,59]	Normalized cross-correlation [60]
	FAST [25,52,55,61]	Corner detection [62]
	Computer vision [55,59]	Derived from OpenCV library [63]
	Canny [25,52]	Edge detector
	Odd-even sorting [57,64,65]	Distributed sorting
	Papabench [66], Rosace [67]	Control apps of drone and plane
	Object tracking [65,68,69]	E.g., Vehicle localization
	3D path planning [70,71]	Avionic collision avoidance
	DemoCar [72]	Gasoline engine ECU

synchronization. Both AutoBench 2.0 and MultiBench are in a form of C/C++ codes intended to be run on a POSIX-compliant operating system. They may also be ported to a bare-metal platform with a custom scheduler, memory driver and thread synchronization mechanisms. Some examples of these benchmarks' licensing costs are provided in [42]. CoreMark-Pro is another set from EEMBC. It consists of five integer and four floating-point workloads including JPEG compression, XML parser, SHA256, Zip, FFT, linear algebra and a neural net. Some of these workloads (e.g., FFT or neural net) exhibit relatively low level of data dependencies and thus are more suitable for many-core systems than others (e.g., XML parser).

SPLASH-2 benchmark suite includes 11 workloads mainly from the high-performance computing (HPC) domain (e.g., Cholesky factorization, FFT, LU decomposition) and graphic synthesis (e.g., Radiocity or Raytrace), which hardly cover the most typical modern usage patterns of parallel processing in many-cores. SPLASH-2 applications are written in C and are optimized to enhance scalability in the large-scale cache coherent nonuniform memory access architectures. In [73], some changes to make the suite compatible with modern programming practices and a number of bug fixes have been performed in order to port the original benchmark suite to a many-core architecture. The authors of [74] found that seven original SPLASH-2 workloads contain data races due to the initial synchronization optimizations. They produced the SPLASH-3 suite, a sanitized version of the SPLASH-2 without data races and performance bugs, compliant with the contemporary C-standard memory model. Despite the year of its release, the SPLASH-2 benchmark suite still remains one of the most popular collections of multithreaded workloads. It has been used for an embedded many-core architecture evaluation in, e.g., [75]. Among the SPLASH-2 workloads, FFT and Cholesky are particularly often considered for many-cores, e.g., in [71,76,77].

PARSEC (Princeton Application Repository for Shared-Memory Computers) benchmark suite [44] contains fundamentally different types of programs than SPLASH-2. Among 13 workloads, there are representative applications from assorted areas such as enterprise servers, computer vision, data mining and animation. They reflect the contemporary computing problems and are not focused on the HPC domain. The applications are written in C and have been parallelized with pthreads and OpenMP. These workloads have been used for embedded many-cores in, e.g., [31,75].

E3S is an embedded system synthesis benchmark set based on the EEMBC benchmarks suite. It includes task graphs of five applications from the automotive industry, consumer, networking, office automation and telecommunication areas without providing their codes (due to the EEMBC licensing restrictions). Consequently, their application is limited to the system-level allocation and scheduling, particularly when applied to the Network-on-Chip based architectures, as shown for example in [78].

MiBench [46] is a set of 35 applications covering the embedded system diversity at the time of its release (2001). The applications range from a sensor system on a simple microcontroller to a smart cellular phone. The whole set is divided into six categories: automotive and industrial control, consumer devices, office automation, networking, security and telecommunications and includes basic math calculations, quick sort, image recognition, Dijkstra's algorithm, Rijndael, SHA,

JPEG encode/decode, MP3 encoder, spelling checker, FFT, CRC32 and many more. The programs are freely available as C source codes with (usually) two data sets: a light-weight but useful embedded application of the benchmark and a large real-world application. Despite their single-thread nature, the benchmarks can be successfully used to evaluate embedded many-core environments, as shown in [79].

The more recent SD-VBS [47] suite includes nine applications from the computer vision domain, namely, disparity map, feature tracking, image segmentation, SIFT, SVM, robot localization, face detection, image stitch and texture synthesis. These applications are composed of over 28 computationally intensive kernels such as principal component analysis (PCA), correlation, Gaussian filter, QR factorization, affine transforms, etc. The codes are provided in both MATLAB® and C. For each benchmark, the data inputs of three different sizes are provided. The SD-VBS suite has been employed in, e.g., [79].

Rodinia (version 3.1) suite contains 23 applications (e.g., Gaussian elimination, K-means, back propagation, leukocyte tracking, BFS, path finder, stream cluster, similarity scores, LU decomposition) targeting heterogeneous architectures with CPUs and GPUs. The domains of these benchmarks range from data mining to fluid dynamics. The diversity of the benchmarks stems from applying various Berkeley Dwarves, such as Dense Linear Algebra, Dynamic Programming, MapReduce, Un/Structured Grid, etc. The CPU-targeted codes are written in C++ where parallelism and synchronization are defined with the OpenMP pragmas. The GPU implementations of the benchmarks are provided as CUDA codes. Additionally, the codes are available in OpenCL and OpenACC.

In [49], a relatively large set of streaming application benchmarks is available as dataflow programs written in the StreamIt language, described in [80]. These benchmarks include DCT, FFT, DES, FM radio, MP3 decoder, Serpent, JPEG decoder/encoder, MPEG2 decoder/encoder, etc. For several benchmarks, the corresponding C codes are also provided. This suite has been used with many-core architectures in [81] or [82].

Despite the abundance of available benchmark suites as presented above, a large number of research is still carried out using other workloads. Some of them implement classic computer science algorithms, such as matrix multiplication in [53–57], odd-even sorting [57,64,65], parallel quick sort in [53], normalized cross-correlation in [50,55,59], etc. The popularity of computer vision many-core applications grows rapidly which is also reflected in the workload selection. The traditional Sobel edge detector filter has been employed in [25,50–52], the Canny edge detector in [25,52] and FAST corner detection in [25,52,55,61]. Various object tracking approaches (including data fusion from multiple sources) have been presented in [65,68,69]. Numerous computer vision algorithms derived from OpenCV library [63] have been studied in [55,59]. Some researchers prefer to work with custom real-world applications. DemoCar, a minimal gasoline engine electronic control unit (ECU), has been presented and studied in [72]. Control applications of a drone and plane have been used as workloads in [66] and [67], respectively. 3D path planning algorithms applied for avionic collision avoidance systems are analyzed in [70,71].

Additionally, tasksets for multi/many-cores can be artificially created using various tools, for example, Task Graph For Free [83], as it is done in [84], or Synchronous

Dataflow 3 [85]. Various automotive ECU can be generated using the AMALTHEA tool platform [86].

5.2 Multi-chip multi/many-core systems

The tools and workloads for multi-chip systems are described in the following subsections.

5.2.1 Tools

Table 5.3 lists various tools employed to evaluate multi-chip multi/many-core systems, as shown in Figure 5.2.

The toolchains/scripts are limited for the evaluation of multi-chip multi/many-core systems. These have been developed to achieve some specific additional purposes.

SystemC based tools are used in [13], where resource allocation approaches are implemented in a C++ prototype and integrated with a SystemC functional simulator. To simulate real situations, it is considered that the number of jobs arriving during peak times is higher than that of off-peak times. All the jobs arriving over a whole day, i.e., 24-h period, are considered to sufficiently stress the data center resources, where a job contains a set of dependent tasks.

Table 5.3 Tools for multi-chip multi/many-core systems

Category	Reference	Comments/Remarks
Toolchains/ Scripts	SystemC-based tool [13]	Configurable number of servers and cores
	Analytical model [87,88]	For fast evaluation
Simulation	CloudSim [89]	Configurable number of nodes (servers)
	CloudAnalyst [90]	Configurable number of nodes (servers)
	GreenCloud [91]	Configurable number of nodes (servers)
	iCanCloud [92]	Configurable number of nodes (servers)
	EMUSIM [93]	Configurable number of nodes (servers)
	GroudSim [94]	Configurable number of nodes (servers)
	DCSim [95]	Configurable number of nodes (servers)
	CloudSched [96]	Configurable number of nodes (servers)
	CDOSim [97]	Configurable number of nodes (servers)
	TeachCloud [98]	Configurable number of nodes (servers)
	SPECI [99]	Configurable number of nodes (servers)
	MDCSim [100]	Configurable number of nodes (servers)
	Dist-Gem5 [101]	Gem5 extension to distributed systems
Commercial tools	CoolSim [102]	Tool for data center managers
	Apache Hadoop [103]	For computer clusters
	OpenMP [104]	For shared memory multiprocessing
	OpenMPI [105]	For multiprocessing
	OpenACC [106]	For heterogeneous CPU/GPU platforms

Analytical models have been used to accelerate the evaluation process [87,88]. In [87], analytical methods for estimating the total data center energy efficiency are proposed. This allows designers to evaluate energy efficiency of various power management approaches. For different approaches, polynomial efficiency models for cooling and power-conversion equipment are used to construct the system-level energy efficiency model. The models are evaluated for various example cases to show their benefits. In [88], an analytical model supports the design and evaluation of various resource allocation controller parameters.

There is a considerable list of simulators to evaluate multi-chip many-core systems and the notable ones are listed in Table 5.3.

CloudSim [89] is a highly generalized and extensible Java-based simulation tool for realizing data centers, virtual machines (VMs), applications, users, computational resources and policies for managing diverse parts of the system like scheduling and provisioning. The data center contains a set of nodes (server), where each node is composed of a many-core chip. It also enables modeling and simulation of large-scale cloud-computing data centers by configuring the number of nodes to a high value. Further, it has support to incorporate user-defined policies for allocating hosts to VMs and include different network topologies.

CloudAnalyst [90] is a GUI-based simulator derived from CloudSim. Therefore, it has some extended features and capabilities. It facilitates evaluation according to the geographical distribution of data centers and users. It is regarded as a powerful simulation framework for deploying real-time data centers and monitoring load balancing. The available extensions in this tool range from enabling GUI features, by saving configurations as XML files to exporting live results in the PDF format. The graphical outputs also include tables and charts, in addition to a large amount of statistical data. It also has a high degree of configuration ability as several entities such as data center size, memory, storage and bandwidth can be easily configured to perform a new set of experiments.

GreenCloud [91] has been developed as an extension to the NS-2 packet-level network simulator. It provides an environment for simulating energy-aware cloud computing data centers. It offers a detailed fine-grained modeling of the energy consumed by the various equipment used in a data center. Examples of these equipment are servers, network switches and communication links. The data center servers, each containing a many-core chip, are created with a help of a script, where data center size can be configured. This simulator can be used to explore methods leading to minimized electricity consumption.

iCanCloud [92] is based on SIMCAN and developed over the OMNeT++ platform. It was developed with the aim of predicting the trade-offs between cost and performance of a given set of applications executed on specific hardware. Further, it supports flexibility, accuracy, performance and scalability and thus has been widely used to design, test and analyze various existing and non-existing cloud architectures. It also provides a user-friendly GUI, which is useful for managing preconfigured experiments/systems and generating graphical reports.

EMUSIM [93] stands for Integrated Emulation and Simulation. It integrates emulation (Automated Emulation Framework) and Simulation (CloudSim) to enable fast and accurate simulations. It is particularly useful when there is limited information regarding the performance of the software under the varied levels of concurrency and parallelism as it accurately models application performance.

GroudSim [94] is designed for scientific applications on grid and cloud environments. It has a rich set of features, e.g., calculation of costs for job executions and background load on resources.

DCSim (data center simulation) [95] is an extensible data center simulator. It facilitates high-end experiments on data center management for the evaluation of data center management policies and algorithms. It also contains a multitier application model that allows the simulation of dependencies and has support for feedback.

CloudSched [96] provides different metrics for load–balance, energy efficiency and utilization, etc. It uses the model suggested by Amazon, where physical machine and VM specifications are predefined. It also supports migration algorithms.

CDOSim [97] is a cloud deployment option (CDO) that can simulate the response times, SLA violations and costs of a CDO. It has the ability to represent the user's rather than the provider's perspective. It can be used to determine trade-off between costs and performance. It also has features to use workload profiles from production monitoring data.

TeachCloud [98] is made specially for education purposes. For students and scholars, it provides a simple graphical interface to modify a cloud's configuration and perform experiments. It uses CloudSim as the basic design platform and introduces many new enhancements on top of it, e.g., a GUI toolkit, a workload generator, new network models and a reconfiguration interface.

SPECI [99] stands for Simulation Program for Elastic Cloud Infrastructures and allows analysis and exploration of scaling properties of large data centers while taking the given design policies of the middleware into account. Due to its elastic nature, it allows exploration of performance properties of future data centers. Thus, the designer can have insights into the expected performance of data centers when they are designed, but not built.

MDCSim [100] is a scalable simulation platform for in-depth analysis of multitier data centers. It captures all the important design specifics of communication paradigm, kernel level scheduling algorithms and the application level interactions among the tiers of the data center.

Dist-Gem5 [101] is a flexible, detailed and open-source full-system simulation infrastructure. It is an extension of Gem5 to model and simulate distributed computer system using multiple simulation hosts.

Commercial tools are also available to evaluate data centers. Such tools provide evaluation on physical real hardware. Some of these tools are listed in Table 5.3 and described as follows.

CoolSim [102] enables the analysis and design refinement of data centers. It offers several benefits such as an easy to use and quick to learn user environment. By using CoolSim, the best data center in terms of price/performance can be designed.

Apache Hadoop [103] is an open-source software framework usually employed for processing of big data applications/data using the MapReduce programming model. The framework contains a set of clusters built from hardware. The processing part in Apache Hadoop is accomplished by employing MapReduce programming model and there is a storage part, known as Hadoop Distributed File System. Hadoop splits files into large blocks and then distributes them across nodes in a cluster to process the data in parallel. Thus, the data is processed fast. Apache Spark is another popular framework providing an interface for programming entire clusters. It allows the developers to efficiently execute the class of applications inappropriate to the Hadoop's MapReduce model, such as iterative jobs, streaming jobs or interactive analysis [107]. Apache Spark can execute applications up to two orders of magnitude faster than Hadoop due to the reduced number of read/write operations. However, Spark usually requires more RAM memory than Hadoop and is perceived as slightly less secure because of limited authentication options.

OpenMP (open multi-processing) [104] is an API that supports multi-platform (multi-chip) shared memory multiprocessing. It is employed with programming languages C, C++, and Fortran and is compatible with most hardware platforms and operating systems such as Solaris, AIX, HP-UX, Linux, macOS and Windows. This API has been implemented in a number of commercial compilers from various vendors (e.g., Intel, IBM), as well as the ones developed by open source communities. It offers a simple and flexible interface to develop parallel applications for platforms of various scales, e.g., desktop computers and supercomputers.

OpenMPI [105] is a MPI library project combining technologies and resources from several other projects. Similarly to OpenMP, it has been implemented in both commercial and open-source compilers. It has been used by several TOP500 supercomputers of the world. Some notable examples include Roadrunner, the world's fastest supercomputer from June 2008 to November 2009, and K computer, the fastest supercomputer from June 2011 to June 2012.

The fastest supercomputer in 2017, Sunway TaihuLight, has its own implementation of OpenACC [106], another directive-based parallel programming model. OpenACC is aimed at heterogeneous HPC hardware platforms with GPU accelerators. In contrast to OpenMP, where the possible parallelisms and data dependencies have to be expressed in the code explicitly, OpenACC can benefit from the user's guidance but is capable of performing automatic parallelization of the user-selected regions (kernels) and off-loading them to GPUs. Commercial compilers supporting OpenACC are available from CRAY and PGI, but this model is also supported by GCC7 and a number of academic compilers.

5.2.2 Workloads

Table 5.4 lists various workloads/benchmarks used to evaluate multi-chip multi/many-core systems. Multithreaded applications are potential benchmarks to evaluate multi-chip systems. However, some of these benchmarks can be used to evaluate single-chip multi/many-core systems as well [11], e.g., PARSEC [44] and SPLASH-2 [43], and have been mentioned earlier in this chapter. Short descriptions of the additional benchmarks listed in Table 5.4 are as follows.

CloudSuite [108] consists of eight applications that have been selected based on their popularity in today's data centers. These benchmarks represent real-world setups and are based on real-world software stacks.

Table 5.4   Benchmarks for multi-chip multi/many-core systems

Category	Reference	Comments/Remarks
Benchmark sets	PARSEC [44]	Modern problems, not HPC
	SPLASH-2 [43]	HPC workloads mainly
	CloudSuite [108]	Several software components
	SPEC Cloud_IaaS [109]	SPEC's first cloud benchmark
	TPCx-V [110]	TPC's data center benchmark
	LINPACK [111]	Currently used to rank the TOP500 computing systems
	HPCG [112]	Proposed to rank the TOP500 computing systems

SPEC Cloud IaaS 2016 benchmark [109] is SPEC's the first benchmark suite to evaluate performance of cloud infrastructures. In addition to academic researchers, the benchmark is targeted for cloud providers, cloud consumers, hardware vendors, virtualization software vendors and application software vendors.

TPC Express Benchmark V (TPCx-V) [110] helps to measure the performance of servers running database workloads. It has features to simulate load variation in cloud data centers with the help of unique elastic workload characteristic. It stresses several resources such as CPU and memory hardware.

The high-performance LINPACK (HPL) benchmark [111] evaluates floating point computing power of a system. For a common task in engineering, they measure how fast a computer system solves a dense system of linear equations. Its latest version is used to evaluate and rank world's most powerful TOP500 supercomputers.

High-performance conjugate gradients (HPCG) benchmark [112] has been proposed to create a new metric for ranking HPC systems. It is a complement to the LINPACK (HPL) benchmark. The benchmark has several basic operations such as sparse matrix-vector multiplication, vector updates and global dot products.

Additionally, the simulators listed in Table 5.3 also contain inbuilt functions to create data center workloads of varying natures. Therefore, they can also be used to stress the data center resources, mainly cores of the chips.

5.3   Discussion

The tools and workloads/benchmarks covered in the earlier sections can be used to evaluate systems of various scales, such as embedded, desktop and data centers. Typically, tools and benchmarks for single-chip systems are used to evaluate embedded systems and desktop computers equipped with many-core CPUs or accelerators. However, some of them, especially having multithreaded applications can be used to evaluate multi-chip systems as well.

Since these benchmarks stress the systems in different ways, i.e., some impose high computation load and some high memory load, they need to be appropriately selected to properly evaluate the considered system. It might also be worth trying a mixture of some of the benchmark applications to cover a broad spectrum of workloads across different resources of a computing system.

In addition to the tools and benchmarks covered in this chapter, there are several developments for GPU-based multi/many-cores systems, e.g., CUDA [113], OpenCL [114], OpenHMPP [115], etc. However, in this chapter, our focus is on CPU-based multi/many-core systems, so we are not detailing GPU-based systems.

5.4 Conclusion and future directions

This chapter presents tools and workloads/benchmarks to evaluate systems containing a set of cores. These cores can be present in a single chip or multiple chips, forming single-chip and multi-chip systems, respectively. Depending upon the requirements such as programming model and evaluating cores stressing, appropriate tools and benchmarks can be chosen to evaluate a system under consideration.

Although there exists a considerable list of tools and workloads to harness the potential of multi/many-core chips, several open problems concerning these need to be addressed to facilitate the multi/many-core computing research for the next era.

5.4.1 Parallelization of real-world applications

Although there are several benchmarks representing computations involved in real-world applications, e.g., PARSEC [44] and SPLASH-2 [43], they cannot be used for deployment in real-world scenarios. This needs consideration of real-world applications to be parallelized in such a way that their parallelized version can be executed on real hardware platforms while processing real-time inputs. Nevertheless, there are some efforts for such parallelization and its usage, e.g., doing image processing by using multithreaded and/or task-graph representation of the application [116,117]. However, a considerable amount of efforts is required to perform parallelization of real-world applications to be executed on real hardware platforms.

5.4.2 Domain-specific unification of workloads

Current workloads/benchmarks contain application from various application domains, e.g., video processing and data mining in PARSEC [44] benchmark. However, researchers, designers and engineers are typically domain specific and thus need application for the respective domain. Therefore, there is a need for unification of the workloads/benchmarks based on the domain that can be achieved by having the domain expertise of researchers, designers and engineers. By putting the unified workloads on a web-page, it will facilitate for easier identification. Additionally, one needing applications from various domains can look into the right categories. This can also prevent creation of a similar benchmarks and thus leading to reduced efforts.

5.4.3 Unification of simulation tools

Similar to the unification of the workloads/benchmarks, unification of the simulation tools is desired. It can be considered from several perspectives, e.g., simulations of small-scale bus-based multicore systems, large-scale NoC-based many-core systems and multi-chip multi/many-core systems. This may help to employ the same simulation tools for similar kind of research, rather than using a different simulator, and thus facilitating for a fair comparison of tools/methodologies.

5.4.4 Integration of tools to real products

Currently, there is widespread development of tools that show significant improvement for various performance metrics when compared to the conventional tools employed in multi/many-core systems [11,118–121]. However, their adoption to real products is missing. There are several reasons for it, e.g., the steps taken to achieve the improvements are not commonly followed by hardware and software engineers in industry and tools are not developed by considering real-world applications. This requires close interaction between academic and industry so that the steps taken can be well communicated for widespread adoption while considering real-world applications.

References

[1] Samsung. Samsung Exynos 5422; 2014. www.samsung.com/exynos/.
[2] Vangal S, Howard J, Ruhl G, *et al.* An 80-Tile 1.28TFLOPS Network-on-Chip in 65nm CMOS. In: Proceedings of IEEE International Solid-State Circuits Conference (ISSCC); 2007. p. 98–589.
[3] Intel. Xeon Phi; 2016. https://ark.intel.com/products/95828/Intel-Xeon-Phi-Processor-7230F-16GB-1_30-GHz-64-core.
[4] Olofsson A, Trogan R, Raikhman O, *et al.* A 1024-core 70 GFLOP/W floating point manycore microprocessor. In: Poster on 15th Workshop on High Performance Embedded Computing HPEC2011; 2011.
[5] TILE-Gx. First 100-Core Processor with the New TILE-Gx Family; 2009. http://www.tilera.com/ (Last visited: 12 February, 2016).
[6] AMD. AMD Opteron 6000 Series Processors; 2011. http://www.amd.com/en-us/products/server/opteron/6000 (Last visited: 12 February, 2016).
[7] De Dinechin BD, Van Amstel D, Poulhiès M, *et al.* Time-critical computing on a single-chip massively parallel processor. In: Proceedings of IEEE Conference on Design, Automation and Test in Europe (DATE); 2014. p. 1–6.
[8] Bohnenstiehl B, Stillmaker A, Pimentel J, *et al.* A 5.8 pJ/Op 115 Billion Ops/sec, to 1.78 Trillion Ops/sec 32nm 1000 processor array. In: IEEE Symposia on VLSI Technology and Circuits; 2016.
[9] Benini L, De Micheli G. Networks on chips: a new SoC paradigm. Computer. 2002;35(1):70–78.

[10] Worm F, Ienne P, Thiran P, *et al.* An adaptive low-power transmission scheme for on-chip networks. In: Proceedings of IEEE/ACM/IFIP Conference on Hardware/Software Codesign and System Synthesis (ISSS+CODES); 2002. p. 92–100.

[11] Reddy BK, Singh AK, Biswas D, *et al.* Inter-cluster thread-to-core mapping and DVFS on heterogeneous multi-cores. IEEE Transactions on Multi-Scale Computing Systems. 2017:4(3):369–382.

[12] Wang X, Singh AK, Li B, *et al.* Bubble budgeting: throughput optimization for dynamic workloads by exploiting dark cores in many core systems. IEEE Transactions on Computers. 2018:67(2):178–192.

[13] Singh AK, Dziurzanski P, Indrusiak LS. Value and energy optimizing dynamic resource allocation in many-core HPC systems. In: IEEE International Conference on Cloud Computing Technology and Science (CloudCom); 2015. p. 180–185.

[14] Smit LT, Smit GJM, Hurink JL, *et al.* Run-time mapping of applications to a heterogeneous reconfigurable tiled system on chip architecture. In: Proceedings of IEEE International Conference on Field-Programmable Technology (FPT); 2004. p. 421–424.

[15] Dick RP, Rhodes DL, Wolf W. TGFF: task graphs for free. In: CODES+ISSS; 1998. p. 97–101.

[16] Stuijk S, Geilen MCW, Basten T. SDF^3: SDF for free. In: Proceedings of IEEE Conference on Application of Concurrency to System Design (ACSD); 2006. p. 276–278.

[17] Xilinx SDK; 2012. https://www.xilinx.com/products/design-tools/embedded-software/sdk.html (Last visited: 04 November, 2017).

[18] Adapteva Inc. Epiphany SDK Reference; 2013.

[19] Brown Deer Technology L. COPRTHR-2 SDK; 2017. Available from: http://www.browndeertechnology.com/coprthr2.htm.

[20] Ross J, Richie D. An OpenSHMEM implementation for the adaptive epiphany coprocessor. In: Workshop on OpenSHMEM and Related Technologies. Springer; 2016. p. 146–159.

[21] Brown N. ePython: an implementation of python for the many-core epiphany coprocessor. In: Proceedings of the 6th Workshop on Python for High-Performance and Scientific Computing. PyHPC'16. Piscataway, NJ, USA: IEEE Press; 2016. p. 59–66. Available from: https://doi.org/10.1109/PyHPC.2016.8.

[22] Agathos SN, Papadogiannakis A, Dimakopoulos VV. Targeting the parallella. In: European Conference on Parallel Processing. Springer; 2015. p. 662–674.

[23] Coduin. Epiphany BSP's Documentation; 2017. Available from: http://www.codu.in/ebsp/docs/.

[24] Tomiyama H, Hieda T, Nishiyama N, *et al.* SMYLE OpenCL: a programming framework for embedded many-core SoCs. In: 2013 18th Asia and South Pacific Design Automation Conference (ASP-DAC); 2013. p. 565–567.

[25] Tagliavini G, Haugou G, Marongiu A, *et al.* A framework for optimizing OpenVX applications performance on embedded manycore accelerators.

In: Proceedings of the 18th International Workshop on Software and Compilers for Embedded Systems. SCOPES'15. New York, NY, USA: ACM; 2015. p. 125–128. Available from: http://doi.acm.org/10.1145/2764967.2776858.

[26]   Ying H, Hollstein T, Hofmann K. GSNoC – the comprehensive design platform for 3-dimensional networks-on-chip based many core embedded systems. In: 2013 International Conference on High Performance Computing Simulation (HPCS); 2013. p. 217–223.

[27]   Lis M, Ren P, Cho MH, *et al.* Scalable, accurate multicore simulation in the 1000-core era. In: (IEEE ISPASS) IEEE International Symposium on Performance Analysis of Systems and Software; 2011. p. 175–185.

[28]   Naruko T, Hiraki K. FOLCS: a lightweight implementation of a cycle-accurate NoC simulator on FPGAs. In: Proceedings of the 3rd International Workshop on Many-Core Embedded Systems. MES'15. New York, NY, USA: ACM; 2015. p. 25–32. Available from: http://doi.acm.org/10.1145/2768177.2768182.

[29]   Jiang N, Balfour J, Becker DU, *et al.* A detailed and flexible cycle-accurate network-on-chip simulator. In: Performance Analysis of Systems and Software (ISPASS), 2013 IEEE International Symposium on. IEEE; 2013. p. 86–96.

[30]   Power J, Hestness J, Orr MS, *et al.* gem5-gpu: a heterogeneous CPU-GPU simulator. IEEE Computer Architecture Letters. 2015;14(1):34–36.

[31]   Nicolas A, Sanchez P. Parallel native-simulation for multi-processing embedded systems. In: 2015 Euromicro Conference on Digital System Design; 2015. p. 543–546.

[32]   Mansour A, Götze J. An OMNeT++ based network-on-chip simulator for embedded systems. In: 2012 IEEE Asia Pacific Conference on Circuits and Systems; 2012.

[33]   Software I. OVP – Open Virtual Platforms; 2017. Available from: http://www.ovpworld.org.

[34]   Technologies M. Multicore Development Environment (MDE); 2017. Available from: http://www.mellanox.com/page/products_dyn?product_family=250.

[35]   Kalray. Kalray Software; 2017. Available from: http://www.kalrayinc.com.

[36]   eSOL Co. Software Development Kit for Many-Core Processors; 2017. Available from: https://www.esol.com/embedded/emcos_sdk.html.

[37]   Oliver K. How-To Guide: Creating and Debugging Linux Applications Using Sourcery Codebench for ARM GNU/Linux; 2012. Available from: http://s3.mentor.com/public_documents/whitepaper/resources/mentorpaper_72367.pdf.

[38]   Rosa F, Ost L, Raupp T, *et al.* Fast energy evaluation of embedded applications for many-core systems. In: 2014 24th International Workshop on Power and Timing Modeling, Optimization and Simulation (PATMOS); 2014. p. 1–6.

[39]   Heckmann R, Ferdinand C. Worst-case execution time prediction by static program analysis. In: In 18th International Parallel and Distributed Processing Symposium (IPDPS 2004). IEEE Computer Society; 2004. p. 26–30.

[40] Technology EE. Erika Enterprise RTOS v3; 2017. Available from: http://www.erika-enterprise.com/.

[41] Poovey JA, Conte TM, Levy M, *et al.* A benchmark characterization of the EEMBC benchmark suite. IEEE Micro. 2009;29(5):18–29.

[42] Halfhill TR. EEMBC's Multibench Arrives; 2008. Available from: http://www.eembc.org/benchmark/pdf/080812_MPRarticle_MultiBench.pdf.

[43] Woo SC, Ohara M, Torrie E, *et al.* The SPLASH-2 programs: characterization and methodological considerations. In: Proceedings 22nd Annual International Symposium on Computer Architecture; 1995. p. 24–36.

[44] Bienia C, Li K. PARSEC 2.0: a new benchmark suite for chip-multiprocessors. In: Proceedings of the 5th Annual Workshop on Modeling, Benchmarking and Simulation; 2009.

[45] Dick R. Embedded System Synthesis Benchmarks Suite (E3S); 2010. Available from: http://ziyang.eecs.umich.edu/dickrp/e3s/.

[46] Guthaus MR, Ringenberg JS, Ernst D, *et al.* MiBench: a free, commercially representative embedded benchmark suite. In: Proceedings of the Fourth Annual IEEE International Workshop on Workload Characterization. WWC-4 (Cat. No. 01EX538); 2001. p. 3–14.

[47] Venkata SK, Ahn I, Jeon D, *et al.* SD-VBS: the San Diego vision benchmark suite. In: 2009 IEEE International Symposium on Workload Characterization (IISWC); 2009. p. 55–64.

[48] Che S, Boyer M, Meng J, *et al.* Rodinia: a benchmark suite for heterogeneous computing. In: 2009 IEEE International Symposium on Workload Characterization (IISWC); 2009. p. 44–54.

[49] Amarasinghe S, Gordon M, Soule R, *et al.* StreamIt Benchmarks; 2009. Available from: http://groups.csail.mit.edu/cag/streamit/shtml/benchmarks.shtml.

[50] Tagliavini G, Haugou G, Benini L. Optimizing memory bandwidth in OpenVX graph execution on embedded many-core accelerators. In: Proceedings of the 2014 Conference on Design and Architectures for Signal and Image Processing; 2014. p. 1–8.

[51] Hollis SJ, Ma E, Marculescu R. nOS: a nano-sized distributed operating system for many-core embedded systems. In: 2016 IEEE 34th International Conference on Computer Design (ICCD); 2016. p. 177–184.

[52] Lepley T, Paulin P, Flamand E. A novel compilation approach for image processing graphs on a many-core platform with explicitly managed memory. In: 2013 International Conference on Compilers, Architecture and Synthesis for Embedded Systems (CASES); 2013. p. 1–10.

[53] Gunes V, Givargis T. XGRID: a scalable many-core embedded processor. In: 2015 IEEE 17th International Conference on High Performance Computing and Communications, 2015 IEEE 7th International Symposium on Cyberspace Safety and Security, and 2015 IEEE 12th International Conference on Embedded Software and Systems; 2015. p. 1143–1146.

[54] Burgio P, Marongiu A, Valente P, *et al.* A memory-centric approach to enable timing-predictability within embedded many-core accelerators. In: 2015

CSI Symposium on Real-Time and Embedded Systems and Technologies (RTEST); 2015. p. 1–8.

[55] Capotondi A, Marongiu A, Benini L. Enabling scalable and fine-grained nested parallelism on embedded many-cores. In: 2015 IEEE 9th International Symposium on Embedded Multicore/Many-Core Systems-on-Chip; 2015. p. 297–304.

[56] Jose W, Neto H, Vestias M. A many-core co-processor for embedded parallel computing on FPGA. In: 2015 Euromicro Conference on Digital System Design; 2015. p. 539–542.

[57] Lai JY, Huang CT, Hsu TS, *et al.* Methodology of exploring ESL/RTL many-core platforms for developing embedded parallel applications. In: 2014 27th IEEE International System-on-Chip Conference (SOCC); 2014. p. 286–291.

[58] Quinn MJ. Parallel programming in C with MPI and OpenMP. McGraw-Hill Higher Education; 2004.

[59] Vogel P, Marongiu A, Benini L. Lightweight virtual memory support for many-core accelerators in heterogeneous embedded SoCs. In: Proceedings of the 10th International Conference on Hardware/Software Codesign and System Synthesis. CODES'15. Piscataway, NJ, USA: IEEE Press; 2015. p. 45–54. Available from: http://dl.acm.org/citation.cfm?id=2830840.2830846.

[60] Magno M, Tombari F, Brunelli D, *et al.* Multimodal abandoned/removed object detection for low power video surveillance systems. In: Proceedings of the 2009 Sixth IEEE International Conference on Advanced Video and Signal Based Surveillance. AVSS'09. Washington, DC, USA: IEEE Computer Society; 2009. p. 188–193. Available from: https://doi.org/10.1109/AVSS.2009.72.

[61] Koutras I, Anagnostopoulos I, Bartzas A, *et al.* Improving dynamic memory allocation on many-core embedded systems with distributed shared memory. IEEE Embedded Systems Letters. 2016;8(3):57–60.

[62] Rosten E, Porter R, Drummond T. Faster and better: a machine learning approach to corner detection. IEEE Transactions on Pattern Analysis and Machine Intelligence. 2010;32(1):105–119.

[63] OpenCV Team. OpenCV: Open Source Computer Vision. Software Library; 2017. Available from: http://opencv.org/.

[64] Huang CT, Tasi KC, Lin JS, *et al.* Application-level embedded communication tracer for many-core systems. In: The 20th Asia and South Pacific Design Automation Conference; 2015. p. 803–808.

[65] Chien HW, Lai JL, Wu CC, *et al.* Design of a scalable many-core processor for embedded applications. In: The 20th Asia and South Pacific Design Automation Conference; 2015. p. 24–25.

[66] Nemer F, Casse H, Sainrat P, *et al.* PapaBench: a free real-time benchmark. In: Mueller F, editor. 6th International Workshop on Worst-Case Execution Time Analysis (WCET'06). vol. 4 of OpenAccess Series in Informatics (OASIcs). Dagstuhl, Germany: Schloss Dagstuhl–Leibniz-Zentrum fuer Informatik; 2006.

[67] Pagetti C, Saussié D, Gratia R, *et al.* The ROSACE case study: from Simulink specification to multi/many-core execution. In: 2014 IEEE 19th Real-Time and Embedded Technology and Applications Symposium (RTAS); 2014. p. 309–318.

[68] Louise S, Dubrulle P, Goubier T. A model of computation for real-time applications on embedded manycores. In: 2014 IEEE 8th International Symposium on Embedded Multicore/Manycore SoCs; 2014. p. 333–340.

[69] Stan O, Sirdey R, Carlier J, *et al.* A GRASP for placement and routing of dataflow process networks on many-core architectures. In: 2013 Eighth International Conference on P2P, Parallel, Grid, Cloud and Internet Computing; 2013. p. 219–226.

[70] Panic M, Quiñones E, Zavkov PG, *et al.* Parallel many-core avionics systems. In: 2014 International Conference on Embedded Software (EMSOFT); 2014. p. 1–10.

[71] Vargas RE, Royuela S, Serrano MA, *et al.* A lightweight OpenMP4 runtime for embedded systems. In: 2016 21st Asia and South Pacific Design Automation Conference (ASP-DAC); 2016. p. 43–49.

[72] Dziurzanski P, Singh AK, Indrusiak LS, *et al.* Benchmarking, system design and case-studies for multi-core based embedded automotive systems. In: 2nd International Workshop on Dynamic Resource Allocation and Management in Embedded, High Performance and Cloud Computing DREAMCloud; 2016. Available from: https://arxiv.org/abs/1601.03708.

[73] Venetis JE, Gao GR. The Modified SPLASH-2 Benchmarks Suite Home Page; 2007. Available from: http://www.capsl.udel.edu/splash/index.html.

[74] Sakalis C, Leonardsson C, Kaxiras S, *et al.* Splash-3: a properly synchronized benchmark suite for contemporary research. In: 2016 IEEE International Symposium on Performance Analysis of Systems and Software (ISPASS); 2016. p. 101–111.

[75] Biswas D, Balagopal V, Shafik R, *et al.* Machine learning for run-time energy optimisation in many-core systems. In: Design, Automation Test in Europe Conference Exhibition (DATE), 2017; 2017. p. 1588–1592.

[76] Ross JA, Richie DA, Park SJ, *et al.* Parallel programming model for the epiphany many-core coprocessor using threaded MPI. In: Proceedings of the 3rd International Workshop on Many-Core Embedded Systems. MES'15. New York, NY, USA: ACM; 2015. p. 41–47. Available from: http://doi.acm.org/10.1145/2768177.2768183.

[77] Nikolakopoulos Y, Papatriantafilou M, Brauer P, *et al.* Highly concurrent stream synchronization in many-core embedded systems. In: Proceedings of the Third ACM International Workshop on Many-core Embedded Systems. MES'16. New York, NY, USA: ACM; 2016. p. 2–9. Available from: http://doi.acm.org/10.1145/2934495.2934496.

[78] Wildermann S, Teich J. Self-integration for virtualization of embedded many-core systems. In: 2014 IEEE Eighth International Conference on Self-Adaptive and Self-Organizing Systems Workshops; 2014. p. 170–177.

[79]   Li Z, He S, Wang L. Prediction based run-time reconfiguration on many-core embedded systems. In: 2017 IEEE International Conference on Computational Science and Engineering (CSE) and IEEE International Conference on Embedded and Ubiquitous Computing (EUC). vol. 2; 2017. p. 140–146.

[80]   Thies W, Karczmarek M, Amarasinghe SP. StreamIt: a language for streaming applications. In: Proceedings of the 11th International Conference on Compiler Construction. CC'02. London, UK, UK: Springer-Verlag; 2002. p. 179–196. Available from: http://dl.acm.org/citation.cfm?id=647478.727935.

[81]   Rouxel B, Puaut I. STR2RTS: refactored StreamIT benchmarks into statically analyzable parallel benchmarks for WCET estimation & real-time scheduling. In: Reineke J, editor. 17th International Workshop on Worst-Case Execution Time Analysis (WCET 2017). vol. 57 of OpenAccess Series in Informatics (OASIcs). Dagstuhl, Germany: Schloss Dagstuhl–Leibniz-Zentrum fuer Informatik; 2017. p. 1:1–1:12. Available from: http://drops.dagstuhl.de/opus/volltexte/2017/7304.

[82]   Selva M, Morel L, Marquet K, *et al.* Extending dataflow programs with throughput properties. In: Proceedings of the First International Workshop on Many-Core Embedded Systems. MES'13. New York, NY, USA: ACM; 2013. p. 54–57. Available from: http://doi.acm.org/10.1145/2489068.2489077.

[83]   Dick RP, Rhodes DL, Wolf W. TGFF: task graphs for free. In: Hardware/Software Codesign, 1998. (CODES/CASHE'98) Proceedings of the Sixth International Workshop on; 1998. p. 97–101.

[84]   de Lima OA, Fresse V, Rousseau F. Evaluation of SNMP-like protocol to manage a NoC emulation platform. In: 2014 International Conference on Field-Programmable Technology (FPT); 2014. p. 199–206.

[85]   Stuijk S, Geilen M, Basten T. Exploring trade-offs in buffer requirements and throughput constraints for synchronous dataflow graphs. In: DAC; 2006. p. 899–904.

[86]   Wolff C, Krawczyk L, Höttger R, *et al.* AMALTHEA – tailoring tools to projects in automotive software development. In: 2015 IEEE 8th International Conference on Intelligent Data Acquisition and Advanced Computing Systems: Technology and Applications (IDAACS). vol. 2; 2015. p. 515–520.

[87]   Malkamäki T, Ovaska SJ. Analytical model of data center infrastructure efficiency for system level simulations. In: Proceedings of the 8th International Conference on Simulation Tools and Techniques. ICST (Institute for Computer Sciences, Social-Informatics and Telecommunications Engineering); 2015. p. 319–326.

[88]   Faraci G, Schembra G. An analytical model for electricity-price-aware resource allocation in virtualized data centers. In: Communications (ICC), 2015 IEEE International Conference on. IEEE; 2015. p. 5839–5845.

[89]   Calheiros RN, Ranjan R, Beloglazov A, *et al.* CloudSim: a toolkit for modeling and simulation of cloud computing environments and evaluation of resource provisioning algorithms. Software: Practice and Experience. 2011;41(1):23–50.

[90]   Wickremasinghe B, Calheiros RN, Buyya R. Cloudanalyst: A cloudsim-based visual modeller for analysing cloud computing environments and applications. In: Advanced Information Networking and Applications (AINA), 2010 24th IEEE International Conference on. IEEE; 2010. p. 446–452.

[91]   Kliazovich D, Bouvry P, Khan SU. GreenCloud: a packet-level simulator of energy-aware cloud computing data centers. The Journal of Supercomputing. 2012;62(3):1263–1283.

[92]   Núñez A, Vázquez Poletti JL, Caminero C, *et al.* iCanCloud: a flexible and scalable cloud infrastructure simulator. Journal of Grid Computing. 2012:10(1):185–209.

[93]   Calheiros RN, Netto MA, De Rose CA, *et al.* EMUSIM: an integrated emulation and simulation environment for modeling, evaluation, and validation of performance of cloud computing applications. Software: Practice and Experience. 2013;43(5):595–612.

[94]   Ostermann S, Plankensteiner K, Prodan R, *et al.* GroudSim: an event-based simulation framework for computational grids and clouds. In: European Conference on Parallel Processing. Springer; 2010. p. 305–313.

[95]   Keller G, Tighe M, Lutfiyya H, *et al.* DCSim: a data centre simulation tool. In: Integrated Network Management (IM 2013), 2013 IFIP/IEEE International Symposium on. IEEE; 2013. p. 1090–1091.

[96]   Tian W, Zhao Y, Xu M, *et al.* A toolkit for modeling and simulation of real-time virtual machine allocation in a cloud data center. IEEE Transactions on Automation Science and Engineering. 2015;12(1):153–161.

[97]   Fittkau F, Frey S, Hasselbring W. Cloud user-centric enhancements of the simulator cloudsim to improve cloud deployment option analysis. In: European Conference on Service-Oriented and Cloud Computing. Springer; 2012. p. 200–207.

[98]   Jararweh Y, Alshara Z, Jarrah M, *et al.* Teachcloud: a cloud computing educational toolkit. International Journal of Cloud Computing 1. 2013; 2(2–3):237–257.

[99]   Sriram I. SPECI, a simulation tool exploring cloud-scale data centres. Cloud Computing. 2009; p. 381–392.

[100] Lim SH, Sharma B, Nam G, *et al.* MDCSim: a multi-tier data center simulation, platform. In: Cluster Computing and Workshops, 2009. CLUSTER'09. IEEE International Conference on. IEEE; 2009. p. 1–9.

[101] Mohammad A, Darbaz U, Dozsa G, *et al.* dist-gem5: distributed simulation of computer clusters. In: Performance Analysis of Systems and Software (ISPASS), 2017 IEEE International Symposium on. IEEE; 2017. p. 153–162.

[102] CoolSim. CoolSim for Data Center Managers; 2017. Available from: http://www.coolsimsoftware.com/.

[103] Foundation AS. Apache Hadoop; 2017. Available from: https://www.apache.org/.

[104] OpenMP. Open Multi-Processing; 2017. Available from: http://www.openmp.org.

[105] OpenMPI. Open Source Message Passing Interface; 2017. Available from: https://www.open-mpi.org/.

[106] org OS. The OpenACC Application Programming Interface; 2017. Available from: https://www.openacc.org/sites/default/files/inline-files/OpenACC. 2.6.final.pdf.

[107] Zaharia M, Chowdhury M, Franklin MJ, *et al.* Spark: cluster computing with working sets. In: Proceedings of the 2nd USENIX Conference on Hot Topics in Cloud Computing. HotCloud'10. Boston, MA, USA; 2010. p. 10.

[108] CloudSuite. Benchmark Suite for Cloud Services; 2017. Available from: http://cloudsuite.ch/.

[109] SPEC. SPEC Cloud_IaaS 2016; 2016. Available from: https://www.spec.org/ benchmarks.html.

[110] TPC. TPCx-V; 2017. Available from: http://www.tpc.org/information/ benchmarks.asp.

[111] LINPACK. LINPACK Benchmark; 2017. Available from: https://www. top500.org/project/linpack/.

[112] HPCG. High Performance Conjugate Gradients (HPCG) Benchmark; 2017. Available from: http://www.hpcg-benchmark.org/.

[113] CUDA. Compute Unified Device Architecture; 2017. Available from: https://developer.nvidia.com/cuda-zone.

[114] OpenCL. Open Computing Language; 2017. Available from: https://www. khronos.org/opencl/.

[115] OpenHMPP. Open Source Hybrid Multicore Parallel Programming; 2017. Available from: http://www.ithistory.org/resource/openhmpp.

[116] Singh AK, Kumar A, Srikanthan T, *et al.* Mapping real-life applications on run-time reconfigurable NoC-based MPSoC on FPGA. In: FPT; 2010. p. 365–368.

[117] Leech C, Kumar C, Acharyya A, *et al.* Runtime performance and power optimization of parallel disparity estimation on many-core platforms. ACM Transactions on Embedded Computing Systems (TECS). 2018;17(2):41.

[118] Prakash A, Amrouch H, Shafique M, *et al.* Improving mobile gaming performance through cooperative CPU-GPU thermal management. In: Proceedings of the 53rd Annual Design Automation Conference. ACM; 2016. p. 47.

[119] Donyanavard B, Mück T, Sarma S, *et al.* Sparta: runtime task allocation for energy efficient heterogeneous manycores. In: Hardware/Software Codesign and System Synthesis (CODES+ ISSS), 2016 International Conference on. IEEE; 2016. p. 1–10.

[120] Gupta U, Patil CA, Bhat G, *et al.* DyPO: dynamic pareto-optimal configuration selection for heterogeneous MpSoCs. ACM Transactions on Embedded Computing Systems (TECS). 2017;16(5s):123.

[121] Singh AK, Prakash A, Basireddy KR, *et al.* Energy-efficient run-time mapping and thread partitioning of concurrent OpenCL applications on CPU-GPU MPSoCs. ACM Transactions on Embedded Computing Systems (TECS). 2017;16(5s):147.

Chapter 6

Hardware and software performance in deep learning

*Andrew Anderson[1], James Garland[1], Yuan Wen[1],
Barbara Barabasz[1], Kaveena Persand[1],
Aravind Vasudevan[1], and David Gregg[1]*

In recent years, deep neural networks (DNNs) have emerged as the most successful technology for many difficult problems in image, video, voice and text processing. DNNs are resource hungry and require very large amounts of computation and memory, which is a particular challenge on IoT, mobile and embedded systems. In this chapter, we outline some major performance challenges of DNNs such as computation, parallelism, data locality and memory requirements. We describe research on these problems, such as the use of existing high-performance linear algebra libraries, hardware acceleration, reduced precision storage and arithmetic and sparse data representations. Finally, we discuss recent trends in adapting compiler and domain-specific program generation techniques to create high-performance parallel DNN programs.

6.1 Deep neural networks

Traditional artificial neural networks (ANNs) consist of a graph of individual *neurons*, which *activate* when some function of their input and an associated weight value crosses a threshold. Appropriate weight values are found by iteratively training the ANN on many thousands of sample inputs. By adjusting the weight values to better match the training input, the network gradually learns to encode features of the inputs. With a sufficiently large training set, the network can learn to identify similar features in new inputs that are not part of the training set. Once the ANN is trained, it can be used to recognize features in real-world data, a process known as *inference*.

ANNs have been studied for decades, but during most of their history, they have been just one approach among many. However, in recent years, neural networks have moved ahead of other approaches for a wide range of problems. Two of the overlapping technologies that underpin this success are convolutional neural networks (CNNs) and DNNs.

---

[1]School of Computer Science and Statistics, Trinity College Dublin, Ireland

CNNs [1] are specifically designed to process data with a spatial component, such as images from a camera. In a traditional ANN, there might be a separate neuron for each pixel of the input image. However, in most image-processing applications, the problem is to detect objects or patterns *somewhere* in the image, not at a particular pixel location. CNNs introduce a convolution operator, which is used to model groups of neurons, each with a certain *receptive field* which covers part of the input data. The convolutional 'neuron' produces as output a mapping of the input image to a new image, by convolving the input with a kernel, which takes the place of a traditional neuron's weight.

The kernel is applied in each spatial location, allowing the same kernel to find a given pattern at any location in the image. By making the patterns location independent, training of the CNN becomes faster and more effective. Every convolutional kernel is adjusted by the training process so that it encodes, either by itself or in concert with other kernels, some feature or features in the input data. CNNs have proven extraordinarily successful at image recognition and classification tasks and have found application in related areas such as object detection, segmentation, captioning and many more.

Another major advance in ANNs has been a move towards deeper networks with more layers. These deep networks became prominent in 2012 when AlexNet [2] beat previous records for object recognition by a significant margin. AlexNet had eight major layers, including five convolutional layers and three of the more old-fashioned *fully connected* layers. In 2015, GoogLeNet [3] again broke all records using more than 70 convolutional layers. It appears that deep networks are able to perform complex operations that, for example, allow the same pattern to be identified in different sizes and orientations, as well as in different locations within an image.

The high classification accuracy of DNNs comes at a significant price however. DNNs require very large amounts of processing capacity, energy and memory both for training and inference. The training process for a DNN is typically conducted offline using graphics processor units (GPUs) or other powerful machines. Training the model to an acceptable degree of classification accuracy may take days or weeks. But using this trained model, inference can be carried out an arbitrary number of times, using new inputs that require classification.

While the ahead-of-time training process can be carried out on powerful computing platforms, inference is typically most useful when deployed in edge computing situations, for example in an automotive context for pedestrian detection, parking assistance, cruise control or lane-keeping functionality. The inputs for inference in edge contexts consist mostly of data from cameras and other environmental sensors. The limited resources available in edge computing scenarios constrain the inference process, making performance, memory requirements and energy efficiency primary concerns.

6.2 DNN convolution

Convolution is the key primitive and accounts for the majority of arithmetic operations performed by many popular CNNs. There are a number of performance obstacles for

DNN convolution. The tensors storing the weight data can be very large, since each weight is a full convolutional filter. The computation of the convolution operator can involve a very large number of multiply–accumulate (MAC) operations. There are also performance opportunities. The large tensor operations that are used to compute DNN convolution can exploit a great deal of data locality to improve performance.

6.2.1 Parallelism and data locality

Figure 6.1 gives a graphical overview of the convolution performed by CNNs operating on two-dimensional images with multiple channels and kernels. The input consists of an image with some number of channels C, each of height and width H, W. Each of the M kernels consists of C two-dimensional $k \times k$ element filters, which are convolved with the corresponding image channels. The C results are then summed pointwise to produce one of the M channels of the output.

Figure 6.2 shows pseudocode for the same operation. The code consists of a six-deep nested loop that scans over the input image and kernels to compute the output. Of the six nested loops, the three outermost loops have a very specific pattern of fully independent loop iterations. In contrast, the three inner loops all contribute to a summation across the three loops. We treat each triple of loops separately.

In DNN convolution, there are always multiple separate kernels, each of which is applied to the input, and this is shown in the outermost loop. Next, the convolution operator scans over each element of the output image traversing by height and width of the result image, which appear in the next two loops. The iterations of these three outer loops that traverse the kernels, height and width are fully independent. These iterations of these loops can be executed in parallel, and the order of these loops can be freely interchanged. These fully independent loop iterations mean that DNN convolution has very large amount of available data parallelism. This data parallelism makes DNN convolution very efficient on multicore CPUs, vector processors and many-core GPUs.

The three inner loops in Figure 6.2 compute a summation. The two innermost loops perform a classical 2D convolution with a kernel of dimensions $K \times K$. In DNNs, each input image has multiple channels, and the result is computed by summing the result of 2D convolution for each channel, which is performed in the third

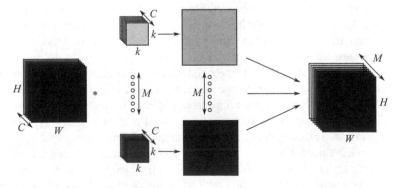

Figure 6.1 Diagram of the convolution operation

```
kernel[KERNELS][CHANNELS][K][K];
image[CHANNELS][HEIGHT][WIDTH];
output[KERNELS][HEIGHT][WIDTH];

for m in 1 to KERNELS {
  for h in 1 to HEIGHT {
    for w in 1 to WIDTH {
      sum = 0
      for c in 1 to CHANNELS {
        for x in 1 to K {
          for y in 1 to K {
            sum += image[c,h+y,w+x] * kernel[m,c,x,y]
          }
        }
      }
      output[m,h,w] = sum
    }
  }
}
```

Figure 6.2   Pseudocode for two-dimensional DNN convolution

innermost loop. Like the three outer loops, the order of the three inner loops can be interchanged arbitrarily. However, unlike the outer loops, the iterations of the three inner loops are not fully independent. There is a cyclic data dependency on the sum variable which limits parallelism. By exploiting the associativity of addition, these inner loops can be parallelized as a parallel reduction tree. However, the parallelism in the three outer loops is so abundant that it may be preferable to exploit the simple parallelism of the outer loops than the reduction parallelism of the inner loops.

Given the large amount of available parallelism, an important question is how best to be exploit it. There are many strategies for dividing the data parallelism in the loops among parallel cores, vector units or GPU threads. In general, the strategies that give the best results are those that both exploit data parallelism *and* maintain high levels of data reuse. A good parallelization strategy requires careful management of data locality.

DNN convolution differs from traditional 2D convolution in which the input images and kernels have multiple channels. Further, DNN convolution always involves simultaneous convolution with multiple different kernels. Thus, DNN convolution contains aspects of classical 2D convolution, aspects of a dot product (or scalar product) reduction across channels and aspects of a many-to-many cross product between blocks of the input image and the multiple convolution kernels. Both convolution and cross-product operations have potential for significant data reuse.

Traditional 2D image convolution offers a good deal of locality. Typically, we convolve a $K \times K$ kernel with an image. To compute a single pixel of output using a 3×3 kernel, we need a $3 \times 3 = 9$ pixel-sized block of input. To compute a 2×2 output block of pixels, we need $((3 + 1) \times (3 + 1)) = 16$ pixel block of input. By computing four output pixels at once, we can exploit a great deal of overlap in the required input points. Further, if we compute a 3×3 output block at a time, we need a $((4 + 1) \times (4 + 1)) = 25$ pixel block of input to compute 9 outputs. This is an average of just 2.78 input pixels per computed output pixel, as compared to 9 input pixels per output if we compute just one output at a time. In summary, classical 2D convolution is very amenable to data reuse and can have excellent data locality.

The third aspect of DNN convolution algorithms is the many-to-many cross product between the multiple kernels and regions of the input image. To compute one output point of a cross product, we need 1 pixel from the image and one kernel value. Given 2 pixel and one kernel point from each of two kernels, we can compute a 2×2 output block. This requires an average of $(2 + 2)/(2 \times 2) = 1$ input point per output computed. With four input pixels and one value from each of four different kernels, we can compute a 2×2 output block, requiring that we load an average of $(4 + 4)/(4 \times 4) = 0.5$ input points per output point. This many-to-many cross-product pattern of computation leads to very large amounts of data reuse and excellent data locality.

This same type of cross-product locality also arises in other problems such as 2D matrix multiplication. As a result, those designing and building parallel software to implement DNNs can draw on existing experience of parallelism and locality in matrix multiplication. However, experience has shown that to achieve maximum performance matrix multiplication routines should not be constructed as normal code. Instead, special-purpose program generators can be used to automatically generate and tune matrix multiplication for the underlying parallel architecture [4]. Given that maximum performance is usually achieved only using program generation, DNN operators are often constructed from existing matrix multiplication libraries, as described in the next section.

6.2.2   GEMM-based convolution algorithms

A popular approach for implementing the convolution operator is by *lowering* to matrix multiplication. High-performance implementations of matrix multiplication are available for a wide range of platforms, often via the Generalized Matrix Multiplication (GEMM) primitive from open-source or vendor Basic Linear Algebra Subprograms libraries. Although GEMM is typically a high-performance operation, lowering convolutions involves a large degree of data replication. This replication hurts locality of access and can drastically inflate memory requirements. Nevertheless, this approach is in widespread use in deep learning frameworks and performs very well on systems which do not have tight constraints on memory usage.

The most widely used lowering scheme, *im2col*, creates a Toeplitz matrix from the input image, which is then multiplied by the kernel matrix to produce the output. Building this Toeplitz matrix expands the input k^2 times. Figure 6.3 shows the main steps of this process. The input matrix is expanded so that each column contains the $k^2 C$ elements needed to compute a single point of the output.

A key tension that exists in GEMM-based implementations of convolution is that the data access pattern in a 2D convolution is fundamentally different from the data access pattern in a matrix multiplication. Lowering convolution into matrix

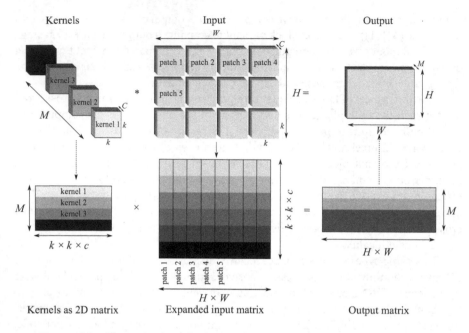

Figure 6.3   The im2col method of convolution using matrix multiplication

multiplications sacrifices a lot of spatial locality of access versus performing the convolution directly. High-performance GEMM implementations are tuned carefully to take advantage of the locality of access in matrix multiplication, but not in convolution.

One solution to this problem is to find different ways to express convolution as matrix multiplication. Cho and Brand propose a *memory-efficient convolution* (MEC) [5] for DNNs. Rather than performing a single GEMM using an input that has been expanded k^2 times, MEC performs k overlapping GEMMs on an input expanded k times.

Vasudevan *et al.* [6] propose an alternative expression of DNN convolution using GEMM that avoids the k^2 growth in the size of the input data, at the cost of k^2 increase in the size of an intermediate matrix. Unlike Cho and Brand, who compute the outputs in complete sections, Vasudevan *et al.* produce k^2 partial results in the result of the matrix multiplication. This *kern2row* method is shown in Figure 6.4. The output of the matrix multiplication is a matrix that is k^2 times larger than the output. In a final post-pass, partial results within this large matrix are summed to produce the correct, smaller output matrix.

Anderson *et al.* [7] proposed a more sophisticated version of *im2row* that uses k^2 separate GEMM calls without replication of the input or output. Each of the k^2 partial result matrices is computed in turn and added to an accumulating result matrix. Their approach becomes very efficient when they use a feature of the GEMM interface to accumulate partial results into a target matrix within the GEMM call.

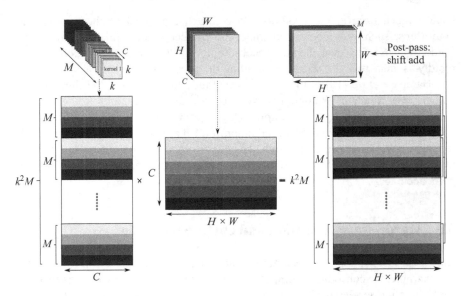

Figure 6.4   The kern2row method of performing convolution using matrix multiplication

6.2.3   Fast convolution algorithms

While direct convolution uses $O(N^2)$ multiplications to convolve two length-N sequences, research in signal processing has yielded *fast* convolution algorithms, which are fast in the sense that they use fewer operations to compute the result.

The well-known Convolution Theorem states that the Fourier transform of the convolution of two sequences is the pointwise product of their individual Fourier transforms. In practice, this allows the convolution to be implemented by taking the Fourier transform of the input and the kernel, performing a pointwise product, and taking the inverse Fourier transform of the result. Fast Fourier transform (FFT) convolution algorithms typically need just $O(N \ log_2(N))$ operations.

Another class of fast convolution algorithms are based on the work of Winograd [8], who proved that the convolution of two sequences of length n and length k can be computed using only $n + k - 1$ *general* multiplications. Winograd's approach does not perform convolution directly, but rather constructs convolution algorithms for a given fixed kernel size. Similar to FFT convolution, a transformation of the input and the kernel is computed, and pointwise multiplications between these transforms yield the result.

Lavin and Gray studied the benefits of Winograd convolution and found that these algorithms can be around twice as fast as direct convolution across a variety of CNNs on different machines [9]. However, fast convolution algorithms are not completely free of drawbacks. For FFT convolution, the computation of the forward and backward transforms can be prohibitively expensive, leading to a net performance decrease in adverse conditions. The kernel size in DNN convolution is typically too small to benefit much from FFT convolution. In contrast, the so-called short convolution algorithms, such as Winograd's method, are perfectly suited to the small kernels found in DNNs. However, the numerical stability of Winograd convolution degrades rapidly as the matrix size increases, limiting the potential benefits.

Barabasz *et al.* [10] propose several methods for improving the floating point numerical accuracy of Winograd convolution for DNNs. Although it is difficult to identify general techniques for improving accuracy, Barabasz *et al.* show that for DNNs, a small number cases are common, and that good solutions can be found for these cases by exhaustive search. They also propose more general methods for improving accuracy, such as exploiting the associativity of addition to improve floating point accuracy.

6.3   Hardware acceleration and custom precision

Hardware acceleration is one solution to the large computations that DNNs require. For example, the convolution computations undertaken in the convolution layers of a CNN are often accelerated by a GPU, a field programmable gate array (FPGA) or an application specific integrated circuit (ASIC) in order to speed up the performance of the overall CNN. However, these accelerators also come with their own advantages and disadvantages which are outlined below.

6.3.1   Major constraints of embedded hardware CNN accelerators

Popular CNNs such as AlexNet [2] and VGG-16 [11], when pretrained, have up to 240 and 552 MB of trained weight data, respectively. This amount of weight data is too large to reside in on-board mobile static random access memory (RAM) (SRAM) or embedded dynamic RAM (DRAM) (edram) and if stored in off-chip DRAM would cause a large energy expense when accessed. If these CNNs are to operate on handheld mobile devices with limited RAM and low power budgets, the weight data must be reduced or compressed.

The first convolutional layer of AlexNet takes an image of dimensions 227×227 pixel and three channels (usually red, green and blue channels). The filter that is used to convolve the image in layer 1 has dimensions 11×11 weight values, and a stride of four. The stride of four means that only elements of every fourth row and fourth column of the output are computed. The output of this first layer is $55 \times 55 \times 96$. Each output point is computed using a kernel of size has $11 \times 11 \times 3$ weights with 1 bias. So the total number of floating point operations (FLOPs) in the first layer alone is $290, 400 \times (363 + 1) = 105, 705, 600$ FLOPs, excessive computation for a low-power, high-latency mobile-embedded platform.

A number of methods have been proposed to reduce the memory footprint and computation intensity whilst increasing efficiency by hardware accelerating certain aspects of the neural network. A few of these methods are discussed below.

6.3.2 Reduced precision CNNs

A much-researched area is that of reducing the precision of the CNNs, i.e. designing the accelerators to use a lower number of bits and different number format. Standard CNNs that are designed to operate in devices that are not constrained by computation or memory usually use 32-bit floating point arithmetic. This number of bits and the large numbers of filter weights and FLOPs is often not feasible in mobile systems. Changing the number format from floating-point to fixed-point integer and reducing the numbers of bits from 32-bit floating point down to 16, 8, 4 or even 2 bits leads to computational and energy efficiency, lower gate counts and smaller area when implemented in ASICs or FPGAs.

Courbariaux *et al.* [12] benchmark floating point, fixed point and dynamic fixed point number formats in neural networks using MNIST [13], CIFAR-10 [14] and other small data sets. They find that multipliers that process inputs as small as 10 bit are not only sufficient for inference but can also be used in the training phase with little impact on classification accuracy.

Substituting the floating-point units with low precision, fixed point 16-bit computations is the focus of the work of Gupta *et al.* [15]. They replace round-to-nearest with stochastic rounding and show little or no classification accuracy effect. This additionally yields significant gains in energy efficiency and throughput when they implement their accelerator in an FPGA.

In order to decrease the training time of neural networks (which can often be very lengthy, hours or even days), one might consider using multiple processors, GPUS or FPGAs to accelerate the training. Dettmers [16] suggests that the communications bottleneck between the multiple accelerators is throttling the potential speedups parallelism offers. They develop 8-bit approximate algorithms to compress the 32-bit gradients and nonlinear activations to better utilize the available bandwidth and show a 50× speedup compared with 32 bit on a 96 GPU accelerator system.

Courbariaux *et al.* go even further, significantly reducing the precision of the CNN to 2 bits and call this BinaryConnect [17]. They reduce the multiplications by 2/3 by forcing the weights used in the forward and backward propagations to be binary; however, values may not necessarily be 1 or 0. They achieve comparable classification results on invariant MNIST, CIFAR-10 and SVHN data sets. This potentially reduces the memory requirements by 16×. They later coin the phrase Binarized Neural Network (BNN) for this reduced precision in their BinaryNet paper [18]. This paper also shows how BNNs can drastically reduce memory size and accesses, and reduce computation by replacing arithmetic operations with bitwise operations which substantially improves power efficiency whilst having comparable classification results on an invariant MNIST, CIFAR-10 and SVHN data sets.

BNNs reduce storage requirements and arithmetic operations, so Zhao *et al.* [19] show they are ideally suited to implementation in an FPGA. They show that input tile and line buffer design constructs are ineffective in BNNs so they propose new constructs such as variable-width line buffers. When compared to other CNN implementations in FPGA, their proposed accelerator yields 208GOPS verses 137GOPS on the next best 16-bit implementation. This gives them 44.2GOPS/Watt verses 14.3GOPS/Watt on the next best implementation.

Going a step further, Umuroglu *et al.* [20] propose FINN, a framework for building fast and flexible FPGA accelerators. When implemented on a ZC706 FPGA development board drawing less than 25 W, they demonstrate 12.3 million image classifications per second with 0.31 s latency on the MNIST data set with 95.8% accuracy, the best to date. Using the CIFAR-10 and SVHN data sets, they show 21,906 image classifications per second with 283 s latency and 80.1% and 94.9% accuracy, respectively, the fastest classification to date in an FPGA at the time of their publication.

With the addition of single bit to a BNN, Li *et al.* propose Ternary Weight Networks (TWNs) [21]. They store the additional bitwidth values $+1, 0$ and -1 and claim that the Euclidean distance between full precision float weights and the ternary weights (with a scaling factor) is minimized. They achieve up to $16\times$ or $32\times$ model compression with fewer multiplications compared with the full float version. They show that TWN achieves a much greater classification accuracy compared to their BNN counterparts. So, where an extra bit of storage per weight is acceptable, ternary weights offer better accuracy.

XNOR-Net proposed by Rastegari *et al.* [22] is a network where both weights and inputs are approximated with binary values. This gains a $32\times$ memory saving compared to a 32-bit floating point when ImageNet (AlexNet) is accelerated with XNOR-Net. The convolutions in the network are approximated with bitwise operations achieving a $58\times$ speed up in inference computations compared to a standard convolution. They also achieve a 44.2% accuracy compared to the 56.7% accuracy of a standard convolution.

6.3.3 Bit slicing

Another method of customizing the precision of data is to bit slice the data and undertake some vector computing on that data. Bit slicing constructs a large n-bit length word of data from smaller or single bitwidth fields or 'slices' to make an arbitrary n-bit word. Bitwise arithmetic operators such as NOR, XOR and NAND can operate on the customized bit precision data. Xu *et al.* [23] implement bitwise operations on arbitrary precision data such as 5 or 9 bit. These arbitrary precision operations would normally only be possible on custom logic such as an FPGA or ASIC; however, Xu *et al.*'s proposal allows for arbitrary precision computation to be performed on Single Instruction Multiple Data (SIMD) processing platforms.

6.3.4 Weight sharing and quantization in CNNs

Weight data of the CNN filters are typically very large and thus would require large amounts of memory accesses to load the complete weight data, data that would be too large to store in local SRAM or eDRAM. By optimizing the locality and bandwidth of the required memory accesses, DianNao proposed by Chen *et al.* [24] implements large CNNs in their accelerator in a 65 nm process ASIC that can perform 496 parallel 16-bit fixed-point operations in 1.02 ns. They claim the accelerator to be

117.87× faster and 21.08× more energy efficient than that of a comparable 128-bit SIMD processor core clocked at 2 GHz.

Later Chen *et al.* propose DaDianNao [25] which implements an accelerator on a 28 nm ASIC. They tackle storing the large weight data by spreading the storage of all weights across multiple accelerator nodes' on-chip eDRAM or SRAM, thus requiring no main memory. They show that their accelerator outperforms a single GPU by up to 450.65× and reduces energy consumption by up to 150.31× when using 64 nodes, taking 6.12 W memory power and 15.97 W total power. However, DaDianNao cannot exploit sparsity or weight sharing of the weights and activations as they need to expand the network to dense form before an operation.

To address the need for reduced power and bandwidth of SRAM accesses of the weight data, Han *et al.* [26] apply pruning, quantization, weight sharing and Huffman code compression methods to the weights of various pipelined networks.

The neurons and synapses (connections between neurons) of a trained network are iteratively pruned and retrained until optimized. This results in a bimodal distribution of the weight data that has been 'smoothed' with the iterative retraining. The weights are clustered using K-means clustering, a type of unsupervised learning that iteratively groups the data into clusters represented by a variable K, the centroids of which can be used to label the data. A code book is generated of weights with similar values. This code book is used to quantize the weights and retrain the code book converting the continuous bimodal weight distribution to a set of discrete weights. Huffman coding (which uses fewer bits to represent data that appears frequently and more bits to represent data that appears less frequently) is used to encode the weights and indexes to the weights. Han *et al.* show that when pruning, quantization and Huffman coding are employed, they obtain compression factors of 35× for AlexNet and 49× for VGG-16. This subsequently reduces AlexNet from 240 to 6.9 MB, and VGG-16 from 552 MB down to 11.3 MB. They also show that even though the fully connected layers dominate the model size by 90%; these layers compress the most by up to 96% of weights pruned in VGG-16 CNN. The newly pruned, quantized and compressed CNNs run 3× to 4× faster on a mobile GPU whilst using 3× to 7× less energy with no loss in accuracy.

Han *et al.* [27] progress further by evaluating a pruned and compressed (weight-shared) inference engine implemented in both a 45 and 28 nm CMOS process ASICs. They call this the Efficient Inference Engine (EIE) hardware accelerator and due to the compression scheme, they can store all weights in on-chip SRAM. They show that compared with DaDianNao, EIE achieves 2.9× better throughput, 19× better energy efficiency and 3× smaller area (μm).

6.3.5   *Weight-shared-with-parallel accumulate shared MAC (PASM)*

Whilst the above accelerators have tackled the large amount of weight data storage and bandwidth, most of these accelerators nonetheless contain huge numbers of MACs units. Each MAC unit contains a multiplier that is both power hungry and consumes large numbers of logic gates on an ASIC or large numbers of hardware multiplier units on an FPGA. Garland *et al.* [28,29], suggest rearchitecting the MAC to exploit

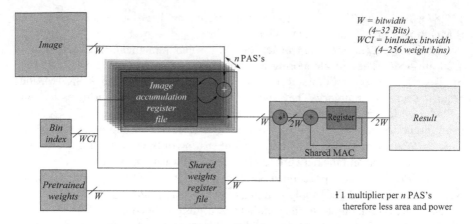

Figure 6.5   PASM block diagram

the quantization or binning of the weights in a weight-shared CNN accelerator. They replace the multiplier in the MAC with counters that count the frequency of each weight and place the corresponding image value in that weight bin. A post-pass multiply phase multiplies the accumulated image values of each weight bin with the corresponding weight value of that bin. They call this rearchitected MAC a parallel accumulate shared MAC (PASM), see Figure 6.5. They implement PASM in a convolutional layer of a CNN and compare its performance to that of standard weight-shared version. For the same clock speed as a standard MAC accelerator, their weight-shared-with-PASM accelerator results in fewer logic gates and reduced power with only a slight increase in latency.

6.3.6   Reduced precision in software

While many approaches to reduced precision inference involve modifications to hardware, or FPGA implementation of customized arithmetic, research has been done on software-only methods which can be used on general purpose processors. Anderson *et al.* [30] propose *flytes*, a scheme for byte-level customizable precision floating point arithmetic which makes use of the SIMD processing capabilities of modern processor architectures to provide a low-overhead software solution. SIMD instructions are used to pack and unpack data efficiently, converting between the custom format and native floating point. Mukunoki *et al.* [31] evaluate a similar technique on GPU architectures and find it effective across a range of operations including linear algebra kernels which find application in deep learning, such as matrix–vector multiplication.

6.4   Sparse data representations

CNNs typically use large numbers of trained parameters to achieve height accuracy. For instance, early networks such as LeNet-300-100 and LeNet-5, have several thousands of parameters, while this number increased to 61 and 138 million in the recent model of AlexNet and VGGNet. The large capacity makes neural networks both computationally and memory intensive, which raises significant challenges for mobile devices, which usually have a tight budget on power consumption and memory size. As redundancy and duplication widely exist in various CNN, pruning weighs and connections that have limited impact on the accuracy can improve computation performance and memory footprint.

6.4.1 L1-norm loss function

In learning algorithm, L1-norm is introduced to loss function as a penalty term to sparse the coefficient matrix. Typically, it is the sum of absolute value of all weights. When performing gradient descent, L1 regularizer penalizes non-zero values towards zeros which can be further pruned because of trivial contribution to the network. The work of [32] uses L1 norm in its training process. Gradually checking the connection value between network layers, when it lower than a threshold, the corresponding connection is going to be dropped.

6.4.2 Network pruning

Pruning has been proven to be a promising approach to increase sparsity of a DNN. The key method is to remove redundancy weights that have trivial impacts on the network. The reduction of resulting parameters lowers the request for computation and memory accessing which improves the performance and power efficiency of the corresponding network.

For a multidimensional tensor, pruning can take place at any level. Normally, a higher level pruning removes a larger number of weights at one go which has a coarser granularity. Methods of pruning in different granularity have their pros and cons which make a compromise more desirable in practice.

6.4.2.1 Fine pruning

A fine sparsity pruning was first proposed in by LeCun *et al.* [33] in 1989. Its strategy is to find parameters with small saliency and delete them from the network. The deletion is a safe process as those parameters with the least saliency will have the least effect on the training error. The network was reported to be reduced by a factor of four after removing unimportant weights. However, extra computation had been spent on performing the second derivatives to identify insignificant weights.

Han *et al.* [32] prune the network in fine granularity by setting a threshold which is a quality parameter multiplied by the standard deviation of a layer's weights. Similar to LeCun's method, the pruning is performed iteratively. Every pruning is followed by retraining to protect the accuracy of the optimized network.

Though the deletion of unimportant weights reduces the size of the parameters remarkably, it brings irregularity at the same time. Irregularity in parameters matrix hurts the computation performance by violating data locality. To enhance computation efficiency, the desired solution is to enforce a structured sparsity after weights removing. Anwar *et al.* [34] bridge the gap between fine pruning and irregularity by a method of intra-kernel strided sparsity. Rather than deleting trivial weights element wise, a stride is cast to each kernel to mask multiple weights at one go. It is a trade-off between model reduction and computation complexity.

6.4.2.2   Coarse pruning

Coarse-grained sparsity is beneficial to hardware acceleration because of the regularity which encourages many works target filter and channel pruning. To determine which filer to remove, Li *et al.* [35]. select the sum of a filter as a guide. Sorting according to the sum of absolute kernel weights for every filter, a preset number of filters with the smallest sum are removed from the output feature maps.

Hu *et al.* [36] believe that a channel is redundant if most of its output weights after activation function are zeros. Therefore, they compute the Average Percentage of Zeros (APoZ) of each channel and retrain the network every time after pruning the one that has the largest APoZ.

Though the sum of the weights and APoZ are two straight methods to guide pruning, neither of them is able to evaluate the relative importance of given filters. In practice, it is possible that a filter with a low APoZ but has a weak connection to the neurons in the next layer. In this case, such filter can be pruned safely though there are many non-zeros within it. Scalpel [37] prunes the network at the filter level by training a mask between each layer of the original network. The values of the mask determine whether or not to prune the corresponding output feature map calculated from the given filter.

6.4.2.3   Discussion

Mao *et al.* [38]. discussed how pruning granularity impacts network accuracy and the efficiency of hardware acceleration. Normally, fine-grained sparsity produces more zeros. However, because of the index saving effect, coarse-grained sparsity can obtain similar or even better compression rate than its finer counterpart. Excepting extreme coarse pruning (filter wise), both coarse and fine sparsity can optimize the network with no obvious loss of prediction accuracy. Because of the regularity, coarse-grained pruning is easier for hardware acceleration.

6.5   Program generation and optimization for DNNs

CNNs have a well-defined dataflow graph structure. The operations at the nodes of this graph are mathematically well understood. In addition, the operations within each node of the graph are matrix and tensor operations, which are suitable for a wide variety of automatic parallelization, vectorization and locality-improving loop optimizations. Given the variety of algorithmic and program-optimization choices that are available at each level of abstraction, domain-specific program generators and optimizers have been found to be effective for improving the performance of DNNs.

6.5.1 Domain-specific compilers

Latte [39] is domain-specific language (DSL) and compiler for DNNs. It provides a simple functional language for defining DNN operations, such a convolution and fully connected layers. The compiler provides domain-specific optimizations of the DSL program. For example, the compiler uses pattern matching to attempt to replace groups of operations that perform matrix multiplication with calls to libraries such as GEMM. The compiler also performs simple cross-layer optimizations. For example, where a convolution layer is immediately followed by a rectified linear activation layer, the compiler merges the loop nests for the two layers.

The Deep Learning Virtual Machine (DLVM) [40] is a DSL and compiler for linear algebra and DNNs. The core of DLVM is an intermediate representation (IR) that allows complex tensor operations to be expressed in just a few high-level instructions. Unlike a compiler for a general-purpose language, DLVM can make use of the data parallelism and locality that are available in high-level tensor operations. The same loop transformation and parallelization infrastructure can also be used to generate code for a variety of parallel architectures, including vector, multicore and GPU architectures. The most popular current DNN frameworks each have their own file formats for DNNs and use a variety of libraries to implement the DNN layers. DLVM offers the alternative of a more expressive IR and more powerful back-end parallel code generation.

6.5.2 Selecting primitives

Even where the DNN framework uses libraries to implement the layers, difficult optimization problems arise when selecting the best primitive function for a particular layer. Given the wide variety of algorithms for convolution, a natural question is how to choose which algorithm should be used for any given layer in the CNN. Some frameworks simply fix a good all-round algorithm to be used for convolutions, while others allow the programmer to select between a number of algorithms when constructing the network. Heuristic models can decide which implementations to use based on properties of the operation being performed, such as the size and shape of input or weight data.

Anderson and Gregg [41] study the problem of optimal selection of layer implementations to minimize the execution time of the whole network. If primitive operations operate on the same input and output data formats, this problem is easy. We simply select the fastest implementation for each layer. However, some algorithms for implementing layers are more efficient on some data layouts than on others, and achieving the best performance may depend on using different data layouts in each layer. For example, in DNNs operating on images, a common data layout is to order the tensor dimensions of the input image as *channel × height × width*, which is also known as *CHW* format. In the C/C++ programming language, the elements of the last dimension of a matrix are contiguous in memory, so the *CHW* format results in items from a row of width W being laid out contiguously in memory.

Many DNN convolution algorithms benefit from the layout in memory matching the spatial traversal of the tensor by the algorithm. However, not all convolution algorithms benefit as much from a memory layout that matches the spatial layout. For example, Winograd convolution algorithms apply a linear transform to sub-blocks of the input as the first step of convolution (see Section 6.2.3). This linear transform scatters the input across memory and breaks up the spatial locality within the input. However, the transform maintains locality across the *channels* dimension, and therefore, Winograd convolution is typically faster when the input is in *HWC* layout rather than *CHW* [41].

When there is a choice of data layouts that can be used in each layer, the problem of selecting the best primitive function to implement each layer becomes much more difficult. It is no longer enough to consider just the execution time of each primitive function that can implement the layer. We must also consider the possibility that data layout transformations are needed to match the different data layouts used by producer and consumer layers. These data layout transformations add to the total execution time and make the optimization problem much more difficult.

Figure 6.6 shows a simple example of a subpart of a DNN containing three convolution layers. For each layer, there is a choice of three different primitive routines, *a*, *b* or *c*, that can implement the layer. In Figure 6.6(a), the cost of each of the three choices is shown to the left of each layer. If we ignore data layout transformation costs, then the optimal selection is simply the fastest implementation of each layer. The example in Figure 6.6(b) shows the effect of data transformation costs. In this example, we assume that each of the three primitive routines operate a different data layout. Therefore, if the same primitive routine is used for successive layers, no data layout transformation is needed, which is indicated by the diagonal zero costs in Figure 6.6(b).

Anderson and Gregg [41] show that this problem can be mapped to the partitioned Boolean quadratic programming (PBQP) problem. Where the graph of layers in the

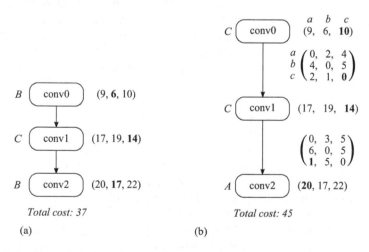

Figure 6.6 Example of simple straight-line primitive selection problem. The cost of optimal selections is highlighted in bold face text. (a) Layer costs only and (b) layer and data transformation costs

DNN is a straight line or tree, this problem can be solved in polynomial time. However, for more general directed acyclic graphs, the problem is NP-hard [42]. However, there is existing off-the-shelf PBQP solvers that can solve many cases that arise in practice in an acceptable amount of time. Using this method, Anderson and Gregg achieve significant speedups compared to using a using just a single algorithm or data layout for each layer of the DNN.

6.6 Conclusion and future directions

In the last decade, DNNs have exceeded the accuracy of other machine learning techniques in classification and recognition problems in image, video and text. DNNs allow difficult, poorly structured problems to be solved using a large number of examples rather than by designing an algorithm specifically to solve the problem. However, DNNs require very large amounts of computation, memory and energy for both training and inference. Inference is particular problem because it must often be performed in the field on embedded and mobile devices rather on powerful servers in data centres.

In this chapter, we have introduced some significant performance challenges of DNNs such as computation, parallelism, data locality and memory requirements. We described several branches of research on these problems, including the use of highly tuned matrix multiplication libraries, hardware accelerators, quantization and dictionary encoding of weights, custom number precision, sparse data representations and the application of compiler and combinatorial optimization techniques to improve the performance of DNNs.

DNNs are one of the most important emerging technologies in modern machine learning. As they are increasingly deployed in autonomous vehicles, drones, handwriting recognition and LIDAR-based systems, new performance challenges will emerge. One particularly important problem will be analysing and classifying 3D data such as clouds of points that are found using laser scanning systems such as LIDAR. DNNs are being used very successfully to analyse 2D images and video-using techniques that operate on mostly dense representations of the input data. In contrast, 3D representations of the world, such as point clouds and meshes, typically contain large amounts of empty space and are therefore almost inherently sparse. DNNs have been successfully applied to the representations of 3D data [43,44]. However, adapting existing DNN algorithms, target hardware and accelerators to very sparse 3D representations is an important problem for both researchers and practitioners who deploy DNNs in autonomous vehicles, drones and robots.

Acknowledgements

Research was supported by Science Foundation Ireland grant 12/IA/1381, and by grant 13/RC/2094 to Lero – the Irish Software Research Centre (www.lero.ie). This research has received funding from the European Union's Horizon 2020 research and innovation programme under grant agreement No 732204 (Bonseyes). The opinions expressed and arguments employed herein do not necessarily reflect the official views of these funding bodies.

References

[1] LeCun Y, Haffner P, Bottou L, *et al.* Object Recognition with Gradient-Based Learning. In: Shape, Contour and Grouping in Computer Vision; 1999. p. 319–345.

[2] Krizhevsky A, Sutskever I, Hinton GE. ImageNet Classification with Deep Convolutional Neural Networks. In: Pereira F, Burges CJC, Bottou L, *et al.*, editors. Advances in Neural Information Processing Systems 25. Curran Associates, Inc., Lake Tahoe, NV; 2012. p. 1097–1105.

[3] Szegedy C, Liu W, Jia Y, *et al.* Going Deeper with Convolutions. Computing Research Repository. 2014;abs/1409.4842. Available from: http://arxiv.org/abs/1409.4842.

[4] Van Zee FG, van de Geijn RA. BLIS: A Framework for Rapidly Instantiating BLAS Functionality. ACM Transactions on Mathematical Software. 2015;41(3):14:1–14:33.

[5] Cho M, Brand D. MEC: Memory-efficient Convolution for Deep Neural Network. In: Proceedings of the 34th International Conference on Machine Learning, ICML 2017, Sydney, NSW, Australia, 6–11 August 2017; 2017. p. 815–824.

[6] Vasudevan A, Anderson A, Gregg D. Parallel Multi Channel Convolution Using General Matrix Multiplication. In: 28th IEEE International Conference on Application-specific Systems, Architectures and Processors, ASAP 2017, Seattle, WA, USA, 10–12 July 2017. IEEE; 2017. p. 19–24.

[7] Anderson A, Vasudevan A, Keane C, *et al.* Low-memory GEMM-based Convolution Algorithms for Deep Neural Networks. Computing Research Repository. 2017;abs/1709.03395. Available from: http://arxiv.org/abs/1709.03395.

[8] Winograd S. Signal Processing and Complexity of Computation. In: IEEE International Conference on Acoustics, Speech, and Signal Processing, ICASSP'80, Denver, Colorado, 9–11 April 1980; 1980. p. 94–101.

[9] Lavin A, Gray S. Fast Algorithms for Convolutional Neural Networks. In: 2016 IEEE Conference on Computer Vision and Pattern Recognition, CVPR 2016, Las Vegas, NV, USA, 27–30 June 2016; 2016. p. 4013–4021.

[10] Barabasz B, Anderson A, Gregg D. Improving Accuracy of Winograd Convolution for DNNs. Computing Research Repository. 2018;abs/1803.10986.

[11] Simonyan K, Zisserman A. Very Deep Convolutional Networks for Large-Scale Image Recognition. Computing Research Repository. 2014;abs/1409.1556.

[12] Courbariaux M, Bengio Y, David J. Low Precision Arithmetic for Deep Learning. Computing Research Repository. 2014;abs/1412.7024. Available from: http://arxiv.org/abs/1412.7024.

[13] Lecun Y, Bottou L, Bengio Y, *et al.* Gradient-based Learning Applied to Document Recognition. Proceedings of the IEEE. 1998;86(11):2278–2324.

[14] Krizhevsky A. Learning Multiple Layers of Features from Tiny Images. University of Toronto; 2009.

[15] Gupta S, Agrawal A, Gopalakrishnan K, *et al.* Deep Learning with Limited Numerical Precision. In: Proceedings of the 32nd International Conference on International Conference on Machine Learning – Volume 37. ICML'15; 2015. p. 1737–1746.

[16] Dettmers T. 8-Bit Approximations for Parallelism in Deep Learning. Computing Research Repository. 2015;abs/1511.04561. Available from: http://arxiv.org/abs/1511.04561.

[17] Courbariaux M, Bengio Y, David JP. BinaryConnect: Training Deep Neural Networks with Binary Weights During Propagations. In: Proceedings of the 28th International Conference on Neural Information Processing Systems – Volume 2. NIPS'15; 2015. p. 3123–3131.

[18] Courbariaux M, Bengio Y. BinaryNet: Training Deep Neural Networks with Weights and Activations Constrained to +1 or −1. Computing Research Repository. 2016;abs/1602.02830. Available from: http://arxiv.org/abs/1602.02830.

[19] Zhao R, Song W, Zhang W, *et al.* Accelerating Binarized Convolutional Neural Networks with Software-Programmable FPGAs. In: Proceedings of the 2017 ACM/SIGDA International Symposium on Field-Programmable Gate Arrays. FPGA'17; 2017. p. 15–24.

[20] Umuroglu Y, Fraser NJ, Gambardella G, *et al.* FINN: A Framework for Fast, Scalable Binarized Neural Network Inference. In: Proceedings of the 2017 ACM/SIGDA International Symposium on Field-Programmable Gate Arrays. FPGA'17; 2017. p. 65–74.

[21] Li F, Liu B. Ternary Weight Networks. Computing Research Repository. 2016;abs/1605.04711. Available from: http://arxiv.org/abs/1605.04711.

[22] Rastegari M, Ordonez V, Redmon J, *et al.* XNOR-Net: ImageNet Classification Using Binary Convolutional Neural Networks. In: Leibe B, Matas J, Sebe N, *et al.*, editors. Computer Vision – ECCV 2016. Cham: Springer International Publishing; 2016. p. 525–542.

[23] Xu S, Gregg D. Bitslice Vectors: A Software Approach to Customizable Data Precision on Processors with SIMD Extensions. In: 2017 46th International Conference on Parallel Processing (ICPP); 2017. p. 442–451.

[24] Chen T, Du Z, Sun N, *et al.* DianNao: A Small-footprint High-throughput Accelerator for Ubiquitous Machine-learning. In: Proceedings of the 19th International Conference on Architectural Support for Programming Languages and Operating Systems. ASPLOS'14; 2014. p. 269–284.

[25]   Chen Y, Luo T, Liu S, *et al.* DaDianNao: A Machine-Learning Super-computer. In: 2014 47th Annual IEEE/ACM International Symposium on Microarchitecture; 2014. p. 609–622.

[26]   Han S, Mao H, Dally WJ. Deep Compression: Compressing Deep Neural Network with Pruning, Trained Quantization and Huffman Coding. Computing Research Repository. 2015;abs/1510.00149.

[27]   Han S, Liu X, Mao H, *et al.* EIE: Efficient Inference Engine on Compressed Deep Neural Network. ACM SIGARCH Computer Architecture News. 2016;44(3):243–254.

[28]   Garland J, Gregg D. Low Complexity Multiply Accumulate Unit for Weight-Sharing Convolutional Neural Networks. IEEE Computer Architecture Letters. 2017;16(2):132–135.

[29]   Garland J, Gregg D. Low Complexity Multiply–Accumulate Units for Convolutional Neural Networks with Weight-Sharing. ACM Transactions on Architecture and Code Optimization. 2018;15(3), Article 31.

[30]   Anderson A, Muralidharan S, Gregg D. Efficient Multibyte Floating Point Data Formats Using Vectorization. IEEE Transactions on Computers. 2017;66(12):2081–2096.

[31]   Mukunoki D, Imamura T. Reduced-Precision Floating-Point Formats on GPUs for High Performance and Energy Efficient Computation. In: 2016 IEEE International Conference on Cluster Computing, CLUSTER 2016, Taipei, Taiwan, 12–16 September 2016; 2016. p. 144–145.

[32]   Han S, Pool J, Tran J, *et al.* Learning both Weights and Connections for Efficient Neural Network. In: Advances in Neural Information Processing Systems 28: Annual Conference on Neural Information Processing Systems 2015, Montreal, Quebec, Canada, 7–12 December 2015; 2015. p. 1135–1143.

[33]   LeCun Y, John S Denker, and Sara A Solla. Optimal Brain Damage. Advances in Neural Information Processing Systems 2 [NIPS Conference, Denver, Colorado, USA, November 27–30, 1989]. Morgan Kaufmann; 1990. p. 598–605.

[34]   Anwar S, Hwang K, Sung W. Structured Pruning of Deep Convolutional Neural Networks. ACM Journal on Emerging Technologies in Computing Systems. 2017;13(3):32:1–32:18.

[35]   Li H, Kadav A, Durdanovic I, *et al.* Pruning Filters for Efficient ConvNets. Computing Research Repository. 2016;abs/1608.08710.

[36]   Hu H, Peng R, Tai Y, *et al.* Network Trimming: A Data-Driven Neuron Pruning Approach towards Efficient Deep Architectures. Computing Research Repository. 2016;abs/1607.03250.

[37]   Yu J, Lukefahr A, Palframan D, Dasika G, Das R, and Mahlke S. Scalpel: Customizing DNN Pruning to the Underlying Hardware Parallelism. In Proceedings of the 44th Annual International Symposium on Computer Architecture (ISCA '17). ACM, New York, NY, USA, 2017; 2017. p. 548–560.

[38]   Mao H, Han S, Pool J, *et al.* Exploring the Granularity of Sparsity in Convolutional Neural Networks. 2017 IEEE Conference on Computer Vision and

Pattern Recognition Workshops (CVPRW), Honolulu, Hawaii, USA; 2017. p. 1927–1934.

[39] Truong L, Barik R, Totoni E, *et al.* Latte: A Language, Compiler, and Runtime for Elegant and Efficient Deep Neural Networks. In: Proceedings of the 37th ACM SIGPLAN Conference on Programming Language Design and Implementation, PLDI 2016, Santa Barbara, CA, USA, 13–17 June 2016; 2016. p. 209–223.

[40] Wei R, Adve VS, Schwartz L. DLVM: A Modern Compiler Infrastructure for Deep Learning Systems. Computing Research Repository. 2017;abs/1711.03016.

[41] Anderson A, Gregg D. Optimal DNN Primitive Selection with Partitioned Boolean Quadratic Programming. In: Proceedings of the 2018 International Symposium on Code Generation and Optimization, CGO 2018, Vösendorf/Vienna, Austria, 24–28 February 2018; 2018. p. 340–351.

[42] Scholz B, Eckstein E. Register Allocation for Irregular Architectures. In: Proceedings of the Joint Conference on Languages, Compilers and Tools for Embedded Systems: Software and Compilers for Embedded Systems. LCTES/SCOPES'02; 2002. p. 139–148.

[43] Lei H, Akhtar N, Mian A. Spherical Convolutional Neural Network for 3D Point Clouds. Computing Research Repository. 2018;abs/1805.07872. Available from: http://arxiv.org/abs/1805.07872.

[44] Camgoz NC, Hadfield S, Koller O, *et al.* Using Convolutional 3D Neural Networks for User-independent Continuous Gesture Recognition. In: 2016 23rd International Conference on Pattern Recognition (ICPR); 2016. p. 49–54.

Part II

Runtime management

Chapter 7

Adaptive–reflective middleware for power and energy management in many-core heterogeneous systems

Tiago Mück[1], Amir M. Rahmani[1,2], and Nikil Dutt[1]

Modern battery-powered and embedded platforms (e.g., mobile devices) need to support highly diverse and complex workloads that typically exhibit dynamically varying resource demands, thus requiring adaptive mechanisms for energy-efficient resource management. To address this trend, emerging mobile are increasingly incorporating heterogeneity in order to provide energy-efficiency while meeting performance requirements with respect to the varying applications demands. For instance, in Arm's big.LITTLE architecture, the big core has a larger cache capacity and higher computational power (i.e., wider out-of-order (OoO) pipeline) compared with the LITTLE core [1].

Effective exploitation of power-performance trade-offs in heterogeneous many-core platforms (HMPs) requires intelligent management at different layers, in particular in the operating system [2]. Operating systems need to continuously analyze the application behavior and find a proper answer for some of the following questions: *What is the most power efficient core type to execute the application without violating its performance requirements?* or *Which option is more power-efficient for the current application: an OoO core at a lower frequency or an in order core at a higher frequency?* Unfortunately, existing operating systems do not offer mechanisms to properly address these questions and therefore are unable to fully exploit architectural heterogeneity for scalable energy-efficient execution of dynamic workloads.

Some existing Linux extensions do address these issues to a limited extent (e.g., Arm's GTS task mapping for big.LITTLE architectures [3]); however, they are customized for certain heterogeneous platforms without being adaptable to other platforms. Furthermore, current solutions exclusively focus on task mapping/scheduling decisions and are oblivious to the behavior of the underlying power-management subsystems (e.g., *cpuidle* and *cpufreq* subsystems control the processing unit's power states and voltage–frequency (VF) scaling, respectively), thus leading the system to an

[1]Department of Computer Science, University of California, Irvine, USA
[2]Institute for Computer Technology, TU Wien, Austria

energy-inefficient state in which the scheduling and power-management subsystems take antagonistic decisions.

In this chapter, we present our vision of a holistic approach for performing resource allocation decisions and power management by leveraging concepts from *reflective software*. The general idea of reflection is to *change your actions based on both external feedback and introspection (i.e., self-assessment)*. In our context, this translates into performing resource-management actuation considering both *sensing information* (e.g., readings from performance counters, power sensors) to assess the current system state, as well as *models* to predict the behavior of other system components before performing an action. The remainder of this chapter is organized as follows: Sections 7.1 and 7.3 describe our Adaptive–Reflective Middleware (ARM) and how it integrates with simulated platforms as well as a full Linux stack on real hardware. Section 7.4 presents three case studies that leverage our ARM toolchain to (1) perform energy-efficient task mapping on heterogeneous architectures (Section 7.4.1), (2) explore the design space of novel HMP architectures (Section 7.4.2), and (3) extend the lifetime of mobile devices (Section 7.4.3).

7.1   The adaptive–reflective middleware framework

Figure 7.1 shows our resource management framework which sits between applications and the operating system kernel and is mainly composed of three parts: **(1) the sensed data** that consists of performance counters and other sensory information (e.g., power, temperature) collected to assess the current system state and to characterize workloads; **(2) the actuators** that generalize components which perform resource allocation and power management; and **(3) the system model** that uses the sensed data to predict how the system state may change given new actuation actions.

The reflective system model is a fundamental part of our framework since it provides actuators with system introspection that is necessary to take informed decisions and provide runtime adaptability. The models interact in a hierarchy defined by the

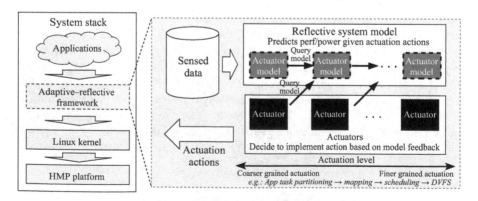

Figure 7.1   Reflective framework for resource management

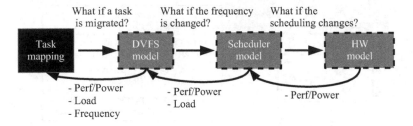

Figure 7.2   Task mapping interacting with finer grained actuators' models

granularity of the actuations performed in the system. For instance, runtime task-to-core mapping and load balancing is typically performed in coarser time periods (e.g., 200 ms) compared with dynamic VF scaling (DVFS) (e.g., 50 ms). DVFS actions are also typically driven by the processing units' load (e.g., Linux's on-demand governors), which are the functions of task mapping. Figure 7.2 illustrates a scenario in which a task-mapping actuator queries the DVFS model in order to make an informed mapping decision. Queries are propagated across the layer to inspect the behavior of all finer grained actuators in the system model.

7.2   The reflective framework

The first step to enable ARM is providing a framework with a well defined, simple, and portable interface to enable designers to develop their own resource management policies and policy models. Figure 7.3 shows a UML class diagram with a simplified overview of the framework and the provided interface.

Our framework is implemented in the C++ language. The central component in the framework is the `ARM_Framework` class which exposes the framework's interface to developer-defined policies (grayed in Figure 7.3). Our framework follows an object-oriented paradigm and user policies are defined as subclasses of `ARM_Framework`. Portability is provided by having `ARM_Framework` inherit all platform-dependent implementation details from one of the available interface implementation classes (the bottom part in Figure 7.3). We support two different implementations of this interface: (1) a lightweight Linux-based implementation for deployment on real systems and (2) an offline implementation for debugging and simulating executions under the control of the management policies. We provide more details on the Linux-based implementation as well as our motivations for an offline interface in Section 7.3.

In order to describe the interface provided by `ARM_Framework` and demonstrate how it is used, we show the implementation of a simple reflective DVFS policy in Figure 7.4. `Simple_DVFS_Policy` attempts to find the most energy-efficient (defined in terms of instructions-per-second (IPS) per Watt of power consumed)

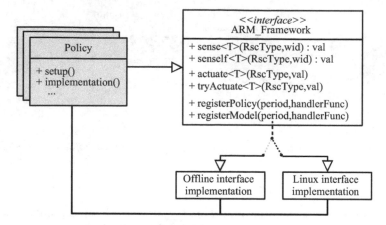

Figure 7.3   Framework UML diagram. Greyed components define policies implemented by the developer

```
1    class Simple_DVFS_Policy : public ARM_Framework {
2      const int PERIOD_MS = 50;
3
4      void setup() {
5        registerPolicy (PERIOD_MS,dvfs);
6      }
7
8      double try_frequency(int wid, frequency_domain &fd, double freq_mhz) {
9        tryActuate <ACT_FREQ_MHZ> (fd,freq_mhz);
10       double ips = senself<SEN_INSTR_TOTAL>(fd,wid)/senself<SEN_TIME_TOTAL_S>(fd,wid);
11       double power = senself<SEN_POWER_W>(fd,wid);
12       return ips / power;
13     }
14
15     void dvfs(int wid){
16       for(auto fd : sys_info. freq_domains)
17       {
18         double best_freq = fd.freq_min;
19         double best_eff = 0;
20         for(auto freq : fd.freqs){
21           double freq_eff = try_frequency(wid,fd,freq);
22           if (freq_eff > best_eff){
23             best_freq = freq;
24             best_eff = freq_eff;
25           }
26         }
27         actuate<ACT_FREQ_MHZ>(fd,best_freq);
28       }
29     }
30   };
```

Figure 7.4   Reflective DVFS actuation policy

frequencies for the system. For simplicity, in this example, we simply try all available frequencies and use model information to select the most energy-efficient one.

The first component the new policy class needs to implement is a mandatory setup() method using which the function that implements the actual behavior registered with the framework. This is done by the registerPolicy function which uses the *policy invocation period* and the function implementing it. The policy invocation period defines how often the registered function is invoked as well as the hierarchy of the policies within the reflective model. The period also establishes a *sensing window* for the policy function. In the example, when the dvfs function (Lines 15–29) is invoked, the sensed information (e.g., performance counters, power sensors) aggregated over 50 ms periods can be obtained.

Within the dvfs function, a special sys_info object provided by the framework is used to iterate through system components. In the example shown, the policy iterates through all *frequency domain resources* (Line 16). For all the supported frequencies, the try_frequency (Lines 8–13) function is called to assess the energy efficiency of the given frequency to select the best settings. The try_frequency function makes use of the actuate/tryActuate and sense/senseIf to perform the following assessment:

- actuate: This function sets a new value for a system actuator. It takes as arguments a reference to the system resource to be actuated upon and the new actuation value. The function's template parameter selects the proper function implementation to perform the requested actuation actions.
- sense: This function takes a reference of a system resource and a sensing window and returns the sense metric for that resource during the window period. Similar to actuate, the function's template parameter selects the proper function implementation to obtain the requested sensed data. For example, in the scope of the try_frequency function in Figure 7.4
  sense<SEN_INSTR_TOTAL>(fd,wid) would return the total number of instructions executed by all processing elements associated to the frequency domain fd in the last 50 ms (defined by the sensing window id—wid)
- tryActuate: Using the same syntax as actuate, this function updates the underlying models used to predict the next system state given the new actuation value (as described in Section 7.1). It does not set the actual actuation value.
- senseIf: This function has the same semantics as sense but returns predicted sensed information for the next sensing window, given a new actuation set by tryActuate.

Note that these functions are implemented using template specialization such that every valid combination of the sensing information/actuation action parameter and resource type has its own specialization. Using this approach, sensing/action requests are mapped to their correct implementation at compile time, thus reducing the framework's runtime overhead. Invalid operations (e.g., setting an invalid frequency level for a power domain) can be also detected at compile time, facilitating the debugging phase.

As described in Section 7.1, queries to the model (done through tryActuate/ senseIf) are propagated to finer grained policies. In our current example, any other policy registered with a period smaller than 50 ms is simulated given the new frequency set in Line 9. This is performed by reexecuting the same policy code registered using registerPolicy. When executing a policy as part of the model, actuate/sense behave like tryActuate/senseIf. Finally, the developer may use the same infrastructure to model the aspects implemented within the underlying system. The registerModel function is provided to facilitate this process (shown in Figure 7.3). When registered using registerModel, the policy code will only be executed as part of the model to predict performance and power, but it will not directly actuate on the system.

7.3 Implementation and tools

In this section, we provide an overview of the environment in which ARM is deployed as well as the toolchain and infrastructure we developed to support portable development and evaluation of runtime resource management policies.

An overview of our toolchain is shown in Figure 7.5. The main component is naturally our ARM framework which encapsulates the resource-management policies. The middleware run as part of a user-space daemon process which monitors the system and triggers the policies as described in the previous sections. As mentioned previously, all interactions between the policies and the system are performed

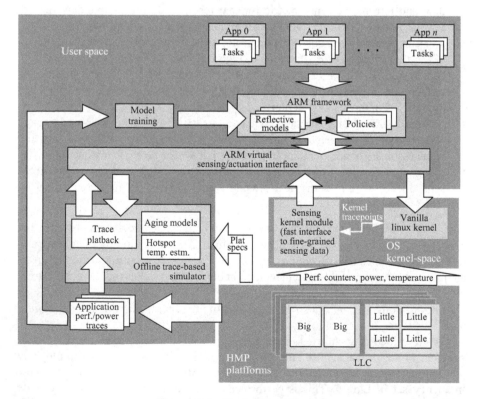

Figure 7.5 Toolchain overview

exclusively through the *virtual sensing/actuation interface*, thus allowing the policies to be instantiated on top of different implementations of the interface.

When the middleware is deployed on top of a real platform, we use the Linux-based implementation of the virtual interface (Figure 7.1). Each interface must provide the mechanisms necessary for the implementation of the *sense* and *actuate* functions, as well as the periodic triggering of the policy functions. Figure 7.6 shows how these functions are implemented on Linux-based systems. Accessing the platform's hardware sensors (performance monitoring units) is done by a portable kernel module. Our current implementation uses kernel tracepoints [4] to enable performance event monitoring on a task-by-task basis, which requires sampling at the granularity of tasks' context switch, creation, and deletion. At the user level, the interface implementation uses `ioctl` system calls to setup the sensing windows for each registered policy function. The policy functions are then executed in the scope of a separate thread that uses blocking `ioctl` calls to synchronize with the kernel module. The kernel module automatically aggregates sensed data on a per-window basis and stores the information in shared memory, so that it can be read directly by `sense` calls with low overhead. The `actuate` functions are implemented on top of standard Linux system calls and modules. For instance, we use CPU affinity system calls to control task-to-core mappings, and the *cpufreq* to control core frequencies.

7.3.1   Offline simulator

The other interface implementation, shown in Figure 7.1, allows our middleware to be deployed as part of a **trace-base offline simulator**, as shown in Figure 7.5. The offline simulator takes traces collected from applications executed on the target system (real platforms or full system simulators) and provides an execution flow that replays those traces considering an arbitrary platform configuration and actuation settings.

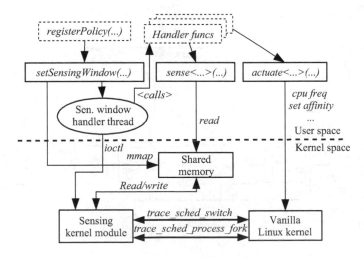

Figure 7.6   Implementation of virtual interface functions in Linux

Our main motivation for providing this offline simulation infrastructure is to allow the evaluation of the new resource-management policies in terms of scalability and generality. Performing this kind of evaluation on top of real platforms is often difficult since real platforms have fixed configurations, and full-system simulations (e.g., gem5 [5]) of large-scale systems are often unfeasible due to extremely long simulation times. Furthermore, an offline simulation allows new policies to be prototyped and debugged more quickly. The idea of using offline simulation in these scenarios has already been explored by previous works. For instance, LinSched [6] and AKULA [7] are useful to easily prototype and debug OS scheduling policies before they are deployed in a real system. However, these works do not directly support generic actuation policies for HMPs. Our toolchain, on the other hand, allows system-level policies to be prototyped and simulated offline under arbitrary execution and scalability scenarios. In the remainder of this section, we provide a brief description on how we perform offline simulation. For more details and a discussion on offline simulation accuracy, please refer to [8].

Figure 7.7 shows the offline simulation flow. Each aspect of the simulation flow is explained in more detail below.

Trace generation: Traces are captured by executing applications individually as a single thread on each core configuration supported in the target system. This includes all architectural variations and all supported actuation settings. For instance, considering the typical HMP mobile platform represented in Figure 7.5 with two core types, one needs a set of traces collected on one of the *big* cores for all supported frequencies, and another set collected on one of the *LITTLE* cores. An application trace consists of a time series that includes performance and power measurements of the application. Trace collection is implemented within the framework itself through a custom policy class which saves the contents of the sensed data across all sensing windows. The length of the sensing window when traces are captured defines the minimum length of the sensing windows supported later by the offline simulation.

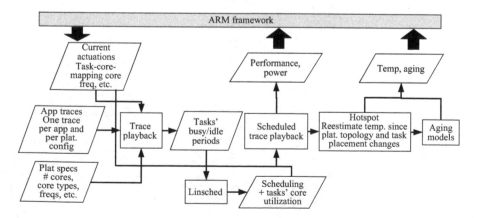

Figure 7.7   Trace-based simulation flow

Offline trace playback: The first step in trace simulation is defining the number of instances of each application to be replayed and their arrival time in the system. The *sys_info* object (Figure 7.4, Line 16) is then created based on the user specification for the platform to be simulated, and the policies are then instantiated. After initialization, the traces are played back at the granularity of the smallest sensing window according to the flowchart shown in Figure 7.7: **(1)** Trace information is used to obtain the maximum amount of processing time a task would use during the sensing window and its duty cycle (i.e., their busy/idle periods for tasks that are not fully CPU-bound). **(2)** If multiple tasks are mapped to the same core, we simulate a scheduler using LinSched [6]; LinSched is used to obtain the CPU time that would be allotted by the Linux scheduler to each task during the simulated sensing window. **(3)** The execution of each task is now emulated again for the allotted time and simulation statistics (e.g., executed instructions, simulated cycles) are collected to update the sensed data for each sensing window before the window handler implementing the policies is called. Once the user policies execute, control returns to the offline simulator and the steps 1–3 are repeated for the next sensing window. The trace that is used for each task on steps 1–3 is selected based on current actuation values set by the policies. When switching traces given a new actuation value, the number of simulated instructions of each task is used to find the appropriate point to continue in the new trace. The offline simulator is also integrated with Hotspot [9] for temperature estimation, since temperature depends on the task placement and cannot be captured by individual traces. We also integrated aging models for transistor delay degradation. This is explored in the case study described in Section 7.4.3. For more details on offline aging simulation, please refer to [10].

7.4 Case studies

In this section, we present multiple incarnations of ARM. SPARTA [11] (Section 7.4.1) illustrates the scenario exemplified previously in Figure 7.2, combining task mapping with reflective models to predict DVFS behavior. Section 7.4.2 illustrates the benefits of the offline simulation infrastructure through the design space exploration (DSE) of novel architectures for mobile HMPs. ADAMANt [10] is presented in Section 7.4.3. ADAMANt also leverages the offline simulator to perform long-term HMP aging simulations and proposes an extension to SPARTA to increase chip lifetime.

7.4.1 Energy-efficient task mapping on heterogeneous architectures

As our first case study, we present SPARTA: a runtime task allocation for energy efficient HMPs, as an instance of our adaptive–reflective framework [11]. SPARTA's runtime adaptivity provides support for workloads that consist of numerous tasks with diverse behavior that may enter and exit the system at any time. In the context of an adaptive–reflective framework, SPARTA achieves energy-efficient allocations by collecting on-chip sensor data, using it to predict task performance/power, and identifying opportunities to maintain a task's performance while reducing its energy consumption.

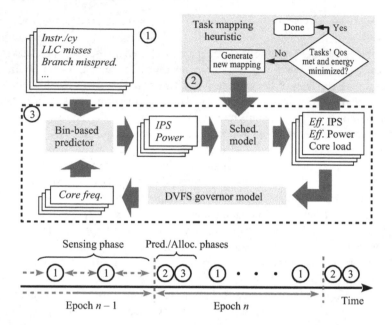

Figure 7.8   Allocating cores to task using ① runtime sensing, ② throughput-aware mapping, and ③ prediction, during periodic epochs

SPARTA is a runtime task allocator for HMPs that consists of three phases as shown in Figure 7.8: *sensing, mapping,* and *prediction.* An *Epoch* (Figure 7.8(b)) is the time period between prediction and mapping phases, while the sensing phase is executed at the same rate as the Linux scheduler, so each epoch covers multiple Linux scheduling periods.

During the sensing phase, hardware performance counters and power sensors are periodically sampled on each core to monitor the characteristics of the executing workload. The following counters are sampled at the same rate as the Linux scheduler (typically 10–20 ms) and individually summed up for each task at the beginning of each epoch: total amount of executed instructions, active cycles (cy_{active}), L1 and last-level cache misses per instruction (mr_{L1I}, mr_{L1D} and mr_{LLC}), and branch mispredictions per instruction (mr_{Br}).

At the beginning of a new epoch, a new global task allocation is determined. The first order goal is to meet the target throughput of the task and then maximize energy efficiency (in terms of IPS per Watt, which can also be thought of as instructions-per-Joule (IPJ)). This is achieved using a list-scheduling heuristic described in details in [11]. During this process, the reflective models shown in Figure 7.8(a) ③, are used to evaluate the impact new candidate task mapping will have in the system. Initially, a bin-based predictor [11] predicts each task's performance and power for all core types in the HMP platform using the sensed information. This is fed to a model of the Linux's completely fair scheduler (CFS) along with the new candidate mapping in order to determine the load each task will impose in the

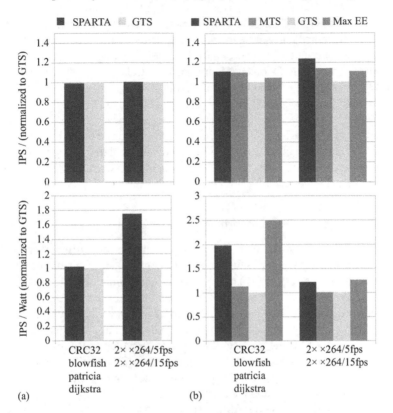

Figure 7.9   SPARTA task mapping results: (a) Odroid and (b) Gem5 simulation.
© 2016 ACM. Data, with permission, from Reference [11]

system [12]. This step is necessary to access the correct behavior of the system since multiple tasks mapped to the same core have their processing time share/load determined by the CFS policy. The final load of each core is then used as input for the DVFS governor model that predicts their execution frequency. Since a new predicted frequency has a side effect on the system load, this prediction loop is repeated as described in [11] to obtain the average effective throughput and power of the new candidate mapping.

Evaluation results. SPARTA's implementation leverages the infrastructure described in Section 7.3 and is evaluated on two different platforms: an 8-core big.LITTLE Exynos SoC (Odroid) and a Gem5-based simulated 8-core system with 4 distinct core types. Figure 7.9 show a subset of our results for two distinct workload mixes with four tasks each (please refer to [11] for a comprehensive evaluation). In the Odroid platform, we compare SPARTA with GTS (the current Linux solution for HMP task mapping) [3], while in the Gem5 simulated platform, we also compare with the MTS heuristic [13] and an optimal energy-efficiency heuristic. Both GTS and MTS attempt to maximize the system performance in this experiment. As shown in the results, SPARTA delivers the same or better performance than GTS and MTS (which are performance-driven heuristics) with better energy efficiency. Across all workload mixes presented in [11], SPARTA achieves average energy reductions of 23% when compared to MTS on Gem5 simulated platforms and 16% when compared to Linux's GTS running on the Odroid platform.

For further reading, the reader may refer to [11] for more details on SPARTA. Run-DMC [12] focuses on performance modeling and describes in details the CFS model employed in SPARTA. An interesting initial work can be found in SmartBalance [14], which is an early task mapping approach for maximizing energy efficiency in HMPs. SmartBalance was our first attempt on using the sense-predict-actuate loop for resource management.

7.4.2 Design space exploration of novel HMPs

Current HMPs used on mobile platforms deploy architecturally different cores with a range of performance capabilities that impact numerous factors in a uniform manner. For instance, in the Odroid-XU3 platform used in our evaluations, the *big* cores have both more cache (4 vs 1 MB L2$) and computational capacity (OoO multi-issue pipeline vs in order pipeline) than the *little* cores. However, as previous work has shown [15,16], memory and computational needs can vary independently across applications, which motivate the use of platforms in which these resources are not treated uniformly. For instance, maintaining a simple CPU while increasing cache capacity can be a more energy efficient approach to increasing performance compared to simply scaling both cache and CPU size together.

In this case study, we use our offline simulator to analyze the energy-efficiency and performance of various workloads on different configurations of HMPs. We consider *four CPU types* ranging from a small in order CPU (*Little CPU*) to a large 8-way OoO CPU with speculative execution (*Huge CPU*). These cores can be paired with private L1 data and L2 caches also ranging from *Little* to *Huge*. Tables 7.1 and 7.2 summarize the parameters of each CPU and cache type considered in our experiments, respectively. A core type is defined as a unique CPU-cache combination (e.g., the *Little–Big* core type combines a little CPU type with a big cache type); therefore, we evaluate platforms consisting of up to 16 core types. Each core type supports multiple VF pairs.

Workloads: Our experimental workloads are constructed using two different approaches. Workloads are made up of benchmarks from MiBench [17] and PAR-SEC [18] benchmark suites, as well as synthetic microbenchmarks proposed by [12]. A microbenchmark is defined as a simple function which exhibits a specific computational and/or memory behavior (e.g., high/low instruction-level parallelism, high/low cache miss rates) [12]. The first set of workloads (Mixes 0–13 in Table 7.3) represent realistic homogeneous use cases. The second set of workloads (Mixes 14–21 in Table 7.3) are diverse: the benchmark mixes comprise a combination of the most compute- and memory-bound benchmarks from PARSEC, as well as synthetic microbenchmarks that exercise different levels of compute and memory boundness.

Table 7.1   Heterogeneous CPU parameters

Parameter	[L]ittle	[M]edium	[B]ig	[H]uge
Issue width	1(In order)	2(OoO)	4(OoO)	8(OoO)
LQ/SQ size	8/8	8/8	16/16	32/32
IQ size	16	16	32	64
ROB size	64	64	128	192
Int/float Regs	64	64	128	256

Table 7.2   Heterogeneous cache parameters

Parameter	[L]ittle	[M]edium	[B]ig	[H]uge
L1$D size (KB)	8	16	32	64
L1$D associativity	1	2	2	2
L2 size (KB)	64	256	512	1,024
L2 associativity	4	4	8	8

Experimental platform: We simulated the execution of all benchmark mixes on multiple platforms composed of different combinations of the 16 possible core types considered in this work using traces generated by gem5 [5] integrated with McPAT [19] to obtain power and chip area information.[1] For each core type and for all operating frequencies, we executed gem5 in full system mode running applications individually in order to collect traces as described in Section 7.3.1.

DSE approach: In order to perform meaningful comparisons, we first define a platform consisting of *four Big–Big* and *four Little–Little* cores as our **baseline** platform (the common configuration of most big.LITTLE implementations) and use area and performance/power information of the baseline to guide our analysis. Our design space exploration steps are outlined below.

1. Using McPAT, we find all possible platforms with the same area (with a tolerance of 1%) as the baseline (to trim our search space, we also limit the number of core types used in the same platform to 4). We consider two different variations of each configuration obtained: a variation in which core with same type are grouped in DVFS clusters, akin to current HMPs, and a variation in which DVFS is performed per-core.

2. We simulate all workload mixes listed in Table 7.3 on all platforms found in Step (1), and we obtain the throughput in terms of IPS and energy efficiency

---

[1]Considering a 22 nm node and the following DVFS pairs: 2 GHz/1 V, 1.5 GHz/0.8 V, 1 GHz/0.7 V, 500 MHz/0.6 V.

Table 7.3 Benchmark Mix composition

Mix 0	Mix 1	Mix 2	Mix 3	Mix 4	Mix 5	Mix 6	Mix 7	Mix 8	Mix 9	Mix 10
CRC32	basicmath	bodytrack	canneal	fluidanimate	streamcluster	jpeg typeset	CB/LU	CB/LU	CB/HU	CB/LU
blowfish	bitcount						CB/MU	MB/MU	CB/MU	
patricia	qsort						(typical)	(typical heavy)	(heavy)	(idle)
dijkstra	susan									

Mix 11	Mix 12	Mix 13	Mix 14	Mix 15	Mix 16	Mix 17	Mix 18	Mix 19	Mix 20	Mix 21
×264 2fps	×264 5fps	×264 15fps	CB/LU	CB/MU	MB/HU	CB/HU	CB/HU	canneal	bodytrack	canneal
×264 5fps	×264 15fps	×264 30fps	MB/LU	MB/MU	MB/LU	CB/LU	CB/LU	fluidanimate	streamcluster	fluidanimate
							MB/HU			bodytrack
							MB/LU			streamcluster

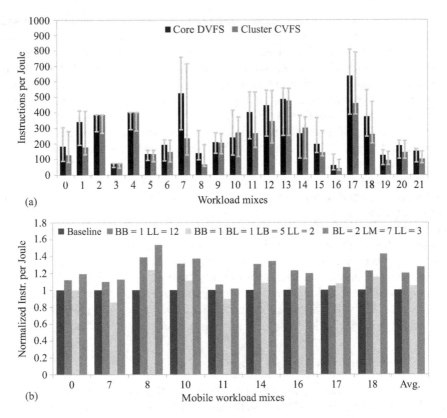

Figure 7.10   *(a) Energy efficiency of the baseline configuration with dynamic*
scheduling for both per-core and per-cluster DVFS. Range bars
represent the energy variability across all configurations that have the
same performance as the baseline. (b) Selected per-cluster DVFS
configurations on typical mobile workloads. © 2017 ACM. Data, with
permission, from Reference [8]

in terms of IPJ for each workload mix on each platform configuration. For all
runs, the total number of threads is half the number of cores in the baseline
configuration.

3. For each workload mix, we keep only the configurations whose IPS is greater
   than or equal to the IPS obtained from the baseline configuration (with a tolerance
   of 1%).

Figure 7.10(a) gives an overview of the energy efficiency design space. In
Figure 7.10(a), the bars indicate the energy efficiency of the baseline configuration ($BB = 4\ LL = 4$), while the range indicators show the minimum and maximum
achievable energy efficiency by all configurations that match the area and performance of the baseline configuration for two different configuration classes (per-core

and per-cluster DVFS). In both cases, the GTS task-mapping policy and an on demand governor are implemented as policies within the ARM framework.

Figure 7.10(b) identifies an opportunity afforded as a result of the observations from the previous analysis. In this set of experiments, we select a subset of workloads that all experience extended periods in which the cores are not completely utilized (low to medium load scenarios, as shown in [20], are the most typical case in the mobile computing domain), and identify three configurations that are more energy-efficient than the baseline for most of these workloads. Two of these configurations ($BB = 1$ $LL = 12$ and $BL = 2$ $LM = 7$ $LL = 3$) are more energy-efficient than the baseline in all cases and save more than 20% energy on average. The $BL = 2$ $LM = 7$ $LL = 3$ configuration consists mostly of smaller CPU/cache types, and are the most efficient for low to medium load scenarios. The $BB = 1$ $LL = 12$ configuration is able to save 20% energy compared to the baseline on average while limited to the same core types. This shows that by reconfiguring contemporary architectures, we can save energy for typical mobile workloads, and with more aggressive heterogeneity, we can improve energy efficiency even further. This DSE study critically depended on the use of our offline simulation infrastructure, demonstrating both the need and versatility of this framework for DSE and rapid system prototyping. For further reading, the reader may refer to [21], which also uses our infrastructure to explore using hybrid memory technology (SRAM+NVM) in on-chip memories of multicore processors.

7.4.3 Extending the lifetime of mobile devices

As extensively discussed in previous sections, effectively exploiting power-performance trade-offs of HMPs requires smart task-management mechanisms that are able to properly map workloads to the appropriate core type. This necessity, however, has the side effect of overutilizing specific core types, which may lead to decreased system reliability due to excessive stress on core of a specific type. This happens due to device-level aging mechanisms such as *bias temperature instability* [22] and *hot carrier injection* [23]. These mechanisms are highly dependent on factors such as temperature and core utilization (i.e., stress), which causes transistor-level delay degradation and reduces core performance throughout its lifetime. In this case study, we describe ADAMANt (Aging **D**riven t**A**sk **MA**ppi**N**g tool) [10], which extends SPARTA [11] with aging awareness. ADAMANt aging, performance, and power sensing and prediction in order to map tasks to the most appropriate core type while balancing out aging toward increased lifetime is shown in Figure 7.11(b).

ADAMANt uses the same task-mapping algorithm and predictive models as SPARTA and takes aging into account by introducing a performance penalty to cores with a high critical-path delay degradation (compared to other cores). We evaluated the effects of aging over a periods of 3 years. Since performing such evaluation using real devices is not feasible, we employed our offline simulation infrastructure. The setup used is the same described in Section 7.4.2 (traces collected from full-system gem5+McPAT simulations); however, the platform configuration is now limited to single 8-core big.LITTLE setup, mimicking the ODROIDXU3 configuration used in SPARTA. Aging is simulated by introducing an additional sensing window that runs

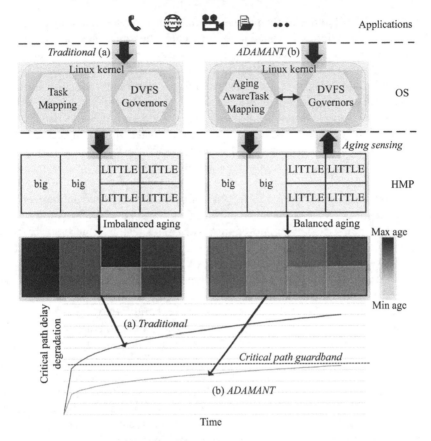

Figure 7.11   Traditional task mapping (a). Aging-aware task mapping with DVFS
(b). Due wear out caused by the aging imbalance in (a), the circuit
critical path delay may violate its operating frequency guardband

the Hotspot to estimate the average temperature of each core over that window. With
the temperature and average core utilization known, the delay degradation of each
core can be estimated using aging models. Since aging is a slow process, it is not
necessary to recompute temperature and delay degradation at the same granularity
we execute the task mapping policies and other models (e.g., once a day vs once
every 200 ms for task mapping), thus mitigating the overheads of running Hotspot.
For more details on the task-mapping policy and aging models, please refer to [10].

Experimental evaluation: In our experimental evaluation, we again define
mobile workloads based on the analysis performed by [20], which characterizes popular mobile applications in terms of potential for thread-level parallelism and core
utilization. They verified that in a typical scenario, only one core is utilized 70%
of the time in an 8-core big.LITTLE platform, even when multiple applications are
running simultaneously. Based on the observations from [20], we used applications

from PARSEC [18] to devise the following core utilization scenarios: **Idle** is a case with all cores utilization $\leq 1\%$ at all times. **Typical** is the typical scenario from [20]. **Typical(heavy)** is the same as typical with one additionally task that always fully utilizes a core. **Light load** has eight tasks that require $\leq 10\%$ LITTLE core utilization each. **Heavy load** has eight tasks that that can fully load any core. **All cores used** has four tasks that that can fully load a big core and four tasks can almost fully load a LITTLE core. The main difference between **Heavy load** and **All cores used**, is that in the former, all tasks tend to be migrated to the big cluster, while in the latter half of the tasks stay in the little cluster since they do not reach the utilization threshold for migration (assuming GTS scheduling), thus leading to a more uniform aging across big/LITTLE cores.

In our results, we compare ADAMANt against Linux GTS scheduling. For fairness of comparison, we also extend *GTS with aging awareness* (GTS AW). GTS AW uses the same aging penalty employed in ADAMANt's task mapping as a baseline *virtual load* when performing load balancing (i.e., aged cores tend to have less compute intensive tasks mapped to them). GTS AW illustrates the case in which aging mitigation is applied only within clusters of cores of the same type. For these experiments, we assume a guardband of 8% with respect to the maximum frequency of each core. Once a core ages beyond the guardband, its maximum frequency is decreased, thus reducing system performance. The aging epoch length is 1 day, task mapping epoch is 200 ms, and the DVFS epoch is 50 ms. We simulate aging for a time frame of 3 years.

Figure 7.12 shows the relative delay degradation. For the *Typical (heavy)* workload (Figure 7.12(a)), GTS violates the guardband within less than a year of runtime. With ADAMANt, we are able to increase the time to guardband violation $\sim 100\%$ (about 8 months). Figure 7.12(b) and (c) shows aging scenarios under high stress. For these cases, the guardband is violated at the very beginning of execution due the simultaneous utilization of all *big* cores. ADAMANt is able to adapt and mitigate aging by prioritizing the use of the *little* cores. It's worth mentioning that under nominal behavior, the system would be throttled due to violation of thermal constraints. Figure 7.12(d)–(f) shows the low stress scenarios.

ADAMANt delay degradation is slightly higher than GTS since the aging penalty is also proportional to the distance of the sensed delay and the guardband violation delay [10]. This adjustment allows ADAMANt to adapt to the available guardband slack and prioritizes other metrics for task mapping (such as IPS and energy efficiency) as shown in Figure 7.13.

Figure 7.13 shows the effects of aging when aging-aware DVFS is applied (i.e., the maximum frequency is scaled down if guardband is violated) and also compares ADAMANt with GTS in terms of performance and energy efficiency. For these cases, the frequency is reduced when the guardband is violated in order to allow continuous operation. In general, ADAMANt yields better performance and energy efficiency. For example, for the *typical* case (no guardband violation) ADAMANt improves performance by $\sim 10\%$. For the case when frequency capping was applied, ADAMANt improves performance by $\sim 7\%$ after 3 years of aging.

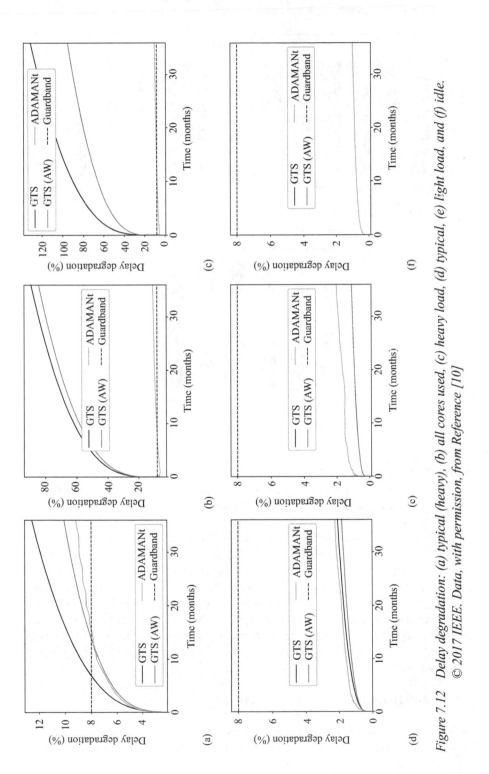

Figure 7.12 Delay degradation: (a) typical (heavy), (b) all cores used, (c) heavy load, (d) typical, (e) light load, and (f) idle. © 2017 IEEE. Data, with permission, from Reference [10]

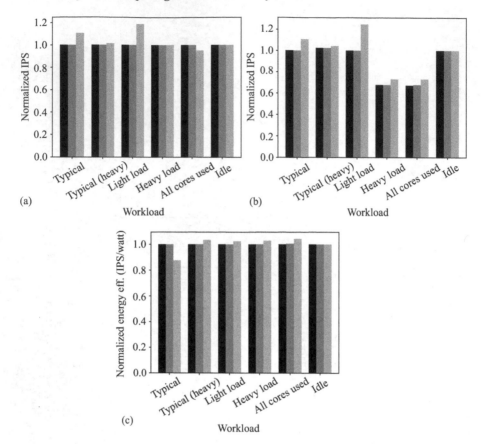

*Figure 7.13   Performance degradation under DVFS frequency capping: (a) initial
IPS, (b) IPS after 3 years, and (c) energy efficiency. © 2017 IEEE.
Data, with permission, from Reference [10]*

Figure 7.13 also shows that GTS and GTS AW yield the same performance and
energy for both aging scenarios. GTS first chooses to which cluster a task will be
migrated and then performs either load balancing (GTS) or aging-aware load balancing (GTS AW) within the cluster, therefore performance and/or power degradation
resulting from forcing a task to a different cluster is not expected since GTS AW
would not take this decision. For the cases, GTS AW is able to reduce the aging rate
(Figure 7.12(a)–(c)), we also observe identical performance after 3 years for both
GTS and GTS AW since both will have the same frequency capping in the big cluster
after 3 years.

7.5   Conclusion and future directions

In this chapter, we described our approach in using the ARM framework for managing
multiple resources in the scope of energy-limited heterogeneous multiprocessors.

We advocate extensive use of models to predict how the system will react to actuations before any action is taken, thus creating a reflective system that can more easily adapt to changes at runtime. The cases studies show that this approach is a promising scheme to pave the path toward more energy efficient heterogeneous systems. While we have presented some of our preliminary work on this topic, we believe that an adaptive reflective middleware opens up several directions for future work:

Increased levels of heterogeneity: We currently support single-ISA heterogeneous architectures, thus a natural progression is to include support for CPU+GPU processing, as well as other accelerators such as FPGAs. Jointly managing performance and power given that applications are already partitioned across the heterogeneous elements (e.g., joint CPU+GPU DVFS) can easily be integrated into our reflective middleware; however, several challenges arise if such partitioning has to be performed at runtime. Runtime systems and languages such as OpenCL provide mechanisms to generate computational kernel code for different processing elements at runtime; however, the partitioning is still fixed by the developer. Fully automating this process would require models with the ability to predict application performance and power across these heterogenous resources such as CPUs, GPUs, and FPGAs. Building these models is extremely challenging since there is no correlation between performance and power across these elements. Some existing solutions attempt to address these problems by providing pre-profiled/pre-generated building blocks to create applications (e.g., the RACECAR framework [24]) or fully profiling the target applications and generating the possible partitioning beforehand (e.g., invasive computing [25]).

Distributed architecture support: Our current implementation for real platforms runs on top of Linux and assumes a coherent shared memory model where the user-level daemon running the policies has a global view of the system. A straightforward implementation of our virtual sensing/actuation interface for a distributed architecture would be to partition the fabric into resource management domains (we partially support this, as shown in Figure 7.2 with the concept of clock domains) and create multiple instances of the daemon for each domain. Naturally, policies may need to be modified for the required coordination. From the infrastructure perspective, each daemon would only be able to access accurate sensing information from its own domain, while information from other domains would be available in an approximated or delayed manner. Trading-off sensing information accuracy for less interconnect traffic or more responsive policies is still an open problem being addressed in the context of Network-on-Chip based many-core systems [26–28].

Memory as a resource: We focus mostly on allocating and managing processing resources. However, whether or not the same approach can be applied to more *passive* components such as memories is still an open issue. The performance and energy efficiency on architectures that rely on noncoherent software-controlled memories is directly affected by the proximity of the processing elements and the data location [29,30]. The same is also true for typical cache-coherent architectures with multiple memory controllers or nonuniform memory access (though caches might be able to hide the latency of accessing far-away controllers) [31,32]. Abstracting memory allocation request as a "task" that needs to mapped to a resource would open up opportunities for optimization.

Self-trained models: Our current reflective model is a combination of regression-based performance and power prediction [10], heuristic-based models [10,11] and analytical models [8]. Given that for any sensing window, the prediction error of the previous window can be computed by keeping information from previous prediction, the models can be improved by including error correction mechanisms. For instance *state-space models* are naturally feedback driven and could be a promising replacement for regression models. However, introducing error correction to heuristics that model highly nonlinear behavior (e.g., the *CFS* model from [10]) is a much greater challenge.

Machine learning: Machine learning is prospective replacement for heuristic-based and analytical models. For instance, [33] uses learning transfer techniques to adapt a trained model to runtime variations. Furthermore, the infrastructure provided by our middleware makes it much easier to collect system performance data at various levels of granularity. Unsupervised machine-learning technique could be used to mine this data and find patterns useful for optimizing existing policies [34].

Policy supervisors: Some applications may require formal or stronger guarantees to ensure that certain parameters of the system do not exceed a limit or remain within a given range of values. Though not addressed in this chapter, our framework provides the infrastructure to easily implement control theory-based policies that provide such guarantees. Furthermore, *supervisory control theory* [35] is also a promising technique to manage policies that require coordination while providing formal guarantees.

Acknowledgments

We would like to thank the authors of the works described in the chapter for their contributions: Bryan Donyanavard, Eli Bozorgzadeh, Santanu Sarma, and Zana Ghaderi. This work was partially supported by NSF grant CCF-1704859 and by CAPES (CSF program). We also acknowledge financial support from the Marie Curie Actions of the European Union's H2020 Programme.

References

[1] Greenhalgh P. big. LITTLE Processing with ARM Cortex-A15 & Cortex-A7. EE Times. 2011;(October 2011):1–8. Available from: http://www.eetimes.com/document.asp?doc_id=1279167.

[2] Rahmani AM, Liljeberg P, Hemani A, Jantsch A, Tenhunen H. The Dark Side of Silicon. 1st ed. Springer, Switzerland; 2016.

[3] ARM. big. LITTLE Technology: The Future of Mobile. ARM; 2013. Available from: https://www.arm.com/files/pdf/big_LITTLE_Technology_the_Futue_of_Mobile.pdf.

[4] Desnoyers M. Using the Linux Kernel Tracepoints; 2015. Available from: https://www.kernel.org/doc/Documentation/trace/tracepoints.txt.

[5] Binkert N, Sardashti S, Sen R, *et al.* The gem5 Simulator. ACM SIGARCH Computer Architecture News. 2011;39(2):1.

[6] Calandrino J, Baumberger D, Li T, Young J, Hahn S. LinSched: The Linux Scheduler Simulator. In: Proceedings of the ISCA 21st International Conference on Parallel and Distributed Computing and Communications Systems; 2008. p. 171–176. Available from: http://happyli.org/tongli/papers/linsched.pdf.

[7] Zhuravlev S, Blagodurov S, Fedorova A. AKULA: A Toolset for Experimenting and Developing Thread Placement Algorithms on Multicore Systems Sergey. In: Proceedings of the 19th International Conference on Parallel Architectures and Compilation Techniques   PACT'10. New York, NY, USA: ACM Press; 2010. p. 249.

[8] Mück T, Donyanavard B, Dutt N. PoliCym: Rapid Prototyping of Resource Management Policies for HMPs. In: 2017 International Symposium on Rapid System Prototyping (RSP); 2017.

[9] Skadron K, Stan MR, Sankaranarayanan K, Huang W, Velusamy S, Tarjan D. Temperature-Aware Microarchitecture: Modeling and Implementation. ACM Transactions on Architecture and Code Optimization. 2004;1(1):94–125.

[10] Muck TR, Ghaderi Z, Dutt ND, Bozorgzadeh E. Exploiting Heterogeneity for Aging-Aware Load Balancing in Mobile Platforms. IEEE Transactions on Multi-Scale Computing Systems. 2017;3(1):25–35.

[11] Donyanavard B, Mück T, Sarma S, Dutt N. SPARTA: Runtime Task Allocation for Energy Efficient Heterogeneous Many-cores. In: Proceedings of the Eleventh IEEE/ACM/IFIP International Conference on Hardware/Software Codesign and System Synthesis – CODES'16. New York, NY, USA: ACM Press; 2016. p. 1–10.

[12] Muck T, Sarma S, Dutt N. Run-DMC: Runtime Dynamic Heterogeneous Multicore Performance and Power Estimation for Energy Efficiency. In: 2015 International Conference on Hardware/Software Codesign and System Synthesis (CODES+ISSS). IEEE; 2015. p. 173–182.

[13] Liu G, Park J, Marculescu D. Dynamic Thread Mapping for High-performance, Power-efficient Heterogeneous Many-core Systems. In: 2013 IEEE 31st International Conference on Computer Design (ICCD). IEEE; 2013. p. 54–61.

[14] Sarma S, Muck T, Bathen LAD, Dutt N, Nicolau A. SmartBalance: A Sensing-Driven Linux Load Balancer for Energy Efficiency of Heterogeneous MPSoCs. In: Proceedings of the 52nd Annual Design Automation Conference on – DAC'15. New York, NY, USA: ACM Press; 2015. p. 1–6.

[15] Van Craeynest K, Jaleel A, Eeckhout L, Narvaez P, Emer J. Scheduling Heterogeneous Multi-cores Through Performance Impact Estimation (PIE). In: 2012 39th Annual International Symposium on Computer Architecture (ISCA). vol. 40. IEEE; 2012. p. 213–224.

[16] Heirman W, Carlson TE, Van Craeynest K, Hur I, Jaleel A, Eeckhout L. Undersubscribed Threading on Clustered Cache Architectures. In: Proceedings – International Symposium on High-Performance Computer Architecture; 2014. p. 678–689.

[17]   Guthaus MR, Ringenberg JS, Ernst D, Austin TM, Mudge T, Brown RB. MiBench: A Free, Commercially Representative Embedded Benchmark Suite. In: IEEE 4th Annual Workshop on Workload Characterization; 2001.

[18]   Bienia C, Kumar S, Singh JP, Li K. The PARSEC Benchmark Suite. In: Proceedings of the 17th International Conference on Parallel Architectures and Compilation Techniques – PACT'08. New York, NY, USA: ACM Press; 2008. p. 72.

[19]   Li S, Ahn JH, Strong RD, Brockman JB, Tullsen DM, Jouppi NP. The McPAT Framework for Multicore and Manycore Architectures. ACM Transactions on Architecture and Code Optimization. 2013;10(1):1–29.

[20]   Gao C, Gutierrez A, Rajan M, Dreslinski RG, Mudge T, Wu CJ. A Study of Mobile Device Utilization. In: 2015 IEEE International Symposium on Performance Analysis of Systems and Software (ISPASS). September 2014. IEEE; 2015. p. 225–234.

[21]   Donyanavard B, Monazzah AMH, Mück T, Dutt N. Exploring Fast and Slow Memories in HMP Core Types. In: Proceedings of the Twelfth IEEE/ACM/IFIP International Conference on Hardware/Software Codesign and System Synthesis Companion – CODES'17. New York, NY, USA: ACM Press; 2017. p. 1–2.

[22]   Bhardwaj S, Wang W, Vattikonda R, Cao Y, Vrudhula S. Predictive Modeling of the NBTI Effect for Reliable Design. In: IEEE Custom Integrated Circuits Conference 2006. CICC. IEEE; 2006. p. 189–192.

[23]   Bravaix A, Guerin C, Huard V, Roy D, Roux JM, Vincent E. Hot-Carrier Acceleration Factors for Low Power Management in DC–AC Stressed 40 nm NMOS Node at High Temperature. In: 2009 IEEE International Reliability Physics Symposium. IEEE; 2009. p. 531–548.

[24]   Wernsing JR, Stitt G, Fowers J. The RACECAR Heuristic for Automatic Function Specialization on Multi-core Heterogeneous Systems. In: Proceedings of the 2012 International Conference on Compilers, Architectures and Synthesis for Embedded Systems – CASES'12. New York, NY, USA: ACM Press; 2012. p. 81.

[25]   Weichslgartner A, Wildermann S, Glaß M, Teich J. Invasive Computing for Mapping Parallel Programs to Many-Core Architectures. 1st ed. Springer, Singapore; 2018.

[26]   Kobbe S, Bauer L, Lohmann D, Schröder-Preikschat W, Henkel J. DistRM: Distributed Resource Management for On-Chip Many-Core Systems. In: Proceedings of the seventh IEEE/ACM/IFIP International Conference on Hardware/Software Codesign and System Synthesis – CODES+ISSS'11. New York, NY, USA: ACM Press; 2011. p. 119. Available from: http://dl. acm.org/citation.cfm?doid=2039370.2039392.

[27]   Pathania A, Venkataramani V, Shafique M, Mitra T, Henkel J. Distributed Fair Scheduling for Many-Cores. In: 2016 Design, Automation & Test in Europe Conference & Exhibition (DATE); 2016. p. 379–384.

[28]   Tsoutsouras V, Anagnostopoulos I, Masouros D, Soudris D. A Hierarchical Distributed Runtime Resource Management Scheme for NoC-Based

Many-Cores. ACM Transactions on Embedded Computing Systems. 2018;17(3):1–26. Available from: http://dl.acm.org/citation.cfm?doid=3185335.3182173.

[29]   Shrivastava A, Dutt N, Cai J, Shoushtari M, Donyanavard B, Tajik H. Automatic management of Software Programmable Memories in Many-core Architectures. IET Computers & Digital Techniques. 2016;10(6):288–298. Available from: http://digital-library.theiet.org/content/journals/10.1049/iet-cdt.2016.0024.

[30]   Shoushtari M, Donyanavard B, Bathen LAD, Dutt N. ShaVe-ICE: Sharing Distributed Virtualized SPMs in Many-Core Embedded Systems. ACM Transactions on Embedded Computing Systems. 2018;17(2):1–25. Available from: http://dl.acm.org/citation.cfm?doid=2933057.2933099%0Ahttp://dl.acm.org/citation.cfm?doid=3160927.3157667   http://dl.acm.org/citation.cfm?doid=3160927.3157667.

[31]   Drebes A, Pop A, Heydemann K, Cohen A, Drach N. Scalable Task Parallelism for NUMA: A Uniform Abstraction for Coordinated Scheduling and Memory Management. In: Proceedings of the 2016 International Conference on Parallel Architectures and Compilation – PACT'16. New York, NY, USA: ACM Press; 2016. p. 125–137. Available from: http://dl.acm.org/citation.cfm?doid=2967938.2967946.

[32]   Caheny P, Casas M, Moretó M, et al. Reducing Cache Coherence Traffic with Hierarchical Directory Cache and NUMA-Aware Runtime Scheduling. In: Proceedings of the 2016 International Conference on Parallel Architectures and Compilation – PACT'16. 1. New York, NY, USA: ACM Press; 2016. p. 275–286. Available from: http://dl.acm.org/citation.cfm?doid=2967938.2967962.

[33]   Shafik RA, Yang S, Das A, Maeda-Nunez LA, Merrett GV, Al-Hashimi BM. Learning Transfer-Based Adaptive Energy Minimization in Embedded Systems. IEEE Transactions on Computer-Aided Design of Integrated Circuits and Systems. 2016;35(6):877–890. Available from: http://ieeexplore.ieee.org/lpdocs/epic03/wrapper.htm?arnumber=7308001.

[34]   Li Y, Chang K, Bel O, Miller EL, Long DDE. Capes: Unsupervised Storage Performance Tuning Using Neural Network-Based Deep Reinforcement Learning. In: Proceedings of the International Conference for High Performance Computing, Networking, Storage and Analysis on – SC'17; 2017. p. 1–14. Available from: http://dl.acm.org/citation.cfm?doid=3126908.3126951.

[35]   Rahmani AM, Donyanavard B, Mück T, et al. SPECTR: Formal Supervisory Control and Coordination for Many-core Systems Resource Management. In: Proceedings of the Twenty-Third International Conference on Architectural Support for Programming Languages and Operating Systems – ASPLOS'18. New York, NY, USA: ACM Press; 2018. p. 169–183. Available from: http://dl.acm.org/citation.cfm?doid=3173162.3173199.

Chapter 8

Advances in power management of many-core processors

Andrea Bartolini[1] and Davide Rossi[1]

Today's power management is the central component of designing a wide range of processing elements (PEs). On the one hand, ultra-low power (ULP) embedded systems, such as micro-controllers and system-on-chips (SoCs), which are at the heart pervasive and "everywhere" Internet-of-Things (IoT) are constrained by their form-factor and consequently by battery capacity or renewable energy power supply. On the other, the power consumption of high-performance computing systems is limited by the finite cooling and power delivery network capacity. As a matter of fact, the entire computing spectrum is affected by the operation under a limited power consumption, which imposes a practical limit to the achievable performance.

It is well known that the power consumption of digital devices is the results of operating conditions and of the computational capacity of the device in a specific moment. Clock frequency which gives the pace at which computation happens in digital devices is also the rate at which internal capacitance is charged and discharged. The strength at which these charges happen depends on the voltage supply. So does the maximum speed at which the device can be clocked and the robustness to process and signal noise. Not all the power consumed is spent in computation, leakage power is wasted for keeping the device on and increases with silicon temperature and supply voltage.

Power management, which involves hardware (HW) design choices in conjunction with software (SW) abstractions and policies, is thus the key component for optimizing the power consumption of the entire spectrum of computing while maximizing the performance and lifetime of wide range of PEs.

This book chapter discusses the advances in power management for two classes of computing systems which sit at the antipodes of the computing spectrum. In the ULP domain, the exploitation of parallel processing over multiple cores has been demonstrated as an effective way to improve the energy efficiency at system level when joined with near-threshold computing (NTC). This approach allows to take advantage of the quadratic dependency of dynamic power with the supply voltage,

[1]Department of Electrical, Electronic, and Information Engineering "Guglielmo Marconi", University of Bologna, Italy

while recovering the related performance degradation through parallelism. However, low-voltage operation magnifies all the effects related to process and temperature variations, which needs to be compensated at runtime to take full benefits from NTC. These topics are covered in Sections 8.2–8.4. On the other hand, high-performance computing multi-cores are designed for performance, they operates in a higher voltage and power consumption regime. For this reason, power management in HPC systems has to handle the side effects of high power consumption being capable of limiting their total power consumption dynamically to be thermally power sustainable. In this domain, heterogeneity in the parallel application running in these cores can be exploited to increase application throughput under total power constraint.

8.1   Parallel ultra-low power computing

IoTs, e-Health, Smart Sensors and wearable consumer gadgets are expected to drive the electronic market of the next decades. These applications rely on the capability of the research community to provide devices that couple ULP behaviour with a reasonable level of performance. Indeed, these applications are characterized not only by an increasingly tighter power budget but also by an increasing demand of computation capabilities. The pace dictated by the Moore's law has slowed down, and CMOS scaling, which drove semiconductor growth during the past decades, is delivering reduced energy gains [1]. In this "Moore's law twilight era", further energy gain can be achieved by moving to the NTC domain [2]. Unfortunately, peak performance is limited to a few tens of MOPS. Some approaches leverage ultra-wide supply voltage scaling to reliably meet performance requirements, at the cost of energy efficiency. The concept of parallel ULP (PULP) computing tackles the performance and energy efficiency challenges in near threshold by leveraging thread-level parallelism over multiple cores to overcome the performance degradation at low voltage, while maintaining flexibility typical of programmable processors and high energy efficiency [3].

However, electronic devices implemented with most advanced technological nodes feature a strong dependency between the ambient temperature and the operating frequency and leakage power. Unfortunately, this dependency increases in the near-threshold operating region, where PULP devices work to provide high energy efficiency. The effects of process variations require a one-time compensation as soon as the chip is fabricated. Contrarily, thermal variations are dependent on the operating environment and hence require a runtime compensation to ensure that chips are able to match the frequency target at low temperatures and leakage targets at high temperatures. A typical means of achieving post-silicon tuning to compensate variations in circuits is through body biasing [4]. As opposed to adaptation of supply voltage, which requires on chip DC/DC converters or voltage regulators, modulation of body biasing can be implemented with simpler and more efficient circuits, as only small transient currents are required to polarize the substrate of the devices [5,6]. Exploiting forward body biasing (FBB), it is possible to increase the operating frequency of a device by avoiding significant growth of dynamic power and making it suitable for compensation of variations causing degradation of the operating frequency. On the other hand, reverse body biasing (RBB) allows to significantly reduce leakage power where the process or operating conditions allow the devices to run faster than the desired frequency, but with excessive leakage power.

Typical means of compensating temperature-induced variations in electronic circuits are through voltage scaling and body biasing [7]. The majority of the works focusing on temperature effects target high-performance devices that are subject to self-heating [8]. These devices necessitate the mitigation of the effects of temperature variation to avoid excessive leakage power dissipation that may lead to thermal runway. However, these works demonstrated the ability to compensate only for relatively small temperature ranges, not representative of the huge amount of scenarios enabled by ULP applications. Indeed, although self-heating does not affect ULP devices due to their extremely small power consumption, compensation of ambient temperature is crucial in this domain as well [9]. In most advanced CMOS technologies, thermal inversion causes an exponential growth of the dependency between temperature and frequency, especially when operating in near-threshold. Some works have addressed this problem, mainly leveraging adaptation of supply voltage [10,11]. On the other hand, the adoption of body biasing to address variation of ambient temperature has not been extensively explored so far, due to the limited capabilities of most advanced technologies such as bulk and FinFET to provide extended body bias ranges suitable for compensation of wide temperature ranges [12,13].

In this chapter, we first analyse the capabilities of UTBB FD-SOI (ultra-thin body and box fully depleted silicon on insulator) technology in compensating temperature variations in the ULP domain. To demonstrate this potential on real silicon, we utilize a test vehicle consisting of an ULP cluster of processors operating in near threshold fabricated in 28-nm UTBB FD-SOI technology. The compensation technique exploits one of the unique features of the UTBB FD-SOI technology: the ability to use a wide range of body bias to modulate the transistors voltage threshold. With respect to traditional bulk technology, UTBB FD-SOI technology enables an extended range of body bias and a better electrostatic control, which provides 85 mV/V of threshold voltage/body bias voltage modulation. Starting from measurements on a multi-core system fabricated in 28-nm UTBB FD-SOI technology, we fit a compact model to extensively evaluate supply voltage and body biasing as knobs for compensation of temperature variations in the ULP domain.

Classical models suitable for describing the impact of physical parameters (i.e. temperature, voltage supply and body-bias) on the performance and energy efficiency of CMOS digital circuits show severe limits when applied to ULP devices [2]. Indeed classical models use different model templates for describing super-threshold and near-threshold operating regions with discontinuities in the interface in between the two regions. Ambient temperature as well as body-bias at the macro-scale can be seen as changes to the overdrive voltage: moving the device from one operating region to the other. As a result, empirical fitting of compact models which learns these dependencies is subjected to numerical errors. Recently, new trans-regional models have been proposed based on EKV and polylogarithm models [2,14]. In this section, we take advantage of these templates for fitting a compact model of the power and performance of a real silicon testchip under a large set of body-bias, voltage supply and ambient temperatures. We then used this model to compensate the ambient temperature variation.

8.1.1 Background

Several approaches in the literature have proposed mechanisms to constraint the power consumption of large-scale computing infrastructures. These can be classified in two main families. Approaches in the first class use predictive models to estimate the power consumed by a job before its execution. At job schedule time, this information is used to let enter jobs in the system that satisfies the total power consumption budget. HW power capping mechanisms like RAPL are used to ensure that the predicted budget is respected during all the application phases and to tolerate prediction errors in the job average power consumption estimation [15–17]. Approaches in the second class distribute a slice of the total system power budget to each computing element which is active. The per-compute element power budget is ensured to HW power capping mechanisms like RAPL. The allocation of the power consumption budget to each compute node can be done statically or dynamically [18–21]. It is the goal of the runtime to trade-off power reduction with application performance loss. The GEOPM [19] runtime developed by Intel is an open source, plugin extensible runtime for power management. GEOPM implements a plugin for power balancing to improve performance in power constraint systems. This is done by reallocating power on sockets involved in the critical path of the application. The authors in [22] quantitatively evaluated RAPL as a control system in terms of stability, accuracy, settling time, overshoot, and efficiency. In this work, the authors evaluated only the proprieties of RAPL mechanism without considering other power capping strategies and how it can vary the application workload.

8.1.2 PULP platform

PULP platform is a multi-core SoC for ULP applications, which operates in near-threshold to achieve extreme energy efficiency on a wide range of operating points [23]. The SoC is built around a cluster featuring: four cores and 16 kB of L2 memory. The cores are based on a highly power optimized micro-architecture implementing the RISC-V ISA featuring a latch-based shared instruction cache to boost energy efficiency of instruction fetching [24]. The cores do not have private data caches, avoiding memory coherency overhead and increasing area efficiency, while they share a L1 multi-banked tightly coupled data memory (TCDM) acting as a shared data scratchpad memory [25]. The TCDM features a parametric number of SRAM banks connected to the processors through a single clock latency, non-blocking interconnect implementing a word-level interleaved scheme minimize banking conflict probability [25]. Off-cluster (L2) memory latency is managed by a tightly coupled DMA featuring private per-core programming channels, ultra-low programming latency and lightweight architecture optimized for low-power and high-transfer efficiency [26].

8.1.3 Compact model

To compare the efficacy of the body-bias and supply voltage knobs in compensating ambient temperature and process variations on next generation ULP devices, we conducted a large data acquisition test directly on the PULP prototypes measuring power and performance metrics at the different corner cases. Based on the measurement results, we have derived a set of empirical models to describe the dependency of the performance metrics to the physical parameters, compensation knobs and environmental conditions.

In the following, the measurements described are performed with an Advantest SoCV93000 tester system, in connection with a Thermonics 2500E temperature forcing system, able to force an environment temperature $-80\,°C$–$220\,°C$. We have then measured the leakage power, total power and maximum frequency achievable by the device when powered at different supply voltages typical of the ULP domain ($V_{DD} = \{0.5, 0.05, 0.8\}V$). For each V_{DD} point, we have applied a different body-biasing voltage ($V_{BB} = \{0, 0.1, 1\}V$). All this measurements have been repeated while forcing a different temperature to the die ($T = \{-40, 10, 120\}\,°C$). For each of them, we have measured the power consumption when the device is not clocked (leakage power P_{LKG}), the power consumption when the device is executing an arithmetic loop at the maximum operating frequency (total power P_{TOT}). The total power accounts for the leakage power (P_{LKG}) and the active dynamic power (P_{DYN}). We extracted the maximum operating frequency (F_{MAX}) empirically as the maximum one for which the arithmetic loop was returning a valid checksum. The entire dataset is composed by the following tuples $\{V_{DD}, V_{BB}, T, P_{TOT}, P_{LKG}, P_{TOT}, P_{DYN}, F_{MAX}\}$. The dynamic power has been derived analytically by subtracting the leakage power from the total power ($P_{DYN} = P_{TOT} - P_{LKG}$). The entire dataset has a cardinality $8 \times 11 \times 17$ for a total of 1,496 tuples.

We used this dataset in combination with empirically learn a set of analytical models:

$$F_{MAX} = b_1 \cdot \log\left[e^{b_2 \cdot V_{DD} - b_3 + b_4 \cdot V_{BB}} + 1\right] \cdot V_{DD} \tag{8.1}$$

$$P_{DYN} = a_1 + a_2 \cdot F_{MAX} \cdot V_{DD}^2 \tag{8.2}$$

$$P_{LKG} = c_1 \cdot e^{c_2 \cdot V_{DD} - c_3 + c_4 \cdot V_{BB}} \cdot e^{c_5 \cdot V_{DD}} + c_6 \tag{8.3}$$

Due to the large operating points covered by the tests, the models templates have to be transregional and cover with continuity NTC and strong inversion domains (8.1). The three models coefficients (a_i, b_i, c_i) have been fitted by mean of a nonlinear least square numerical optimization. We obtained a set of different constants for each temperature. To validate the model, we computed for each dataset point the relative error of the model output and the real measurements. We report here the root mean square of the modelling error which is $RMS_{F_{MAX}} = 0.0239$, $RMS_{P_{DYN}} = 0.0287$, $RMS_{Pleak} = 0.0106$. In average the error is below the 3 per cent.

This model can be used as a baseline for analytical optimization and SW-based runtime compensation. It is indeed used to compute the required amount of supply voltage and body biasing to compensate for temperature variation in the experiments that follow.

8.1.4 Process and temperature compensation of ULP multi-cores

This section describes the experimental results elaborated with the model described previously. For the sake of clarity, we present the problem of process compensation separately from the temperature compensation one. The results presented in the two explorations can be easily generalized to the more generic case where devices are in presence of both process and temperature variation. Indeed, as demonstrated in [7], the optimal body bias voltages for process and temperature compensation can be computed as the sum of the voltages obtained by compensating for process and temperature variations independently of each other.

8.1.4.1   Compensation of process variation

This section presents the results of the exploration performed to evaluate the effectiveness of the two performance knobs to compensate chips for process variation exploiting supply voltage and body biasing.

Figure 8.1 shows with bars the histogram of the maximum frequency achievable by 60 PULP chips operating at 0.6 V of V_{DD} with no body-bias at ambient temperature (20 °C). The solid line reports the Gaussian fit of the maximum clock frequency distribution ($\mu = 25$ MHz, $\sigma = 2.52$ MHz). We used this distribution in conjunction with the maximum frequency model (8.1) to compute the relative threshold voltage (b_3/b_2) for different process variation realization. With this perturbed threshold voltage, we inverted the maximum frequency model (8.1) and computed the V_{DD} and V_{BB} level which compensate for the process variation, within a range of $[-3\sigma, 3\sigma]$, bringing the maximum frequency equal to the nominal one.

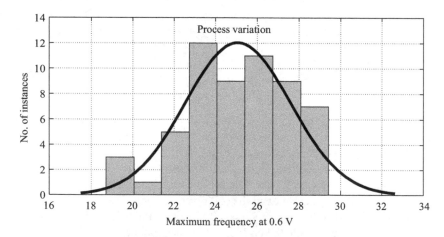

Figure 8.1   Distribution of maximum operating frequency of 60 PULP chips at the supply voltage of 0.6 V

Figure 8.2 shows the percentage of voltage increment (y-axis) to compensate different levels of process variations (x-axis) at the different voltage levels (different lines). From the plot, we can notice that for slowest silicon (negative variation), the process can be compensated by increasing the voltage level, whereas for fast silicon, the process can be compensated by reducing the voltage level. Moreover decreasing the nominal voltage supply increases the process variation sensitivity requiring larger increments of V_{DD} to compensate the performance loss or gain. Figure 8.3 also shows the V_{BB} level (y-axis) which compensates for the different process variation levels (x-axis). We notice that the body-bias which compensates a given process variation

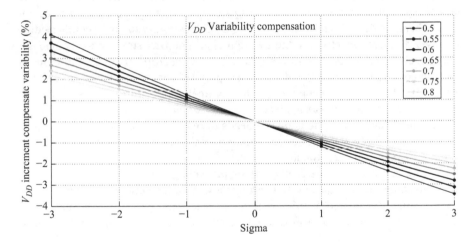

Figure 8.2   Compensation of process variation with supply voltage

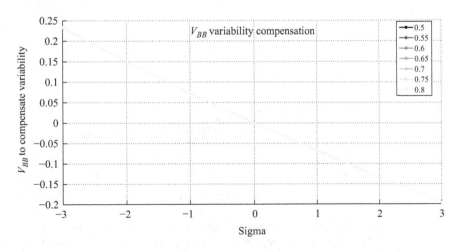

Figure 8.3   Compensation of process variation with body biasing

level is independent to the nominal voltage level. As a consequence the body-bias forms an ideal knob to compensate variability in the near-threshold domain.

8.1.5 Experimental results

This section describes the results of the exploration performed to achieve compensation against temperature variation by adapting the supply voltage and body-bias voltage on the PULP silicon. As shown in Figure 8.4, depending on the variation of operating temperature with respect to the nominal temperature, which we consider 20 °C, the maximum frequency of a device may increase or decrease due to thermal inversion. At the same time, the exponential dependency between temperature and leakage power causes devices to dissipate much more power at high temperatures, where the devices are faster. This opens the possibility to apply compensation with two different objectives in the two domains. The first strategy for compensation, namely *frequency compensation* applies at *low temperatures* (temperatures lower than the nominal) and leads to increase the supply voltage, or apply FBB in order to achieve the *nominal frequency* (i.e., at the nominal temperature). The second kind of compensation, namely *leakage power compensation* applies at *high temperatures* (temperatures higher than the nominal), leads to reduce the supply voltage or apply RBB in order to reduce the power consumption with the constraints of achieving the *nominal frequency* at each voltage.

Figure 8.5 shows the percentage of supply voltage increase (or decrease) that allows to compensate frequency and leakage power for temperature variation. At the lowest voltage considered of 0.5 V, a frequency decrease of ∼100 per cent, which occurs at the temperature of −40°C, can be compensated with a 12-per-cent increase

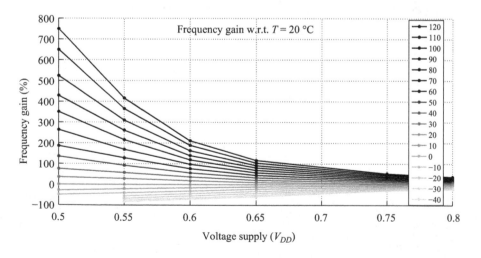

Figure 8.4   Effect on thermal inversion on maximum frequency achieved by the PULP silicon prototype within the voltage range of 0.5–0.8 V and temperature range of −40 °C–120 °C

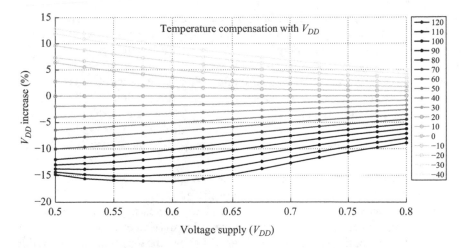

Figure 8.5 Percentage of voltage supply increase (and decrease) required to compensate for frequency degradation at low temperatures and leakage increase at high temperatures

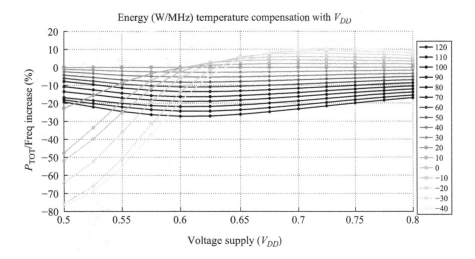

Figure 8.6 Percentage of ratio between energy per cycle of non-compensated and compensated silicon exploiting adaptation of supply voltage

of supply voltage, leading to a supply voltage of 0.56 V after compensation. At the same voltage, and the temperature of 120°C, the nominal frequency can be achieved by decreasing the supply voltage by 17 per cent, leading to a voltage of 0.415 V. The effect of compensation through adaptation of supply voltage on the energy is shown in Figure 8.6. In the *high temperatures* range, the effect of compensation is always beneficial from an energy perspective, as it allows to achieve the target frequency with a smaller supply voltage, leading to a reduction of both leakage and dynamic power. On the other hand, in the *low temperatures* range, there are two regions. At very low voltage (0.5–0.6 V), the compensation has a beneficial effect on energy, despite the increase of dynamic power caused by the increase of supply voltage. Indeed, operating at a higher frequency, the contribution of leakage power (which is dominant) is integrated over a smaller period, and its impact on the energy dramatically decreases. When the supply voltage increases (above 0.65 V), the contribution of dynamic power on the energy increases and becomes dominant. In this voltage range, the energy of compensated devices increases due to the quadratic dependency between dynamic power and supply voltage.

Compensation with body biasing can be achieved in a similar way. When the operating temperature leads to a reduction of the maximum frequency, FBB can be applied to reduce the threshold voltage of transistors increasing performance. When the operating temperature leads to an increase of the maximum frequency, RBB can be applied to reduce the leakage power. Figure 8.7 shows the results of the exploration. At the lowest nominal voltage of 0.5 V, where the effect of temperature inversion is larger, the reduction of maximum frequency occurring at the temperature of −40°C can be theoretically achieved by applying 0.8-V FBB. However, at the supply voltage of 0.5 V, the technology supports the maximum FBB of 0.55 V. Thus, the minimum temperature that can be compensated with body biasing at the supply voltage of 0.5 V is −20°C, on the PULP chip prototype. Moving the focus on leakage power, thanks to the extended RBB supported by conventional well technology, it is possible to compensate power up to 120°C, with a RBB of up to 1.1 V. The energy saving related to compensation with body biasing is shown in Figure 8.8. The first observation is

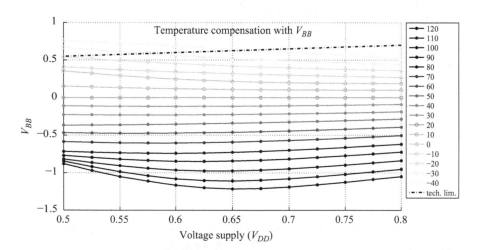

Figure 8.7   Body biasing required to compensate for frequency degradation at low temperatures and leakage increase at high temperatures

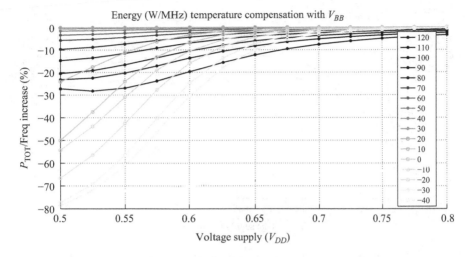

Figure 8.8 *Percentage of ratio between energy per cycle of non-compensated and compensated silicon exploiting adaptation of body bias voltage*

that as opposed to compensation with supply voltage, the adoption of compensation with body biasing is always beneficial, from an energy perspective, for all voltages and temperatures. For *high temperatures*, the gain in energy efficiency is given by the leakage power reduction associated with RBB, which leads to a reduction of energy of up to 23 per cent at 0.5 V, 120°C. The key advantage of compensation through body biasing with respect to supply voltage can be seen in the *low temperatures* range, where the slower operating frequency needs to be compensated. Applying FBB leads to an increase of leakage power, but not dynamic power. Hence, even for high voltage supply ($\geq$0.65 V), an energy reduction with respect to the non-compensated case is visible.

Figure 8.9 shows the percentage of energy per cycle achieved compensating for temperature variation with body biasing with respect to supply voltage. The energy of compensation through body biasing is smaller than the energy of compensation through voltage scaling in all the *low temperature* range thus in all the points where a frequency degradation need to be compensated, by up to 15 per cent. When the leakage power has to be compensated, due to operation at *high temperatures*, for a wide range of voltages and temperatures ($T \leq 80°C$; VDD ≥ 0.55 V) compensation through voltage scaling is more energy efficient than compensation through body biasing. In extreme high temperatures and low voltage conditions ($T \geq 80°C$; VDD ≤ 0.55 V), where leakage dominates dynamic power, compensation of power through VBB provides better energy than compensation of through VDD, due to the effectiveness of body biasing in reducing leakage.

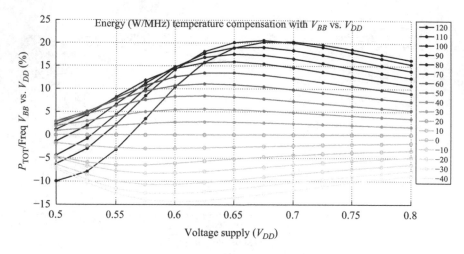

Figure 8.9   Comparison between energy per cycle required to compensate using body biasing with respect to supply voltage

8.2   HPC architectures and power management systems

In this section, we focus on the opposite compute domain. The high-performance computing clusters are among the fastest computing systems in the world. Periodically, the Top500 lists the 500 most powerful computing clusters worldwide based on their double precision floating point operations per second (FLOPS) [27]. These computers are "big enough" to be considered supercomputer-class.

8.2.1   Supercomputer architectures

High-performance computing systems are composed of clusters of thousands of computing nodes. Each computing node features several computing engines. Most of the computing nodes of supercomputing systems (398/500 supercomputers in the Top500 November 2017 list) are based on multi-core processors, 22 use accelerators. Overall 471 supercomputers in the Top500 November 2017 list use Intel multi-core processors.

On these machines, users submit their applications through a batch queue system which guarantees exclusive access to the exact number of resources requested during the application submission.

HPC applications are single program multiple data codes, the same application's executable is replicated multiple times on different nodes of the cluster. Each instance works on a partition of the problem domain and data and communicates with the other instances intermediate results to globally solve the different computational steps composing the application. For this reason, a HPC application can be seen as the composition of several tasks executed in a distributed environment which exchanges messages among all the instances. Communication latencies and unbalance in the work done by each task can delay the synchronization's points as well as the application execution time. Barriers based on spin locks are thus preferred over interrupt based synchronization primitives as they are faster, causing each node to never "rest" even during waiting periods. Power management solutions are thus sought to reduce the energy wasted during these periods.

High power and energy consumption is an important challenge for the evolution of HPC systems. Indeed, today's most powerful supercomputer, TaihuLight, reaches 93.01 PetaFLOPS with 15.37 MW of only IT power consumption [28]. Its predecessor Tianhe-2, reaches 33.2 PetaFlops with 17.8 MW of power dissipation that increases to 24 MW when considering also the cooling infrastructure [29]. However, [30] shows that an acceptable value for the power consumption of future supercomputer's data centre is 20 MW. Moreover, each processing engine is power limited itself. Indeed, today the power consumption of processors is limited by both the heat dissipation, and the maximum current flowing through the power supply pins. As an example, an increase in the leakage power consumption caused by an increased ambient temperature has the direct effect of reducing the processor clock speed [31]. It is thus central for HPC processors to dynamically manage the power consumption. The next section introduces the mechanisms at the base of the control of power consumption in HPC systems.

8.2.2 Power management in HPC systems

The Advanced Configuration and Power Interface (ACPI) [32] defines an open standard interface between operating systems and different HW power managers. Today's CPU architectures are composed of multiple PEs which communicate through a network subsystem that interconnect PEs, Last Level Cache, Integrated Memory Controllers and other uncore components. Taking as an example an Intel® multi-cores' CPU for the HPC market (more than 86 per cent of supercomputers listed in [27] are based on Intel CPUs), ACPI specification defines different component's states which a CPU can use to reduce power consumption. Intel architecture optimizes ACPI using different power saving levels for cores and uncore components. The ACPI standard defines P-states to select DVFS operating points to reduce the active power consumption while also defines specific C-states to reduce both static and active power consumption during idle and unintensive CPU activities.

Figure 8.10 show the Intel P-States. These are defined by levels ranging from 0 to *n* where *n* is the lowest frequency and 0 is a speculative operating point characterized by the highest frequency, namely Turbo Boost frequency. Turbo Boost is an Intel technology that enables processors to increase their frequency beyond the nominal value. In each moment, the maximum turbo frequency at which the processor can be clocked is limited by its power consumption, temperature and the number active cores. The P-state can be changed in SW for each core of the CPU independently since the Haswell family of processors.

8.2.2.1 Linux power management driver

The choice of which P-state to select in each moment is a task of the operating system. P-states are managed by a power governor implemented as a Linux kernel

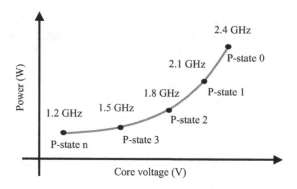

Figure 8.10   DVFS levels and Intel P-states

driver. Recent Intel architectures on Linux system are managed by a kernel module called *intel_pstate* by default.

This driver implements a proportional–integrated–derivative (PID) feedback controller. Every 10 ms the PID controller computes an error value as the difference between a desired set-point and the measured CPU load in that period. The PID controller compensates this error by adapting the P-state value accordingly. Only two governors are implemented inside the *intel_pstate* driver: *powersave* (default) and performance. *Performance* always maintains the CPU at maximum frequency, while *powersave* can choose a different level depending on the machine workload. A notable limitation of today *intel_pstate* implementation is that all the cores under the same O.S. instance (node) are selected by the driver to run at the same P-state. For this reason when the *intel_pstate* is selected, heterogeneous clock frequencies between cores of the same O.S. domain can only happen as effect of lower HW power controller.

Differently, the standard power management driver of Linux *acpi-cpufreq*, namely *acpi-cpufreq*, includes the capability of changing the core's clock frequency independently as well as implementing a wider set of governors. The available governors are as follows:

1.   *powersave*: This governor runs the CPU always at the minimum frequency.
2.   *performance*: This governor runs the CPU always at the maximum frequency.
3.   *userspace*: This governor runs the CPU at user specified frequencies.
4.   *ondemand*: This governor scales the frequency dynamically according to current load [33].
5.   *conservative*: This governor is similar to *ondemand* but scales the frequency more gradually.

In opposition, ACPI C-states represent low-power operating points targeting the power reduction when the system is underutilized or idle. The Linux kernel takes advantage of these states with two main components/strategies: the idle task and the cpuidle subsystem. The idle task is a special task of the Linux kernel which is executed all the time that in a specific core there are no runnable processes available. By default, this task releases the core in which is running and enters in wait-for-interrupt mode. The entrance in more depth low power states is then demanded either to HW logic which may enter in deeper power states opportunistically, or to the cpuidle subsystem which defines time thresholds after which activating deeper low power states.

Table 8.1 shows which low power states for cores and package correspond to a given C-state for an Intel Processor. As for the P-states, C-states are numbered from 0 to n. Higher C-state means higher power saving but also longer transitions. C-states are defined independently for cores and uncore (package) region. As the table shows uncore C-states are bounded by the core C-states. The uncore cannot be in a deeper C-state that the core.

To quantify the power associated to each C and P state we took as target one node of the *Galileo* cluster running at CINECA [34], which is a Tier-1 HPC system based on an IBM NeXtScale technology. Each node of GALILEO is equipped with 2 Intel Haswell E5-2630 v3 CPUs, with 8 cores with 2.4 GHz nominal clock speed and 85 W thermal design power (TDP, [35]).

On the node we executed a constant power load under different configurations (number of cores executing the constant workload, turbo enabled/disabled; different frequencies) while limiting C-states.[1] We maintained each configuration for 10 min, and we measured the power consumed by each CPU. We replicated the same test with Intel turbo enabled and disabled, and by keeping the system idle but while limiting the C-states. From the collected data, we then extracted the power values for the core and uncore parts under the different ACPI states.

Tables 8.2 and 8.3 report these results. Table 8.2 reports the power consumed in the different P-states (C0=active) (Turbo, Max, Min Frequency), while Table 8.3 reports the power consumed in the different C-states. From Table 8.2, we can notice first that at full performance, the uncore power weights almost as three cores of an eight cores platform. Thus it is one-fourth of the total power of the socket. Moreover, the power of the uncore in saturated at *C0 – Max Freq* and does not increases in *C0 – Turbo*, while the power of the core increases in *C0 – Turbo*. Indeed, the clock speed of

Table 8.1   C-states

		Core C-states				
		C0	**C1**	**C3**	**C6**	
Package	C0	+++++	+++++	+++++	+++++	Active state
C-states	C1E	——	+++++	+++++	+++++	Lower P-state
	C2	——	——	+++++	+++++	Only L3 snoop
	C3	——	——	+++++	+++++	Flush L3 – off
	C6	——	——	——	+++++	Low voltage
		Active state	Clock gated	Flush L1,L2 off	Power gated	

"+++++" cells represent a valid configuration for Core and Package C-states, "——" are invalid ones.

[1] C-states in Intel architectures can be limited through dedicated machine specific registers.

Table 8.2   *Power model – active*

	C0 – Turbo	C0 – Max Freq	C0 – Min Freq
Puncore (W)	17.13	17.13	12.76
Pcore (W)	6.38	5.47	3.16

Table 8.3   *Power model – idle*

	C1	C3	C6
Puncore (W)	12.76	11.90	11.84
Pcore (W)	1.32	0.38	0.00

the uncore component differently from the cores does not increase with the turbo frequency. However, reducing the frequency (Min freq) reduces both the uncore and the core power. From the table, we can also notice that core power decreases proportionally with the frequency.

Focusing now on the C-states, the idle power (Table 8.3) in *C1* is the 42 per cent of the *C0 – Min Freq* for the core. *C3* further reduces the core idle power to 12 per cent of the *C0 – Min Freq*, but only marginally for the uncore. *C6* instead zeroes the core power but reduces the uncore power only of the 1 per cent. In deepest idle power state, the uncore components still cost as two cores in full activities. We can conclude this analysis remarking the importance of considering in power management solutions both the core and uncore parts, as well as the C and P states.

8.2.3   Hardware power controller

As previously discussed, HPC systems require fine grain power control as the power consumption of a given device can cause thermal issues as well as energy provisioning issues. For this reason, processors targeting this market embed control units for the power dissipation and performance in the chip, as well as power monitoring capabilities. One common feature of the HW controller aims at maximizing the overall performance while constraining the power consumption. Intel architectures implement this through an HW power controller called Running Average Power Limit (RAPL). Its scheme is depicted in Figure 8.11. RAPL is a control system, which receives as input a power limit and a time window. As a consequence, RAPL continuously tunes the P-states to ensure that the limit is respected in average in the specified time window. RAPL can override the intel-pstate specified P-states by scaling down and up the cores' frequencies when the power constraint is not respected. RAPL can be dynamically configured and inspected through a set of machine specific registers. From this interface, it is possible to configure the RAPL power budget and time window. Inspect the maximum and minimal values for both power budget and time window. These values are represented as multiple of a reference unit contained in a

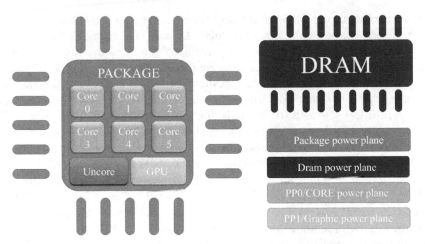

Figure 8.11   Intel RAPL design with the identification of power domains

specific architectural register. At the machine start-up, RAPL is configured using TDP as power budget with a 10-ms time window. RAPL also provides 32-bit performance counters for each power domain to monitor the total throttled time and the energy consumption. RAPL allows the independent configuration of four power domains:

1. *Package domain*: This power domain limits the power consumption for the entire package of the CPU, this includes cores and uncore components.
2. *DRAM domain*: This power domain limits the power consumption of the DRAM memory. It is available only for server architectures.
3. *PP0/Core domain*: This power domain limits the power consumption of the cores of the CPU only.
4. *PP1/Graphic domain*: This power domain limits the power consumption of the graphic component of the CPU if present.

8.2.4   The power capping problem in MPI applications

While RAPL controller is useful to constraint the total power consumption of the CPUs, it is agnostic to workload properties. As discussed earlier, HPC applications are characterized by parallel workload which is extremely sensitive to unbalance in the computation. This can be brought by several factors, and it can be related to the application domain. For instance, different algorithms in the application can scale differently with the number of cores. For this reason, often HPC codes take advantages of configuration parameters which leave to the users to choose on how to partition the workload. These let the same application to adapt to different datasets and different architectures but may result in an additional complexity and workload imbalance.

To study this concept in a real application, we took as an example a real application that is widely used in supercomputers worldwide. Quantum ESPRESSO (QE) [36] is an integrated suite of computer codes for electronic-structure calculations and nanoscale materials modelling. It is freely available to researchers around the world under the terms of the GNU General Public License. Quantum ESPRESSO runs on a significant portion of high-end supercomputers around the world. The main computational kernels of QE include dense parallel linear algebra (LA) and 3D parallel fast Fourier transform (FFT). In addition, the LA and FFT mathematical kernels are typical in other applications which make the study general for other HPC codes. In our tests, we use a Car–Parrinello (CP) simulation, which prepares an initial configuration of a thermally disordered crystal of chemical elements by randomly displacing the atoms from their ideal crystalline positions.

We executed QE-CP in the target node with 16 MPI tasks. For each MPI task, we extracted for each 10 s the ratio between the average time spent in the application code and the time spent in the MPI runtime. This is reported in Figure 8.12 with different lines for each MPI process. From it, we can directly see that one MPI process spends less time in the MPI runtime than the others MPI tasks. Indeed, the MPI task 0 spends more time in the application with respects to the others. This suggests that slowing down the core running the MPI task 0 will slow down the application execution total time more than any of the other cores. This introduces the concept of task criticality. With this term, we describe the MPI task that in a given period of time is more critical to the entire application progress, which makes all the other cores to wait for its computation completion.

Globally the interplay between critical tasks and power management decisions can be seen in Figure 8.13 which depicts the results of a set of tests where the QE-CP problem is solved on two nodes (nodes0, node1) of the target supercomputer with 32 MPI tasks. We executed the same problem 35 times. Each time we changed a power management setting. We run the test with all the cores at ACPI P0 (#33 – all 2,400 MHz) (nominal frequency 2,400 MHz+turbo), all the cores at ACPI PN (#34 – all

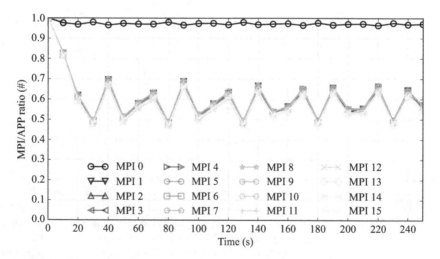

Figure 8.12   Ratio of the time spent in application phases and MPI phases for each core and every 10 s

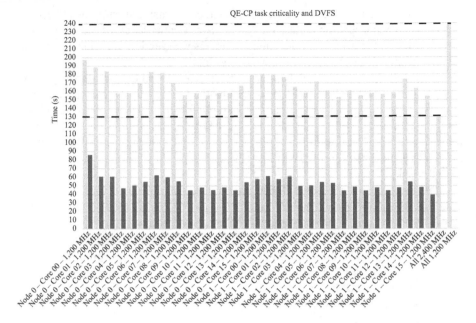

Figure 8.13   Unbalance jobs

1,200 MHz) (minimum frequency 1,200 MHz), all the cores at ACPI P0 but one at ACPI PN (#1–32 – Node X – core Y – 1,200 MHz); all the cores at ACPI P0 and profiling enabled (#35). We profile the time spent in the MPI runtime and in active computation by each process using v-tune.

The figure reports the results of these testes. Light Green bars refer to the total execution time of the application, while the darker grey bars refer to the time spent by each MPI task on the barrier measured in test. Tests #33 and #34 represent the upper and the lower bound for the application execution time. From the figure, we can notice that reducing the frequency for different cores/MPI task results in different total execution times. The cores that slow-down the application the most have a larger computation-to-communication ratio. The core 0, which is also from the previous plot has the largest amount of communication, leads to the larger penalty in the total execution when its frequency is reduced. As a matter of fact when cores frequency needs to be reduced to preserve a safe power budget, not all of them have the same impact to the final application performance, and thus, it is important to detect the critical task.

The task criticality level can be calculated from the time spent by the task in the application and in waiting the global synchronization points. It is not sufficient to consider only the total time spent by each MPI task in the application during the last interval to compute a criticality level. We need to consider each global synchronization point, and for each of them, compute the waiting time of each task. With waiting time we express the time that a given MPI task waits the latest MPI task to reach the synchronization point.

We introduce a mathematical model to extract the task criticality level between two global synchronization points. We define the criticality level for each task in this interval time as the average of the criticality levels weighted by the time which lasts between each pair of global synchronization points.

Figure 8.14 shows a general application phase enclosed by two global synchronization points where all the MPI tasks are involved. Every time a MPI task reaches a global synchronization point, it must wait all other tasks reaching the same point to continue its execution. For each task, we identify three major time events, on which we base our model: the exit time of the last MPI call T_l; the start time of the current MPI call T_s; the exit time of the current MPI call T_e. We use [i] as the index to identify the MPI task.

The last task that enters the global synchronization point unlocks all the waiting tasks which can now restart their execution. T_{ls}, in (8.4), is the time at which the last task enters in the synchronization point. For each application section and for each task [i], we define as computation time $T_{comp[i]}$ in (8.5) as the time spent in the application code and MPI time the time spent in the MPI library. The latter is composed by two factors: (i) $T_{slack[i]}$ in (8.6), which represents the time that a task spends in the MPI library waiting the last task reaching the synchronization point, (ii) $T_{comm[i]}$ in (8.7), which identifies the time spent to exchange data.

$$T_{ls} = MAX(T_{s[i]}) \tag{8.4}$$

$$T_{comp[i]} = T_{s[i]} - T_{l[i]} \tag{8.5}$$

$$T_{slack[i]} = T_{ls} - T_{s[i]} \tag{8.6}$$

$$T_{comm[i]} = T_{e[i]} - T_{ls} \tag{8.7}$$

$$T_{avg} = AVG(T_{s[i]}) \tag{8.8}$$

$$F_{OPT[i]} = F_{NOM} \cdot \frac{T_{avg} - T_{l[i]}}{T_{comp[i]}} = F_{NOM} \cdot \frac{T_{avg} - T_{l[i]}}{T_{s[i]} - T_{l[1]}} \tag{8.9}$$

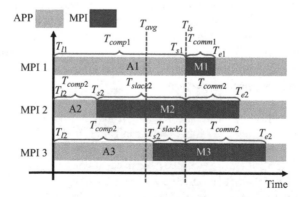

Figure 8.14   General HPC application section with our naming convention for the mathematical model to calculate the criticality for each MPI task

T_{avg} in (8.8) is the average of all the $T_{comp[i]}$. Assuming a linear dependency of the $T_{comp[i]}$ and the frequency at which the task is executed as well as a linear dependency of the power with the core's frequency, the T_{avg} represents the minimum execution time for the given application phase under the same power consumption. Assuming to reduce the clock speed of the cores running tasks which have $T_{comp[i]}$ larger than T_{avg} and assuming to increase the clock speed of tasks which have $T_{comp[i]}$ shorter than T_{avg} preserving the same average frequency between the cores. T_{avg} is the minimum execution time which correspond to the case of no communication slack $T_{slack[i]}$, for each i.

The optimal frequency at which executing each core $F_{OPT[i]}$ can be computed as in as the nominal frequency F_{NOM} multiplied by the ratio between the T_{avg} and the $T_{comp[i]}$ (8.9). This approach can be used at runtime to minimize the communication slack under a power budget, leading overall to an increase execution time.

This model can be used to drive application-aware power-capping strategies in multi-core systems for high-performance computing servers.

References

[1] Dreslinski RG, Wieckowski M, Blaauw D, *et al.* Near-Threshold Computing: Reclaiming Moore's Law Through Energy Efficient Integrated Circuits. Proceedings of the IEEE. 2010;98(2):253–266.

[2] Markovic D, Wang CC, Alarcon LP, *et al.* Ultralow-Power Design in Near-Threshold Region. Proceedings of the IEEE. 2010;98(2):237–252.

[3] Rossi D, Pullini A, Loi I, *et al.* Energy-Efficient Near-Threshold Parallel Computing: The PULPv2 Cluster. IEEE Micro. 2017;37(5):20–31.

[4] Tschanz JW, Kao JT, Narendra SG, *et al.* Adaptive Body Bias for Reducing Impacts of Die-to-Die and Within-Die Parameter Variations on Microprocessor Frequency and Leakage. IEEE Journal of Solid-State Circuits. 2002;37(11):1396–1402.

[5] Sundaresan K, Allen PE, Ayazi F. Process and Temperature Compensation in a 7-MHz CMOS Clock Oscillator. IEEE Journal of Solid-State Circuits. 2006;41(2):433–442.

[6] Gammie G, Wang A, Chau M, *et al.* A 45 nm 3.5G Baseband-and-Multimedia Application Processor using Adaptive Body-Bias and Ultra-Low-Power Techniques. In: 2008 IEEE International Solid-State Circuits Conference – Digest of Technical Papers; 2008. p. 258–611.

[7] Kumar SV, Kim CH, Sapatnekar SS. Body Bias Voltage Computations for Process and Temperature Compensation. IEEE Transactions on Very Large Scale Integration (VLSI) Systems. 2008;16(3):249–262.

[8] Oh C, Kim HO, Seomun J, *et al.* Thermal-Aware Body Bias Modulation for High Performance Mobile Core. In: 2012 International SoC Design Conference (ISOCC); 2012. p. 147–150.

[9] Alioto M. Ultra-Low Power VLSI Circuit Design Demystified and Explained: A Tutorial. IEEE Transactions on Circuits and Systems I: Regular Papers. 2012;59(1):3–29.

[10]   Lee W, Wang Y, Cui T, *et al.* Dynamic Thermal Management for FinFET-Based Circuits Exploiting the Temperature Effect Inversion Phenomenon. In: 2014 IEEE/ACM International Symposium on Low Power Electronics and Design (ISLPED); 2014. p. 105–110.

[11]   Ono G, Miyazaki M, Tanaka H, *et al.* Temperature Referenced Supply Voltage and Forward-Body-Bias Control (TSFC) Architecture for Minimum Power Consumption [Ubiquitous Computing Processors]. In: Proceedings of the 30th European Solid-State Circuits Conference; 2004. p. 391–394.

[12]   Jacquet D, Hasbani F, Flatresse P, *et al.* A 3 GHz Dual Core Processor ARM Cortex TM -A9 in 28 nm UTBB FD-SOI CMOS With Ultra-Wide Voltage Range and Energy Efficiency Optimization. IEEE Journal of Solid-State Circuits. 2014;49(4):812–826.

[13]   Yeap G. Smart Mobile SoCs Driving the Semiconductor Industry: Technology Trend, Challenges and Opportunities. In: 2013 IEEE International Electron Devices Meeting; 2013. p. 1.3.1–1.3.8.

[14]   Garca-Snchez FJ, Ortiz-Conde A, Muci J, *et al.* A Unified Look at the Use of Successive Differentiation and Integration in MOSFET Model Parameter Extraction. Microelectronics Reliability. 2015;55(2):293–307. Available from: http://www.sciencedirect.com/science/article/pii/S0026271414004843.

[15]   Borghesi A, Bartolini A, Lombardi M, *et al.* Predictive Modeling for Job Power Consumption in HPC Systems. In: International Conference on High Performance Computing. Springer; 2016. p. 181–199.

[16]   Sîrbu A, Babaoglu O. Predicting System-Level Power for a Hybrid Supercomputer. In: High Performance Computing & Simulation (HPCS), 2016 International Conference on. IEEE; 2016. p. 826–833.

[17]   Borghesi A, Conficoni C, Lombardi M, *et al.* MS3: A Mediterranean-Stile Job Scheduler for Supercomputers-Do Less When it's Too Hot! In: High Performance Computing & Simulation (HPCS), 2015 International Conference on. IEEE; 2015. p. 88–95.

[18]   Marathe A, Bailey PE, Lowenthal DK, *et al.* A Run-Time System for Power-constrained HPC Applications. In: International Conference on High Performance Computing. Springer; 2015. p. 394–408.

[19]   Eastep J, Sylvester S, Cantalupo C, *et al.* Global Extensible Open Power Manager: A Vehicle for HPC Community Collaboration Toward Co-Designed Energy Management Solutions. In: Supercomputing PMBS. 2016.

[20]   Sarood O, Langer A, Gupta A, *et al.* Maximizing Throughput of Overprovisioned HPC Data Centers Under a Strict Power Budget. In: Proceedings of the International Conference for High Performance Computing, Networking, Storage and Analysis. IEEE Press; 2014. p. 807–818.

[21]   Gholkar N, Mueller F, Rountree B. Power Tuning HPC Jobs on Power-Constrained Systems. In: Proceedings of the 2016 International Conference on Parallel Architectures and Compilation. ACM; 2016. p. 179–191.

[22]   Zhang H, Hoffman H. A Quantitative Evaluation of the RAPL Power Control System. In: Feedback Computing. 2015.

[23]   Conti F, Rossi D, Pullini A, *et al.* Energy-Efficient Vision on the PULP Platform for Ultra-Low Power Parallel Computing. In: 2014 IEEE Workshop on Signal Processing Systems (SiPS); 2014. p. 1–6.

[24]   Loi I, Capotondi A, Rossi D, *et al.* The Quest for Energy-Efficient I$ Design in Ultra-Low-Power Clustered Many-Cores. IEEE Transactions on Multi-Scale Computing Systems. 2017;4(2):99–112.

[25]   Rahimi A, Loi I, Kakoee MR, *et al.* A Fully-Synthesizable Single-Cycle Interconnection Network for Shared-L1 Processor Clusters. In: 2011 Design, Automation Test in Europe; 2011. p. 1–6.

[26]   Rossi D, Loi I, Haugou G, *et al.* Ultra-Low-Latency Lightweight DMA for Tightly Coupled Multi-Core Clusters. In: Proceedings of the 11th ACM Conference on Computing Frontiers. CF'14. New York, NY, USA: ACM; 2014. p. 15:1–15:10. Available from: http://doi.acm.org/10.1145/2597917.2597922.

[27]   TOP500.Org. Top 500 Supercomputer Sites; 2017. Available from: http://www.top500.org.

[28]   Fu H, Liao J, Yang J, *et al.* The Sunway TaihuLight Supercomputer: System and Applications. Science China Information Sciences. 2016;59(7): 072001.

[29]   Dongarra J. Visit to the national university for defense technology Changsha. China, University of Tennessee. 2013;199.

[30]   Bergman K, Borkar S, Campbell D, *et al.* Exascale computing study: Technology challenges in achieving exascale systems. Defense Advanced Research Projects Agency Information Processing Techniques Office (DARPA IPTO), Tech Rep. 2008;15.

[31]   Moskovsky AA, Druzhinin EA, Shmelev AB, *et al.* Server Level Liquid Cooling: Do Higher System Temperatures Improve Energy Efficiency? Supercomputing Frontiers and Innovations. 2016;3(1):67–74.

[32]   Hogbin EJ. ACPI: Advanced Configuration and Power Interface. In: CreateSpace Independent Publishing Platform; 2015.

[33]   Pallipadi V, Starikovskiy A. The Ondemand Governor. In: Proceedings of the Linux Symposium. 2006;2(00216):215–230.

[34]   Conficoni C, Bartolini A, Tilli A, *et al.* Integrated Energy-Aware Management of Supercomputer Hybrid Cooling Systems. IEEE Transactions on Industrial Informatics. 2016;12(4):1299–1311.

[35]   Hammarlund P, Kumar R, Osborne RB, *et al.* Haswell: The Fourth-Generation Intel Core Processor. IEEE Micro. 2014;34(2):6–20.

[36]   Giannozzi P, Baroni S, Bonini N, *et al.* QUANTUM ESPRESSO: A Modular and Open-Source Software Project for Quantum Simulations of Materials. Journal of Physics: Condensed Matter. 2009;21(39):395502.

Chapter 9

Runtime thermal management of many-core systems

Anup Das[1] and Akash Kumar[2]

Many-core systems are widely deployed for embedded and high-performance computing. With matured technological advances in the deep submicron technology nodes, it is now possible to integrate 100s to 1,000s of cores per system-on-chip die. However, growing core count results in thermal hot spots and large temperature gradients, which significantly impact system reliability, performance, cost and leakage power. A primary design optimization objective for many-core systems is, therefore, to efficiently manage thermal overheads of applications while satisfying their performance requirements. This improves system reliability leading to higher mean-time-to-failure.

This chapter presents approaches to runtime thermal management for embedded systems looking from two perspectives—management in a conventional many-core system and that designed in evolving three-dimensional (3D) integrated circuit (IC) technology. Specifically, this chapter first introduces the design of a runtime manager for a many-core system, which uses workload statistics from the processing cores to efficiently allocate resources in order to alleviate thermal emergencies. The impact of workload uncertainty is characterized using machine-learning techniques. Next, this chapter presents a fast thermal-aware approach for mapping throughput-constrained streaming applications on 3D many-core systems. In this approach, to avoid slow thermal simulations for every candidate mapping, a thermal model of the 3D IC is used to derive an on-chip power distribution (PD) that minimizes the temperature before the actual mapping is done. This distribution is then used in a resource allocation algorithm to derive a mapping that meets the throughput constraint while approaching the target PD and minimizing energy consumption. This way, in contrast to most existing approaches, a mapping can be derived in the order of minutes.

9.1 Thermal management of many-core embedded systems

Multimedia applications, such as video encoding and decoding, are characterized by different execution phases, which are defined as a group of consecutive frames.

[1]Department of Electrical and Computer Engineering, Drexel University, USA
[2]Institute of Computer Engineering, Department of Computer Science, Technische Universität Dresden, Germany

The average workload of the frames comprising a phase (inter) varies significantly across the different phases; however, the workload variation within each phase (intra) is relatively low. Proactive power and thermal management involves predicting these dynamic workloads a priori to determine the most appropriate frequency for every phase such that performance constraint is satisfied while minimizing the power consumption, which in turn leads to a reduction of average temperature [1–6]. Studies have been conducted recently to use machine learning to determine the minimum frequency through continuous feedback from the hardware performance monitoring unit (PMU) [7–15]. These approaches suffer from the following limitations.

First, some of the practical aspects of many-core systems are ignored in the existing works. Specifically, the CPU cycle count for a frame, obtained by reading the PMU registers at runtime, is assumed to be a true indicator of the frame workload. However, as we show in this chapter, the PMU register readings contain a certain amount of uncertainty, influenced by factors such as cache contention, dynamic random access memory (DRAM) access, that can have a significant impact on thermal management. This uncertainty is difficult to estimate at runtime due to the unpredictability associated with these factors, especially for many-core systems with a realistic assumption of concurrently executing routine applications. Thus, although workload estimation based on CPU cycle count leads to efficient thermal management using dynamic voltage/frequency scaling (DVFS), a significant improvement is possible by estimating the uncertainty as show in this chapter. Second, the existing approaches do not consider voltage and frequency switching overhead, which is significant in modern many-core systems. Last, the classical workload prediction-based power/thermal minimization techniques work in an ad hoc manner by predicting the workload and deciding the frequency based on this predicted workload. On the other hand, workload history-based statistical classification approaches determine the probability that a sudden spike (positive or negative) in the workload is due to a change in the phase of the workload that needs to be processed at a different frequency. Thus, instead of acting instantaneously, the classifier evaluates the probability distribution of the different classes based on the workload change, and the most probable frequency is selected such that the scaling leads to thermal improvement for future workloads. However, these classifiers require characterization using training data, i.e., a supervised learning approach. Modern many-core operating systems, such as Linux and Android, also support dynamic frequency scaling during application execution. The default and the most popular *ondemand* power governor [16] uses the current workload to determine the voltage-frequency value to process the future workload (a reactive approach). As we show in this chapter, thermal improvement using the *ondemand* power governor can be outperformed using a naive predictive heuristic.

9.1.1 Uncertainty in workload estimation

Conventionally, the minimum frequency for an application is determined based on the CPU cycle count (henceforth, referred to as workload) read from the PMU registers. The underlying assumption is that the CPU cycle count corresponds to frame processing only. In modern many-core systems, there are a number of applications that continue to operate in the background. Some of these applications are user controlled such as web page rendering, email checking and virus scanning. There are also system-related applications that are routinely executed on the processing cores. Some of these applications are beyond the knowledge of the users and cannot be forcefully exited. As a result, the PMU register readings are not always a true indicator of the actual frame workload. This can be seen in a recent work by Das *et al.* [17].

To estimate the impact of workload uncertainty on the frequency value, let $\tilde{w}$ and w denote the observed and the actual frame workloads, respectively, with $\tilde{w} = w + e$, where e is the workload uncertainty. The observed and the required workload frequencies are related according to

$$\frac{f_{required}}{f_{observed}} = \frac{\tilde{w} - e}{\tilde{w}} \leq 1 \tag{9.1}$$

Clearly, estimating the uncertainty in the observed workload leads to further scope for energy improvement. Thus, the problem we are addressing is as follows. Given the workload obtained from the PMU registers at runtime, how to estimate the workload uncertainty (e), being agnostic of its probability distribution, such that the voltage-frequency value corresponding to the actual workload w can be applied on the system. This is the objective of the next section.

9.1.2 Learning-based uncertainty characterization

Statistical classification is the process of identifying a class (from a set of discrete classes) for a new observation, based on a training set of observations, whose class is known a priori [18]. In this work, we focus on a discriminative classifier—logistic regression applied to a multinomial variable [19]. This type of classifier predicts the probability distribution over a set of classes from a sample input to learn a direct mapping from the input sample to the output class. The logistic regression based classification is composed of two steps—modeling to estimate the probability distribution of the different classes for a given input, and parameter fitting to estimate the parameters of the logistic regression model. These are described next.

9.1.2.1 Multinomial logistic regression model

Assumptions

$\mathscr{A}_1$: There are K discrete frequencies supported by the hardware. The incoming workload is assigned to one of these values, depending on which frequency results in the least energy consumption while satisfying the performance requirement. This is same as classifying into one of K classes.

$\mathscr{A}_2$: The class of the next video frame is predicted based on the workloads of the N previous frames. These are identified by $X = (x_1 \; x_2 \; \cdots \; x_N) \in \mathbb{R}^{1 \times N}$, where x_i is the workload of the ith previous frame.

$\mathscr{A}_3$: The workload class is denoted by the variable $y \in [1, 2, \ldots, K]$ and the logistic regression model is represented by the hypothesis h_θ, with parameter $\theta \in \mathbb{R}^{(K-1) \times N}$.

It can be shown that for a given input *feature* set X, the logistic regression model outputs $h_\theta(X)$ is given by

$$
h_\theta(X) = \begin{bmatrix} p_1 \\ p_2 \\ \vdots \\ p_{K-1} \end{bmatrix} = \left(\frac{e^{\left(\theta^{(1)^T} \cdot x\right)}}{\sum_{j=1}^{K} e^{\left(\theta^{(j)^T} \cdot x\right)}} \cdots \frac{e^{\left(\theta^{(K-1)^T} \cdot x\right)}}{\sum_{j=1}^{K} e^{\left(\theta^{(j)^T} \cdot x\right)}} \right) \tag{9.2}
$$

The output class y is given by

$$
y = \underset{l}{\mathrm{argmax}} \{ p_l \; \forall \, l \in [1, 2, \dots, K] \} \tag{9.3}
$$

9.1.2.2   Maximum likelihood estimation

We consider a training set of M samples generated independently and identically. For each of these samples, the input *feature* X and the output class y are known a priori and the input–output pairs are identified as $(X^{(i)}, y^{(i)}) \; \forall i \in [1, 2, \dots, M]$. The maximum likelihood estimation is a technique to estimate the parameters (θ in our case) of a model by maximizing the likelihood of the joint probability distribution of the different observations. This is given by

$$
\ell(\theta) = \ln\left(\mathscr{L}(\theta)\right) = \sum_{i=1}^{M} \sum_{l=1}^{K} \mathscr{I}(y^{(i)} = l) \cdot \ln \left(\frac{e^{\left(\theta^{(l)^T} \cdot X^{(i)}\right)}}{\sum_{j=1}^{K} e^{\left(\theta^{(j)^T} \cdot X^{(i)}\right)}} \right) \tag{9.4}
$$

9.1.2.3   Uncertainty interpretation

First we define two new terms—observed class and actual class. The observed class (denoted by $\tilde{y}$) is the class perceived at the output of the logistic regression model corresponding to input X and includes the uncertainty. Let the variable y denote the actual class as before. Using the basic principles of probability theory, the probability of the observed class is

$$
P(\tilde{y} = i \mid X) = \sum_{r=1}^{K} P(\tilde{y} = i \mid y = r) \cdot P(y = r \mid X) = \sum_{r=1}^{K} \gamma_{i,r} \cdot p_r \tag{9.5}
$$

where $\gamma_{i,r}$ is the probability that the actual class r is flipped to the observed class i. Using this probability and the definition of the likelihood function, the log likelihood function is[1]

$$
\ell(\theta, \gamma) = \sum_{i=1}^{M} \sum_{l=1}^{K} \mathscr{I}(\tilde{y}^{(i)} = l) \ln \left(\sum_{r=1}^{K} \gamma_{l,r} \cdot p_r \right) \tag{9.6}
$$

Finally, the output of the hypothesis is modified as

$$
h_\theta(X) = \left[\left(\sum_{r=1}^{K} \gamma_{1,r} \cdot p_r \right) \cdots \left(\sum_{r=1}^{K} \gamma_{K-1,r} \cdot p_r \right) \right]^T \tag{9.7}
$$

---

[1]The derivation steps are omitted for space limitation.

9.1.3 Overall design flow

Figure 9.1 shows the adaptive thermal minimization methodology for a many-core system. An overview is provided on the interaction of the different blocks of this methodology.

Application: Typically, multimedia applications are characterized with a performance constraint specified as *frames per second*, reciprocal of which gives the timing constraint for processing a frame. The application source code is annotated to include this timing requirement.

Operating system: The operating system is responsible for coordinating the application execution on the hardware. After processing every frame of an application, the operating system stalls execution and triggers the classifier, which predicts the class for the next frame. This class is translated to a frequency value for the CPU cores. The operating system applies this frequency on the CPU cores using the cpufreq utility.

Hardware: The hardware consists of processing cores with a PMU to record performance statistics. Of the different performance statistics available, we focus on CPU cycle count. After processing every frame, the PMU readings are collected using the perfmon utility. Subsequently, the readings are reset to allow recording for the next frame. Finally, before the start of the next frame, the frequency value set by the operating system is first converted to a corresponding CPU clock divider setting and is then written into appropriate CPU registers. The frequency is scaled to execute the next frame.

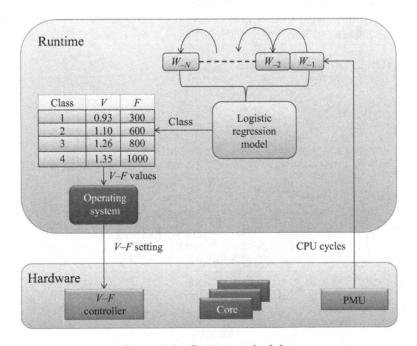

Figure 9.1   Design methodology

9.1.4 Early evaluation of the approach

The proposed run-time approach is evaluated on Texas Instrument's PandaBoard featuring ARM A9 cores and Intel quad-core system running Linux.

9.1.4.1 Impact of workload uncertainty: H.264 case study

To signify the impact of the workload uncertainty on the thermal behavior, an experiment is conducted using two 30 s video sequences—"ducks" and "sta_launch" [20]. The H.264 decoder application is restricted to execute on only one core using the `cpu-affinity` feature of the operating system. Further, we let all other routine applications execute freely on any cores. The videos are decoded ten times each and the CPU cycles consumed for each run is recorded. The CPU cycles count are normalized with respect to the maximum obtained for the ten readings. These results are shown in Figure 9.2 corresponding to the label *single core*. The minimum, maximum, the median value and the 80% distribution (as box) of the CPU cycles count for the runs are shown as box plots for both the videos. Furthermore, the percentage difference between minimum and the maximum CPU cycles count of the ten runs (referred to as the variation) is reported on top of each box. Next, the same experiment is repeated by allowing the H.264 decoder application to run on two and four cores of the system. These results are also plotted in Figure 9.2.

As seen from the figure, when the H.264 decoder runs on single core, there is a variation of 3.5% and 6.7% in CPU cycles count for the two videos, respectively. It is to be noted that, even though the H.264 application executes on one core, some of the threads from other routine applications are also scheduled on this core by the operating system. Thus, there is an amount of uncertainty in the observed CPU cycle count. Hence, the voltage-frequency value obtained based on this observed CPU cycle count

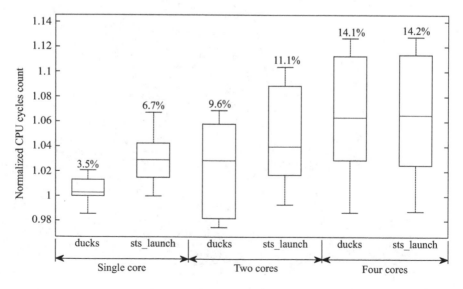

Figure 9.2   Variation in CPU cycles count due to workload uncertainty

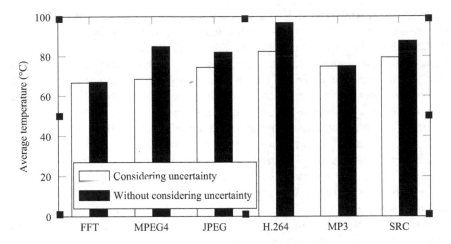

Figure 9.3 Thermal improvement using our proposed approach

is not optimal, implying that there is a performance slack that enables the operating system to schedule more threads on this core. When the H.264 application is allowed to execute on two cores, the percentage variation for the two videos increases to 9.6% and 11.1%, respectively. This is because, as the application uses more cores, there are more cache conflicts due to other background threads, increasing the workload uncertainty. Finally, when all the four cores are used by the H.264 decoder, the variation increases to 14%. It can thus be concluded that, workload uncertainty can result in as high as 14% variation in the observed CPU cycles count, clearly motivating our approach to model the uncertainty and mitigate it using the runtime manager.

9.1.4.2 Thermal improvement considering workload uncertainty

Figure 9.3 reports the thermal improvement obtained by considering workload uncertainty. Results are shown for six applications. For some applications such as FFT and MP3, the average temperature are similar, while for others, there are significant difference in the temperature by considering workload uncertainty. Thermal reduction considering uncertainty is between 1 °C and 20 °C. These results clearly show the potential of thermal improvement considering workload uncertainty and allocation of frequency based on this uncertainty estimation.

This concludes our proposal for thermal management for conventional 2D many-core systems. In the remainder of the chapter, we present heuristics for thermal management of systems in 3D IC technology.

9.2 Thermal management of 3D many-core systems

3D ICs provide interesting possibilities to implement promising many-core systems in advanced technology nodes. In a 3D IC, multiple layers of logic (or memory) are stacked vertically; these layers are interconnected using vertical interconnect accesses, commonly referred as through silicon vias (TSVs). Figure 9.4 illustrates a 3D IC with two layers and two TSVs. Stacking multiple layers of processing and/or memory elements into a 3D IC structure can significantly reduce the die size and average interconnect wire length. This in turn can reduce communication delays and interconnect energy, while increasing the interconnect flexibility [21,22]. However, stacking active layers increases the power density, which can cause serious thermal problems, affecting both the performance and reliability of a system.

In this section, we introduce an integrated thermal-aware approach for mapping streaming applications on a 3D many-core system. A streaming application, such as video decoding, typically has a throughput requirement, which possibly cannot be guaranteed in combination with unexpected thermal emergencies in a 3D IC. The goal of the proposed approach is to map and schedule multiple applications, satisfying their throughput requirements, communication and storage constraints, while minimizing the peak-temperature and temperature gradients across the chip. Since simulating the thermal process with a high temporal resolution is a time-consuming activity, the approach described in this work is split into two main steps. In the first step, thermal characteristics of the 3D IC are extracted from a simple but flexible model of the physical chip. Then, the extracted profile is passed to the actual resource allocation algorithm, which does not require iterative temperature simulations. This causes runtime of the total flow to be in the order of minutes, in contrast to most existing thermal-aware mapping approaches.

The many-core system is assumed to contain a 3D mesh of (homogeneous or heterogeneous) processing tiles. Since networks-on-chip (NoCs) are widely regarded

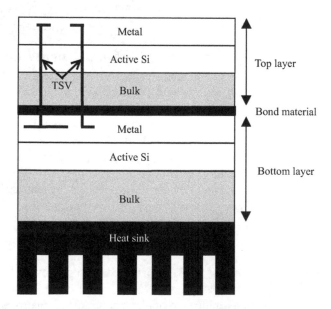

Figure 9.4   Two stacked layers connected by TSVs [23]

as the most promising communication architecture for many-core 3D architectures [22], a 3D NoC is assumed to provide the communication between these tiles. The streaming applications are modeled as synchronous dataflow graphs (SDFGs) [24]. Since there are multiple trade-offs involved, for example, between optimizing for energy consumption or peak temperature in the 3D IC [25], a set of parameters has been used to steer the optimization process by providing varying weights to the optimization criteria. This results in a flexible thermal-aware mapping flow. The thermal process resulting from the mapping is simulated using the *HotSpot* thermal simulator [26], which is extended to consider thermal effect of TSVs.

To evaluate performance, the proposed flow is used to map and schedule a set of synthetic benchmark applications as well as realistic multimedia streaming applications on a NoC-based 3D many-core systems. The performance evaluations show that compared to the load-balancing (LB) strategy, the peak temperature and energy consumption are reduced by 7% and 47%, respectively, while meeting all timing and storage constraints.

9.2.1 Recent advances on 3D thermal management

Thermal-aware mapping and scheduling on 3D many-core systems is a well-studied topic. Multiple approaches have been proposed, which can be split into dynamic (runtime) and static (design-time) thermal-aware mapping techniques. Dynamic approaches measure or estimate instantaneous thermal distribution in the chip and initiate actions in order to minimize hotspots and thermal gradients (spatial, temporal or both). In [27], several dynamic mechanisms such as temperature-triggered DVFS, clock gating and hot-task migration are reviewed, and a runtime task assignment algorithm is proposed that takes the thermal history of cores into account. A thermal-aware OS-level scheduler for 3D many-core system is proposed in [28]. These methods share the goal of minimizing the peak temperature and thermal gradients without sacrificing performance too much. Constraints such as deadlines or memory requirements are, however, not taken into account, as well as the effect of inter-task communication. Recent studies have shown that NoCs can dissipate a substantial part of the power budget, and the dissipation depends on the traffic [29]. Therefore, ignoring the interconnect thermal contribution can lead to underestimation of temperature, leading to system failures before they are anticipated. For 2D ICs, a thermal-aware task assignment and scheduling technique for real-time applications is proposed in [30], which is based on mixed integer linear programming. However, the techniques for 2D ICs cannot simply be applied to 3D ICs due to significantly different thermal behavior of 3D ICs. Skadron *et al.* [26] developed the HotSpot thermal simulator to evaluate the steady state and dynamic temperature distribution in ICs.

Static mapping approaches aim at finding a thermal-aware mapping at design time, by using a model of the physical chip, or by using general knowledge about the thermal behavior of 3D ICs. In [29], both temperature and communication load are considered, and a genetic algorithm is used to generate static mappings. Cheng *et al.* [25] show that a trade-off exists when minimizing energy usage as well as peak temperature and use a combination of heuristics, simulated annealing and a greedy algorithm to find optimal static mappings. However, application constraints such as throughput requirements are not taken into account. The authors of [31] propose an approach to find optimal mappings in a thermal sense for applications with deadlines. First, a power balancing algorithm is used to find an initial mapping. The initial mapping is then iteratively improved by simulating the temperature distribution and migrating tasks. Communication between tasks as well as memory constraints are not taken into account. Thiele *et al.* [32] argue that being able to guarantee the maximum peak temperature in a many-core system and analyzing real-time applications early in the design process (i.e., analyzing at design-time) is important, since it removes the need for unpredictable runtime mechanisms. Toward this, the authors use formal methods in a tool to find optimal static mappings of SDFG-modeled applications on heterogeneous 2D many-core systems while guaranteeing performance and peak temperature. The communication overhead is taken into account, but the power dissipation of the NoC has not been considered. Since vertical communication in a 3D NoC can be considerably faster and energy efficient than horizontal communication [25], a straightforward extension of their methods to 3D many-core systems will not provide optimal mapping solutions. In contrast to above strategies, our approach performs thermal-aware mapping of throughput-constraint applications on 3D many-core systems while taking memory as well as communication constraints into account. Further, our approach considers the effect of TSVs on the temperature distribution and power dissipation and minimizes the energy consumption.

Next to thermal-aware mapping, thermal-aware floorplanning can also help to mitigate thermal problems. Thermal-aware floorplanning techniques have been developed for 2D ICs [33] as well as for 3D stacked ICs [34,35]. There are also some research studies on efficient floorplanning to mitigate thermal problems.

9.2.2 Preliminaries

3D ICs have gained significant research attention in recent years. However, experimental platforms for 3D ICs are not yet available to research community. In the absence of real platforms, abstract models of 3D ICs are used for analysis and design space exploration. This section covers the application model, multiprocessor platform model and the 3D IC model.

9.2.2.1 Application model

To model streaming applications with a throughput constraint, synchronous dataflow graphs (SDFGs) [24] are used. In a SDFG, an application is modeled as a set of tasks, called *actors*, that communicate chunks of data with a predefined size, called *tokens*. An example SDFG that models an H.263 decoder is depicted in Figure 9.5. The nodes correspond to the actors and the edges represent data dependencies, referred to as connections, between the actors. The H.263 decoder is modeled with four actors *vld*, *iq*, *idct* and *mc* and four edges d_1, d_2, d_3 and d_4. An actor has fixed input and output rates on every connection. The input rate corresponds to the number of tokens that the actor consumes from the incoming connection when fired once. Similarly, the output rate defines the number of tokens that are produced on the outbound connection

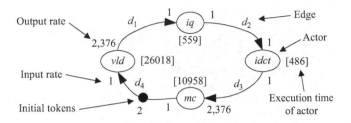

Figure 9.5   SDFG of a H.263 decoder

during one firing of the actor. An initial number of tokens might be available on the connection. An actor fires as soon as sufficient tokens are available at all its incoming connections, and enough buffer space is available to store the produced tokens. The size of a token may be different for every connection.

The input and output rates of the actors in an SDFG determine the relative frequency in which the actors can fire, which can be represented by a unique repetition vector. In the application model, the worst case execution times (in time units) and memory requirements (in bits) of all actors on all possible processing elements are specified. For example, an actor performing encoding may have worst case execution times of 10,000 time units on an ARM7 or 2,000 time units on dedicated encoder hardware. Specifying requirements for all possible mappings enables the use of heterogeneous architectures. For all connections, the size of the tokens (in bits) is specified, as well as the memory required when mapping the connection to memory, or the bandwidth required when mapping the connection to interconnect. If actors are fired as soon as they are ready to fire (self-timed execution), the execution pattern of a consistent, strongly connected SDFG is always periodic after an initial start-up period [36]. The time between two recurring states in the execution of an SDFG defines the throughput of the application. An application may have a throughput requirement, fixing the maximum time between two recurring states. The throughput of a SDFG may be calculated by simulating the execution until a recurrent state is found [36].

9.2.2.2   Multiprocessor platform model

In this work, a regular 3D mesh of tiles connected by a NoC is considered, as depicted in Figure 9.6. Every tile contains at least a network interface (NI), connecting the tile to the interconnect network. Furthermore, a tile may contain a processing element (*P*) of some type *PT* (processor type), for example, an ARM core and a memory. Different types of processors are possible, allowing the modeling of heterogeneous architectures. Such an architecture can be modeled by an architecture graph consisting of tiles and connections as defined below.

Definition 9.1 (Tile). *A tile t is a 9-tuple (pt, w, m, c, i, o, pa, pi, pm) with $pt \in PT$ the processor type, $w \in \mathbb{N}_0$ the TDMA timewheel size, $m \in \mathbb{N}_0$ the available memory (in bits), $c \in \mathbb{N}_0$ the maximum number of supported connections, $i, o \in \mathbb{N}_0$ the maximum i/o bandwidth (in bits), $pa, pi \in \mathbb{R}$ the active and idle power (in W) and $pm \in \mathbb{N}_0^3$ the position of the tile in the mesh.*

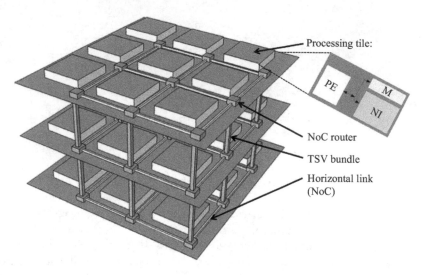

Figure 9.6 Example 3D mesh of tiles [23]

Tiles are connected by an NoC. In the architecture graph, the NoC is abstracted to a set of point-to-point connections between tiles.

Definition 9.2 (Connection). *A connection c is a 5-tuple (u, v, l, h_h, h_v) with $u \in T$ the source tile, $v \in T$ the destination tile, $l \in \mathbb{N}_0$ the latency (in time units), and $h_h, h_v \in \mathbb{N}_0$, respectively, the number of horizontal and vertical hops between u and v.*

The set of tiles T and the set of connections C together define the architecture graph. A tile is assumed to consume pa W of power when active, and pi W when idle.

Vertical links between tiles are generally implemented using TSVs. As reported in [25], TSVs can often provide faster and more energy efficient communication compared to horizontal links, mainly because of their short length. The differences in delay and energy per bit depend on the technology and the NoC topology. For example, the NoC switches can simply be extended with two extra ports for up/down communication, or the vertical links can be implemented as a shared bus. This work does not treat all these options in detail, but the latency (l) and horizontal and vertical hop count (h_h, h_v) properties of a connection do provide some room for modeling different 3D NoC implementations in the architecture graph. For example, the latency of a connection can be specified such that it is dependent on the direction of the communication.

9.2.2.3 3D IC model

To be able to simulate the on-chip temperature for a given execution trace, a model describing the thermal characteristics of the 3D IC is required. The model is also used to extract information about the thermal behavior of the chip, which can be used by the mapping algorithm. The model used in this work is based on the 3D grid model available in the HotSpot thermal simulator [26]. The model contains all relevant physical properties of the IC and the heat sink, as well as a set of active and

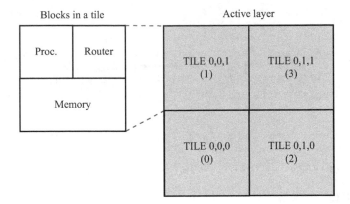

Figure 9.7   Active layer floorplan illustration

inactive layer specifications. Active layers correspond to layers that actually dissipate power, while inactive layers are used to model the bonds (glue, thermal interface material (TIM)) between the active layers. Figure 9.7 illustrates the floorplan of an active layer. For every layer, the thickness, material properties and a floorplan are specified. Floorplans of the active layers consist of tiles, all of which contain one or more blocks (e.g., processor, memory, router), specified by the floorplan of the specific tile type. Execution of the application models is tracked at the tile level. The power, that is dissipated in a tile, is assumed to be distributed over the blocks of that tile. For example, 80% may be dissipated in the processor block, 10% in the router block and 10% in the memory. Blocks can correspond to function blocks of the processor, but the processor can also be modeled as one block. This enables the use of both fine (detailed) and course-grained models.

TSVs are generally made of copper, which has significantly different thermal properties than silicon. To take the thermal effect of TSVs into account, the size, position and material properties of the TSVs are also specified in the 3D IC model. To be able to simulate the thermal impact of the TSVs, the HotSpot simulator is extended to take TSVs into account. This is done by changing the thermal properties (conductance and heat capacity) of grid cells in the internal HotSpot model that contain TSV material, based on the ratio of the grid cell volume that is occupied by TSV material.

9.2.3   Thermal-aware mapping

This section introduces the proposed mapping flow. The general structure of the flow is depicted in Figure 9.8. The flow consists of two main steps: a *"thermal profiling"* step and the actual mapping algorithm. In the *"thermal profiling"* step, the physical model of the 3D IC is used to derive a PD among the tiles that minimizes the peak temperature and spatial temperature gradients. For example, in the power distribution that minimizes the peak temperature, tiles that are on the layer closest to the heat sink are likely to dissipate more power than tiles far away from the heat sink. This is due to

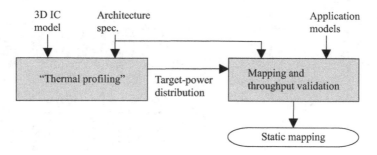

Figure 9.8   Overview of the thermal-aware mapping flow [23]

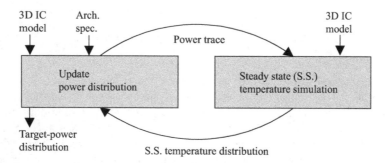

Figure 9.9   Structure of the "thermal profiling" algorithm [23]

the fact that the layers close to heat sink are able to get rid of the heat faster; therefore, they are able to handle more load/power without overheating. Thus, they get a higher target power ratio. The power density, the floorplan and the absolute position of a tile in the horizontal plane will also influence its target power ratio. The resulting "*target PD*" assigns a power ratio to every tile and is passed to the mapping algorithm. The mapping algorithm tries to find a mapping that approaches this distribution while minimizing the energy and meeting all timing and storage constraints.

The two step structure is based on the observation that (high resolution) thermal simulations have a long running time, making it impossible to simulate the temperature for every candidate mapping within a limited running time. A lot of existing approaches avoid iterative thermal simulations by just applying heuristics to optimize for temperature. However, these heuristics are often not very accurate in a quantitative way, requiring the designer to tune the heuristics by hand in order to match the actual chip properties and find good mappings. In our approach, this tuning is done automatically in the first step of the flow. In the mapping step, no thermal simulations are required, which drastically reduces the runtime compared to methods that simulate the temperature for a lot of candidate mappings. The remainder of this section discusses the steps of the flow in more detail.

9.2.3.1   Thermal profiling

The structure of the *thermal profiling* step is depicted in Figure 9.9. The update algorithm adjusts the power ratios R_t of the tiles based on the steady state temperature distribution resulting from the previous PD. The power ratio R_t of a tile corresponds to the ratio between the total chip power P and the power dissipated in tile t. The power dissipated in tile t, $P_t = R_t \times P$, is distributed among the blocks in that tile based on an intra-tile PD, which may be constant in simple models. This way, a power trace is generated for every block in the chip. To limit the number of thermal simulations, a heuristic is used for updating the PD. The power ratios of tiles with a peak temperature above the average are decreased, while the power ratios of tiles with a peak temperature below the average are increased in the update step. This way, temperature differences among tiles are decreased, resulting in a lower peak temperature and smaller temperature gradients. The adaptation rate of the power ratios is defined by constant α. The update algorithm is summarized in Algorithm 1.

Algorithm 1: Thermal profiling algorithm

Input: 3D IC model, stopping criterion $\delta \in \mathbb{R}$, max. # of iterations $I_{\max} \in \mathbb{N}$, adaptation constant $\alpha \in \mathbb{R}$, total chip power $P \in \mathbb{R}$.
Output: Target power ratios R_t, $t \in [0, N_{tiles} - 1]$.
Initialize power ratios $\forall t \in [0, N_{tiles} - 1] : R_t = 1/N_{tiles}$;
$T_{avg} = 0$, $T_{prev.\max} = \infty$, $T_{\max} = 1,000$;
$i = 0$;
while $(T_{prev.\max} - T_{\max}) \geq \delta$ **and** $i \leq I_{\max}$ **do**
   Generate power traces for all blocks based on P, R_t and the intra-tile power distribution;
   Simulate steady state temperature dist.;
   $T_{avg} \leftarrow$ average chip temperature;
   $\forall t \in [0, N_{tiles} - 1] : T_{peak,t} \leftarrow$ max. temp. in tile t;
   $T_{\max} \leftarrow \max(T_{peak})$;
   if $(T_{prev.\max} - T_{\max}) < \delta$ **then**
     | **break**
   end
   if $T_{prev.\max} < T_{\max}$ **then**
     | $\alpha = \alpha/2$;
     | Restart algorithm;
   end
   for *all tiles* $t \in [0, N_{tiles} - 1]$ **do**
     | $d = (T_{peak,t} - T_{avg})/T_{avg}$;
     | $R_t = \max(0, R_t * (1.0 - (\alpha * d)))$;
   end
   Renormalise power ratios R_t;
   $T_{prev.\max} = T_{\max}$;
   $i++$;
end
return power ratios R_t

In agreement with observations described in related literature [27,28], some general observations can be made regarding the PD after convergence of the algorithm:

1. Tiles on layers farther away from the heat sink get hotter than tiles closer to the heat sink with the same power dissipation. Hence, algorithm will in general assign smaller power ratios to tiles further away from the heat sink.
2. The thermal conductance in the vertical direction is generally high compared to the horizontal direction, because the layers are thin (typically 20–100 μm). As a result, blocks with a high power density that are stacked on top of each other generate high temperatures. Because of this, the combined power dissipation of horizontally aligned blocks in different layers will be limited.
3. TSVs increase the thermal conductance between layers. As a result, temperature differences between layers get decreased. The magnitude of this effect depends on the TSV material, size and density.
4. Blocks that are near the edges/corners of the die tend to get hotter than blocks farther away from the edges, since there is less material for the heat to spread to.

The above observations are used to develop heuristics in some thermal-aware mapping approaches, for example, by assigning higher costs to mappings that use tiles that are further away from the heat sink or by balancing computational load over "stacks" of vertically adjacent tiles [28]. However, these heuristics are generally not tuned to the specific IC that is considered, possibly resulting in suboptimal solutions. In our approach, the temperature-related observations are modeled implicitly in the *target PD*, which is derived directly from a model of the 3D IC. This results in assumptions that are more representative for the specific 3D IC that is considered.

9.2.3.2 Runtime

The steady state temperature is iteratively simulated by the modified HotSpot thermal simulator, which determines the runtime of the algorithm. The simulation time depends on the spatial resolution and the number of layers. For an IC with three active layers and a grid resolution of 32×32, one simulation takes 117s on a 2.3 GHz Intel i7 CPU (single threaded). With a well-chosen value for the adaptation constant α, the algorithm converges to a static PD in 6–10 iterations, resulting in a total runtime of up to 1,170 s. Note that the running time is independent from the number of tiles on a layer, since the thermal simulator internally uses a grid with a fixed resolution.

An overview of the mapping flow is depicted in Figure 9.10. The application graphs, the architecture specification and the target PD serve as inputs to the flow. For the memory dimensioning, constraint refinement and communication scheduling steps, existing implementations available in the SDFG[3] tool set [37] are applied. The other steps are described subsequently.

9.2.3.3 Application merging

In practical situations, use cases consisting of multiple applications running simultaneously are common. To support the mapping of multiple applications, in the first step of the flow, all application graphs are merged into one application graph using the rate control principle. In this approach, a *rateControl* actor is inserted to control the

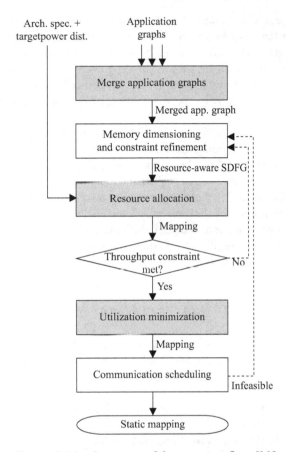

Figure 9.10   Overview of the mapping flow [23]

relative execution rates of the different applications that are merged into one graph. Connections between the *rateControl* actor and one actor in every application are added, with input and output rates that force the execution rates of the applications to synchronize in a desired ratio. For example, application *A* might have a throughput requirement twice as high as that of application *B*. In that case, the rate controller will force the execution of application *B* to stall until *A* has executed twice, and vice versa. The throughput constraint of the merged application is the minimum of the original individual throughput constraints, and the individual applications can have throughput constraints that are a multiple of the overall throughput constraint.

9.2.3.4   Resource allocation

In the resource allocation step, every actor of the merged application is bound to a tile in the architecture graph. As a result of binding the actors, the connections between the actors will be bound to either memory (in case both connected actors are bound to the same tile) or to a set of NoC links (in case the actors are bound to different tiles). Since the tile binding defines the computational load distribution and thus the

PD within the many-core system, it is the most important step in the thermal-aware mapping flow. A feasible tile binding binds all actors to a tile and all connections to a memory or interconnect link such that no storage, connection count or bandwidth limitation is violated. After a feasible tile binding is found, a static-order schedule is generated for each tile, defining the order of execution of the actors mapped on that tile. Note that the resulting resource allocation is not guaranteed to be able to meet the throughput constraint.

An extension of the heuristic-based resource allocation strategy introduced in [38] is used to find a feasible mapping that results in a PD close to the target PD. The binding algorithm is summarized in Algorithm 2. First, all actors are sorted on criticality in descending order. The criticality is calculated as a measure for the worst case. Next to approaching the target PD, there might also be other optimization targets, such as computational LB among the tiles, memory usage balancing or communication balancing/minimization. Function $cost(t, a)$, defined in (9.8), assigns a cost to binding actor a to tile t, which is used in the binding algorithm. Constants $c_1, \ldots, c_6$ weight the costs of the different optimization criteria:

$$cost(t, a) = c_1 \times P(t, a) + c_2 \times M(t, a) + c_3 \times C(t, a) + c_4 \times L(t, a)$$
$$+ c_5 \times PDT(t, a) + c_6 \times PDS(t, a) \qquad (9.8)$$

- $P(t, a) \in [0, 1]$ is the normalized processor load when binding actor a to tile t;
- $M(t, a) \in [0, 1]$ is the ratio of allocated memory when a is bound to t;
- $C(t, a) \in [0, 1]$ is the ratio of allocated connections on tile t when a is bound to t;
- $L(t, a) \in [0, 1]$ is the normalized average latency of all connections from/to a when a is bound to t;
- $PRT(t, a) \in [0, 1]$ is the normalized cost for the power ratio of tile t when a is bound to t

$$PRT(t, a) = c \cdot \left(\frac{r_t}{R_t} \right)$$

where r_t is the estimated power ratio of tile t when binding a to t and R_t is the target power ratio of tile t. c is a normalizing constant to scale the cost to $[0, 1]$ for all tiles; and

- $PRS(t, a) \in [0, 1]$ is the normalized cost for the power ratio of the tile stack s containing tile t when mapping a to t.

$$PRS(t, a) = c \cdot \left(\frac{r_s}{R_s} \right)$$

where r_s is the estimated power ratio of stack s when binding a to t and R_s is the target power ratio of stack s. c is a normalizing constant to scale the cost to $[0, 1]$ for all stacks. A tile stack is a set containing all tiles that are in the same horizontal position at different layers. The target power ratio of a stack is defined by the sum of the ratios of the tiles it contains.

Algorithm 2: Tile binding algorithm

Input: tiles T, actors A, connections C.
Output: Feasible resource allocation.
// Find an initial binding
Sort all actors $a \in A$ on criticality, **descending**;
for *all sorted actors $a \in A$* **do**
  Sort all tiles $t \in T$ on $cost(t, a)$, ascending (see (9.8));
  for *all sorted tiles $t \in T$* **do**
    if *binding actor a to tile t is feasible* **then**
      Bind actor a to tile t;
      Bind connections to/from a;
      break;
    end
  end
  if *actor a not bound* **then**
    return "Unable to find feasible binding";
  end
end

// Try to improve the binding
Sort all actors $a \in A$ on criticality, **ascending**;
for *all sorted actors $a \in A$* **do**
  Unbind actor a;
  Unbind connections to/from a;
  Sort all tiles $t \in T$ on $cost(t, a)$, ascending (see (9.8));
  for *all sorted tiles $t \in T$* **do**
    if *binding actor a to tile t is feasible* **then**
      Bind actor a to tile t;
      Bind all related connections;
      break;
    end
  end
end

Note that there are two terms related to the PD: $PRT(t, a)$ and $PRS(t, a)$. PRT represents the deviation from the original target power ratios of the individual tiles. Since we observed that there is a large thermal correlation between vertically adjacent tiles, it makes sense to also take the target power ratios of stacks of tiles into account, which is captured by the PRS term. If the PD among stacks would not be included, deviations from the target PD in the vertical direction would result in the same cost as deviations in the horizontal direction, leading to worse results in a thermal sense.

The tile power ratios resulting from a candidate binding can be calculated since the active and idle powers of all tiles are known, along with the execution time of every actor on every possible tile.

9.2.3.5   Throughput computation

When a feasible resource allocation has been found, the maximum throughput of the mapped application has to be calculated in order to validate the throughput constraint. This is done by modeling the mapped application as a binding-aware SDFG and performing a state-space exploration by simulating the self-timed execution of the graph [36]. The throughput is calculated as soon as a recurrent state is found during the execution.

9.2.3.6   Utilization minimization

It is possible that the maximum throughput of the mapped application is higher than the throughput constraint. From an energy and temperature perspective, it makes sense to slow down the execution as long as the throughput constraint is satisfied. This is done in the utilization minimization step. It is assumed that every processor contains a TDMA system, in which a time slice can be reserved during which the processor is idle. To slow down execution, an idle timeslice is inserted in the TDMA schedule of every active processor. The appropriate sizes of the idle time slices are determined by performing a binary search and recalculating the throughput after every step. The search is terminated once the actual throughput is not more than 10% above the throughput constraint.

9.2.4   Experimental results

The performance of the proposed approach is tested by applying it to a set of synthetic benchmark applications as well as a set of real-life multimedia applications.

9.2.4.1   Benchmark applications

To evaluate the performance of the thermal-aware mapping approach, a set consisting of four application graphs is generated. Every application consists of eight actors with random (Gaussian distributed) execution times and storage requirements. To evaluate the effect of the weights in the tile binding cost function, multiple mappings are generated for each set of applications, based on different cost function weights. To eliminate the effects of the random generator, three sets of applications are generated. Next to the synthetic benchmark application set, a real-life application set consisting of four independent H.263 encoders (five actors each) with a throughput constraint of 60 frames per second is constructed.

9.2.4.2   Target 3D many-core system

The sets of benchmark applications are mapped on a tile-based 3D many-core system consisting of three layers of 2×2 identical tiles. Each tile consists of a processor, memory and NI, all modeled as a single block as depicted in Figure 9.7. The active power of each tile is set to 1.5 W, the idle power is set to 10% of the active power. For the placement of blocks in a tile, two different tile floorplans are used, such that the processor blocks do not overlap. Tile floorplan 1 is used on the bottom and top layer, while floorplan 2 is used on the middle layer to avoid stacking all processor blocks exactly on top of each other, since the power density is the highest in that block. The heat sink is connected (via a heat spreader) to the bottom layer. The other active (power dissipating) layers are thinned down to 50 μm. Between two active layers, a 10 μm thin layer containing TIM is modeled. The most important physical properties of the 3D IC model are listed in Table 9.1. In the center of the NI block of every tile, a bundle of 8 × 9 TSVs is placed. For the interconnect, a hybrid NoC-Bus design is assumed, consisting of a regular NoC in the horizontal plane and a multi-drop shared bus for vertical communication [25]. In this setup, every tile is assumed to have its own NoC switch, and every stack of tiles contains a shared bus. In the architecture graph, communication links are modeled as point-to-point connections. The latencies of all possible tile-to-tile connections are calculated based on the delay of the shortest path between the tiles. A hop in the horizontal plane is modeled as a delay of 2 time units, a hop in the vertical direction as 1 time unit.

9.2.4.3 Temperature simulation

For every mapping, an execution trace of 0.5 s is generated. The execution patterns are periodic with a period much shorter than 0.5 s, making longer simulations obsolete. From the execution trace and the architecture specification, power traces are derived for every block. The power traces are used in the modified HotSpot 5.02 thermal simulator to simulate the temperature with a grid resolution of 32 × 32 and a temporal resolution of 10 μs. First, a steady state simulation is performed to find a representative initial temperature distribution. Next, the transient temperature simulation is performed. Table 9.1 lists the most important HotSpot parameters.

Table 9.1   Physical properties and HotSpot parameters

Parameter	Value
Tile size [mm]	2×2
Silicon thermal conductance [W/(m K)]	150
Silicon specific heat [J/(m^3 K)]	$1.75 \cdot 10^6$
TIM thermal conductance [W/(m K)]	4
TIM specific heat [J/(m^3 K)]	$4 \cdot 10^6$
TSV thermal conductance [W/(m K)]	300
TSV specific heat [J/(m^3 K)]	$3.5 \cdot 10^6$
TSV diameter [μm]	10
TSV pitch [μm]	20
Bottom layer thickness [μm]	200
Non-bottom layer thickness [μm]	50
TIM layer thickness [μm]	10
Convection resistance to ambient [K/W]	3.0
Heat sink side/thickness [mm]	$14 \times 14 \times 10$
Heatsink conductance [W/(m K)]	400
Heat sink specific heat [J/(m^3 K)]	$3.55 \cdot 10^6$
Ambient temperature [K]	300

9.2.4.4 Interconnect energy computation

Since the interconnect energy consumption can be a significant part of the total energy consumption [39], it is also interesting to investigate the communication intensity and interconnect energy consumption resulting from different mappings. Note that the computational energy consumption will be close to identical for all mappings, since a homogeneous architecture is considered and every application is slowed down to match the throughput constraint.

The interconnect consumes energy to facilitate communication between the titles and consumed energy is also referred to as communication energy. In between two tiles, communication has to take place when actors (tasks) mapped on them need to communicate with each other. The communication energy depends on the data volume and the relative locations of the communicating task (actor) pair. For each communicating task pair mapped to tile i and tile j and connected by edge e, the communication energy is estimated by the product of the number of transferred bits ($nrTokens[e] \times tokenSize[e]$) and the energy required to transfer one bit between tiles i and j ($E_{bit}(i,j)$), as defined in (9.9). The value of $E_{bit}(i,j)$ is calculated based on the energy required for horizontal link traversals, vertical link traversals and the energy consumed in routers between tiles i and j, as shown in (9.10). Vertical interconnects are implemented as shared buses, so no intermediate routers are involved when traversing multiple layers. Therefore, hops in the vertical direction will increase the total number of routings by just 1, independent of the number of vertical hops. The total communication energy is estimated by summing over all communicating task pairs (edges).

$$E_{comm}(e) = \left(nrTokens[e] \times tokenSize[e]\right) \times E_{bit}(i,j) \tag{9.9}$$

$$E_{bit}(i,j) = \left(E_{bit}^{horizontal} \times hops_{horizontal}(i,j)\right) + \left(E_{bit}^{vertical} \times hops_{vertical}(i,j)\right) \\ + \left(E_{bit}^{router} \times numOfRouters(i,j)\right) \tag{9.10}$$

In our 3D IC model, the horizontal link energy per bit, $E_{bit}^{horizontal}$, is taken as 0.127 PJ, which is estimated from [25]. The vertical link energy per bit, $E_{bit}^{vertical}$, is determined by the used TSVs and is therefore referred to as E_{bit}^{TSV}. E_{bit}^{TSV} is estimated to be 9.56×10^{-3} PJ [40]. For a horizontal link length of 2 mm, the per bit router energy E_{bit}^{router} is approximately 70% of $E_{bit}^{horizontal}$ [41]. E_{bit}^{TSV} is only 7.5% of $E_{bit}^{horizontal}$, providing substantial space for communication energy optimization by exploiting the low link energy in the vertical direction. However, using more vertical links may result in a higher peak temperature due to increased power density because of mapping communicating tasks on stacked tiles.

9.2.4.5 Thermal profiling results

The target PD obtained by running the thermal profiling algorithm on the considered 3D IC is given in Table 9.2. It is observed that the power is almost completely balanced in the horizontal plane, indicating that the power dissipated in a stack of tiles is

Table 9.2   Target power distribution for the considered 3D IC

	Tile position in the horizontal plane			
	(0,0)	**(0,1)**	**(1,0)**	**(1,1)**
Top layer (%)	2.8	2.8	2.7	2.4
Middle layer (%)	7.5	7.6	7.4	6.9
Bottom layer (%)	15.0	15.3	15.0	14.7

minimized. In the static PD that minimizes the peak temperature on this specific 3D IC, about 60% of the total chip power is dissipated in the bottom layer. About 29% is dissipated in the middle layer, and the remaining 11% is dissipated in the top layer. Further experiments show that this distribution mainly depends on the PD within the tiles, the layer thickness and the interlayer bonds. Although the thermal properties of the heat sink have a large impact on the average chip temperature, the optimal PD is almost independent from it.

9.2.4.6   Benchmark application results

To evaluate the performance of the resource allocation strategy, five different combinations of tile-binding cost-function weights are evaluated, corresponding to the following different optimization objectives:

1. **Load balancing (LB):**
   $(c_1, c_2, c_3, c_4, c_5, c_6) = (1, 0, 0, 0, 0, 0)$. Balance the computational load as much as possible.
2. **Communication latency minimization (CLM):**
   $(c_1, c_2, c_3, c_4, c_5, c_6) = (0, 0, 0, 1, 0, 0)$. Minimize the interconnect latency.
3. **Load balancing + latency minimization (LB+CLM):**
   $(c_1, c_2, c_3, c_4, c_5, c_6) = (1, 0, 0, 1, 0, 0)$. Combine computational LB and latency minimization with equal weights.
4. **Power balancing by stack (PBS):**
   $(c_1, c_2, c_3, c_4, c_5, c_6) = (0, 0, 0, 0, 0, 1)$. The power ratios of all tile stacks are set equal, causing power balancing in the horizontal plane.
5. **Optimize power distribution (PD):**
   $(c_1, c_2, c_3, c_4, c_5, c_6) = (0, 0, 0, 0, 1, 1)$. Optimize for a PD close to the target distribution.
6. **Optimize power distribution + latency minimization (PD+CLM):**
   $(c_1, c_2, c_3, c_4, c_5, c_6) = (0, 0, 0, 1, 1, 1)$. Combine PD optimization with latency minimization.

Temperature results

Figure 9.11 shows the lowest and highest observed temperatures resulting from mapping the benchmark application set using the different optimization objectives. All mappings result in a throughput within 10% above the constraint. The results are averaged over the three application sets to remove effects of the random generator.

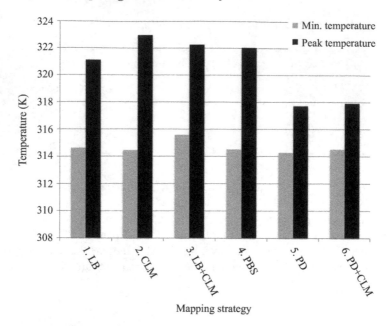

*Figure 9.11   Minimum and peak temperature resulting from mappings with
different optimization objectives [23]*

It is clear that trying to minimize the communication latency alone (scenario 2) results in the highest peak temperature. This is due to the fact that vertically adjacent tiles have smaller communication delays, which results in communicating actors being mapped on vertically adjacent tiles. This can cause a power imbalance in the horizontal plane, explaining the increased temperature. Including the target power ratio terms leads to a peak temperature decrease of 5.3K compared to the latency minimization case and 3.4K compared to the computational LB case. It is clear that only balancing the load in the horizontal plane (scenario 4) does not result in the minimum temperature.

Interconnect usage and energy consumption results
Figure 9.12 depicts the average normalized number of bit hops, as well as the average interconnect power consumption for different optimization criteria. A bit hop is defined as 1 bit of data that is transferred 1 hop through the NoC. The interconnect power is estimated as the average communication energy per second. It can be observed that including the latency cost term results in a significant decrease in interconnect utilization. This can be explained by the observation that the latency cost term assigns high costs to mappings in which communicating actors are mapped on tiles that are far apart in the 3D NoC. In scenario 6, the interconnect utilization is roughly halved compared to scenario 5, with almost no increase in peak temperature (Figure 9.11).

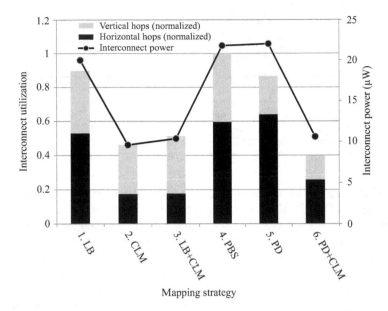

Figure 9.12 Average normalized horizontal/vertical interconnect utilization and interconnect power [23]

The average interconnect power depends on the usage of the horizontal and vertical interconnect links, as can be seen in Figure 9.12. A couple of observations can be made from Figure 9.12. First, the total power consumption is mainly governed by the usage of horizontal links, as they consume much more power than the vertical links. Second, the power consumption for the *CLM* and *LB+CLM* strategies are low due to more usage of vertical links than horizontal links, but they show high peak temperatures (Figure 9.11). This indicates that using more vertical links instead of horizontal links facilitates lower interconnect power consumption at the cost of a higher peak temperature due to more power stacking within the chip. Thus, a trade-off exists between minimizing interconnect energy consumption and peak temperature. Third, the *PD+CLM* strategy shows almost the same power consumption as the *CLM* and *LB+CLM* strategies, along with lower interconnect utilization and peak temperature. This indicates that the *PD+CLM* strategy results in a good balance between peak temperature, interconnect utilization and interconnect energy consumption. The absolute interconnect energy reduction highly depends on the communication intensity of the applications as well as the NoC type and technology.

9.2.4.7 Case-study for real-life applications

To test the applicability of our approach for real-life applications, four independent H.263 encoder applications are mapped on the 3D many-core system using our mapping flow. Two different mapping strategies are applied: *LB+CLM* and *PD+CLM*, as introduced earlier. The *LB+CLM* strategy tries to balance the computational load

Table 9.3   *Average interconnect power consumption,*
minimum and maximum temperature for four
independent H.263 encoder applications

	LB+CLM	PD+CLM
Interconnect power consumption (μW)	166.62	85.10
Minimum temperature (K)	310.75	310.15
Maximum temperature (K)	317.05	314.25

while minimizing the interconnect latency, whereas the *PD+CLM* strategy aims at optimizing the PD while also minimizing interconnect latency.

Table 9.3 shows the average interconnect power consumption, minimum and maximum temperature when the mapping strategies *LB+CLM* and *PD+CLM* are employed. Strategy *PD+CLM* outperforms strategy *LB+CLM* for all the performance figures, i.e., it results in a lower interconnect power consumption, minimum temperature and maximum temperature. Minimizing the communication latency (*CLM*) results in a significant reduction in interconnect utilization and interconnect power consumption (Figure 9.12), making it an important optimization criterion to be considered. The results in Table 9.3 indicate that in addition to minimizing the communication latency, optimizing the *PD* is a better choice than balancing the computational load (*LB*).

9.3   Conclusions and future directions

We proposed a flexible and fast approach for thermal-aware mapping of throughput-constrained streaming applications on 3D many-core systems. As compared to the LB case, the proposed approach reduces the peak temperature by 7% (in °C) and interconnect energy consumption by 47% for a set of benchmark applications on a three-layer IC, while meeting all storage and throughput constraints. We showed that the approach can also be used in combination with other optimization criteria, such as interconnect utilization minimization. The average runtime of the total flow is 20 min, with about 90% being spent in the thermal profiling step. The runtime of the resource allocation and throughput validation step highly depends on the size and complexity of the application graph.

Despite the significant progress on thermal management for 2D and 3D ICs, there are open challenges that need to be addressed in future. One emerging challenge is the dissipation of heat in the absence of atmosphere, e.g., when systems are employed in space. Specifically, it is important to manage the thermal aspects more aggressively in such situations, otherwise a simple task can lead to the system temperature to surpass the safe limit, leading to damaging the system. Recently, significant efforts are been made to improve the thermal dissipation of many-core systems. A thermal management of battery system using novel phase-change materials is proposed in [42].

Two-phase liquid cooling is proposed for 3D systems [43]. Optimal placement of liquid microchannels for heat management of 3D ICs is discussed in [44]. Integrated flow cells are used in [45] for quick heat dissipation. Integrated microfluidic power generation and cooling is described in [46]. For a comprehensive study of these techniques, readers are referred to [47].

Another possible solution is to harvest useful energy from heat, mitigating the impact. In [48,49], energy harvesting from thermoelectrics is discussed for thermal management of many-core systems. Self-powered distributed networks is proposed in [50]. A new design of energy-harvesting systems is proposed in [51]. A scheduling technique for mixed critical tasks is discussed in [52] for heterogeneous many-core systems powered by energy harvesting sources. There is also approach for scheduling sporadic tasks on systems with energy harvesting sources [53]. Readers are referred to [54] for a survey on recent advances in thermal management using energy-harvesting sources.

For a 3D IC, the positive/negative impact of increasing the number of stacked layers on the temperature needs to be addressed in future. Simultaneous multilayer access in a 3D system is discussed in [55]. Placement of the 3D layers is described in [56]. Simulated annealing-based layer placement is proposed for 3D systems in [57]. Readers are referred to [58] for a survey of the challenges in layers optimization of 3D many-core systems.

Finally, the design-space exploration needs to be extended to consider emerging design principles such as approximate computing. An online quality-management system for approximate computing is discussed in [59]. A hardware–software framework for approximate computing is proposed in [60]. Recent works that propose approximate arithmetic blocks such as multiplier and adders may also be considered for low-area and low-power implementations of the DSE algorithms [61,62]. Readers are referred to [63] for a survey of architectural techniques for approximate computing.

References

[1] Jung H, Pedram M. Continuous frequency adjustment technique based on dynamic workload prediction. In: Proceedings of the International Conference on VLSI Design; 2008. p. 249–254.

[2] Das A, Al-Hashimi BM, Merrett GV. Adaptive and hierarchical runtime manager for energy-aware thermal management of embedded systems. ACM Transactions on Embedded Computing Systems (TECS). 2016;15(2):24.

[3] Das A, Shafik RA, Merrett GV, et al. Reinforcement learning-based inter-and intra-application thermal optimization for lifetime improvement of multicore systems. In: Proceeding of the Annual Design Automation Conference (DAC). ACM; 2014. p. 1–6.

[4] Das A, Kumar A, Veeravalli B. Reliability and energy-aware mapping and scheduling of multimedia applications on multiprocessor systems. IEEE Transactions on Parallel and Distributed Systems. 2016;27(3):869–884.

[5]   Ma Y, Chantem T, Dick RP, *et al.* Improving system-level lifetime reliability of multicore soft real-time systems. IEEE Transactions on Very Large Scale Integration (VLSI) Systems. 2017;25(6):1895–1905.

[6]   Yang Z, Serafy C, Lu T, *et al.* Phase-driven learning-based dynamic reliability management for multi-core processors. In: Proceeding of the Annual Design Automation Conference (DAC). ACM; 2017. p. 46.

[7]   Dhiman G, Rosing TS. Dynamic voltage frequency scaling for multi-tasking systems using online learning. In: Proceedings of the ACM/IEEE International Symposium on Low Power Electronics and Design (ISLPED). New York, NY, USA: ACM; 2007. p. 207–212.

[8]   Shen H, Lu J, Qiu Q. Learning based DVFS for simultaneous temperature, performance and energy management. In: Proceedings of the International Symposium on Quality Electronic Design (ISQED); 2012. p. 747–754.

[9]   Shen H, Tan Y, Lu J, *et al.* Achieving autonomous power management using reinforcement learning. ACM Transactions on Design Automation of Electronic Systems (TODAES). 2013;18(2):24:1–24:32.

[10]   Ye R, Xu Q. Learning-based power management for multicore processors via idle period manipulation. IEEE Transactions on Computer-Aided Design of Integrated Circuits and Systems (TCAD). 2014;33(7):1043–1055.

[11]   Dhiman G, Kontorinis V, Tullsen D, *et al.* Dynamic workload characterization for power efficient scheduling on CMP systems. In: Proceedings of the ACM/IEEE International Symposium on Low Power Electronics and Design (ISLPED); 2010. p. 437–442.

[12]   Jung H, Pedram M. Supervised learning based power management for multicore processors. IEEE Transactions on Computer-Aided Design of Integrated Circuits and Systems (TCAD). 2010;29(9):1395–1408.

[13]   Cochran R, Hankendi C, Coskun AK, *et al.* Pack & Cap: Adaptive DVFS and thread packing under power caps. In: Proceedings of the IEEE/ACM International Symposium on Microarchitecture (MICRO). ACM; 2011. p. 175–185.

[14]   Cochran R, Hankendi C, Coskun A, *et al.* Identifying the optimal energy-efficient operating points of parallel workloads. In: Proceedings of the International Conference on Computer Aided Design (ICCAD); 2011. p. 608–615.

[15]   Mercati P, Bartolini A, Paterna F, *et al.* Workload and user experience-aware dynamic reliability management in multicore processors. In: Proceeding of the Annual Design Automation Conference (DAC). ACM; 2013. p. 2:1–2:6.

[16]   Pallipadi V, Starikovskiy A. The ondemand governor. In: Proceedings of the Linux Symposium. vol. 2; 2006. p. 215–230.

[17]   Das A, Kumar A, Veeravalli B, *et al.* Workload uncertainty characterization and adaptive frequency scaling for energy minimization of embedded systems. In: Proceedings of the Conference on Design, Automation and Test in Europe (DATE). IEEE; 2015. p. 43–48.

[18]   Michie D, Spiegelhalter DJ, Taylor CC. Machine Learning, Neural and Statistical Classification. New York, NY: Ellis Horwood; 1994.

[19]   Anderson JA, Richardson SC. Logistic discrimination and bias correction in maximum likelihood estimation. Technometrics. 1979;21(1):71–78.

[20]   Derf. Test Media; 2014. Available from: http://media.xiph.org/video.

[21]   Knickerbocker JU, Patel CS, Andry PS, *et al.* 3-D silicon integration and silicon packaging technology using silicon through-vias. IEEE Journal of Solid-State Circuits. 2006;41(8):1718–1725.

[22]   Feero BS, Pande PP. Networks-on-chip in a three-dimensional environment: A performance evaluation. IEEE Transactions on Computers. 2009;58(1):32–45.

[23]   Cox M, Singh AK, Kumar A, *et al.* Thermal-aware mapping of streaming applications on 3D Multi-Processor Systems. In: IEEE Symposium on Embedded Systems for Real-time Multimedia (ESTIMedia). IEEE; 2013. p. 11–20.

[24]   Lee EA, Messerschmitt DG. Static scheduling of synchronous data flow programs for digital signal processing. IEEE Transactions on Computers. 1987;100(1):24–35.

[25]   Cheng Y, Zhang L, Han Y, *et al.* Thermal-constrained task allocation for interconnect energy reduction in 3-D homogeneous MPSoCs. IEEE Transactions on Very Large Scale Integration (VLSI) Systems. 2013;21(2): 239–249.

[26]   Skadron K, Stan MR, Sankaranarayanan K, *et al.* Temperature-aware microarchitecture: Modeling and implementation. ACM Transactions on Architecture and Code Optimization (TACO). 2004;1(1):94–125.

[27]   Coskun AK, Ayala JL, Atienza D, *et al.* Dynamic thermal management in 3D multicore architectures. In: Design, Automation & Test in Europe Conference & Exhibition, 2009. DATE'09. IEEE; 2009. p. 1410–1415.

[28]   Zhou X, Yang J, Xu Y, *et al.* Thermal-aware task scheduling for 3D multicore processors. IEEE Transactions on Parallel and Distributed Systems. 2010;21(1):60–71.

[29]   Addo-Quaye C. Thermal-aware mapping and placement for 3-D NoC designs. In: SOC Conference, 2005. Proceedings. IEEE International. IEEE; 2005. p. 25–28.

[30]   Chantem T, Hu X, Dick RP. Temperature-aware scheduling and assignment for hard real-time applications on MPSoCs. IEEE Transactions on Very Large Scale Integration (VLSI) Systems. 2011;19(10):1884–1897.

[31]   Sun C, Shang L, Dick RP. Three-dimensional multiprocessor system-on-chip thermal optimization. In: Hardware/Software Codesign and System Synthesis (CODES+ ISSS), 2007 5th IEEE/ACM/IFIP International Conference on. IEEE; 2007. p. 117–122.

[32]   Thiele L, Schor L, Bacivarov I, *et al.* Predictability for timing and temperature in multiprocessor system-on-chip platforms. ACM Transactions on Embedded Computing Systems. 2013;12(1s):48:1–48:25. Available from: http://doi.acm.org/10.1145/2435227.2435244.

[33]   Nookala V, Lilja DJ, Sapatnekar SS. Temperature-aware floorplanning of microarchitecture blocks with IPC-power dependence modeling and transient analysis. In: Proceedings of the 2006 International Symposium on Low Power Electronics and Design. ACM; 2006. p. 298–303.

[34] Zhou P, Ma Y, Li Z, *et al.* 3D-STAF: Scalable temperature and leakage aware floorplanning for three-dimensional integrated circuits. In: Computer-Aided Design, 2007. ICCAD 2007. IEEE/ACM International Conference on. IEEE; 2007. p. 590–597.

[35] Pathak M, Lim SK. Thermal-aware Steiner routing for 3D stacked ICs. In: Computer-Aided Design, 2007. ICCAD 2007. IEEE/ACM International Conference on. IEEE; 2007. p. 205–211.

[36] Ghamarian AH, Geilen M, Stuijk S, *et al.* Throughput analysis of synchronous data flow graphs. In: Application of Concurrency to System Design, 2006. ACSD 2006. Sixth International Conference on. IEEE; 2006. p. 25–36.

[37] Stuijk S, Geilen M, Basten T. SDF^3: SDF for free. In: Application of Concurrency to System Design, 2006. ACSD 2006. Sixth International Conference on. IEEE; 2006. p. 276–278.

[38] Stuijk S, Basten T, Geilen M, *et al.* Multiprocessor resource allocation for throughput-constrained synchronous dataflow graphs. In: Design Automation Conference, 2007. DAC'07. 44th ACM/IEEE. IEEE; 2007. p. 777–782.

[39] Hoskote Y, Vangal S, Singh A, *et al.* A 5-GHz mesh interconnect for a teraflops processor. IEEE Micro. 2007;27(5):51–61.

[40] International Technology Roadmap for Semiconductors; 2010. Available from: http://www.itrs.net/reports.html.

[41] Bhat S. Energy Models for Network-on-Chip Components [MSc. thesis]. Eindhoven University of Technology; 2005.

[42] Wang Q, Rao Z, Huo Y, *et al.* Thermal performance of phase change material/oscillating heat pipe-based battery thermal management system. International Journal of Thermal Sciences. 2016;102:9–16.

[43] Chiou HW, Lee YM. Thermal simulation for two-phase liquid cooling 3D-ICs. Journal of Computer and Communications. 2016;4(15):33.

[44] Dash R, Pangracious V, Risco-Mart JL, *et al.* Thermal management in 3D homogeneous NoC systems using optimized placement of liquid microchannels. In: Embedded Multicore/Many-core Systems-on-Chip (MCSoC), 2017 IEEE 11th International Symposium on. IEEE; 2017. p. 37–44.

[45] Andreev AA, Sridhar A, Sabry MM, *et al.* PowerCool: Simulation of cooling and powering of 3D MPSoCs with integrated flow cell arrays. IEEE Transactions on Computers. 2018;67(1):73–85.

[46] Sabry MM, Sridhar A, Atienza D, *et al.* Integrated microfluidic power generation and cooling for bright silicon MPSoCs. In: Design, Automation and Test in Europe Conference and Exhibition (DATE), 2014. IEEE; 2014. p. 1–6.

[47] Murshed SS, de Castro CN. A critical review of traditional and emerging techniques and fluids for electronics cooling. Renewable and Sustainable Energy Reviews. 2017;78:821–833.

[48] Jayakumar S, Reda S. Making sense of thermoelectrics for processor thermal management and energy harvesting. In: Low Power Electronics and Design (ISLPED), 2015 IEEE/ACM International Symposium on. IEEE; 2015. p. 31–36.

[49] Lee Y, Kim E, Shin KG. Efficient thermoelectric cooling for mobile devices. In: Low Power Electronics and Design (ISLPED, 2017 IEEE/ACM International Symposium on. IEEE; 2017. p. 1–6.

[50] Brunelli D, Passerone R, Rizzon L, *et al.* Self-powered WSN for distributed data center monitoring. Sensors. 2016;16(1):57.

[51] Merrett GV, Al-Hashimi BM. Energy-driven computing: Rethinking the design of energy harvesting systems. In: Proceedings of the Conference on Design, Automation & Test in Europe. European Design and Automation Association; 2017. p. 960–965.

[52] Xiang Y, Pasricha S. Mixed-criticality scheduling on heterogeneous multicore systems powered by energy harvesting. Integration. 2018;61:114–124.

[53] Housseyni W, Mosbahi O, Khalgui M, *et al.* Real-time scheduling of sporadic tasks in energy harvesting distributed reconfigurable embedded systems. In: Computer Systems and Applications (AICCSA), 2016 IEEE/ACS 13th International Conference of. IEEE; 2016. p. 1–8.

[54] Zhang Y. Improving the Efficiency of Energy Harvesting Embedded System. Syracuse University; 2016.

[55] Lee D, Ghose S, Pekhimenko G, *et al.* Simultaneous multi-layer access: Improving 3D-stacked memory bandwidth at low cost. ACM Transactions on Architecture and Code Optimization (TACO). 2016;12(4):63.

[56] Banerjee S, Majumder S, Varma A, *et al.* A placement optimization technique for 3D IC. In: Embedded Computing and System Design (ISED), 2017 7th International Symposium on. IEEE; 2017. p. 1–5.

[57] Zhu HY, Zhang MS, He YF, *et al.* Floorplanning for 3D-IC with through-silicon via co-design using simulated annealing. In: 2018 IEEE International Symposium on Electromagnetic Compatibility and 2018 IEEE Asia-Pacific Symposium on Electromagnetic Compatibility (EMC/APEMC). IEEE; 2018. p. 550–553.

[58] Chan WTJ, Kahng AB, Li J. Revisiting 3DIC benefit with multiple tiers. Integration, the VLSI Journal. 2017;58:226–235.

[59] Khudia DS, Zamirai B, Samadi M, *et al.* Rumba: An online quality management system for approximate computing. In: Computer Architecture (ISCA), 2015 ACM/IEEE 42nd Annual International Symposium on. IEEE; 2015. p. 554–566.

[60] Mishra AK, Barik R, Paul S. iACT: A software-hardware framework for understanding the scope of approximate computing. In: Workshop on Approximate Computing Across the System Stack (WACAS); 2014.

[61] Ullah S, Rehman S, Prabakaran BS, *et al.* Area-optimized low-latency approximate multipliers for FPGA-based hardware accelerators. In: Proceedings of the 55th Annual Design Automation Conference. ACM; 2018. p. 159.

[62] Ullah S, Murthy SS, Kumar A. SMApproxlib: Library of FPGA-based approximate multipliers. In: Proceedings of the 55th Annual Design Automation Conference. ACM; 2018. p. 157.

[63] Mittal S. A survey of techniques for approximate computing. ACM Computing Surveys (CSUR). 2016;48(4):62.

Chapter 10

Adaptive packet processing on CPU–GPU heterogeneous platforms

Arian Maghazeh[1], Petru Eles[1], Zebo Peng[1], Alexandru Andrei[2], Unmesh D. Bordoloi[3], and Usman Dastgeer[4]

General processing on graphics processing units (GPGPUs) has been widely deployed in different categories of computing devices from supercomputers to embedded mobile systems [1]. In the era of big data, where traditional CPUs cannot bear the computation demand any further, GPUs have been the righteous representatives for general-purpose class of computing devices to fill the gap. Thanks to the tremendous computing power of GPUs, algorithms that decades ago would require a large number of CPUs to execute can now run on a mobile platform powered by a GPU.

Inspired by the success stories of mainstream GPGPU applications (like in the fields of artificial intelligence, computer vision, finance, etc.), researchers have sought to deploy GPUs in other less-conventional applications [2]. One such example is in the domain of packet processing, which deals with operations that need to be performed on a packet as it traverses the network. The throughput-oriented nature of packet processing applications and the recent paradigmatic shift towards software-based networking are the two primary factors which have made packet processing an attractive case of study for GPGPU. However, the stringent timing requirements of these applications – something that GPUs are not particularly designed for – have cast doubts on the actual deployment of GPU-based networking devices in future. This chapter discusses some of the academic attempts made in response to this challenge.

In continuation, we first provide a quick overview of GPU architecture and GPGPU. We then discuss some of the related work in packet processing on GPUs. Sections 10.2 and 10.3 explain the throughput–latency trade-off, which is at the heart of the challenge, and propose an adaptive GPU-based packet processing approach that improves the latency of the packets while maintaining the throughput at the required level. In Section 10.4, we choose the packet classification application as a case study to demonstrate the benefit of the proposed technique.

[1]Department of Computer and Information Science, Linköping University, Sweden
[2]Ericsson, Sweden
[3]General Motors, USA
[4]Sectra, Sweden

10.1   Background on GPU computing

In the following sections, we briefly review the architecture of high-end and mobile GPUs from the GPGPU perspective and discuss two important performance factors specific to GPUs.

10.1.1   GPU architecture

Hardware perspective. GPUs are massively parallel processors that were originally designed for rendering graphics. In such applications, a lightweight process is required to run on a large number of pixels. To address this demand, GPUs were designed to have a large number of cores each capable of running simple arithmetic operations. Unlike CPU cores where significant chip space is dedicated to the control unit, a group of GPU cores (e.g. 16 or 32) share the same control unit. Each GPU core in the group executes the same instruction in a lock-step execution fashion, but with a different input (i.e. single instruction multiple data (SIMD)). The cores are further divided into one or more identical streaming multiprocessors (SMs). Each SM also contains several load/store units and special function units for performing operations like floating-point transcendental functions. To keep the power consumption at reasonable level, GPU cores run at lower frequencies compared to their CPU counterparts. Due to the simple control unit and lower core frequency, the processing time of a single unit (e.g. a pixel) on a GPU core is larger than that on a CPU core. However, the GPU delivers much higher throughputs than the CPU thanks to the large number of cores and high amount of parallelism.

GPUs use a hierarchical memory model to accelerate distribution of data to the cores. At the lowest level, each thread[1] can access a limited number of registers at high speed. Registers are *private* memory units that can be accessed only by the individual threads. Each SM also contains a fast on-chip memory which is used partly as *shared* memory (a software-managed scratchpad memory) and partly as the SM's L1 cache. The shared memory is evenly partitioned between the blocks on each SM. Threads within the same block may access the same shared memory partition. At higher level, there are *global*, *local*, *texture* and *constant* memory units each for a different purpose. All of these units reside on an off-chip memory module. As compared to on-chip private and shared memory units, off-chip units are larger but slower. In a high-end GPU, the off-chip memory is dedicated to the GPU (which in turn connects to the system memory via PCI (peripheral component interface) express channel), while in an embedded GPU the memory is shared by the CPU. In addition, all SMs share a single L2 cache.

Software perspective. A *thread* is the smallest software execution unit that represents execution of the kernel. A *kernel* is a small program that runs on the GPU. A group of 32 threads form a *warp*. Threads in a warp execute instructions in the lock-step fashion. A group of warps are organised into a one-, two- or three-dimensional *thread block*. A block is executed on an SM. Blocks execute independently from each

---

[1]In this chapter, we use CUDA (compute unified device architecture) terminology to address GPU related concepts [3].

other and are further organised into a one-, two- or three-dimensional *grid* of thread blocks. The minimum grid size is one block. A kernel is specified by the grid size and block size.

Kernel execution. A GPU is a slave device and therefore the execution of kernels must be initiated by the host (CPU). In conventional high-end GPUs, kernel execution is typically performed in three stages: (1) the CPU prepares and transfers the input data to the GPU memory (via PCI express bus), (2) the CPU launches the kernel and GPU performs the execution and (3) the CPU reads the output back from the GPU memory. In a heterogeneous platform, however, the first and third stages are not required since the memory is shared between the CPU and GPU. Instead, the CPU only transfers the data pointer to the GPU. At runtime, the GPU uses the pointer to access the data. In this method, there is no need to explicitly copy the data between the CPU and GPU memory (aka, zero-copy).

10.1.2 Performance considerations

Occupancy. When the kernel is launched, the GPU driver distributes each kernel block to one of the SMs for execution. A block/warp is considered active (aka, resident) from the time resources, such as registers and shared memory (known at compile-time), are allocated to its threads until all threads have exited the kernel. The number of active blocks/warps on an SM is limited by several factors imposed by the kernel launch configuration and the capabilities of the GPU. The limiting factors include: (1) maximum number of warps per SM that can be active simultaneously; (2) maximum number of blocks per SM that can be active simultaneously; (3) number of registers per SM and (4) amount of shared memory per SM. The ratio of active warps on an SM to the maximum number of active warps supported by the device is known as theoretical *occupancy*.[2] Maintaining high occupancy is often necessary to achieve high throughput on the GPU. The reason lies in the fact that when an active warp is stalling for a long latency instruction to be completed (e.g. a memory operation), the GPU immediately replaces it with another *eligible* warp ready to issue an instruction. Therefore, to hide latencies between dependent instructions, it is desirable to have as many active warps as possible.

Memory coalescing. Memory latency is the most important performance considera-tion in GPGPU [4]. To reduce global memory accesses, the GPU combines multiple memory accesses into one single transaction. The memory access pattern required for achieving coalescing and the number of transactions depend on the architecture of the GPU, e.g. the target cache that is going to hold the data (L1 or L2), and the size of the cache line (e.g. 128 bytes for L1 and 32 bytes for L2). For example, every successive 128 bytes of memory can be accessed by the threads in a warp in one coalesced 128-byte L1 transaction or four 32-byte L2 transactions.

---

[2]This is the maximum occupancy that can be achieved. The true achieved occupancy often varies at runtime and depends on various factors, like workload distribution within and across blocks.

10.1.3   CPU–GPU heterogeneous platforms

In addition to lower power consumption in these systems as compared to high-end GPUs, the main distinguishing factor is that the GPU resides on the same chip as the CPU[3] and the system memory is shared between the CPU and GPU, as opposed to the high-end GPU where the GPU has its own dedicated memory. In such an architecture, both devices have the same view of the memory (virtual memory). Therefore, instead of explicitly transferring the data, the CPU can pass the pointer to the input data to the GPU. Data coherency is managed either by the software at the beginning and end of the kernel launch, or by the user. Recently, cache coherent interconnects have emerged which ensure data coherency between the CPU and GPU at hardware level [5]. The unified memory architecture together with the cache coherent interconnect of the heterogeneous platforms facilitate the producer–consumer type applications where the CPU and GPU cooperatively process a stream of data.

10.2   Packet processing on the GPU

In digital communication networks, packet processing refers to the various algorithms applied on the packet as it traverses the network. These algorithms are typically enforced by intermediate networking devices such as routers and switches. Examples of packet processing applications include forwarding, encryption/decryption, transcoding, pattern recognition, etc.

Traditionally, packet-processing applications were implemented in hardware, for example by using application-specific integrated circuits (ASICs). However, recently, the trend has been shifted towards using software implementation of packet processing applications on general purpose processors [6]. As compared to hardware, software can deliver more flexibility by providing fine-grained control over network functionalities, faster time-to-deploy by shortening development cycle, programmability (to facilitate network management) and reduced network hardware costs. Moreover, a software router allows for experimenting with new protocols that are not used currently. On the downside, general purpose processors lag behind application- and domain-specific hardware with respect to computing capability and power consumption. Although recent technological advances have helped reduce this performance gap, it is still crucial to carefully design and optimise packet processing algorithms to meet the stringent requirements of networking applications.

As each packet passes through a router, it is manipulated by a number of applications. Since a router typically processes millions of packets per second, this results in a huge amount of data parallelism. GPUs are ideal for this purpose. In the past, researchers have proposed GPU-based techniques to achieve high performance that is on par with a custom-made network processor [7–13]. GPU-offloaded processing tasks include IP routing, encryption/decryption, string matching, etc.

---

[3]In a heterogeneous system, the CPU typically contains multiple cores.

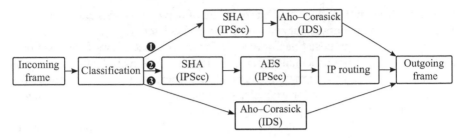

Figure 10.1   A sample packet flow inside a router

Figure 10.1 shows a simplified high-level view of the packet flow inside a GPU-accelerated router. The flow contains several processing nodes (algorithms), where each node can be accelerated on a GPU device. The classification node classifies the packet according to multiple fields in the packet's headers. In Section 10.4, we discuss a GPU implementation for a classification algorithm. The SHA (secure hash algorithm) node, used in the IPsec protocol, provides integrity and authentication for the packet [11]. The AES node, also used in IPsec, provides confidentiality by encrypting the packet [11,14]. The Aho–Corasick node performs pattern matching for an intrusion detection system (IDS) [12]. Finally, the IP routing node provides routing information about the next hop that the packet needs to be forwarded to [8–10]. In the example, the incoming packets (Ethernet frames to be more precise) are first classified into one of the three traffic flows and then processed successively by the nodes in their corresponding flows. In such a router, similar nodes from different flows (e.g. SHA nodes from the first and second flows) can, potentially, be combined and processed in one kernel launch, which leads to higher GPU utilisation.

10.2.1   Related work

PacketShader [7] is the first GPU-accelerated software router to reach a multi-10 Gb/s (precisely, 40 Gbps/s) performance. It achieves this by providing significant I/O optimisations at operating system level and efficiently processing the packets on GPU. The GPU-accelerated applications include IPv4/6 lookup, classification, packet encryption and authentication.

Li *et al.* [10] propose GAMT, a GPU-based IPv4/6 lookup engine that can smoothly handle high update frequencies of the routing table. The proposed method encodes a multi-bit trie into a state-jump table efficiently represented in the GPU.

Zhu *et al.* [9] propose an integrated CPU–GPU microarchitecture to optimise QoS metrics. Their work addresses two problems in GPU-based packet processing, namely the communication overhead between the CPU and GPU and the throughput vs latency trade-off. To eliminate the CPU–GPU communication overhead, the authors propose the use of a shared memory system (an available feature in today's integrated CPU–GPU platforms). As for the latter, they propose a hardware-based adaptive warp issuing mechanism that adapts to the arrival rate of network packets and maintains a balance between the throughput and worst case packet latency.

Sun *et al.* [15] propose Snap, a flexible framework that allows for packet processing tasks being implemented as modular elements. The main feature of Snap is its ability to efficiently support complex pipelines, where packets can be split across divergent processing paths; for example, some packets can take the path through a lookup function while others pass through a pattern matching function.

Zhou *et al.* [16] and Varvello *et al.* [13] present techniques to implement packet classification on GPU. A packet classifier matches each packet against the rules in a rule-set and treats the packet according to the actions of the highest priority matching rule [17]. The proposed technique in [16] uses a two-phase algorithm. In the first phase, each thread examines a set of rules and produces a local classification result using a binary range-tree search technique. Then in phase two, the rule with the highest priority among the local results is identified. The performance of this technique is limited by the size of shared memory and does not scale well with the number of rules. In [13], the authors propose GPU-accelerated implementations of several algorithms to perform multi-layer packet classification, including linear search, tuple search and tuple search enhanced by Bloom filters. The proposed algorithms are integrated with a high-speed packet I/O engine.

Kang *et al.* [18] propose another GPU-accelerated packet classification algorithm, which is based on a linear search framework. The core of the framework is a metaprogramming technique that compiles the rules into fragments of C code in order to avoid high-latency memory accesses normally needed to fetch the rules.

One common pitfall in most of the previous studies is that they mainly focus on the throughput aspect of performance and pay less attention to packet latency [19], perhaps due to the fact that GPUs are throughput-oriented machines and achieving a higher throughput is regarded as a more desirable goal. This, however, has implications on the residence time of the packet inside the networking device. The next section discusses the throughput–latency trade-off in more details.

10.2.2 Throughput vs latency dilemma

The throughput–latency dilemma stems from two distinguishing characteristics of packet processing applications: first, the amount of computation that needs to be performed on a single packet is far below the amount required to efficiently utilise GPU cores – regardless of the particular packet processing application. Second, packet-processing applications are latency-sensitive and the quality of communication is greatly affected by the amount of delay it takes to process the packet. In contrast, the mainstream GPGPU applications are usually not latency-sensitive but throughput dominated.

To deal with the first problem and increase GPU utilisation, one common approach is to wait and collect a large batch of packets before launching the GPU kernel. Increasing the batch size provides higher degree of data-level parallelism and improves the throughput, until the throughput saturates. However, this method incurs additional latency on the packet. First, it increases the average queueing delay at the

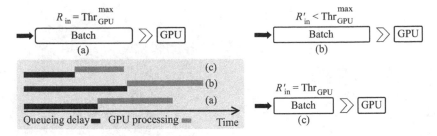

Figure 10.2   The impact of batch size on maximum packet latency when: (a) the network is fully loaded and throughput is at its peak; (b) network is underloaded and throughput is larger than the input rate; (c) network is underloaded and throughput is adjusted down

input port because packets have to wait longer before they can be dispatched to the GPU. Second, it leads to larger pipeline processing time due to larger workload.[4]

Most of the existing software-based GPU solutions ignore the fact that achieving high throughputs usually comes at the cost of larger packet latency. These techniques rely on accumulating a fixed number of packets, large enough to achieve (near to) maximum throughput [9,13,16]. The drawback of such *fixed-size batch-processing* approaches is that regardless of the packet arrival rate, the system always has to collect the same number of packets before it can start the actual processing on the GPU. Therefore, if the arrival rate is lower than the maximum throughput, the system waits longer to build the batch, which also takes longer to process, whereas a smaller batch size could actually provide the required throughput with smaller queueing delay and processing time. Figure 10.2 illustrates the problem of fixed-size batch processing. Comparing cases (a) and (b), we can see that (b) results in a larger worst case latency, even though the input rate is lower. This is due to a larger queueing delay in (b). Also note that the GPU processing time has not changed because the batch sizes are the same. In case (c), the batch size is adapted to the input rate. As a result, both the queueing delay and processing time have dropped.

10.2.3   An adaptive approach

One way to circumvent the latency issues of the fixed-size method is to dynamically adjust the throughput by changing the batch size according to the traffic rate [20]. Towards this, a runtime algorithm monitors the packet arrival rate at regular intervals. Based on the current rate, the algorithm then selects an appropriate batch size that can satisfy the traffic load demand. The batch size is selected from a table that contains a list of batch sizes and their respective throughputs. From this point forward, until the next batch size switch occurs, the GPU processes the packets in batches of the selected size. Figure 10.3 shows the steps involved in an adaptive packet processing

---

[4]Here we assume that the batch size has no impact on the queueing delay at the output port.

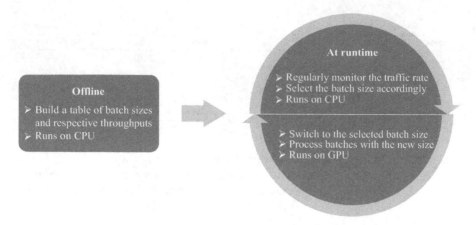

Figure 10.3   High-level view of a latency-aware adaptive technique

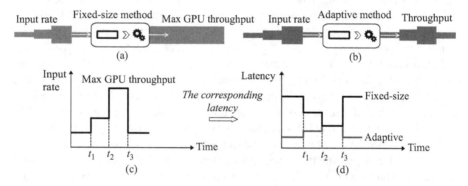

Figure 10.4   Fixed-size method vs adaptive method: (a) the fixed-size method always collects as many packets as required to provide a maximum GPU throughput, while (b) the throughput of the adaptive method varies with the input rate; (c) sample of an input traffic with varying rate; (d) the average packet latency of each method under the sample input traffic

technique. In Sections 10.2.4, 10.2.5 and 10.2.6, we, respectively, explain the details of how the batch size table is built, how the best batch size is selected, and how the switching from one batch size to another takes place. But before that let us look at the advantage of the adaptive method over the fixed-size method.

Performance comparison. Figure 10.4 compares the latency performance of the fixed-size method with the adaptive method. The fixed-size method sets the throughput at the maximum level (Figure 10.4(a)), while the adaptive method maintains the throughput at a level slightly higher than the current input rate at all time (Figure 10.4(b)). This is to avoid any packet loss due to buffer overflow. Note that for the adaptive method, latency follows the same pattern as the input rate, such that when the rate is low latency is also low and vice versa. This is due to the capability of the method to adapt to the changes of the input traffic. In contrast, the latency of the fixed-size method follows an inverse pattern of the input rate, as illustrated in Figure 10.4(d). This is due to the fact that the queueing delay is larger when the input rate is smaller, while the GPU processing time remains unchanged. Only when the input rate is high, the fixed-size method can batch sufficient number of packets quickly enough to maintain a low latency. Moreover, as load increases, the adaptive method switches to larger batch sizes and the latency gap between the two methods diminishes, as shown in Figure 10.4(d) during time interval t_2–t_3.

10.2.4   Offline building of the batch-size table

At runtime, the algorithm refers to a batch-size table to select the next batch size based on the current traffic rate. This table is built offline and each of its rows contains a pair of a batch size and the maximum GPU throughput that can be obtained for the corresponding batch size. Building the table is straightforward. For each batch size, the buffer is initially filled up with multiple batches of the given size. This is done to exclude the queueing delay at the input port. Then, we run the kernel with the given batch size, let it process all the batches and measure the average throughput. The table is unique for every GPU model and depends on its compute capability and amount of resources. Figure 10.5 shows such a table. Note that the batch size factor is a factor that determines the batch size by multiplying it with the GPU block size. Therefore, the minimum batch size corresponds to the factor of value one, when each GPU thread processes one packet.

Typically, the size of the table is quite small. For the test platform used in the case study given in Section 10.4 (i.e. Jetson TX1 development board with Nvidia GM20B GPU), the table contains (at most) 16 entries. Because the throughput saturates after a certain batch size, the table only needs to store batch sizes below the saturation point. Additionally, if needed, the size of the table may further be reduced by eliminating entries where throughput gain between consecutive batch sizes is regarded as insignificant.

10.2.5   Runtime batch size selection

The core idea to achieve an adaptive technique is to change the batch size at runtime. Smaller batches provide shorter queuing and processing delay (assuming that the throughput is higher than the input rate so that no additional queuing delay is caused

Batch size factor	Throughput (Gbps)
⋮	⋮
12	13.5
13	15
14	16.2
⋮	⋮

Figure 10.5   A sample batch-size table

by the backlogged traffic) at the expense of lower throughput. Therefore, in order to minimise packet latency while avoiding any packet loss due to buffer overflow, we should select the smallest batch whose throughput value in the table is not less than the input rate.

Selection is performed by a governor thread that runs on the CPU. This thread measures the average input rate during a given time interval (e.g. 5 ms) and accordingly selects the suitable batch size factor by referring to the batch-size table. For example, considering the table in Figure 10.5, if the input rate is 14 Gbps, the governor selects the batch size factor 13 with throughput 15 Gbps.

10.2.6   Switching between batch sizes

Once a new batch size is selected by the CPU thread, it needs to be communicated to the GPU and adopted. This leads to some issues starting with the following: how to make the switching process swift and smooth so that the throughput is minimally compromised?

One intuitive way is to invoke a separate GPU kernel launch for every new batch, with a grid size that is a function of the batch size (as opposed to constant batch sizes in the fixed-size method). However, this solution is crude for two reasons. The first reason is the kernel launch overhead. For typical GPU kernels with execution times in the order of milliseconds or higher, kernel launch overhead is negligible. However, for packet processing applications with latency requirements in the order of microseconds, kernel launch overhead can become a significant factor. The effect is even more remarkable for smaller batches with lower execution time. The second reason is the workload imbalance across blocks. This happens when some blocks finish earlier and need to wait before all kernel blocks end and only then new kernel blocks can be scheduled. Similar to launch overhead, workload imbalance is more detrimental when the workload is small. Below, we discuss the *persistent* kernel, an unconventional type of kernel that can mitigate these issues.

10.3   Persistent kernel

The main characteristic of a persistent kernel is that it is launched only once and runs continuously (in an infinite loop) until terminated by the host. The kernel is composed of a few number of blocks that are resident (active) at all time during lifetime of the kernel, as opposed to a conventional kernel where old active blocks are replaced by new blocks that are waiting to be executed. Each batch is processed by the blocks in a collaborative manner. In other words, a batch is fully processed when all blocks have done their parts in processing the batch. After a block processed a batch, it busy-waits until the next batch becomes available. Blocks are notified about the arrival of a new batch by a host thread via shared variables.

A persistent kernel does not suffer from the performance issues of frequent launching. First, the kernel launch overhead is eliminated since the kernel is launched only once. Second, unlike normal kernels, where there is an implicit synchronisation point at the end of the kernel, here different blocks can work on different batches concurrently (more details in Section 10.3.2). Thus, in this method, workload imbalance does not have the same negative impact on throughput as it has on conventional kernels. According to our experiments, for the minimum sized batches, using persistent kernel yields 50 per cent higher throughput than the conventional method [20].

10.3.1 Persistent kernel challenges

Designing a persistent kernel creates some challenges that need to be addressed. First, the communication between the CPU and GPU must be synchronised. In conventional GPU programming, the host prepares the data and sends it to the GPU memory before the kernel is launched and then reads back the results after the kernel is finished. In the case of a persistent kernel, however, the communication needs to take place while the kernel is running, to inform the GPU about the newly selected batch size, and to move around the data in the shared buffers between the host and GPU. In the next section, we discuss a software architecture that exploits the shared memory architecture in integrated CPU–GPU platforms to synchronise data communication.

Another challenge is to maintain a high theoretical occupancy on the GPU. In a persistent kernel, the task of processing a batch must be distributed among a few blocks, as opposed to conventional kernels where the task may be broken into a large number of blocks with each block carrying out a small portion of the processing. Having more workload on a block may increase its resource usage and limit the number of active blocks on each SM[5] (see Section 10.1.2 for the relation between resource usage of the block and GPU occupancy). Therefore, the kernel must be designed diligently so that the benefit of using a persistent kernel is not cancelled out by the low utilisation of the GPU.

Moreover, to reduce the latency of each batch, workload should be distributed evenly across the resident blocks. The reason is that for a given amount of workload and a number of identical compute resources (here, blocks), the minimum computation time is achieved when the workload is distributed evenly among the resources. Note that this is different from the effect of workload imbalance on throughput.

10.3.2 Proposed software architecture

In this section, we describe the software architecture that serves as the basis for realising the persistent kernel. It exploits the unified memory architecture in GPU-based heterogeneous systems to process the packets in cooperation with the CPU. Figure 10.6(a) shows the main components of the proposed architecture, some of which are described below. Figure 10.6(b) shows the structure of the transmit (TX) and receive (RX) buffers for the case study explained in Section 10.4.

CPU threads. On a multi-core CPU the following threads are running concurrently: *main thread*, which initialises the system and launches the GPU kernel and other

---

[5]At the same time, having fewer blocks increases the shared memory size for each block, which may be used to improve kernel performance by storing more data on the on-chip memory.

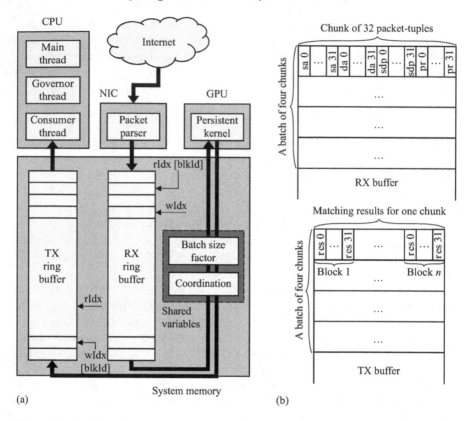

Figure 10.6　(a) Software architecture of a persistent kernel; (b) structure of receive (RX) and transmit (TX) buffers

CPU threads; *consumer thread*, which reads the results from the output buffer, i.e. TX buffer, and takes the corresponding actions; *governor thread*, which monitors the traffic rate and decides the appropriate batch sizes.

System memory. As discussed in Section 10.1.3, in a heterogeneous platform the system memory is shared between the CPU and GPU. Using the unified memory architecture, the GPU can directly access the memory to read the packet headers that are stored in the RX buffer earlier by the host. Likewise, the CPU can directly access the results from the GPU that are stored in the TX buffer. Moreover, we use this feature to seamlessly (1) inform the GPU of the selected batch sizes at runtime, represented by the *batch size factor* variable in the figure and (2) coordinate the start and termination time of the infinite kernel loop between the CPU and GPU, as represented by the *coordination* variables in the figure.

RX buffer. As packets arrive, particular fields of theirs are extracted by the network parser and stored in the RX buffer to be processed by the GPU. For example, in the case of the packet classification algorithm, each packet is represented in the buffer as a five-tuple containing the source and destination IP addresses, source and destination ports, and transport protocol.

Writing into the RX buffer is managed by the host using one write index. Reading from the buffer, however, is managed by the GPU using multiple read indices. The reason is as follows: in the conventional case, reading packet-tuples from the buffer requires only one index. The index points to the beginning of the batch and is advanced once at the end of every kernel launch [13]. Recall that here each kernel launch processes one batch. In contrast, the proposed persistent kernel crunches the batches continuously. Therefore, unlike the conventional case, we need a mechanism to move the index while the kernel is running. Using one read index requires to wait for all blocks to finish processing the same batch before advancing the index. The drawback is that the blocks that finish their tasks earlier have to idle, and this hurts GPU utilisation. Instead, we assign one read index to every block so that the blocks can work on different batches independently. Each read index points to the beginning of the batch currently being processed by the corresponding block and is advanced by the block when the processing is over. The buffer is full when the write index meets any of the read indices, in which case subsequent packets are dropped. Read indices are checked by the host to determine if the buffer is full. Each GPU thread uses its own local index to keep track of the next tuple to process (Section 10.4.4).

TX buffer. Results are written into the TX buffer by the GPU threads and read by the consumer thread. The exact details regarding managing this buffer are specific to the application and kernel implementation. For example, each thread may process a packet individually or together with threads from other blocks. In Section 10.4.4, we elaborate on this buffer in the context of a packet classification algorithm.

10.4 Case study

In this section, we investigate a packet classification algorithm as a case study to illustrate the application of the adaptive method. But first let us explain the packet classification problem and a state-of-the-art GPU-accelerated implementation of this application.

10.4.1 The problem of packet classification

The packet classification problem is defined as follows [17]: for any input packet, find the matching rule with the highest priority in the rule-set and treat the packet according to the action associated with the rule. Each rule is basically a set of fields used to find a match with an incoming packet. A rule also contains an additional field that encodes the action to be taken if there is a match. Figure 10.7 shows a simple rule-set with five rules, where each rule has two fields (source and destination addresses) and an associated action. Each field in a rule (except the action field) contains two entries: a network prefix and a prefix length. For the source address field of rule R_1 in our example, the network prefix is 192.168.153.0. The prefix length is 24 because the last eight bits in the network prefix are zeros. Given the prefix, a subnet mask

Rule	Source address (network prefix/prefix length)	Destination address (network prefix/prefix length)	Action
R1	192.168.153.0/24	10.120.0.0/16	Deny
R2	192.168.144.0/20	10.120.0.0/16	Deny
R3	172.129.240.0/24	150.25.0.0/16	Permit
R4	158.70.112.0/20	192.168.0.0/16	Deny
R5	192.168.0.0/16	10.0.0.0/8	Permit

(a)

Class tuple	Hash tables
(24, 16)	{R1, R3}
(20, 16)	{R2, R4}
(16, 8)	{R5}

(b)

Source address	Destination address	Best match, action
192.168.152.17	10.120.133.1	R2, Deny

(c)

Figure 10.7   (a) An example classifier with two fields, (b) three hash tables corresponding to three tss-class tuples, (c) an example packet header P

can be defined for each field. For example, the corresponding subnet mask of prefix length 24 is 255.255.255.0.

A match between a packet and a rule is based on the outcome of masking, i.e. a bitwise AND operation performed between the fields of the packet and the subnet masks in the corresponding fields in the rule. In our example, we need two masking operations; one bit-wise AND operation between each of the source and destination fields of the input packet and their corresponding subnet masks. For our example, packet P does not match R1 because the source address of the packet does not match the network prefix of the rule, i.e. 192.168.152.17 AND 255.255.255.0 = 192.168.152.0 ≠ 192.168.153.0. On the other hand, using the same logic, P matches R2 and R5.

10.4.2   The tuple space search (TSS) algorithm

One popular sequential algorithm to solve the above problem is the tuple space search (TSS) algorithm [21]. The basic TSS algorithm first assigns an n-element tuple to each rule, where the ith element is the prefix-length specified in the ith field of the rule. All the rules with similar prefix lengths are mapped to the same tuple and belong to the same *tss-class*. For example, in the classifier given in Figure 10.7, R_1 and R_3 belong to the class with tuple (24,16). For every tss-class there is a hash table containing the rules in the class. When building the hash table, the index of each rule in the table is determined by applying a hash function over the network prefixes defined in the rule fields. Queries are answered by performing lookups on each hash table in the following way: for each table, the packet header is first masked using the prefix lengths specified in the class tuple (hereafter, referred to as *class mask*). The result is then processed by the same hash function that was used earlier to build the hash table. An exact match operation is performed using the index provided as the hash result. Among the matches found in all the hash tables, the classifier selects the one with the highest priority and handles the packet according to its action. In the example, R_2 and R_5, from two different classes, match P. But R_2 has higher priority and is therefore selected as the final match.

There are two levels of parallelism inherent in the basic TSS algorithm, which make it a suitable candidate for SIMD architectures, and in particular for GPUs. They include (1) packet level parallelism, where several packets are processed in parallel by different threads and (2) tss-class level parallelism, where a single packet is matched against the rules in multiple classes in parallel. Both potentials are exploited by the following GPU-based implementation to accelerate the TSS algorithm.

10.4.3 GPU-based TSS algorithm

In [13], the authors propose a GPU-accelerated implementation of TSS (hereafter, referred to as GPU-TSS). This method is based on the fixed-size batch-processing scheme, where packets are typically processed in batches of 8k. The rules in each tss-class are handled by a separate block. Threads in each block match all the headers against the rules in the class as follows: initially, the class hash table and the class mask are loaded into the shared memory. Then, each thread performs the lookup, iteratively, for at most $\lceil batch\text{-}size/block\text{-}size \rceil$ iterations. In every iteration, a GPU thread i performs the following: first, it loads a header and masks it using the tss-class mask. Second, it applies a hash function over the result of masking to calculate an index in the hash table. Then, the thread performs a matching operation between the header and the indexed location (as explained in Section 10.4.1). Finally, it writes the result to a unique memory location allocated for that header. This memory location contains both the global id of the matched rule and its priority. The thread writes into this location only if it finds a match with a higher priority than the one already in the location. Note that the ith threads of all blocks work on the same header and write to the same location using atomic write operations.

Despite achieving high throughput, this method suffers from the problems of the fixed-size approach (Section 10.2.2). Following, we discuss a modified version of this algorithm that is compatible with the adaptive-method approach.

10.4.4 TSS persistent kernel

As explained in Section 10.3.2, the adaptive method exploits the RX and TX shared buffers for processing the packet-tuples. The exact structure of the buffers is, however, dependent on the specific application. Figure 10.6(b) illustrates the layout the of TX and RX buffers for the TSS persistent kernel.

In the TSS algorithm, a packet-tuple consists of five fields including source and destination IP addresses, source and destination ports, and transport protocol. Each tuple in the RX buffer is represented by four 32-bit memory words (source and destination ports are 16-bits long each and are merged together). In the figure, these fields are denoted as *sa, da, sdp,* and *pr,* respectively. Each RX buffer slot contains a chunk of 32 packet-tuples, with similar fields located adjacent to each other for better memory coalescing. Several chunks are batched together for processing by the GPU. As for the TX buffer, note that the result for every packet-tuple is found cooperatively by several blocks; the *i*th threads of different blocks match the same tuple against the rules covered by their blocks. Conventionally, such threads share the same memory location to store their results. Therefore, for every packet-tuple in the RX buffer there is a 32-bit word in the TX buffer, which stores the global id of the highest priority rule that matches the tuple. Upon finding a match, each thread *i* of a block uses an atomic operation to overwrite this location if it has a higher priority match. However, this method decreases the throughput because the number of atomic operations that can be used in parallel by several threads is limited, and this occasionally leads to serialization of accesses. To avoid using atomic operations, each thread in a block writes its best found result to a separate memory location exclusively allocated for that thread. Therefore, given *n* blocks, there are *n* words in the TX buffer for every packet-tuple in the RX buffer, as shown in Figure 10.6(b). The consumer thread then collects all the partial results and selects the one with the highest priority. Note that the additional amount of memory is not significant (6 MB out of 4 GB for our case).

Before going into the details of the implementation, let us also discuss another challenge in designing a persistent kernel, i.e. workload distribution across the blocks. In GPU-TSS [13], each tss-class is assigned to one block. The GPU can handle a large number of tss-classes by replacing the blocks that have finished their jobs with the new ones. However, the persistent kernel runs continuously and blocks are used to iteratively process the packet-tuples from different batches. Therefore, multiple tss-classes must be assigned to one block. This has negative performance implications because processing against each tss-class separately (as in GPU-TSS) introduces an overhead due to thread synchronisations. To reduce the number of iterations, we combine the rules in multiple classes into one bigger *mixed hash table.* For faster memory accesses, the mixed table is loaded into the shared memory (once for each batch). Typically, the amount of shared memory per block is not sufficient to accommodate all block rules in one table. Hence, the rules are packed into smaller mixed tables, each of the size of the available shared memory. This is a one-time process which is performed offline, for a given rule-set.

Now let us explain how the packet-tuples in a batch are assigned to the threads in each block. For a batch-size-factor f and a block size b, any GPU thread i of block j is responsible for matching the $(i \bmod 32)$th packet-tuples of the batch chunks $\lfloor i/32 \rfloor, \ldots, \lfloor i/32 \rfloor + (f - 1) \times (b/32)$ against the jth portion of the rule-set. For example, assuming that $f = 4$ and $b = 256$, thread 32 processes the zeroth tuples of the batch chunks 1, 9, 17, 25. Note that in this configuration, each tuple is processed cooperatively by all blocks.

The algorithm. Algorithm 10.1 shows the TSS persistent kernel. In the beginning, each GPU thread initialises its local read and write indices using its id (denoted as *tid*). They are used to keep track of the advances of the buffer indices without having

---

Algorithm 1: The persistent kernel

---

    input   : hash tables, tss-class masks and other shared variables
    output : partial matching results stored in the TX buffer

1 *rIdxLocal* ← *tid*/*chunkSize*;
2 *wIdxLocal* ← *tid*/*chunkSize*;
3 *SyncThreads*(); // let all block threads enter the loop together
    /* The main loop starts here   */
4 **while** *true* **do**
5   **if** *tid* = 0 **then** load batch size factor into shared memory;
6   *SyncThreads*() ;   // wait for the load to be completed
7   *batchSizeFactor* ← Read from shared memory;
8   **while** *the whole batch is not ready* **do**
9   **if** *glFlag* = TERM **then** exit;
10   **end**
        /* batch is ready, start processing by going through all
           tables   */
11   **for** *i* ← 0 **to** *numMixedTablesPerBlock* **do**
12   *SyncThreads*(); // wait until previous table is still used
13   Load *mixedTable* into shared memory;
14   Load *classMasks* into shared memory;
15   *SyncThreads*();   // wait for all loads to complete
           /* Match the tuples in the batch against the current
              table   */
16   **for** *j* ← 0 **to** *batchSizeFactor* **do**
17   Read a *packetTuple* using *rIdxLocal* and *tid*;
18   Advance *rIdxLocal* and keep it in range;
19   **foreach** *class in hashTable* **do**
20   Load *classMask* from shared memory;
21   Apply *classMask* over *packetTuple*;
22   Hash *maskedTuple* to get *index*;
23   Lookup using *index*;
24   Update *partialRes*[*j*] if improves;
25   **end**
26   **end**
27   Put back *rIdxLocal* at the start of the batch;
28   **end**
29   Advance *rIdxLocal* to the start of the next batch;
30   **for** *j* ← 0 **to** *batchSizeFactor* **do**
31   Store *partialRes*[*j*] in the TX buffer using *wIdxLocal*;
32   Advance *wIdxLocal*;
33   **end**
34   *SyncThreads*();   // wait for all threads to commit their
        results
35   **if** *tid* = 0 **then**
36   *wIdxTxBuff*[*blkId*] = *wIdxLocal*;
37   *rIdxRxBuff*[*blkId*] = *rIdxLocal*;
38   **end**
39 **end**

---

to frequently access the global memory (lines 1–2). In lines 5–7, the latest value of the batch size factor is loaded into the shared memory (by thread 0 of each block) and broadcast to the threads. This is to ensure that all block threads see the same value of the batch size factor. Then, the threads wait until the required number of packets have arrived and the batch is ready (lines 8–10). Meanwhile, the host (i.e. the main thread) may declare the end of the loop by setting a shared flag.

Once the batch is ready, each block starts matching the packet-tuples against the rules it covers (lines 11–28). Each thread is potentially responsible for handling more than one packet-tuple as described above. At the beginning of each iteration, the mixed hash table and the corresponding tss-class masks are loaded into the shared memory (lines 12–15). In doing so, all block threads cooperatively read the data from the system memory using memory-coalesced accesses. Then each thread matches its assigned tuples in the batch against all the classes in the current mixed table (lines 16–26). The matching procedure is similar to that in Section 10.4.3. After the tuples are matched against the current mixed table, the local read index is reset to point to the thread's first tuple in the batch so that the algorithm can continue with the next mixed table (line 27). When the whole batch is processed, each thread stores its partial results (for the tuples that it has processed) in the TX buffer to be used by the consumer thread (lines 30–33). Once all threads have committed their results, the block updates its global buffer indices (lines 35–38).

10.4.5   Experimental results

In this section, we experimentally show that the proposed adaptive technique is able to provide lower packet latency compared to the fixed batch size algorithm (GPU-TSS). The results are based on an accurate measurement scheme and realistic traffic traces, as elaborated below.

Experimental setup. We use a Jetson-TX1 development board as our experimental platform. Jetson-TX1 features an Nvidia Maxwell GPU with 256 Nvidia CUDA Cores (two SMs each containing 128 cores), a Quad-core ARM Cortex-A57 Processor and a 4-GB LPDDR4 Memory. We fix the GPU and memory frequencies at 1 and 1.6 GHz, respectively.

The kernel configuration is as follows: four blocks (two per SM), 512 threads per block, 32 kB of shared memory per block and 16 k chunks for each of the TX and RX buffers. To compute the throughput, we consider the minimum 84-byte Ethernet frames (i.e. 64-byte minimum payload size plus 20-byte Ethernet overhead). The batch size factor can take a value from $\{1, 2, 4, 6, \ldots, 16\}$. Therefore, the batch size varies from 512 to 8k packet-tuples. We used a rule-set composed of 128 tss-classes with each class containing 128 rules. For this setting, the maximum throughput of the persistent kernel is 16.5 Gbps. Note that for all traces, we assume that the ingress traffic is shaped according to the network capacity and hence the input rate is lower than the maximum GPU throughput.

Realistic traffic simulation. We introduce a so-called producer thread on one of the cores in the CPU to generate the packets that enter the system memory. We use

ClassBench [22], a packet classification benchmark, to generate the packet-tuples and the rule-set, as the approach used in [13]. For each experimental run, we let the kernel process the packets arriving during a 1-min interval. To create realistic traffic conditions, we schedule the arrival times such that the input rate follows a pattern similar to the actual traces obtained from a public network trace repository [23].

Latency measurement. For the experiments, we need to measure the latency of each packet. Note that all 32 packets of a chunk arrive at the same time, namely the chunk arrival time. Therefore, they will have the same latency, namely the chunk latency. The chunk latency is derived by subtracting the chunk arrival time from its departure time (which is the same for all the chunks in the same batch). Chunk arrival is an event in the CPU and the time is logged by the producer thread. Thus, the arrival time is obtained by recording the actual host time, in microseconds, at the moment of arrival. Chunk departure is an event in the GPU. Thus, the departure time is defined by the GPU, in terms of the number of elapsed GPU clock cycles, immediately after the batch has been processed. Accurate measurement, in this context, implies that the CPU and GPU clocks must be synchronised. Towards this, we introduce a so-called synchroniser thread, which performs the regular synchronisation of the GPU clock with CPU time.

Results. We evaluate the performance of the adaptive method under various traffic loads, i.e. light, medium and high, where the input rate varies in the range of 2.1–7.5, 3–16 and 12–16 Gbps, respectively. We accurately measure the latency of every single chunk. The three plots in Figure 10.8 compare the chunk latency of the proposed persistent kernel with GPU-TSS during a 1-min interval. A point on the plots shows the average chunk latency measured during the past sampling interval (2 ms). We make the following observations: (1) for all the three plots, using the persistent kernel, the latency follows the same pattern as the input rate, meaning that when the rate is low the latency is low and vice versa. This is due to the capability of the method to quickly adapt (within 5 ms) to the changes of the input traffic. In contrast, GPU-TSS follows the inverse pattern of the input rate. The reason is that GPU-TSS always runs with a fixed batch size (8k packet-tuples). Therefore, when the input rate is low, the system has to wait longer to build the batch, which results in a larger queuing delay. Only when the input rate is high, GPU-TSS can batch sufficient packet-tuples quickly enough to maintain a low latency. (2) As the load increases, the adaptive method switches to larger batch sizes and the latency gap between the two methods gradually decreases. For example, in Figure 10.8(b) at second 42 the gap closes. (3) In all cases, the adaptive method provides lower packet latency than GPU-TSS, except in Figure 10.8(c) between seconds 31 and 50 under the maximum load. For the light, medium and heavy traffic, the average packet latency of the adaptive method is 147, 197 and 490 μs, while for GPU-TSS it is 1381, 930 and 594 μs, respectively. Following the same reasoning explained in the first remark, GPU-TSS performs the worst at the light load condition, whereas the adaptive method delivers its best performance at this load (Figure 10.8(a)).

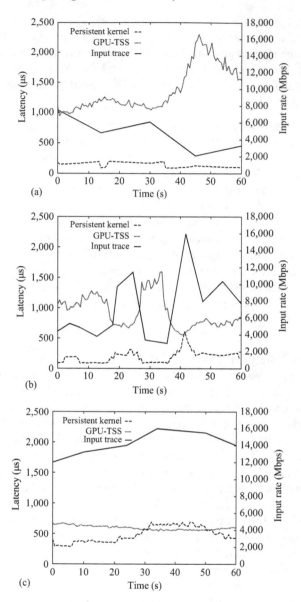

Figure 10.8   Packet latency under various traffic conditions: (a) light, (b) medium, (c) heavy load

10.5   Conclusion and future directions

In this chapter, we reviewed some of the academic research in the area of packet processing on GPUs. We discussed how the computing power of GPUs can be exploited to fulfil the high throughput demand of these applications. We also showed that setting the throughput to the maximum level, paradoxically, results in higher latency for lower traffic loads. To address this issue, we presented an adaptive method that at runtime adjusts the throughput according to the current input rate and by doing so reduces both the queuing delay and the processing time of packets.

The current work deals with implementing one packet processing application (i.e. packet classification) using a persistent kernel on the GPU. In further research, it may be worthwhile to implement other applications that manipulate the packet inside the router, using the same approach. The next natural step is then to map a part or the entirety of the packet flow diagram (such as the one shown in Figure 10.1) on the GPU. This can be achieved by implementing each application as a distinct persistent kernel residing alongside other persistent kernels on the GPU. In this way, the flow can be seen as a pipeline and each application as a stage of the pipeline. In addition to the advantages of the persistent kernel (discussed in Section 10.3) and lower packet latency, this approach may also increase the throughput due to pipelining. However, further work is required to investigate if the achieved performance gain can outweigh the detrimental effects caused by imbalance among pipeline stages and the possible reduction of GPU utilisation due to persistent kernels (see Section 10.3.1).

In another direction of future research, persistent kernels can be used in scenarios where several applications with different priorities share the same GPU. For example, one application may perform packet classification on high priority voice packets while the other performs pattern matching on low priority media packets. GPUs are non-preemptive devices, meaning that once the execution starts it has to end before the next kernel can be executed. This property can cause a problem for the high priority packets as they may be delayed due to the ongoing processing of the low priority packets. Running the packet classification algorithm as a persistent kernel allows us to circumvent this problem by allocating some of the GPU resources to the high priority task at all time. This way we can ensure minimal processing delay for the voice packets. As an alternative to this approach, we note that recently CUDA introduced support for prioritising the kernels dispatched into different CUDA streams (a stream in CUDA is a sequence of operations that execute on the GPU in the order in which they are issued by the host code). However, prioritising delay-sensitive packets in this way has a major drawback: At runtime, when resources become available, waiting blocks in the high priority stream are scheduled to be executed first. However, a high priority block still may not preempt a low priority block and needs to wait until the running block finishes. This waiting time increases the average latency of the high priority packets. Additionally, the amount of the added delay is not fixed, hence increasing the undesirable jitter effect over the voice packets.

References

[1]   Nickolls J, Dally WJ. The GPU Computing Era. IEEE Micro. 2010;30(2): 56–69.

[2]   Maghazeh A, Bordoloi UD, Eles P, *et al.* General Purpose Computing on Low-Power Embedded GPUs: Has It Come of Age? In: 2013 International

Conference on Embedded Computer Systems: Architectures, Modeling, and Simulation; 2013. p. 1–10.

[3]   Wilt N. The CUDA Handbook: A Comprehensive Guide to GPU Programming. Addison-Wesley, Crawfordsville, IN; 2013.

[4]   CUDA C Best Practices Guide [user guide]. NVidia; 2018 [cited 2018-02-10]. Available from: http://docs.nvidia.com/cuda/cuda-c-best-practices-guide.

[5]   HSA Platform System Architecture Specification Version 1.0. HSA foundation; 2015.

[6]   Kreutz D, Ramos FMV, Veríssimo PE, et al. Software-Defined Networking: A Comprehensive Survey. Proceedings of the IEEE. 2015;103(1):14–76.

[7]   Han S, Jang K, Park K, et al. PacketShader: A GPU-Accelerated Software Router. In: Proceedings of the ACM SIGCOMM Conference; 2010. p. 195–206.

[8]   Mu S, Zhang X, Zhang N, et al. IP Routing Processing with Graphic Processors. In: Proceedings of the Conference on Design, Automation and Test in Europe; 2010. p. 93–98.

[9]   Zhu Y, Deng Y, Chen Y. Hermes: An Integrated CPU/GPU Microarchitecture for IP Routing. In: Proceedings of the 48th Design Automation Conference; 2011. p. 1044–1049.

[10]   Li Y, Zhang D, Liu AX, et al. GAMT: A Fast and Scalable IP Lookup Engine for GPU-based Software Routers. In: Proceedings of the Ninth ACM/IEEE Symposium on Architectures for Networking and Communications Systems; 2013. p. 1–12.

[11]   Park J, Jung W, Jo G, et al. PIPSEA: A Practical IPsec Gateway on Embedded APUs. In: Proceedings of the 2016 ACM SIGSAC Conference on Computer and Communications Security; 2016. p. 1255–1267.

[12]   Tumeo A, Villa O, Sciuto D. Efficient Pattern Matching on GPUs for Intrusion Detection Systems. In: Proceedings of the 7th ACM International Conference on Computing Frontiers; 2010. p. 87–88.

[13]   Varvello M, Laufer R, Zhang F, et al. Multi-Layer Packet Classification with Graphics Processing Units. In: Proceedings of the 10th ACM International on Conference on Emerging Networking Experiments and Technologies; 2014. p. 109–120.

[14]   Harrison O, Waldron J. Practical Symmetric Key Cryptography on Modern Graphics Hardware. In: Proceedings of the 17th Conference on Security Symposium; 2008. p. 195–209.

[15]   Sun W, Ricci R. Fast and Flexible: Parallel Packet Processing with GPUs and Click. In: Proceedings of the Ninth ACM/IEEE Symposium on Architectures for Networking and Communications Systems; 2013. p. 25–36.

[16]   Zhou S, Singapura SG, Prasanna VK. High-Performance Packet Classification on GPU. In: 2014 IEEE High Performance Extreme Computing Conference (HPEC); 2014. p. 1–6.

[17]   Gupta P, McKeown N. Algorithms for Packet Classification. IEEE Network. 2001;15(2):24–32.

[18]   Kang K, Deng YS. Scalable Packet Classification via GPU Metaprogramming. In: Design, Automation Test in Europe Conference Exhibition; 2011. p. 1–4.

[19]   Kalia A, Zhou D, Kaminsky M, *et al.* Raising the Bar for Using GPUs in Software Packet Processing. In: Proceedings of the 12th USENIX Conference on Networked Systems Design and Implementation; 2015. p. 409–423.

[20]   Maghazeh A, Bordoloi UD, Dastgeer U, *et al.* Latency-Aware Packet Processing on CPU–GPU Heterogeneous Systems. In: Proceedings of the 54th Annual Design Automation Conference 2017; 2017. p. 41:1–41:6.

[21]   Srinivasan V, Suri S, Varghese G. Packet Classification Using Tuple Space Search. SIGCOMM Computer Communication Review. 1999;29(4):135–146.

[22]   Taylor DE, Turner JS. ClassBench: A Packet Classification Benchmark. IEEE/ACM Transactions on Networking. 2007;15(3):499–511.

[23]   Internet Traffic Trace. WAND Network Research Group; 2018 [cited 2018-02-10]. Available from: http://wand.net.nz/wits/ipls/3/.

Chapter 11

From power-efficient to power-driven computing

Rishad Shafik[1] and Alex Yakovlev[1]

The dramatic spread of computing, at the scale of trillions of ubiquitous devices, is delivering on the pervasive penetration into the real world in the form of Internet of Things (IoT). Today, the widely used power-efficient paradigms directly related to the behaviour of computing systems are those of real-time (working to deadlines imposed from the real world) and low-power (prolonging battery life or reducing heat dissipation and electricity bills). None of these addresses the strict requirements on power supply, allocation and utilisation that are imposed by the needs of new devices and applications in the computing swarm – many of which are expected to be confronted with challenges of autonomy and battery-free long life. Indeed, we need to design and build systems for survival, operating under a wide range of power constraints; we need a new power-driven paradigm called real-power computing (RPC).

This chapter provides an overview of this emerging paradigm with definition, taxonomies and a case study, together with a summary of the existing research. Towards the end, the overview leads to research and development challenges and opportunities surfacing this paradigm. Throughout the chapter, we have used the power and energy terms as follows. From the supply side, the *energy* term will be used to refer to harvesters with built-in storage, while the *power* term will indicate instantaneous energy dispensation. For the computing logic side, the energy term will define the total *power* consumed over a given time interval.

11.1 Computing is evolving

Computing systems continue to be at the core of our everyday life – from large-scale infrastructure server systems to small-scale implanted electronics or swarms of wireless sensing nodes pervading in smart cities. Based on design considerations, their domains can be classified into six major applications: high-performance server systems, desktop computing, portable computing, mobile systems, embedded systems and ubiquitous systems. Figure 11.1 depicts different design and optimisation requirements of these application domains.

---

[1]Electrical and Electronic Engineering, School of Engineering, Newcastle University, UK

	Typical population	Power supply	Operating power	Supply variation	Energy efficiency (h/Joule)
Ubiquitous system Energy constrained and survivability driven	Trillions+	Energy harvesters	μW–mW+	5–40×	>3
Embedded system Energy constrained	Billions+	Batteries	MW–W+	3–5×	<1
Personal mobile Energy and performance constrained	Billions	Batteries	0.1–10W+	2–3×	~0.1
Portable computing Energy and performance constrained	Billions	Batteries + line	10W+	2×+	0.01
Desktop computing Power and performance constrained	Millions	Line	20–100W+	>1×	≪1
High-perf. computing Power constrained	Thousands+	Generators + line	KW–MW+	~1×	≪1

Power/performance (downward arrow, left) — *Energy efficiency* (upward arrow, right)

Figure 11.1   Major computing application domains and their typical system design and optimisation requirements [1–3]

For line-supply-powered computing applications, such as servers and desktop computing systems, performance is achieved by provisioning higher computing resources in the form of many cores. Maximum allowable performance for these systems is formulated using the thermally safe limits of operating clock frequencies [4]. As thermal behaviour is directly related to the power density of the parallel cores, design considerations are dominated by power constraints, which ranges from tens of watts to several megawatts. For battery-powered systems with limited energy, such as portable computing devices and embedded systems, extending operating lifetime is a key requirement [5]. Performance is often compromised in favour of energy minimisation, especially when there is no strict time constraint.

For energy or power minimisation, scaling the supply voltage is a key mechanism as any reduction in voltage decreases power/energy quadratically [6]. However, lower voltage increases the transistor gate delay, which necessitates the operating frequency to be scaling down to a suitable value. This coupling between voltage and frequency, commonly termed voltage/frequency scaling (VFS), is fundamental to energy-efficient computing. A key aspect of achieving energy efficiency is the ability to operate with multiple supply voltages (i.e. V_{dd}), from sub-threshold to super-threshold [7,8]. The V_{dd} range between minimum (V_{min}) to maximum (V_{max}) point also tends to be higher when more controls need to be leveraged for energy efficiency [9]. Significant research has been carried out in the past two decades that deeply embed VFS decisions in circuits and systems at design- and/or run-time [10].

In many embedded systems real-time constraints are common, which can either be hard (i.e. the constraint must be adhered to) or soft (i.e. the constraint can be occasionally violated) [11]. To extend operating lifetime, the energy is typically minimised within the envelope of these constraints. The key aim is to exploit the VFS opportunity dynamically to reduce slack time (i.e. the time between task execution time and its real-time deadline) as best as possible. Figure 11.2 shows a demonstration of performance-constrained energy minimisation in embedded systems.

Swarms of small-scale ubiquitous computing systems, at the scale of trillions, are expected to dominate future generations of data-driven IoT devices [12,13]. Examples include implantables or wearables, cybernetics and *fire-and-forget* systems in smart cities and offices. For low-cost, low-maintenance and light-weight considerations, these systems offer limited feasibility of integrating batteries. In fact, with the development of new energy scavenging devices, there is now considerable interest in developing these systems with harvested energy from the real world through vibration [14], thermal [15], solar or kinetic energy [15,16]. However, harvesting sources have natural fluctuations in their physical properties, which are typically characterised by high variation of the available energy over time [17]. This makes the operation of these devices challenging, particularly when the available energy is unreliable, but the device needs to complete useful computations in part or in full [18].

Given the unprecedented power variations, a desirable property for these emerging systems is to have natural survival instincts defined by the instantaneous energy levels. In other words, they should continue to provide a required computation capacity at limited energy, even if it requires gracefully degrading the computation quality or retaining the computation states for resumption when more energy is available. Biological organisms and systems, such as microbes, work with similar principles as

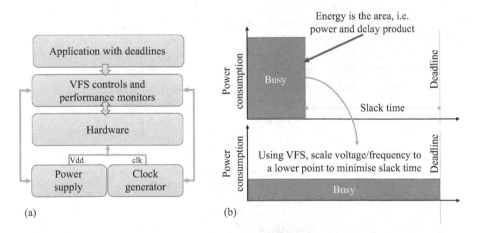

(a)   (b)

Figure 11.2 *(a) Hardware/software interaction in real-time embedded systems, and (b) demonstration of energy minimisation using VFS. The real-time application is annotated with deadlines, which are serviced by exercising the hardware with different VFS options. The VFS options are either pre-characterised or determined at run-time [10]*

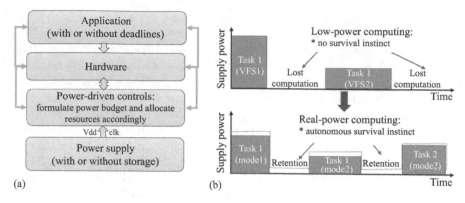

Figure 11.3 (a) A block diagram of real-power computing consisting of feedback based power-constrained control of hardware and software resources, and (b) traditional low-power computing compared to real-power computing. Low-power computing does not guarantee the completion tasks when supply power varies dynamically, leading to lost computation and re-executing the computation tasks at different VFS; real-power computing has autonomous survivability that allows the system to guarantee completion of tasks based on power availability by suitably choosing computation mode [22]

they morph and adapt for carrying out useful synthesis and regenerative processes for their survival under varying sunlight [19].

Traditional low-power computing approaches do not provide such survival instincts under varying supply energy levels [18]. In low-energy situations, these approaches react by scaling operating voltage/frequency to extend lifetime, which does not guarantee retention or completion of computation tasks before the system is depleted of energy [20]. In fact, due to lack of survival instincts, the direct application of existing approach can cause loss of computation in such an event, as shown in Figure 11.3. This calls for a change in the computing paradigm to design computing systems with natural survivability and adaptability instincts going beyond the traditional approaches for dealing with unreliable power supply. Power-driven design and run-time adaptation offer a disruptive paradigm that has promising prospects in terms survivability and energy efficiency under variable supply envelopes. The next section introduces this paradigm as RPC with its definition, manifestations and taxonomies.

11.2 Power-driven computing

For autonomous survivability of computing under variable power envelope, a key question is as follows: *Can we guarantee computation continuum under unreliable power supplies, mitigating computation uncertainties?* One particular form of computational uncertainty is performance uncertainty in terms of the time it takes to perform the computation when power is variable. While we have the definite power level, what we can also have is a definite computation (hardware, algorithm, data and sequence of actions), but with uncertain performance [21]. Another form would be to have both definite power or energy budget and time deadlines, but then accept the possibility of the temporary termination of the computation when either energy or time limits has been reached.

Existing real-time (compute by deadlines) and low-power (prolonging battery life or throttling for power densities) approaches cannot address the computational certainty concerns raised above. However, a simple reversal of design thinking, from power efficient, performance driven to power driven, can address these uncertainties and provide with the envisioned computing continuum. We refer to this new thinking as *RPC*, akin to *real-time computing*, but different in the way instantaneous power is considered as a constraint rather than time constraints derived from the real world. The definition and taxonomies of RPC are stated in the following subsection.

11.2.1   Real-power computing

RPC can be defined as follows [22]:

> *Real-power computing (RPC), or energy-driven computing, describes hardware and software systems subject to a "real-power constraint", for example availability of energy from a power source, or restriction on power dissipation. Real-power applications must guarantee performance within specified power constraints, referred to as "power bands" Systems of this type are linked to the notion of survivability, which depends on their power aspects as well as their ability to morph functional aspects to ensure continued computation. Real-power systems are not simply low-power systems which are optimised to the criterion of minimum power consumption.*

Based on how energy is stored and dispensed, RPC can be classified as hard and soft RPC as described next. The implications of performance constraints are discussed following their definitions.

11.2.1.1   Hard real-power computing

In hard RPC systems, the scavenged power is delivered directly into the circuits and systems, i.e. the system does not have any energy storage. The input power is strictly budgeted by the power delivery mechanism. If the estimated computation power is lower than the power budget, computation is carried out; however, if the estimated power is higher, remaining computation tasks are deferred and current states are retained (Figure 11.4). Examples of hard real-power systems include autonomous cybernetic or signal-processing systems that have to carry out non-critical data sensing and computations. A key requirement for these systems is to have high predictability of supply power so that power scheduling policies can be predetermined at design-time against different power budgets, which we will refer to as power-compute co-design (see Section 11.3).

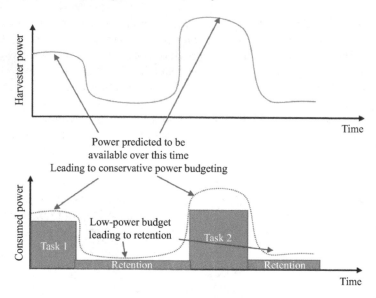

Figure 11.4 *An example demonstration of hard real-power computing for two
tasks. When power is predicted to be available over a time, the system
formulates a strategy to control power with the aim of allowing these
tasks to be carried out, strictly meeting the power budget. However,
when the available energy is low, the system skips computation and
switches to retention mode*

11.2.1.2 Soft real-power computing

Soft RPC has built-in energy buffers (e.g. supercapacitors) with limited capacity.
Unlike hard real-power systems, it does not strictly control computations against
a power budget derived from the scavenged power. Instead, these systems allow for
partial computation to be carried out, even if these violate the power budget. Examples
of soft real-power applications include data ingestion or dynamic sensing systems,
which can tolerate partial loss of periodic computations. Soft RPC systems can use
a combination of power-compute co-design and run-time to maximise computation
continuum (Figure 11.5).

11.2.2 *Performance constraints in power-driven systems*

Besides delivering computation based on the incoming power, some applications
inherently require certainty in performance. This certainty can be ensured by imposing either hard or soft real-time deadlines. With an additional real-time deadline, the
problem of devising power scheduling is reduced to identify the least energy (the product of average power budget and time deadline) that can be parsimoniously utilised
to deliver the best quality of computation (which can be application-dependent).

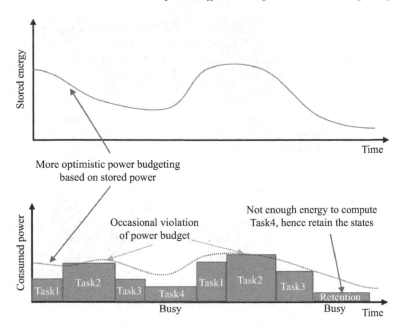

*Figure 11.5   A demonstration of soft real-power computing showing four tasks.
When energy is available, the system proceeds with more optimistic
power budgeting to allow for the tasks to be carried out allowing
occasional violations. When energy level is low, computation states
are retained*

Considering different scenarios, a number of different optimisation taxonomies are given below.

1. *Hard real-power hard real-time computing:* For systems with no energy storage, there exists a variant of computation functionality, when the power budget is higher than the minimum computation power level. The choice of functionality will ensure the best possible computation quality within the power budget and also strictly meet the real-time deadline. When available power is low, the computation is skipped to the next available power cycle.

2. *Hard real-power soft real-time computing:* For systems with no energy storage, there exists a variant of computation functionality, when the power budget is higher than the minimum computation power level. The choice of functionality will ensure the best possible computation quality within the power budget and also approximately meet the real-time deadline, if necessary by completing part of the functionality.

3. *Soft real-power hard real-time computing:* With limited storage for scavenged energy, there exists a variant of computation functionality, which will approximately meet the power budget at any given time. The choice of functionality will ensure that energy consumption is always less than the available stored energy

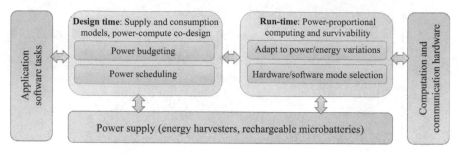

Figure 11.6 A block diagram of the real-power computing paradigm showing
design and run-time considerations for power-constrained controls.
Design-time considerations facilitate power budget formulations at
different available power levels and scheduling the supply power to
the hardware/software mode selection through extensive
characterisations and co-design. For soft real-power systems, this is
often coupled with continuous run-time optimisation to ensure
survivability of the computation tasks under variable energy
availability using hardware/software knobs and feedback monitors

and strictly meet the given real-time deadline, while also providing with the best possible computation quality.

4. *Soft real-power soft real-time computing:* With some storage for scavenged energy, there exists a variant of computation functionality, which will approximately meet the power budget at any given time. The choice of functionality will ensure that energy consumption is always less than the available stored energy and approximately meet the given real-time deadline, while also providing with the best possible computation quality.

Meeting power, performance and quality requirements in RPC can be challenging due to the large system space during optimisation. A systematic and cross-layer approach is needed to reduce this design space through design-time power-compute co-design and co-optimisation, particularly for hard real-power systems. In soft real-power systems, this can be coupled with run-time support for power-driven adaptation as described in Figure 11.6. The design- and run-time optimisation and adaptation aspects are described in the following two sections.

11.3 Design-time considerations

At design-time, the available and computation power levels are modelled and co-optimised through a process called power-compute co-design. It can be defined as *a set of design tools that models the available power and computation/communication power consumptions, thereby deriving efficient power scheduling and co-optimisation policies between them* [22]. The co-design process requires explicitly modelling the supply and consumption powers, followed by the power-proportional scheduling between them, as follows.

11.3.1 Power supply models and budgeting

Energy harvesters typically have large spatial and temporal variations in instantaneous power levels [23]. Understanding and modelling these variations is core to power-driven, RPC. Spatial variation models characterise the power supply voltages and their variations and determine the maximum and minimum operating points [24]. Since harvested power is typically a function of the operating environment, realistic assumptions must be made to derive accurate spatial variation models. Additionally, temporal variations also need to be modelled to establish high predictably of the available energy over a given time. Hard real-power systems can use more pessimistic assumptions of the available energy to avoid any power violation. However, soft RPC can leverage deviations in assumptions to a run-time adaptation problem. Power-supply models are used to design power controllers that can suitably allocate maximum available power as the power budget to govern computation/communication tasks [25].

11.3.2 Power-proportional systems design

To enable RPC, hardware and software systems must be designed to provide computation capability at variable power levels. In other words, the systems must be designed with heterogeneity, which can offer different performance-energy-quality (PEQ) trade-offs for a given functionality. The PEQ trade-offs must also be appropriately reasoned for to facilitate power-scheduling to different computation and communication tasks under different constraints [26]. In the following, the design considerations of these tasks are further detailed.

11.3.2.1 Computation tasks

With a power-driven view, the computation hardware and software must be designed to first establish proportionality in the power envelope. The basic premise is to ensure computation continuum by hardware/software mode selection, essentially leveraging the PEQ trade-offs. When there is a good power availability, it may be more convenient to perform the tasks using high-complexity computing resources for better quality outcomes [27]. However, when the power is scarce, they can be performed by more constrained resourcing policies, gracefully degrading the quality by using low-complexity computing resources [20,27].

Alongside supply power models, the power or energy estimation of the computation tasks needs to be either accurate or approximate, depending on hard or soft RPC. For example, hard real-power systems requires accurate estimation at instruction or micro-architectural level as underestimation can lead to violation of the power budgets imposed by the power controller. Microcontrollers and application-specific integrated circuits (ASICs) typically have deterministic computational behaviour [28], and hence these are well suited for accurate energy-transparency models using worst case power consumption estimations. On the other hand, soft real-power systems can leverage approximations in energy estimations and adapt during run-time. Microprocessors with hierarchical caches and reconfigurable logic circuits and systems tend to exhibit variations in their energy consumptions [29], and as such, they are suitable for power-compute co-design using expected power consumption models.

11.3.2.2   Communication tasks

Communication tasks are carried out in parallel or in an interleaved manner along-side computation [30]. In ubiquitous systems, these tasks are deterministic (in regular patterns of sense, process and communicate data). However, the energy consumption of these tasks can vary due to network behaviour [31]. As such, to generate power or energy models for these tasks, a key requirement is to study the detailed network characteristics (including traffic, channel or network availability and congestion sce-narios) [32]. Based on these characteristics, the expected energy consumed for each of the communication packets can be estimated. Similar to computation tasks, these esti-mations can be carried out optimistically for soft real-power systems or pessimistically for hard real-power systems.

11.3.3   Power scheduling and optimisation

Given the supply and computation power/energy models, power-compute co-design needs to identify the appropriate power scheduling and optimisation policies to ensure that a fixed power budget can be effectively allocated among the computation and communication task/resources. Using these policies, multiple layers of the system architecture can turn on/off at different power levels (see Figure 11.7). As power goes lower, computation at deeper layers (i.e. survival layers with lower accuracy and computation capacity) stay on, while the surface layers (i.e. higher accuracy and more computation capacity) turn off; this is where systems' natural survival instincts come to effect! The more effectively the system manages these layers, the more energy efficient and survivable it is [33].

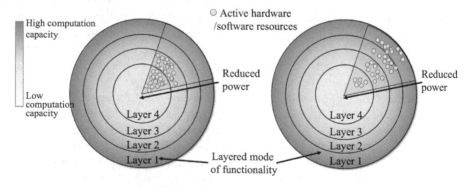

Figure 11.7   Layered mode of computational functionality reacting to two different power budgets. The inner layers have lower computational capacity and hence less power, while the outer layers have higher power/computation capacity

11.4 Run-time considerations

Run-time support is crucial for real-power systems to warrant survivability and continued execution adapting to power variations (see Figure 11.6). Survivability ensures the capability of the system to identify the right energy-level and time to retain the states of computation and continuing when more energy is available. Below, we provide further details of power adaptation and retention, two important aspects of the run-time system.

11.4.1 Adapting to power variations

A given energy, when applied to a computational device, can be converted into a corresponding amount of computation activity by selecting the appropriate mode of computation. Run-time adaptation ensures this through computational mode selection at different power levels (see Section 11.3 and Figure 11.7).

Servicing a known functionality (a set of computation and communication tasks) in different modes and types is a key to achieving power proportionality [20,27]. One mode of this could be computing (and communicating) with heterogeneous resources. These resources can provide similar functionality but with different energy/performance trade-offs. When there is good energy availability, it may be more convenient in terms of controllability, precision and programmability to perform functionality using traditional computing resources, such as CPUs with DSPs. However, when the energy is scarce, similar functionality can be provided through more customised resources, such as FPGAs/ASICs for better quality of service at low energy. The decision of performing computation (and communication) through a resource will be strictly governed by design-time rules and run-time adaptation algorithms built in the system based on the energy availability and proportionality [34,35].

In extreme energy conditions, computing can be challenging using these traditional computing resources. To ensure useful computation (and communication), tasks can still be carried out; the traditional definition of functionality, whereby the output data and their quality can be deterministically related to a given set of input data, will need to be relaxed. This leads to another mode of computing using power-proportional approximate computing. To enable this promising mode, new computational units need be designed to meet the ultra-low-energy computing requirements at gracefully degraded quality of the functionality [36]. The impact of trading quality off in favour of energy can be strictly application specific, and hence these will need to be carefully analysed at design-time during power-compute co-design (see Section 11.3).

11.4.2 Dynamic retention

When power levels become uncertain or scarce, retention becomes incumbent. During such an event, the system will need to 'consciously' switch between a full functionality mode to a low-latency hibernating mode primarily depending on the data processing and application requirements. In traditional computing systems, such switching is carried out through check-pointing process that requires saving the instruction and data states in special purpose registers and memory units. The check-pointing process is governed by a special software routine that is triggered on demand when the system encounters any known hardware/software anomalies.

In RPC systems, traditional approaches of check-pointing can prove challenging due to the following two reasons. First, the requirement to retain data can be aperiodic and on demand, and second, the typical latency of check-pointing can result in diminish returns in terms of energy efficiency and performance [37]. A promising approach to integrating dynamic retention is deeply embedding non-volatile logic or storage registers in the electronic system. This will require additional knobs and controls raised to the system software or firmware.

11.5   A case study of power-driven computing

In this section, we present a case study as an exemplar to demonstrate our research in the development of real-power systems. The study represents a soft real-power system with the aim to maximise computation under variable power supply levels ignoring the impact of delays.

Concurrency in electronic circuits improves computing performance and/or energy efficiency. In this case study, a self-timed micropipeline is designed based on [23] to maximise the amount of compute per energy unit through dynamically variable concurrency. The processing of the data tokens in the micropipeline of a given computation functionality will be favourably completed in part or in full following a power budget derived from the available energy.

A C-element-based micropipeline architecture is shown in Figure 11.8. The elements are connected in an unrolled configuration, feeding the last stage output back to

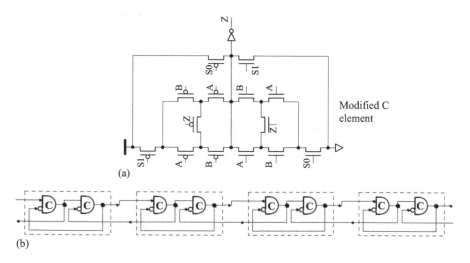

*Figure 11.8   (a) A self-timed, modified C element and (b) micropipeline
architecture with unrolled C elements, featuring set/reset functions*

the first stage input [38]. Each element can be set or reset by S1 or S0 inputs. The data *tokens* are identified as '01' or '10' input to the pair of C elements shown in dashed boxes, while '00' is considered as non-data. Due to causality of events, it is possible to have an old copy of the token, called a *bubble*. As more *tokens* move forward, the *bubbles* move backward. An N-stage pipeline can process $(N - 1)$ maximum number of tokens to free one stage to hold a bubble. Token deadlock takes place when there are N and 0 tokens.

The soft real-power micropipeline is evaluated using a five-stage ring of C-elements. In each experiment, concurrency levels are varied (i.e. 1, 2, 3, 4 tokens) at different voltages (1.0, 0.8, 0.6, 0.4, 0.35, 0.25, 0.2, 0.16 V) with the available energy of 600, 700 and 800 PJ. The resulting amount of computation is counted for each run in terms of a unit, defined as one pulse generated in the pipeline. Figure 11.9 shows the outcome of these experiments.

As can be seen from Figure 11.8, the micropipeline concurrency adapts to the incoming energy levels and the data availability. For example, under 600 PJ @1 V with one data item, the power budget was adjusted to ensure 1,276 computations (Figure 11.9(a)). However, with two data available at the same energy and voltage in each concurrent stage, the power budget and pipeline are set to deliver the highest concurrency (1,299 computations), which is a minor increase. However, the delay reduces by more than 50%.

At the same energy, when V_{dd} drops to 0.8 V, the amount of computations for the most concurrent case increases by 61.7%, with >50% increase in delay and a similar computation outcome. The power budget is 387 μW at 0.8 V compared to 968 μW at 1 V, about a 60% lower. When further reducing V_{dd} to 0.2 V, exhausting the same amount energy, the amount of computation is increased 23 times, and it takes about more than 10,000 times. For the same amount of computation, more than 380 time is required while working at the nominal V_{dd}. In this case, the power figure goes from 968 μW down to 110 nW. Figure 11.9(b) shows the corresponding delay for different computation voltages.

Figure 11.10 demonstrates computations versus concurrency trade-offs at different V_{dd}s with one to four tokens. As can be seen, the maximum computations happens at the same condition of the optimum throughput, which is at $N/2$ tokens when N is even or $(N - 1)/2$ tokens when N is odd; the higher the concurrency, the greater the amount of computation. At the nominal voltage, change from the lowest extreme (four tokens) to the optimum point (two tokens) results in a 5% improvement in computations per unit energy. But at a sub-threshold voltage, the effect on the computation is considerable – nearly 1.7×. Theoretically, at a fixed V_{dd}, under the same amount energy, the optimum case will halve the execution time. Over a shorter period the leakage is lower, which results in the improvement.

The results (Figure 11.10) further suggest that above threshold voltage, the amount of computation per given amount of energy is practically insensitive to the degree of concurrency, but below threshold, the dependency on the degree of concurrency and thereby also the energy efficiency goes up significantly due to the dynamic power adaptation in this case study.

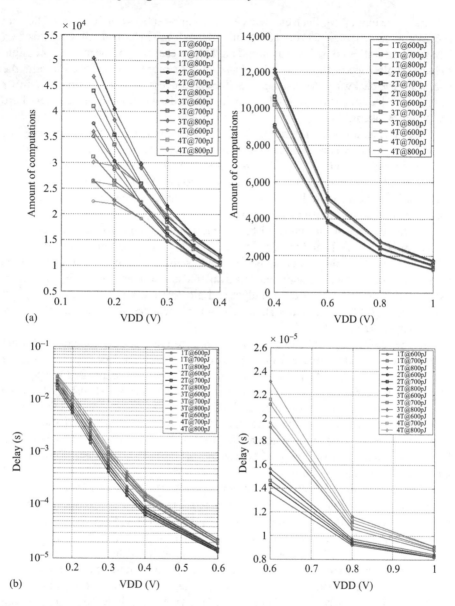

Figure 11.9   (a) Computation at different supply voltage levels and (b) computation latencies for these voltage levels

11.6   Existing research

Power-driven computing has recently received significant attention from academic and industrial research community. Researchers have used the following terminologies in similar vein: transient computing [39–41], power-/energy-neutral

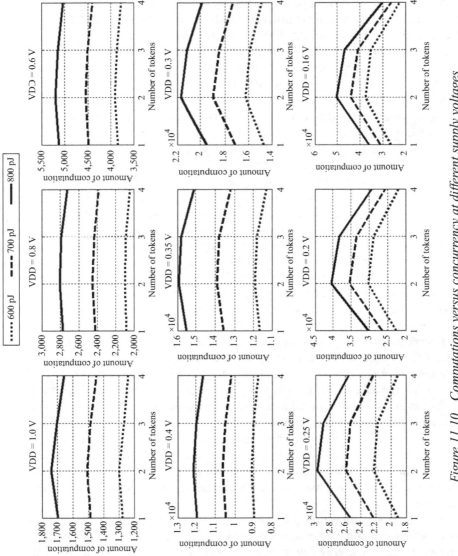

Figure 11.10   Computations versus concurrency at different supply voltages

computing [42], power-/energy-proportional computing [20,43], energy-modulated computing [27], ultra-low-power computing [44] and normally-off computing [45,46]. Their research highlights challenges surfacing around the overall need to design electronic systems with energy or power as the first control derivative [47]. A brief account of previous research works is given as follows.

Balsamo *et al.* proposed a *power-neutral computing* paradigm in [42]. The computation tasks in this system are instantaneously adapted based on available power using dynamic frequency scaling. For an uninterrupted operation, the system also needs to have state retention feature enabled by on-demand check-pointing [48]. A variant of power-neutral computing is energy-neutral computing, which assumes the presence of supercapacitors or small batteries with limited energy storage. Energy-neutral computing needs power controllers that interact with these supercapacitors or batteries to ensure uninterrupted computation under varying energy situations.

Transient computing has been proposed by Gomez *et al.* [41], which refers to opportunistic computing for energy harvesting systems. The aim is to ensure computation and communication tasks can be carried out based on the available energy in the battery or the supercapacitor. Faster wake up and reaction times are critical for transient computing as these allow for better predictions of harvested energy availability [40]. To enable computation at challenging energy levels, the ability to operate at ultra-low-power is also of profound importance [44].

An ultra-low-power microcontroller architecture, named PULP,[1] is proposed by Conti *et al.* in [49] using the principle of transient computing. The processor has built-in parallelisation features, and integrated power controller that can react to energy critical situations with check-pointing support. The check-pointing routine is controlled by a run-time routine, which automatically initiates state retention modes when the power is low [50,51].

Recently *energy- or power-proportional computing* has been proposed using the similar principles of transient computing. The transparency of energy usage profile of every system component is a core component for this power-proportionality [20,27]. The aim is to achieve tighter control over the energy consumption of hardware/ software systems when subjected to different workloads. Liqat *et al.* and Kerrison *et al.* proposed software energy modelling and verification approach using execution statistics together with instruction set architecture (ISA) in [26,52], showing minor deviation with from hardware energy measurements. The model elaborated the impact of different instructions on the hardware components, including processors, arithmetic/logic units, memories and pipelines for multithreaded XMOS-based embedded systems.

Flinn and Satyanarayanan proposed a modelling tool in [53], called *Power-scape*, which can combine execution statistics and hardware instrumentation to generate a detailed energy transparency. Tools like this can reason for better hardware/software energy efficiency using a number of different approaches. For example, a compiler-based approach for optimised register cache sizing for modern

---

[1] http:/www.pulp-platform.org

superscalar processors is proposed in [54]. Using the energy/performance profiles from ISA simulators, the authors demonstrate energy- and performance-proportional architectural optimisations.

Recently, *energy-modulated computing* was proposed by [9,27], which argues that computing systems must have the capability to adapt to input energy constraints. The computation must continue to provide intended functionality of its equivalent even when energy is scarce. Energy-modulated computing capability can be achieved via a layered design with heterogeneous computing resources. When more energy is available, the layer with high-complexity and high-accuracy hardware/software resources is active. However, at low energy, the layer of low-complexity, energy-efficient and less-accurate resources becomes active, powering off the other layers [55] (see Figure 11.7). A key aspect of achieving dynamic controllability in the power-performance envelope is approximate systems design that can operate with variable quality-compromised mode when energy is low [56].

Normally-off computing has been proposed by Nakamura *et al.* [45,46]. Design of computing systems with faster non-volatile memories is a key concept in this mode of computing. When circuits and systems are designed with these memories, they enable aggressive shutting down the computing components when energy/power is low. The power management features are incorporated at micro-architectural-level, providing the system with survivability.

We are already seeing the penetration of survivability-based systems design in industrial products, increasingly following the real-power approach. Two relevant examples are (a) modern smartphones, in which services are reduced progressively when the battery is low or unreliable [57] and (b) autonomous drones or vehicles, in which reduced flying/driving capabilities would still be required to ensure safe landing/parking when the power supply is about to fail [58]. Although these products do not have autonomous survival instincts reacting to instantaneous power supply variations, real-power approach is expected to make this possible.

11.7 Research challenges and opportunities

Power-driven computing in the realm of RPC continues to be an exciting direction for future research and development. The full-scale design and implementation will need concerted efforts across the entire system stack: from power supply controllers to on-chip sensing and from computation/communication hardware to application/system software. In the following subsection, we highlight some important research challenges and opportunities.

11.7.1 Power-proportional many-core systems

The current trend of many-core embedded computing is largely motivated by energy/performance trade-offs. The power envelope for the computing cores is small and as such they do not lend themselves to dynamic power proportionality, which is required to leverage the wider power variations in modern ubiquitous systems. As such, we need to design new heterogeneous architectures that can offer wider power proportionality [59]. Approximate circuits and systems design is a promising direction as low-complexity and low-accuracy circuits can drastically cut down power/energy consumption, with meagre loss of quality [56]. The new architectures will also need to integrate hardware/software support (such as non-volatile registers or tightly coupled flash memories) for faster dynamic retention capabilities.

11.7.2   Design flow and automation

Power-driven management introduced in RPC is clearly a departure from the existing power-agnostic controls. As such, existing electronic design automation (EDA) tools will not be able to meet the needs of the new paradigm, largely due to the power constraints. New design flows and EDA tools will need to be developed to facilitate power-compute co-design, validation and verification. These tools will use power-compute co-design policies to integrate power budgeting as part of the power regulation systems.

11.7.3   On-chip sensing and controls

Real-power systems will need careful instrumentation of on-chip sensors and knobs to tightly couple power scheduling and resource allocation policies based on the incoming power. New knobs and monitors need to be developed to sense the incoming power supply and accurately estimate the power consumption of the hardware and software resources. Moreover, to seamlessly integrate resource allocation and controls, hardware-enabled context-switching methods are needed [47]. The context switching controls can be either reactive [60] or proactive [61,62] using low-cost machine-learning principles.

11.7.4   Software and programming model

New software and programming models are needed that can reason for power schedulability at hierarchical levels (i.e. more accurately at micro-architectural-level and less accurately at architectural-level). These models will consist of a set of annotations and run-time routines. Annotations will dictate the power budgets of modular tasks in heterogeneous computing resources, either statically (for hard real-power systems) or dynamically (for soft real-power systems), while run-time routines will manage the system (and its survivability) based around the given power budgets. Interacting with knobs and monitors will be exposed to the run-time through application programming interfaces.

11.8   Conclusion and future directions

Existing low-power design methods largely use performance-constrained energy minimisation under reliable energy supply. For new generation of ubiquitous systems with highly variable and unreliable energy supply, we need to design and build systems that can operate uninterruptedly under a wide range of power constraints. Underpinning these motivations, we defined and proposed a new, power-driven computing paradigm, named *RPC*. Our definitions have been complemented with different case studies and exemplars, coupled with reflections and experiences from existing research efforts.

Power-/energy-driven computing is a popular research topic. To date, research has made piece-meal advances, considering the hardware and software issues in different silos [27,41–46] (see Section 11.6). Nonetheless, for RPC to make strides towards energy autonomy, significant research efforts are needed with holistic considerations (see Section 11.7). These include design and automation of new hardware architectures, software support at application and run-time layers for cross-layer system management. Unlike traditional low-power systems, the hardware/software coupling in these systems will need to be transparent within and across the layers. In other words, the cost of any resource utilisation at hardware and/or software must be explicitly known. A fundamental approach to achieving this transparency is power-compute co-design discussed in Section 11.3. To match the varying energy constraints, new power delivery and control systems must be designed to operate over a dynamic energy envelope.

Real-power paradigm has a direct relevance to current and future generations of ubiquitous systems. However, we believe that there is a strong impetus for this paradigm to be useful in other computing applications for cost and energy-efficiency considerations. We are already witnessing the emergence of new technologies that are growing without strict cost and energy bounds, such as big data, artificial intelligence and cryptocurrencies. Real-power paradigm can permeate into these technologies with tight control over cost through energy parsimony, i.e. the system optimises computation for a given energy budget.

References

[1] Hong I, Kirovski D, Qu G, *et al.* Power optimization of variable-voltage core-based systems. IEEE Transactions on Computer-Aided Design of Integrated Circuits and Systems. 1999;18(12):1702–1714.

[2] Venkatachalam V, Franz M. Power Reduction Techniques for Microprocessor Systems. ACM Computing Surveys. 2005;37(3):195–237.

[3] Bauer M, Bui N, Jardak C, Nettsträter A. In: Ch. The IoT ARM Reference Manual, in Enabling Things to Talk: Designing IoT solutions with the IoT Architectural Reference Model. Springer, Berlin, Heidelberg; 2013. p. 213–236.

[4] Hardavellas N, Ferdman M, Falsafi B, *et al.* Toward dark silicon in servers. IEEE Micro. 2011;31(4):6–15.

[5] Simunic T, Benini L, De Micheli G. Energy-efficient design of battery-powered embedded systems. IEEE Transactions on Very Large Scale Integration (TVLSI) Systems. 2001;9(1):15–28.

[6] Shafik RA, Al-Hashimi BM, Chakrabarty K. Soft error-aware design optimization of low power and time-constrained embedded systems. In: DATE; 2010. p. 1462–1467.

[7]   Zhai B, Blaauw D, Sylvester D, *et al.* Theoretical and practical limits of dynamic voltage scaling. In: Proc. of the 41st Annual Design Automation Conference (DAC). ACM; 2004. p. 868–873.

[8]   Xia F, Rafiev A, Aalsaud A, *et al.* Voltage, throughput, power, reliability, and multicore scaling. Computer. 2017;50(8):34–45.

[9]   Yakovlev A. Energy-modulated computing. In: Design, Automation & Test in Europe Conference & Exhibition (DATE); 2011. p. 1–6.

[10]   Shafik RA, Yang S, Das A, *et al.* Learning transfer-based adaptive energy minimization in embedded systems. IEEE Transactions on Computer-Aided Design of Integrated Circuits and Systems (TCAD). 2016;35(6):877–890.

[11]   Andrei A, Eles P, Peng Z, *et al.* Energy optimization of multiprocessor systems on chip by voltage selection. IEEE Transactions on Very Large Scale Integration (VLSI) Systems. 2007;15(3):262–275.

[12]   Lyytinen K, Yoo Y. Ubiquitous computing. Communications of the ACM. 2002;45(12):63–96.

[13]   Iyer R, Ozer E. Visual IoT: Architectural challenges and opportunities; toward a self-learning and energy-neutral IoT. IEEE Micro. 2016;36(6):45–49.

[14]   Beeby SP, Torah R, Tudor M, *et al.* A micro electromagnetic generator for vibration energy harvesting. Journal of Micromechanics and Microengineering. 2007;17(7):1257.

[15]   Paradiso JA, Starner T. Energy scavenging for mobile and wireless electronics. IEEE Pervasive Computing. 2005;4(1):18–27.

[16]   Chalasani S, Conrad JM. A survey of energy harvesting sources for embedded systems. In: SouthEastCon. IEEE; 2008. p. 442–447.

[17]   Mateu L, Moll F. Review of energy harvesting techniques and applications for microelectronics (Keynote Address). In: Microtechnologies for the New Millennium 2005; 2005. p. 359–373.

[18]   Raghunathan V, Kansal A, Hsu J, *et al.* Design considerations for solar energy harvesting wireless embedded systems. In: Proc. IPSN. IEEE Press; 2005. p. 64.

[19]   Haruta S, Kanno N. Survivability of microbes in natural environments and their ecological impacts. Microbes and Environments. 2015;30(2):123–125.

[20]   Barroso LA, Hölzle U. The case for energy-proportional computing. Computer. 2007;40(12):33–37.

[21]   Lhermet H, Condemine C, Plissonnier M, *et al.* Efficient power management circuit: From thermal energy harvesting to above-IC microbattery energy storage. IEEE Journal of Solid-State Circuits. 2008;43(1):246–255.

[22]   Shafik R, Yakovlev A, Das S. Real-power computing. IEEE Transactions on Computers. 2018;67(10):1–17.

[23]   Baz A, Shang D, Xia F, *et al.* Energy efficiency of micropipelines under wide dynamic supply voltages. In: 2014 IEEE Faible Tension Faible Consommation; 2014. p. 1–4.

[24]   Weddell AS, Magno M, Merrett GV, *et al.* A survey of multi-source energy harvesting systems. In: DATE. EDA Consortium; 2013. p. 905–908.

[25] Li Y, Henkel J. A framework for estimating and minimizing energy dissipation of embedded HW/SW systems. In: DAC; 1998. p. 188–193.

[26] Liqat U, Kerrison S, Serrano A, *et al.* Energy consumption analysis of programs based on XMOS ISA-level models. In: Intl. Sym. on Logic-Based Program Synth. & Transf.; 2013. p. 72–90.

[27] Ramezani R, Sokolov D, Xia F, *et al.* Energy-modulated quality of service: New scheduling approach. In: Faible Tension Faible Consommation (FTFC), 2012 IEEE. IEEE; 2012. p. 1–4.

[28] Cheng BH, Eder KI, Gogolla M, *et al.* Using models at runtime to address assurance for self-adaptive systems. In: Models@ run. time. Springer; 2014. p. 101–136.

[29] Walker MJ, Diestelhorst S, Hansson A, *et al.* Accurate and stable run-time power modeling for mobile and embedded CPUs. IEEE Transactions on Computer-Aided Design of Integrated Circuits and Systems. 2017;36(1):106–119.

[30] Tozlu S, Senel M, Mao W, *et al.* Wi-Fi enabled sensors for Internet of Things: A practical approach. IEEE Communications Magazine. 2012;50(6):134–143.

[31] Xia F, Yakovlev AV, Clark IG, *et al.* Data communication in systems with heterogeneous timing. IEEE Micro. 2002;22(6):58–69.

[32] Chen YK. Challenges and opportunities of Internet of Things. In: Design Automation Conference, 2012 17th Asia and South Pacific (ASP-DAC). IEEE; 2012. p. 383–388.

[33] Yakovlev A. In: Ch. Enabling Survival Instincts in Electronic Systems: An Energy Perspective, in Transforming Reconfigurable Systems. Imperial College Press, London; 2015. p. 237–263.

[34] Liu Q, Mak T, Luo J, *et al.* Power adaptive computing system design in energy harvesting environment. In: Embedded Computer Systems (SAMOS), 2011 International Conference on. IEEE; 2011. p. 33–40.

[35] Beigne E, Vivet P, Thonnart Y, *et al.* Asynchronous circuit designs for the Internet of Everything: A methodology for ultralow-power circuits with GALS architecture. IEEE Solid-State Circuits Magazine. 2016;8(4):39–47.

[36] Sokolov D, Yakovlev A. Quality of Service in Power Proportional Computing. Newcastle University; 2011.

[37] Chabi D, Zhao W, Deng E, *et al.* Ultra low power magnetic flip-flop based on checkpointing/power gating and self-enable mechanisms. IEEE Transactions on Circuits and Systems I: Regular Papers. 2014;61(6):1755–1765.

[38] Williams TE. Self-timed Rings and Their Application to Division. Stanford, CA, USA; 1991. UMI Order No. GAX92-05744.

[39] Rodriguez A, Balsamo D, Das A, *et al.* Approaches to transient computing for energy harvesting systems.... In: ENSsys 2015; 2015.

[40] Spenza D, Magno M, Basagni S, *et al.* Beyond duty cycling: Wake-up radio with selective awakenings for long-lived wireless sensing systems. In: Computer Communications (INFOCOM), 2015 IEEE Conference on. IEEE; 2015. p. 522–530.

[41]   Gomez A, Sigrist L, Magno M, *et al.* Dynamic energy burst scaling for transiently powered systems. In: DATE; 2016. p. 349–354.

[42]   Balsamo D, Das A, Weddell AS, *et al.* Graceful performance modulation for power-neutral transient computing systems. IEEE Transactions on Computer-Aided Design of Integrated Circuits and Systems. 2016;35(5):738–749.

[43]   Hoffmann H, Sidiroglou S, Carbin M, *et al.* Dynamic knobs for responsive power-aware computing. In: ACM SIGPLAN Notices. vol. 46. ACM; 2011. p. 199–212.

[44]   Abnous A, Rabaey J. Ultra-low-power domain-specific multimedia processors. In: VLSI Signal Processing, IX, 1996 [Workshop on]. IEEE, San Francisco, CA, USA; 1996. p. 461–470.

[45]   Nakada T, Nakamura H. In: Ch. Normally-Off Computing, in Normally-Off Computing. Springer; 2017. p. 57–63.

[46]   Nakada T, Shimizu T, Nakamura H. Normally-off computing for IoT systems. In: SoC Design Conference (ISOCC), 2015 International. IEEE; 2015. p. 147–148.

[47]   Christmann JF, Beigné E, Condemine C, *et al.* Energy harvesting and power management for autonomous sensor nodes. In: DAC. ACM; 2012. p. 1049–1054.

[48]   Balsamo D, Weddell AS, Merrett GV, *et al.* Hibernus: Sustaining computation during intermittent supply for energy-harvesting systems. IEEE Embedded Systems Letters. 2015;7(1):15–18.

[49]   Conti F, Rossi D, Pullini A, *et al.* PULP: A ultra-low power parallel accelerator for energy-efficient and flexible embedded vision. Journal of Signal Processing Systems. 2016;84(3):339–354.

[50]   Tagliavini G, Marongiu A, Rossi D, *et al.* Always-on motion detection with application-level error control on a near-threshold approximate computing platform. In: ICECS. IEEE; 2016. p. 552–555.

[51]   Rusci M, Rossi D, Lecca M, *et al.* An event-driven ultra-low-power smart visual sensor. IEEE Sensors Journal. 2016;16(13):5344–5353.

[52]   Kerrison S, Eder K. Energy modeling of software for a hardware multithreaded embedded microprocessor. ACM Transactions on Embedded Computing Systems (TECS). 2015;14(3):56.

[53]   Flinn J, Satyanarayanan M. Powerscope: A tool for profiling the energy usage of mobile applications. In: Mobile Computing Systems and Applications, 1999. Proc. WMCSA'99. Second IEEE Workshop on. IEEE; 1999. p. 2–10.

[54]   Jones TM, O'Boyle MF, Abella J, *et al.* Energy-efficient register caching with compiler assistance. ACM Transactions on Architecture and Code Optimization. 2009;6(4):13.

[55]   Larsen KG, Laursen S, Zimmermann M. Limit your consumption! Finding bounds in average-energy games. In: Proc. of QAPL, The Netherlands, April 2–3, 2016; 2016. p. 1–14.

[56]   Qiqieh I, Shafik R, Tarawneh G, *et al.* Energy-efficient approximate multiplier design using bit significance-driven logic compression. In: DATE; 2017. p. 7–12.

[57] Elnashar A, El-Saidny MA. Extending the battery life of smartphones and tablets: A practical approach to optimizing the LTE network. IEEE Vehicular Technology Magazine. 2014;9(2):38–49.

[58] Schiller I, Draper JS. Mission adaptable autonomous vehicles. In: Neural Networks for Ocean Engineering, 1991. IEEE Conference on. IEEE; 1991. p. 143–150.

[59] Toffoli T. In: Ch. Action, or the Fungibility of Computation, in Feynman and Computation. Ed. Anthony Hey, Perseus Books, Cambridge, MA, USA; 1999. p. 349–392.

[60] Das A, Shafik RA, Merrett GV, *et al.* Reinforcement learning-based inter-and intra-application thermal optimization for lifetime improvement of multicore systems. In: DAC. ACM; 2014. p. 1–6.

[61] Yang S, Shafik RA, Merrett GV, *et al.* Adaptive energy minimization of embedded heterogeneous systems using regression-based learning. In: PATMOS. IEEE; 2015. p. 103–110.

[62] Das A, Kumar A, Veeravalli B, *et al.* Workload uncertainty characterization and adaptive frequency scaling for energy minimization of embedded systems. In: DATE. IEEE; 2015. p. 43–48.

Part III

System modelling, verification, and testing

Chapter 12

Modelling many-core architectures

Guihai Yan[1], Jiajun Li[1], and Xiaowei Li[1]

Architectural modelling has two primary objectives: (1) navigating the design space exploration, i.e. guiding the architects to arrival at better design choices, and (2) facilitating dynamic management, i.e. providing the functional relationships between workloads' characteristics and architectural configurations to enable appropriate runtime hardware/software adaptations. In the past years, many-core architectures, as a typical computing fabric evolving from the monolithic single-/multicore architectures, have been shown to be scalable to uphold the staggering the Moore's Law. The many-core architectures enable two orthogonal approaches, scale-up and scale-out, to utilize the growing budget of transistors. Understanding the rationale behind these approaches is critical to make more efficient use of the powerful computing fabric.

12.1 Introduction

The research on architectural modelling always goes alone with the architecture evolution over the past two decades. There are two major types of modelling methodologies: (1) simulation-based modelling and (2) regression-based modelling.

The basic principle of simulation-based modelling is to mimic the detailed hardware behaviour given a benchmark (workload). It is more like a "white-box" test bed. The outputs are the corresponding trace of architectural and microarchitectural event statistics such as instruction per cycle (IPC), cache miss rate, branch predictor accuracy, number of cache accesses, memory bandwidth utilization. This style of modelling approach is always represented as kinds of simulators. For instance, SimpleScalar [1] is for modelling superscalar processors, Wattch [2] is for modelling processor power, CACTI [3] is for cache hierarchies, Hotspot [4] is for chip-level thermal distribution, gem5 [5] is for system-level architectural simulation, to name a few. These simulators are basically software products implemented with a mix of high-level programming languages such as C/C++, Python.

Clearly, this style of modelling is quite accurate to model the target architectures, because all of the simulator features are abstracted from their architectural

[1]State Key Laboratory of Computer Architecture, Institute of Computing Technology, Chinese Academy of Sciences, China

counterparts. These simulators can even run the workloads from real application scenarios in a cycle accurate way. However, the advantage on accuracy comes at significant costs. Almost all of these detailed simulators are notorious for high complexity. This fact is inevitable given the modern architectures are already at extremely high complexity. Consequently, these simulators are usually quite slow to execute the benchmarking workloads so that we have to pinpoint some "interested" regions [6] to execute, excepting to keep the simulation in an acceptable time horizon. Another disadvantage of this type of methodology is poor scalability. For example, simulating one core (multicore) in detail can not necessarily extend to multicore (many-core) scenarios because of the absence of the core-level interactions.

In contrast to the white-box simulator, the regression-based methodology is more like a black-box test bed. The primary goal is to build the functions between independent (explanatory) variables (such as the number of cores, the core data path width, and memory bandwidth) and the dependent responses (such as the system-level throughput and performance speedup). However, two fundamental challenges render such models not so gracefully. (1) How to justify the comprehensiveness of independent variables? and (2) How to justify the function between the explanatory and dependent variables?

To some extent, this style of modelling methodology adopts a statistical learning approach, a classical branch of machine learning. These models are built up on rigorous data sampling and learning algorithms. Determining the set of explanatory variables often mingles with the intuitions from experienced architects and therefore is regarded as an empirical, rather than mathematical, process. This 'non-graceful' rationale behind these types of models usually seems not that mathematically solid, but the effectiveness of the result models is undeniable. The regression-based models are intrinsically data-driven approach, and we accept that 'all models are wrong but some are useful'.[1]

Such a regression-based approach has significant advantages over its simulation-based counterpart. First, it is of low complexity because of the intrinsic black-box nature. The low complexity makes the simulation time not a concern any more. Instead, data sampling and model training, which is more manageable than simulation time, would be more critical. The data sampling can be conducted at runtime with various performance counters and program instrumentations [7], and model training can be conducted offline. Second, the models, either parametric or non-parametric, can serve as a 'controller' to guide architectural dynamic optimization. The models can be interpreted as a kind of function between the architectural configuration and resultant performance, and therefore the expected response can be tuned by manipulating the hardware/software configurations.

In this chapter, we focus on the regression-based modelling methodology to study the many-core architectures. Specifically, we will target a more general heterogeneous many-core which has been a hot topic in the computer-architecture community.

---

[1]This is a common aphorism in statistics and is generally attributed to the statistician George Box. In Box's widely cited book *Statistics for Experimenters*, the second edition, published in 2005, was co-authored with William Hunter and J. Stuart Hunter.

Heterogeneous many-core architectures play an increasingly important role in heterogeneous data centres for enhancing power efficiency. Such architectures consist of various types of cores with different microarchitectural configurations but with a single instruction set architecture (ISA) [8], or more radically, with different ISAs. Accelerator-rich architecture [9] stands at an extreme end of the spectrum of the heterogeneous many-core architectures, where each type of core is customized for a specific workload type to maximize the energy efficiency. These cores are dedicated for very specific computing patterns so that some of them even do not have any explicit ISA at all. These issues are supposed to be beyond the scope of this chapter.

This chapter is devoted to study the single-ISA heterogeneous architectures, and, particularly, hctcrogeneous processors comprised many small and few large cores. This type of 'big–LITTLE' architecture [10] can outperform its homogeneous counterparts in terms of performance, power, and energy efficiency in many scenarios [11]. We model such architecture from two orthogonal perspectives: scale-out and scale-up. Note that such perspectives are applicable for modelling not only heterogeneous many-cores but also heterogeneous data centres which host many various computing nodes [12].

The rest of this chapter is organized as follows. First, we introduce the scale-up and scale-out architectural implications. Second, we introduce the approaches to modelling scale-out many-core and scale-up many-core, respectively. Third, we study the interaction between scale-up and scale-out. Finally, we demonstrate how the model can be used for dynamic management.

12.2 Scale-out vs. scale-up

In many-core context, scale-out implies more core-level parallelism such as from 2×2 scale to 4×4 scale of cores, as Figure 12.1 shows. The goal of scale-out is always associated with the quest for coarse-grained (e.g. thread-level) parallelism. Scale-out is also represented as the 'horizontal' scalability which is of low design and implementation overhead.

By contrast, scale-up always implies more aggressive single-thread performance with more sophisticated microarchitecture innovations such as instruction dynamic scheduling, sophisticated cache hierarchy, data prefetch, VLIW (very long instruction word) techniques. For these reasons, the scale-up, a.k.a. 'vertical' scalability, is always associated with high complexity, low marginal benefits, and poor scalability.

In some words, scale-out tends towards multithread performance, while scale-up towards single-thread performance. Both orientations are attractive but each with very different 'utility' functions and applicable conditions. Empirically, the cost of scale-out approach is more scalable than that of scale-up approach, but the roof of performance for the non-parallel applications is hard to elevate by scale-out approach. By contrast, the scale-up is viable for the non-parallel workloads even though at the expense of usually disproportional cost. Hence, we cannot reach any meaningful conclusions without specifying the workload characteristics and optimizing objective functions.

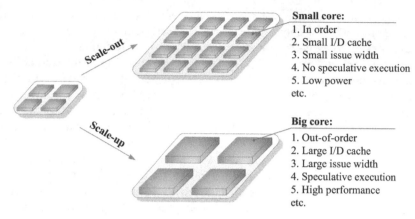

Small core:
1. In order
2. Small I/D cache
3. Small issue width
4. No speculative execution
5. Low power
etc.

Big core:
1. Out-of-order
2. Large I/D cache
3. Large issue width
4. Speculative execution
5. High performance
etc.

Figure 12.1   Conceptual view of scale-out and scale-up

Note that even the scale-out and scale-up are conceptually orthogonal to each other, but this merit may not perfectly hold in practise because the workload-threading seldom only affects the number of threads without involving subtle thread interactions. Take the speedup ratio Φ as an example, which comes from the scale-out speedup α and scale-up speedup β, we have

$$\Phi = \alpha \times \beta + \varepsilon(\alpha, \beta), \tag{12.1}$$

where ε is a higher order component determined by specific scale-out and scale-up configurations. However, we find that to accurately model ε is very hard, if not totally impossible. Fortunately, we find the subtle component is relative small so that the orthogonality assumption is approximately hold, which can greatly simplify the modelling process. Section 12.5.1 will give an in-depth discussion.

12.3   Modelling scale-out many-core

In this section, we describe two popular regression approaches to modelling scale-out many-core: (1) composable performance regression (CPR) and (2) α model.

12.3.1   CPR model

The overview of CPR [13] is shown in Figure 12.2. CPR uses the combination of three models to estimate the multiprocessor performance: (1) the uniprocessor model, (2) the contention model, and (3) the penalty model. First, CPR uses the uniprocessor model to predict the baseline performance of each core. At the same time, the contention model is used to predict the interfering accesses from the other cores. Finally, the outputs of the uniprocessor and contention model are composed by a penalty model to produce the final multiprocessor performance estimate.

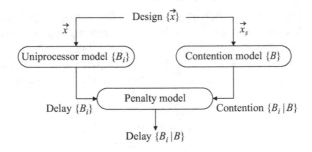

Figure 12.2 The overview of CPR [13]

Specifically, in Figure 12.2, $\vec{x}$ denotes the vector of parameter values that characterize a design, while $\vec{x}_s \subset \vec{x}$ is a sub-vector of $\vec{x}$ in which the values characterize the resources shared between processors. When an n-core multiprocessor executes a set of benchmarks, denoted as $B = \{B_1, \ldots, B_n\}$, the CPR framework iteratively predicts the performance of each benchmark. For example, consider that B_i is executed on the core of interest, while the other benchmarks $B_{\neq i} = \{B_1, \ldots, B_{i-1}, B_{i+1}, \ldots, B_n\}$ are all contending with B_i. Under this condition, CPR predicts the baseline uniprocessor performance of B_i executing on design $\vec{x}$ and meanwhile predicts contention indicators for B_i when it contends with $B_{\neq i}$ for shared resources $\vec{x}_s$. Finally, CPR uses a penalty model to compute a linear combination of baseline performance and contention indicators to estimate the performance of B_i when contending with $B_{\neq i}$ benchmarks in a symmetric multiprocessor with n cores of design $\vec{x}$.

12.3.2 α Model

Another approach to modelling the scale-out speed-up is α model [14], which assumes that the scale-out speed-up of many-core architectures is only determined by multithreading configuration. The α model is defined as the performance of target multithreading configuration over current multithreading configuration on the same type of cores:

$$\alpha = \frac{T_{current}}{T_{target}}, \tag{12.2}$$

where T is the execution time on current and target multithreading configuration, respectively. Generally,

$$T = T_{serial} + T_{parellel} + T_{penalty}, \tag{12.3}$$

where T_{serial} is the serial portion, which determines the upper bound of scale-out speed-up [15]. $T_{parallel}$ is the parallel portion, which can be eaten away by spawning more threads. For on-line usage, T_{serial} and $T_{parallel}$ can be accurately obtained by loop-peeling method [16] that finishes executions repeatedly and learns the ratio of the serial portion, or, instrumentation technique [17] that inserts bottleneck-identification instructions at the entry and exit of serial and parallel portions to record elapsed cycles. As the distinctive part of α model, multithreading overhead $T_{penalty}$ indeed reveals the bottleneck of scale-out speed-up [17]. It is determined by (1) synchronization contentions, such as inter-thread locks and barriers, and (2) communication contentions, happened on communication-related hardware resources such as Last Level Cache (LLC), memory controller, and shared memory buses. Unfortunately, how to accurately model $T_{penalty}$ is still an open question.

One feasible solution is using univariate analysis. First, we assume a contention-free scenario by over-provisioning communication-related hardware resources, and then study the performance impact only from synchronization contentions. Figure 12.3(a) shows the relationship between time penalty and number of threads. We choose the applications with the largest amounts of lock and barrier synchronizations. No matter what type of synchronization happens, the penalty can be tracked and returned by the bottleneck-identifying instructions (`BottleneckCall`, `BottleneckReturn` and `BottleneckWait`) already used in [17]. Basically, the penalty correlates linearly with thread number, even though with different slope owing to different intensity of locks and barriers. The more synchronization operations are involved, the steeper the slope is. For example, both contention-intensive `freqmine` and `fluidanimate` exhibit steeper slopes. Hence, we reckon that $T_{penalty} \propto a_1 \times k_1 \times n$. The n is the thread number. The k_1 represents the synchronization intensity measured by synchronization-induced waiting cycles per kilo-instructions (SPKI). SPKI is calculated by accumulating the penalties from both locks and barriers. The a_1 is a modulating constant.

Second, we tight the communication-related hardware resources to match the reality by logging the stall cycles from communication contentions. The communication-related hardware resources include Translation Look-aside Buffer (TLB), Network on Chip (NoC), memory controller, bus, disk, etc. The communication contention-induced penalty is measured by the incremental penalty over the hardware resource-unlimited scenario. Unlike in synchronization contention scenario,

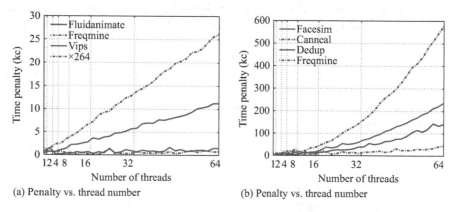

(a) Penalty vs. thread number

(b) Penalty vs. thread number

Figure 12.3   The absolute time penalty from (a) synchronization contentions and (b) communication contentions

we choose the applications with highest communication intensity, e.g. with the largest working set. We find that contention-induced penalty increases much faster with increasing thread number n, roughly following a quadratic trend, as Figure 12.3(b) shows. Hence, inspired by the this trend, we extrapolate that $T_{penalty} \propto a_2 \times k_2 \times n^2$. The quadratic trend is fitted by the term n^2. k_2 is miss-induced waiting cycles per kilo-instructions (MPKI). Because there are always misses happened before communication-related contentions, MPKI can faithfully take the communication intensity into account. It proportionally weighs the quadratic trend. MPKI is obtained by aggregating the penalty of L1 miss, LLC miss, TLB miss, and page fault trans-action. Note that MPKI is a time-varying, online-obtained parameter, so MPKI can capture communication contention variations over application phases changing. a_2 is a modulating constant and obtained by offline regression.

So far, the overall penalty can be obtained by combining above synchronization-related penalty and communication-related penalty,

$$T_{penalty} = a_0 \times k_0 + a_1 \times k_1 \times n + a_2 \times k_2 \times n^2, \tag{12.4}$$

where k_0 is an application-specific bias gotten by redundant computations [18]. For PARSEC benchmark, we use line of code in the parallel region of interest to substitute the redundant computations. It is obtained offline and modulated by a_0.

12.4   Modelling scale-up many-core

The scale-up approach boosts power efficiency by enabling thread migration between heterogeneous many-cores. The heterogeneous many-core architectures are typically composed of small (e.g. in order) power-efficient cores and big (e.g. out-of-order) high-performance cores. The effectiveness of heterogeneous multicores depends on how well a scheduler can map workloads onto the most appropriate core type. In general, small cores can achieve good performance if the workload inherently has high levels of instruction level parallelism (ILP). On the other hand, big cores provide good performance if the workload exhibits high levels of memory level parallelism (MLP) or requires the ILP to be extracted dynamically. Hence, accurate models for scale-up many-core are also highly required. In this section, we describe two popular approaches: (1) performance impact estimation (PIE) and (2) β model.

12.4.1   PIE model

PIE [19] is a runtime statistics-based model to estimate performance differences between small in-order and big out-of-order cores. PIE is established on the differ-ent design characteristics of big and small cores. Specifically, big cores are usually designed for the workloads that have a large amount of MLP, while small cores are particularly suitable for workloads which contain intensive inherent ILP. This differ-ence implies that the performance on the two types of cores can be estimated by the amount of MLP and ILP prevalent in the workload. For example, memory-intensive workloads usually require big cores and will incur significant slowdown on small cores if they do not expose MLP. Meanwhile, compute-intensive workloads with intensive ILP may have reasonable performance degradation and need not require big cores. Hence, PIE estimates the workload performance on different core types by analysing the workload characteristics. Specifically, PIE accomplishes this by using cycle per instruction (CPI) stacks, which contain two major components: the base component and the memory component; the former lumps together all non-memory related components:

$$CPI = CPI_{base} + CPI_{mem}. \tag{12.5}$$

It has been confirmed by experiments that MLP and ILP ratios can provide good indicators on the performance difference between big and small cores. Therefore, PIE collects CPI stack, MLP and ILP profile information, to develop the model (see Figure 12.4). Specifically, PIE estimates the performance on a small core while executing on a big core in the following manner:

$$\begin{aligned}
CPI_{small} &= \widetilde{CPI}_{base\_small} + \widetilde{CPI}_{mem\_small} \\
&= \widetilde{CPI}_{base\_small} + CPI_{mem\_big} \times MLP_{ratio}.
\end{aligned} \tag{12.6}$$

Similarly, the performance on a big core while executing on a small core is estimated as follows:

$$\begin{aligned}
CPI_{big} &= \widetilde{CPI}_{base\_big} + \widetilde{CPI}_{mem\_big} \\
&= \widetilde{CPI}_{base\_big} + CPI_{mem\_small}/MLP_{ratio}.
\end{aligned} \tag{12.7}$$

In the above formulas, $\widetilde{CPI}_{base\_big}$ denotes the base CPI component on the big core estimated from the execution on the small core; $\widetilde{CPI}_{base\_small}$ is defined similarly. The memory CPI component on the big (small) core is computed by dividing (multiplying)

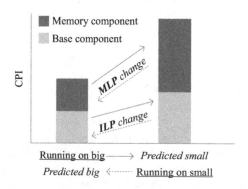

Figure 12.4   Illustration of the PIE model [19]

the memory CPI component measured on the small (big) core with the MLP ratio. MLP and ILP ratios are defined as follows:

$$MLP_{ratio} = \frac{MLP_{big}}{MLP_{small}} \tag{12.8}$$

$$ILP_{ratio} = \frac{CPI_{base\_big}}{CPI_{base\_small}} \tag{12.9}$$

with MLP defined as the average number of outstanding memory requests if at least one is outstanding, and CPI_{base} as the base (non-miss) component of the CPI stack.

12.4.2 β Model

Another approach to modelling the scale-out speed-up is β model [14]. β model uses single thread's average CPI of an application with the same thread number as the performance metric. Based on the definition, we have

$$\beta = \frac{CPI_{current}}{CPI_{target}}. \tag{12.10}$$

Given a multithreaded application, the primary goal is to accurately predict its single thread's average CPI on different types of cores.

Similar to PIE, the β model also relies on the change of ILP and MLP to differentiate heterogeneous cores but builds a more essential analytical model with them. Although CPI is also impacted by other architectural components, β model prefers embracing these two principal components to make a trade-off between the accuracy and complexity for on-line usage.

The β model is approximated with a power-exponent law based on the following observation. We first hold W and study the CPI sensitivity to R. As Figure 12.5(a) shows, the CPI reduction gets less significant with larger reorder buffer (ROB) size. Initially, CPI reduces dramatically when ROB size is smaller than 32 entries but quickly flats out when ROB size increases beyond 32 entries. This trend can be

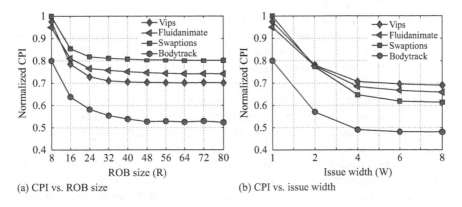

(a) CPI vs. ROB size   (b) CPI vs. issue width

Figure 12.5 The relative performance impact from (a) ROB size R and (b) issue width W

Table 12.1   Model parameters

Coefficients	Description	Value	Implementation
a_0	Modulating constant	1.837e−003	Offline regression
a_1	Modulating constant	0.05312	Offline regression
a_2	Modulating constant	−2.025e−005	Offline regression
k_0	Redundant computing	Volume of parallel codes	Offline measurement
k_1	Synchronization intensity	Synchronization waiting cycles per kilo-instructions	Bottleneck instructions recording
k_2	Communication intensity	Miss-induced waiting cycles per kilo-instructions	Performance counters reading
b_0	Modulating constant	0.2837	Offline regression
b_1	Modulating constant	1.1675	Offline regression
b_2	Modulating constant	1.8427	Offline regression
i	Formula bias	Intrinsic CPI	CPI_{base}
m	Memory intensity	CPI_{mem}/CPI	CPI stack calculation
c	Computing intensity	CPI_{base}/CPI	CPI stack calculation
μ	Modulating constant	0.2046	Offline regression
$P_{W,R}$	Maximum power	Platform dependent	Offline measurement

approximated well by a power law. We then hold R and study the CPI sensitivity to W. As Figure 12.5(b) shows, CPI also decreases along with issue width increasing. This trend fits an exponential function well (with negative exponent). Therefore, we build a new CPI prediction model for core heterogeneity, as (12.11) shows

$$CPI = i + m \times R^{-c \times W}. \tag{12.11}$$

Equation (12.11) is in accordance with prior knowledge: the marginal performance will decrease (with lower slope of CPI) when running on more aggressive cores, because larger machine parallelism (larger issue width, ROB size, etc.) mismatches the available program parallelism (inherent instruction parallelism and concurrent memory access, etc.) [20,21].

Meanwhile, the performance sensitivity to W and R shows subtle difference. For instance, if front-end capacity (represented by W) is too small, saying 1 or 2, and then expanding back end (represented by R) will be ineffective. That is because the pipeline becomes unbalance if instructions issued in front-end underfeed the back end. Thus, we put W in exponent function instead of power function in (12.11), because exponent function can show higher first-order gradient than power function in most cases, which is appropriate for modelling front-end performance impact.

Coefficient m and c are two application-specific constants. They correlate with memory (or communication) intensity and computing intensity, respectively. As Figure 12.5(a) shows, comparing to `fluidanimate`, the CPI of `vips` is more sensitive to R, i.e. shows deeper slope, because `vips` is more memory intensive than `fluidanimate`. Meanwhile, m, the coefficient of R, scales the effect of R. Based on first-order derivative, the deeper the slope, the bigger the m. Likewise, in Figure 12.5(b), `swaptions`, a financial analysis benchmark with higher computing intensity, is more sensitive to W. c, the coefficient of W, scales the effect of W. The deeper the slope, the bigger c. Hence, m and c are weights, weighing the memory and computing intensity, respectively. Moreover, i represents an application's intrinsic CPI. In Figure 12.5, `bodytrack`, with similar ratio of computing and memory intensity to `fluidanimate`, shows a steady lower bias. The higher intrinsic CPI, the larger i. Thus, it serves as a bias of CPI.

These coefficients are calculated as follows. Given that the CPI comes from the sum of two components: CPI_{base}, the base CPI without any stalls from memory access and CPI_{mem}, the penalty of data waiting or pipeline stalls [22]. We define

$$\eta = \frac{CPI_{mem}}{CPI_{mem} + CPI_{base}} \tag{12.12}$$

to reveal the memory-related overhead in CPI. Then, m can be calculated by

$$m = b_1 \times \eta \tag{12.13}$$

which highlights the memory intensity. It implies that the memory intensity linearly correlates with CPI, no matter which type of cores is used. c is calculated by

$$c = b_2 \times (1 - \eta), \tag{12.14}$$

which negatively weighs the computing intensity on the exponent. As c is the coefficient of issue width W and scales the effectiveness of W, the calculation of c implies that the CPI of computing intensive application can be reduced more by powerful front end. Bias i reflects the intrinsic CPI once running on oracle core with infinite R and W [20,23]. It is approximated by CPI_{base} in this paper, calculated by $b_0 \times CPI_{base}$. b_0, b_1 and b_2 are modulating constants.

12.5 The interactions between scale-out and scale-up

Scale-out and scale-up can change performance and power profile in different ways and to different application-specific extents. This section presents the interactions between them. First of all, the relationship between scale-out and scale-up is better explained with the following example.

Figure 12.6(a) shows a typical heterogeneous many-core architecture [11] built by gem5 full-system simulator [5]. It is consisted of three types of cores – A (issue width: 8; ROB size: 128), B (issue width: 6; ROB size: 96), and C (issue width: 4; ROB size: 64), clustered on one piece of silicon. Core details are listed in Table 12.2. A cluster is interconnected with 2-D mesh NoC, which also provides communication fabric to main memory and I/O devices. The banked LLC and the peripheral memory controllers are logically centralized but physically distributed. Figure 12.6(b) illustrates the α (X-axis) and β (Y-axis) with four representative PARSEC benchmarks [18]. Supposing current state is 8-threads on core C, then we study α and β under target states of 16 and 32 threads on core B and core A, respectively.

The results in Figure 12.6(b), called Φ space, illustrate how the overall performance responds to scale-out and scale-up configurations, respectively. Taking the

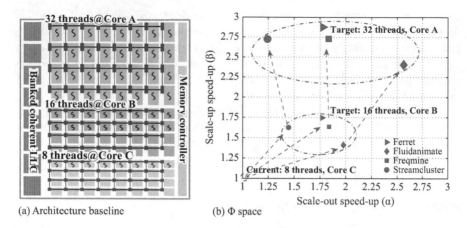

(a) Architecture baseline　　　(b) Φ space

Figure 12.6　(a) An illustrative example of heterogeneous many-core architecture and (b) Φ space: scale-out speed-up (α) and scale-up speed-up (β)

Table 12.2　Microarchitectural parameters

Parameter	OoO	In order
Issue width	8(A), 6(B), 4(C)	1(D), 2(E), 4(F)
ROB size	128, 96, 64	8 (constant)
I/D cache	64 KB, 2-way	32 KB, direct
I-L1/D-L1 access time	2/4 ns	2/4 ns
LLC access/miss time	12/54 ns	12/54 ns
Branch predictor	Hybrid 2-level	Static, 2k

fluidanimate, for example, when state changes from 8-threads to 16-threads on core C, the scale-out way boosts performance by about 2×, while changing from core C to core B with 8-threads, the scale-up speed-up contributes to about 1.4×. Surprisingly, if changing from current state of 8-threads with core C to target state of 16-threads with core B, overall performance speed-up approximates to 2.8× (i.e. 2×1.4). Also, we run lots of other cases with different applications and scale-out/scale-up configurations, and all their results confirm that the overall performance approximates the product of scale-out and scale-up speed-up.

The Φ space illustrates that different multithreaded applications show diverse scale-out and scale-up speed-up. It also clearly indicates how to improve the overall performance. First, according to the Amdahl's Law [24], spawning more threads not necessarily yields higher scale-out speed-up. For example, multithreading from 16-threads to 32-threads brings no speed-up for ferret, freqmine and even hurts the performance of streamcluster. Second, choosing more powerful cores does improve scale-up speed-up, but to application-specific extents because of their diverse boundness to computing or memory intensity [19].

12.5.1 Φ *Model*

The α model and the β model are orthogonal to each other, which makes the overall performance modelling a trivial issue: the resultant performance speed-up, Φ, can be readily modelled by the product of α and β, according to the following equation:

$$\Phi = \alpha \times \beta. \tag{12.15}$$

The key advantage of the orthogonality assumption is to greatly simplify the prediction: scale-out and scale-up speed-up can be totally regarded as two independent performance boosting ways, obtained just by profiling the performance impact to multithreading, and core heterogeneity, respectively.

Actually, scale-out and scale-up speed-up are occasionally correlated to each other, because the synchronization happened in multithreading inevitably interferes each thread's behaviour, which further impacts scale-up speed-up. For example, lots of locks between the threads can result in high overhead of thread waiting, which increases the CPI of all threads and therefore hurts the effectiveness of scale-up. Nonetheless, we confirm that scale-out and scale-up are nearly orthogonal to each other. The error brought by orthogonality assumption is small, which is validated by the following experiments.

Figure 12.7(a) illustrates the cumulative distribution function of Φ model's errors. The results (up to 1,080 configurations randomly picked out from whole population: $633{,}600 \times 18{,}000$) show that for most benchmarks, applying Φ model always results in less than 10% prediction error, or for more than 80% samples of `facesim`, `fluidanimate`, and 90% samples of `blackscholes`, `x264`. The average error (dash-dotted line) is below 12%. Although Φ has shown to be more comprehensive and accurate than state-of-the-art models, we should note that Φ is not perfect. In some corner cases, the prediction error is up to 30% and even higher, such as `dedup`, `swaptions`.

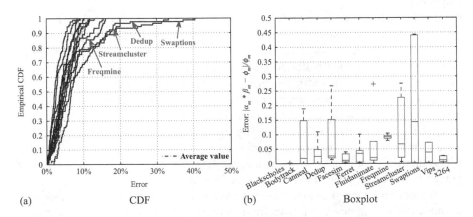

(a) CDF (b) Boxplot

Figure 12.7 *(a) The cumulative distribution function (CDF) of Φ model error and (b) evaluate the orthogonality between α and β*

12.5.2   *Investigating the orthogonality assumption*

The main error derives from the orthogonality assumption. Although we deliberately assume that α and β are completely orthogonal to each other, α and β are often weakly correlated. Figure 12.7(b) evaluates the orthogonality between α and β. In each interval, we measure the three kinds of speed-up by gem5 simulator, i.e. α_m, β_m, and Φ_m. If α and β are orthogonal, then $|\alpha_m \times \beta_m - \Phi_m|$ should be zero. Hence, we use the normalized correlation *Cor* defined by

$$Cor = \frac{|\alpha_m \times \beta_m - \Phi_m|}{\Phi_m} \tag{12.16}$$

to evaluate the orthogonality.

First, we run one thread on baseline core A and then T threads on core A. By measuring the billions instructions per second (BIPS), we can obtain the scale-out speed-up α_m. Second, we run one thread on core B and measure the scale-up speed-up β_m by using BIPS. Finally, measuring the speed-up of T threads on core B can obtain the overall speed-up Φ_m. Following this measurement, we randomly sample 2,268 cases from the 12 benchmarks. The results are shown in Figure 12.7(b) with 'boxplot' which show central mark for median, interquartile range, and possible outliers. These results justify our orthogonality assumption; the *Cor* values are below 5% for most benchmarks.

The prominent non-orthogonal cases happen on swaptions, stream cluster and dedup, whose results are in line with their performance errors in Figure 12.7(a). We say that the more impact on the average CPI of threads from multithreading, the higher error of orthogonality assumption, which is further explained.

The scale-up speed-up definition is single thread' average CPI on current cores over the one on target cores under the same number of threads. However, if target thread number is changed, the average CPI on target cores will be inevitably impacted. The impact degree determines application's synchronization and memory contentions, respectively.

Let us analyse swaptions first which shows the largest error in Figure 12.7(a) and the weakest independence in Figure 12.7(b). The swaptions threads have few locks and no barriers at all, which makes itself appropriate to do multithreading. However, swaptions has coarse-grained data-parallelism (memory contention). This leads to heavy cache traffic that grows very fast as thread number increases. For example, spawning too many threads can easily result in severe access contentions of memory controllers and buses. Its threads hence suffer more waiting cycles, which inevitably increases their CPI. Differently, the threads of streamcluster and dedup have too large amount of synchronization primitives (locks and barriers). When increasing thread number, threads' waiting overheads from synchronization gradually dominant, which in turn increases their average CPI.

To sum up, since β model does not have the variable of thread number n, it cannot explicitly capture CPI impact from memory and synchronization contentions. Nonetheless, the results in Figure 12.7(b) confirm that the orthogonality assumption is a good approximation.

12.6 Power efficiency model

The growing energy cost and thermal concern are leading the quest of higher power efficiency [25–28]. Generally, power efficiency is defined as the ratio of performance and power [24]. When multithreaded application changes from current to target configuration, its power efficiency speed-up, denoted as γ, is expressed by

$$\gamma = \frac{E_{target}}{E_{current}} = \frac{Perf_{target}}{Perf_{current}} \times \frac{P_{current}}{P_{target}}, \tag{12.17}$$

where E_{target} and $E_{current}$ are the power efficiency of target and current configuration; $Perf_{target}$ and $Perf_{current}$ are the performance in BIPS, for example, $P_{current}$ and P_{target} are the average power. The performance speed-up $Perf_{target}/Perf_{current}$ is calculated by Φ model, while $P_{current}/P_{target}$ remains a question to be addressed—that is the purpose of the power modelling detailed as follows.

12.6.1 Power model

Power modelling is also very challenging. For example, multithreading and thread migration can change the number and types of active cores, the communication between cores, and the core utilization. Every factor can result in power variation of the heterogeneous many-cores.

The average power consumption of a multithreaded application can be calculated by the cumulated energy over the elapsed time [29]. Figure 12.8(a) exemplifies the power trace of a four-thread application during consecutive serial and parallel phases. Assume that each thread occupies one core at a time (assuming the core with simultaneous multithreaded support is also possible at higher complexity), and thread stalling is only caused by lock-based synchronization.

In the beginning of serial portion, when slave threads have not been spawned, the power is only consumed by one master thread and therefore relatively low. Once it enters the parallel portion where four threads are spawned, the power instantly quadruples because four cores are active. Then these threads compete for a critical section in parallel portion; only one thread can execute at a time and the other three become stalling [16,17]. The power therefore drops immediately, because the power of stalling is much smaller than the power of executing [30].

The above example clearly indicates how to model the power. For multithreaded application i with n threads, its average power consumption P_i can be calculated by

$$P_i = \frac{P_{ex}T_{serial} + nP_{ex}T_{parallel} + (P_{ex} + (n-1)P_{st})T_{penalty}}{T}, \tag{12.18}$$

where T_{serial}, $T_{parallel}$, $T_{penalty}$ and T have been all described in (12.3). P_{ex} and P_{st} are thread's average power in executing and stalling state, respectively.

Ma *et al.* proposed a simple and efficient way to model P_{ex} and P_{st}. Intuitively, bigger core exhibits higher P_{ex} and P_{st} and they positively correlate with the computing intensity. Specifically, P_{ex} and P_{st} are determined by (1) the intrinsic power of heterogeneous cores and (2) the computing intensity in execution and stall. First, they

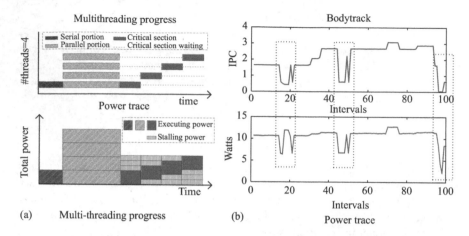

Figure 12.8 *(a) An example of multithreading progress with corresponding power trace. The thread stalling is only caused by lock-based synchronization between threads. (b) We observe the parallel portion of bodytrack for 100 continuous intervals (10 ms per interval) with four threads spawned. The IPC and power are sampled from one core of a Xeon E5335 like quad-core processor*

introduce a hardware-dependent constant to represent the core's maximum power. As issue width W and ROB size R are two representative parameters [19], they denote core's maximum power as $P_{W,R}$. Second, because maximum power is only achieved in theoretically maximum computing intensity, the actual executing and stalling power is proportional to the actual computing intensity. P_{ex} and P_{st} hence can be calculated as

$$P_{ex} = \theta_{ex}P_{W,R}, \quad P_{st} = \theta_{st}P_{W,R}, \tag{12.19}$$

where θ_{ex} and θ_{st} are proportion factors that represent the ratio of instant computing intensity to maximum theoretical computing intensity. Meanwhile, they are application specific; the larger the θ, the more intensive computation.

For describing the proportion factors, we refer to the contribution of Jacobson *et al.* [31]. They find a core's runtime power strongly correlates to its IPC. Conversely, when a thread is stalling, its IPC declines a lot, and the power also comes down. Therefore, proportion factors θ are determined by IPC, that is $\theta = \mu IPC$, where μ is the modulating constant. This expression can capture power variation induced by thread migration between heterogeneous cores and also differentiates the power in execution and stall. Figure 12.8(b) confirms this positive correlation between IPC and power. We can see that the trace of IPC and the trace of power are correlated well.

Although only correlating IPC to proportion factor is a first order approximation [32,33], IPC is the most comprehensive data to reflect the utilization of power-hungry components. Meanwhile, the simplicity of the formula can greatly facilitate the online usage where heavy computational complexity is unaffordable because of real-time constraint.

12.6.2 Model calculation

Compared to Φ model, power model is easier to implement, because all its variables can be reused from the performance model. First, the time-related terms T_{serial}, $T_{parallel}$, $T_{penalty}$, and T have been obtained in α model. Second, as the CPI has been used in calculating η of β model (Equation (12.12)), the IPC required by proportion factors can be calculated as $1/(CPI_{base} + CPI_{mem})$. The maximum power $P_{W,R}$ can be obtained offline with power virus benchmarks [34].

So far, we can see that the power efficiency, composed by the performance and power model, is the function of thread number n, issue width W, and ROB size R. All the coefficients are easy to obtain on the fly, as detailed in Table 12.1. Before presenting the model validation results, we shall demonstrate the runtime usage of these models in the next section.

12.7 Runtime management

With the preparation of performance and power models for many-core architectures, this section further demonstrate the runtime management that exploits both scale-up and scale-out to boost power efficiency.

A generic runtime management for heterogeneous many-cores can be divided into three steps:

- Step 1: Predict performance speed-up and power efficiency improvement.
- Step 2: Invoke scheduling algorithm to figure out the optimal scale-out and scale-up configurations for power efficiency.
- Step 3: The operating system (OS) triggers the corresponding configurations of multithreading and thread migration.

The models presented in the previous sections take charge of the first step. To demonstrate the model application in the second step, two scheduling algorithms are presented to explore maximum performance and power efficiency. The third step is a basic OS functionality and is detailed in Section 12.7.3.

12.7.1 MAX-P: performance-oriented scheduling

Generally, to maximize performance needs exhaustive search of the number and type of cores for each application. Achieving such goal on heterogeneous many-core processor is an NP-complete problem [35]. MAX-P is a heuristic algorithm that ensures the low complexity for online usage, as shown in Algorithm 1. The goal of MAX-P scheduling is to maximize the overall throughput of heterogeneous many-core processor. The aggregated BIPS of all applications is used as the overall throughput metric.

Specifically, MAX-P is divided into two decisions, D_{out} and D_{up}, which decide the thread number and core type for each application.

Algorithm 1: *Scale-out (D_{out}) and scale-up (D_{up})*

Input: thread number n, issue width W and ROB size R
Output: configurations of scale-out and scale-up
Model scale-out α and scale-up β for each application;
Calculate the expectations of $E[\alpha]$ and $E[\beta]$;
Allocate the thread number according to: $n_i = \frac{E[\alpha_i]}{\sum_{i=1}^{N} E[\alpha_i]} \times N$;
Sort the array $E[\beta_1 \cdots \beta_M]$ and then set priority for each application;
repeat
    $E_{\max}[\beta]$ chooses the fastest cores;
    Pop $E_{\max}[\beta]$ from array $E[\beta_1 \cdots \beta_M]$;
until *Array $E[\beta_1 \cdots \beta_M] = \emptyset$*;

First, D_{out} follows the strategy that an application with higher scale-out speed-up should spawn more thread. Therefore, we make the thread number of an application proportional to its scale-out speed-up, i.e.

$$n_i = \frac{E[\alpha_i]}{\sum_{i=1}^{N} E[\alpha_i]} \times N, \tag{12.20}$$

where n_i is the thread number of application i. N is the number of all available heterogeneous cores. $E[\alpha_i]$ is the scale-out expectation of application i. It refers to the average scale-out speed-up calculated by the following equation:

$$E[\alpha_i] = \frac{1}{|U|} \sum_{j \in U} \alpha_{i,j}, \tag{12.21}$$

where $\alpha_{i,j}$ is the scale-out speed-up of application i with multithreading configuration j. U is the set of all possible thread number for scale-out. The size of U, $|U|$, is 33 in this paper ($\{1\} \bigcup \{2 : 2 : 64\}$).

After D_{out} finishes, D_{up} allocates available heterogeneous cores to the threads of each application. D_{up} follows the policy that an application with larger $E[\beta]$ (calculated similar to $E[\alpha]$) should be allocated with faster cores. So we rank the $E[\beta]$ of all applications in descending order and then follow the iterations: the application with maximum $E[\beta]$ always gets highest priority to choose the fastest cores available, until all available cores are allocated.

12.7.2 MAX-E: power efficiency-oriented scheduling

Generally, power budget is viewed as limited resource because of the huge energy cost and power wall [36,37]. So in the following, the goal is to exploit maximum power efficiency under a certain power budget.

MAX-E is a power efficiency-oriented scheduling method. Under power-constrained scenarios, MAX-E follows a hierarchical two-layer framework: Layer1 ($L1$) allocates power quota to each multithreaded application and Layer2 ($L2$) searches the optimal configuration of each application for scale-out and scale-up and then enables corresponding scale-out and scale-up configurations. The procedures of $L1$ and $L2$ are detailed as follows.

First, $L1$ regulates the instant power with respect to power budget. At the end of current interval, $L1$ calculates the average power consumption. If it exceeds the power budget, $L1$ cuts off the extra power in next interval to reduce the risk of thermal violation. If the opposite happens, $L1$ compensates the power headroom for further improving performance. Note that power violations brought by application phase change are possible, because the predicted power is an average value. However, the accuracy of the power prediction ensures that the spike magnitude is quite small. Therefore, such short transient power spikes would not endanger the reliability of processors.

Second, $L1$ allocates corresponding power quota to each application. Generally, traditional method, such as multi-variable nonlinear programming, can solve how to allocate power resource to each application for maximizing power efficiency. However, the fairness of this method is poor. For example, the application with low power efficiency is always starved for power. MAX-E is hence designed to strike a trade-off between global maximum and fairness.

$L1$ follows the policy that each application's power quota is proportional to its power efficiency improvement. For application i, its power quota Q_i is given by

$$Q_i = \frac{E[\gamma_i]}{\sum_{i=1}^{M} E[\gamma_i]} P_{Budget}, \tag{12.22}$$

where P_{Budget} is the power budget. $E[\gamma_i]$ is the expectation of power efficiency improvement of application i. M is the number of applications. By doing so, the applications showing less power efficiency also have chance to obtain, rather than starving for, reasonable power resource.

When each application's power quota is allocated, $L2$ finds the optimal configurations of scale-out and scale-up for each application and then enables the corresponding multithreading or thread migration. $L2$ follows the policy that each application searches for maximum performance speed-up under its power quota. So given application i, its objective is expressed by the nonlinear programming problem:

$$\begin{aligned} &\text{Maximize } (\Phi_i), \\ &\text{Subject to } P_i \le Q_i, \end{aligned} \tag{12.23}$$

where Φ_i is the performance speed-up. P_i is the predicted average power.

Note that the search for optimal solutions is time-efficient with pruning. Branch-and-cut is used to accelerate the solving progress. For example, if the power of `blackscholes` with four-thread running on core A exceeds its power quota, then all the cases in which the thread number is more than four with the same core type, or the core is bigger than core A with the same threading should be cut off, because its power absolutely overflows the allocated budget. Algorithm 2 gives the overview of MAX-E scheduling.

Algorithm 2: *Place Layer1 (L1) and Layer2 (L2)*

Input: thread number n, issue width W, ROB size R and power budget
$\quad P_{Budget}$
Output: configurations of scale-out and scale-up
Model the power, and then obtain γ for each application;
Calculate the expectations $E[\gamma]$;
Allocate power quota according to: $Q_i = \frac{E[\gamma_i]}{\sum_{i=1}^{M} E[\gamma_i]} \times P_{Budget}$;
Sort the array $E[\gamma_1 \cdots \gamma_M]$ and then set priority for each application;
repeat
$\quad E_{max}[\gamma]$ starts the non-linear programming;
$\quad max . \Phi_{max}$;
$\quad s.t. P_{max} \leq Q_{max}$;
$\quad$ Pop $E_{max}[\gamma]$ from array $E[\gamma_1 \cdots \gamma_M]$;
until *Array* $E[\gamma_1 \cdots \gamma_M] = \emptyset$;

12.7.3 The overview of runtime management

The overview of the whole framework is presented in Figure 12.9. This heterogeneous many-core instance is organized as same as the one in Figure 12.6(a). In the beginning of interval $N + 1$, OS takes charge of inputting the application-specific coefficients. OS calls (1) PDH interface (`PdhCollectQueryData()`) from the performance counters for MPKI, front-end and back-end misses; (2) bottleneck-identification interface (`BottleneckCall()`, `BottleneckReturn()`, `BottleneckWait()`) from trace instructions for the SPKI sampled in interval N. Other coefficients are prepared offline by regression for a_* and b_* and measurement for k_0 and $P_{W,R}$.

After finishing the performance and power predictions, MAX-P or MAX-E scheduling calculates the optimal scale-out and scale-up configurations. Then OS begins (1) triggering OpenMP interface (`omp_set_dynamic()`, `omp_set_num_threads()`) to dynamically change the corresponding thread number for scale-out and (2) activating thread migration interface (`processor_bind()`) for scale-up simultaneously.

The runtime interval must be in order of second's magnitude. This considers not only the penalty of runtime management but also the effectiveness of management depended on interval granularity [38]. The interval is set to one second. The OS actions (blue-labelled in Figure 12.9), the calculations about power efficiency and scheduling, are tightly finished within 50 ms, which can be amortized well (5% of the total interval).

The overheads of multithreading and thread migration are quite small. First, the reconfiguration of multithreading, i.e. dynamically changing the thread number, has to manipulate the active dataset and generates or kills some threads. Although these operations inevitably introduce some workload-dependent overheads, the multi-threading overhead from the OpenMP, up to 32 threads in this paper, is much less than 10 ms [39], which can be amortized well in typical OS time slice (10 ms). Second,

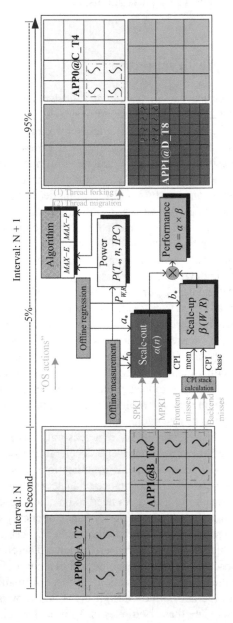

Figure 12.9 *The whole framework includes power efficiency prediction and runtime management. Assuming this heterogeneous many-core instance is consisted of four cores: A (upper left), B (lower right), C (upper right), and D (lower left). Their microarchitectures are listed in Table 12.2. In interval N, application 0 runs on core A with 2 threads, labelled as APP0@A_T2; application 1 runs on core B with 6 threads, labelled as APP1@B_T6. In interval N + 1, their configurations transfer to APP0@C_T4 and APP1@D_T8, respectively*

thread migration mainly expends on thread context switch, data movement, and data warm-up in the cache hierarchy. These workload-dependent overheads are also quite small. PIE has comprehensively evaluated the overheads of thread migration [19]. Even for a fine-grained migration interval, such as 2.5 ms, the performance overhead is less than 0.6%.

12.8   Conclusion and future directions

Architectural modelling plays a critical role in architectural design and optimization. The models can help navigate the architectural design space, which is especially useful in the early design phase. Targeting many-core architectures, this chapter describes two orthogonal modelling approaches, scale-up and scale-out, to characterize the performance responses dependent on the architectural/microarchitectural settings. By investigating the orthogonality of the two scaling approaches, we found that the orthogonality assumption can greatly simplify the model integration without compromising significant accuracy. When using the models, the scale-up and scale-out approaches are not supposed to replace each other but give mutual complement. Finally, this chapter demonstrates how to use the models to facilitate runtime management for maximizing performance and power efficiency, respectively.

The emerging new computing devices and the design of new algorithms in different fields have posed a great challenge for architectural modelling. Nowadays parallel applications significantly differ from traditional ones, as they have lower ILP, more challenging branches for the branch-predictors and more irregular data access patterns. Meanwhile, it is observed that processors evolute towards heterogeneous many-cores especially special-purpose accelerators. Therefore, the future directions for architectural modelling lie in two folds: (1) being more device specific and therefore more accurate and (2) being more agile to cope with various domain-specific accelerators without dictating considerable accuracy degradation, and more importantly, short time-to-validation design cycles.

With the end of Dennard scaling, architects have increasingly turned from general purpose architectures to special-purpose hardware accelerators to improve the performance and energy efficiency for domain-specific applications. Upon this trend, understanding the factors which dictate the performance of an accelerator are crucial for both architects and programmers. Programmers need to be able to predict when offloading a kernel will be worthwhile in terms of performance or energy efficiency. Similarly, architects need to understand how the interactions between accelerators and host machines will affect the achievable accelerator performance. Therefore, performance models for special-purpose accelerators have emerged as a hot research topic. These models help both programmers and architects identify performance bounds and design bottlenecks early in the accelerator design cycle and provide insights into which optimizations may alleviate these bottlenecks. To model special-purpose hardware accelerators, programmer and architects can employ either complex or simple modelling techniques. Complex modelling techniques and full-system simulation can provide highly accurate performance estimates. Unfortunately, they often require low-level system details which are not available till late in the design cycle. Simple models, such as analytical models, abstract away these low-level system details and provide key insights early in the design cycle that are useful for experts and non-experts alike. The key problem in accelerator architecture modelling is how to strike the right balance between overly simple models and the detailed sophistication of modern parallel systems.

Some recent studies have been devoted to address these open problems. Ajam *et al.* [40] reviews the performance modelling of existing heterogeneous systems and their development frameworks and addresses the emerging issues that affect the performance of these devices and associated techniques employed for simulation and evaluation. Lopez-Novoa *et al.* [41] surveys the performance modelling and simulation techniques for accelerator-based computing. LogCA [42] is a high-level performance model for hardware accelerators, providing sufficient simplicity such that programmers and architects can easily reason with it. The goal of LogCA is to develop a simple model that supports the important implications of application analysis and use as few parameters as possible while providing sufficient accuracy. Charm provides domain-specific language support for architecture modelling in a way that leads to more flexible, scalable, shareable, and correct analytic models. Lopes *et al.* [43] explores the GPU performance, power and energy efficiency bounds with cache-aware roofline modelling. Bombieri *et al.* [44] proposed a fine-grained performance model for GPU architectures that allows accurately estimating the potential performance of the application under tuning on a given GPU device, and it also provides programmers with interpretable profiling hints. SmartShuttle [45] proposed an energy model based on off-chip memory accesses for deep-learning accelerators. These models play an important role in the design and optimization of special-purpose accelerator architectures.

Acknowledgements

This work is supported by the National Natural Science Foundation of China under Grant Nos. 61872336, 61572470, 61532017, 61432017, 61521092 and in part by Youth Innovation Promotion Association, CAS under grant No.Y404441000.

References

[1] Austin TM, Larson E, Ernst D. SimpleScalar: An Infrastructure for Computer System Modeling. IEEE Computer. 2002;35(2):59–67.

[2] Brooks DM, Tiwari V, Martonosi M. Wattch: A Framework for Architectural-level Power Analysis and Optimizations. International Symposium on Computer Architecture. 2000;28(2):83–94.

[3] Naveen M, Rajeev B, Norman PJ. CACTI 6.0: A Tool to Understand Large Caches. 2008.

[4]   Huang W, Ghosh S, Velusamy S, Sankaranarayanan K, Skadron K, Stan MR. HotSpot: A Compact Thermal Modeling Methodology for Early-stage VLSI Design. IEEE Transactions on Very Large Scale Integration Systems. 2006;14(5):501–513.

[5]   GEM5. The gem5 Simulator System. http://wwwm5simorg. 2012.

[6]   Sherwood T, Perelman E, Hamerly G, Calder B. Automatically Characterizing Large Scale Program Behavior. In: ASPLOS; 2002. p. 45–57.

[7]   Yan G, Sun F, Li H, Li X. CoreRank: Redeeming "Sick Silicon" by Dynamically Quantifying Core-Level Healthy Condition. IEEE Transactions on Computers. 2016;65(3):716–729.

[8]   Mogul JC, Mudigonda J, Binkert N, Ranganathan P, Talwar V. Using Asymmetric Single-ISA CMPs to Save Energy on Operating Systems. IEEE Micro. 2008;28(3):26–41.

[9]   Cong J, Ghodrat MA, Gill M, Grigorian B, Reinman G. Architecture Support for Accelerator-rich CMPs. In: Proceedings of the 49th Annual Design Automation Conference. DAC'12. New York, NY, USA: ACM; 2012. p. 843–849. Available from: http://doi.acm.org/10.1145/2228360.2228512.

[10] EETimes. ARM Reveals 'Little Dog' A7 Processor. http://wwweetimescom/electronics-news/4229867/ARM-reveals-little-dog-A7-processor. 2011.

[11] Borkar S, Chien AA. The Future of Microprocessors. Communications of the ACM. 2011:67–77.

[12] Yan G, Ma J, Han Y, Li X. EcoUp: Towards Economical Datacenter Upgrading. IEEE Transactions on Parallel and Distributed Systems. 2016;27(7):716–729.

[13] Lee BC, Collins J, Wang H, Brooks D. CPR: Composable Performance Regression for Scalable Multiprocessor Models. In: MICRO; 2008. p. 270–281.

[14] Ma J, Yan G, Han Y, Li X. An Analytical Framework for Estimating Scale-Out and Scale-Up Power Efficiency of Heterogeneous Manycores. IEEE Transactions on Computers. 2016;65(2):367–381.

[15] Hill MD, Marty MR. Amdahl's Law in the Multicore Era. Computers. 2008;41(7):33–38.

[16] Suleman MA, Qureshi MK, Patt YN. Feedback-Driven Threading: Power-Efficient and High-Performance Execution of Multi-threaded Workloads on CMPs. In: ASPLOS; 2008. p. 277–286.

[17] Joao JA, Suleman MA, Mutlu O, Patt YN. Bottleneck Identification and Scheduling in Multithreaded Applications . In: ASPLOS; 2012. p. 223–234.

[18] Bienia C, Kumar S, Singh JP, Li K. The PARSEC Benchmark Suite: Characterization and Architectural Implications. In: PACT; 2008. p. 72–81.

[19] Craeynest KV, Jalee A, Eeckhout L, Narvaez P, Emer J. Scheduling Heterogeneous Multi-cores Through Performance Impact Estimation (PIE). In: ISCA; 2012. p. 213–224.

[20] Jouppi NP. The Nonuniform Distribution of Instruction-level and Machine Parallelism and Its Effect on Performance. Computers. 1989;38(12):1645–1658.

[21] Eyerman S, Eeckhout L, Karkhanis T, Smith JE. A Mechanistic Performance Model for Superscalar Out-of-Order Processors. ACM Transactions on Computer Systems. 2009;27(2):1–37.

[22] Eyerman S, Eeckhout L, Karkhanis T, Smith JE. A Performance Counter Architecture for Computing Accurate CPI Components. In: ASPLOS; 2006. p. 175–184.

[23] Noonburg DB, Shen JP. Theoretical Modeling of Superscalar Processor Performance. MICRO; 1994. p. 52–62.

[24] Woo DH, Lee HHS. Extending Amdahl's Law for Energy-Efficient Computing in the Many-Core Era. Computers. 2008;41(12):24–31.

[25] Karpuzcu UR, Sung KN, Torrellas J. Coping with Parametric Variation at Near-Threshold Voltages. IEEE Micro. 2013;33(4):6–14.

[26] Paul I, Manne S, Arora M, Bircher WL, Yalamanchili S. Cooperative Boosting: Needy versus Greedy Power Management. In: ISCA; 2013. p. 285–296.

[27] Barroso LA, Hlzle U. The Case for Energy-Proportional Computing. Computer. 2007;40(12):33–37.

[28] Lubin B, Kephart JO, Das R, Parkes DC. Expressive Power-based Resource Allocation for Data Centers. In: IJCAI; 2009. p. 1451–1456.

[29] Martin AJ. ET2: a metric for time and energy efficiency of computation. Power aware computing. Springer, 2002;p. 293–315.

[30] Bhattacharjee A, Martonosi M. Thread Criticality Predictors for Dynamic Performance, Power, and Resource Management in Chip Multiprocessors. In: ISCA; 2009. p. 290–301.

[31] Jacobson H, Buyuktosunoglu A, Bose P, Acar E, Eickemeyer R. Abstraction and Microarchitecture Scaling in Early-Stage Power Modeling. In: HPCA; 2011. p. 394–405.

[32] Ganesan K, John LK. MAximum Multicore POwer (MAMPO): An Automatic Multithreaded Synthetic Power Virus Generation Framework for Multicore Systems. In: SC; 2011. p. 1–12.

[33] Wang D, Ren C, Sivasubramaniam A. Virtualizing Power Distribution in Datacenters. In: ISCA; 2013. p. 595–606.

[34] Reddi VJ, Kanev S, Wonyoung K, *et al.* Voltage Noise in Production Processors. IEEE Micro. 2011;31(1):20–28.

[35] Winter JA, Albonesi DH, Shoemaker CA. Scalable Thread Scheduling and Global Power Management for Heterogeneous Many-Core Architectures. In: PACT; 2010. p. 29–39.

[36] Monchiero M, Canal R, Gonz A. Design Space Exploration for Multicore Architectures: A Power/Performance/Thermal View. In: ICS; 2006. p. 177–186.

[37] Wang Y, Ma K, Wang X. Temperature-Constrained Power Control for Chip Multiprocessors with Online Model Estimation. In: ISCA; 2009. p. 314–324.

[38] Isci C, Contreras G, Martonosi M. Live, Runtime Phase Monitoring and Prediction on Real Systems with Application to Dynamic Power Management. In: MICRO; 2006. p. 359–370.

[39] OpenMP. OpenMP. http://openmporg/wp/. 2013.

[40] Ajam H, Agyeman MO. A Study of Recent Contributions on Performance and Simulation Techniques for Accelerator Devices. In: 2017 4th International Conference on Electrical and Electronic Engineering (ICEEE); 2017. p. 256–260.

[41] Lopez-Novoa U, Mendiburu A, Miguel-Alonso J. A Survey of Performance Modeling and Simulation Techniques for Accelerator-Based Computing. IEEE Transactions on Parallel and Distributed Systems. 2015;26(1): 272–281.

[42] Altaf MSB, Wood DA. LogCA: A High-level Performance Model for Hardware Accelerators. In: 2017 ACM/IEEE 44th Annual International Symposium on Computer Architecture (ISCA); 2017. p. 375–388.

[43] Lopes A, Pratas F, Sousa L, Ilic A. Exploring GPU Performance, Power and Energy-efficiency Bounds with Cache-aware Roofline Modeling. In: 2017 IEEE International Symposium on Performance Analysis of Systems and Software (ISPASS); 2017. p. 259–268.

[44] Bombieri N, Busato F, Fummi F. A Fine-grained Performance Model for GPU Architectures. In: 2016 Design, Automation and Test in Europe Conference and Exhibition (DATE); 2016. p. 1267–1272.

[45] Li J, Yan G, Lu W, *et al.* SmartShuttle: Optimizing Off-chip Memory Accesses for Deep Learning Accelerators. In: 2018 Design, Automation and Test in Europe Conference and Exhibition (DATE); 2018. p. 343–348.

Chapter 13

Power modelling of multicore systems

Matthew J. Walker[1], Geoff V. Merrett[1], and Bashir Al-Hashimi[1]

In recent years, energy-efficiency has become the primary design objective in modern CPUs. From mobile and Internet-of-Things devices where battery-life is limited, to servers and cloud computing where energy bills and cooling system costs must be minimised, the key design focus is reducing power consumption while achieving the required level of performance. Fundamental to improving energy-efficiency is managing the various energy-saving techniques efficiently to find the optimum trade-off under the current operating conditions. To achieve this effectively, online access to accurate knowledge of the run-time power consumption is required. Furthermore, a device's performance is limited by its thermal envelope and, therefore, by carefully monitoring the power consumption and considering this envelope, a greater peak performance can be achieved.

In addition, the slowdown of technology scaling means that processor architects cannot solely rely on semiconductor process improvements and must look to innovative design enhancements. Accurate architecture and system-level power modelling is therefore required to evaluate the trade-offs in new techniques and for design-space exploration, as well as for software and compiler energy efficiency evaluation.

This chapter first gives a brief overview of how power is consumed in CPUs (Section 13.1) before exploring the various energy-saving techniques and power management considerations (Section 13.2). A description of different power modelling approaches and applications is presented (Section 13.3) before *top-down*, run-time power models are described in detail, highlighting many important, but often-overlooked, considerations (Section 13.4). Bottom-up approaches, their accuracy, and methods of improving their representativeness are then discussed (Section 13.5) and finally, hybrid approaches are proposed (Section 13.6).

13.1 CPU power consumption

Modern CPUs are implemented using complementary metal–oxide–semiconductor (CMOS), which is also used to implement the dynamic random access memory (DRAM) and other components. The power consumption of a CPU can be broadly

[1]Electronics and Computer Science, University of Southampton, United Kingdom

split into three key components: static power (P_{static}), short-circuit power (P_{sc}), and dynamic power (P_{dyn}) [1,2]. Dynamic power consumption is caused by the charging and discharging of capacitive loads when the transistors change state (C). Not every transistor changes state on every clock cycle, and so an activity factor (α) is used to indicate the fraction of activity:

$$P_{dyn} = \alpha C V^2 f \tag{13.1}$$

When a gate changes state there will be a short period of time where both the P-type metal-oxide-semiconductor (PMOS) and N-type metal-oxide-semiconductor (NMOS) transistor will conduct due to the non-zero transistor transition time and a short-circuit current will flow, causing short-circuit power dissipation. This is called short-circuit power consumption, P_{sc}, (also known as *glitching* power consumption). It is often omitted from the CMOS power equation as it is smaller than the dynamic and static components [1]. While dynamic power remains the dominant consumer, increasingly aggressive technology scaling means that static power is becoming a larger contributor. The static power consumption is caused by leakage currents (13.2) which are dependent on the temperature [2].

$$P_{static} = I_{leak} V \tag{13.2}$$

13.2 CPU power management and energy-saving techniques

In order to maximise energy-efficiency and satisfy performance and power requirements for the specific workloads and situations, the operation of the CPU must be controlled effectively. Modern CPUs implement a number of energy-saving techniques, perhaps the most common of which is dynamic voltage–frequency scaling (DVFS), which allows the maximum performance to be traded-off for energy-efficiency. It was shown in (13.1) that the dynamic power is proportional to the square of the voltage multiplied by the clock frequency ($V^2 f$); therefore, reducing the voltage alone results in a quadratic reduction in power consumption. Many applications, particularly those that are memory intensive, cannot make effective use of a CPU running at the maximum frequency due to the memory latency, which results in slack (stalled CPU cycles). The DVFS level can therefore be reduced, saving energy, without any significant impact on performance.

Another common technique is to employ CPU core idle states, also known as dynamic power management (DPM), where the CPU core is switched into a lower power mode where no instructions are executed. As technology scaling progresses, a larger proportion of power consumed is static (leakage) power, making it more viable to execute at a high DVFS level to finish the task in a smaller amount of time, and then go into an idle state. The choice of when to employ DVFS scaling or when to use idle states (i.e. *race-to-idle*) has been the topic of much research [3–5].

Single-ISA (instruction set architecture) heterogeneous processing architectures, such as ARM *big.LITTLE* technology [6], utilise multiple types of CPU cores optimised for different performance-power operating points [7]. For example, ARM big.LITTLE configurations combine CPUs optimised for high-performance (e.g. ARM Cortex-A15, or Cortex-A73) with CPUs optimised for power efficiency (e.g. ARM Cortex-A7 or Cortex-A53). This enables energy-saving opportunities to be exploited while also having high-peak performance when required. Together with DVFS and DPM, single-ISA heterogeneous architectures provide a large potential for performance, power, energy, and temperature optimisation through intelligent-management algorithms [8–11].

While intelligent management is important for saving energy, it is also necessary for ensuring that the CPU remains within its thermal-operating envelope. The thermal design power (TDP), also known as the thermal design point, is used to define the maximum power a CPU can draw for a thermally significant time period and remain within the upper limit of the thermal profile to ensure reliability [12]. Due to the thermal capacitance of the package and the heat sink, the TDP can be exceeded for a short period of time (i.e. by increasing the DVFS level), therefore providing superior performance. For example, Intel's Turbo Boost technology takes advantage of any thermal headroom available to provide performance when needed [13]. Therefore, careful modelling, understanding, and management of run-time power potentially enables higher peak performance as well as greater energy efficiency.

13.3 Approaches and applications

Power modelling is required for various scenarios, each with different requirements, including the different stages of the CPU design process, software and compiler optimisation, as well as system run-time management.

13.3.1 Power measurement

The most accurate method of obtaining run-time power consumption is by measuring the device power directly. However, it is usually not practical for devices to contain power sensors due to cost and the physical space required. For estimating the power of CPUs in development and design-space exploration, power measurement is usually not possible as the finalised device does not exist, and it may be too costly and time-consuming to create prototypes for design-space exploration for future ideas.

13.3.2 Top-down approaches

Alternatively, the power consumption of a CPU can be characterised offline using external power analysis instruments and modelled using available online metrics. A simple metric is the CPU utilisation, which is an OS statistic describing the amount of time the CPU is spent busy, as opposed to being idle. While utilisation-based power models have been proposed [14,15], it is a very simple metric and the CPU power consumption depends largely on the type of workload, for example, what function units are being used, how memory and caches are being accessed, and utilisation-based models, therefore, have limited accuracy.

Performance monitoring counters (PMCs) are registers built into the CPU that can be set to count specific architectural and microarchitectural events, such as the number of integer operations executed, or the number of L1 data cache misses, and can, therefore, provide information on the current workload. While principally intended for performance analysis, PMCs have been widely shown to be effective in estimating the run-time CPU power consumption [16–23]. Regression analysis is typically used to create a set of linear equations relating several PMC events to the CPU power consumption; however, other techniques such as workload classification [24] and neural networks [25] have also been proposed. PMC-based power models have been implemented for some Intel CPUs, and power estimations are available through Intel's Running Average Power Limit interface. Such approaches that measure the overall CPU power of an existing device to create power models are known as *top-down* approaches and are potentially very accurate. However, they must be formulated correctly to work effectively with a wide range of workloads, and some key considerations are often overlooked [23], as will be demonstrated in Section 13.4.

13.3.3   Circuit, gate, and register-transfer level approaches

When designing and developing a new device, the power and energy-efficiency must be analysed at various points during the design flow before a prototype or final device is available. Designers can use different power estimation techniques depending on the accuracy required and the current stage in the design flow, including circuit-level techniques, such as the use of SPICE modelling; transistor-based approaches, such as PowerMill [26]; gate-level simulation using foundry-supplied standard-cell libraries and gate-level netlists; or register-transfer level (RTL) simulation.

However, all of these techniques require CPU intellectual property which is typically only available to commercial customers and partners. Furthermore, even the relatively fast RTL simulation requires much processing time even for very small workloads. For this reason, the remainder of this chapter will focus on top-down and *bottom-up* approaches.

13.3.4   Bottom-up approaches

For CPU and system design exploration, higher level simulation frameworks and component models are widely used in research. These high-level *bottom-up* approaches are not as accurate as top-down approaches or lower level circuit, gate, or RTL approaches. However, they are faster and more accessible than lower level approaches and are very flexible (i.e. allowing many different architectural and system-level configurations to be tested), unlike top-down approaches (Figure 13.1(a)). Typical examples of bottom-up power modelling frameworks include Wattch [27], a framework for architectural power analysis; CACTI [28], a cache timing, power and area model; and McPAT [29], a multicore and many-core system power, area, and timing modelling framework. Such tools require a system specification and an indication of CPU behaviour (e.g. activity statistics) as inputs. A system performance simulator, such as SimpleScalar [30] or *gem5* [31], is typically used to provide architectural and microarchitectural performance statistics to a power simulation tool (Figure 13.1(b)). A recent survey presents a detailed comparison of various architecture simulators [32]. Due to its active design community and support for many ISAs (Alpha, ARM, SPARC, MIPS,

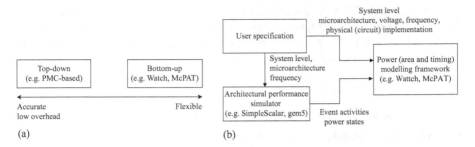

Figure 13.1   Top-down and bottom-up modelling approaches: (a) top-down vs. bottom-up power models and (b) bottom-up simulation workflow

POWER, RISC-V, and ×86), gem5 has become a widely used simulation framework. Its advanced features include DRAM modelling, support for DVFS, GPU modelling, Kernel-based virtual machine support, and elastic traces. A distributed version of gem5, called *dist-gem5*, can model and simulate distributed many-core systems using multiple simulation hosts. gem5 is commonly coupled with McPAT for energy analysis (discussed in Section 13.5).

Their flexibility and reconfigurability mean that bottom-up approaches are better suited for design-space exploration, whereas the accuracy and low overhead of top-down approaches makes them better suited for run-time power estimation and software energy profiling. However, depending on the use case, the accuracy and validity of bottom-up approaches can be insufficient. Section 13.5 focusses on the accuracy of bottom-up techniques, while Section 13.6 looks at combining bottom-up and top-down techniques.

13.4   Developing top-down power models

This section gives a detailed approach on developing and validating top-down, PMC-based power models for use in run-time power estimation and software profiling. The models produced by these techniques are specific to the platform they were developed on, but the methodology can be applied to any CPU that has PMCs.

Top-down approaches are potentially very accurate. However, they must be formulated correctly to work effectively with a wide range of workloads and some key considerations are often overlooked in typical top-down modelling methods. Furthermore, typically used validation techniques are insufficient in identifying key issues with the models, and their quality is typically assessed and reported with simple metrics, which are misleading and insufficient without other information.

This section describes the various stages required to develop top-down power models and covers some key considerations, including model stability, appropriate model specification, training and validation workload set choice, heteroscedasticity, validation techniques, modelling the thermal effects on power consumption, and the effect of nonideal voltage regulators.

The *Powmon* [33] software tool implements many of the methods discussed in this section, which were originally presented in [23,34]. While this section uses a mobile ARM-based CPU as an example, approaches based on the ones outlined in this chapter have been applied to ×86 architectures [35].

13.4.1   Overview of methodology

There are three main stages to develop empirical power models:

Empirical data collection: Workloads are first run on the device under test to exercise the CPU while recording PMC data and measured CPU power and voltage.

Model development: The relationship between the CPU frequency, voltage, and PMC data must be modelled (simple regression techniques are typically employed).

Validation: The model must be carefully validated to ensure the accuracy and confidence are within the required level.

The Performance Monitoring Unit (PMU) allows a wide range of architectural and microarchitectural events to be counted using PMCs. There are typically only a small number of PMCs (e.g. four to six), and so the optimum events to use as model inputs needs to first be identified and assigned to a PMC. The model development flow therefore gets split into the following two stages:

PMC event selection: Experiments are first conducted to measure the full set of PMC events for a large set of workloads and the optimum ones are chosen.

Model formulation: Once the events have been identified, experiments can be run across all the DVFS level (and perhaps under different temperature conditions, etc.) for training the model itself.

13.4.2   Data collection

The quality of the models produced inherently depends on the quality of data used to build them. This section outlines techniques for extracting power, voltage, and PMC data.

13.4.2.1   Power and voltage measurements

There are several approaches to obtain CPU power measurements depending on the device and granularity of power required. For desktop and server computers, the power consumption is typically measured from the power sockets, therefore collecting power for the whole system as opposed to the CPU alone [16–18]. Some works measure the motherboard power from the ATX (Advanced Technology eXtended) connector using a hall-effect current sensor or the voltage drop across a sense resistor. However, for accurate power modelling, it is important to accurately isolate the CPU power from other devices. The most accurate results on desktop platforms can be obtained from accessing the CPU voltage regulator itself [36].

Experiments on mobile CPUs are usually carried out on a development board. The most accurate method of estimating power on a mobile development board is to modify the board by placing a sense resistor between the voltage regulator and the CPU, and measuring both current and voltage with a power analyser (Figure 13.2(a)). As well as providing accurate results, it allows high frequency sampling that can capture individual workload spikes. Some mobile development boards, such as the Hardkernel ODROID-XU3 board (Figure 13.2(b)) [37], include built-in current and voltage sensors which have been utilised in many works, including [23,38]. However, the sensors only provide readings at 3.8 Hz (they internally sample at a higher frequency and provide an average) and this must be taken into account for repeatable and accurate results, for example, by running workloads for a long time so enough samples can be collected [39]. While it is possible to increase the update rate of the sensors, it comes at the cost of overhead.

13.4.2.2 PMC event collection

PMCs have long been accessible and used on ×86 desktop and server class systems via tools such as *perf* [41]. However, on ARM-based mobile systems, PMCs have been more difficult to obtain, leading to a lack of work considering power modelling on mobile systems, despite energy consumption being of particular importance on such devices. An early example of the use of PMCs in ARM platforms for power modelling uses a custom loadable kernel module to allow user-space access to the PMU registers and then accesses those registers directly [40]. More recently, support has improved and some newer development platforms now have in-built support for the *perf* tool. The open-source *GemStone-Profiler* [42] allows low-overhead recording of PMCs on ARMv7 and ARMv8 without requiring OS support. Furthermore, it works on big.LITTLE platforms and optionally automates the running of workloads at various DVFS levels and on different cores.

13.4.3 Multiple linear regression basics

Multiple linear regression is a method of modelling the relationship between a dependent variable y and multiple-independent variables (or predictors), X, using a linear predictor function:

$$y_i = \beta_0 + x_{i1}\beta_1 + x_{i2}\beta_2 + \cdots + x_{ip}\beta_p \tag{13.3}$$

where y_i is the dependent, or response, variable; $x_{i1}, x_{i2}, \ldots, x_{ip}$ are the independent variables; and $\beta_0, \ldots, \beta_p$ are the regression coefficients.

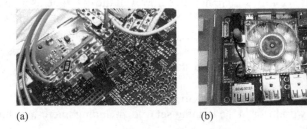

(a) (b)

Figure 13.2 Power and voltage measurement of development boards: (a) sense resistor [40] and (b) power sensors

Once specified, the model can be fitted (i.e. the regression coefficients calculated) using an estimator, such as ordinary least squares (OLS). The estimator aims to minimise the fitted line and the data points; in the case of an OLS estimator, the sum of the squared residuals are reduced. While often overlooked, estimation techniques make several assumptions that must be considered, including [43,44]

1. correct specification of the model,
2. the relationship between the independent variables and the dependent variable must be linear,
3. the elements of β are constants (parameters),
4. there must be little or no multicollinearity in the data,
5. there must be no autocorrelation, e.g. in time-series data, a value must not be dependent on a previous (historic) value, and
6. homoscedasticity (constant variance of the errors, e.g. no *heteroscedasticity*).

The *goodness-of-fit* of the regression model is measured using the *coefficient of determination*, denoted R^2 [45]. The R^2 can be inflated by increasing the number of independent variables, even if they are not statistically significant. Another metric, known as the *adjusted R^2*, denoted $\overline{R}^2$, which takes the number of independent variables into account, is commonly used.

13.4.4   Model stability

A CPU power model accuracy is typically assessed using the mean percentage error (MPE) or mean absolute percentage error (MAPE). While these are easy to interpret, they can be misleading and biased towards the validation workloads. In practical run-time power estimation applications, it is important that the power model is able to predict a wide range of workloads accurately, including the ones that are not well represented in the training set. For example, while a MAPE of under 7 per cent may appear reasonable for some applications, the same model could still predict the power of certain types of workloads with an error of over 45 per cent [23]. Furthermore, while the error for a whole workload may seem reasonable, often power models are required to estimate workload phases or micro-phases, which are typically more diverse and therefore more difficult to predict. The most important property of a power model is therefore its stability, which indicates how well the coefficients individually capture the influence of a particular model input (independent variable) on the power consumption, allowing the model to reliably predict power consumption on a wide range of workloads, even if they are not covered well in the training workload set.

There are two key requirements for a stable model:

1. little or no multicollinearity between the model inputs and
2. a diverse set of workloads in the training set (e.g. including micro-benchmarks).

The importance of considering stability is experimentally demonstrated in the next section.

13.4.5 PMC event selection

As only a few PMC events can be monitored simultaneously, a small selection of PMC events must be chosen as inputs to the model. For a regression model to be stable, there must be low errors in the coefficients. A key assumption of the OLS estimator is that there is little or no multicollinearity present (Section 13.4.3); if independent variables are correlated with each other, it is said that *intercorrelation* or multicollinearity exists among them. With the presence of intercorrelation between the independent variables, it is not possible to establish how each independent variable *individually* affects the dependent variable. A model with multicollinearity is therefore unreliable at predicting the response for a set of inputs that do not directly correspond to a sample data point (observation) and interpretations based on individual coefficients cannot be made [43,46]. Multicollinearity problems often go unnoticed as a good R^2 value can still be achieved.

Typical power modelling approaches simply choose PMC events that correlate well with the CPU power consumption [17,21,22,40,47,48]. However, there is much interaction between different components of a CPU, and therefore PMC events inherently have high intercorrelation.

The variance inflation factor (VIF) is a formal method of detecting and measuring multicollinearity and has been proposed for use in the PMC event selection process [23]. It is a measure of how the variance of the estimated regression coefficient is inflated compared to the case of there being no multicollinearity. The square root of the variance is the standard error. A common rule-of-thumb states that a VIF over five or ten suggests multicollinearity problems [49]. A method of automatically selecting PMC events using regression techniques and the VIF has been demonstrated to be effective at selecting events that provide the model with a large amount of information for predicting power with minimum intercorrelation [23]. A *forward-selection* approach (see [43,46]) using the $\overline{R}^2$ value is first used to select a new PMC event, one by one. After each PMC event is added to the model, the *p-value* (indicating the statistical significance) is checked and the VIF is calculated. Events that were known to be required but not necessarily automatically chosen first (e.g. the cycle count) were forced as the first choice to improve the selection process, which selects the next event *given* the information in the previous events.

As the number of selected PMC events included in the model increases, the $\overline{R}^2$ value (labelled *Adj. R^2*) increases before it plateaus, while the average VIF of all chosen events (labelled *VIFb*) increases (Figure 13.3(a)). After adding the fifth event (0×73), the average VIF increases significantly, suggesting that the optimum number of events to choose is four. However, analysing the change in the VIF of all PMCs before and after adding the fifth event shows that the increase is due to intercorrelation between 0×73 and $0\times1B$ (not shown). Event $0\times1B$ counts the number of instructions speculatively executed while event 0×73 counts the number of integer instructions speculatively executed; when 0×73 increments, $0\times1B$ also increments, causing this correlation between the two. Transforming $0\times1B$ to $0\times1B-0\times73$ therefore resolves this problem. Making such transformation allows more events to be used (providing the model with more information) while maintaining stability (the new VIF, labelled

VIF, remains low in Figure 13.3(a)); after the transformation was made in this example, all seven (maximum that can be measured simultaneously) could be used in the model, improving the MAPE from 5 to 3 per cent while keeping the average VIF to under 2.5 (and the maximum individual VIF to under 4).

The importance of stability and reducing collinearity between the model inputs can be experimentally demonstrated by considering two models that are identical with the exception of their selected events (Figure 13.3(b)): *Model i*, which has PMC events chosen using correlation and does not consider multicollinearity (VIF ≫ 10,000); and *Model ii*, which uses the described PMC event selection methodology (VIF < 10). Three different training and validation workload scenarios are considered:

1. training and validating the models with a small set of typical workloads (MiBench and MediaBench);
2. training and validating with a small set of diverse workloads (random selection including microbenchmarks); and
3. training with the small set of diverse workloads and validating with a large set of 60 workloads.

In scenario **1**, both models achieve a low MAPE. However, this reported MAPE value is optimistic and misleading as the next two scenarios show. Scenario **2** shows how the more stable model is better able to capture information from the diverse set of workloads (due to smaller coefficient errors). And when this same model is validated on a large set of 60 workloads (scenario **3**), the stable model (Model ii) is able to maintain a low MAPE, while the MAPE of the unstable Model i increases to over 8 per cent. Furthermore, the maximum MAPE (considering individual workloads) in scenario **3** for *model i* and *model ii* is 45 and 15 per cent, respectively.

13.4.6   Model formulation

Once PMC events have been chosen, the next stage is to formulate the model and estimate the coefficients. This requires experimental data to be collected for those

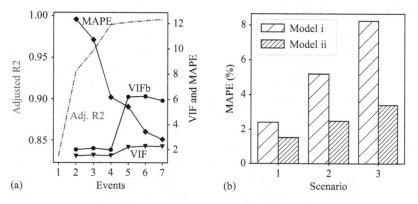

(a)   (b)

Figure 13.3   PMC event selection: (a) number of events and (b) unstable vs. stable.
© 2016. Adapted, with permission, from Reference [23]

fixed PMC event values but at multiple DVFS levels and with multiple CPU cores being utilised. While most works develop a model for each voltage-frequency point, a more effective way is to use a voltage and frequency-independent model formulation, allowing the model to be trained at a single DVFS level but applied to all levels [23,50]. One of the assumptions of OLS (Section 13.4.3) was that the model is correctly specified; error caused by the model being incorrectly specified is known as *specification error*. A simple example of a misspecified model is where a variable is included when in fact the dependent variable is related to the square of that variable, and therefore the square of the variable should be included instead [34]. The equation used in this section is based on the equations in Section 13.1 and separates the power into different components [34]:

$$P_{cluster} = \underbrace{\left(\sum_{n=0}^{N-1} \beta_n E_n V^2 f_{clk} \right)}_{\text{dynamic activity}} + \underbrace{\beta_b V^2 f_{clk}}_{\text{BG dynamic}} + \underbrace{f(V, T)}_{\text{static}} \tag{13.4}$$

where $P_{cluster}$ is the power consumed for the CPU cluster (e.g. ARM Cortex-A15 quad-core cluster), f_{clk} is the CPU clock frequency, V is the CPU supply voltage, and N is the total number of PMC events used in the model. The power consumption is broken down into three parts:

Dynamic activity: The dynamic power consumed due to the activity as indicated by the PMC events. $E_0, \ldots, E_{N-1}$ are the PMC event rates (events per second) divided by the clock frequency. $\beta_0, \ldots, \beta_{N-1}$ are the regression coefficients.

Background (BG) dynamic: A constant dynamic power component that is independent of the PMC events.

Static: The static power equation, which is a function of the CPU voltage and the temperature (T).

In many situations, the CPU temperature, T, is not available and so a different model is first considered:

$$P_{cluster} = \underbrace{\left(\sum_{n=0}^{N-1} \beta_n E_n V^2 f_{clk} \right)}_{\text{dynamic activity}} + \underbrace{f(V, f_{clk})}_{\text{static and BG dynamic}} \tag{13.5}$$

The model equation in (13.5) models the dynamic power due to the activity (as measured by the performance counters) and the static and background (constant) dynamic components separately. At a given DVFS level, the *static and BG dynamic* components of the equation are constant (assuming an ideal voltage regulator, see Section 13.4.9).

Table 13.1 shows the independent variables and corresponding coefficients (as estimated using OLS) of a power model for an ARM Cortex-A15 quad-core CPU cluster. The *dynamic activity* contains the selected PMC event rates (divided by f_{clk} to make them independent of the clock frequency) and multiplies them by $V^2 f$ as this is the relationship the CPU activity has on the dynamic CPU power (13.1). The static power consumption is proportional to V. However, it is also dependent on temperature (Section 13.1), which is not included as an input into this model. If the

Table 13.1   Model coefficients

Component	Coefficient name	Weight	*p*-Value
Dyn. activity	$(0\times11)V^2f$	5.721E−10	$p < 0.0001$
Dyn. activity	$(0\times1B - 0\times73)V^2f$	7.297E−10	$p < 0.0001$
Dyn. activity	$(0\times50)V^2f$	8.115E−09	$p < 0.0001$
Dyn. activity	$(0\times6A)V^2f$	1.606E−08	$p < 0.0001$
Dyn. activity	$(0\times73)V^2f$	8.574E−11	$p < 0.0001$
Dyn. activity	$(0\times14)V^2f$	1.083E−09	$p < 0.0001$
Dyn. activity	$(0\times19)V^2f$	2.505E−09	$p < 0.0001$
Static and BG dyn.	Intercept	−7.526E+02	$p < 0.0001$
Static and BG dyn.	f	1.516E−01	$p < 0.0001$
Static and BG dyn.	V	2.506E+03	$p < 0.0001$
Static and BG dyn.	Vf	−6.025E−01	$p < 0.0001$
Static and BG dyn.	V^2	−2.774E+03	$p < 0.0001$
Static and BG dyn.	V^2f	7.65E−01	$p < 0.0001$
Static and BG dyn.	V^3	1.021E+03	$p < 0.0001$
Static and BG dyn.	fV^3	−3.14E−01	$p < 0.0001$

Source: Data published in [23], downloaded from [33].

ambient temperature remains constant, the CPU temperature is mostly dependent on the current CPU operating voltage V, the switching speed (f), and also the amount of dynamic activity. The dynamic activity is already included in the model. The remaining components in the model *absorb* the effect of temperature due to DVFS level by including terms such as V^3 and Vf (constant ambient temperature is assumed). These terms were identified by trial-and-error while carefully monitoring the $\overline{R}^2$, MAPE, and *p-values*. All model coefficients in the final model have a *p-value* lower than 0.0001, showing that they are statistically very significant. Section 13.4.7 describes how a model using temperature measurements can be formulated. The next section describes how to validate the power models.

13.4.7   Model validation

The very first step in validating the model is to check the residual plots to confirm whether the model is appropriate for the data. A residual, e_i, is the difference between the observed value, y_i, and the fitted value $\hat{y}_i$:

$$e_i = y_i - \hat{y}_i \tag{13.6}$$

The model should have captured all of the available information from the independent variables in and the errors should therefore be stochastic. Therefore, there should not be any predictable patterns in the residuals when they are plotted against the fitted values, independent variables and available metrics not included in the model. Any patterns could mean that some important variables have been omitted from the model or that the incorrect relationship has been specified for some variables (e.g. perhaps x_p^2 is required instead of x_p). In this example, there is no pattern between the residuals and the fitted values (Figure 13.4(a)) or any other independent variable, as desired.

However, the cone shape shows the presence of non-constant variance of the error terms, which is known as heteroscedasticity; constant variance (homoscedasticity) is one of the assumptions of linear regression (Section 13.4.3). Heteroscasticity is inherent in some scenarios. A typical example is the relationship between family food expenditure and family income. Families with a low income will consistently spend a smaller amount on food, whereas families with a larger income will sometimes spend little on food but also sometimes spend a larger amount on a meal; there is a higher variance in money spent on meals in families with a higher income than families with a lower income. In CPU power models, the error variance is inherently larger in observations that consume more power (e.g. at higher DVFS levels, more activity, and utilising more cores).

The OLS estimator is still unbiased and consistent in the presence of heteroscedasticity. However, the OLS estimator is not as efficient with heteroscedasticity and the usual formulae for coefficient standard errors are inaccurate (depending on the degree of the problem) [44]. While this problem is inherent in PMC-based power modelling, it has not been addressed in existing works (with the exception of [23,34]), and many of the reported statistics from regression tools (e.g. standard errors, confidence intervals, p-values) are inaccurate without taking it into account. One solution is to use a heteroscedasticity-consistent standard error estimator of OLS parameter estimates [51].

Another overlooked consideration in power models is the uncertainly in the predictions. As explained at the beginning of this section, the MAPE does not give a good indication of how accurate a specific observation will be. It is usually important to know how much confidence can be placed on a prediction's accuracy being in a particular range. The prediction interval (PI) is a range where a new observation is likely to fall given the independent variables. The PI depends on the specific independent variables for a given observation, and many statistical packages provide the ability to calculate the PIs.

It is not good practice to calculate the MAPE from the same workloads used to train the model. A common approach is to use *k-fold cross validation* which involves

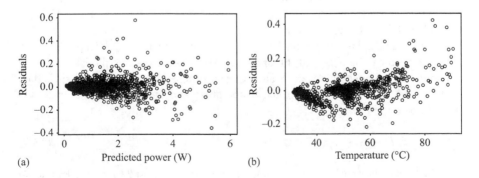

Figure 13.4   Residual plots. (a) Residuals vs predicted power and (b) Residuals vs temperature

randomising the order of the observations, splitting them into k groups, then using $k - 1$ of the groups to build the model (training dataset) and the one remaining group to validate the model (testing dataset). This process is repeated k times, with each group of observations being used to validate the model. For the example model, the average cross-fold validated MAPE was 2.81 per cent. The standard deviation between each k-fold group error (per cent) was 0.022 per cent. This shows the consistency and stability of the model across various workloads. Of the 60 workloads, only one had an error larger than 6.5 per cent.

Due to the model formulation, it is possible to build a model by only running the workloads at a single DVFS level and just sampling the idle voltage at every DVFS level. Additionally, due to the enhanced stability of the method shown in this chapter, fewer workloads are required. A MAPE of only 3.4 per cent (compared to 2.8 per cent) was achieved when using only 30 workloads at one DVFS level to train the model and validating on the full set of 60 workloads across nine DVFS levels. This shows the effectiveness of the model formulation and how the assumptions (e.g. breakdown of static and dynamic power) hold true. It also shows the terms included to absorb the effect of temperature (without using the measured temperature) are effective, as the temperature when running workloads at different DVFS levels varies significantly.

13.4.8   Thermal compensation

The CPU static power consumption is highly dependent on the CPU temperature (Section 13.1). The model formulated in Section 13.4.6 indirectly compensates for the effect of temperature due to the current voltage and frequency by including extra terms related to V and f (that were found to be statistically significant). This section demonstrates how more accurate models can be built, which works with extreme ambient temperature changes, if temperature is available as a model input (e.g. from a thermal sensor). The example in this section uses the temperature-compensated power model presented in [34].

The first step is to remove the terms used to indirectly absorb the temperature effects from the previous model. Without the higher order V terms, this model is not able to accurately estimate the power consumption under varying temperature conditions. For example, under three different fan settings, the power MAPE of a workload at 1.6 GHz is 1.6, 2.7, and 25 per cent when the temperature is 43.5 °C, 40.2 °C, and 73.6 °C, respectively.

The residuals of this new model are plotted against the measured temperature and a clear pattern can be observed (Figure 13.4(b)), showing that the model is missing valuable data included in the temperature measurements. Regression analysis is then used to predict the residuals from the temperature and the resulting relationship is found to be optimum:

$$e = \alpha_a T^2 + \alpha_b T + c \tag{13.7}$$

Therefore, the static power equation requires terms related to T, T^2, V, and an intercept. Including every combination results in a model with the lowest R^2 and apparent MAPE. However, doing so reduces the quality of the model as these mechanisms are being overfitted. Using the same method described in Section 13.4.6 using the *p*-values, six terms are selected to predict the static power. The new model has no observed patterns in the residuals and achieves a MAPE of 3.7 per cent, using 10-fold cross validation on over 1,000 observations under three different ambient temperature conditions.

13.4.9   CPU voltage regulator

In the previously described top-down models, the measured voltage is used as the voltage input into the model. However, the voltage supplied to the CPU from the (nonideal) voltage regulator actually varies with CPU load and has a significant effect on the power consumption. For example, when evaluating the model described in Section 13.4.6 at 1,800 MHz the MAPE is 2.6 per cent when using the measured voltage for each observation, but rises to 8.5 per cent when using the idle voltage instead. The measured voltage is not typically available at run-time and therefore a model predicting the actual voltage from the idle voltage and the estimated dynamic power consumption is presented in [23] and shown to reduce the MAPE to 3.0 per cent.

13.5   Accuracy of bottom-up power simulators

While top-down power models are profiled on a specific device, bottom-up power models use theoretical knowledge of each component to model a CPU based on a user's specification. CPU power consumption is determined by the number of transistors switching and the physical properties of the specific transistors switching. To determine this accurately, the simulator needs to know the CPU design (i.e. the size and complexity of each component), which functional units are activated, the physical properties of transistors used in different parts of the design, and how energy-saving techniques are implemented (e.g. clock gating, power gating, current voltage, and frequency). Creating a tool that is able to take a design specification from a user and to provide realistic and representative power estimations is therefore a challenging task.

Because bottom-up power modelling requires an architectural performance simulator to provide CPU activity statistics to the power modelling framework, the accuracy of the power models are therefore dependent on both the power-modelling and the performance-modelling frameworks. The remainder of this section focusses on the accuracy of bottom-up techniques.

While such simulation tools are invaluable to research, they inherently contain errors which can impact the conclusions drawn from research, particularly if the sources of error are not well understood. This potentially affects the quality and integrity of research that relies on the tools [39]. Recent works have focussed on these errors and their effects [39,52–55]. Three key categories of errors encountered in performance and power simulation tools include modelling error (model is incorrectly implemented by the developer), specification error (the model developer does not have access to detailed enough information about the CPU), and abstraction error (the simulator simplifies certain components) [38,54,56].

Butko *et al.* [57] compare the accuracy of a gem5 model against a hardware device with a dual-core ARM Cortex-A9 CPU, find an average error of between 1.4 and 17.9 per cent, and conclude that an overly simple DRAM model is a key source of the error. Gutierrez *et al.* [54] model and validate a dual-core Cortex-A15 CPU (with some complex-to-model features, such as prefetching, indirect branch predicting disabled) in gem5 and make improvements to the model to achieve an execution time MAPE of 13 and 17 per cent for SPEC2006 and dual-core PARSEC, respectively. They identify specification error to be the dominant cause of divergence between the model and the hardware platform. A later work by Butko *et al.* [38] presents an up-to-date gem5 model of an Exynos-5422 SoC. They find an execution time MAPE of 20 per cent using the Rodinia benchmarking suite and also identify specification error as the key source of error. They then use McPAT to conduct energy analysis and find a MAPE of 25 per cent when compared with the hardware platform.

Lee *et al.* [55] compare gem5 and McPAT with a hardware platform and present a learning-based methodology for calibrating the power estimations using the reference platform. A MAPE of 4.4 per cent was achieved when validating on 15 workloads and employing 15-fold cross validation. However, it does not correct inaccuracies in modelling of individual components.

A recently presented methodology and corresponding open-source software tool called *GemStone* [42] automatically compares a gem5 model with a reference hardware platform, identifies sources of error, and evaluates the impact of that error on the estimated performance and energy (assuming a power model is used) for different groups of workloads [39]. Hierarchical Cluster Analysis (HCA), correlation analysis and regression analysis are employed to identify sources of error without requiring detailed CPU specifications, therefore addressing the problem of specification error raised by Gutierrez *et al.* [54] and Butko *et al.* [38].

The gem5 simulation framework has a large and active development community and it is constantly becoming more capable and improving. However, one side effect is that it is becoming more complex and bugs can occasionally be unintentionally introduced. For example, when comparing a gem5 model of an ARM Cortex-A15 to a hardware platform using GemStone, the execution time MPE was initially found to be −51 per cent (performance is underestimated). A later version of gem5 included a bug fix that improved the MPE to +10 per cent [39] (Figure 13.5). This shows the importance of an automated tool to compare reference performance models against hardware platforms and analysing the errors.

This shows that the gem5 performance simulator can achieve good accuracy across a large set of workloads if the models have been specified well and tested for errors [39]. However, power modelling frameworks have a less active development community, use simpler CPU models, are more difficult to validate, and concerns have been raised over their accuracy [52]. The next section briefly describes coupling a performance simulator with top-down power models for more accurate power analysis.

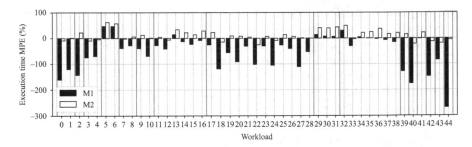

Figure 13.5   *GemStone evaluation of two versions (M1 and M2) of the same gem5*
model. Thick vertical lines group workloads deemed to be similar by
HCA of the PMC events. © 2017. Adapted, with permission, from
Reference [39]

13.6   Hybrid techniques

When evaluating research ideas or conducting design-space exploration, accurate
performance and power reference models are key to ensure representative results and
correct conclusions. For example, a common use case of a full-system simulator is
evaluating a proposal for a specific part of the system (e.g. the out-of-order scheduling,
branch predictor, L1I cache size, using non-volatile memory technology). To do this,
a baseline model is first used, the changes then applied, and the differences measured
and evaluated. A reference model based on a typical system is therefore an important
component of a simulation framework [39]. If there are significant errors in the
reference model, it may not respond in a representative way to the change under test.

While the gem5 performance simulator can achieve good accuracy if validated
and specified appropriately, there are questions regarding commonly used power simulation frameworks [52]. A recent work [39] validates gem5 models against hardware
platforms, creates top-down power models on hardware optimised for events available
in gem5, integrates the models into gem5, and presents software tools for applying
the power models to gem5 results statistics. Furthermore, a demonstration of how
errors in the gem5 models impact the power and energy estimations, including how
the models scale with frequency compared to hardware, is presented.

13.7   Conclusion and future directions

This chapter first described how power is consumed in a CPU and how energy-
efficiency can be maximised by controlling power-management techniques such as
DVFS, DPM, and single-ISA heterogeneous multiprocessing cores. Fundamental
to finding the optimum trade-offs are accurate and stable run-time power models.
Techniques for developing such models are presented, including solutions to some
typically overlooked problems such as improving coefficient stability, correctly specifying the equation to work across multiple DVFS levels, addressing heteroscedasticity,

modelling the effects of temperature on power consumption, and understanding the nonideal effects of the voltage regulator. Furthermore, effective validation techniques were presented, as well as an experimental demonstration of the importance of considering the variance inflation and using effective training and testing datasets.

As well as guiding run-time management decisions, accurate power modelling is fundamental for evaluating the energy efficiency of proposed hardware and software improvements and for system-level optimisation. This chapter has highlighted the importance of high-level bottom-up modelling frameworks (such as gem5 and McPAT) as well as some of their shortcomings and described techniques for improving their accuracy and applicability for typical use cases. Furthermore, the merits of combining flexible performance modelling frameworks (such as gem5) with empirical top-down power models have been outlined. Further work is needed to provide accurate, hardware-validated reference models for a variety of modern CPUs for multi- and many-core performance and energy simulation.

Modern systems are continuing to employ higher numbers of single-ISA heterogeneous cores, and are utilising new technologies, such as ARM DynamIQ [58] which allows cores with different microarchitectures to be within the same cluster, to be more tightly coupled, and to be on a separate DVFS domain to other cores in the cluster. Such improvements provide more energy-saving opportunities but require more complex run-time management guided by more accurate and sophisticated run-time power models in order to be effectively exploited. In recognition of the growing problems, energy-aware scheduling (EAS) [59], which unified the power management and scheduling decisions in Linux and uses run-time power models to guide them, has recently been introduced. Accurate and stable run-time power models must be built for every device utilising EAS using the techniques and advice shared in this chapter. To ensure forward progress in run-time management, methods of predicting the effects of switching heterogeneous cores and DVFS level on performance, power consumption, and temperature must be derived to ensure the energy-aware scheduler can make optimum decisions at run-time and proactively respects thermal and power limits. Furthermore, as run-time modelling advances, PMCs will be required for multiple purposes and the power model will therefore have to share its critical PMC event selection. Methods of effectively extracting as much microarchitectural information as possible, dynamically adapting power model input features and reducing multicollinearity at run-time must be explored to ensure forward progress.

References

[1]   Kaxiras S, Martonosi M. Computer Architecture Techniques for Power-Efficiency. 1st ed. Morgan and Claypool Publishers; 2008.

[2]   Kim NS, Austin T, Baauw D, *et al.* Leakage Current: Moore's Law Meets Static Power. Computer. 2003;36(12):68–75.

[3]   Irani d, Shukla S, Gupta R. Algorithms for Power Savings. In: Proceedings of the Fourteenth Annual ACM-SIAM Symposium on Discrete Algorithms. SODA'03. Philadelphia, PA, USA: Society for Industrial and

Applied Mathematics; 2003. p. 37–46. Available from: http://dl.acm.org/citation.cfm?id=644108.644115.

[4]   Albers S, Antoniadis A. Race to Idle: New Algorithms for Speed Scaling with a Sleep State. ACM Transactions on Algorithms. 2014;10(2):9:1–9:31. Available from: http://doi.acm.org/10.1145/2556953.

[5]   Bhatti K, Belleudy C, Auguin M. Power Management in Real Time Embedded Systems through Online and Adaptive Interplay of DPM and DVFS Policies. In: 2010 IEEE/IFIP International Conference on Embedded and Ubiquitous Computing; 2010. p. 184–191.

[6]   ARM Ltd. White Paper: big.LITTLE Technology, The Future of Mobile; 2013. Available from: https://www.arm.com/files/pdf/big_LITTLE_Technology_the_Futue_of_Mobile.pdf.

[7]   Kumar R, Farkas KI, Jouppi NP, *et al.* Single-ISA Heterogeneous Multi-core Architectures: The Potential for Processor Power Reduction. In: Proceedings. 36th Annual IEEE/ACM International Symposium on Microarchitecture, 2003. MICRO-36; 2003. p. 81–92.

[8]   Zhu Y, Reddi VJ. High-performance and Energy-efficient Mobile Web Browsing on Big/little Systems. In: 2013 IEEE 19th International Symposium on High Performance Computer Architecture (HPCA); 2013. p. 13–24.

[9]   Muthukaruppan TS, Pricopi M, Venkataramani V, *et al.* Hierarchical Power Management for Asymmetric Multi-core in Dark Silicon Era. In: 2013 50th ACM/EDAC/IEEE Design Automation Conference (DAC); 2013. p. 1–9.

[10] Kim M, Kim K, Geraci JR, *et al.* Utilization-aware Load Balancing for the Energy Efficient Operation of the big.LITTLE Processor. In: 2014 Design, Automation Test in Europe Conference Exhibition (DATE); 2014. p. 1–4.

[11] Chronaki K, Moretó M, Casas M, *et al.* POSTER: Exploiting Asymmetric Multi-core Processors with Flexible System Software. In: 2016 International Conference on Parallel Architecture and Compilation Techniques (PACT); 2016. p. 415–417.

[12] Intel Corporation. White paper: Measuring Processor Power, TDP vs. ACP; 2011. Available from: https://www.intel.com/content/dam/doc/white-paper/resources-xeon-measuring-processor-power-paper.pdf.

[13] Rotem E, Naveh A, Ananthakrishnan A, *et al.* Power-Management Architecture of the Intel Microarchitecture Code-Named Sandy Bridge. IEEE Micro. 2012;32(2):20–27.

[14] Zhang Y, Liu Y, Zhuang L, *et al.* Accurate CPU Power Modeling for Multicore Smartphones; 2015. Available from: https://www.microsoft.com/en-us/research/publication/accurate-cpu-power-modeling-for-multicore-smartphones/.

[15] Yoon C, Lee S, Choi Y, *et al.* Accurate Power Modeling of Modern Mobile Application Processors. Journal of Systems Architecture. 2017;81(Supplement C):17–31. Available from: http://www.sciencedirect.com/science/article/pii/S1383762117301947.

[16] Bellosa F. The Benefits of Event: Driven Energy Accounting in Power-sensitive Systems. In: Proceedings of the 9th Workshop on ACM SIGOPS

European Workshop: Beyond the PC: New Challenges for the Operating System. EW 9. New York, NY, USA: ACM; 2000. p. 37–42. Available from: http://doi.acm.org/10.1145/566726.566736.

[17]   Singh K, Bhadauria M, McKee SA. Real Time Power Estimation and Thread Scheduling via Performance Counters. ACM SIGARCH Computer Architecture News. 2009;37(2):46–55. Available from: http://doi.acm.org/10.1145/1577129.1577137.

[18]   Bertran R, Gonzalez M, Martorell X, *et al.* Decomposable and Responsive Power Models for Multicore Processors Using Performance Counters. In: Proceedings of the 24th ACM International Conference on Supercomputing. ICS'10. New York, NY, USA: ACM; 2010. p. 147–158. Available from: http://doi.acm.org/10.1145/1810085.1810108.

[19]   Costa GD, Hlavacs H. Methodology of Measurement for Energy Consumption of Applications. In: 2010 11th IEEE/ACM International Conference on Grid Computing; 2010. p. 290–297.

[20]   Bircher WL, John LK. Complete System Power Estimation Using Processor Performance Events. IEEE Transactions on Computers. 2012;61(4):563–577.

[21]   Rodrigues R, Annamalai A, Koren I, *et al.* A Study on the Use of Performance Counters to Estimate Power in Microprocessors. IEEE Transactions on Circuits and Systems II: Express Briefs. 2013;60(12):882–886.

[22]   Su B, Gu J, Shen L, *et al.* PPEP: Online Performance, Power, and Energy Prediction Framework and DVFS Space Exploration. In: 2014 47th Annual IEEE/ACM International Symposium on Microarchitecture; 2014. p. 445–457.

[23]   Walker MJ, Diestelhorst S, Hansson A, *et al.* Accurate and Stable Run-Time Power Modeling for Mobile and Embedded CPUs. IEEE Transactions on Computer-Aided Design of Integrated Circuits and Systems. 2017;36(1): 106–119.

[24]   Mair J, Huang Z, Eyers D, *et al.* PMC-Based Power Modelling with Workload Classification on Multicore Systems. In: 2014 43rd International Conference on Parallel Processing Workshops; 2014. p. 129–138.

[25]   Alawnah S, Sagahyroon A. Modeling of Smartphones' Power Using Neural Networks. EURASIP Journal on Embedded Systems. 2017;2017(1):22. Available from: https://doi.org/10.1186/s13639-017-0070-1.

[26]   Huang CX, Zhang B, Deng AC, *et al.* The Design and Implementation of PowerMill. In: Proceedings of the 1995 International Symposium on Low Power Design. ISLPED'95. New York, NY, USA: ACM; 1995. p. 105–110. Available from: http://doi.acm.org/10.1145/224081.224100.

[27]   Brooks D, Tiwari V, Martonosi M. Wattch: A Framework for Architectural-level Power Analysis and Optimizations. In: Proceedings of 27th International Symposium on Computer Architecture (IEEE Cat. No.RS00201); 2000. p. 83–94.

[28]   Shivakumar P, Jouppi NP, Shivakumar P. CACTI 3.0: An Integrated Cache Timing, Power, and Area Model; 2001.

[29]   Li S, Ahn JH, Strong RD, *et al.* McPAT: An Integrated Power, Area, and Timing Modeling Framework for Multicore and Manycore Architectures.

In: Proceedings of the 42Nd Annual IEEE/ACM International Symposium on Microarchitecture. MICRO 42. New York, NY, USA: ACM; 2009. p. 469–480. Available from: http://doi.acm.org/10.1145/1669112.1669172.

[30] Burger D, Austin TM. The SimpleScalar Tool Set, Version 2.0. ACM SIGARCH Computer Architecture News. 1997;25(3):13–25. Available from: http://doi.acm.org/10.1145/268806.268810.

[31] Binkert N, Beckmann B, Black G, *et al.* The Gem5 Simulator. ACM SIGARCH Computer Architecture News. 2011;39(2):1–7. Available from: http://doi.acm.org/10.1145/2024716.2024718.

[32] Akram A, Sawalha L. A Comparison of ×86 Computer Architecture Simulators. Computer Architecture and Systems Research Laboratory (CASRL). 2016.

[33] Walker MJ, Diestelhorst S, Hansson A, *et al.* Powmon: Run-Time CPU Power Modelling; 2017. [Online; accessed 06-Nov-2017]. http://www.powmon.ecs.soton.ac.uk/powermodeling.

[34] Walker MJ, Diestelhorst S, Hansson A, *et al.* Thermally-aware Composite Runtime CPU Power Models. In: 2016 26th International Workshop on Power and Timing Modeling, Optimization and Simulation (PATMOS); 2016. p. 17–24.

[35] Chadha M, Ilsche T, Bielert M, *et al.* A Statistical Approach to Power Estimation for ×86 Processors. In: 2017 IEEE International Parallel and Distributed Processing Symposium Workshops (IPDPSW); 2017. p. 1012–1019.

[36] Spiliopoulos V, Kaxiras S, Keramidas G. Green Governors: A Framework for Continuously Adaptive DVFS. In: 2011 International Green Computing Conference and Workshops; 2011. p. 1–8.

[37] Hardkernel. ODROID-XU3; 2013. [Online; accessed 30-Nov-2017]. http://www.hardkernel.com.

[38] Butko A, Bruguier F, Gamatié A, *et al.* Full-System Simulation of big.LITTLE Multicore Architecture for Performance and Energy Exploration. In: 2016 IEEE 10th International Symposium on Embedded Multicore/Many-core Systems-on-Chip (MCSOC); 2016. p. 201–208.

[39] Walker MJ, Diestelhorst S, Bischoff S, *et al.* Hardware-Validated CPU Performance and Energy Modelling. 2018 IEEE International Symposium on Performance Analysis of Systems and Software (ISPASS); 2018. https://ieeexplore.ieee.org/document/8366934.

[40] Walker MJ, Das AK, Merrett GV, *et al.* Run-time Power Estimation for Mobile and Embedded Asymmetric Multi-core CPUs. In: HIPEAC Workshop on Energy Efficiency with Heterogenous Computing; 2015. Available from: https://eprints.soton.ac.uk/372827/.

[41] perf. Linux Profiling with Performance Counters; 2015. [Online; accessed 30-Nov-2017]. https://perf.wiki.kernel.org.

[42] Walker MJ, Diestelhorst S, Bischoff S, *et al.* GemStone; 2017. [Online; accessed 30-Jan-2018]. http://gemstone.ecs.soton.ac.uk/.

[43] Freund RJ, Minton PD. Regression Methods: A Tool for Data Analysis. vol. 30 of Statistics, Textbooks and Monographs. New York, NY: Marcel Dekker Inc.; 1979.

[44]   Fox J. Applied Regression Analysis, Linear Models, and Related Methods. SAGE Publications; 1997.

[45]   Kutner M, Nachtsheim C, Neter J. Applied Linear Regression Models. 4th ed. McGraw-Hill Education; 2004.

[46]   Kutner MH. Applied Linear Statistical Models. McGraw-Hill International ed. McGraw-Hill Irwin; 2005.

[47]   Bircher WL, Valluri M, Law J, *et al.* Runtime Identification of Microprocessor Energy Saving Opportunities. In: ISLPED'05. Proceedings of the 2005 International Symposium on Low Power Electronics and Design, 2005; 2005. p. 275–280.

[48]   Pricopi M, Muthukaruppan TS, Venkataramani V, *et al.* Power-performance Modeling on Asymmetric Multi-cores. In: 2013 International Conference on Compilers, Architecture and Synthesis for Embedded Systems (CASES); 2013. p. 1–10.

[49]   Jr JFH, Black WC, Babin BJ, *et al.* Multivariate Data Analysis. 7th ed. Prentice Hall, Harlow, Essex; 2009.

[50]   Spiliopoulos V, Sembrant A, Kaxiras S. Power-Sleuth: A Tool for Investigating Your Program's Power Behavior. In: 2012 IEEE 20th International Symposium on Modeling, Analysis and Simulation of Computer and Telecommunication Systems; 2012. p. 241–250.

[51]   Hayes AF, Cai L. Using Heteroskedasticity-consistent Standard Error Estimators in OLS Regression: An Introduction and Software Implementation. Behavior Research Methods. 2007;39(4):709–722. Available from: https://doi.org/10.3758/BF03192961.

[52]   Xi SL, Jacobson H, Bose P, *et al.* Quantifying Sources of Error in McPAT and Potential Impacts on Architectural Studies. In: 2015 IEEE 21st International Symposium on High Performance Computer Architecture (HPCA); 2015. p. 577–589.

[53]   Nowatzki T, Menon J, Ho CH, *et al.* gem5, GPGPUSim, McPAT, GPUWattch, "Your favorite simulator here" Considered Harmful; 2014.

[54]   Gutierrez A, Pusdesris J, Dreslinski R, *et al.* Sources of Error in Full-system Simulation; 2014.

[55]   Lee W, Kim Y, Ryoo JH, *et al.* PowerTrain: A Learning-based Calibration of McPAT Power Models. In: 2015 IEEE/ACM International Symposium on Low Power Electronics and Design (ISLPED); 2015. p. 189–194.

[56]   Black B, Shen JP. Calibration of Microprocessor Performance Models. Computer. 1998;31:59–65.

[57]   Butko A, Garibotti R, Ost L, *et al.* Accuracy Evaluation of GEM5 Simulator System. In: 7th International Workshop on Reconfigurable and Communication-Centric Systems-on-Chip (ReCoSoC); 2012. p. 1–7.

[58]   Arm Developer. DynamIQ; 2018. [Online; accessed 08-Mar-2018]. https://developer.arm.com/technologies/dynamiq.

[59]   Arm Developer. Energy Aware Scheduling; 2018. [Online; accessed 08-Mar-2018]. https://developer.arm.com/open-source/energy-aware-scheduling.

Chapter 14

Developing portable embedded software for multicore systems through formal abstraction and refinement

Asieh Salehi Fathabadi[1], Mohammadsadegh Dalvandi[1], and Michael Butler[1]

14.1 Introduction

Run-time management (RTM) systems [1,2] are used in embedded systems to dynamically adapt hardware performance to minimise energy consumption. An RTM system implementation is coupled with the hardware platform specifications and is implemented individually for each specific platform. A significant challenge is that RTM software can require laborious manual adjustment across different hardware platforms due to the diversity of architecture characteristics. Hardware specifications vary from one platform to another and include a number of characteristic such as the number of supported voltage and frequency (VF) settings.

Formal modelling offers the potential to simplify the management of platform diversity by shifting the focus away from handwritten platform-specific code to platform-independent models from which platform-specific implementations are automatically generated. Formal models can provide reusability and portability through abstraction and refinement. Developing RTM systems in a way that is independent of the platform specification diversity, making RTM designs portable across different platforms. Furthermore, the use of formal verification provides the means to ensure correctness.

Formal methods are mathematically based techniques used for specifying and reasoning about software and hardware systems [3]. We use the Event-B formal method [4] to model and verify RTM systems. Our methodology in designing the RTM systems uses the Event-B high-level mathematical language, which can describe systems at different abstraction levels. Code generation has been introduced in the Event-B formal method to bridge the gap between abstract specifications and implementation [5]. The code generation tool is used to translate platform-independent Event-B RTM models to platform-specific implementations in C. The platform

[1] Faculty of Engineering and Physical Sciences, University of Southampton, United Kingdom

parameters are instantiated to prepare the independent model for specific translation. Formal verification is used to ensure correctness of the Event-B models.

The portability offered by the methodology is validated by modelling a learning-based RTM for video decoder applications and generating implementations for three different platforms (ARM Cortex-A8, A7, and A15) that all achieve energy savings on the respective platforms.

In addition, formal modelling is associated with the verification techniques which can ensure the correctness of the RTM design. The use of formal methods helps to reduce costs by identifying specification and design errors at early development stages when they are cheaper to fix [4].

The rest of this chapter is organised as follows: Section 14.2 presents an overview of the motivations for this work. Section 14.3 overviews the RTM architecture and requirements. Section 14.4 introduces the Event-B formal method and its tool support. Section 14.5 describes the Event-B model of two different RTMs. Section 14.6 presents the portability support provided by formal modelling and code generation. Section 14.7 reviews the verification and experimental results. Finally, Section 14.8 concludes the chapter.

14.2 Motivation

Our RTM-modelling approach utilises the formal abstraction technique and supports portability, which are introduced in this section.

14.2.1 From identical formal abstraction to specific refinements

Formal abstraction, using Event-B, is adopted to abstract away complexities within the RTM in embedded systems. In the abstract levels, we focus on main functionality of the RTM. This approach of abstraction results in an identical formal abstraction for different types of RTM (top box of Figure 14.1). In Section 14.5.1, we present more details of the shared abstract model (e.g. see diagrammatic representation in Figure 14.6 of the actions within the RTM Event-B models).

Details of run-time algorithms are added through refinement levels which are specific to each RTM procedure (bottom boxes of Figure 14.1). Here, two RTM systems, within a cross-layer architecture, are demonstrated that share two levels

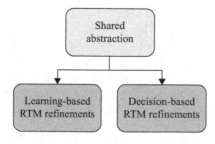

Figure 14.1　From identical abstraction to specific refinements

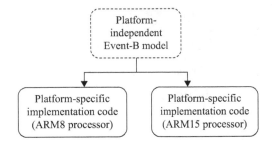

Figure 14.2   From platform-independent formal model to platform-specific implementation

of abstraction. Sections 14.5.2 and 14.5.3, respectively, present details of the two different refinements (see Figures 14.7 and 14.9 for a diagrammatic representation of the events of the two refined models).

14.2.2   From platform-independent formal model to platform-specific implementations

The RTM algorithms can be highly dependent of the hardware specifications. However, in our approach, the design model is independent of the platforms while the generated code is specific to each platform, as illustrated in Figure 14.2.

For example, an Event-B model is parameterised by the number of supported VFs, which is different from one platform to another, and makes it independent of this number. The model is instantiated with the specific number of VFs and is translated to a C implementation tailored to one specific platform. Details of this are explained in Section 14.6.

Shared abstraction facilitates reusing of model across different RTMs, and therefore saving time and modelling efforts. Properties of shared abstraction are preserved by refinements. In addition, platform-independent modelling aids portability across different platforms. The RTM model is built once and is atomically translated to RTM codes specific to each platform architecture. It can reduce the time and effort of developing RTMs tailored to each specific platform.

14.3   RTM cross-layer architecture overview

Figure 14.3 shows the RTM architecture adopting a cross-layer approach, interacting with the application and device layers. The application layer is any software program running on the system and the device layer includes the physical hardware and any low-level drivers. Communication between layers is indicated by arrows. The RTM is aiming to meet the performance constraint (required by the application), while saving power by tuning the controls (e.g. VF, thread-to-core mapping) of the device and monitoring core activities (e.g. workload, temperature).

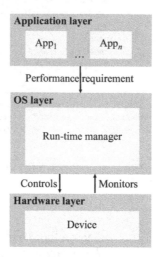

Figure 14.3   Run-time management, cross-layer architecture

Different RTMs adopted different algorithms to facilitate trade-offs between power and performance. We applied our formal approach to two types of RTM: a learning-based RTM [6] and a static decision-based RTM [7]. The former uses Q-learning as a decision-making algorithm to select the optimal value of VF which meets the deadline, set by the application. Our learning-based RTM monitors the CPU-cycles (actual workload) for each epoch to learn an improved choice of VF for future epochs. Details are presented in Section 14.5.2. The latter RTM uses offline and static information to select the optimal value of VF and thread-to-core mapping. It monitors the Memory Read Per Instruction (MRPI) for each epoch to adjust the VF for the future epochs. Details are presented in Section 14.5.2. Both RTMs share a single abstract model (in two levels of abstraction) including representation of cross-layer interactions (Section 14.5.1). Each RTM is refined differently to model the distinct details of its algorithm (Sections 14.5.2 and 14.5.3).

14.4   Event-B

Event-B is a formal language for system-level modelling based on set theory and predicate logic for specifying, modelling and reasoning about systems, introduced by Abrial [4].

In the rest of this section, the Event-B method is described. The structure of Event-B models, stepwise refinement, and proof obligations are discussed in more details.

14.4.1   Structure and notation

A model in Event-B consists of two main parts: context and machine. The static part (types and constants) of a model is placed in a context and is specified using carrier

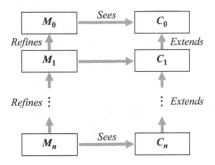

Figure 14.4   Event-B model structure

sets, constants and axioms. The dynamic part (variables and events) is specified in a machine by means of variables, invariants, and events. A context, say C, can be seen by one or more machines, and it can be extended by another context D. A machine, say M, can be refined by another machine N. In this case, it is said that N is a refinement of M and M is an abstraction of N. If machine M can see context C, then N can see context C too. Figure 14.4 illustrates the relations between machines and contexts in an Event-B development, where machine M_0 is the most abstract machine and M_n is the most concrete machine in the development.

14.4.1.1   Context structure

To describe the static part of a model there are four elements in the structure of a context: *carrier sets, constants, axioms,* and *theorems.* Carrier sets are represented by their name, and they are disjoint from each other. Constants are defined using axioms. Axioms are predicates that express properties of sets and constants. Theorems in contexts should be proved from axioms.

14.4.1.2   Machine structure

A machine in Event-B consists of three main elements: (1) a collection of *variables,* which defines the states of a model; (2) a collection of *invariants,* which is a set of conditions on state variables that must hold whenever a variable is changed by an event; and (3) a collection of *events* which model the state change in the system. Each event may have a number of assignments called *actions.* Each event may also have a number of *guards.* Guards are predicates that are implicitly conjoined forming the necessary overall enabling condition of an event. Enabled events are selected non-deterministically and executed atomically. Note that an event might not have any guards; in this case, that event will always be enabled. An event may have a number of parameters. Event parameters are considered to be local to the event. In the following, we denote the variables and invariants by v and $I(v)$, respectively. An event may have one of the following forms:

$$\text{Evt} \triangleq \textbf{when } P(v) \textbf{ then } S(v) \textbf{ end}$$

$$\text{Evt} \triangleq \textbf{any } t \textbf{ when } P(t,v) \textbf{ then } S(t,v) \textbf{ end}$$

Table 14.1   Event types

Type	Assignment	Example
Deterministic	$x := E(t, v)$	$x := x + 1$
Non-deterministic	$x : \in E(t, v)$	$x : \in A \cup \{y\}$
Non-deterministic	$x : \mid Q(t, v, x')$	$x, y : \mid x' > y \wedge y' > x' + z$

The difference between above events is that the first event does not have any parameters, while the second one has one or more parameters represented by t. $P(v)$ and $P(t, v)$ denote guards and $S(v)$ and $S(t, v)$ denote actions.

As mentioned above, actions are assignments describing the associated state change with an event. An assignment may have one of the following types: (1) deterministic assignment, (2) non-deterministic assignment of a value from a set, or (3) non-deterministic assignment of a value satisfying a predicate. There may also be no action in an event which in that case it is shown by skip. Table 14.1 shows these three types and a simple example for each. x is a variable, $E(t, v)$ is an expression, and $Q(t, v, x')$ is a predicate.

14.4.2   Refinement

Modelling a complex system in Event-B benefits from refinement as modelling a system in different levels of abstraction helps to tackle the complexity of design. Refinement is a stepwise process of building a large system starting from an abstract level towards a concrete level [8,9]. This is done by a series of steps in which new details of functionality are added to the model in each step. The abstract level represents key features and the main purpose of the system. The abstract model does not include implementation details and how the goal of the system is going to be achieved. Instead, it focuses on what the goal of the system is.

Refining an Event-B model may involve context extension and machine refinement. When a context is extended, new sets, constants, and axioms are added and sets and constants in abstract context will be kept in the extension.

All abstract events must be refined by one or more concrete events. New events can be added in a refined machine. All new events refine a dummy skip event in the abstract machine. The new events must converge which is verified by proving that they decrease a variant (VAR).

Each refinement may involve introducing new variables to the model. This usually results in extending abstract events or adding new events to the model. It is also possible to replace abstract variables by newly defined concrete variables.

Refinement of a machine may consist of refining existing events, adding new events, and adding new variables and invariants. Refining an existing abstract event may have one of the following two forms: (1) extending the abstract event with new parameters, guards, and actions (*horizontal refinement*) or (2) modifying parameters, guards, and actions of the abstract event (*vertical refinement*). In the former, abstract parameters, guards, and actions do not change. In the latter, however, replacing and adding new parameters, guards, and actions are allowed. In both cases, guards of concrete event should be stronger than guards of abstract event.

Concrete variables are connected to abstract variables through gluing invariants. A gluing invariant associates the state of the concrete machine with that of its abstraction. All invariants of a concrete model including gluing invariants should be preserved by all events.

14.4.3   Proof obligations

For proving different formal properties of a model, a number of proof obligations are defined [4]. In order to verify a model, all proof obligations should be discharged. This can be done with the help of automatic or interactive provers. The different kinds of proof obligations are as follows:

- **Invariant preservation (INV):** This proof obligation ensures that each invariant in a machine is preserved by all events in that machine.
- **Feasibility:** This is to ensure that each non-deterministic action is feasible, i.e. there is an after state satisfying the corresponding before–after predicate.
- **Guard strengthening:** This proof obligation is to guarantee that the guards of a concrete event are stronger than the guards of its abstract event. This means that whenever the concrete event is enabled, the abstract event is enabled as well.
- **VAR:** This proof obligation guarantees that each convergent event decreases a proposed VAR expression. A convergent event is proved to terminate by specifying that it decreases a VAR with lower bound.
- **Well definedness:** This proves that guards, actions, invariants, axioms, theorems, and VARs are *well defined*. A well-defined expression is an expression that its definition assigns it a unique interpretation or value. If an expression is not well defined, its meaning is ambiguous.

14.4.4   Rodin: event-B tool support

Modelling in Event-B is facilitated by a tool called Rodin [10,11]. Rodin is an open-source tool which is built on top of the Eclipse IDE. It is an extensible and adaptable modelling tool. Various plug-ins have been developed in order to perform different tasks in Rodin. The ProB animator [12], the decomposition plug-in [13], the code generator plug-in [14], and many other plug-ins are representative examples of Rodin extensibility.

Rodin provides feedback about model text by detecting possible syntactic and semantic errors. One of the most important tasks which Rodin performs automatically is generating proof obligations. As mentioned in Section 4.3, proof obligations define what should be proved about the model. By trying to discharge proof obligations, developers can find possible semantic errors in their design. A proof obligation can prove either automatically by the Rodin provers or interactively with the Rodin support for interactive proving. Also ProB animator can help to find counterexamples by

Figure 14.5   A screenshot of the Rodin Platform

offering model checking facilities. Figure 14.5 is a screenshot of Rodin platform. A comprehensive guide on the Rodin tool can be found in [11,15].

14.5   From identical formal abstraction to specific refinements

14.5.1   Abstraction

To present the Event-B model of RTMs, we utilise a visualisation technique within Event-B called ERS (event refinement structures) [16]. This technique helps us to demonstrate the formal model without getting too involved with the details of Event-B mathematical language.

Figure 14.6 presents the two levels of abstraction in the RTM Event-B model using an ERS hierarchical diagram. Each node indicates an event in the Event-B model and the oval contains a name for the overall flow of events in the model. The nodes are read from left to right indicating the ordering between them. In the top region, there are three actions representing the abstract view of the RTM interactions with the application and device layers. First the *get_app_perf* event (RTM gets required performance from the application) executes, followed by execution of the *set_dev_controls* event (where an RTM controls settings in the device) and *get_dev_monitors* executes to monitor the device activity.

The bottom region presents a further level of modelling where abstract details of the *set_dev_controls* event are introduced as a refinement. The types of lines in the diagram indicate whether a sub-node is a refining event (solid line) or a new event (dashed line). The *set_dev_controls* event is refined by two sub-events: *select_dev_controls* (to model the specific RTM algorithm to decide on the value of the device parameters in the future refinements) and *set_dev_controls*.

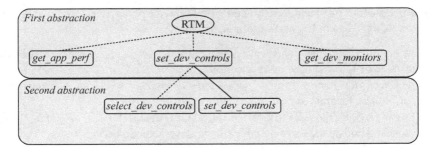

Figure 14.6   RTM abstraction

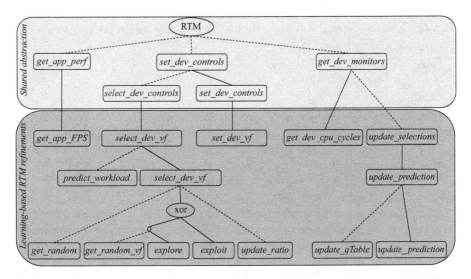

Figure 14.7   Learning-based RTM refinement

RTM-dependent details are not included in the abstraction. Each RTM is separately refined to include such details (see the following sections). The learning-based RTM (Section 14.5.2) controls dynamic VF scaling (DVFS) using a learning-based procedure (appears in the refinements of the *select_dev_controls* abstract event), while the decision-based RTM (Section 14.5.3) controls both DVFS and thread-to-core mapping using offline profiling and static information. All properties proved for the shared abstraction are guaranteed, by refinement, to be preserved by both of the refined RTMs (Sections 14.5.2 and 14.5.3).

14.5.2   Learning-based RTM refinements

Figure 14.7 presents the shared abstraction (top region) and specific refinements to model the learning-based RTM (bottom region). There are three levels of refinements. The first level of refinement provides details of specific performance requirement (frame per second (FPS) required by application), device parameters (VF), and device monitors (CPU cycles). Events are refined as below:

- The *get_app_perf* abstract event is refined by the *get_app_fps* event (RTM gets the value of FPS required by application).
- The *select_dev_controls* and *set_dev_controls* events are refined to specifically control the VF parameter.
- The *get_dev_monitors* event is refined to get CPU cycles (the *get_dev_cpu_cycles* event) and update the learning table (the update_selections event).

In the first level of refinement of the bottom region, the value of the VF is decided non-deterministically from the constant set VF. Below is the Event-B specification of the *select_dev_vf* event. Here action *act*1 indicates the body of the event where the value of VF is non-deterministically assigned to a value from the set VF:

> **Event** *select_dev_vf*
> **then**
> > act1: *freq* $:\in VF$
>
> **End**

Non-deterministic assignment allows the selection of VF to be specified in an abstract way without getting involved with the details of selection algorithm.

The set VF is assigned specifically for each device in an Event-B context which is seen by the Event-B machine including the abstract events. For example, for the ARM Cortex-A8, which provides four values of VF, it is defined as follows: $VF :=$ $\{FREQ1, FREQ2, FREQ3, FREQ4\}$

Our learning-based RTM includes workload prediction and machine learning. There are two refinement levels to introduce the details of the prediction and learning algorithms. We are using refinement to separate the details of prediction and machine-learning algorithms and deal with each of them in separate refinement levels.

The details of the prediction algorithm are added to the following two abstract events: *select_dev_vf* and *update_selections*. The *select_dev_vf* event is refined into two concrete events: *predict_workload*, where the workload is predicted and *select_dev_vf*, where the value of VF is decided based on the prediction. The *update_selections* event is also refined into two events: *get_dev_cpu_cycle* (monitoring the actual workload) and *update_prediction* (updating the prediction factors).

The prediction algorithm estimates the workload for the next frame using a modified form of *Exponential Weighted Moving Average* (EWMA). The specification of the *predict_workload* and *update_prediction* events are as follows:

> **Event** *predict_workload*
> **then**
> > act1: *pwl* $:= avgwl$
>
> **End**
> **Event** *update_prediction*
> **then**
> > act1: $avgwl := update(l, w, avgwl)$
>
> **End**

In the new *predict_workload* event, the predicted workload variable (*pwl*) is assigned to the average workload variable (*avgwl*), where *avgwl* is updated in the refining *update_prediction* event, according to the definition of update operator in the EWMA theory.

A theory is an Event-B component where we can introduce additional mathematical operators which can be seen from the Event-B machine/context components. In this development, we have defined a theory of EWMA where the prediction operators are defined. The *update* operator is defined as below:

Theory *EWMA*
operator $update(l \in \mathbb{Z}, w \in \mathbb{Z}, avgwl \in \mathbb{Z}) = l * w + (1 - l) * avgwl$

The value of *freq* is calculated based on the predicted workload in *select_dev_vf* event:

Event *select_dev_vf*
refines *select_dev_vf*
then
     act1: *freq* := *pwl* * *fps*
End

This event is refined in the next refinement where the *freq* is selected based on the learning algorithm.

The last level of refinement is providing details of the learning algorithm. The learning algorithm works in two phases: exploration and exploitation. In the exploration stage, random VF values are selected and the corresponding responses (rewards or penalties) are recorded in a lookup table called *QTable*. In the exploitation stage, the VF decisions that can achieve the highest rewards from the QTable are applied.

To model these details, the *select_dev_vf* event is further refined. First the *get_random* event non-deterministically chooses a value. Comparing this chosen value with the exploration–exploitation ratio (ε), either the explore or exploit event are executed, and this is followed by updating ε (the *update_ratio* event). The oval containing XOR represents an exclusive choice between its branches. In the case of exploration, first the *get_random_vf* event non-deterministically chooses a VF value within the available VFs to be used in the explore event. The transition from exploration to exploitation is not immediate but is a gradual change, defined as the ε-greedy strategy, in which the exploration–exploitation ratio (ε) is gradually increased to reduce the random decisions in favour of decision-based knowledge gained from observations by the learning-based algorithm.

Below is the Event-B description of the *explore* and *exploit* events. These events are guarded based on the value of the random variable (non-deterministically chosen in the *get_random* event). If random is greater than the exploration–exploitation ratio (ε), the explore event executes, otherwise the *exploit* event executes. In the body of the *explore* event, the value of *freq* is assigned to a random VF value (generated in the *get_random_vf* event). The *exploit* event assigns the value of *freq* to the optimal value of VF according to the predicted workload (*pwl*). *optimalVF* is an operator defined in a theory where all of the necessary learning operators are defined.

> **Event** *explore*
> **refines** *select_dev_vf*
> **where**
>   grd1: *random* > *epsilon*
> **then**
>   act1: *freq* := *randomVF*
> **End**

> **Event** *exploit*
> **refines** *select_dev_vf*
> **where**
>   grd1: *random* ≤ *epsilon*
> **then**
>   act1: *freq* := *optimalVF*(*QTable, pwl*)
> **End**

Knowledge generated from learning is stored as values in a QTable, which is a lookup table. At each decision epoch, the decision taken for the last epoch is evaluated; the reward or penalty computed is added to the corresponding QTable entry, thereby gaining experience on the decision. To model the QTable update, the *update_prediction* event is refined where the workload is rewarded or penalised:

> **Event** *update_qTable*
> **any** *i*
> **where**
>   grd1: $i \in 1..NF(i1) < freq \leq F(i)$
> **then**
>   act1: *qTable* := *updateArray*(*qTable, row, i, re_pe*)
> **End**

The *update_qTable* event specifies that a value *i* (indicated by the keyword *any*) should be selected that satisfies the event guard (indicated by the keyword when) and the update action (indicated by the keyword then) should be performed with the selected value for *i*. Here *i* represents an index for a frequency value and determines which column of the *qTable* gets updated with the value of the reward/penalty (*re_pe*). *N* is the number of VFs and *F* is an ordering function specifying the values of frequencies (voltage is paired with frequency).

In the body of the event, the value of the variable *qTable* is updated, where *qTable* is defined as a two-dimension array; *row* specifies the row number, *i* specifies the column number, and *re_pa* is the reward or penalty of the most recent decision. The value of the *row* and *re_pe* are assigned in separated events.

The *update_qTable* event is an example of a dependency between the RTM algorithm and the platform specification (number of VFs here). The event parameter

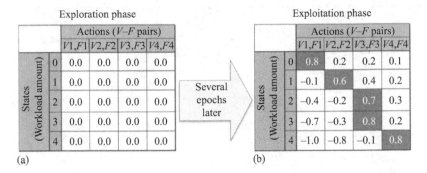

Figure 14.8   Learning table during (a) exploration and (b) exploitation phases

(*i* here) constrains the choice of frequency. This event is discussed in depth in the next section.

Figure 14.8 shows the evolution of the QTable. Initially, the values in the QTable are all zeros (Figure 14.8(a)). In the exploration phase, the QTable will be filled with values indicating rewards or penalties. In the exploitation phase, the optimal value of VF is determined based on the QTable entries with highest rewards (highlighted in Figure 14.8(b)).

14.5.3   Static decision-based RTM refinements

Figure 14.9 presents the refinements for the decision-based RTM. Comparing Figures 14.7 and 14.9 shows how both RTMs share a single abstraction (top region) to model the general interactions, while the refinements are specific to each RTM algorithm. The learning-based RTM is modelled for single core platforms and one application to manage DFVS, while the decision-based RTM supports heterogeneous multicore platforms that contain different types of cores, organised as clusters and multiple applications having different performance requirements, executing concurrently. To support multicore, in the refinement, an event is allocated to specify the thread-to-core mapping. Also, a refining event specifies setting changes when the set of applications changes. The static decision-based RTM uses offline profiling and static workload classification to build a decision table, whereas the learning-based RTM updates the QTable at runtime based on observations and learning from these through rewards and penalties.

Figure 14.9 represents three levels of refinement for the static decision-based RTM. The first level of refinement provides details of specific performance requirement (instruction per second (IPS)), device parameters (illustrated as a choice between thread-to-core mapping and VF), and device monitors (MRPI). Events are refined as follows:

- The *get_app_perf* abstract event is refined by the *get_app_IPS* event (RTM gets the value of IPS required by application).

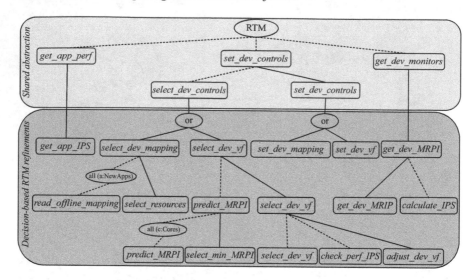

Figure 14.9   Decision-based RTM refinements

- The *select_dev_controls* and *set_dev_controls* events are refined to specifically control the thread-to-core mapping and VF parameters. The *or* constructor represents a choice between its branches. RTM controls VF for each epoch, while thread-to-core mapping is only changed when the set of applications changes; for example, in the case of introducing a new application during runtime.
- The *get_dev_monitors* event is refined to get the MRPI (the *get_dev_MRPI* event).

The decision-based RTM first selects a thread-to-core mapping based on the performance requirements and resource availability. Then, it applies online adaptation by adjusting the VF levels to achieve energy optimisation, without trading-off application performance. For thread-to-core mapping, offline profiled results are used, which contain performance and energy characteristics of applications when executed on the heterogeneous platform by using different types of cores in various possible combinations. For an application, thread-to-core mapping defines the number of used cores and their type, which are situated in different clusters. The online adaptation process classifies the inherent workload characteristics of concurrently executing applications. The classification of workload is performed using the metric MRPI. The adaptation process proactively selects an appropriate VF pair for a predicted workload. Subsequently, it monitors the performance loss, quantified by IPS, and adjusts the chosen VF to compensate.

In the next level of refinement, details of the selection of device parameters (refining *select_dev_mapping* and *select_dev_vf* events) and also of monitoring the device (refining *get_dev_MRPI*) are added.

- The *select_dev_mapping* event is refined by execution of *read_offline_mapping* for all of the newly introduced applications (using the all constructor), followed by execution of *select_resources* (which is refined in the next refinement).

- To select the VF value (the *select_dev_vf* event), first MRPI is predicted, then the optimal value of VF is selected based on the predicted value of MRPI.
- The *get_dev_MRPI* event is also refined to include a new event which calculate the IPS, *calculate_IPS*.

Further details of prediction and VF selection are added in the last refinement. To predict the MRPI, first its value is predicted for each core, then a minimum value is selected per cluster of cores. Selection of VF includes selecting the VF based on the predicted value of MRPI, followed by checking the IPS and adjusting the VF value if needed. If 'required IPS < actual IPS', the VF value is reduced; if 'required IPS > actual IPS', VF value is increased.

14.6 Code generation and portability support

The refined Event-B model of the RTM system is automatically translated to executable C code using the code generation plugin of the Rodin toolset. The run-time algorithms can be highly dependent on hardware platform specifications. However, the Event-B models of the RTMs are independent of these specifics. The platform-independent model of an RTM is parameterised by the hardware specific characteristics, and a specific implementation code is generated automatically.

For example, from the refined model of the learning-based RTM, we are able to generate three separate C implementations for each of three platforms: ARM Cortex-A8, A7, and A15. The number of supported VFs in each platform can influence the implementation of the learning algorithm, for example the size of the QTable is different for each platform because of the difference in the number of VFs. The column number of the QTable is equal to the number of supported VFs. Cortex-A8 supports four values of VF, while the Cortex-A7 and Cortex-A15 support 13 and 19 VFs, respectively.

Figure 14.10 shows how part of a platform-independent model is instantiated by defining concrete values for the model parameters for the Cortex-A8 platform and the Cortex-A7 platform. For the Cortex-A8 on the left, the number of VF pairs is 4, whereas for the Cortex-A7 on the right, it is 13.

The RTM events are independent of the number of supported VFs, while the generated code is specific for each platform. This is presented on top of Figure 14.10 for the *update_qTable* event. The *update_qTable* event is indexed by N indicating the number of VFs. Here i represents an index for a frequency value (voltage is paired with frequency) and determines which column of the QTable gets updated with the value of the reward/penalty.

Finally, (bottom of Figure 14.10), the code generation result contains the data definition (*Common.c* file) and the C code of the RTM algorithms (*Controller.c* file). As explained earlier in this section, the number of frequencies corresponds to the number of *qTable* columns.

The Event-B model is independent of these platform parameters but *Controller.c* depends on the number of frequencies. The event is translated to a set of 'if–then–else' branches in the number of frequencies (number of *qTable* columns)

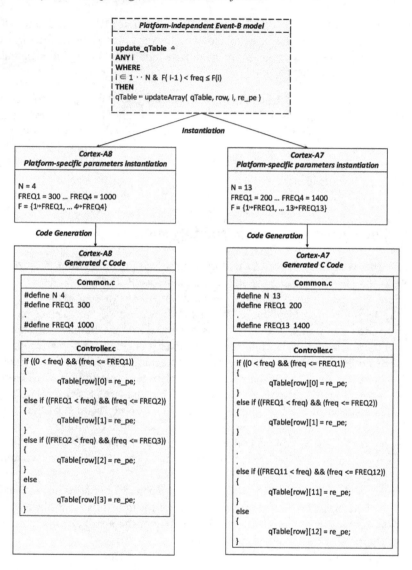

Figure 14.10   Code generation and portability

to modify the *qTable*. The left *Controller.c* box presents the generated implementation for the Cortex-A8 by four branches, modifying the four columns of the *qTable* depending on the value of selected frequency. For the Cortex-A7 (left box), there are 13 branches to modify the columns of QTable by 13 columns. The variable *row*, specifying the appropriate row of the *qTable*, has been assigned in a separated event according to the value of the predicted workload.

Both implementations are automatically generated from the same model, even though one has 4 branches and the other has 13. In contrast to the automatic generation, modifying one version of an implementation to a different number of branches manually would require recoding and can be error-prone.

The portability of the Event-B model is provided as the result of abstraction and parametrisation. The RTM model abstracts away from the specific platform settings and so is identical across different platform architecture. An example of this was presented in this section where an event parameter allows the event to be indexed. The single event parameterised by i gives rise to N if–then–else branches in the generated C code corresponding to the distinct values of i. Multiple implementations are generated from an identical model by the use of parameter instantiation. The generic Event-B model is instantiated by specific platform parameters (number of VFs here) before applying the code generation.

14.7 Validation

We validated the modelling and code generation in two main ways: through formal verification of properties of the model and through experimental performance analysis of the generated code.

The Event-B model of the RTM was verified using Rodin theorem proving. In the last refinement of the learning-based RTM model, 76 proof obligations were generated, of which 96% are proved automatically, mostly associated with correct sequencing of events. The rest are proved interactively using the interactive proving facilities provided by the Rodin prover.

We also analysed our model using ProB to ensure that the model is deadlock free and convergent. At any point during model checking, at least one of the events of the model should be enabled to ensure that the model is deadlock free. For each new event added in the refinements, we have verified that it would not take control forever (convergence). Also, INV POs ensure that the new events keep the existing ordering constrains between the abstract events. The ordering between events are specified as invariants, the PO associated with each invariant ensures that its condition is preserved by each event.

In terms of validation of the code generation, we generated code for the learning-based RTM for three different platforms and two applications and performed experiments to measure performance and power-consumption savings. Experiments were conducted on the BeagleBoard-xM with Cortex-A8 processor and the ODROID-XU3 with both Cortex-A7 and Cortex-A15 processors. Both platforms were running the Linux operating system, and we compared the performance and energy usage achieved by our generated RTM with the performance and energy usage achieved with the Linux on-demand governor. The learning-based RTM targets applications with soft deadlines including multimedia and computer-vision applications. For our experiments, the test applications were a video decoder and a Jacobian matrix solver.

From the experimental results [17], comparing with the Linux on-demand governor, our generated RTM for all three platforms (ARM Cortex-A8, A7, and A15) provides better energy saving while maintaining the required performance.

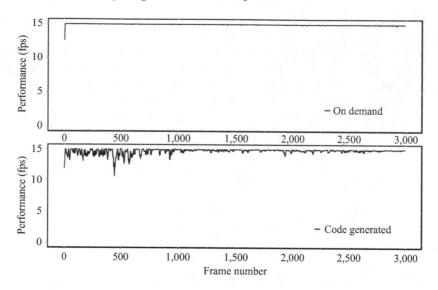

Figure 14.11   Cortex-A7, performance comparison

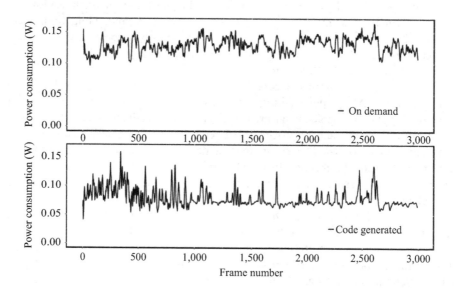

Figure 14.12   Cortex-A7, power comparison

Figures 14.11 and 14.12 (from [17]) show the comparison of performance and power consumption for the Cortex-A7 (video decoding application) when using our code-generated RTM against the Linux on-demand governor. Figure 14.11 shows the effectiveness of the generated RTM with a performance constraint of 15 FPS. The on-demand governor occasionally misses the deadline, while our generated RTM performs worse in the beginning (because of learning) but gradually improves to achieve almost the same performance as the on-demand governor. Figure 14.12 shows the power consumption for our generated RTM and the Linux on-demand governor. The graph shows that during the exploitation phase, the generated RTM achieves significant power savings when compared to the on-demand governor while achieving close to the same performance as the on-demand governor: for the Cortex-A7 the generated RTM achieves 98% of the performance of the on demand while using 61% of power used with the on-demand governor.

14.8 Conclusion and future directions

In this chapter, we presented a model-based approach addressing complexities in RTM software programming due to the diversity of runtime algorithms and diversity of hardware platform characteristics. In our approach, different RTM algorithms share identical abstract models while are refined specifically depending on the specification of the runtime algorithm. In addition, automatic code generation facilitates generating platform-specific RTM code from platform-independent RTM model.

Although the designer needs to know the formal language and the associated toolset to build formal models, the formal model is built once for an RTM algorithm and specific RTM software for different platforms is automatically generated from an identical formal model. In addition, different RTM models can reuse a common abstract model. This automatic generation of implementations from platform-independent models can result in time saving compared to manual adjustment of the RTM implementation for different platforms.

In addition to automatic code generation, formal modelling is augmented by verification techniques. The correctness of the RTM design specifications and consistency of the refinement levels can be ensured by theorem proving and model checking. We have verified the Event-B model of RTM using the Rodin provers for theorem proving and ProB animator for model checking.

We have experimented with our generated learning-based RTM for three platforms, with different characteristics, and two applications. The impact analysis shows energy saving on the respective platforms.

In the broader context, there are a number of open problems that set the future direction for this work. One important problem that still requires further research is the construction of executable programs from mathematical models. Due to the large abstraction gap between mathematical models and the executable program code, automatic transformation from model to code is not straightforward. Furthermore, proving the correctness of the transformation in many cases is not trivial and often complex. One possible solution for this can be the use of different verification techniques at different levels of abstraction. For instance, high-level properties of the system can be modelled and verified in a high level specification language, and low-level code properties can be verified using a static program verifier [18–20].

The case studies presented in this chapter involve machine-learning algorithms. Machine-learning algorithms typically rely on very complex decision making procedures. Providing rigorous specifications for these algorithms is usually difficult due to their complex and unpredictable nature. While a machine-learning algorithm can be very efficient and effective in many environments with different input data, the output in some other environments might be completely unpredictable and unreliable. This fact poses another broad open challenge, which is how to ensure safety of autonomous systems that rely on artificial intelligence algorithms. More specifically, in future, we are interested in looking at how code generation can be used to derive policing functions for intelligent systems [21,22].

References

[1]   Bang SY, Bang K, Yoon S, *et al.* Run-time adaptive workload estimation for dynamic voltage scaling. IEEE Transactions on Computer-Aided Design of Integrated Circuits and Systems. 2009;28(9):1334–1347.

[2]   Moeng M, Melhem R. Applying statistical machine learning to multicore voltage & frequency scaling. In: Proceedings of the 7th ACM International Conference on Computing Frontiers. ACM; 2010. p. 277–286.

[3]   Abrial JR. Formal methods: theory becoming practice. Journal of Universal Computer Science. 2007;13(5):619–628.

[4]   Abrial JR. Modeling in Event-B: system and software engineering. Cambridge University Press, Cambridge; 2010.

[5]   Edmunds A, Butler M. Linking Event-B and concurrent object-oriented programs. Electronic Notes in Theoretical Computer Science. 2008;214:159–182.

[6]   Maeda-Nunez LA, Das AK, Shafik RA, *et al.* PoGo: an application-specific adaptive energy minimisation approach for embedded systems. HiPEAC Workshop on Energy Efficiency with Heterogenous Computing (EEHCO); 2015.

[7]   Reddy BK, Singh A, Biswas D, *et al.* Inter-cluster thread-to-core mapping and DVFS on heterogeneous multi-cores. IEEE Transactions on Multiscale Computing Systems. 2017;4(3):1–14.

[8]   Butler M. Incremental design of distributed systems with Event-B. Engineering Methods and Tools for Software Safety and Security. 2009;22(131):131–160.

[9]   Butler M. Mastering system analysis and design through abstraction and refinement; 2013. Available from: http://eprints.soton.ac.uk/349769/.

[10]   Abrial JR, Butler M, Hallerstede S, *et al.* Rodin: an open toolset for modelling and reasoning in Event-B. International Journal on Software Tools for Technology Transfer. 2010;12(6):447–466.

[11]   Abrial JR, Butler M, Hallerstede S, *et al.* An open extensible tool environment for Event-B. In: International Conference on Formal Engineering Methods. Springer; 2006. p. 588–605.

[12]   Leuschel M, Butler M. ProB: an automated analysis toolset for the B method. International Journal on Software Tools for Technology Transfer. 2008;10(2):185–203.

[13]   Silva R, Pascal C, Hoang TS, *et al.* Decomposition tool for event-B. Software: Practice and Experience. 2011;41(2):199–208.

[14]   Edmunds A, Butler M. Tasking Event-B: an extension to Event-B for generating concurrent code; 2011. Event Dates: 2nd April 2011. Available from: https://eprints.soton.ac.uk/272006/.

[15]   Jastram M, Butler PM. Rodin User's handbook: covers Rodin v.2.8; 2014.

[16]   Fathabadi AS, Butler M, Rezazadeh A. Language and tool support for event refinement structures in Event-B. Formal Aspects of Computing. 2015;27(3):499–523.

[17]   Fathabadi AS, Butler MJ, Yang S, *et al.* A model-based framework for software portability and verification in embedded power management systems. Journal of Systems Architecture. 2018;82:12–23.

[18]   Dalvandi M, Butler M, Rezazadeh A. From Event-B models to Dafny code contracts. In: International Conference on Fundamentals of Software Engineering. Springer; 2015. p. 308–315.

[19]   Dalvandi M, Butler M, Rezazadeh A. Derivation of algorithmic control structures in Event-B refinement. Science of Computer Programming. 2017;148:49–65.

[20]   Dalvandi M, Butler M, Rezazadeh A, *et al.* Verifiable code generation from scheduled Event-B models. In: International Conference on Abstract State Machines, Alloy, B, TLA, VDM, and Z. Springer; 2018. p. 234–248.

[21]   Hoang TS, Sato N, Myosin T, *et al.* Policing functions for machine learning systems. Workshop on Verification and Validation of Autonomous Systems: Satellite Workshop of Floc 2018, Oxford, United Kingdom; 2018.

[22]   Bogdiukiewicz C, Butler M, Hoang TS, *et al.* Formal development of policing functions for intelligent systems. In: Software Reliability Engineering (ISSRE), 2017 IEEE 28th International Symposium on. IEEE; 2017. p. 194–204.

Chapter 15

Self-testing of multicore processors

Michael A. Skitsas[1,2], Marco Restifo[3], Maria K. Michael[1,2],
Chrysostomos Nicopoulos[2], Paolo Bernardi[3],
and Ernesto Sanchez[3]

The era of nanoscale technology has ushered designs of unprecedented complexity and immense integration densities. Billions of transistors now populate modern multicore microprocessor chips, and the trend is only expected to grow, leading to single-chip many-core systems [1]. However, a side effect of this deep technology scaling is the exacerbation of the vulnerability of systems to unreliable components [2]. Beyond the static variation of transistors that can occur during the fabrication, which is expected to get worse, current and future technologies also suffer from dynamic variations. Single-event upsets (soft errors) are another source of concern with a direct impact on the system's reliability. Finally, a third source of unreliable hardware operation that can lead to permanent system failures is the increased sensitivity to aging (time-dependent device degradation) and wear-out artifacts, due to the extreme operating conditions.

The issue of increased vulnerability and the expected increase in the occurrence of transient and permanent failures—as a result of future technologies—render the one-time factory testing of the system inadequate to guarantee the in-field reliability of the system. The new state of affairs necessitates the use of mechanisms that can enable protection against undesired system behavior by facilitating detection, mitigation, and/or recovery from faults throughout the lifetime of the system [3]. Several fault-tolerant techniques have been proposed in order to detect faults during the normal lifetime of the chip. Such schemes broadly fall into two categories: (a) concurrent methods relying on fault-tolerant mechanisms (i.e., redundancy techniques) [4] and (b) nonconcurrent periodic on-line testing [5], which aims to detect errors that are, subsequently, addressed using various techniques.

Multi/many-core microprocessor chips with an abundance of identical computational resources would appear to be ideal for implementing high-availability solutions on-chip, due to the inherent replication of resources (i.e., the processing cores). Multicore systems should remain operational despite the occurrence of

[1] KIOS Research and Innovation Center of Excellence, University of Cyprus, Cyprus
[2] Department of Electrical and Computer Engineering, University of Cyprus, Cyprus
[3] Dipartimento di Automatica e Informatica, Politecnico di Torino, Italy

permanent and/or transient faults. Detection and diagnosis of such faults constitute the first and perhaps the most important step toward the implementation of self-healing multicore systems. The already proposed self-testing techniques for simple and even more complex microprocessors have matured enough, while current and future trends in the self-testing research area are adapting these techniques to multi-/many-core processors. Considering the huge range of today's applications that require many and different types of computational systems, researchers aim to develop self-testing techniques targeting either general-purpose multicore microprocessors, or embedded microprocessors and microcontrollers that constitute application-specific systems-on-chip (SoC).

The purpose of this chapter is to develop a review of state-of-the-art techniques and methodologies for the self-testing of multicore processors. The chapter is divided into two main sections: (a) self-testing solutions covering **general-purpose** multicore microprocessors such as chip multiprocessors (CMPs) and (b) self-testing solutions targeting **application-specific** multicore designs known as SoCs. In the first section (general-purpose), a taxonomy of current self-testing approaches is initially presented, followed by a review of the state-of-the-art for each class. The second section (application-specific) provides an overview of the test scheduling flows for multicore SoCs, as well as the testing strategies for the individual components (sub-systems) of such systems.

15.1 General-purpose multicore systems

15.1.1 Taxonomy of on-line fault detection methods

Over the last several years, a number of approaches have been proposed toward reliable and dependable multicore microprocessor systems. On-line fault detection techniques can be broadly categorized into non-self-test- and self-test-based methods, as shown in Figure 15.1. When considering the abstraction level in which a technique is employed, as well other operational and implementation details, different classes of approaches can be defined for each of the two categories. Inspired by the taxonomy presented in [3], the non-self-test-based techniques can be further classified into three

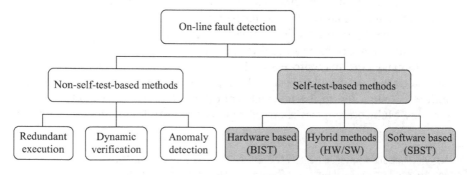

Figure 15.1   Taxonomy of on-line fault detection methods

subclasses: (a) *redundant execution*, where the exploitation of "spare" processing elements (i.e., cores) for the replication of normal workload can lead to the detection of failures, (b) *dynamic verification*, where the fault detection is based on the validation of program invariants during runtime, and (c) *anomaly detection* where the system is monitored for the detection of symptoms of faults. On the other hand, self-test-based methods—whereby on-line fault detection is done by the application of test patterns and/or programs—can be further divided into three categories, based on the level of implementation of each technique: (a) *hardware (HW) based*, (b) *software (SW) based*, and (c) *hybrid methods*.

The main characteristic of self-test-based methods is that the detection of faults is achieved by exploiting the normal workload that is applied in the system. As a result of these approaches, in fault-free executions, the imposed performance overheads in normal workloads is almost zero, while hardware overhead exists either using additional hardware components (i.e., using checkers) or by increasing (i.e., doubling) the resources for the execution of the workload (i.e., redundant execution). In self-test-based techniques, the detection of faults is achieved by the application of test patterns either by using hardware support (i.e., scan chains), in hardware-based techniques, or by exploiting the available resources and instruction set architecture (ISA) to execute test programs, in software-based techniques.

During self-testing, tests are applied in field, while the system is operational. As a result, the normal operation of a module under test (i.e., core) is suspended and turned into testing mode. Therefore, self-test-based approaches can potentially impose significant performance overhead in the system, and scheduling must be performed carefully in order to minimize this cost. In the era of multi/many-core architectures with multiple homogeneous cores on the same chip, despite the suspension of the normal operation of a core under test, the entire system can remain operational as normal workloads can be scheduled in one of the remaining available resources.

15.1.2 Non-self-test-based methods

One fault detection approach targeting microprocessor cores involves running two, or more, identical copies of the same program (different executions either at the thread, or process levels) and comparing their outputs. Such **redundant execution** is feasible both at the hardware and software levels. In the era of multi/many-core architectures with multiple homogeneous cores integrated on the same chip, and the capability to execute multiple threads (or processes) simultaneously, the hardware-based redundant techniques can be applied with significantly reduced performance overhead, targeting both transient and permanent faults. The application of these hardware-based redundant techniques is feasible because of the rather improbable simultaneous utilization of all the processing resources at any given time, due to the dark-silicon as well as parallel programming effects. In literature, two forms of redundancy techniques at hardware level can be found: structural and temporal.

In structural redundancy, identical cores are working in close synchronization either at the instruction level, or at the cycle level, known as lockstep configuration. Aggarwal *et al.* [6] propose dual modular redundancy (DMR) and triple modular redundancy configurations for CMPs, which provide error detection and error recovery through fault containment and component retirement. LaFrieda *et al.* [7] present a dynamic core coupling technique that allows arbitrary CMP cores to verify each other's execution. Unlike existing DMR techniques that require a static binding of adjacent cores via dedicated communication channels and buffer, this technique avoids the static binding of cores. Li *et al.* [8] propose a variation-aware core-level redundancy scheme in order to achieve robust computation in many-core systems with inter-core variations and mixed workloads.

In temporal hardware-based redundancy approaches, several redundant multithreading (RMT) techniques have been proposed targeting single-core chips that support simultaneous multi-threading (SMT) [9,10]. The evolution of technology and the era of multicore systems forced researchers to develop techniques exploiting the nature of CMPs. Mukherjee *et al.* [11] study RMT techniques in the context of both single- and dual-processor SMT and propose a chip-level redundant threading for CMP architectures. Wang *et al.* [12] present a software-based RMT approach for transient fault detection targeting general-purpose CMPs. Furthermore, Chen *et al.* [13] explore how to efficiently assign the tasks onto different cores with heterogeneous performance properties in order to achieve high reliability and satisfy the tolerance of timeliness. Mitropoulou *et al.* [14] proposes a compiler-based technique that makes use of redundant cores within a multicore system to perform error checking.

As already mentioned, redundant execution techniques can be found at the software level as well. In this case, the redundant execution of workloads at different architectural levels (i.e. instruction, thread, process) is based on re-execution using the same resources. As a result, redundant techniques at this level are primarily used to detect transient faults. Oh *et al.* [15] propose a pure software technique, called error detection by duplicated instructions that duplicates instructions during compilation and uses different registers and variables for the new instructions. Reis *et al.* [16] present SWIFT, a novel, software-only transient fault detection technique. SWIFT efficiently manages redundancy by reclaiming unused instruction-level resources present during the execution of most programs. Recently, Mushtaq *et al.* [17] propose an error-detection mechanism that is optimized to perform memory comparisons of the replicas efficiently in user-space. Kuvaiskii *et al.* [18] present HAFT, a fault tolerance technique using hardware extensions of commodity CPUs to protect unmodified multi-threaded applications against such corruptions. HAFT utilizes instruction-level redundancy for fault detection and hardware transactional memory for fault recovery.

The second category of non-self-test-based approaches is **Dynamic Verification**. The basic operation of these approaches is based on the run-time verification of specifically selected/developed invariants that in a fault free execution are true. The verification is typically based on dedicated hardware checkers. The research challenge faced for these approaches, beyond maintaining a low-cost in terms of hardware implementation, is to provide a comprehensive set of invariants aiming to increase the number of possibly detected faults. Dynamic verification was first introduced by Austin in [19], where a novel micro-architecture-based technique that permits detection and recovery of all transient and permanent faults in the processor core, called DIVA (Dynamic Implementation Verification Architecture) is proposed. DIVA uses a simple checker core to detect errors in a speculative, super-scalar core. Despite the low-cost implementation requirements compared with a complex super-scalar core, in multicore systems with simpler microprocessors the overhead becomes significant. Meixner *et al.* [20] propose Argus, a low-cost, comprehensive fault detection scheme targeting simple cores. Based on dynamic verification, Argus uses four invariants that guarantee the correct operation of a core, control flow, computation, dataflow and memory. Additionally, Meixner and Sorin [21] propose dynamic dataflow verification, another approach of dynamic verification using a high-level invariant. In this case, faults are detected by verifying at runtime the dataflow graph.

The last category of non-self-test-based approaches is **anomaly detection**, where faults are detected by monitoring the hardware and/or software for anomalous behavior, or symptoms of faults. Anomaly detection approaches may, or may not, use invariants. Based on the level of symptoms that can be detected, anomaly detection approaches can be further classified in three classes [3]: (a) those that detect data value anomalies, (b) those that detect micro-architectural behavior anomalies, and (c) those that detect software behavior anomalies. Hari *et al.* [22] propose SWAT, a low-cost solution that handles hardware faults by treating the resulting software anomalies. SWAT uses near zero cost always-on symptom monitors for error detection. Racunas *et al.* [23] dynamically predict the valid set of values that an instruction will produce, and consider a departure from this prediction as a symptom of a (transient) fault. Wang and Patel [24] propose ReStore to detect transient faults without significant overhead by utilizing symptoms. Example symptoms include exceptions, control flow mis-speculations, and cache or translation look-aside buffer misses. Feng *et al.* [25] in Shoestring enhance ReStore by selectively duplicating some vulnerable instructions with simple heuristics. Li *et al.* [26] propose the detection of faults by deploying low overhead monitors for simple software symptoms at the operating system level. Their approach relies on the premise that micro-architectural structures eventually propagate symptoms to the operating system.

15.1.3   Self-test-based methods

The second main category of the considered taxonomy in Figure 15.1 refers to **self-test-based** methods, where the detection of faults is based on the application of tests. Self-test-based methods are further classified in three subclasses: (a) hardware-based methods, known as built-in self-test (BIST), where self-testing is performed exclusively by hardware components, (b) software-based methods, known as software-based self-testing (SBST), where the application of tests is achieved using software programs applied in the processor's functional mode, and (c) hybrid approaches, where self-testing is supported both by hardware and software techniques.

Table 15.1 presents a summary of the main characteristics of self-test-based methods for CMP systems over the most important test-related evaluation metrics. The various self-test-based methods are classified according to the taxonomy of Figure 15.1, i.e., based on the implementation type: hardware, software, and hybrid. For each salient metric, Table 15.1 first provides a brief summary of the characteristics that affect the specific metric, followed by a qualitative comparison between the related works.

Table 15.1 A summary of the main characteristics of self-test-based methods for CMP systems

		Hardware overhead	Testing time overhead	Detection latency	System performance overhead	Fault coverage
Hardware-based (BIST)		*HW for storing and/or generating test patterns, scan chains, checkers, test controllers, output signature compressors, etc.*	*Save and restore current state, load/generate/apply test patterns, collect/compress responses*	*Depends on test triggering method: periodic, idle cores, on-demand*	*Core(s) under test are off-line*	*High*
	[27]	Moderate	Low to moderate	Periodic	High	Very high
	[28]	Moderate to high	Low	Periodic/Idle Cores	Low to moderate	Very high
	[29]	Low to moderate	Low	n/a	High	Very high
Software-based (SBST)		*None to Low (for system monitoring)*	*Depends on test program size, test triggering and scheduling approach*	*Depends on test triggering: periodic, idle cores, on-demand*	*Low to high: time-multiplexing of test programs and normal workload*	*Moderate to high: Depends on test programs*
	[30]	None	Low	Periodic	High	High
	[31]	None	Moderate	n/a	High	High
	[32]	None	Moderate to high	Periodic	Low to high	n/a
	[33]	Very low	Low	Adaptive period	Low	High
	[34]	Negligible	n/a	On-demand	Low	Moderate
	[35]	Negligible	Very low to moderate	On-demand	Very low	High
Hybrid methods (HW/SW)		*Hardware modifications are required, ISA enhancements*	*Combination of SBST and BIST*	*Depends on test triggering: periodic, idle cores, on demand*	*Low to high: core(s) under test are off-line*	*High*
	[36]	Low	Low to moderate	Periodic	Low to moderate	Very high
	[37]	Low	Low	Periodic	Low to moderate	Very high
	[38]	Very low	Low to moderate	Periodic	Negligible	Very high
	[39]	Low	Low	Periodic	Low to moderate	Very high

15.1.3.1 Hardware-based self-testing

BIST approaches, coupled with scan chain infrastructure which is used to access the embedded BIST instruments, can perform nonconcurrent error detection in microprocessors during their entire lifetime. The BIST approach exploits special circuits located on the chip that produce, monitor, and evaluate the tests needed by the cores. Traditionally, BIST techniques have been proposed for manufacturing testing, building on scan-based automatic test pattern generation (ATPG), and including multicore designs in which embedded IP cores can be accessed via a surrounding test logic known as test-wrappers. The overall concept can be also applied to non-IP-protected cores and any other partition of logic. Current advancements in technology necessitate the application of such techniques during the lifetime and normal operation of the system, targeting beyond faults caused by manufacturing defects, such as transient, intermittent, and wear-out/aging-related induced permanent faults.

Shyam *et al.* [27] utilize existing distributed hardware BIST mechanisms to validate the integrity of the processor components in an on-line detection strategy. For each of the pipeline components, a high-quality input vector set is stored in an on-chip ROM, which is fed into the modules during idle cycles. A checker is also associated with each component to detect any defect(s) in the system.

Li *et al.* [28] present CASP, concurrent autonomous chip self-test using stored test patterns, which is a special kind of self-test where the system tests itself during normal operation, without any downtime visible to the end-user. The operation of CASP is based on two main functions: (a) the storage of very thorough test patterns in nonvolatile memory and (b) the architectural and system-level support for autonomous testing of one, or more, cores in a multicore system, without suspending the normal system operation. The testing procedure under the CASP solution is composed of four phases: (a) test scheduling, where one, or more, cores may be selected for testing; (b) the preprocessing phase, where the core under test is temporarily isolated, saving the current state; (c) testing, where test patterns are loaded and applied to the core under test, and, finally, (d) restoration of the state and resumption of the operation of the tested core(s). The evaluation of the proposed technique is done using the OpenSPARC T1 multicore processor, where a fault coverage of more than 99% is achieved, using 5 MB of stored patterns.

Lee *et al.* [29] propose a self-test architecture that achieves high-fault coverage by using deterministic scan-based test patterns. The main idea of this work is the compression and storage on the chip, while the decompression and application to the circuits under test will take place during the testing. As the testing is performed based on deterministic patterns, pseudorandom patterns are not required, and this results in the reduction of testing time. Experimental results on OpenSPARC T2, a publicly accessible 8-core processor containing 5.7 M gates, show that all required test data—for 100% testable stuck-at fault coverage—can be stored in the scan chains of the processor with less than 3% total area overhead for the whole test architecture.

15.1.3.2 Software-based self-testing

The SBST technique is an emerging new paradigm in testing that avoids the use of complicated dedicated hardware for testing purposes. Instead, SBST employs the existing hardware resources of a chip to execute normal (software) programs that are designed to test the functionality of the processor itself. The test routines used in this technique are executed as normal programs by the CPU cores under test. The processor generates and applies functional-test programs using its native instruction set. In recent years, several active research teams have been working in the area of SBST, focusing on different approaches. The two main phases of SBST for the detection of a fault are (a) test-program development and (b) the execution of the test program on the system.

Test program development for multicore architectures

Several research teams are working on the development of test programs with multi-dimensional scope, such as to increase the fault coverage, extend the considered fault models, reduce the test-program size, achieve savings in testing time overhead, etc. [40]. More recently, in the age of CMPs and multi-threading, the development of test programs also focuses on the effective adoption of the underlying hardware to yield self-test optimization strategies that benefit from the targeted architectures.

Foutris *et al.* [41] propose a multi-threaded SBST (MT-SBST) methodology targeting multi-threaded multicore architectures. The proposed MT-SBST methodology generates an efficient multi-threaded version of the test program and schedules the resulting test threads into the hardware threads of the processor to reduce the overall test execution time, and—at the same time—increase the overall fault coverage. The MT-SBST approach significantly speeds up testing time at both the core level ($3.6\times$) and the processor level ($6\times$) compared to single-threaded execution, while improving the overall fault coverage.

Kaliorakis *et al.* [30] propose a test-program parallelization methodology for many-core architectures, in order to accelerate the on-line detection of permanent faults. The proposed methodology is based on the identification of the memory hierarchy parameters of many-core architectures that slow down the execution of parallel test programs, in order to identify the parts that can be parallelized and, therefore, improve the performance. The evaluation of the methodology in [30] is done using Intel's Single-chip Cloud Computer (SCC), showing up to $47.6\times$ speedup, compared to a serial test program execution approach.

Test program scheduling

One salient aspect of on-line testing, and specifically of SBST, is the scheduling of the test program(s). In light of the rapid proliferation of multi/many-core microprocessor architectures, the test scheduling issue becomes even more pertinent. One approach is to periodically initiate testing on the system targeting individual cores, or all the cores simultaneously. In any case, the interruption of the current execution of normal workloads is unavoidable. Another approach is the execution of test programs on cores that have been observed to be idle for some time. Recent techniques have proposed the monitoring of the utilization of the system and subsequent selection of specific cores to be tested.

Apostolakis *et al.* [31] proposed a methodology that allocates the test programs and test responses into the shared on-chip memory and schedules the test routines among the cores aiming at the reduction of the total test application time and, thus, the test cost for the processor. This is achieved by increasing the execution parallelism and reducing both bus contentions and data-cache invalidations. The proposed solution is demonstrated with detailed experiments on several multicore systems based on the OpenRISC 1200 processor.

A recent test-scheduling study for online error detection in multicore systems is discussed in [43]. The authors evaluate the performance of test programs applied on Intel's 48-core SCC architecture. Due to possible congestion within common hardware resources used by the various cores, the test time can be quite large with a significant impact on performance. As a result, the authors of [43] develop effective test scheduling algorithms to expedite the test process in such systems.

Skitsas *et al.* [32,42] investigate the relation between system test latency and test-time overhead in multi/many-core systems with shared last-level cache for periodic SBST, under different test scheduling policies. The investigated scheduling policies primarily vary the number of cores concurrently under test in the overall system test session. Under given system test-latency constraints, which dictate the recovery time in the event of error detection, the proposed exploration framework identifies the scheduling policy under which the overall test-time overhead is minimized and, hence, system availability is maximized. Figure 15.2 gives a high-level overview of the considered scheduling policies: (a) the test scheduler invokes all the test programs simultaneously, in order to test all the cores of the system at the same time, (b) test scheduling scenarios that vary the number of cores concurrently under test, and (c) the scheduling scenario that considers a serial execution of test programs during each testing session. For the evaluation of the test-scheduling process, the authors propose test scheduling scenarios that vary the number of cores concurrently under test. Additionally, the authors propose a new methodology aiming to reduce the extra overhead related to testing that is incurred as the system scales up (i.e., the number of on-chip cores increases).

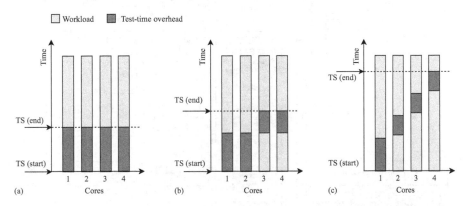

Figure 15.2   High-level overview of the scheduling policies explored in [32,42]: (a) all the cores may be under test simultaneously, (b) the number of cores concurrently under test may be varied, and (c) the test programs may be serially executed during a testing session (TS)

Monitoring system activity

The test triggering mechanism is an important aspect which determines the effectiveness and efficiency of SBST executed during the lifetime of a system. Traditionally, self-test is triggered periodically (both in H/W- and S/W-based approaches). In the multicore arena, idle cores can also serve as a trigger. Recently, several techniques propose the monitoring of the system status over time as an indicator for the initiation of a testing procedure. Power, utilization, and performance are among the parameters used to define triggers for test.

Gupta *et al.* [33] propose an adaptive online testing framework aiming to significantly reduce the testing overhead. The proposed approach is based on the ability to assess the hardware health and apply detailed tests. Hardware health assessment is done using in-situ sensors that detect the progress of various wear-out mechanisms. The results show a reduction in software test instructions of about 80%, while the sensor area overhead for a 16-core CMP system is 2.6%.

Haghbayan *et al.* [34] proposed a power-aware nonintrusive online testing approach for many-core systems. The approach schedules SBST routines on the various cores during their idle periods. The scheduler selects the core(s) to be tested from a list of candidate cores. The selection is based on a criticality metric, which is calculated considering the utilization of the cores and power budget availability.

Skitsas *et al.* [35,44] investigate the potential of SBST at the granularity of individual microprocessor core components in multi/many-core systems. While existing techniques monolithically test the entire core, the proposed approach aims to reduce testing time by avoiding the over-testing of under-utilized units. To facilitate fine-grained testing, the authors of [35] introduce DaemonGuard, a framework that enables the real-time observation of individual sub-core modules and performs on-demand selective testing of only the modules that have recently been stressed. Figure 15.3

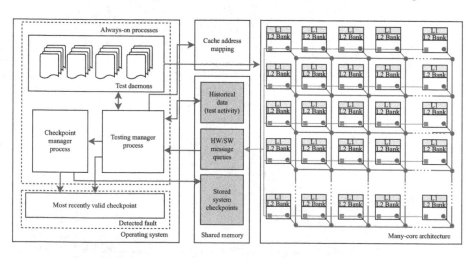

Figure 15.3 *Architectural overview of the DaemonGuard Framework proposed in [35,44], which enables the real-time observation of individual sub-core modules and performs on-demand selective testing of only the modules that have recently been stressed*

depicts the architectural overview of the DaemonGuard Framework. The monitoring and test-initiation process is orchestrated by a transparent, minimally intrusive, and lightweight operating system process that observes the utilization of individual datapath components at run-time. The results indicate substantial reductions in testing overhead of up to $30\times$. Moreover, the framework can be extended to support on-line recovery using efficient check-pointing and roll-back mechanisms, as discussed in [45].

15.1.3.3 Hybrid self-testing methods (hardware/software)

Beyond self-test-based methods that are purely implemented either in hardware or in software, there is a different approach that spans both the hardware and software levels. The purpose of these hybrid approaches is to further improve the performance of self-test-based methods, by reducing the testing time, increasing the fault coverage, etc. The hardware architectural support provides the necessary substrate to facilitate testing, while the software makes use of this substrate to perform the testing. For the implementation of such approaches, modifications of the ISA and/or the extension of hardware components may be required.

Inoue *et al.* [36] propose a Virtualization-Assisted concurrent, autonomous self-test (VAST) that enables a multi/many-core system to test itself, concurrently during normal operation, without any user-visible downtime. VAST is a hardware and software codesign of on-line self-test features in a multi/many-core system through integration of BIST (i.e., CASP [28]) methods with virtualization software. Testing can be done in two ways, stop-and-test and migrate-and-test. Experimental results from an actual multicore system demonstrate that VAST-supported self-test policies enable extremely thorough on-line self-test with very small performance impact.

Constantinides *et al.* [37] proposed an online testing methodology using an enhanced ISA with special instructions for fault detection and isolation. Structural tests are performed by applying test patterns using software routines. The test routines are executed periodically, after a number of executed instructions have committed, and checkpoints are used for recovery. The technique of Constantinides *et al.* is software assisted, but it requires various hardware modifications. These intrusive modifications are needed, because the goal is to enable very detailed structural testing through the existing scan-chain infrastructure.

A hardware and software codesign methodology for functional testing is proposed by Khan *et al.* [38]. The testing methodology is based on the redundancy concept, whereby two cores execute the same program and capture corresponding footprints. The results of the executions are compared for fault detection. The choice of the test program is based on profiling that can be done offline, or online. In [46], the authors propose a thread relocation methodology that uses dynamic profiling based on phase tracking and prediction.

In [39], a self-test mechanism for online testing of many-core processors has been proposed. Several hardware components are incorporated in the many-core architecture that distribute software test routines among the processing cores, monitor behavior of the processing cores during test routine execution, and detect faulty cores. The results indicate a good fault coverage in a limited number of test cycles, while the scalability—in terms of hardware and timing overhead—is maintained.

15.2   Processors-based systems-on-chip testing flows and techniques

Modern multicore systems manufacturing encompasses several steps. Similarly, their test is constituted by several phases, the characteristics of which are often dominated by the constraints imposed by the current manufacturing step and the available testing equipment [47].

In every test phase (or corner), the device is binned according to the test result, and the test history is updated by storing the collected data-log in proper databases; collected data are key for the successive analysis of failing samples, carefully selected among the population of discarded devices. The next subsections describe the manufacturing flow and discusses the test scheduling along the production phase, concluding with some indication about in-field [48] testing. As well, methods and concepts related to the classification of the tested population behaviors are illustrated. Each device in a population of semiconductor products must undergo a sequence of test phases that take place at different stages of the manufacturing process. Figure 15.4 shows a typical industrial manufacturing flow [49].

The first test step is performed at wafer level, and it is called electrical wafer sort (EWS) [50]; in this phase, a special contacting equipment, called probe card, is used to drive the device to execute a test. As the devices belonging to a wafer are not yet separated from each other and the pin distance is very small, a major testing issue of this phase is related to:

- the number of pins to be contacted at the same time, which is limited and
- the insertion time that need to be minimized due to the high cost per time.

In fact, the probe cards cannot touch all pins at the same time; therefore, the test needs to rely only on a reduced number of pins; low pin count interfaces can be used, such as JTAG, I2C, SPI, to feed data and commands to the device. Preferable test methods at this level are based on BIST approaches; in particular, logic and memory BISTs afford a fast test activation and a quick execution with quite high coverage; each core may be equipped with its own logic BIST, or the test flow relies on a shared resource. Functional methods like SBST of SW memory test are often considered too slow because of the time required to upload a microcode into an available memory resource. Direct scan-chain-based approaches are usually not practicable because of the limitation in terms of contacted pins and access speed, which can be constrained to low frequency due to physical contacting that degrades signals. At the EWS, an important issue is also related to power consumptions; as a matter of fact, excessive current requirements by the test can have the negative fall-outs of entering a thermal runaway status, finally leading to test uncertainties and chip damage. Therefore, a careful selection of patterns and a test scheduling that maximizes the amount of test done in parallel without exceeding the power budget are needed.

As shown in Figure 15.4, the outcome of the EWS phase can be either the release of Known Good Dies to be shipped to market or progression to packaging or the discard of devices; concerning the last category, the discarded devices are seldom both failing devices and outliers. Outliers, a currently working chips, are anyway

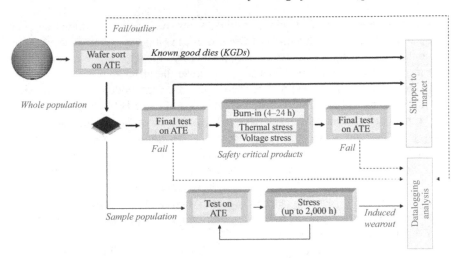

Figure 15.4   A typical manufacturing flow including the main test steps

suspected to be imperfect and therefore to fail with high probability in the next test phases. A trace of all the discarded devices is stored in the system of data-log, a sample of them is subject to failure analysis.

After the packaging process, the device population runs the so-called final test. This test phase is performed on high-performance testing equipment, with low parallelism (the tester may host a limited number of chips, e.g., 1-2-4), full pin contacting, and high frequency in driving pins value. At this test step, the scan-chain-based methods are the most used because high coverage is demanded. Such raw-test strategies need to consider power issues [51]; most commonly, effective pattern selection aims at controlling the amount of logic gate toggling, especially during pattern shift in, to be not excessive. In the multicore scenario, a device can be subdivided into several scan domains, which can be driven in a fully parallel mode or partially, meaning one at a time. Such a subdivision is eventually supported by infrastructural DfT like wrappers (i.e., ieee 1500 wrappers, IJTAG, etc. …). At this stage, the functional methodologies are often used to target performance evaluation [52]. SBST can be run at the nominal frequency with the support of phased locked loop peripherals to detect delay-related marginalities, which are difficult to detect with scan patterns. Such methods also permits to perform a speed binning of the population, not discarding devices with reduced performance but selling them with explicit indication of a lower operating frequency.

Devices passing the final test may be shipped to market or undergo some more test steps. This is case of chips used in safety-critical environments, like all devices used in automotive, medical, avionics, and space. Additional test phase is shown in Figure 15.4; in particular, a quite long phase called burn-in (BI) phase is performed to screen out all devices that will fail during the first months of life of the device. The BI process consists in the execution of several test and stress steps: FLASH cores are erased and verified several times, while BIST and SBST procedures make the logic circuits working [53]. The BI equipment drives a massively parallel stimulation of up to thousands of devices at the time and also provides voltage and thermal stress as an additional, external source of stress. High parallelism makes the power issues even more important than in the previous steps, because the tester is required to supply many devices (up to hundreds) with the same power driver module. Such a physical limitation makes the application of scan patterns and logic BIST quite dangerous, while functional modes are more suitable as they naturally respects the power limits of the device and do not ask to much current to the equipment. Scan chain usage is also limited by the number of pins that can be contacted per chip, which is usually low because of the high parallelism, and by the limitations in terms of speed and signal integrity over large BI board hosting up to 100 devices. In the context of multicore devices, the SBST [50] strategy can be effectively used to create temperature gradients inside the device, e.g., by activating only a limited number of cores per time in such a way that the device area is strained.

To conclude the overview of the test methods, the reliability evaluation of a device need to be detailed. This is the phase shown the bottom of Figure 15.4, which is performed on a subset of the population. Such samples are sacrificed in order to assess the reliability of the product by undergoing a very long stress/test process similar to BI (thermal/voltage stress). The number of hours of stress may reach up to 2,000, which is estimated to be a sufficient time to bring the device to wear-out. This special test is therefore oriented to complete the failure rate analysis which is limited to infant mortality in the BI stage.

Almost all electronic devices shipped to market are self-tested during their useful life. Most of them undergo self-test often based on DfT and especially on BISTs execution. This is different for devices used in safety-critical environment, as they need also run-time self-test. The next subsections describe generation techniques to generate SBST procedures and illustrate how to manage the coexistence of the Self-Test execution with the mission application.

15.2.1   On-line testing of CPUs

This subsection aims at providing a guideline to be able to effectively generate and run test programs for in-field testing of microprocessor cores used in safety-critical applications [54,55]. In particular, this section highlights the important constraints that need to be considered when devising test programs to be used for in-filed testing. Finally, a comparison is provided by checking the obtained results made by using three different SBST strategies on an industrial processor core.

SBST is one of the preferred solutions when it is required to periodically monitor the health of the different cores in the device while the normal applications are running. A standard solution adopted by the industry is the periodic application of the test programs exploiting a SBST library composed of a set of different programs. The general approach consists of periodically forcing the different processors to execute the SBST test programs aiming at detecting the possible occurrence of permanent faults in the different processor cores and the peripherals connected to them.

The different SBST test programs are designed to activate possible faults in very well-defined modules, then compress and store the computed results in an available memory space, or raise a signal when the test is terminated wrongly. The goal of the SBST test library is to increase the multicore system reliability requirements, as imposed by standards such as the ISO 26262, which requires a constant monitoring for the possible occurrence of permanent faults in the system along its operational life.

15.2.1.1 SBST test library generation constraints

The main constraints related to the use of SBST libraries for in-field testing of multicore systems stem from the necessity to share the available resources with the mission applications, i.e., the OS which is managing mission tasks; the coexistence between SBST test libraries with the Operating Systems introduces very strong limitations for these test libraries:

- SBST test programs need to be compliant with standard interfaces, enabling the OS to handle them as normal processes.
- The SBST test programs need to be generated following execution-time constraints, due to the resources occupation that can be afforded by the actual environment.
- Memory resources impose strong limitations, then, it is recommended to
  - provide the SBST test programs as a set of precompiled programs stored as binary images to be run during in-field testing,
  - not to refer to any absolute addresses for branching and accessing memory variables, and
  - identify memory constraints imposed by the coexistence with the OS.

Moreover, targeting effort reduction, the SBST tests should be created taking into account the characteristics of the general processor family, in order to reduce code modifications when transferring the test libraries to other processor cores belonging to the same production family.

15.2.1.2 Execution management of the SBST test program

The most relevant constraints related to test program execution are considered here.

Encapsulation of the test programs
It is important to consider the cooperation with other software modules while running the test program. In fact, it is essential to include key features enabling the test program to be launched, monitored, and, in the given case, interrupted by a higher priority process.

In order to be compliant with the actual application software environment, a good solution is the adoption of the embedded-application binary interface (EABI) [56]. EABIs specify standard conventions for file formats, data types, register usage, stack frame organization, and function parameter passing of a software program. Thus, every SBST test program includes an EABI prologue and epilogue, in charge of saving and restoring the mission status.

In addition, we propose for every SBST test program the inclusion of additional information such as

- stack frame size,
- special purpose registers (SPR) setup,
- memory protection setup,
- test duration, and
- final signature.

Context switching to test procedure

Every time a SBST test program is scheduled to be run, it is important to assure that the context of the actual application is not modified by the execution of the test program. In particular, three general cases have been identified, and every one of them demands for proper metadata to be used in the related setup procedures:

- Run-time tests: These are the most flexible test programs since these programs can be interrupted by almost all the mission requests; in general, these test programs include tests covering computational modules such as the arithmetic ones.
- Non-exceptive tests: Usually, these test programs require to use and modify some SPR, for example, during a procedure testing some parts of the Register Bank.
- Critical tests: These test programs cannot be interrupted since they are intended to test critical parts of the processor cores that intentionally raise interrupts, make use of peripheral cores, or need special synchronous requirements to effectively perform the intended test. For example, a procedure for testing modules managing software exceptions.

Interruption management and robustness

Synchronous and asynchronous exceptions need to be handled with extreme attention, then it is necessary to develop the SBST test programs considering additional constraints when these may require to coexist with processor interrupts. Three types of exceptions are detailed:

- Intentionally provoked exceptions, i.e., SBST test programs that test processor exceptions.
- Unexpected, these exceptions are induced by an erroneous execution provoked by a faulty situation.
- Mission mode interruptions.

One of the most critical aspects to be handled during the in-field test of processors is to test the processor exceptions; it is necessary to carefully rise and manage them. If the modules managing the interrupt have not been modified by a fault, each single exception is correctly managed. It means that a test interrupt service routine (ISR) is accessed, executed, and then the CPU control returns back to the main program. Clearly, such ISR should be properly configured at every time the SBST test scheduler prepares the environment for the test program execution, by replacing the mission ISR with the test ISR.

Interestingly, the exception management implemented is also crucial for detecting faults producing execution flow deviations that lead to an unexpected processors internal status or cause unexpected synchronous interruptions.

Exploiting exceptions for checking program flow deviations make the test code quite robust, but additional work is needed if the processor status become unstable. In this case, an external mechanism has to be implemented in order to bring the system into a safe status, i.e., by watchdog timer.

For example, Figure 15.5(a) depicts the program flow followed by a processor core while executing a test program oriented to test the exception mechanisms through a test ISR. In the figure, a special instruction, called an excepting instruction, triggers a synchronous exception that should be served by a test ISR. In the case, there is not a fault causing an atypical behavior, the test ISR normally returns the processor control to the main program.

However, as depicted in Figure 15.5(b), in case, a fault is present, a series of abnormal behaviors may arise due to the fault. This situation requires to add additional code barriers able to handle unexpected behaviors; for example, it may happen that the fault prevents the excepting instruction to actually activate the exception, then the next instruction after the excepting one is executed without activating the test ISR. Therefore, it is necessary to include a special assert able to detect this particular situation.

Figure 15.5(b) also depicts other necessary to implement instruction asserts in specific places that may be executed in the case a faulty behavior modifies the expected program flow. When dealing with multicore systems.

15.2.1.3 Comparison of SBST techniques for in-field test programs development

In the following subsections, a comparison of three of the most common strategies for developing SBST programs, presented in [40], is illustrated.

ATPG based

This methodology guarantees the highest possible coverage, given the fact that test patterns for a specific module are automatically generated by means of an ATPG engine. Especially for combinational blocks, ATPG is able to reach 100% test coverage, while it may be harder (in terms of computational effort) for complex sequential circuits.

These patterns are intended to be applied to the primary input signals of the block under test and are usually provided in text format (e.g., STIL). Further work is needed to parse the text file and transform the signal values to a sequence of assembly instructions. Such step is trivial for simple blocks but can be more challenging in other cases, where selection signals have to be properly interpreted. This requires the knowledge of the processors microarchitecture.

A little coverage loss is typically observed when transforming ATPG patterns to SBST, due to masking effects and aliasing during the signature computation. Effort: medium-low (minutes to hours), depending the functional block complexity. In the best case, it requires a single fault simulation.

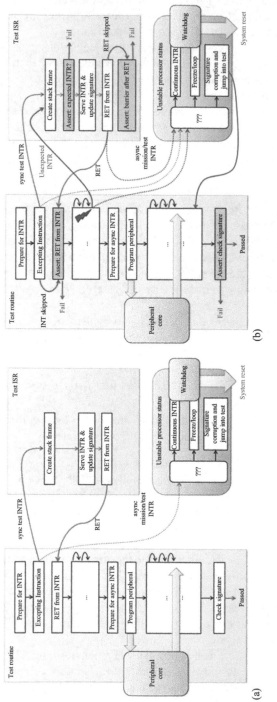

Figure 15.5 Interrupt exception flow (a) fault free behavior and (b) faulty behavior

Deterministic

It consists in the implementation of a documented algorithm or methodology. This is a functional methodology, which does not highly depend on the internal structure of the module under test.

The expected fault coverage level is medium to high. However, the resulting program can be highly redundant in terms of test patterns applied to the module under test. This redundancy is mainly present to effectively adapt the program to the whichever implementation of the module.

These kind of techniques are really useful when the netlist is missing or not hierarchical (e.g., flattened, obfuscated). Moreover, they are suitable for such modules that are too complex for ATPG-based methods. Effort: low (minutes to hours). In some cases, it requires several adjustments and fault simulations, until an appropriate level of fault coverage is reached.

Evolutionary based

This methodology uses an evolutionary engine to continuously generate test programs. The effectiveness of this technique depends both on the number of test programs generated and the skills of the test engineer, which has to guide the evolutionary engine. Briefly, the test engineer has to build the basic blocks of the test programs, where some parameters such as register contents are unknown. The evolutionary engine starts by assigning random values to such parameters. Later on, after the fault coverage level of the generated programs is evaluated, the engine is able to combine previously generated programs and to generate new ones [57].

The fault coverage can be very high, but it requires the generation if many programs.

This technique is highly useful for distributed parts of the processor, which is quite difficult to group the logic into a well-defined module. In this case, the fault list is enough to guide the evolution. Even for flattened or obfuscated circuits, it can be used to cover the corner cases as the last generation process (i.e., after deterministic approaches).

Effort: Medium-high (hours to days). Since each program is fault simulated, the time required for a single fault simulation is a key parameter for the effectiveness of this method. The preliminary steps of preparing the program skeletons require additional effort, but typically this is not very high.

Table 15.1 provides the results in terms of number of code lines, clock cycles required to execute the programs, and the obtained FC% while using the three described techniques, targeting the shifter module included in the ALU of an industrial processor core. The shifter counts with 4,196 gates.

The column labeled as # lines provides two values (A and B) showing the number of lines of the obtained test program. The A value counts the number of lines of a loop-based version of the final program, whereas the B value shows the number of lines of the unrolled version of the same program.

Table 15.2   SBST generation techniques comparison

Technique	#Lines	#Clock cycles	Stuck-at FC%
ATPG based	110/708	3,549	98.0
Deterministic	42/533	41,326	90.1
Evolutionary based	164/188	1,651	91.9

15.2.2   On-line testing of application-specific functional units

This section provides to the reader meaningful examples of functional-based test regarding external functional units. More in details, test of the floating-point unit (FPU), direct memory access (DMA), and error correction code (ECC) are described. These test strategies can be a starting point or can suggest good ideas for developing a software-based self-test concerning external modules.

15.2.2.1   Floating-point unit

Modern safety-critical applications usually use FPU to compute arithmetic operations more precisely. For this reason, safety-critical system requires to test the FPU both during the manufacturing process and during the mission mode. From a structural point of view, FPU contains several integer functional units, such as adders, multipliers, shifters, etc., which are coupled with control modules that perform normalization, rounding, and truncation operations.

The floating-point representation follows the standard IEEE 754-2008 [58]. A floating-point number consists of three different fields: the sign (S), the exponent (E), and the mantissa (M). The leading one of mantissa is implied and is not stored in the mantissa field. In addition, the standards define values for positive and negative infinity, a negative zero, exceptions to handle invalid results like division by zero, special values called not a numbers for representing these exceptions, denormalized numbers to represent numbers lower than the minimum, and rounding methods.

15.2.2.2   Test for FPU

The research community focused on FPU test by using SBST during the latest years. Online periodic testing of microprocessors supporting FP processor must be considered differently from those without FP support because FP units are more complex than their integer counterparts and require more test patterns to reach a satisfactory fault and test coverage.

The approach of [59] generates effective test patterns by means of ATPG tools, then patterns are converted into loop-based sequences of instructions. The authors of [60] applied the technique used in [59] to a commercial and industrial FPU. The result of [60] outlined the efficiency for the FPU pipelined the data-path (i.e., composed by a multiplier and adder) and the weakness of the approach on iterative data-paths (i.e., the divider). Reference [61] presents the development of the first SBST according to the requirements of periodic online testing using an ATPG loop-based approach, but with the same issues on iterative data-paths of [60]. Current FPUs implement different formats described by the standard, an example is a single-precision FPU that supports the half-precision format. For this reason, FPU contains specialized modules in charge of converting values. In this case, the authors of [62] suggest performing conversions from single-precision to half-precision, and then the result is converted again to single-precision. This allows to detect the fault related to the conversion logic. In addition, FPU is involved in checking and alerting erroneous FP operations. The same paper proposes to implement a test program which includes FP operations that create erroneous results to detect the faults of the checking and alerting error logic.

15.2.2.3 Direct memory access

DMA is a peripheral and can perform large data movements between memory and peripheral (or between two memories) with minimal intervention from the host processor. In presence of a DMA, the CPU initiates the transfer configuring the DMA registers, and then, it may do other operations while the transfer is in progress. Once the DMA register are programmed, a transfer can be started to relocate data from one memory location to another or write data to/from a peripheral depending on the application requirements. The inclusion of a DMA into a SoC reduces the microprocessor workload, since different devices can transfer data without requiring the microprocessor intervention. The CPU usually receives an interrupt from the DMA controller when the transfer ends. The generation of a functional test concerning to DMA peripheral is not a trivial task. The number of all possible test set configurations explodes exponentially. The methodology presented in [63] targets the complexity reduction for the test sets generation, whereas guaranteeing the observability of the resulting test set.

First, an initial analysis on the description of the DMA must be done. This step identifying the main elements devoted to the configuration of the device and the possible cover metrics. Then, the second step identifies the shared and unshared resources. We define a resource shared if it is involved in more than one component operating configuration. Once shared and unshared modules are labeled, based on them functionalities, a series of specific test algorithms are developed. The test algorithms for the unshared modules might require some specific restrictions regarding the configuration of the complete device. All possible configurations are represented in a configuration graph where each path is a different configuration. The upper bound is $2\hat{n}$ where $\hat{n}$ is the number of bits contained in the configuration registers. To purge this graph, it is necessary to remove impossible configuration and to exploit the shared/unshared information. Finally, the reduced configuration graph is build, and real test programs must be developed considering the whole device configuration up to the expected coverage.

15.2.2.4 Error correction code

ECC techniques are widely used in the industry to afford safety standards on large memory cuts [64]. ECC works concurrently to the system application and checks whether permanent or transient faults corrupt the memory content. The ECC code

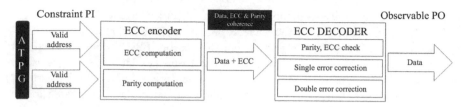

Figure 15.6   ATPG framework for testing ECC logic

augments the current information, thus providing detection and correction abilities. The ECC logic modules are the encoder and the decoder, which perform the ECC computations. The encoder generates the ECC bits every time a write operation occurs, and the decoder verify the integrity of the data using the ECC bits during a read access. Examples are data storage and load, or instruction fetching.

It is a common perception that a permanent fault in this logic can only produce false positives (e.g., the memory content is fault-free, but the decoder is either correcting or signaling an error). This assumption is not always true, and many more misbehaviors can arise with potentially very dangerous effects especially in harsh environment of safety-critical application. For example, a fault affecting the ECC logic can fetch an instruction that might be misinterpreted. The authors in [65] proposed to use SBST for testing the ECC logic. The methodology addresses the whole ECC logic fault universe including "latent" faults. A latent fault is a special type of fault that is excited only when the ECC logic detects a memory content corruption (i.e., a bit-flip). The methodology presented in [65] uses a debugger, which inserts corruption inside the memory matrix during a write operation. The presence of corruptions allows to excite latent faults of decoder logic during a read operation.

In addition, [65] proposes to detect faults using an ATPG technique, which is depicted in Figure 15.6. The ATPG forces a valid address and data. The address is constrained to a value matching the memory map. The data is more difficult because it is necessary to preserve the integrity between data and the related ECC bits. For this reason, the encoder outputs are connected directly to the decoder inputs.

15.3   Conclusion and future directions

This chapter performs a review of state-of-the-art techniques and methodologies for the self-testing of multicore processors. The main characteristic of self-test-based methods is that the detection of faults is achieved by exploiting the normal workload that is applied in the system. Based on the application purpose of multicore systems, the chapter focuses on two main areas: (a) general-purpose multicore microprocessors and (b) application-specific multicore designs. Despite the fact that this domain has been significantly researched, more research challenges remain open toward more efficient techniques in terms of overhead, performance, coverage, and detection latency.

In recent years, extensive work on the development of test programs targeting different architectural levels (e.g., cores, sub-core granularity, interconnections) have been proposed, accompanied with high-quality results in terms of performance and fault coverage [40,41]. Moreover, test scheduling approaches that monitor system activity and initiate the testing activity—aiming to reduce the testing overhead and improve detection latency—have also been studied [31,32].

A high-level monitoring mechanism that can enable testing at different system granularities using multiple test programs (and aiming to improve fault coverage at the system level) constitutes an open problem in the area of self-testing of multicore systems [34,35]. Additionally, the assessment and evaluation of the testing process using different reliability metrics (instead of merely testing overhead and detection latency) is still an open research challenge in this area. A reliability model that includes the test quality (i.e., test coverage), system characteristics and requirements (i.e., critical/non-critical systems), detection latency, aging and wearout, etc. can be integrated in a framework to improve the testing procedure [66,67].

The research in self-testing methodologies is mainly focused on the generation and execution of test programs. However, a reliable system able to remain operational despite the presence of hardware failures should also incorporate recovery and reconfiguration mechanisms [45,54]. While the two research areas have been extensively studied, the combination and the integration of both in a single system are a promising and challenging research field.

The self-test-based approaches discussed in this chapter show that individual techniques and methodologies (i.e., test development, test scheduling, etc.) have already reached a significant level of maturity. Recent research efforts are focused on the combination of existing work and on further developments toward self-healing reliable multicore processor systems. This should also be the goal of future efforts in this research field.

References

[1] Borkar S. Thousand Core Chips: A Technology Perspective. In: Proceedings of the 44th Annual Design Automation Conference. DAC'07. New York, NY, USA: ACM; 2007. p. 746–749. Available from: http://doi.acm.org/10.1145/1278480.1278667.

[2] Borkar S. Designing Reliable Systems From Unreliable Components: The Challenges of Transistor Variability and Degradation. IEEE Micro. 2005;25(6):10–16.

[3] Gizopoulos D, Psarakis M, Adve SV, *et al.* Architectures for Online Error Detection and Recovery in Multicore Processors. In: Design, Automation & Test in Europe Conference & Exhibition (DATE), 2011; 2011. p. 1–6.

[4] Mitra S, McCluskey EJ. Which Concurrent Error Detection Scheme to Choose? In: IEEE International Test Conference (ITC), 2010; 2000. p. 985–994.

[5] Nicolaidis M, Zorian Y. On-Line Testing for VLSI – A Compendium of Approaches. Journal of Electronic Testing. 1998;12(1–2):7–20.

[6]   Aggarwal N, Ranganathan P, Jouppi NP, Smith JE. Configurable Isolation: Building High Availability Systems with Commodity Multi-Core Processors. In: Proceedings of the 34th Annual International Symposium on Computer Architecture. ISCA'07. New York, NY, USA: ACM; 2007. p. 470–481. Available from: http://doi.acm.org/10.1145/1250662.1250720.

[7]   LaFrieda C, Ipek E, Martinez JF, Manohar R. Utilizing Dynamically Coupled Cores to Form a Resilient Chip Multiprocessor. In: 37th Annual IEEE/IFIP International Conference on Dependable Systems and Networks (DSN'07); 2007. p. 317–326.

[8]   Li HT, Chou CY, Hsieh YT, Chu WC, Wu AY. Variation-Aware Reliable Many-Core System Design by Exploiting Inherent Core Redundancy. IEEE Transactions on Very Large Scale Integration (VLSI) Systems. 2017;25(10): 2803–2816.

[9]   Rotenberg E. AR-SMT: A Microarchitectural Approach to Fault Tolerance in Microprocessors. In: Digest of Papers. 29th Annual International Symposium on Fault-Tolerant Computing (Cat. No. 99CB36352); 1999. p. 84–91.

[10] Reinhardt SK, Mukherjee SS. Transient Fault Detection via Simultaneous Multithreading. In: Proceedings of 27th International Symposium on Computer Architecture (IEEE Cat. No. RS00201); 2000. p. 25–36.

[11] Mukherjee SS, Kontz M, Reinhardt SK. Detailed Design and Evaluation of Redundant Multi-Threading Alternatives. In: Proceedings 29th Annual International Symposium on Computer Architecture; 2002. p. 99–110.

[12] Wang C, s Kim H, Wu Y, Ying V. Compiler-Managed Software-Based Redundant Multi-Threading for Transient Fault Detection. In: International Symposium on Code Generation and Optimization (CGO'07); 2007. p. 244–258.

[13] Chen KH, Chen JJ, Kriebel F, Rehman S, Shafique M, Henkel J. Task Mapping for Redundant Multithreading in Multi-Cores with Reliability and Performance Heterogeneity. IEEE Transactions on Computers. 2016;65(11):3441–3455.

[14] Mitropoulou K, Porpodas V, Jones TM. COMET: Communication-Optimised Multi-Threaded Error-Detection Technique. In: Proceedings of the International Conference on Compilers, Architectures and Synthesis for Embedded Systems. CASES'16. New York, NY, USA: ACM; 2016. p. 7:1–7:10. Available from: http://doi.acm.org/10.1145/2968455.2968508.

[15] Oh N, Shirvani PP, McCluskey EJ. Error Detection by Duplicated Instructions in Super-Scalar Processors. IEEE Transactions on Reliability. 2002;51(1): 63–75.

[16] Reis GA, Chang J, Vachharajani N, Rangan R, August DI. SWIFT: Software Implemented Fault Tolerance. In: International Symposium on Code Generation and Optimization; 2005. p. 243–254.

[17] Mushtaq H, Al-Ars Z, Bertels K. Efficient Software-Based Fault Tolerance Approach on Multicore Platforms. In: 2013 Design, Automation Test in Europe Conference Exhibition (DATE); 2013. p. 921–926.

[18] Kuvaiskii D, Faqeh R, Bhatotia P, Felber P, Fetzer C. HAFT: Hardware-assisted Fault Tolerance. In: Proceedings of the Eleventh European Conference on

Computer Systems. EuroSys'16. New York, NY, USA: ACM; 2016. p. 25:1–25:17. Available from: http://doi.acm.org/10.1145/2901318.2901339.

[19] Austin TM. DIVA: A Reliable Substrate for Deep Submicron Microarchitecture Design. In: MICRO-32. Proceedings of the 32nd Annual ACM/IEEE International Symposium on Microarchitecture; 1999. p. 196–207.

[20] Meixner A, Bauer ME, Sorin D. Argus: Low-Cost, Comprehensive Error Detection in Simple Cores. In: 40th Annual IEEE/ACM International Symposium on Microarchitecture (MICRO 2007); 2007. p. 210–222.

[21] Meixner A, Sorin DJ. Error Detection Using Dynamic Dataflow Verification. In: 16th International Conference on Parallel Architecture and Compilation Techniques (PACT 2007); 2007. p. 104–118.

[22] Hari SKS, Li ML, Ramachandran P, Choi B, Adve SV. mSWAT: Low-Cost Hardware Fault Detection and Diagnosis for Multicore Systems. In: 2009 42nd Annual IEEE/ACM International Symposium on Microarchitecture (MICRO); 2009. p. 122–132.

[23] Racunas P, Constantinides K, Manne S, Mukherjee SS. Perturbation-Based Fault Screening. In: 2007 IEEE 13th International Symposium on High Performance Computer Architecture; 2007. p. 169–180.

[24] Wang NJ, Patel SJ. ReStore: Symptom-Based Soft Error Detection in Microprocessors. IEEE Transactions on Dependable and Secure Computing. 2006;3(3):188–201.

[25] Feng S, Gupta S, Ansari A, Mahlke S. Shoestring: Probabilistic Soft Error Reliability on the Cheap. In: Proceedings of the 15th Edition of ASPLOS on Architectural Support for Programming Languages and Operating Systems. ASPLOS XV. New York, NY, USA: ACM; 2010. p. 385–396. Available from: http://doi.acm.org/10.1145/1736020.1736063.

[26] Li ML, Ramachandran P, Sahoo SK, Adve SV, Adve VS, Zhou Y. Understanding the Propagation of Hard Errors to Software and Implications for Resilient System Design. In: Proceedings of the 13th International Conference on Architectural Support for Programming Languages and Operating Systems. ASPLOS XIII. New York, NY, USA: ACM; 2008. p. 265–276. Available from: http://doi.acm.org/10.1145/1346281.1346315.

[27] Shyam S, Constantinides K, Phadke S, Bertacco V, Austin T. Ultra Low-cost Defect Protection for Microprocessor Pipelines. In: Proceedings of the 12th International Conference on Architectural Support for Programming Languages and Operating Systems. ASPLOS XII. New York, NY, USA: ACM; 2006. p. 73–82. Available from: http://doi.acm.org/10.1145/1168857.1168868.

[28] Li Y, Makar S, Mitra S. CASP: Concurrent Autonomous Chip Self-Test Using Stored Test Patterns. In: 2008 Design, Automation and Test in Europe; 2008. p. 885–890.

[29] Lee KJ, Tang PH, Kochte MA. An On-Chip Self-Test Architecture With Test Patterns Recorded in Scan Chains. In: 2016 IEEE International Test Conference (ITC); 2016. p. 1–10.

[30]   Kaliorakis M, Psarakis M, Foutris N, Gizopoulos D. Accelerated Online Error Detection in Many-Core Microprocessor Architectures. In: VLSI Test Symposium (VTS), 2014 IEEE 32nd; 2014. p. 1–6.

[31]   Apostolakis A, Gizopoulos D, Psarakis M, Paschalis A. Software-Based Self-Testing of Symmetric Shared-Memory Multiprocessors. IEEE Transactions on Computers. 2009;58(12):1682–1694.

[32]   Skitsas MA, Nicopoulos CA, Michael MK. Exploring System Availability During Software-Based Self-Testing of Multi-Core CPUs. In Springer Journal of Electronic Testing – Theory and Applications (JETTA). 2018;34(1):67–81.

[33]   Gupta S, Ansari A, Feng S, Mahlke S. Adaptive Online Testing for Efficient Hard Fault Detection. In: Proceedings of the 2009 IEEE International Conference on Computer Design. ICCD'09. Piscataway, NJ, USA: IEEE Press; 2009. p. 343–349. Available from: http://dl.acm.org/citation.cfm?id=1792354.1792420.

[34]   Haghbayan MH, Rahmani AM, Miele A, *et al.* A Power-Aware Approach for Online Test Scheduling in Many-Core Architectures. IEEE Transactions on Computers. 2016;65(3):730–743.

[35]   Skitsas MA, Nicopoulos CA, Michael MK. DaemonGuard: Enabling O/S-Orchestrated Fine-Grained Software-Based Selective-Testing in Multi-/Many-Core Microprocessors. IEEE Transactions on Computers. 2016;65(5):1453–1466.

[36]   Inoue H, Li Y, Mitra S. VAST: Virtualization-Assisted Concurrent Autonomous Self-Test. In: 2008 IEEE International Test Conference; 2008. p. 1–10.

[37]   Constantinides K, Mutlu O, Austin T, Bertacco V. A Flexible Software-Based Framework for Online Detection of Hardware Defects. IEEE Transactions on Computers. 2009;58(8):1063–1079.

[38]   Khan O, Kundu S. Hardware/Software Codesign Architecture for Online Testing in Chip Multiprocessors. IEEE Transactions on Dependable and Secure Computing. 2011;8(5):714–727.

[39]   Kamran A, Navabi Z. Hardware Acceleration of Online Error Detection in Many-Core Processors. Canadian Journal of Electrical and Computer Engineering. 2015;38(2):143–153.

[40]   Psarakis M, Gizopoulos D, Sanchez E, Reorda MS. Microprocessor Software-Based Self-Testing. IEEE Design Test of Computers. 2010;27(3):4–19.

[41]   Foutris N, Psarakis M, Gizopoulos D, Apostolakis A, Vera X, Gonzalez A. MT-SBST: Self-Test Optimization in Multithreaded Multicore Architectures. In: ITC 2010; 2010. p. 1–10.

[42]   Skitsas MA, Nicopoulos CA, Michael MK. Exploration of System Availability During Software-Based Self-Testing in Many-Core Systems Under Test Latency Constraints. In: 2014 IEEE International Symposium on Defect and Fault Tolerance in VLSI and Nanotechnology Systems (DFT); 2014. p. 33–39.

[43]   Kaliorakis M, Foutris N, Gizopoulos D, Psarakis M, Paschalis A. Online Error Detection in Multiprocessor Chips: A Test Scheduling Study. In: 2013 IEEE 19th International On-Line Testing Symposium (IOLTS); 2013. p. 169–172.

[44] Skitsas MA, Nicopoulos CA, Michael MK. DaemonGuard: O/S-Assisted Selective Software-Based Self-Testing for Multi-Core Systems. In: 2013 IEEE International Symposium on Defect and Fault Tolerance in VLSI and Nanotechnology Systems (DFTS); 2013. p. 45–51.

[45] Skitsas MA, Nicopoulos CA, Michael MK. Toward Efficient Check-Pointing and Rollback Under On-Demand SBST in Chip Multi-Processors. In: 2015 IEEE 21st International On-Line Testing Symposium (IOLTS); 2015. p. 110–115.

[46] Khan O, Kundu S. Thread Relocation: A Runtime Architecture for Tolerating Hard Errors in Chip Multiprocessors. IEEE Transactions on Computers. 2010;59(5):651–665.

[47] Appello D, Bernardi P, Bugeja C, et al. An Optimized Test During Burn-In for Automotive SoC. IEEE Design & Test. 2018;35(3):46–53.

[48] Abraham JA, Gu X, MacLaurin T, et al. Special Session 8B #x2014; Panel: In-Field Testing of SoC Devices: Which Solutions by Which Players? In: 2014 IEEE 32nd VLSI Test Symposium (VTS); 2014. p. 1–2.

[49] Sadi M, Kannan S, Winemberg L, Tehranipoor M. SoC Speed Binning Using Machine Learning and On-Chip Slack Sensors. IEEE Transactions on Computer-Aided Design of Integrated Circuits and Systems. 2017;36(5):842–854.

[50] Zhang Y, Peng Z, Jiang J, Li H, Fujita M. Temperature-Aware Software-Based Self-Testing for Delay Faults. In: 2015 Design, Automation Test in Europe Conference Exhibition (DATE); 2015. p. 423–428.

[51] Kapoor B, Edwards JM, Hemmady S, Verma S, Roy K. Tutorial: SoC Power Management Verification and Testing Issues. In: 2008 Ninth International Workshop on Microprocessor Test and Verification; 2008. p. 67–72.

[52] Kampmann M, Kochte MA, Schneider E, Indlekofer T, Hellebrand S, Wunderlich HJ. Optimized Selection of Frequencies for Faster-Than-at-Speed Test. In: 2015 IEEE 24th Asian Test Symposium (ATS); 2015. p. 109–114.

[53] Bernardi P, Cantoro R, Gianotto L, et al. A DMA and CACHE-Based Stress Schema for Burn-In of Automotive Microcontroller. In: 2017 18th IEEE Latin American Test Symposium (LATS); 2017. p. 1–6.

[54] Bernardi P, Cantoro R, Luca SD, Sánchez E, Sansonetti A. Development Flow for On-Line Core Self-Test of Automotive Microcontrollers. IEEE Transactions on Computers. 2016;65(3):744–754.

[55] Lin CW, Chen CH. A Processor and Cache Online Self-Testing Methodology for OS-Managed Platform. In IEEE Transactions on Very Large Scale Integration (VLSI) Systems; 2017;25(8):2346–2359.

[56] Sobek S, Burke K. PowerPC Embedded Application Binary Interface (EABI): 32-Bit Implementation, 2014. Available from: http://www.freescale.com/files/32bit/doc/app_note/PPCEABI.pdf.

[57] Squillero G. Artificial Evolution in Computer Aided Design: From The Optimization of Parameters to the Creation of Assembly Programs. Computing. 2011;93(2):103–120. Available from: https://doi.org/10.1007/s00607-011-0157-9.

[58]   IEEE Standard for Floating-Point Arithmetic. IEEE Std 754-2008. 2008 Aug; p. 1–70.

[59]   Tupuri RS, Abraham JA. A Novel Functional Test Generation Method for Processors Using Commercial ATPG. In: Proceedings International Test Conference 1997; 1997. p. 743–752.

[60]   Bayraktaroglu I, d'Abreu M. ATPG Based Functional Test for Data Paths: Application to a Floating Point Unit. In: Proceedings. Ninth IEEE International High-Level Design Validation and Test Workshop (IEEE Cat. No. 04EX940); 2004. p. 37–40.

[61]   Xenoulis G, Gizopoulos D, Psarakis M, Paschalis A. Instruction-Based Online Periodic Self-Testing of Microprocessors with Floating-Point Units. IEEE Transactions on Dependable and Secure Computing. 2009;6(2):124–134.

[62]   Cantoro R, Piumatti D, Bernardi P, Luca SD, Sansonetti A. In-Field Functional Test Programs Development Flow for Embedded FPUs. In: 2016 IEEE International Symposium on Defect and Fault Tolerance in VLSI and Nanotechnology Systems (DFT); 2016. p. 107–110.

[63]   Grosso M, H WJP, Ravotto D, Sanchez E, Reorda MS, Medina JV. Functional Test Generation for DMA Controllers. In: 2010 11th Latin American Test Workshop; 2010. p. 1–6.

[64]   Hamming RW. Error Detecting and Error Correcting Codes. The Bell System Technical Journal. 1950;29(2):147–160.

[65]   Restifo M, Bernardi P, Luca SD, Sansonetti A. On-Line Software-Based Self-Test for ECC of Embedded RAM Memories. In: 2017 IEEE International Symposium on Defect and Fault Tolerance in VLSI and Nanotechnology Systems (DFT); 2017. p. 1–6.

[66]   Oboril F, Tahoori MB. ExtraTime: Modeling and Analysis of Wearout Due to Transistor Aging at Microarchitecture-Level. In: Dependable Systems and Networks (DSN), 2012 42nd Annual IEEE/IFIP International Conference on; 2012. p. 1–12.

[67]   Karl E, Blaauw D, Sylvester D, Mudge T. Reliability Modeling and Management in Dynamic Microprocessor-based Systems. In: 2006 43rd ACM/IEEE Design Automation Conference; 2006. p. 1057–1060.

Chapter 16

Advances in hardware reliability of reconfigurable many-core embedded systems

Lars Bauer[1], Hongyan Zhang[1], Michael A. Kochte[2],
Eric Schneider[2], Hans-Joachim Wunderlich[2],
and Jörg Henkel[1]

The continued need for performance increase in face of the end of Dennard scaling made many-core architectures with dozens of cores mainstream, and architectures with hundreds or even thousands of cores have already been investigated [1–5]. A typical tiled many-core architecture is shown in Figure 16.1 [6]. It consists of multiple tiles interconnected by a network-on-chip (NoC). Memory tiles and I/O tiles handle storage requests and periphery communications, whereas compute tiles host the actual cores including their caches (see right part of Figure 16.1). In addition to homogeneous processing cores, a tile may also host one or multiple *heterogeneous* cores. Heterogeneity allows to optimize the system for specific workloads and increases the efficiency over homogeneous cores. As a special case, *runtime reconfigurable* processors even allow the dynamic optimization of this specialization by customization of the hardware organization for changing workload requirements during runtime. This combines the advantages of high performance and low energy consumption only achievable in hardware, with the flexibility of software to customize the hardware resources at runtime. The *i*-Core reconfigurable processor [7,8] is an example of such an architecture. It is sketched in Figure 16.1 and will be used as baseline in this chapter (details in Section 16.2.1).

Runtime reconfigurable processors based on field-programmable gate arrays (FPGAs) are a promising augment to conventional processor architectures and have gained economical relevance [9,10]. They consist of a general purpose processor and a *reconfigurable fabric* that are interconnected over a communication infrastructure. The reconfigurable fabric is partitioned into multiple *reconfigurable regions* that can be reconfigured at runtime to implement *accelerators* that perform compute-intensive functions to speed up the execution of applications. However, modern FPGAs are manufactured in the latest technology nodes and the reliable operation of their reconfigurable fabric is increasingly threatened by dependability issues. While higher

[1]Chair for Embedded Systems, Karlsruhe Institute of Technology, Germany
[2]Institute of Computer Architecture and Computer Engineering, University of Stuttgart, Germany

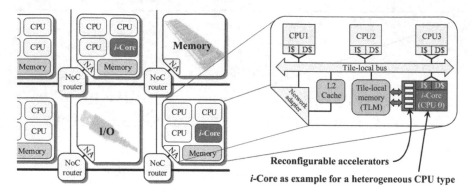

*Figure 16.1   Typical NoC-based many-core architecture (left) with heterogeneous
            cores in the tiles (right)*

transistor density, higher performance, and lower energy consumption are the major
benefits and the driving force of ever shrinking nano-CMOS devices, dependability
poses as a serious challenge lying ahead of continued scaling [11]. Reconfigurable
fabrics are especially threatened by transient errors caused by environmental conditions. For instance, radiation emitted from the environment may generate a transient
current in the circuit. This current pulse may flip a stored value in a memory cell,
called *soft error* or *single event upset* (SEU, details in Section 16.1.2) [12]. If such
an erroneous value in a memory cell holding data is used in a computation, the result
may be erroneous as well. If the erroneous value is overwritten, however, the error
has no impact. For reconfigurable processors, the situation is very different, as their
reconfigurable fabric contains a relatively large memory array (typically SRAM) to
store the configuration data. A single bit flip in the configuration memory may actually alter the circuit of a reconfigurable accelerator and thus its functionality. This
effect is *permanent* until a reconfiguration takes place.

For applications with strict reliability constraints, highly reliable operation of the
reconfigurable accelerators is required despite the threats of soft errors. Concurrent
error detection (CED) techniques such as modular redundancy (details in Section
16.1.4) are therefore obligatory, even though they incur high resource usage and
performance loss due to overprotection. On the other hand, runtime reconfigurable
processors also provide a high degree of *flexibility and adaptivity* that can be exploited
to solve the demanding reliability requirements. A runtime strategy is able to adapt
itself to changing environmental conditions in a way that optimized decisions, trading-
off performance and reliability, can be made during runtime, compared to a static and
pessimistic worst case design decision. For instance, to guarantee a required level
of reliability at minimal performance cost, a runtime system can dynamically select
and activate the appropriate level of redundancy and protection for each accelerator,
depending on the vulnerability of individual accelerators, reliability constraints of the
application, and the environmental radiation level.

In the following, this chapter discusses the background for the most demanding
dependability challenges for reconfigurable processors and presents a dependable

runtime reconfigurable processor for high reliability. By exploiting the inherent flexibility provided by runtime reconfiguration, an *adaptive* modular redundancy technique is realized for high reliability at minimal hardware and runtime overhead.

16.1 Background

16.1.1 Runtime reconfigurable processors

This chapter targets fine-grained reconfigurable fabrics that employ established FPGA technologies and have already been widely adopted [9,10]. FPGAs are composed of a two-dimensional array of configurable logic blocks (CLBs) and programmable switching matrices (PSMs). CLBs are the basic reconfigurable resources that contain look-up tables, registers, etc., and PSMs provide the interconnect between the CLBs. The logic function of a reconfigurable region is determined by configuration bits, called its bitstream, stored in the configuration memory. Modern FPGAs support partial reconfiguration, i.e. the runtime reconfiguration of a part of the FPGA without interrupting the operation in other parts [13]. This allows to maximize performance at very low energy consumption.

Typically, a reconfigurable processor consists of a general-purpose processor and a reconfigurable fabric, partitioned into multiple reconfigurable regions and interconnected via a communication infrastructure [8]. During runtime, these regions can be reconfigured (without interrupting the operation in other parts) to implement accelerators that speed up applications. As shown in Figure 16.2, an application with computationally intensive parts, so-called kernels, is accelerated on a reconfigurable processor by executing them using dedicated hardware accelerators in the reconfigurable fabric. A runtime system dynamically selects the required accelerators and performs their reconfiguration for optimal adaptation to different application requirements. An accelerated function (AF) in a kernel (see Figure 16.2(b)) is implemented by one or multiple accelerators of potentially different types [8]. An AF is represented

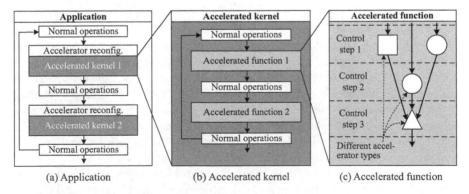

(a) Application   (b) Accelerated kernel   (c) Accelerated function

Figure 16.2   A typical application model, showing how applications can use reconfigurable accelerators

by a data-flow graph where each node corresponds to an accelerator. The example in Figure 16.2(c) shows an AF with four accelerators of three different types (represented by different shapes). Before executing a kernel, all required accelerator types need to be configured into the reconfigurable fabric. Otherwise, the AF needs to be executed in software on the processor without acceleration, which can be done transparent to the application programmer by using an 'unimplemented instruction' trap [8].

16.1.2   Single event upset

Ionizing particles (i.e. due to radiation [14]) can induce transient current pulses in nano-electronic devices that may alter the values of logic signals. These so-called SEUs threaten the dependability of SRAM-based reconfigurable fabrics, leading to *soft errors*. The amount of ionizing radiation, in particular of the neutrons, provoked by cosmic rays, is a strong function of altitude, geomagnetic location, and solar activity [15]. For example, going from sea level to the cruising altitude of commercial flights (around 10 km), the neutron flux increases 500× [15]. Depending on the affected site of particle striking in the circuit, the current pulse has different impact on the circuit operation [12]. If the current pulse is generated at a node in combinational logic, it will cause a transient voltage change (i.e. a change of logic value). Such a value change may propagate to a (pseudo-)primary output and lead to an error, or it can get masked by the down-cone logic of the circuit. On the other side, if a register is affected, then the stored logic value may flip, leading to a transient erroneous logic state that can produce wrong data in the data path or wrong states in *finite state machines*.

Because the functionality of a circuit implemented on an FPGA is defined by the configuration bits stored in the configuration memory, a soft error altering a configuration bit can modify the circuit implementation. Thus, a 'soft' error in the configuration bits can be considered as a 'hard' fault in the circuit which persists until the corrupted bits are corrected.

16.1.3   Fault model for soft errors

Soft errors in the configuration memory caused by SEUs are stochastic processes. The location (i.e. which bits) and the occurrence time of a soft error are nondeterministic. Although SEUs may affect multiple neighbouring memory cells and cause multiple erroneous configuration bits, experiments from flight tests [16] and radiation chambers [17] showed that the dominating soft errors were single bit errors. The susceptibility of the configuration memory of an FPGA to SEUs is typically reported by the device vendor as *soft-error rate* (SER) [18]. It is measured in *failures in time per megabit* and provides the expected number of erroneous configuration bits in an FPGA operating for 10^9 h. For the SER, it is assumed that the error probabilities of the configuration bits are all equal and constant over time.

A continuous-time Markov model can be used to describe the stochastic behaviour of the soft error of a configuration bit [19], which can either be erroneous or error-free. Without fault tolerance and recovery mechanisms, once a configuration bit is erroneous, it stays erroneous. Thus, the transition rate from the error-free state to the erroneous state is the SER of one configuration bit, denoted as λ. The probability that a configuration bit that is error-free at time t_0 remains error-free till time $t_0 + t$ is given by the Poisson distribution:

$$P(\text{error-free at } t + t_0 | \text{error-free at } t_0) = e^{-\lambda t} \tag{16.1}$$

The *critical bits* of an accelerator are those configuration bits that define its functionality [20]. A functional failure of the accelerator may occur if those bits are altered due to SEU. In this chapter, it is conservatively assumed that an accelerator operates correctly only when all of its critical bits are error-free, otherwise it is considered as faulty. If an accelerator A is (re-)configured without errors at time t_0, the reliability $R(A, t)$ after some time t is equal to the probability that none of its critical bits is affected by soft errors from t_0 to $t_0 + t$, such that

$$R(A, t) = \prod^{n} e^{-\lambda t} = e^{-\lambda n t} \tag{16.2}$$

where n is the number of critical bits and t the *resident time* of A. It is assumed here that the soft errors of individual configuration bits are independent of each other.

Functionally used memory elements in FPGAs, such as Block RAMs, are readily protected by an error correcting code (ECC) [21] combined with physical interleaving in the recent FPGA generations, which reduces their SER well below their permanent failure rate [22]. Also regarding the number of flip-flops contained in an FPGA, the amount of configuration bits is two to three orders of magnitude higher. Therefore, this chapter focuses on SEUs in configuration bits.

16.1.4 Concurrent error detection in FPGAs

In safety- and mission-critical system, soft errors caused by SEUs often need to be immediately detected and corrected on site to prevent propagation into the system. *CED* [23] techniques typically utilize a certain degree of redundancy with comparison for error detection. CED schemes utilizing *spatial redundancy* compare outputs from replicated circuits with identical computations or information redundancy from prediction circuits (i.e. parity bits). The most widely used redundancy technique for error detection *and* correction for FPGAs is *triple modular redundancy* (TMR) [24]. Three replicas of the same circuit are fed with a common input, and the outputs are compared by a majority voter. The majority output is forwarded as the final result, while the minority output is considered as corrupted. As long as only a single replica is corrupt, TMR produces correct outputs, as error detection and correction is performed simultaneously. The corrupted replica can be repaired by partial reconfiguration without interrupting system operation. Only when two or more replicas are corrupt, reliable system operation cannot be guaranteed anymore as the voter cannot identify the correct output.

Similar to TMR, another common redundancy technique for error detection is *duplication with comparison* (DWC), which consists of two replicas of the same circuit whose outputs are compared by a checker that asserts an error signal upon output mismatching. If no error is detected, one of the two identical outputs can be used as the result. However, in case of a mismatch, it is not possible to derive which replica is corrupt. Hence, both need to be reconfigured and the computation has to be re-executed. Reference [25] proposes to use a SEU-resistive processor executing a software version of the replicas to identify corrupted units.

The TMR and DWC redundancy schemes require at least $3\times$ and $2\times$ more area and power than an unprotected circuit, respectively. While over-protected systems might provide high reliability beyond the application requirements, the contributed area and power cost could have been saved or diverted to increase the performance. Thus, the trade-off between spatial redundancy and performance in high-reliable reconfigurable processors needs to be taken into account (see Section 16.2).

16.1.5 Scrubbing of configuration memory

Scrubbing is a technique for SEU mitigation in FPGAs [26] by periodically scrutinizing the configuration memory to ensure that any erroneous configuration bits will be corrected, allowing to prevent accumulation of errors. Scrubbing is categorized into two types: *blind* and *readback*. Blind scrubbing uses a 'golden' bitstream of an SEU-protected (e.g., with ECC) secured external memory to constantly overwrite the configuration memory of the FPGA. Readback scrubbing reads the configuration data of the FPGA and checks the ECC bits for errors. In case of a single-bit error, it will be corrected and the configuration bits are written back to the configuration memory. If multiple bits are corrupted, ECC may only be able to detect (but not correct) erroneous configuration bits. Between two consecutive scrubbing cycles, corrupted configuration bits may lead to circuit malfunctioning. CED mechanisms such as TMR are thus typically coupled with scrubbing to achieve seamless protection for highest reliability. To the configuration port of the FPGA, scrubbing poses a non-functional workload besides the (partial) configuration of accelerators. Conflicts may occur when scrubbing and accelerator configuration are executed at the same time or when blind scrubbing overwrites configuration bits that are just being reconfigured to implement a different accelerator. Therefore, the write access to the configuration data should be carefully scheduled to prevent these conflicts [27].

16.2 Reliability guarantee with adaptive modular redundancy

16.2.1 Architecture for dependable runtime reconfiguration

The target reconfigurable processor is an extension of the *i*-Core [7,8]. The extended version is shown in Figure 16.3. It consists of a *core pipeline* that executes instructions that are not accelerated in the reconfigurable fabric, a *runtime system* that performs reconfiguration decisions and dependability management, *multiple reconfigurable regions* into which different accelerators can be reconfigured, a *memory controller* handling memory accesses from the processor pipeline and the reconfigurable regions, and a *bitstream loader* that performs reconfiguration requests of the runtime system. The core pipeline is extended to support AFs that are identified as special assembler instructions for application-specific computations such as transformations, filters, or

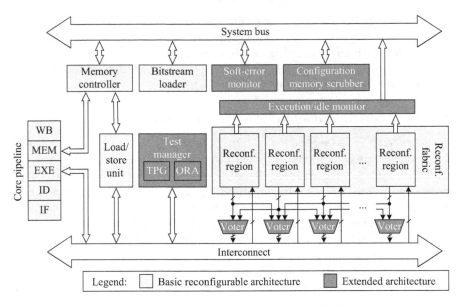

Figure 16.3   Target reconfigurable processor

encryptions. An AF is either implemented by accelerators or is executed in software on the core pipeline if not all accelerators are available (see Section 16.1.1).

In scope of the OTERA project [28–31], the *i*-Core is extended to support dependable operation by online testing, workload/stress monitoring, resource management for reliability/graceful degradation, and CED and correction using the following components (see also Figure 16.3):

- a test manager including test pattern generator and output response analyser to perform structural tests on the reconfigurable fabric and functional tests on the reconfigured accelerators [28],
- a configuration memory scrubber to detect and correct errors in the configuration memory by periodical readback and check of the configuration data,
- a soft-error monitor that estimates the currently experienced SER by using two indicators, the SER in the configuration bits obtained from periodic scrubbing and the SER in Block RAMs protected by error detecting codes,
- voters supporting disparity checking and majority voting of accelerator outputs when neighbouring accelerators are setup for error detection and masking using modular redundancy, and
- runtime system extensions for dynamic dependability management by environmental monitoring, self-awareness, test, and reliability management [29–31].

We focus on SEUs in the reconfigurable fabric in this chapter, as it is the most demanding threat for reconfigurable processors. Soft errors in the configuration memory are defended by the combination of modular redundancy and periodic scrubbing. The configuration memory scrubber periodically reads back the configuration data of each configured accelerator, which will eventually correct a flipped configuration bit. Additionally, error detection and masking needs to be ensured at accelerator level to bridge the time until the scrubber has corrected an SEU. This is achieved by configuring neighbouring reconfigurable regions with identical accelerators and by using voters to detect or correct errors in accelerator outputs.

16.2.2   Overview of adaptive modular redundancy

Due to changing SERs (see Section 16.1.2), application requirements, and the system state (available/used resources), it is not possible to *statically* determine the best suitable error-detection method for a given target reliability at minimal cost. A static optimization *has* to be pessimistic since it must consider the worst case. But when the error rate is lower than that, the system is over protected at corresponding hardware and/or performance cost. In contrast to a static selection of fault-tolerance methods, this chapter presents a method for adaptive modular redundancy for reconfigurable processors. It *guarantees* an application-specified minimum level of reliability of the accelerated computation at minimal performance overhead. This is achieved by using monitoring information to dynamically reconfigure between different redundancy modes, such that the error-detection overhead is minimized.

As shown in Section 16.1.1 and Figure 16.2, AFs may use multiple different accelerator types. Figure 16.4(a)(i) shows an example that consists of three types and thus requires at least three reconfigurable regions to be implemented. The example in Figure 16.4(a)(i) uses exactly three regions and thus has to execute the instances A_2 and A_3 of the same type in different *control steps*. Figure 16.4(a)(ii) shows a different implementation variant of the same AF that uses an additional region to execute A_2 and A_3 in parallel, thus leading to a reduced AF execution latency. It is also possible to provide a partially or completely fault-tolerant variant. Figure 16.4(a)(iii) needs altogether five regions, has the same execution latency as Figure 16.4(a)(i) with three regions, but therefore triplicates A_2 and A_3, which protects these regions against SEUs.

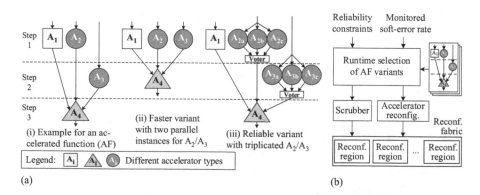

Figure 16.4   Different hardware implementation variants of an accelerated function (AF) and an overview of our proposed adaptive modular redundancy: (a) hardware implementation alternatives and (b) method overview

The reliability requirement of an application specifies the upper bound of its error probability. The reliability of a system depends on the reliability of its components. It is assumed that the processor core is a reliable computing base and an AF is error free during its execution if none of its accelerators are affected by soft errors. An AF that is executed as a software routine (see Section 16.1.1) is considered as reliable. The reliability of an AF that is executed on the reconfigurable fabric depends on the following factors:

Current error rate: It is determined by the environment.

System state: It corresponds to the time since a region was last known to be error free because it was tested, reconfigured, or scrubbed.

Hardware usage: It depends on the number of critical bits (see Section 16.1.3) needed to implement the accelerators of the AF.

In order to guarantee a given target reliability while optimizing the performance, the runtime system (see Figure 16.4(b)) needs to address the following challenges:

1. If a target reliability is specified for an AF, then whenever that AF shall execute, its needs to be guaranteed that it meets that target for the current error rate and system state. If the target reliability cannot be satisfied at that moment, then the AF needs to be executed on the reliable computing base.

2. If a target reliability is specified for the application itself, its needs to bc decomposed into proper target reliabilities for the individual AFs.

3. For all AFs to be executed, its needs to be decided which implementation variant shall be reconfigured such that the target reliability is ensured while maximizing performance for the monitored error rate and system state.

4. For each region, it needs to be decided when/how often to perform scrubbing. After scrubbing, an accelerator is known to be error-free, but scrubbing also reduces performance, as no other region can be reconfigured during scrubbing.

16.2.3 Reliability of accelerated functions (AFs)

The reliability of an AF depends on the SER, the type, structure and size of the used accelerators and the *resident time* the accelerators have been instantiated without errors in the reconfigurable fabric, i.e. the time elapsed since the last reconfiguration or scrubbing event of the regions. As already established in Section 16.1.3 and (16.2) the reliability $R(A, t)$ of an accelerator A with n critical bits and resident time t is $e^{-\lambda n t}$, which decreases with increasing resident time. For accelerators without any fault-tolerance method, the reliability of an AF (probability that it produces the correct result) is

$$R(AF, t, \tau) = \prod_i^{A_i \in AF} e^{-n_i \lambda (t_i + \tau_i)} = e^{-\lambda \sum_i n_i (t_i + \tau_i)} \tag{16.3}$$

where t_i is the resident time of accelerator A_i until AF starts to execute, and τ_i denotes the time period until A_i finishes all its executions. Since $\tau_i \ll t_i$, τ is ignored in the following calculation. It is assumed conservatively that an accelerator computes the correct results only if all its critical bits are correct. In a similar manner, it is assumed that an AF produces correct results only if all of its accelerators compute correctly, and an application operates correctly only when all its AFs are correct.

Frequent scrubbing improves the reliability of accelerators by checking and repairing errors in short periods. It is limited by the bandwidth of the configuration port of the FPGA. When a reconfigurable fabric with N reconfigurable regions is periodically scrubbed, the minimum scrubbing period (i.e. the time between two scrubbing operations) of an accelerator is $N \cdot T_S$, where T_S denotes the time required to scrub one reconfigurable region. In other words, the correctness of the critical bits of an accelerator can only be checked in a period longer than or equal to $N \cdot T_S$. By scrubbing alone, the reliability of an AF_j (Equation (16.3)) is maximized when all of its accelerators are scrubbed at the fastest period $N \cdot T_S$. In this case, it holds that $\forall A_i \in AF : t_i \leq N \cdot T_S$. This is shown in (16.4), where the right-most term expresses the lower bound of the reliability of the AF_j.

$$R(AF_j) = e^{-\lambda \sum_i n_i t_i} \geq e^{-\lambda (\sum_i n_i) N \cdot T_S} \tag{16.4}$$

Implementation variants of accelerators may include partially or completely protected accelerators based on duplication or triplication (see Section 16.2.2). For accelerators in TMR mode with a hardened voter, the probability that it delivers the correct output is the probability that at most one of the three replicated accelerators is affected by soft errors in their critical bits. For accelerators in DWC mode, the AF is re-executed on the hardened processor if an error is detected, i.e. it equals to the probability that at most one of the replicated accelerators is erroneous. The probabilities of correct results for TMR and DWC are shown in (16.5) and (16.6), where $R(A_i)$ and t_i denote the reliability and resident times of the replicated accelerators.

$$R(A_i^{TMR}) = (1 - R(A_a)) R(A_b)R(A_c) + (1 - R(A_b)) R(A_a)R(A_c) \tag{16.5}$$
$$+ (1 - R(A_c)) R(A_a)R(A_b) + R(A_a)R(A_b)R(A_c)$$
$$= e^{-n\lambda(t_a+t_b)} + e^{-n\lambda(t_a+t_c)} + e^{-n\lambda(t_b+t_c)} - 2e^{-n\lambda(t_a+t_b+t_c)}$$
$$R(A_i^{DWC}) = e^{-n\lambda t_a} + e^{-n\lambda t_b} - e^{-n\lambda(t_a+t_b)} \tag{16.6}$$

16.2.4   Reliability guarantee of accelerated functions

When a *reliability constraint* is specified for each AF, it requires that the error probability of every execution of AF_j, i.e. $1 - R(AF_j, t_j)$, is less than or equal to a statically or dynamically given threshold, usually written in powers of ten as 10^{-r_j}, i.e. $\forall j : 1 - R(AF_j, t_j) \leq 10^{-r_j}$. For instance, when $r_j = 5$, the error probability of each execution of AF_j must be less than 10^{-5}. In the above equations, the values of n_i and τ_i are derived from AF implementations at design time. λ, t_i, and the target reliability r_j are variables whose values may dynamically change during runtime.

16.2.4.1 Maximum resident time

To satisfy the reliability constraint, the runtime system must ensure that unprotected accelerators used in the next execution of AF_j are still sufficiently reliable. This requires that the resident times of non-redundant accelerators in AF_j satisfy (16.7).

$$\sum_{i, \, A_i \in AF_j} n_i t_i \leq -\frac{1}{\lambda} \log\left(1 - 10^{-r_j}\right) \tag{16.7}$$

By making t_i small enough, e.g., by scrubbing accelerators more frequently, the reliability constraint can be fulfilled. However, there are many combinations of resident times t_i that satisfy (16.7). To find the optimal combination which maximizes every t_i so that the scrubbing overhead is minimized, the runtime system has to solve a max–min problem involving $\|AF_j\| + 2^{\|AF_j\|}$ constraints, where $\|AF_j\|$ is the number of accelerators required by AF_j. This is too complex for the runtime system and would decrease its responsiveness to other important tasks. To simplify the problem, let $t_{\max}$ denote the maximum resident time of all accelerators required by AF_j, i.e. $t_{\max} = \max_i\{t_i\}$. Then, (16.7) is automatically satisfied when (16.8) is satisfied. T_j^{up} denotes the upper bound of $t_{\max}$ for AF_j. With the above *tightening*, the runtime system only needs to schedule scrubbing for non-redundant accelerators such that $t_{\max}$ satisfies (16.8), which is stricter than required.

$$t_{\max} \leq \frac{1}{\sum_i^{A_i \in AF_k} n_i}\left(-\frac{1}{\lambda} \log\left(1 - 10^{-r_k}\right)\right) = T_j^{up} \tag{16.8}$$

For an AF_j consisting of only triplicated accelerators and applying tightening by $t_{\max} = \max\{t_a, t_b, t_c\}$, the reliability constraint $1 - R(A_i^{TMR}) \leq 10^{-r_j}$ becomes $3e^{-2n\lambda t_{\max}} - 2e^{-3n\lambda t_{\max}} \geq 1 - 10^{-r_j}$. This can be easily solved by substitution to obtain the bound for $t_{\max}$. But it becomes difficult when we compute $t_{\max}$ for partially fault-tolerant variants as shown in Figure 16.4(a)(iii). However, we can always find a suitable q (usually < 1) such that (16.9) holds for all $t_{\max}$ where $e^{-n\lambda t_{\max}}$, the reliability of a non-redundant accelerator, is assumed to be larger than a very conservative value such as 0.99. Therefore, the reliability constraint for an arbitrary AF combining non-redundant and triplicated accelerators is tightened to (16.10), where $t_{\max}$ is the maximum resident time of all accelerators. In a similar way, tightening is also applied to AFs with accelerators in duplicated mode.

$$3e^{-2n\lambda t_{\max}} - 2e^{-3n\lambda t_{\max}} \geq e^{-qn\lambda t_{\max}} \tag{16.9}$$

$$t_{\max} \leq \frac{1}{\sum_i^{\text{non-red.}} n_i + \sum_i^{\text{TMR}} qn_i}\left(-\frac{1}{\lambda} \log\left(1 - 10^{-r_j}\right)\right) = T_j^{up} \tag{16.10}$$

16.2.4.2 Acceleration variants selection

When the application requests to execute AFs in the reconfigurable fabric, then the runtime system has to select from a large set of acceleration variants that have distinct resource usage, performance, and reliability characteristics. We have conducted a case study for a complex H.264 video encoder application, in which nine AFs are implemented. The different variants utilize between 1 and 24 reconfigurable regions, and their absolute performance ranges from $6.3\times$ to $70.2\times$ (relative to software execution). The error probabilities even differ by more than three orders of magnitude.

Due to the large search space, it is computationally inviable to obtain an exact solution fast at runtime. Instead, a greedy algorithm is proposed here that selects the appropriate variants for requested AFs such that the target reliability and resource constraints are satisfied and the performance of the whole application is maximized. Its worst case complexity is $\mathcal{O}(n^2)$, where n is the number of variants to be selected.

The variant selection is guided by a *performance score*, which ensures that the selection is resource efficient and the performance of the whole application increases. At first, a set $\mathscr{C}$ is used to collect those acceleration variants for the requested AFs that are able to meet the reliability constraint, i.e. the upper bound of t_{max} for the variant is greater or equal to the minimum scrubbing period of the system. Then, $\mathscr{C}$ is filtered to keep the smallest derived variant per base variant, i.e. the variant using the fewest regions. In the next step, a loop iteratively selects the variant with the highest *performance score* in $\mathscr{C}$ that still fits into the available regions. The performance score is calculated as the weighted speedup gain compared to a previously selected variant for the same AF. The weight is the monitored execution frequency of the AF divided by the number of regions required by the variant. If there is no previously selected variant, the speedup gain is calculated relative to the software execution. The variant with the highest score is added to the result set $\mathscr{R}$ if there is no faster variant of the same AF already in $\mathscr{R}$. The loop continues until $\mathscr{C}$ is empty, or no variant with the targeted reliability fits into the remaining regions.

Before the actual execution of an AF, the runtime system checks if the selected hardware variant is configured and if it still satisfies the reliability constraint for the current error rate (both might have changed since the last execution of the selection). If that is not the case, the AF is executed in software by the hardened processor.

16.2.4.3   Non-uniform accelerator scrubbing

The scrubbing rate for each region is determined by the accelerator implemented in it. If the accelerator belongs to an accelerator variant that requires a short resident time to satisfy the reliability constraint, the region must be scrubbed more frequently. More precisely, if t_{max} of a variant has to satisfy (16.10), then all the regions it uses are scrubbed as soon as the resident time exceeds $(T_j^{up} - N \cdot T_S)$. In this way, t_{max} of every implemented variant is guaranteed to satisfy the tightened reliability constraint and the scrubbing overhead is minimized.

16.2.5   *Reliability guarantee of applications*

When a reliability constraint is specified for the whole application instead of individual AFs, then the error probability of the outputs from the application must be lower than a given bound. Using multiple kernels in the application (see Section 16.1.1) brings another layer of complexity to the reliability-performance trade-off. Consider the execution of an application with two kernels, targeting maximum performance, as shown in Figure 16.5(a). Kernel 1 requires a large amount of resources and finishes in relatively short time (compared to kernel 2), while kernel 2 has a lower resource

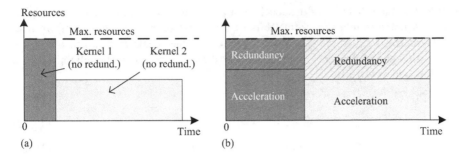

Figure 16.5   Execution of kernels with different degrees of redundancy: (a) kernel execution without redundancy and (b) kernel execution with redundancy

utilization and needs more time. When the application is imposed by a reliability constraint, then redundancy might be needed for the accelerators. This is shown in Figure 16.5(b), where some accelerators in kernel 1 and all accelerators in kernel 2 are protected by DWC. However, due to the limited amount of available resources (marked by the dashed horizontal line), resources devoted to redundancy are not available for acceleration, which leads to longer execution time of kernel 1. This implies a higher chance of being affected by soft errors for protected and unprotected accelerators during the execution. Therefore, the protection strategy in Figure 16.5(b) does not necessarily fulfil the error probability required by the application. If just kernel 2 is protected, while considering the intrinsic low error probability of kernel 1 due to its short execution time, then the reliability constraint of the application may be met without any loss of performance.

Overall, multiple factors need to be considered simultaneously to target the reliability of an application: the kernel execution time, the implementation variants of AFs, the vulnerability of accelerators and their impact on each other. This chapter presents a resource budgeting method to maximize the system performance under a given application reliability constraint. This is achieved by budgeting the *effective critical bits*, which is a metric that allows to capture all reliability impacting factors as one single value. Budgeting of effective critical bits is performed by the following three steps: (1) Transform the reliability constraint of the application (i.e. its allowed error probability) to the number of allowed effective critical bits of the application; (2) Theses allowed effective critical bits are then assigned to the kernels based on their resource requirement and expected execution time; (3) Based on that, the run-time system selects the redundancy modes for the AFs to maximize the performance within the budget.

16.2.5.1   Effective critical bits of accelerators

By scrubbing with maximum frequency, the reliability of an accelerator pair in DWC, i.e. (16.6) with $t_a = t_b = N \cdot T_S$, can be maintained as shown in (16.11). By solving (16.12) for α, we obtain (16.13), where α is a number that is always less than 1 for $0 < u < 1$. Equation (16.13) can be interpreted in a way that by introducing redundancy with DWC, the reliability of the accelerator pair can be maintained at a much higher level, as if the number of critical bits of the accelerator were reduced from n to αn. Here, αn is called the *effective critical bits* of the accelerator pair in DWC. By duplicating one of the accelerators for DWC, the lower bound of the reliability of an AF_j is raised to (16.14).

$$R(A^{DWC}) \geq 2e^{-\lambda nN \cdot T_S} - e^{-2\lambda nN \cdot T_S} \tag{16.11}$$

$$2e^{-\lambda nN \cdot T_S} - e^{-2\lambda nN \cdot T_S} = e^{-\lambda \alpha nN \cdot T_S} \tag{16.12}$$

$$\alpha(n) = \log_u (2u - u^2) \text{ with } u = e^{-\lambda nN \cdot T_S} \text{ and } R(A^{DWC}) \geq e^{-\lambda \alpha nN \cdot T_S} \tag{16.13}$$

$$R(AF_j) \geq e^{-\lambda (\sum_{i \neq 1} n_i + \alpha(n_1)n_1) N \cdot T_S} \tag{16.14}$$

By comparing (16.4) and (16.14), it can be observed that after introducing DWC for an accelerator with n_i critical bits, the total number of effective critical bits of AF_j is reduced by $(1 - \alpha(n_i))n_i$. When three instances of accelerators with n critical bits each are paired to implement TMR, based on the similar derivation, the effective critical bits βn of the TMR pair can be obtained:

$$\beta(n) = \log_u (3u^2 - 2u^3) \text{ and } u = e^{-\lambda nN \cdot T_S} \tag{16.15}$$

16.2.5.2 Reliability of accelerated kernels

The correct functionality of a kernel depends on the error-free execution of its AFs. It is assumed that a kernel delivers correct results only when all its AFs are executed error-free. The reliability of a kernel K_k, i.e. the probability that it delivers correct results, can be formulated as (16.16). Since the configuration bits of accelerators in AF_j are independent of each other, the probability of error-free execution of an AF can be decomposed into the product of the probability of error-free execution of its accelerators, as shown in (16.17).

$$R(K_k) = \prod_{AF_j \in K_k} P(\text{every exec. of } AF_j \text{ is error-free}) \tag{16.16}$$

$$P\left(\begin{array}{c} \text{every execution of} \\ AF_j \text{ is error-free} \end{array}\right) = \prod_{A_i \in AF_j} P\left(\begin{array}{c} \text{every execution of} \\ A_i \text{ is error-free} \end{array}\right) \tag{16.17}$$

The example shown in Figure 16.6 is used to illustrate the calculation of the probability of error-free execution of an accelerator. It shows an execution series of an AF consisting of three accelerators. Short solid lines on the time axis represent the time points at which the scrubbing process of respective accelerators is finished. Long solid lines with circles represent the time points (t_1 to t_5) at which the AF is executed. The time difference between the consecutive execution of different accelerators (few tens of cycles) is ignored since it is negligible in comparison to the scrubbing period (thousands of cycles).

The error-free execution of A_1 requires that all five executions of A_1 at t_1 to t_5 are error-free. The probabilities of error-free consecutive executions of A_1, e.g. at t_1 and t_2, cannot be considered independent, as they rely on the same configuration bits. The error-free execution at t_2 implies that the configuration bits are error-free throughout

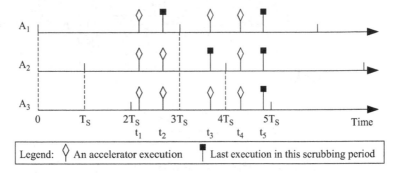

Figure 16.6   Illustrative execution series of an accelerated function

the time period from 0 to t_2 and therefore also implies the error-free execution of A_1 at t_1, as shown in (16.18). But after scrubbing at time point $3T_S$, the configuration bits are ensured to be error-free and thus independent of those before scrubbing. Therefore, the executions of A_1 at t_3 to t_5 are independent of those at t_1 and t_2 and their correctness is implied by the correctness at t_5. The probability of error-free execution of A_1 from t_3 to t_5 is shown in (16.19) and its probability from time 0 throughout t_5 is given in (16.20). In general, the probability that every execution of an accelerator is error-free within one scrubbing period is equal to the error-free probability of the last execution of the accelerator within that scrubbing period (marked by the long solid lines with filled circles in Figure 16.6).

$$P\left(\begin{array}{c}\text{error-free execution}\\\text{of }A_1\text{ at }t_1\text{ and }t_2\end{array}\right) = P\left(\begin{array}{c}\text{error-free execution}\\\text{of }A_1\text{ at }t_2\end{array}\right) = e^{-\lambda n_1 t_2} \qquad (16.18)$$

$$P\left(\begin{array}{c}\text{error-free execution}\\\text{of }A_1\text{ at }t_3\text{ to }t_5\end{array}\right) = P\left(\begin{array}{c}\text{error-free execution}\\\text{of }A_1\text{ at }t_5\end{array}\right) = e^{-\lambda n_1 (t_5 - 3T_S)} \quad (16.19)$$

$$P(\text{every execution of }A_1\text{ is error-free}) = e^{-\lambda n_1 (t_2 + t_5 - 3T_S)} \qquad (16.20)$$

16.2.5.3 Effective critical bits of accelerated kernels and applications

The execution of an accelerator A_i that occurs just before the next scrubbing period starts has the lowest error-free probability $e^{-\lambda n_i N \cdot T_S}$. For an arbitrary execution series of an accelerator A_i in a kernel K_k with total execution time T_k, the lower bound of its error-free probability can be obtained in (16.21), where $T_k / N \cdot T_S$ represents the number of scrubbing periods occurred during the execution of A_i. Therefore, the lower bound of the kernel reliability can be derived from (16.16), (16.17), (16.21) as (16.22), where n_k denotes the effective critical bits of kernel K_k, which is dependent on its own execution time T_k. An application *App* delivers error-free results when all of its accelerated kernels $\{K_k\}$ are executed error-free. With (16.22), the lower bound of the reliability of the application and its effective critical bits n_{app} is obtained as shown in (16.23).

$$P(\text{every execution of }A_i\text{ is error-free}) \geq e^{-\lambda n_i (T_k / N \cdot T_S) N \cdot T_S} \qquad (16.21)$$

$$R(K_k, T_k) \geq e^{-\lambda n_k N \cdot T_S} \quad \text{with} \quad n_k(T_k) = \frac{T_k}{N \cdot T_S} \sum_{AF_j \in K_k} \sum_{A_i \in AF_j} n_i \qquad (16.22)$$

$$R(App) = \prod_k R(K_k) \geq e^{-\lambda n_{app} N T_S},$$

$$n_{app} = \sum_k n_k = \frac{1}{N T_S} \sum_k T_k \sum_{AF_j \in K_k} \sum_{A_i \in AF_j} n_i \qquad (16.23)$$

16.2.5.4   Budgeting of effective critical bits

Equation (16.23) shows that the reliability of an application is able to stay above a certain lower bound depending on the application's effective critical bits. The reliability constraint r of an application denotes that the probability to obtain an error-free result is greater than $1 - 10^{-r}$ and it is satisfied when its reliability lower bound satisfies (16.24). If the number of effective critical bits of the application is lower than the value given in (16.24), then the reliability requirement is automatically satisfied. This chapter proposes a two-step budgeting method that assigns the maximum allowable number of effective critical bits of the application to kernels and AFs. In the first step, the number of effective critical bits of each kernel is determined such that the application performance is maximized. In the second step, the number of effective critical bits of each AF in the kernels is calculated, which indirectly determines the required redundancy for each AF.

$$e^{-\lambda n_{app} N \cdot T_S} \geq 1 - 10^{-r} \Leftrightarrow n_{app} \leq -\frac{1}{\lambda N \cdot T_S} \log(1 - 10^{-r}) \qquad (16.24)$$

16.2.5.5   Budgeting for kernels

To find the number of effective critical bits allowed for individual kernels, it is necessary to determine the relationship between the number of accelerators and the kernel execution time. The amount of resources available for hardware acceleration is limited by the number of reconfigurable regions, which can be devoted to (1) accelerators of different types to accelerate different functions, (2) accelerators of the same type for parallel execution, and (3) accelerators of the same type paired to compose DWC or TMR. All these different scenarios of resource usage lead to different reliability-performance trade-offs. It is assumed here that a reliability-*unaware* runtime system for a reconfigurable processor is optimized to maximize the application performance for the given reconfigurable regions. The execution time $T_k(N)$ of individual kernels k is determined offline for different numbers N of regions in the reconfigurable fabric. When more regions are available for acceleration, then more independent accelerators can be configured and the execution time of the kernel is reduced. When accelerators are paired to implement modular redundancy, then the number of used regions devoted to acceleration is reduced. The acceleration provided by two/three accelerators paired in DWC/TMR is as much as only one accelerator. In other word, M DWC or TMR pairs of accelerators reduce the number of regions available for acceleration by M or $2M$, respectively.

Given the maximum number of effective critical bits of the application determined by (16.24), the problem of finding the number of effective critical bits of each kernel K_k while maximizing the application performance, i.e. minimizing the execution time of all kernels $\sum_k T_k$, is formulated as follows:

$$\text{minimize} \quad \sum_k T_k(N_k^{acc})$$

$$\text{subject to} \quad \sum_k (n_k(T_k) - \Delta_k) \leq -\frac{\log(1 - 10^{-E})}{\lambda N \cdot T_S}$$

$$\Delta_k \approx (1 - \alpha(\mu_k)) \mu_k M_k + \mu_k \max(M_k - (N - ||K_k||), 0)$$

$$\mu_k = \frac{n_k(T_k)}{||K_k||}$$

$$N_k^{acc} = \min(||K_k||, N - M_k)$$

$$M_k \leq \min(||K_k||, \lfloor N/2 \rfloor)$$

where M_k denotes the number of redundancy pairs (here DWC) in kernel K_k, $||K_k||$ denotes the number of regions used by the kernel without any redundancy, and μ denotes the average number of critical bits in one region before applying DWC. Δ_k estimates the reduction of the effective critical bits in kernel k after introducing M_k DWC pairs. N_k^{acc} denotes the number of regions available for acceleration. In the above formulation, it is assumed that accelerator redundancy is achieved by DWC. If TMR is chosen, then Δ_k, N_k^{acc} and M_k need to be changed as follows:

$$\Delta_k \approx (1 - \beta(\mu_k)) \mu_k M_k + \mu_k \max(2M_k - (N - ||K_k||), 0)$$

$$N_k^{acc} = \min(||K_k||, N - 2M_k)$$

$$M_k \leq \min(||K_k||, \lfloor N/3 \rfloor)$$

The number of redundancy pairs M_k needed in each kernel is determined by iterating through all possible combinations of M_k. The complexity of solving the problem is thus $(N/2)^{||K||}$ for DWC or $(N/3)^{||K||}$ for TMR, where $||K||$ denotes the number of kernels. This search process is performed before the application starts and when the SER changes. Since the number of kernels is typically small, in spite of the exponential time complexity, the runtime overhead is low, as evaluated in Section 16.2.6. After determining M_k, the number of effective critical bits of each kernel after budgeting, i.e. $n'_k = n_k - \Delta_k$, can be calculated. It determines the maximum total number of effective critical bits of AFs in each kernel: $\sum_{AF_j \in K_k} n'_j = n'_k N \cdot T_S / T_k$ (see (16.22)).

16.2.5.6 Budgeting for accelerated functions

During the execution of each kernel, the accelerators to implement the AFs coexist in the reconfigurable fabric at the same time. They share the reconfigurable regions among each other. The runtime system selects the appropriate implementation variants for each AF, such that the performance of the kernel is maximized for a given number of reconfigurable regions. More effective critical bits budgeted to an AF allow it to be implemented with more accelerators for higher performance. Therefore, AFs that contribute more to the computation in the kernel or require complex accelerators (more intrinsic critical bits) shall be assigned with more effective critical bits. Given the total number of effective critical bits $n'_k N \cdot T_S/T_k$ that are budgeted to all AFs in each kernel, the budgeted critical bits of each AF n'_j are calculated by solving (16.25), where w_j and n_j denote the proportion of the execution time of AF_j in the kernel and the number of critical bits of AF_j obtained from the reliability-unaware kernel profiling, respectively. Before the start of each kernel, the reliability-unaware runtime system then selects from those AF implementations, whose number of effective critical bits are within the budget, to maximize the kernel performance.

$$\frac{n'_j}{n'_k N \cdot T_S/T_k} = \frac{w_j n_j}{\sum_{AF_j \in K_k} w_j n_j} \tag{16.25}$$

16.2.6 Experimental evaluation

The presented method is evaluated in a reconfigurable processor that is prototyped on a Xilinx Virtex-5 FPGA with an H.264 video encoder as target application. The application consists of three kernels that contain multiple AFs that are composed from nine distinct accelerators. The number of critical bits per accelerator are obtained from the Xilinx `bitgen` tool and range from 19,036 to 86,796 bits. The reliability requirement specifies the upper bound of the error probability of one encoded frame. The algorithm for finding the effective critical bits for kernels and AFs is implemented in fixed-point arithmetic and integrated into the runtime system. The reliability model presented in Section 16.2.3 is integrated into the *i*-Core architectural simulator to evaluate the application reliability. To evaluate the response of the system to different environmental conditions, the SER is changed from 0.1 to 10 errors per Mb per month to simulate realistic cases [16].

For the performance evaluation, the method of critical bits budgeting is applied with reliability requirements from $r=6$ to $r=9$ (see Section 16.2.5.4), i.e. the error probability of each encoded frame must be less than 10^{-r}. DWC is applied as the redundancy mode and we compare the execution time for encoding one frame to an approach that applies DWC to all used accelerators in the AFs (full DWC). The error probability of a full DWC system is close to zero. To evaluate the achieved application reliability, we use the ratio of the calculated application error probability (see Section 16.2.3) and the required error probability ($P_{err}/10^{-r}$). A value smaller than 1 implies that the reliability requirement is satisfied.

Figure 16.7 shows the results under different SERs in a system with eight regions. When the SERs and the reliability requirements are low, it is not necessary to duplicate all accelerators to achieve high reliability, which translates to about 20% performance improvement against full DWC while still satisfying the required reliability. When the SER raises, more accelerators need to be duplicated to compensate the increasing error rate. In worst case, almost all accelerators are duplicated and the resulting error probability is lower than 10^{-15}, as shown in the upper part of Figure 16.7, where the bars for $r=9$ are too small to be visible for SERs higher than 4 Mb^{-1} month^{-1}. The resulting reliability and performance of the system converges to a full DWC system.

To achieve these improvements, the budgeting of effective critical bits introduces two types of runtime overhead. They are due to the computation of budgeted critical

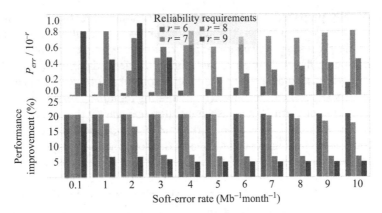

Figure 16.7 Ratios of error probability and performance improvement under different soft-error rates and reliability requirements

bits for each kernel (Type 1) and each AF (Type 2). Type 1 overhead occurs before the start of an application and when the SER changes. In the worst case, which corresponds to a system with 13 regions, it takes 4.1 ms on a SPARC V8 LEON3 processor running at 100 MHz. Type 2 overhead occurs before the start of each kernel by solving (16.25) and takes only 0.07 ms.

16.3 Conclusion and future directions

This chapter discussed the background for the most demanding dependability challenges for reconfigurable processors in many-core systems and presented a dependable runtime reconfigurable processor for high reliability. It uses an adaptive modular redundancy technique that *guarantees* an application-specified level of reliability under changing SEU rates by budgeting the *effective critical bits* among all kernels and all accelerators of an application. This allows to deploy reconfigurable processors in harsh environments without statically protecting them.

The key open problem in this area is to simplify the usage of dependability-aware reconfigurable processors. Significant effort was spent in the past on automating the generation of complex accelerators from given application source code [32]. But specifying the dependability *demand* of applications and accelerators was left to the programmer, who is actually concerned about the functional correctness of the application code instead of being supposed to know the underlying hardware architecture in sufficient detail to be able to provide the demanded dependability parameters. Providing an abstract interface or programming model for the programmer to specify the dependability demands for the entire application (or some application variables or some memory arrays) without having to know about the reconfigurable accelerator details would simplify the usage of dependable reconfigurable systems significantly. A first attempt to specify dependability demands for variables and then to automatically propagate these requirement to data-dependent variables and calculations was made in [33], but it is not comprehensive enough to allow targeting reconfigurable processors. Given a comprehensive transparent or explicit dependability description, the challenge remains to infer the dependability demands for the accelerators, which also depends on the application control flow, e.g. the execution frequency of these accelerators. Similarly, annotating minimal performance demands or maximal power or thermal budgets would allow navigating the embedded system along the scenario-specific sweet spot at runtime by using cross-layer optimizations.

Another key optimization potential lies in the combination of approximate computing [34] and dependable reconfigurable systems. For an application that tolerates approximating some of its calculations, it actually also tolerates certain SEUs or even certain permanent faults. Instead of using an accurate voter to identify differences in a modular-redundant implementation of accelerators, the voter could actually check whether an observer deviation is within the limits of the approximation to decide whether or not costly recalculation/repair is needed. Altogether, despite key enhancements were made for architectures and runtime systems of dependable reconfigurable processors, additional optimization potentials exist and additional efforts w.r.t. tools are needed to ease their widespread usage.

Acknowledgements

This work is supported in parts by the German Research Foundation (DFG) as part of the priority program 'Dependable Embedded Systems' (SPP 1500 – http://spp1500.itec.kit.edu) and of the Transregional Collaborative Research Center 'Invasive Computing' (SFB/TR 89).

References

[1] Borkar S. Thousand core chips: a technology perspective. In: Design Automation Conference (DAC); 2007. p. 746–749.

[2] Kurian G, Miller JE, Psota J, *et al.* ATAC: a 1000-core cache-coherent processor with on-chip optical network. In: International Conference on Parallel Architectures and Compilation Techniques (PACT); 2010. p. 477–488.

[3] Sodani A, Gramunt R, Corbal J, *et al.* Knights Landing: Second-Generation Intel Xeon Phi Product. IEEE Micro. 2016;36(2):34–46.

[4] Kalray. MPPA2-256 Bostan Processor–Kalray's 2nd Generation 288-Core Processor; 2017. http://www.kalrayinc.com/download/4640/.

[5] NVIDIA Corporation. NVIDIA Tesla V100 GPU Architecture; 2017. http://images.nvidia.com/content/volta-architecture/pdf/volta-architecture-white paper.pdf.

[6] Henkel J, Herkersdorf A, Bauer L, *et al.* Invasive manycore architectures. In: Asia and South Pacific Design Autom. Conf. (ASP-DAC); 2012. p. 193–200.

[7]   Henkel J, Bauer L, Hübner M, *et al.* i-Core: a run-time adaptive processor for embedded multi-core systems. In: International Conference on Engineering of Reconfigurable Systems and Algorithms (ERSA); 2011. p. 1–8.

[8]   Bauer L, Shafique M, Henkel J. Concepts, architectures, and run-time systems for efficient and adaptive reconfigurable processors. In: NASA/ESA Conference on Adaptive Hardware and Systems (AHS); 2011. p. 80–87.

[9]   Hansen L. Unleash the Unparalleled Power and Flexibility of Zynq UltraScale+ MPSoCs. Xilinx, Inc.; 2016. WP470 (v1.1).

[10]   Gupta PK. Xeon+FPGA platform for the data center. In: Workshop on the Intersections of Computer Arch. and Reconf. Logic; 2015.

[11]   Henkel J, Hedrich L, Herkersdorf A, *et al.* Design and architectures for dependable embedded systems. In: Int. Conference on Hardware/Software Codesign and System Synthesis (CODES+ISSS); 2011. p. 69–78.

[12]   Ferlet-Cavrois V, Massengill LW, Gouker P. Single Event Transients in Digital CMOS—A Review. IEEE Transactions on Nuclear Science. 2013;60(3): 1767–1790.

[13]   Xilinx. Partial Reconfiguration User Guide. Xilinx, Inc.; 2012. UG702 (v14.1).

[14]   Baumann RC. Radiation-induced Soft Errors in Advanced Semiconductor Technologies. IEEE Transactions on Device and Materials Reliability. 2005;5(3):305–316.

[15]   JEDEC Standard. Measurement and Reporting of Alpha Particles and Terrestrial Cosmic Ray-Induced Soft Errors in Semiconductor Devices. JEDEC Solid State Technology Association; 2006.

[16]   Quinn H, Graham P, Morgan K, *et al.* Flight Experience of the Xilinx Virtex-4. IEEE Transactions on Nuclear Science. 2013;60(4):2682–2690.

[17]   Wirthlin MJ, Takai H, Harding A. Soft Error Rate Estimations of the Kintex-7 FPGA within the ATLAS Liquid Argon (LAr) Calorimeter. Journal of Instrumentation. 2014;9(01):C01025.

[18]   Xilinx. Device Reliability Report. Xilinx, Inc.; 2016. UG116 (v10.4).

[19]   Su SYH, Koren I, Malaiya YK. A Continuous-Parameter Markov Model and Detection Procedures for Intermittent Faults. IEEE Transactions on Computers. 1978;C-27(6):567–570.

[20]   Le R. Soft Error Mitigation Using Prioritized Essential Bits. Xilinx, Inc.; 2012. XAPP 538 (v1.0).

[21]   Xilinx. 7 Series FPGAs Memory Resources User Guide. Xilinx, Inc.; 2016. UG473 (v1.12).

[22]   Hussein J, Swift G. Mitigating Single-Event Upsets. Xilinx, Inc.; 2015. WP 395 (v1.1).

[23]   Mukherjee S. Architecture Design for Soft Errors. Morgan Kaufmann Publishers, San Francisco, CA, USA; 2008.

[24]   Carmichael C. Triple Module Redundancy Design Techniques for Virtex FPGAs. Xilinx, Inc.; 2006. XAPP 197 (v1.0.1).

[25] Ilias A, Papadimitriou K, Dollas A. Combining duplication, partial reconfiguration and software for on-line error diagnosis and recovery in SRAM-based FPGAs. In: Int. Symp. on FCCM; 2010. p. 73–76.

[26] Berg M, Poivey C, Petrick D, *et al.* Effectiveness of Internal versus External SEU Scrubbing Mitigation Strategies in a Xilinx FPGA: Design, Test, and Analysis. IEEE Transactions on Nuclear Science. 2008;55(4):2259–2266.

[27] Heiner J, Sellers B, Wirthlin M, *et al.* FPGA partial reconfiguration via configuration scrubbing. In: International Conference on Field Programmable Logic and Applications (FPL); 2009. p. 99–104.

[28] Bauer L, Braun C, Imhof ME, *et al.* Test Strategies for Reliable Runtime Reconfigurable Architectures. IEEE Transactions on Computers. 2013;62(8): 1494–1507.

[29] Zhang H, Kochte MA, Imhof ME, *et al.* GUARD: GUAranteed reliability in dynamically reconfigurable systems. In: Design Automation Conference (DAC); 2014. p. 32:1–32:6.

[30] Zhang H, Bauer L, Henkel J. Resource budgeting for reliability in reconfigurable architectures. In: Design Automation Conference (DAC); 2016. p. 111:1–111:6.

[31] Zhang H, Bauer L, Kochte MA, *et al.* Aging Resilience and Fault Tolerance in Runtime Reconfigurable Architectures. IEEE Transactions on Computers. 2017;66(6):957–970.

[32] Haaß M, Bauer L, Henkel J. Automatic custom instruction identification in memory streaming algorithms. In: Int. Conference on Compilers, Architecture, and Synthesis for Embedded Systems (CASES); 2014. p. 6:1–6:9.

[33] Engel M, Schmoll F, Heinig A, *et al.* Unreliable yet useful – reliability annotations for data in cyber-physical systems. In: Workshop on Software Language Engineering for Cyber-physical Systems (WS4C); 2011. p. 1–15.

[34] Shafique M, Hafiz R, Rehman S, *et al.* Cross-layer approximate computing: From logic to architectures. In: Design Automation Conference (DAC); 2016. p. 99:1–99:6.

Part IV

Architectures and systems

Chapter 17

Manycore processor architectures

Prasenjit Chakraborty[1], Bharath Narasimha Swamy[1],
and Preeti Ranjan Panda[2]

17.1 Introduction

Trade-offs between performance and power have dominated the processor architecture landscape in recent times and are expected to exert a considerable influence in the future. Processing technologies ceased to provide automatic speedups across generations, leading to the reliance on architectural innovation for achieving better performance. This trend is observed in Figure 17.1, which shows the variation in clock frequencies of Intel processors over recent decades. The frequencies are seen to increase exponentially with time, in line with Moore's law until about 2005, after which the frequencies taper off around 3.5 GHz. With power constraints limiting the complexity of individual CPUs in their quest to achieve higher levels of instruction level parallelism (ILP), the focus shifted to the integration of larger numbers of processing elements on the same chip, each being relatively simple so as to keep the total power dissipation under control. In spite of single-thread performance tapering off, the overall performance continues to improve because of the presence of a large number of processor cores in a manycore system.

Manycore processor systems have found their way into various computing segments ranging from mobile systems to the desktop and server space. With the advent of graphics processing units (GPUs) with a large number of processing elements into the computing space, manycore systems have become the default engine for all target computing domains. We have focused in this chapter on mainly the desktop and system-on-chip (SoC) domain, but the architectural possibilities blend in a seamless way into the other domains also.

The chapter is organised as follows. In Section 17.2, we outline a high-level classification of manycore processors. In Section 17.3, we describe the major architectural components typically expected in modern and future processors, with a focus on the computing elements. Issues arising out of the integration of the various components are outlined in Section 17.4. Future trends are identified in Section 17.5.

[1]Intel, India
[2]IIT Delhi, India

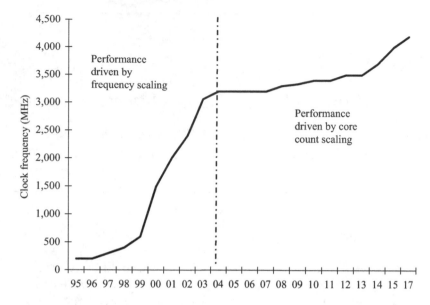

Figure 17.1   Clock frequency scaling in Intel processors over the years

17.2   Classification of manycore architectures

Before studying the processor architectures in detail, let us first develop a high-level classification of the architecture categories. Such a generic classification has to focus on some architectural parameters and abstract away several others. Our focus here is on the way the processor cores and cache levels are organised, along with other major components such as accelerators. This view simplifies several other components and mechanisms such as interconnection structure and I/O. In later sections, we take a more detailed look at several example processor systems.

17.2.1   Homogeneous

Homogeneous CPU architecture refers to the simplest multiprocessor architecture which has all identical CPU cores. The cores have attached to them private first level (L1) instruction and data caches, and often, a private second level (L2) cache also. These are connected over an interconnection structure to a shared last level cache (LLC or L3), and through it, to the external main memory (Figure 17.2(a)). The interconnection network could range from a simple bus or ring structure, to a mesh-based network-on-chip.

17.2.2   Heterogeneous

In heterogeneous CPU architectures, the multiprocessor system has a mix of different types of CPU cores. The heterogeneity could be in terms of complexity or instruction

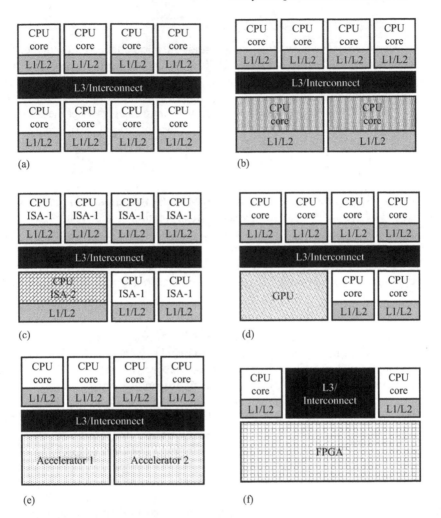

Figure 17.2   *(a) Homogeneous CPUs, (b) heterogeneous CPUs: same ISA,
different complexities, (c) heterogeneous CPUs: multi-ISA,
(d) GPU-enhanced, (e) accelerators and (f) reconfigurable*

set architecture (ISA). Figure 17.2(b) shows a heterogeneous architecture in which
processor cores with different levels of complexity coexist in the same system, permitting the runtime system to exercise a performance/power trade-off. Figure 17.2(c)
shows heterogeneity along an orthogonal direction, where processor cores running
different ISA reside in the same multiprocessor system. Such an organisation would
cater to different functionalities executed by different software components (such as
computation and control) of a larger system.

17.2.3   GPU enhanced

The GPU has emerged in recent times as an important component contributing to heterogeneity in multicore processors (Figure 17.2(d)). Even though originally designed for specific graphics rendering tasks, the GPU has found favour in various general purpose applications where parallelism is explicitly identified by the programmer. We have classified GPU-enhanced architecture as a separate category because of strong similarities in the different prevalent GPUs, and the specific class of programmer interventions that are expected for efficient utilisation of such processing cores.

17.2.4   Accelerators

Accelerators are processing blocks in modern MPSoCs that are designed to perform specific tasks efficiently. With the increasing incorporation of accelerators (machine learning, computer vision, analytics, etc.) in mainstream processors, these hardware blocks are becoming increasingly relevant in general-purpose systems, and their interaction with other components and interface with the interconnection networks need to be considered more carefully in system design decisions (Figure 17.2(e)).

17.2.5   Reconfigurable

The final category of heterogeneous processors is reconfigurable processors, where the architecture platform includes a field programmable gate array (FPGA), that can be configured to realise different hardware functions at run time (Figure 17.2(f)). This leads to flexibility in a different direction and significantly enhances the processing options available for application execution, since the FPGA could be programmed to offer a wide range of different functionalities depending on the demands of the application scenario.

17.3   Processor architecture

We discuss the major processor architectures in this section, with an emphasis on the major computing elements. We take a deeper look at the various architectural categories, identifying the chief internal blocks and outlining the major functionalities.

17.3.1   CPU architecture

17.3.1.1   Core pipeline

The drive towards higher performance of the modern processors is enabled through the concept of ILP. Early CPUs demonstrated one instruction per cycle (1 IPC) throughput attained by the classic five-stage pipeline. There is no consensus on an optimal pipeline depth, and over the years the number of pipeline stages in state-of-the-art commercial processors varied greatly across different architectures based on the performance requirements and power budget. As a rule of thumb, a shallower pipeline reduces power and area, whereas a deeper pipeline leverages the parallelism better leading to better performance.

- *Instruction fetch*

  Figure 17.3 shows the main stages of a modern CPU pipeline employed by most of the commercial vendors today. Though the first step is to fetch the instructions, it is equally important to know which address to fetch the next instruction from. A branch prediction logic described below, utilising various techniques, directs the fetch unit to the address of the next instruction, commonly known as speculation. The application instruction and data addresses are referenced in the

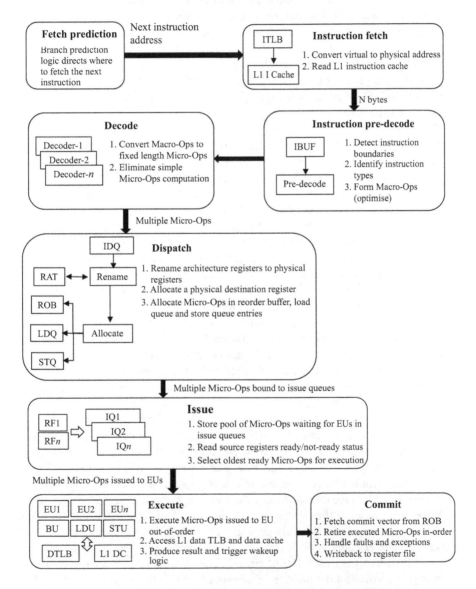

Figure 17.3 Pipeline stages of a typical modern CPU

virtual address (VA) space which are converted into real physical address (PA) using the memory management unit. Once the instruction translation lookaside buffer (ITLB) converts the address, it is looked up in the first level instruction cache (L1 I cache) which provides the instruction to the next pipeline stage. The instruction cache and ITLB are looked up in parallel avoiding any performance penalty in the VA to PA conversion. If the instructions referenced are not present in the L1 cache, then the memory system fetches it from the lower agents (L2, LLC cache) in the memory hierarchy and may result in additional delay in providing the requested instructions. A contiguous set of instruction bytes is read from the instruction cache and stored in an instruction buffer (IBUF) in preparation for decoding. Latest generations of Intel Xeon processors such as Broadwell and Skylake [1] fetch 16 bytes from the L1 I cache every cycle whereas the IBM Power8 [2] fetches 8 fixed length instructions. ARM's high performance Cortex-A72 64-bit processors [3] fetch 3 ARMv8 instructions.

- *Instruction decode*
  Owing to the ever-increasing number of instructions and complexity of instruction encoding (e.g. variable length, multiple format) across all major ISAs, decoding in a single cycle at higher frequencies has become very challenging. A portion of the instruction decoding tasks, such as demarcating the instruction boundaries, identifying instruction categories, types, properties, etc., is performed in the Pre-Decode or Early-Decode stage. In this stage, some high-level optimisation opportunities are also leveraged by merging/fusing-related instructions and forming groups of operations commonly known as Macro-Ops or Complex-Ops. A very common example of this grouping performed by Intel microarchitectures is fusing the individual compare and branch instructions into a fused compare-jump instruction, thereby saving pipeline resources downstream. The real decoding of the instructions is performed in the Decoding stage of the pipeline where the complex Macro-Ops are broken down into simpler and targeted constituent operations better known as Micro-Ops (μOps). To handle instruction categories of various encoding complexities, a set of different decoding mechanisms is employed. A majority of instructions can be easily decoded using simple decoders, which generally maps a Macro-Op to a Micro-Op whereas complex decoders are used to crack instructions that result in multiple Micro-Ops. Yet, there are cases requiring separate treatment by passing them through a Microcode engine which sequences them into a series of several Micro-Ops. Following the decoder stage, the machine operates at the Micro-Ops granularity. To keep the actual execution stages of the pipeline busy, the Fetch to Decoder interface is very carefully designed. The Skylake microarchitecture has a maximum throughput of 6 Macro-Ops per cycle in the Pre-Decode stage with a caveat of consuming the complete 16 bytes in IBUF before commencing the next set of 16 bytes leading to a reduced throughput unless exactly 6 instructions are packed into the 16 bytes. It has four simple and one complex decoder logic for parsing up to five Macro-Ops and converting to five Micro-Ops per cycle. The Microcode engine works in a mutually exclusive manner with the decoder logic and emits four Micro-Ops per cycle. While ARM's A-72 supports a 3 wide decode, on the other hand, Power8 maintains a consistent

8-instruction Pre-Decode and Decode throughput to feed the later stages of the pipeline.

- *Dispatch*

  The Micro-Ops are written to the Instruction Decode Queue (IDQ) which formally begins the process of dispatch and register renaming. One of the most daunting obstacles in the way of high ILP is the presence of data dependences between the neighbouring instructions. False data dependencies, a ramification of limited architectural registers, cause stalls in in-order-cores (INO) until all dependencies are resolved but are bypassed by out-of-order (OOO) cores. Register renaming eliminates false dependencies by mapping architected source and destination registers onto a large pool of physical registers. The exact mapping information is contained in a Register Alias Table and drives the renaming decisions. A hardware structure called reorder buffer (ROB) not only enables the OOO cores to appear sequential to software but also works as a recovery mechanism for misspeculation where the branch has been wrongly predicted. A high-end processor typically performs 4–8 register renaming and ROB allocations per cycle. All Micro-Ops must reserve an entry in ROB before starting execution. Similarly, to enable memory level parallelism (MLP) and avoid data hazards occurring due to memory addressing, all memory instructions are allocated slots in the load (LDQ) and store (STQ) queues before commencing their execution.

- *Execution*

  Following dispatch, Micro-Ops are issued to instruction queues or reservation stations where they wait for execution until a matching execution unit (EU) is available and all its source operands are ready. Issue queues can be unified such as in Skylake, split as in AMD's Zen, or can hold a group as in Power8. A non-ready Micro-Op waits and is considered for execution either when the value is marked available in the register file or can be bypassed from some other EU. In an in-order core, the dispatch and issue can be much simpler as register renaming is not present and instructions are executed from the head of the issue queue when ready. Actual execution of the Micro-Op is performed in the various EUs; once they finish execution, the result may need to be sourced to other waiting instructions and also to be written to the register file. Finally, the instructions are considered for retirement (commit) by deallocating in program order from ROB. In practice, all processors today employ a large number of EUs executing instructions in parallel. Skylake has seven ports that stack up various EUs to each of them and can issue up to seven Micro-Ops but retire six of them per cycle. Besides, to maintain high MLP it dedicates four of those ports to memory instructions. Similarly, the Power8 backend comprises 16 execution engines and supports 10 issues and 8 commits per cycle. Cortex-A72 has five Micro-Ops dispatch width and can issue eight to the various EUs.

  To reduce the pressure on the front end of the pipeline, modern processors are also equipped with some common caching structures such as the Micro-Op cache and Loop-Cache that eliminates the redundant repeated fetch and decode of the same instructions, thereby improving efficiency. In Skylake, a hit in the 1.5K Micro-Ops cache allows six Micro-Ops to be sent to the IDQ directly. Similarly, when a loop is locked in the Loop-Cache the Micro-Ops can be fed directly to the Dispatch without involving the previous stages of the pipeline.

17.3.1.2 Branch prediction

As branches disrupt the flow of instructions to the pipeline, deciding the location of the next instruction becomes practically critical and many hardware structures are provisioned for this purpose. Unconditional branches (jump, call return) can be easily detected and their target can be predicted using a branch target buffer accessed during the fetch of every instruction. To tackle nested subroutine calls, the return address stack, a last-in first-out structure is employed. However, the most sophisticated micro-architectural strategies have been invested towards predicting the direction and target of conditional branches. A dynamic branch prediction logic uses a table that captures the past history of the branch using a small saturation counter. The table is indexed using a combination of the instruction address along with the outcome of previous and neighbouring branches. Once the actual outcome of the branch is determined, the table is further updated to reflect the history correctly. When a branch is mis-predicted, the pipeline needs to be flushed to discard the operations from the wrong path, the speculative state of the registers and queues need to be restored, and the fetch restarted with the correct address. This rollback often involves tens of cycles of penalty, impacting the overall efficiency of the processor significantly.

17.3.1.3 Data parallelism

A simple way to increase the performance of single core processors is through the application of data parallelism realised in single instruction multiple data (SIMD) – performing the same operation on different data. For example, a single vector add instruction can add multiple pairs of array elements, thereby improving the performance and efficiency of the core. Most modern processors architect SIMD by employing wide EUs and register files such as 128, 256 and even 512 bytes, supporting various lengths of integer and floating point (FP) arithmetic concurrently. The latest Skylake Xeon processors implement two 512-bit SIMD EUs to support Intel AVX-512 extensions. PowerPC supports AltiVec with Power9 implementing the most recent VSX-3 ISA capable of handling 2–4 128-bit vector operations. Similarly, ARM supports NEON with the Cortex-A72 capable of executing two 128-bit vector instructions per cycle. The wider execution is supported by wider load and store memory instructions that can read and write a full cache line using only a single instruction in a single cycle. Though the SIMD mechanism of data parallelism fits very well for processing contiguous data elements aligned to its natural boundary, current generation vector ISAs and architectures allow operations on unaligned and non-contiguous data using scatter-gather mechanisms. The limit to performance improvement using SIMD is largely dependent on the inherent data parallelism exhibited by the application. Applications from domains such as high performance computing (HPC) and machine learning, which are rich in dense linear algebra, are promising candidates for speedup using SIMD whereas applications from traditional server and desktop space have limited opportunity to benefit from SIMD.

17.3.1.4 Multi-threading

With a large number of finely balanced structures and logic to improve the performance of single threaded applications, small disruptions such as translation lookaside buffer (TLB) or cache misses are often sufficient to dent the performance drastically. Moreover, not all applications exhibit large degrees of ILP, leaving the pipeline resources idle. Adding more threads of instructions and leveraging thread level parallelism (TLP) is an effective way to keep all the pipeline resources completely utilised, thereby boosting throughput and efficiency. Current processors allow anywhere from a single thread context to several thread contexts (simultaneous multi-threading – SMT) to be active at any point of time. The hardware tax associated with the management is reasonable in terms of duplicating the architectural state of the machine visible to the software, such as registers and the additional space to hold many contexts simultaneously such as for IBUF, IDQ, etc. Intel Xeon processors allow 2-way SMT whereas Power8 and 9 have 4-way and 8-way SMT mode of execution.

17.3.2 GPU architecture

GPUs are highly parallel programmable processing engines that can sustain extremely high arithmetic and memory throughput rates. They are ideal for applications with large computational requirements and are currently the preferred architecture for accelerating massively parallel applications [4]. State-of-the-art GPUs today can deliver several teraflops of double precision performance and sustain memory bandwidth upwards of several hundred GB/s.

GPUs originated as fixed function hardware pipelines targeted at accelerating 3D graphics APIs. While fixed function GPUs helped realise the graphics rendering pipeline in real time, they were not capable of supporting advanced shading and lighting techniques necessary for rendering complex graphics effects. In the first step towards programmability, Nvidia Geforce 7800 replaced fixed function vertex and pixel operations with specialised programmable units which could execute user specified programs [5]. The number of vertex or pixel processors required was dependent on the workload, and managing different programmable engines in a single 3D pipeline led to bottlenecks, requiring additional effort to balance the throughput of pipeline stages.

17.3.2.1 Unified shading architecture

Today, beginning with the first Xenos/Xbox 360, modern GPUs are organised around a unified shader architecture model with various hardware stages in the pipeline sharing a single type of programmable processing unit [6]. Separate processors specialised for vertex and pixel operations are instead replaced with a single unified processor, which is capable of executing both types of shader programs. From a graphics perspective, the unified shader architecture supports enhanced programmability for advanced graphics effects and simplifies the load balancing problem. Even on emerging workloads with varying kernel types and distribution, execution of shader programs can be distributed among all available processors. From a compute perspective, the unified shader simplifies the programming model allowing general purpose programmers to directly target the unified programmable unit, instead of mapping and dividing the compute problem onto multiple heterogeneous units.

Figure 17.4 illustrates the high-level chip architecture of a contemporary GPU. Modern GPUs are fully programmable processors with additional special purpose graphics functionality implemented as fixed function units. GPUs consist of a large number of simple but specialised cores instead of a few large general purpose cores. Programmable cores are organised into independently executing clusters, each connecting to high bandwidth memory (HBM) controllers through an on-chip interconnection network. The on-chip L2 cache is physically banked and logically shared across the execution clusters. GPUs are throughput machines which leverage independently executing threads to saturate execution resources and are hence tolerant of the memory access latency. Unlike CPUs, GPUs do not implement the traditional hierarchy with large on-chip cache memories. To support a large number of threads executing, GPU memory systems are designed for data throughput with wide memory buses (such as GDDR5 and HBM) and support bandwidths six to eight times that of typical CPUs.

Figure 17.5 illustrates the organisation of an execution cluster. Each graphics execution cluster is a fully capable rendering pipeline consisting of fixed function graphics hardware, programmable shader cores, scheduler and special purpose functional units interconnected by a local fabric. Graphics fixed function hardware units perform setup and post shader activities such as input assembly and vertex fetch, rasterising triangles, depth testing and blending, while the shader cores handle all programmable calculations in the GPU.

A shader core forms the fundamental building block of a programmable GPU. It is a unified processing element that supports the execution of both 3D and compute

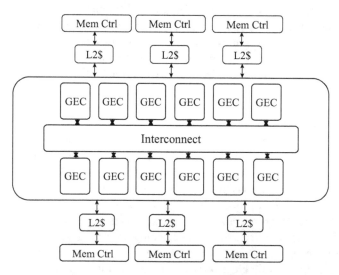

Figure 17.4   Chip architecture of a contemporary GPU

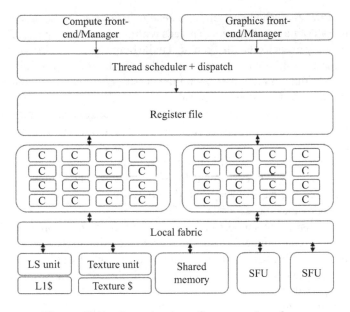

Figure 17.5   Organisation of an execution cluster

programs. Programmable vertex, geometry and pixel stages of the graphics pipeline spawn 3D shader programs that are all executed on the unified core. In addition, general purpose compute is also supported through the execution of compute shaders.

An instruction fetch and decode unit feeds into ALU/Processing elements arranged in the form of independent execution lanes, with each lane supporting FP and integer (INT) general purpose operations [7]. Specialised functional units support complex operations required for graphics rendering such as transcendental functions and interpolation for calculation of pixel attributes. Load store units handle access to graphics global memory and a specialised texture unit handles access to graphics texture memory.

17.3.2.2   Single instruction multiple thread (SIMT) execution model

GPUs are reliant on massive multithreading to deliver high throughput. Recent GPUs can have in excess of 10,000 threads executing in parallel to hide EU latency and memory access latency. Threads are created, scheduled and executed in the form of thread-groups – also called warps (NVIDIA) [8] or quads (ARM) [9]. A thread-group consists of threads of the same type and starting at the same instruction pointer address. Concurrent scheduling and execution of thread-groups of different types is supported. A scoreboard structure tracks the ready status of in-flight groups and selects the next group on a priority algorithm based on thread-group type, instruction type and fairness of execution.

The shader core supports the single instruction multiple-thread (SIMT) model of execution where all execution lanes share a single instruction front end. At each instruction issue, the scheduler selects a ready thread-group and issues the same instruction to all of its active threads. Threads within a thread-group execute together, but independently of each other. In order to handle branches, executions for individual threads are masked off due to predication. If threads of a group take different paths through a conditional branch, then each branch path is executed separately until all threads reconverge to the same branch path.

To sustain peak execution rates, the shader core manages a pool of thread-groups concurrently and interleaves their execution. To implement fast switching between instruction streams, execution contexts for all threads in flight are stored in a large and unified register file. A multi-banked architecture is used to share the register file across thread-groups and to provide high operand read bandwidth, with operands from different register banks brought to the appropriate compute unit/lane through crossbar networks and operand collectors [10].

Along with hardware support for low overhead thread creation and scheduling, GPUs provide several unique features that make fine-grained parallel programming easy and efficient. Threads within one thread-block can allocate and share data in the local shared memory and synchronise with fast barrier synchronisation operations. Using shared memory results in very low latency compared to using global memory and can reduce off-chip global memory pressure. To efficiently manage access to shared data and support parallel computing operators such as reductions, a set of atomic memory operations is supported. These standard ALU instructions, namely integer addition, minimum, maximum, swap and compare-and-swap, perform the atomic operation directly resulting in several orders of magnitude faster memory read–modify–write operations in comparison to conventional semaphore-based synchronisation methods.

17.3.3 DSP architecture

Digital signal processors (DSP) are processors targeted at and optimised for processing of digitally represented analogue signals [11]; nearly all architectural features included in a DSP are associated with specific algorithms whose computation improves by the addition of the feature. For applications that are still evolving, DSPs provide a middle-point in architecture design between a custom ASIC fixed function hardware block and general purpose processors. Due to their specialisation, DSPs provide high performance programmable logic blocks to implement newer standards and yet are more efficient at execution compared to a CPU. DSPs are employed in a number of applications such as voice processing, audio processing, image processing and video processing.

DSPs are targeted at cost (area) and power-sensitive applications. From a high-level processor organisation perspective, DSPs are more focused on exploiting ILP rather than TLP, with the design objective being maximising the work done per cycle for performance, but targeting slower clock speeds to achieve low power execution. Almost all modern commercially successful DSPs are based on a statically scheduled VLIW architecture. VLIWs avoid expensive and power hungry dynamic scheduling techniques and instead rely on the compiler to extract ILP. VLIW instruction packets are variable sized and contain multiple instructions (typically up to four instructions) which are executed in parallel. Additionally, conditional execution may be employed to remove branches through if-conversion.

Despite their evolution during the last decade to address newer application segments, DSPs have several characteristic features when compared to general purpose CPUs, as listed in [12]. DSPs support a fast single-cycle multiply-accumulate (MAC) instruction, since multiplication and a subsequent accumulation of products is a common operation in signal processing. A hardware feature called zero overhead loops provides an instruction to specify the loop count and the loop-start address, which enables low overhead loop execution without the need to update and test the loop counter or branching back to the loop-start instruction. Address generation units support several special addressing modes for efficient handling of predictable memory access patterns in DSP algorithms. Register-indirect addressing with post-increment automatically increments the address pointer and is useful for accessing data that is stored sequentially in memory. Circular addressing allows access to a sequential block of data followed by automatic wrap around to the starting address. Without these features, explicit instructions are required to update the address pointer. Finally, DSPs support variable data width and fixed precision data formats. Fixed point processing is cheaper and less power consuming than FP processing, and the variable data widths enable using the shortest data word that can provide the required accuracy for target applications, thus enabling cost-sensitive use-cases.

DSP instructions sets are targeted for a specific application domain in order to realise high performance and energy efficiency. Hexagon DSP from Qualcomm [13] has two variants, the modem DSP (mDSP) with instructions customised for modem processing and the application DSP (aDSP) for multimedia acceleration. The aDSP has several domain-specific instructions that accelerate the important multimedia algorithms such as variable length encode/decode, sliding window filters, linear feedback shift, cyclic redundancy check calculation and elliptic curve cryptography. Similarly, the C5 Vision DSP from Cadence [14] provides several instructions targeted for accelerating convolutional neural networks.

17.3.4 ASIC/accelerator architecture

With transistor technology scaling not keeping with the historical pace, the quest for performance and energy efficiency has fallen back more on architectural improvements. Hardware optimisation in the control and data path applied to common yet specific patterns of operation has contributed to the rise of accelerator ASICs that provide substantial improvement in efficiency over CPU and GPU. Pieces of acceleration logic can be placed at suitable locations of the overall system, guided by the integration cost and the use case benefits. At a high level, accelerators integrated in MPSoC can be categorised as shown in Figure 17.6.

- An accelerator acting as another EU added to the core pipeline operates at the instruction granularity and benefits from the low latency of accesses and is tightly coupled with the core. A suitable example of such a model is the cryptography

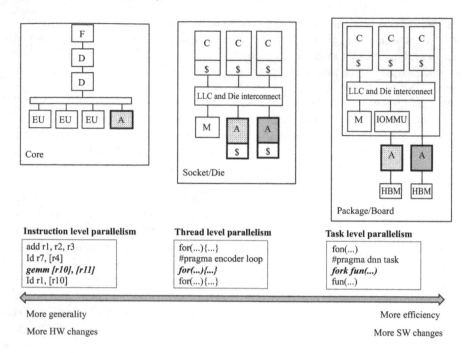

Figure 17.6   Categorising accelerators in MPSoCs

logic present to extend Intel AES ISA and the addition of Tensor Cores to
NVIDIA's latest Volta GPU [15].
* Raising the granularity a little further, an accelerator can be coupled at the same
  level as a CPU or GPU in the same coherent memory space, capable of performing somewhat more complex routines such as FFT, convolution and speech
  processing. Current generation GPUs with media encoder/decoder is a pertinent
  example of such an architecture.
* Finally, accelerator logic dedicated completely towards a specific task can be
  integrated through existing IO links in the system. Currently such systems are
  prevalent to solve problems such as deep neural networks (DNN) and computer
  vision and are available generally as a separate PCIe card. Once the task is
  offloaded, these units perform independently of their own or system memory
  and require minimal changes to the rest of the system. Examples of such configurations are Google's tensor processing unit (TPU) [16] and Intel Quickassist
  Adapters [2].

Contrary to CPU and GPU's generic architecture and principle of working, a hardware
accelerator is optimised for a specific application and follows no generic framework.
We illustrate a high-level approach to design an accelerator for Matrix–Matrix multiplication (GEMM) operations which are heavily used for many HPC and DNN
applications and are the focus of current generation of hardware designers.

Optimised GEMM implementation involves decomposing large matrices into smaller ones that fit into the cache, reusing the elements maximally as shown in Figure 17.7(a). A vectorised GEMM (4 × 4 matrix) implementation for CPU is also shown in Figure 17.7(b). Apart from the memory operations, the performance of the code is dependent on the FP multiply/accumulate (FMA) throughput. We observe that several hardware resources in the core pipeline, such as fetch, decode, branch prediction, register renaming and issue logic, are unnecessary for this application and can be safely discarded. With carefully orchestrated static instruction scheduling the power hungry OOO logic can be avoided and an in-order core would perform equally well. GPUs with much simpler processing pipeline can accommodate many such simple cores within the same power and area budget and perform much more efficiently than a classical CPU. However, both CPU and GPU would need to read 3 vector registers and write 1 register for each FMA instruction, resulting in 48 reads and 12 writes to the register file. A simple optimisation of reading the row once can avoid three extra register reads per iteration of the loop. Latching the FMA result internally in the EU can avoid the writes and eventually result in only 20 register reads for the whole operation, with significant energy savings. Factoring the memory operations performed, the overhead of read and write to cache can be significantly reduced by organising a simple scratchpad customised to the specific access pattern. It is now clearly evident that a hardware logic architected along these optimisations can easily provide much better energy and area efficiency compared to CPU and GPU.

Recently, Google revealed the architecture of a custom-built ASIC called TPU [16] for speeding up the inference of neural network applications in their datacentres. Running at a modest 700 MHz, it is capable of performing 64K 8-bit FMAs

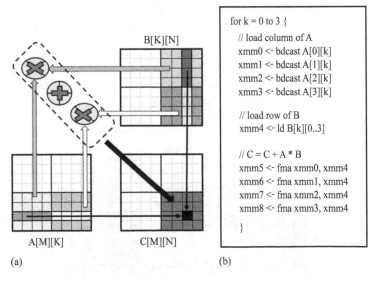

(a)   (b)

Figure 17.7   (a) Blocked matrix multiply and (b) vectorisation in matrix multiply (4 × 4)

and delivering 92 TeraOps/second within a 75-W power budget. This extracts 30–80 times higher efficiency than a CPU or GPU. It is a PCIe connected card with four pipeline stages and possesses a massive matrix multiply unit performing 256×256 8-bit multiply-add operations in a systolic fashion suited for inference algorithms. The rest of the resources such as data paths and queue sizes are balanced to keep the multiply array busy.

17.3.5 Reconfigurable architecture

In reconfigurable architectures, on-chip FPGA modules permit the creation of hardware functionalities at run time that could be customised for different application scenarios. The FPGA could serve as an accelerator, but with the added advantage that the accelerator functionality could be different for different programs. While FPGA acceleration has been attempted in the past, the tight integration of FPGA blocks close to the processor core creates new opportunities for more efficient acceleration, through increased communication bandwidth and shorter latencies. We study two commercial examples of reconfigurable architectures: the Xilinx Zynq [17] and the Intel ARRIA 10 [18].

The Xilinx Zynq 7000 Series is a heterogeneous platform consisting of a processing system consisting of ARM processor cores and a programmable logic fabric. Figure 17.8 depicts a view of the architecture family, where the processing system consists of one or two ARM cores, and the programmable fabric is of various sizes. Such architecture leads to improved performance because of the much higher interface

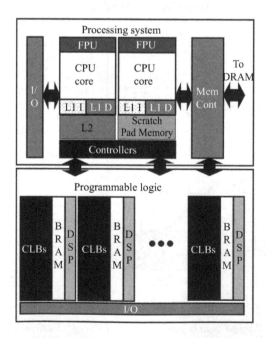

Figure 17.8   Reconfigurable architectures: the Xilinx Zynq 7000 Series

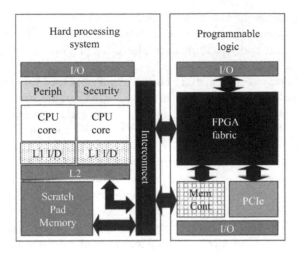

Figure 17.9   Reconfigurable architectures: Intel Arria 10

bandwidth and latency between the processor and FPGA sections than what could be possible using separate chips. Software running on the processors manages the over-all system, including the configuration and high-level power management functions of the programmable logic. The programmable logic consists of regular FPGA fab-ric elements such as look-up tables, Block RAMs (BRAMs: on-chip SRAMs), DSP slices and programmable interconnections. The programmable logic has independent access to the external memory controllers, permitting independent access to off-chip DRAM and on-chip Scratch Pad Memory for the customised logic without interfering with the processors.

The Intel Arria 10 SoC device (Figure 17.9) embodies a philosophy similar to the Zynq. It has a hard processing system (HPS) consisting of ARM CPUs and an accompanying FPGA. A number of peripherals are connected to the HPS, as in the Zynq processing system. The on-chip memory system consists of levels of caches and Scratch Pad Memory. Memory controllers interfacing with off-chip DRAM are accessible both from the HPS and FPGA subsystems. Upon powering on, the booting up of the system can be done either through the FPGA or the HPS.

17.4   Integration

Fabrication and overall integration was relatively simpler in earlier processor gen-erations, with relatively few homogeneous components, and the classical growth in processor performance has been fuelled by the progress made in IC integration and packaging technology. With the primary focus today being the inclusion of many distinct functionalities as closely as possible in a cost-efficient way, integration chal-lenges have become formidable. The key parameters that dictate integration choices depend not only on performance and power but also equally on cost and time-to-market considerations. The issues of IP (intellectual property) design, verification of the SoC, chip size and yield of the manufacturing process are critical for overall success of a product.

In a monolithic integration, every component is packaged using the same manufacturing technology in a single die. This provides the best performance, power and form factor advantage and often used in mobile, laptop and desktop chips as shown in Figure 17.10(a). However, it is often practically infeasible for a sizable chip due to IP unavailability for a specific process node caused by different vendors. To surmount these requirements, a larger system is broken down into smaller groups and these groups are connected and assembled in a single chip, known as multi-chip-module (MCM), shown in Figure 17.10(b). The IPs are clustered as per their performance, inter-IP communication requirements, and process readiness. For example, if two IPs need high speed communication then it is beneficial to place them in a single group. Each group is fabricated separately into a smaller die and finally integrated into a unifying substrate to reconstitute the large and complex chip. For example, a CPU, FPGA, HBM and a network interface card can be integrated into a MCM chip. AMD's new product combines 4 silicon dies each containing 8 CPUs to build a 32 cores EPYC server processor.

The breathtaking pace of wider and faster data communication needs fuelled by the emerging applications imposes the requirements of very high data transfer rates at low latency and power at the same time. The low speed and high-power links in current generation MCM components becomes a bottleneck for future use cases. As a next

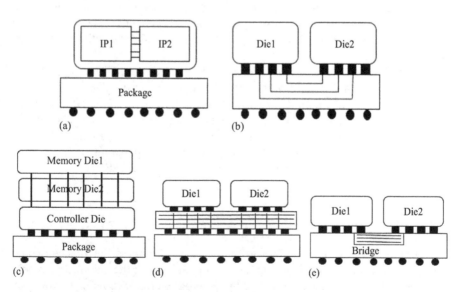

Figure 17.10   *(a) Monolithic die integration, (b) multi-chip-module (MCM), (c) 3D integration of HBM, (d) 2.5D integration using Si interposer and (e) Intel EMIB-based integration*

generation integration solution, chip manufacturers are shifting towards a stacked solution by either stacking dies on top of each other (3D stacking) or using a silicon interposer. In 3D IC integration, active chips (homogenous or heterogeneous) are stacked on top of each other and connected vertically using through-silicon-vias all the way down to the package substrate. The most prevalent usage of this technology is in the manufacture of HBM, stacking 8–9 layers of memory over a bottom die with the controller logic as represented in Figure 17.10(c). This means of integration enables HBM to pack memory and logic in a dense array to provide bandwidth and power advantages that are not possible using traditional manufacturing methodologies. This integration is also quite favourable in the low-power mobile domain where SoC and the WideIO memory are stacked to reap the additional benefits of smaller form factor [19]. However, due to stacking, heat dissipation is inefficient, and applying pure 3D stacking for high-power chips turns out to be problematic, with thermal challenges. A recent research paper from IBM discussed the performance, power issues in 3D stacking [20].

The 2.5D integration method using passive silicon interposers (Figure 17.10(d)), a rich interconnection mechanism between dies, provides a suitable integration alternative to 3D-IC. Silicon interposers can be thought of as consisting of conductive material and connection wires while allowing the connection of the active dies with the silicon substrate using microbumps. Although silicon interposers enable today's integration, they pose challenges regarding the handling of signal and scalability for large die sizes and constitute an expensive solution. New emerging technologies such as Intel's embedded multi-die interconnect bridge (EMIB) alleviate these problems and facilitate a simple yet high-density interconnection. Instead of using a large silicon interposer straddling every die (resulting in longer wires), EMIB uses a small silicon bridge die (short wires) embedded in the underlying package substrate to realise a dedicated connection between the edges of the dies as shown in Figure 17.10(e). Intel's Kaby Lake G processor integrates Intel Core, HBM and GPU from AMD using EMIB. Also, Intel's Stratix10 FPGA and SoC employ EMIB to realise a high-performance FPGA product.

17.5 Conclusion and future directions

17.5.1 CPU

CPU core due to its wide applicability and flexibility to execute all kinds of applications will continue to remain a critical component in a computer system. Traditional research targeting various stages of the core pipeline frontend, backend and branch prediction will persist as usual [21–29]. Though performance is paramount, the shift to energy efficiency has dominated its improvement in last decade and will contribute to its evolution at a much faster pace in future. A recent study from Intel [30] discusses the impact of architectural features and future improvement possibilities. Power-saving mechanisms such as dynamic voltage and frequency scaling and clock/power gating would constitute the bottom line for all digital circuit design.

Existing CPU architecture has already been segmented to suit the demands of target application use cases. With the fast-changing application profile for every segment the improvement in core pipeline will be adopted by majority of the CPU vendors. The spirit of delivering increased performance with lower power has led to a lot of recent research focused on the pipeline stages and structures.

Vital understanding of the actual reasons for OOO core benefits [31] has motivated to propose mechanisms that let only those critical instructions receive OOO treatment and rest enjoy the power benefit of INO execution. Such a hybrid mechanism is either leveraged using modified and granular ISA changes [32,33], extending the pipeline to accommodate hybrid structures [34–37], and fine-tuning instruction scheduling [38–40]. A more coarse scheduling of application phases on to suitable cores has been commercially employed in ARM's Big.LITTLE architecture [41] employed by Qualcomm's Snapdragon processors. On the research side, many heterogeneous architectures have been proposed [42–44] with either the same ISA or multi-ISA [45] to realise the opportunity of varying performance and power characteristics [46]. Such architectures are accompanied by the major challenge of modifying the associated software but are worth the investment considering the benefits [47,48]. Alleviating programming challenges would be critical to the success of heterogeneous architectures. The recent research thrust towards automated identification of opportunities and scheduling of amenable portions is in the right direction [49–51]. An alternative to constitute such architecture is through deployment of reconfigurable hardware resources. Providing fine-grain configurability to tailor hardware structures as per application needs can improve CPU utilisation and efficiency further [52–54].

17.5.2 Graphics processing units

Due to their high-memory bandwidth and compute capabilities, GPUs are now found in a range of HPC application areas such as molecular dynamics, weather modelling, computational finance, medical imaging, and oil and gas exploration. GPU-based machine architectures are now consistently featuring in the Top 500 supercomputer list. Despite their impressive raw compute capabilities, GPUs are extremely energy efficient and are hence attractive platforms to run applications in the data centre where energy consumed is a primary cost factor.

As GPUs gear up to support newer demanding applications in deep learning, data analytics, computer vision and several other emerging areas, scaling GPU performance while maintaining energy efficiency remains a challenge [55]. Towards this, beyond the gains that come from moving to newer fabrication technologies, architectural innovations to reduce inefficiencies in instruction execution and overheads of data movement are needed.

SIMT model of execution introduces several inefficiencies. Researchers have proposed hardware techniques [56–59] to efficiently execute redundant scalar computations. Techniques to improve utilisation of SIMD execution [60–62] and control-divergence aware scheduling techniques [63,64] have been proposed to mitigate the impact of branch divergence in the SIMT model.

Data movement contributes significantly to the energy consumed both at the memory interface and on-chip. Locality aware memory hierarchy [65] and cache management techniques [66,67], data compression and compressed execution techniques [68–70], coordinated thread scheduling and prefetching [71] and locality aware thread scheduling techniques [72,73] have been proposed to reduce data movement and improve energy efficiency.

GPUs have traditionally relied on transistor scaling to increase the SIMT core count with corresponding improvements to memory bandwidth, as the path to improved performance. However, with the slowing of Moore's law, performance scaling of single-socket and single-die (monolithic) GPU will plateau out. Package level integration techniques that build a logical GPU using multiple smaller GPU modules [74] and multi-socket designs techniques [75,76] are likely to be the way forward to meet the growing demand for GPU computation power.

17.5.3 Accelerators

Architects and researchers have been debating for some time now about what the future heterogeneous multicore architecture would look like. The work in [77] considers the various designs discussed in this chapter and compares them on the basis of various metrics. As discussed earlier, ASICs are able to improve efficiency to an extent unmatched by CPU due to the reasons mentioned in this chapter (and illustrated beautifully in [78]). On similar lines, the work mentioned in [79] explores the design space for architecting ASIC for visual computing. ASIC being too targeted lacks the flexibility provided by the CPU. A programmable accelerator, as a middle ground, has been proposed in [80]. At a system level, employing ASIC brings many challenges commonly applicable for all classes of accelerator design. A recent research proposes building datacentres using a large array of ASICs [81]. A methodology is presented to determine the optimal system configuration based on use cases. Reference [82] discusses the design challenges faced in architecting an ASIC-dominated computer system (data transfer, scheduling, etc.) and proposes tools to perform rapid accelerator-based system design.

ASICs have already started being employed in a broad range of devices from low-end mobile to high-end server, encompassing practically every market segment – finance, health care, manufacturing, telecommunication, etc. The major thrust area where accelerators are deployed is in the field of machine learning due to their prevalent usage in image recognition, analytics, driverless vehicles and speech recognition. Consequently, a large volume of research has proposed deep learning accelerator design targeting optimisation for training and inference in DNNs [83–88]. Presently, Google's TPU [16] and NVIDIA's Volta GPU [15] are commercial production systems; several other vendors are expected to enter the market soon with similar offerings [89,90]. Otherwise, accelerating networking applications, big data, computer vision and parallel graph processing are other areas where ASICs are being deployed.

In our opinion, despite programming challenges, ASIC-based systems will continue to grow owing to the overwhelming efficiency advantages. Though the level of integration will be generally use-case driven, it is not difficult to envisage a balanced system design employing ASIC at every level analogous to the memory hierarchy evolution. Also, keeping pace with the hardware development, the software toolchain to program such machines easily would continue to rise. As in the graphics ecosystem, these optimisations will be available at all levels of the software stack with varying performance and productivity trade-offs.

17.5.4   Field programmable gate array

What does the future hold for FPGAs as compute components? The heterogeneous systems discussed in this chapter may have scratched only the surface of the possibilities. Whereas the current generation of systems are clearly divided into the processor sub-system and programmable hardware sub-system, future architectures could have a lot more tightly integrated FPGAs that are distributed throughout the manycore system. Just as accelerators are likely to be scattered throughout a system in the interest of reducing data transfer latencies between them and the compute cores, the programmable logic could also be similarly located at strategic positions, leading to very high data bandwidths and low latencies. We envisage an architectural shift of the manycore system towards an array of tiles, each tile consisting of CPUs, some levels of the memory hierarchy, augmented by accelerator and FPGA components.

This brings us to an important question: that of accelerator vs. FPGA for implementing a specific functionality. The accelerator has the obvious advantage of being more efficient for carrying out the task it was designed for, while the FPGA's programmability advantage ensures that it can be dynamically personalised to offer different functionalities. Since the total area is limited, a trade-off is likely to play out here, with the general purpose system leaning towards the most common functions anticipated to run on them being implemented as accelerator, with all the less common functions mapped into the FPGA. The SoC space is likely to veer closer towards a larger custom implementation component, and smaller emphasis on programmable hardware. The FPGAs on the heterogeneous manycore systems are likely to witness a number of innovative applications, such as verification and security, in addition to the traditional role of accelerating functionality.

17.5.5   Emerging architectures

* Autonomous driving – The industry push towards driverless cars is driving semiconductor companies such as Nvidia and Intel to provide solutions with unprecedented features, performance and reliability requirements. Nvidia's DRIVE PX system is a leading product in this segment that merges various sensors with high computation capabilities. It hosts a wide range of sensors such as multiple cameras, ultrasonic sensors, lidars and radars to gauge the complete surrounding of the vehicle. The data from these devices is fed in real time to a powerful GPU optimised for deep learning inferencing to estimate the path forward and the next set of correct actions. As vehicles become more and more autonomous in the future, the computing system would not only need to process an enormous volume of data from a multitude of sensors but also need to provide the decisions at very low latency in real time. The system design would need to

balance critically both the throughput and latency aspects along with the stringent requirement of very high levels of functional safety. Consequently, the complexity to build such systems would dramatically increase in future.

- Internet of things (IoT) – The projected explosion of smart and connected devices encompassing every aspect of human life is already beginning to dictate how future hardware systems are designed. Although the devices will have distinct functionality and would require diverse sets of components, they would embed certain common elements to meet the IoT concerns and challenges. First, due the possible inclusion of both analogue and digital sensors, SoC and CPU designers will need to architect solutions such that integrating these sensors of wide variety with the rest of the system components would become simple. Second, owing to the connected nature, every device would need to enable the basic networking stack and specifications. Finally, due to the connected and critical nature of these devices, they will be mandated to implement rigorous security mechanisms to thwart any malicious threats. As always, all these need to be managed at a reasonable performance and power budget and will spur innovative solutions for future SoC design.

References

[1] Intel® 64 and IA-32 Architectures Optimization Reference Manual – https://software.intel.com/en-us/articles/intel-sdm, Accessed 2018.

[2] Alex Mericas. Performance Characteristics of the POWER8 Processor – 2014 IEEE Hot Chips 26 Symposium (HCS'14).

[3] A Walk Through of the Microarchitectural Improvements in Cortex-A72 – community.arm.com, Accessed 2018.

[4] John Nickolls and William J. Dally. 2010. The GPU computing era. IEEE Micro 30, 2, 56–69. DOI=http://dx.doi.org/10.1109/MM.2010.41.

[5] NVIDIA's Fermi: The First Complete GPU Computing Architecture. 2009. NVIDIA White Paper http://www.nvidia.com/content/PDF/fermi_white_papers/P.Glaskowsky_NVIDIA's_Fermi-The_First_Complete_GPU_Architecture.pdf, Accessed 2018.

[6] John D. Owens, Mike Houston, David Luebke, Simon Green, John E. Stone, and James C. Phillips. 2008. GPU computing. Proc. IEEE. 96, 5, 879–899. doi: 10.1109/JPROC.2008.917757.

[7] NVIDIA's Next Generation CUDATM Compute Architecture: Fermi. NVIDIA White Paper. 2009. http://www.nvidia.in/content/PDF/fermi_white_papers/NVIDIA_Fermi_Compute_Architecture_Whitepaper.pdf, Accessed 2018.

[8] Erik Lindholm, John Nickolls, Stuart Oberman, and John Montrym. 2008. NVIDIA tesla: a unified graphics and computing architecture. IEEE Micro 28, 2, 39–55. DOI=http://dx.doi.org/10.1109/MM.2008.31.

[9] Jem Davies. 2016. The bifrost GPU architecture and the ARM Mali-G71 GPU. In 2016 IEEE Hot Chips 28 Symposium (HCS), Cupertino, CA, 1–31. doi: 10.1109/HOTCHIPS.2016.7936201.

[10]   Jingwen Leng, Tayler Hetherington, and Ahmed ElTantawy, *et al.* 2013. GPUWattch. In Proceedings of the 40th Annual International Symposium on Computer Architecture – ISCA'13.

[11]   Edwin J. Tan and Wendi B. Heinzelman. 2003. DSP architectures: past, present and futures. SIGARCH Comput. Archit. News 31, 3, 6–19. DOI=http://dx.doi.org/10.1145/882105.882108.

[12]   Jennifer Eyre and Jeff Bier. 2000. The evolution of DSP processors. IEEE Signal Proc. Mag. 17, 2, 43–51. doi: 10.1109/79.826411.

[13]   L. Codrescu, W. Anderson, S. Venkumahanti, *et al.* 2014. Hexagon DSP: an architecture optimized for mobile multimedia and communications. IEEE Micro 34, 2, 34–43. doi: 10.1109/MM.2014.12.

[14]   David Kanter. May 30, 2017. Cadence C5 flexes for neural networks. Linley Newsl.

[15]   NVIDIA Volta – https://www.nvidia.com/en-us/data-center/volta-gpu-architecture/, Accessed 2018.

[16]   Norman P. Jouppi, Cliff Young, Nishant Patil, *et al.* 2017. In-datacenter performance analysis of a tensor processing unit. In Proceedings of the 44th Annual International Symposium on Computer Architecture (ISCA'17).

[17]   Intel® QuickAssist Technology – https://www.intel.in/content/www/in/en/architecture-and-technology/intel-quick-assist-technology-overview.html, Accessed 2018.

[18]   Xilinc Inc, Zynq-7000 All Programmable SoC Data Sheet: Overview. Datasheet DS190(v1.11), June 2017. http://www.xilinx.com.

[19]   Intel Inc., Intel® Arria 10® Hard Processor, System Technical Reference Manual, Version a10_5v4, July 2017. http://www.intel.com.

[20]   Young Jun Yoon, Byung Deuk Jeon, Byung Soo Kim, *et al.* 18.4 An 1.1V 68.2GB/s 8Gb Wide-IO2 DRAM with non-contact microbump I/O test scheme. In Proceeding of IEEE International Solid-State Circuits Conference (ISSCC'16).

[21]   Philip Emma, Alper Buyuktosunoglu, and Michael Healy. 2014. 3D Stacking of high-performance processors. In Proceedings of High Performance Computer Architecture (HPCA'14).

[22]   David J. Schlais, Mikko H. Lipasti. BADGR: a practical GHR implementation for TAGE branch predictors. In Proceeding of IEEE International Conference on Computer Design (ICCD'16).

[23]   André Seznec, Joshua San Miguel, and Jorge Albericio. 2015. The inner most loop iteration counter: a new dimension in branch history. In Proceedings of the 48th International Symposium on Microarchitecture (MICRO-48).

[24]   Dibakar Gope and Mikko H. Lipasti. 2014. Bias-free branch predictor. In Proceedings of the 47th Annual IEEE/ACM International Symposium on Microarchitecture (MICRO-47).

[25]   Mitchell Hayenga, Vignyan Reddy Kothinti Naresh, Mikko H. Lipasti. Revolver: processor architecture for power efficient loop execution. In Proceedings of the 2013 IEEE 19th International Symposium on High Performance Computer Architecture (HPCA) (HPCA'14).

[26]   Zichao Xie, Dong Tong, Mingkai Huang, Xiaoyin Wang, Qinqing Shi, Xu Cheng. TAP prediction: reusing conditional branch predictor for indirect branches with Target Address Pointers. In Proceeding of IEEE International Conference on Computer Design (ICCD'11).

[27]   Furat Afram, Hui Zeng, and Kanad Ghose. 2013. A group-commit mechanism for ROB-based processors implementing the X86 ISA. In Proceedings of the 2013 IEEE 19th International Symposium on High Performance Computer Architecture (HPCA) (HPCA'13).

[28]   Michael Ferdman, Cansu Kaynak, and Babak Falsafi. 2011. Proactive instruction fetch. In Proceedings of the 44th Annual IEEE/ACM International Symposium on Microarchitecture (MICRO-44).

[29]   Shantanu Gupta, Shuguang Feng, Amin Ansari, and Scott Mahlke. 2011. Bundled execution of recurring traces for energy-efficient general purpose processing. In Proceedings of the 44th Annual IEEE/ACM International Symposium on Microarchitecture (MICRO-44).

[30]   Mayank Agarwal, Nitin Navale, Kshitiz Malik, and Matthew I. Frank. 2008. Fetch-criticality reduction through control independence. In Proceedings of the 35th Annual International Symposium on Computer Architecture (ISCA'08).

[31]   Kenneth Czechowski, Victor W. Lee, Ed Grochowski, *et al.* 2014. Improving the energy efficiency of big cores. In Proceeding of the 41st annual international symposium on Computer architecture (ISCA'14).

[32]   Sandeep Navada, Niket K. Choudhary, and Eric Rotenberg. 2010. Criticality-driven superscalar design space exploration. In Proceedings of the 19th International Conference on Parallel Architectures and Compilation Techniques (PACT'10).

[33]   Ziqiang Huang, Andrew D. Hilton, and Benjamin C. Lee. 2016. Decoupling loads for nano-instruction set computers. In Proceedings of the 43rd International Symposium on Computer Architecture (ISCA'16).

[34]   Daniel S. McFarlin and Craig Zilles. 2015. Branch vanguard: decomposing branch functionality into prediction and resolution instructions. In Proceedings of the 42nd Annual International Symposium on Computer Architecture (ISCA'15).

[35]   Faissal M. Sleiman and Thomas F. Wenisch. 2016. Efficiently scaling out-of-order cores for simultaneous multithreading. In Proceedings of the 43rd International Symposium on Computer Architecture (ISCA'16).

[36]   Trevor E. Carlson, Wim Heirman, Osman Allam, Stefanos Kaxiras, and Lieven Eeckhout. 2015. The load slice core microarchitecture. In Proceedings of the 42nd Annual International Symposium on Computer Architecture (ISCA'15).

[37]   Amin Ansari, Shuguang Feng, Shantanu Gupta, Josep Torrellas, and Scott Mahlke. 2013. Illusionist: transforming lightweight cores into aggressive cores on demand. In Proceedings of the 2013 IEEE 19th International Symposium on High Performance Computer Architecture (HPCA) (HPCA'13).

[38]   Andreas Sembrant, Trevor Carlson, Erik Hagersten, *et al.* 2015. Long term parking (LTP): criticality-aware resource allocation in OOO processors.

In Proceedings of the 48th International Symposium on Microarchitecture (MICRO-48).

[39]   Arthur Perais, André Seznec, Pierre Michaud, Andreas Sembrant, and Erik Hagersten. 2015. Cost-effective speculative scheduling in high performance processors. In Proceedings of the 42nd Annual International Symposium on Computer Architecture (ISCA'15).

[40]   Görkem Aşılığlu, Zhaoxiang Jin, Murat Köksal, Omkar Javeri, and Soner Önder. 2015. LaZy superscalar. In Proceedings of the 42nd Annual International Symposium on Computer Architecture (ISCA'15).

[41]   Erika Gunadi and Mikko H. Lipasti. 2011. CRIB: consolidated rename, issue, and bypass. In Proceedings of the 38th Annual International Symposium on Computer Architecture (ISCA'11).

[42]   Big.LITTLE processing with ARM Cortex-A15 & Cortex-A7, ARM White Paper, 2011.

[43]   Andrew Lukefahr, Shruti Padmanabha, Reetuparna Das, *et al.* 2012. Composite cores: pushing heterogeneity into a core. In Proceedings of the 2012 45th Annual IEEE/ACM International Symposium on Microarchitecture (MICRO-45).

[44]   Ganesh Venkatesh, Jack Sampson, Nathan Goulding, *et al.* 2010. Conservation cores: reducing the energy of mature computations. In Proceedings of the 15th Edition of ASPLOS on Architectural Support for Programming Languages and Operating Systems (ASPLOS XV).

[45]   Ganesh Venkatesh, Jack Sampson, Nathan Goulding-Hotta, Sravanthi Kota Venkata, Michael Bedford Taylor, and Steven Swanson. 2011. QsCores: trading dark silicon for scalable energy efficiency with quasi-specific cores. In Proceedings of the 44th Annual IEEE/ACM International Symposium on Microarchitecture (MICRO-44).

[46]   Ashish Venkat and Dean M. Tullsen. 2014. Harnessing ISA diversity: design of a heterogeneous-ISA chip multiprocessor. In Proceeding of the 41st Annual International Symposium on Computer Architecture (ISCA'14).

[47]   Nagesh B. Lakshminarayana and Hyesoon Kim. Understanding performance, power and energy behavior in asymmetric multiprocessors. In Proceeding of IEEE International Conference on Computer Design (ICCD'08).

[48]   Ting Cao, Stephen M. Blackburn, Tiejun Gao, and Kathryn S. McKinley. 2012. The yin and yang of power and performance for asymmetric hardware and managed software. In Proceedings of the 39th Annual International Symposium on Computer Architecture (ISCA'12).

[49]   Yuhao Zhu and Vijay Janapa Reddi. 2013. High-performance and energy-efficient mobile web browsing on big/little systems. In Proceedings of the 2013 IEEE 19th International Symposium on High Performance Computer Architecture (HPCA) (HPCA'13).

[50]   Shruti Padmanabha, Andrew Lukefahr, Reetuparna Das, and Scott Mahlke. 2017. Mirage cores: the illusion of many out-of-order cores using in-order hardware. In Proceedings of the 50th Annual IEEE/ACM International Symposium on Microarchitecture (MICRO-50'17).

[51] Daniel Shelepov, Juan Carlos Saez Alcaide, Stacey Jeffery, *et al.* 2009. HASS: a scheduler for heterogeneous multicore systems. SIGOPS Oper. Syst. Rev. 43, 2, 66–75.

[52] Shruti Padmanabha, Andrew Lukefahr, Reetuparna Das, and Scott Mahlke. 2015. DynaMOS: dynamic schedule migration for heterogeneous cores. In Proceedings of the 48th International Symposium on Microarchitecture (MICRO-48).

[53] Yanqi Zhou, Henry Hoffmann, and David Wentzlaff. 2016. CASH: supporting IaaS customers with a sub-core configurable architecture. In Proceedings of the 43rd International Symposium on Computer Architecture (ISCA'16).

[54] Yanqi Zhou and David Wentzlaff. 2014. The sharing architecture: sub-core configurability for IaaS clouds. In Proceedings of the 19th International Conference on Architectural Support for Programming Languages and Operating Systems (ASPLOS'14).

[55] Matthew A. Watkins and David H. Albonesi. 2010. ReMAP: a reconfigurable heterogeneous multicore architecture. In Proceedings of the 2010 43rd Annual IEEE/ACM International Symposium on Microarchitecture (MICRO'43).

[56] Stephen W. Keckler, William J. Dally, Brucek Khailany, Michael Garland, and David Glasco. 2011. GPUs and the future of parallel computing. IEEE Micro 31, 5, 7–17. DOI=http://dx.doi.org/10.1109/MM.2011.89.

[57] Kai Wang and Calvin Lin. 2017. Decoupled affine computation for SIMT GPUs. In Proceedings of the 44th Annual International Symposium on Computer Architecture (ISCA'17). ACM, New York, NY, USA, 295–306. DOI: https://doi.org/10.1145/3079856.3080205.

[58] Sylvain Collange, David Defour, and Yao Zhang. 2009. Dynamic detection of uniform and affine vectors in GPGPU computations. In Proceedings of the 2009 International Conference on Parallel Processing (Euro-Par'09), Hai-Xiang Lin, Michael Alexander, Martti Forsell, Andreas Knüpfer, Radu Prodan, Leonel Sousa, and Achim Streit (Eds.). Springer-Verlag, Berlin, Heidelberg, 46–55.

[59] Yi Yang, Ping Xiang, Michael Mantor, *et al.* 2014. A case for a flexible scalar unit in SIMT architecture. In Proceedings of the 2014 IEEE 28th International Parallel and Distributed Processing Symposium (IPDPS'14). IEEE Computer Society, Washington, DC, USA, 93–102. DOI=http://dx.doi.org/10.1109/IPDPS.2014.21.

[60] Zhongliang Chen and David Kaeli. 2016. Balancing scalar and vector execution on GPU architectures. In 2016 IEEE International Parallel and Distributed Processing Symposium (IPDPS), Chicago, IL, 973–982. doi: 10.1109/IPDPS.2016.74.

[61] Minsoo Rhu and Mattan Erez. 2013. Maximizing SIMD resource utilization in GPGPUs with SIMD lane permutation. SIGARCH Comput. Archit. News 41, 3, 356–367. DOI: http://dx.doi.org/10.1145/2508148.2485953.

[62] Aniruddha S. Vaidya, Anahita Shayesteh, Dong Hyuk Woo, Roy Saharoy, and Mani Azimi. 2013. SIMD divergence optimization through intra-warp

compaction. In Proceedings of the 40th Annual International Symposium on Computer Architecture (ISCA'13). ACM, New York, NY, USA, 368–379. DOI: http://dx.doi.org/10.1145/2485922.2485954.

[63]   Yunsup Lee, Vinod Grover, Ronny Krashinsky, Mark Stephenson, Stephen W. Keckler, and Krste Asanović. 2014. Exploring the design space of SPMD divergence management on data-parallel architectures. In Proceedings of the Annual International Symposium on Microarchitecture, MICRO. 2015. 101–113. 10.1109/MICRO.2014.48.

[64]   Nicolas Brunie, Sylvain Collange, and Gregory Diamos. 2012. Simultaneous branch and warp interweaving for sustained GPU performance. ACM SIGARCH Comput. Archit. News 40, 49–60. 10.1109/ISCA.2012.6237005.

[65]   Minsoo Rhu and Mattan Erez. 2012. CAPRI: prediction of compaction-adequacy for handling control-divergence in GPGPU architectures. SIGARCH Comput. Archit. News 40, 3, 61–71. DOI=10.1145/2366231.2337167 http://doi.acm.org/10.1145/2366231.2337167.

[66]   Minsoo Rhu, Michael Sullivan, Jingwen Leng, and Mattan Erez. 2013. A locality-aware memory hierarchy for energy-efficient GPU architectures. In Proceedings of the 46th Annual IEEE/ACM International Symposium on Microarchitecture (MICRO-46). ACM, New York, NY, USA, 86–98. DOI=http://dx.doi.org/10.1145/2540708.2540717.

[67]   Gunjae Koo, Yunho Oh, Won Woo Ro, and Murali Annavaram. 2017. Access pattern-aware cache management for improving data utilization in GPU. In Proceedings of the 44th Annual International Symposium on Computer Architecture (ISCA'17). ACM, New York, NY, USA, 307–319. DOI: https://doi.org/10.1145/3079856.3080239.

[68]   Yunho Oh, Keunsoo Kim, Myung Kuk Yoon, *et al.* 2016. APRES: improving cache efficiency by exploiting load characteristics on GPUs. SIGARCH Comput. Archit. News 44, 3, 191–203. DOI: https://doi.org/10.1145/3007787.3001158.

[69]   Sangpil Lee, Keunsoo Kim, Gunjae Koo, Hyeran Jeon, Murali Annavaram, and Won Woo Ro. 2017. Improving energy efficiency of GPUs through data compression and compressed execution. IEEE Trans. Comput. 66, 5, 834–847. DOI: https://doi.org/10.1109/TC.2016.2619348.

[70]   Sangpil Lee, Keunsoo Kim, Gunjae Koo, Hyeran Jeon, Won Woo Ro, and Murali Annavaram. 2015. Warped-compression: enabling power efficient GPUs through register compression. SIGARCH Comput. Archit. News 43, 3, 502–514. DOI: https://doi.org/10.1145/2872887.2750417.

[71]   Gennady Pekhimenko, Evgeny Bolotin, Nandita Vijaykumar, Onur Mutlu, Todd Mowry, and Stephen W. Keckler. 2016. A Case for Toggle-Aware Compression for GPU Systems. 188–200. 10.1109/HPCA.2016.7446064.

[72]   Adwait Jog, Onur Kayiran, Asit K. Mishra, *et al.* 2013. Orchestrated scheduling and prefetching for GPGPUs. In Proceedings of the 40th Annual International Symposium on Computer Architecture (ISCA'13). ACM, New York, NY, USA, 332–343. DOI: http://dx.doi.org/10.1145/2485922.2485951.

[73]   Jin Wang, Norm Rubin, Albert Sidelnik, and Sudhakar Yalamanchili. 2016. LaPerm: locality aware scheduler for dynamic parallelism on GPUs. SIGARCH Comput. Archit. News 44, 3, 583–595. DOI: https://doi.org/ 10.1145/3007787.3001199.

[74]   Shin-Ying Lee, Akhil Arunkumar, and Carole-Jean Wu. 2015. CAWA: coordinated warp scheduling and cache prioritization for critical warp acceleration of GPGPU workloads. SIGARCH Comput. Archit. News 43, 3, 515–527. DOI: https://doi.org/10.1145/2872887.2750418.

[75]   Akhil Arunkumar, Evgeny Bolotin, Benjamin Cho, *et al.* 2017. MCM-GPU: multi-chip-module GPUs for continued performance scalability. SIGARCH Comput. Archit. News 45, 2, 320–332. DOI: https://doi.org/ 10.1145/3140659.3080231.

[76]   Ugljesa Milic, Oreste Villa, Evgeny Bolotin, *et al.* 2017. Beyond the socket: NUMA-aware GPUs. In Proceedings of the 50th Annual IEEE/ACM International Symposium on Microarchitecture (MICRO-50'17). ACM, New York, NY, USA, 123–135. DOI: https://doi.org/10.1145/3123939.3124534.

[77]   NVIDIA Tesla P100, The Most Advanced Datacenter Accelerator Ever Built. 2017. NVIDIA Whitepaper – WP-08019-001_v01.1 | 1.

[78]   Eric S. Chung, Peter A. Milder, James C. Hoe, and Ken Mai. 2010. Single-chip heterogeneous computing: does the future include custom logic, FPGAs, and GPGPUs? In Proceedings of the 2010 43rd Annual IEEE/ACM International Symposium on Microarchitecture (MICRO'43).

[79]   Rehan Hameed, Wajahat Qadeer, Megan Wachs, *et al.* 2010. Understanding sources of inefficiency in general-purpose chips. In Proceedings of the 37th Annual International Symposium on Computer Architecture (ISCA'10).

[80]   Aqeel Mahesri, Daniel Johnson, Neal Crago, and Sanjay J. Patel. 2008. Tradeoffs in designing accelerator architectures for visual computing. In Proceedings of the 41st Annual IEEE/ACM International Symposium on Microarchitecture (MICRO 41).

[81]   Kevin Fan, Manjunath Kudlur, Ganesh Dasika, and Scott Mahlke. 2009. Bridging the computation gap between programmable processors and hardwired accelerators. In International Symposium on High Performance Computer Architecture (HPCA'09).

[82]   Ikuo Magaki, Moein Khazraee, Luis Vega Gutierrez, and Michael Bedford Taylor. 2016. ASIC clouds: specializing the datacenter. In Proceedings of the 43rd International Symposium on Computer Architecture (ISCA'16).

[83]   Jason Cong, Mohammad Ali Ghodrat, Michael Gill, Beayna Grigorian, Karthik Gururaj, and Glenn Reinman. 2014. Accelerator-rich architectures: opportunities and progresses. In Proceedings of the 51st Annual Design Automation Conference (DAC'14).

[84]   Angshuman Parashar, Minsoo Rhu, Anurag Mukkara, *et al.* 2017. SCNN: an accelerator for compressed-sparse convolutional neural networks. In Proceedings of the 44th International Symposium on Computer Architecture (ISCA'17).

[85]　Ali Shafiee, Anirban Nag, Naveen Muralimanohar, *et al.* 2016. ISAAC: a convolutional neural network accelerator with in-situ analog arithmetic in crossbars. In Proceedings of the 43rd International Symposium on Computer Architecture (ISCA'16).

[86]　Yu-Hsin Chen, Joel Emer, Vivienne Sze. Eyeriss: a spatial architecture for energy-efficient dataflow for convolutional neural networks. In Proceedings of the 43rd International Symposium on Computer Architecture (ISCA'16).

[87]　Jongse Park, Hardik Sharma, Divya Mahajan, Joon Kyung Kim, Preston Olds, and Hadi Esmaeilzadeh. 2017. Scale-out acceleration for machine learning. In Proceedings of the 50th Annual IEEE/ACM International Symposium on Microarchitecture (MICRO-50'17).

[88]　Michaela Blott, Thomas Preusser, Yaman Umuroglu, *et al.* Scaling neural network performance through customized hardware architecture. In Proceeding of IEEE International Conference on Computer Design (ICCD'17).

[89]　Tianshi Chen, Zidong Du, Ninghui Sun, *et al.* 2014. DianNao: a small-footprint high-throughput accelerator for ubiquitous machine-learning. In Proceedings of the 19th International Conference on Architectural Support for Programming Languages and Operating Systems (ASPLOS'14).

[90]　Intel Nervana – https://www.intelnervana.com/, Accessed 2018.

[91]　Graphcore – https://www.graphcore.ai/, Accessed 2018.

Chapter 18
Silicon photonics enabled rack-scale many-core systems

Peng Yang[1], Zhehui Wang[1], Zhifei Wang[1], Xuanqi Chen[1], Luan H.K. Duong[1], and Jiang Xu[1]

The increasingly higher demands on computing power from scientific computations, big data processing and deep learning are pushing the emergence of exascale computing systems. Tens of thousands of or even more manycore nodes are connected to build such systems. It imposes huge performance and power challenges on different aspects of the systems. As a basic block in high-performance computing systems, modularized rack will play a significant role in addressing these challenges.

In this chapter, we introduce rack-scale optical networks (RSON), a silicon photonics enabled inter/intra-chip network for rack-scale many-core systems. RSON leverages the fact that most traffic is within rack and the high bandwidth and low-latency rack-scale optical network can improve both performance and energy efficiency. We codesign the intra-chip and inter-chip optical networks together with optical internode interface to provide balanced data access to both local memory and remote note's memory, making the nodes within rack cooperate effectively. The evaluations show that RSON can improve the overall performance and energy efficiency dramatically. Specifically, RSON can deliver as much as 5.4× more performance under the same energy consumption compared to traditional InfiniBand connected rack.

18.1 Introduction

Scientific computation, big data and deep-learning applications are demanding higher performance and more energy-efficient computing systems. The emerging exascale system is planned to fulfill these requirements. However, it is widely acknowledged that the way toward exascale will be significantly more challenging [1]. On the one hand, as Moore's law stops affecting the semiconductor technology, it will be harder to integrate more transistors on given die size. Many chips/nodes are organized to undertake distributed workloads. Tens of thousands of multicore processors

[1]Department of Electronic and Computer Engineering, Hong Kong University of Science and Technology, Hong Kong

and memory/storage resources are organized together to provide higher parallelism and throughput in a warehouse or high-performance computing system. On the other, rack becomes the main assemble and standardized unit for cloud computing and high performance computing (HPC) [2], but its structure has changed little during the last decades. The performance-cost effectiveness of rack architecture is becoming more important than that of a sole node and plays a significant role in approaching the efficient exascale system.

As much as 80% servers generated traffic stays within rack in cloud-computing area [3], and the power consumed by interconnection network is expected to grow correspondingly and contributes almost one-quarter of overall system power consumption [4,5]. The required energy efficiency on the high-bandwidth interconnect side implies 20 pJ/bit for exascale systems [6]. Traditional electrical links are difficult to meet the requirement because of its high-power consumption and capability to transmit high data rate for long distance. Optical fibers are used for connecting nodes in a rack and between racks for its low loss at long distance data transmission. Optical interconnect can also achieve ultra-high data rate without bring much extra energy consumption. It can transmit data at near light speed, decreasing considerable latency for internode and inter-rack communication. These advantages make optical interconnect a promising candidate to replace traditional interconnect architectures.

Optical interconnect are also studied extensively for inter-chip and intra-chip architectures by academia. These works demonstrate interesting features and result from different aspects, but the remaining weaknesses are not well addressed. First, most works focus on either intra-chip or inter-chip optical network. Although a few works put forward codesigned inter/intra-chip networks, they do not present details on how to connect the two parts and how they interact with each other. Second, they do not emphasize much on dedicated and efficient optical data channel assignment and control. This could be a severe issue for optical interconnects since circuit switching is usually used, which could occupy certain paths for a long time and result in serious responsive delay. Third, most existing optical interconnects fail to analyze and optimize the inter-chip and inter-chip communication flow and traffic characteristics, which could diminish the benefits of optical interconnect if not thoroughly considered. Lastly, those designs are well analyzed for interconnect features, but it is unclear how it impacts on large-scale applications and system performance.

In this chapter, we introduce RSON [7], a rack-scale optical network architecture to address the aforementioned issues. RSON codesigns the inter-chip and intra-chip optical network and develops optical internode interface to provide balanced connection of them. We provide detailed internode interface and optical transceiver design to fulfill such a function. Internode communication requires the collaboration of inter-chip and intra-chip networks. We develop elaborate channel partition scheme to make the data channel arbitration overhead low and scalable. Dynamic weight control scheme is proposed to resolve the imbalanced traffic load between memory controller and internode interface. We also analyze and optimize the communication protocol based on the intra-rack traffic characteristics, ensuring that different types of traffic can be served by the optical network architecture efficiently. Apex benchmarks [8] and machine-learning-based benchmarks are used for the evaluation since these benchmarks are designed for large-scale computing system and suitable for evaluating our proposed rack-scale high-performance computing architecture. The results show RSON achieves 5.4× and 2.2× more performance under the same energy consumption compared to the traditional InfiniBand connected and optical link connected many-core rack architecture, respectively. It demonstrates that the silicon photonics enabled rack architecture shows promising performance and energy-efficiency advantages toward the future many-core rack systems over the state-of-the-art InfiniBand and optical fiber interconnection solutions. For clarity, we use Trad. IB to stand for the rack architecture with InfiniBand connected traditional server nodes and electrical Top-of-Rack switch, and Trad. OS to stand for the rack architecture with optical links and switch connected traditional server nodes.

The rest of this chapter is organized as follows. Section 18.2 briefly reviews related works. Section 18.3 presents the RSON architecture and components design details. The communication flow and arbitration is presented in Section 18.4. Section 18.5 shows the evaluations. We conclude this chapter in Section 18.6.

18.2 Related work

There exists numerous works that use optical interconnect architectures to cope with the performance and power issues in manycore processor and large-scale computers. References [9,10] targeted on hybrid optical-electrical on-chip interconnects. Ring/loop-based topologies have been examined for using low-radix switches and more scalable optical ring path in [11,12]. The optical ring is basically used for global interconnect, reducing overhead on optical related overhead. Except for such an electrical-optical hybrid design method, all optical intra-chip networks were also investigated in [13–15], removing the necessity to do power-hungry and latency overhead of O/E/O conversion. It is common that these designs take fair consideration on control scheme, but they omit the design of detailed optical network interface to convert signals between electrical and optical domain. Mesh-based optical on-chip networks are also studied by [16–18]. These works considered the design of optical router and the detailed routing technique for on-chip optical communication. Nonetheless, the previously mentioned works focus only on intra-chip optical interconnects. In these systems, the off-chip communication, such as external memory and chip-to-chip communication, is realized by electrical links, which leads to a critical performance bottleneck. The concept of off-chip optical interconnects were also investigated in [19–21]. But these works focused on the inter-chip channel design and did not thoroughly investigate the inter-chip optical networks topology, switch and control.

Different types of passive optical interconnects were presented in [22]. The lack of flexibility and scalability of passive optical interconnects could be a problem for larger scale systems. An all-optical ultra-low latency server-to-remote memory/storage data center connection was shown by [23]. A scalable photonic interconnection network architecture for data center applications was proposed in [24]. In [25], the authors presented an ASIC switch that is able to sustain 8.2 TB/s, which was designed for all-optical networks using the InfiniBand protocol. The ASIC has a 25-Gb/s optical transceiver per channel bandwidth. Optical switch is essential to provide high-bandwidth and low-latency interconnect for the rack scale communication architecture. In [26], it experimentally demonstrates a 75-ns end-to-end latency in an optical ToR switch. Reference [27] exploited wavelength routing characteristics of a switch fabric to resolve contention in the wavelength domain based on arrayed waveguide grating router. The proposed optical switch achieved significantly better performance than electrical switch. These works showed optical switch fabric promising to fulfill the performance and power requirements for rack-scale interconnect. Different from the above rack-scale optical architectures, RSON considers both the intra-chip (Optical Network-on-Chip or ONoC) and inter-chip optical networks, providing high-bandwidth and low-latency interconnection for both on-chip and off-chip traffic.

18.3   RSON architecture

RSON targets high-performance and energy-efficient rack-scale architecture for data centers and exascale computing systems. Different from the traditional electrically connected racks, RSON is an intra-rack communication architecture enabled by the emergence of silicon photonics. It aims to achieve high performance and energy efficiency for rack-scale computing systems. RSON provides a novel connection for local processing cores, caches/memory and remote node's counterparts via the high-radix low-loss optical switch and ONoC. The internode and ONoC optical domains are efficiently interconnected by the integrated internode interface. In addition to these detailed architectural designs, RSON also implements a scalable and efficient control scheme and communication flow optimization to improve the functionality of hardware components.

18.3.1   Architecture overview

The overview structure is as shown in Figure 18.1. Similar to traditional rack systems using Trad. IB and Trad. OS, each rack contains tens of even more many-core nodes, which these server nodes. However, in RSON, these server nodes are fully connected via optical fibers and integrated silicon photonic switch fabric to replace the traditional electrical ToR switch. This switch is a staged switch proposed by [28], as shown on the right hand side of Figure 18.1. It is composed of input stage, middle stage and output stage with similar stage structure built by waveguides and BOSE. It can realize high-throughput, low-latency and low-loss switching function. Tens of multicore server nodes reside within the rack, each node composed of multiple cores, and several memory controllers. It is worth noting that the on-chip or on-node resources are interconnected by two on-chip networks, electrical network-on-chip (ENoC) for general on-chip traffic and ONoC connecting the memory controllers and internode interface for off-chip memory and remote node memory access. For clearness, we omit the ONoC in Figure 18.1. The ONoC can deliver large amount of data from one

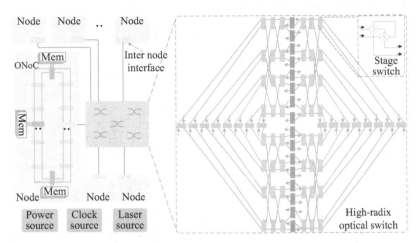

*Figure 18.1   RSON architecture overview. The nodes are connected with high-radix
low-loss integrated optical switch. Each node contains multicore
chips, local memory and internode interface. ONoC is designed to
thread memory controllers and internode interface [7]*

local DRAM to another local DRAM without the involvement of ENoC, relieving the
burden of traffic flood and increasing shortage of on-chip bandwidth.

The detailed server node architecture together the aforementioned ENoC and
ONoC are shown in Figure 18.2. Each core has a private L1 data and instruction
cache and four cores form a core cluster, sharing a L2 cache slice. The last level
cache (LLC) is shared by all core clusters. The number of LLC slices is the same
as that of memory controllers. These core clusters, LLC slices, memory controllers
together with the internode interface are fully connected by the traditional electrical
network-on-chip (ENoC) through ENoC interface. We do not change much on ENoC
topology and functional units since we want to keep the proposed silicon photonics
enabled rack-scale architecture more feasible. Besides the ENoC, a dedicated ONoC is
designed to provide high-bandwidth, low-latency communication service for memory
controllers and the internode interface, benefiting both local memory copy and remote
memory access. We try to make the internal rack structure as efficient as possible,
avoiding unnecessary overheads, such as unnecessary I/O ports and inter-rack header
processing. So the internode interface is designed to realize connection between
the inter-chip and intra-chip optical networks, which eliminates the inter/intra-chip
performance bottleneck.

18.3.2   ONoC design

The traditional electrical on-chip interconnect is becoming the performance bottleneck as the off-chip interconnection keeps involving high-bandwidth and low-latency
silicon photonics links. More and more computing cores and caches are integrated

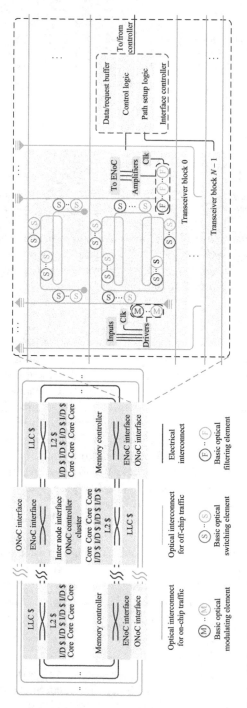

Figure 18.2 Server node architecture. The organization of on-chip components, ENoC, ONoC, internode interface, ONoC controller cluster and the optical transceivers [7]

into a single core also generates more on-chip traffic and limit the precious area leaving for on-chip interconnects. We propose ONoC to relieve the ENoC burden and at the same time provide streamlined connection for both inter-chip and intra-chip optical network. As shown in Figure 18.2, the proposed ONoC for each server node is to provide high-bandwidth and low-latency interconnection for data movement between different local memory copy and remote memory access. It is an important supplement for the existing ENoC. The dedicated ONoC is designed to connect on-chip memory controllers and internode interface so that the data copy among local memories and remote direct memory access (RDMA) operations, which directly moves data from one node's memory to another node's memory and plays indispensable role in large-scale systems. The local memory copy and RDMA usually involve huge amount of data movement. By introducing ONoC, they can "bypass" the ENoC, relieving the increasingly limited electrical bandwidth.

Specifically, the ONoC is composed of multiple parallel closed-loop bidirectional waveguides. These waveguides are the data channels, except one for control signals among ONoC interfaces. These data channels connect memory controllers and internode interface via the corresponding ONoC interfaces. A certain number of waveguides can be grouped together to the designed on-chip optical link bandwidth. For example, four waveguides should work together to provide 200 Gbps bandwidth when a single waveguide can provide 50 Gbps data rate. What's more, each transceiver block in the ONoC interface are shared by several parallel waveguides as shown on the right hand side in Figure 18.2. Under each transaction, only one waveguide can be used for data transmission by a pair of transceiver blocks. The transceiver blocks choose to use different waveguides for different transactions based on channel section assignment under the control of ONoC interface. The total number of waveguides should follow the number of transceiver blocks N within an ONoC interface and the number of waveguides attached to each transceiver block. Each ONoC data channel could be virtually divided into multiple sections and each section could work independently. The proposed ONoC allows two dimensions of flexibility, adjusting bandwidth by changing number of transceiver blocks and reducing contention by utilizing different data channels for different ONoC interface. By the design of channel partition and control scheme, we can achieve efficient and scalable management on the ONoC data channels. The design of ONoC control scheme is detailed in Section 18.4.

18.3.3   Internode interface

The on-chip optical network and inter-chip optical links and switch fabric have enabled the optical communication from local node to remote node except that the off-chip interface, where usually PCIe links and network interface controller (NIC) reside. As the deep-learning acceleration demands more GPU resources, the off-chip PCIe links also become scarce. Although optical switch connected rack architecture and on-chip optical networks have been investigated by extensive works, they failed to consider the impact of traditional off-chip links and discrete NIC. Extra communication hop is needed to connect the inter-chip and intra-chip optical networks. This incurs extra latency and power overhead on the power hungry O/E or E/O conversion and diminishes the benefits of high-bandwidth ONoC and inter-chip optical interconnection network. Our results show that if not eliminating the bottleneck between intra-chip and inter-chip networks and optimizing the internal communication flow, the optical switch and links connected rack-scale architecture (Trad. OS) design brings little performance gain, less than 12% on an average as shown in Figure 18.3, compared to InfiniBand connected traditional rack-scale many-core system (Trad. IB) under different interconnection bandwidth.

To this end, we design the optical internode interface and integrate it into the chip, working as an interface to connect inter-chip optical network and the ONoC. Similar to memory controllers, internode interface also contains ENoC and ONoC interface to interact with ENoC and ONoC. The internode interface communicate with both on-chip and off-chip traffic, either by ENoC or ONoC. Two typical types of internode/chip traffic are handled by internode interface, as shown in Figure 18.5. The first type is channel semantic, Send/Receive, which sends data via ENoC first and converts data to optical signals in internode interface. This will not involve ONoC. It receives data from ENoC interface, modulates data to corresponding optical signals and sends data out under the grant of inter-chip network. The second type is memory semantic, RDMA, which needs the cooperation of ONoC and inter-chip optical network and realizes direct data movement between local and remote memories.

Basically, all request packets initiated by the host process is transported via the ENoC to internode interface. The internode interface decodes these incoming requests and takes right actions based on the request information. For channel semantic, the packets from ENoC already contain the payload, the internode interface should store the data and forward the request to the high-radix switch for grant. For memory semantic, the packets does not contain the data and the data location is decided by the

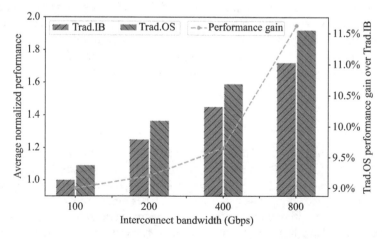

Figure 18.3   The averaged performance normalization of different benchmarks for Trad. IB and Trad. OS. under different interconnect bandwidth

packet information. The difference of channel semantic case lies in that the data chunk will be fetched from corresponding memory and that the data transmission will need readiness of path in local ONoC, optical switch and remote ONoC. Therefore, the internode interface should coordinate the local ONoC through the ONoC controller and forward the path reservation request toward optical switch and remote ONoC. That is one of the reasons that we place the ONoC controller cluster in the internode interface so that the ONoC and the inter-chip interconnect path control cooperate efficiently. The ONoC control will be illustrated in Section 18.4.4.

18.3.4   Bidirectional and sharable optical transceiver

The transceiver block is essential for functions of ONoC interface and internode interface. The ONoC interface serves as an efficient "bridge" for ENoC, ONoC and off-chip links, enabled by the bidirectional and sharable optical transceiver block. Its functionality illustration is in Figure 18.4. As we can see from channel 0 and 1, it realizes bidirectional transmission by changing the basic optical switching element (BOSE) status. These two cases show the data movement between local memory and other nodes. The data from ENoC can be sent out to local memory or other nodes directly without switching. Another important feature is that each data channel is virtually sectioned and sections are independent from each other so that they can conduct communication simultaneously. The drawback of channel section is that it results in huge traffic patterns even on a single channel, incurring dramatic control complexity when the number of controllers is large. We propose a scalable and low overhead

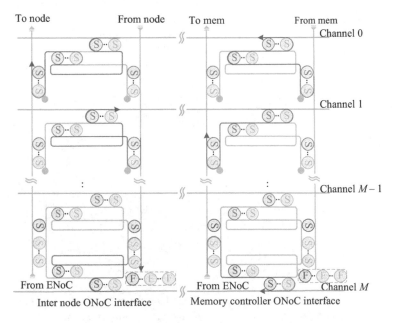

Figure 18.4   Illustration of optical transceiver block's functionality [7]

algorithm in Section 18.4 to mitigate this issue. Figure 18.4 shows that channel N is implemented for the purpose of control signals. Each interface owns one unique wavelength, so control signals from/to different interfaces can be transmitted without blocking and interfering. This is important for efficient arbitration and signaling.

18.4   Communication flow and arbitration

The internode communication requires the cooperation of different domains, including local node, off-chip optical switch and remote node. What's more, different types of traffic could ask for different resources and behave differently. These needs particular analysis and optimization on communication flow and all kinds of control strategy.

18.4.1   Communication flow

We conduct thorough analysis of the complete communication flow between two server nodes. Two typical kinds of internode communication are issued by applications: channel and memory semantic (RDMA). Generally, channel semantic operation (Send/Receive) is used to exchange small messages between local and remote application's internal buffers. On the other hand, RDMA exchanges large messages between local and remote memory. These two types of traffic are fully supported by internode interface. As shown in Figure 18.5, the channel semantic send/receive operation and memory semantic RDMA operation involves different subsystems and procedures. In send/receive scenario, the payload and request packet originating from host process's internal buffers is sent to internode interface via the ENoC. Then the internode interface decodes the packet and convert electrical signals to optical signals and transmit

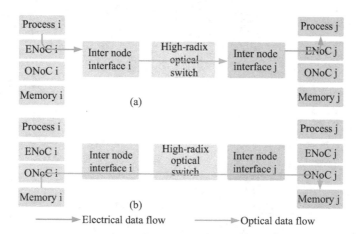

Figure 18.5   *The involvement of resources on two typical traffic types of message passing in internode communication: (a) send/receive traffic and (b) RDMA traffic*

to optical switch with the help of optical transceivers. In RDMA scenario, as shown in Figure 18.5(b), all data are transmitted in optical domain, except that the request packets are generated by host process, which is omitted in this figure. No extra buffer and hop are needed in the optical path from the source memory to the destination memory. However, this demands to set up corresponding optical paths in ONoC *i*, optical switch and ONoC *j* before real-data transmission. The internode interface should coordinate local ONoC and optical switch. It's quite different from the send/receive scenario. These differences are carefully considered during the design of control and arbitration system.

18.4.2   Optical switch control scheme

The optical switch arbitrates and setups the corresponding switch path based on the incoming requests, regardless of the send/receive and RDMA operation. Based on previous discussion, in the optical switch, no data buffer is necessary. This saves plenty area and power. Each port consists of data links and control links, boosting control signaling efficiency. The data and control links for each port operate independently. Since in memory semantic it involves the complete path reservation of relevant components, we provide the internal "bypass" function to forward the path reservation request to the destination. This can easily implement but can greatly improve the optical path reservation process. We adopt a tree-based round-robin arbiter for switch arbitration. The request buffer depth is 8 for each input port and the synthesized dynamic power is around 0.25 W for 64-port switch, which corresponds to a small fraction of the total interconnection energy. Besides the inter-chip interconnect, the ONoC control and arbitration also plays an important role in the communication flow because of the frequent on-chip traffic and the huge possible traffic patterns.

18.4.3   Channel partition

As stated above, the traffic patterns could lead to a performance and scalability issues for the control channel. To improve the channel control efficiency and lower the overhead, we adopt channel partition to divide data channels into different partitions. Only specific traffic patterns are allowed in each partition. The scheme is illustrated in Figure 18.6. Specifically, the allowed traffic pattern in partition *i* is defined as $[(3^i - 1)/2, 3^i]$, and there are at least 3^i waveguides for partition *i*. For example, in group 1, traffic with distance of 2 and 3 is allowed. Three waveguides are necessary to cover all traffic with distance of 2 and 3. It is easy to observe that contention only happens in "neighboring" nodes in each partition. In this way, there are only limited requesters valid for one channel section; therefore the arbitration overhead is quite low. The channel section reservation can be realized in $O(1)$ time for different channel sections. This alleviates much on the ONoC channel arbitration.

18.4.4   ONoC control subsystem

Basically, all memory controllers have the similar possibility to communicate with other nodes via the optical internode interface. The internode interface tends to be

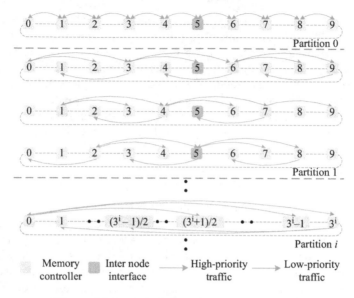

Figure 18.6   ONoC data channel partition [7]

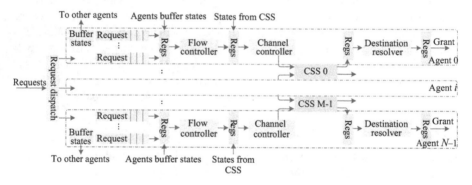

Figure 18.7   ONoC controller cluster implementation diagram. There are N agents and M channel section solvers (CSS), where N and M vary according to the number of memory controllers and the configuration of ONoC [7]

a hot-spot on the on-chip optical data channel. We need to solve the original imbalance. The traffic related to internode interface is assigned higher weights over other traffic patterns in channel partition. The high weight traffic patterns are marked with green line in Figure 18.6. Based on channel partition and the analysis, we design Algorithm 1 and implement the algorithm as shown in Figure 18.7. The controller mainly contains two parts: interface agents and channel section solvers (CSS). Interface agent is corresponding to one ONoC interface and deals with requests from that ONoC interface. CSS is responsible for resolve the contention for the specific channel section. When a request arrives, the agent should first assign channel partition and

---

Algorithm 1: ONoC channel control algorithm

1: Initialize buffer and weight status
2: Incoming request packet
3: *RequestBuffer.push*()
4: Select requests, *RequestBuffer.pop*()
5: Decide channel partition and check channel states
6: Forward request to channel section solver S
7:     **for** All requests $P(i)$ forwarded to S **do**
8:         **if** $P(i)$ for internode interface **then**
9:             Assign weight $W1$ to $P(i)$
10:        **else**
11:            Assign weight $W2$ to $P(i)$
12:        **end if**
13:    **end for**
14:    Arbitrate among requests for S
15:    Update $W1$ and $W2$
16:    Forward reservation results R to agents
17: Destination collision check D
18: **if** ($R == True$ AND $D == True$) **then**
19:    *Grant == True*
20: **else**
21:    *Grant == flase*
22:    *RequestBuffer.push*()
23:    Release reserved link
24: **end if**
25: Return *Grant*

---

section based on the request's source and destination, as illustrated in the design of channel partition. The interface will iteratively check the request buffer to select requests to be issued, in round-robin method. The selected requests then are forwarded to corresponding CSS i. The agents for different ONoC interfaces can work relatively independently, only sharing limited information, buffer status, CSS status. For each CSS, only requests belonging to this channel section will be forwarded to it. Only limited requesters go for this CSS so the arbitrate overhead is quite low. The synthesis result shows that the controller power is around 0.06 W when using 16 ONoC interfaces.

18.5 Evaluations

In this section, we will conduct evaluation on RSON and the baseline designs, traditional node with InfiniBand (Trad. IB) and traditional node with optical switch (Trad. OS), because of their wide usage by industry and extensive study by academia.

Table 18.1   Basic configurations

Item	Configuration
Core cluster	8, 4 cores/cluster
L1 I/D $	64 kB/core, private
L2 $	512 kB/cluster, shared
LLC	2.5 MB/slice
Coherence protocol	Directory-based MOSI
Electrical link	128-bit width/direction
Memory bandwidth	480 GB/s/port
Memory capacity	16 GB/port

We develop and model the proposed architecture and baseline designs on a simulation platform [29]. By using this simulation platform, we consider the processor microarchitecture, cache subsystem and memory other than the interconnect itself. According to InfiniBand roadmap, the link bandwidth is evolving to 200 Gbps when adopting 4× port widths, which is the common practice. We scale InfiniBand's interconnect bandwidth beyond 200 Gbps, to be 400 and 800 Gbps for comparison with Trad. OS and RSON. Benchmarks from both data center and high-performance computing are considered in the evaluation. We do not include all benchmarks when evaluating each metric. We set the processor frequency to 4 GHz, since it is reasonable to expect the emergence of 4-GHz process-operating frequency. The following evaluations are carried out for 64-node system scale and 4-GHz processor frequency, unless otherwise stated. The more detailed architectural configurations are listed in Table 18.1.

18.5.1 Performance evaluation

First, we present the achieved overall system performance per energy consumption (PPE). Higher PPE means more performance are achieved under the same power consumption. Figure 18.8 shows that RSON obtains higher PPE for different applications and interconnect bandwidths. More specially, RSON achieves 5.4× higher PPE than Trad. IB when running GTC under 800 Gbps. This is because GTC is communication intensive and is more sensitive to the interconnect technology. It is also interesting to observe that RSON's PPE scales much better than Trad. IB and Trad. OS regarding the interconnect bandwidth. Similar trend is observed on performance measurement in Figure 18.9. It's obvious that RSON benefits applications quite differently. This is because of the various traffic patterns from applications. For example in Figure 18.10, high-performance conjugate gradient (HPCG) shows more burst traffic imposing heavy burden on optical path and incurring more queue delay because of optical path reservation, while GTC's traffic is more dispersive and the path reservation's impact is amortized. So their performance expresses quite different trends. These results demonstrate that RSON brings joint benefits on performance and the PPE, which is crucial for the emerging exascale system which is expected to have much higher performance under strict power constraint.

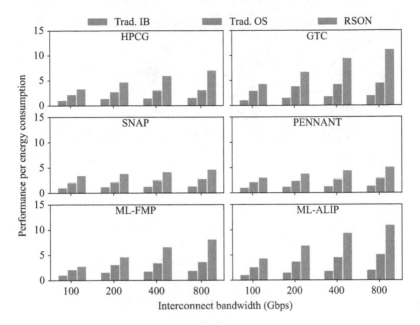

*Figure 18.8   Performance per energy consumption under 64-node system scale and
6 GHz processor frequency for HPCG, GTC, SNAP, PENNANT,
ML-FMP and ML-ALIP applications*

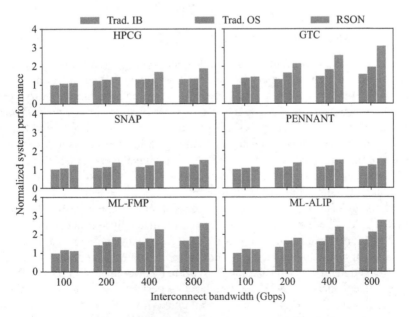

*Figure 18.9   The normalized performance comparison under different interconnect
bandwidths for different applications*

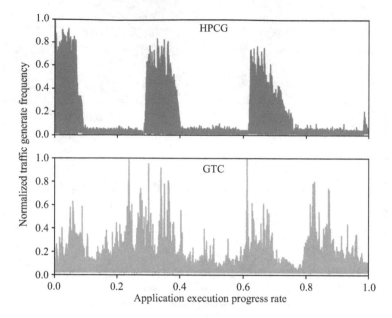

Figure 18.10   The profiled traffic generation frequency and pattern for HPCG and GTC

18.5.2   Interconnection energy efficiency

Interconnect is a big contributor to the overall system energy consumption. It deserves to evaluate the interconnect energy efficiency thoroughly. We consider energy from electrical and optical domain. Optical power is measured as minimum power generated by laser source to compensate the loss induced by optical devices, as shown in Table 18.2. The energy efficiency is shown in Figure 18.11. Both RSON and Trad. OS achieve much better energy efficiency, consuming almost 85% less energy for transmitting one bit compared to Trad. IB. RSON maintains the energy efficiency under 20 pJ/bit even considering optical devices loss variation. It marks an impressive step on reducing interconnection energy consumption.

Technology's impact on interconnect energy is shown in Figure 18.12. It clearly shows that Trad. IB energy efficiency decreases dramatically as process node evolves from 22 to 7 nm, while RSON and Trad. OS's trend is slower. The reason lies in that the advance of technology node brings corresponding power reduction to electrical circuits-related interconnect technology, but optical power lowers little since they are relatively independent on technology node. The performance and energy benefits from CMOS technology evolution come to an end as Moore's law stops taking effect. It is harder to achieve high-bandwidth and energy-efficient interconnection using the traditional electrical methods. RSON is a promising rack-scale computer design choice fulfill the performance and energy requirements toward exascale systems.

Table 18.2   Parameters for optical interconnect

Item	Value
Laser efficiency	0.33 [30,31]
MR insertion loss	1–3 dB
MR passing loss	0.06–0.3 dB
Edge coupling loss	1–3 dB
Waveguide crossing loss	0.3–0.8 dB
Waveguide propagation loss	0.8–1.3 dB/cm
Photodetector sensitivity	−15 to −20 dBm

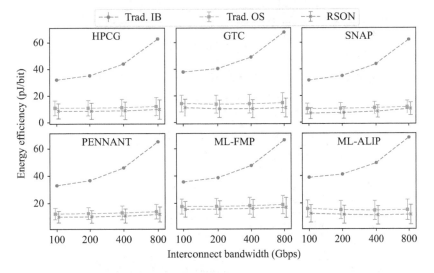

Figure 18.11   The interconnect energy efficiency for Trad. IB, Trad. OS and RSON under different applications

18.5.3   Latency analysis

Latency is an important factor to judge the interconnection architecture and it affects much on task's turnaround and response time. We measure the latency from network level for these three designs and break into several parts as shown in Figure 18.13. The main trend indicates that higher bandwidth can lessen the average latency. Closer look reveals that further bandwidth increase will not lower Trad. IB and Trad. OS latency much. Request issue delay dominates latency in higher bandwidth for Trad. IB and Trad. OS. It is their chip I/O and protocol designs that lag behind the bandwidth progress. It is reasonable to see that queue and arbitration delay takes up a major part of RSON's packet latency since circuit switching is used for RSON's inter/intra-chip

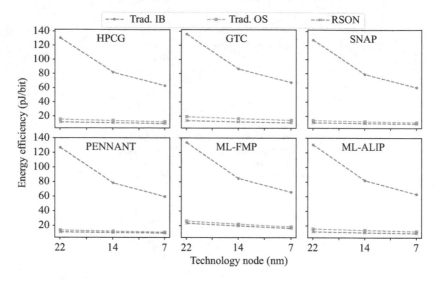

Figure 18.12   *Energy efficiency vs. Technology nodes*

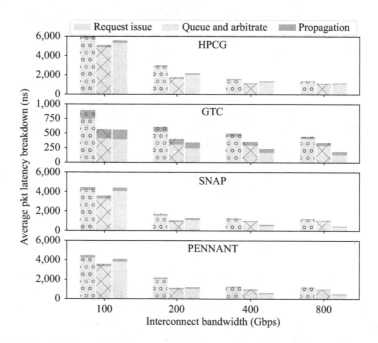

Figure 18.13   *Latency breakdown. The bars in each group stand for Trad. IB, Trad. OS and RSON from left to right hand side*

optical network, making packets wait for the release of requested path. It deserves further investigating on inter/intra-chip optical network with cooperative control and improving this architecture's potential.

18.6 Conclusions and future directions

In this chapter, we have introduced RSON, an inter/intra-chip rack-scale optical network for rack-scale computing systems. RSON codesigns the inter-chip and intra-chip optical network and uses the optical internode interface to relieve their performance gap. Scalable and fast control schemes for inter-chip and ONoC are also proposed, dealing with channel semantic and memory semantic traffic efficiently. The evaluation demonstrates that silicon photonics enabled rack-scale many-core system is advantageous on both performance and energy consumption compared to traditional Infiniband and optical switch connected rack architectures, promising a silicon photonics enabled rack-scale solution for reaching exascale systems.

However, some critical issues regarding the optical interconnects for rack-scale high-performance computing systems are remaining to be investigated. First, the circuit switching used in the inter/intra-chip rack-scale optical networks requires efficient message scheduling and path reservation across multiple optical network domains. These operations are complicated and time-consuming, directly affecting the interconnect latency and throughput. Most previous works adopt passive switching to avoid the path control and scheduling in optical networks. But this method is less of scalability on both bandwidth and system size due to the limited usable optical wavelengths. The active control of rack-scale optical networks have not been explicitly studied. The speculative fashion scheduling and allocation of network resources, such as the speculative reservation protocol proposed by [32] and the channel reservation protocol in [33] to resolve both the intermediate channel and endpoint congestion, could provide insights on this issue in optical interconnects.

Second, as dense rack becomes more and more popular, hundreds of or even more servers could exist in a single rack and should be interconnected efficiently. This requires high-radix and low-loss optical switch fabric to fulfill both interconnection demand and power consumption budget. Most available integrated optical switch fabric designs are limited to tens of ports due to the signal loss incurred by optical devices. Research efforts have been put on reducing the optical signal loss by optimizing the design strategy and floorplan of integrated waveguide, BOSE on the switch fabric. In [28,34], the integrated switch fabric can support as much as thousands of ports with acceptable average signal loss and low port-to-port latency. These promise a good direction to devise high-radix optical switch fabrics to fulfill the ultra-high bandwidth requirements by future large-scale applications. But how to tune so many integrated optical devices to suitable work range still needs further exploration and study.

Third, the optical device level characteristics, such as crosstalk noise, thermal effect and process variation, also deserve more attentions. These effects could severely affect optical interconnect's functionality, even make the network malfunction. They are quite different from the electrical devices, which have been thoroughly studied. Moreover, bottom up models and analyses are necessary to demonstrate how these effects could impact on the optical networks from both device level and system level. This will make the rack-scale optical interconnects more feasible in the future.

References

[1] Rumley S, Nikolova D, Hendry R, *et al.* Silicon photonics for exascale systems. Journal of Lightwave Technology. 2015;33(3):547–562.

[2] Costa P, Ballani H, Razavi K, *et al.* R2C2: a network stack for rack-scale computers. In: ACM SIGCOMM Computer Communication Review. vol. 45. ACM; 2015. p. 551–564.

[3] Benson T, Akella A, Maltz DA. Network traffic characteristics of data centers in the wild. In: Proceedings of the 10th ACM SIGCOMM Conference on Internet Measurement. ACM; 2010. p. 267–280.

[4] Minkenberg C. Interconnection Network Architectures for High-Performance Computing. IBM Research, Zurich; 2013.

[5] Hoefler T. Software and hardware techniques for power-efficient HPC networking. Computing in Science & Engineering. 2010;12(6):30–37.

[6] Rumley S, Polster RP, Hammond SD, *et al.* End-to-end modeling and optimization of power consumption in HPC interconnects. In: Parallel Processing Workshops (ICPPW), 2016 45th International Conference on. IEEE; 2016. p. 133–140.

[7] Peng Y, Zhengbin P, Zhifei W, *et al.* RSON: an inter/intra-chip silicon photonic network for rack-scale computing systems. In: Design, Automation and Test in Europe Conference and Exhibition; 2018.

[8] Benchmark Distribution & Run Rules. http://www.nersc.gov/research-and-development/apex/apex-benchmarks/. Accessed on 2017.

[9] Cianchetti MJ, Kerekes JC, Albonesi DH. Phastlane: a rapid transit optical routing network. In: Proceedings of the 36th Annual International Symposium on Computer Architecture. New York, NY, USA: ACM; 2009. p. 441–450.

[10] Pan Y, Kim J, Memik G. FlexiShare: channel sharing for an energy-efficient nanophotonic crossbar. In: High Performance Computer Architecture, IEEE 16th International Symposium on; 2010. p. 1–12.

[11] Kirman N, Kirman M, Dokania RK, *et al.* Leveraging optical technology in future bus-based chip multiprocessors. In: Proceedings of the 39th Annual IEEE/ACM International Symposium on Microarchitecture. Washington, DC, USA: IEEE Computer Society; 2006. p. 492–503.

[12] Bahirat S, Pasricha S. UC-PHOTON: a novel hybrid photonic network-on-chip for multiple use-case applications. In: Quality Electronic Design (ISQED), 2010 11th International Symposium on; 2010. p. 721 –729.

[13] Koohi S, Hessabi S. All-optical wavelength-routed architecture for a power-efficient network on chip. IEEE Transactions on Computers. 2014;63(3): 777–792.

[14] Bartolini S, Lusnig L, Martinelli E. Olympic: a hierarchical all-optical photonic network for low-power chip multiprocessors. In: Digital System Design (DSD), 2013 Euromicro Conference on; 2013. p. 56–59.

[15] Browning M, Li C, Gratz PV, *et al.* LumiNOC: a low-latency, high-bandwidth per Watt, photonic network-on-chip. In: System Level Interconnect Prediction (SLIP), 2013 ACM/IEEE International Workshop on; 2013. p. 1–4.

[16] Mirza-Aghatabar M, Koohi S, Hessabi S, *et al.* An empirical investigation of mesh and torus NoC topologies under different routing algorithms and traffic models. In: Digital System Design Architectures, Methods and Tools, 2007. DSD 2007. 10th Euromicro Conference on; 2007. p. 19–26.

[17] Mo KH, Ye Y, Wu X, *et al.* A hierarchical hybrid optical-electronic network-on-chip. In: VLSI (ISVLSI), 2010 IEEE Computer Society Annual Symposium on; 2010. p. 327–332.

[18] Kirman N, Martínez JF. A power-efficient all-optical on-chip interconnect using wavelength-based oblivious routing. SIGPLAN Notices. 2010;45(3): 15–28. Available from: http://doi.acm.org/10.1145/1735971.1736024.

[19] Vantrease D, Schreiber R, Monchiero M, *et al.* Corona: system implications of emerging nanophotonic technology. In: Computer Architecture, 35th International Symposium on; 2008. p. 153–164.

[20] Kim J, Dally WJ, Scott S, *et al.* Cost-efficient dragonfly topology for large-scale systems. In: Optical Fiber Communication - Incudes Post Deadline Papers, 2009. OFC 2009. Conference on; 2009. p. 1–3.

[21] Wu X, Xu J, Ye Y, *et al.* An inter/intra-chip optical network for manycore processors. IEEE Transactions on Very Large Scale Integration (VLSI) Systems. 2015;23(4):678–691.

[22] Chen J, Gong Y, Fiorani M, *et al.* Optical interconnects at the top of the rack for energy-efficient data centers. IEEE Communications Magazine. 2015;53(8):140–148.

[23] Saridis G, Hugues-Salas E, Yan Y, *et al.* DORIOS: demonstration of an all-optical distributed CPU, memory, storage intra DCN interconnect. In: Optical Fiber Communication Conference. Optical Society of America; 2015. p. W1D–2.

[24] Rumley S, Glick M, Dongaonkar G, *et al.* Low latency, rack scale optical interconnection network for data center applications. In: Optical Communication (ECOC 2013), 39th European Conference and Exhibition on. IET; 2013. p. 1–3.

[25] Krishnamoorthy A, Torudbakken O, Müller S, *et al.* From chip to cloud: optical interconnects in engineered systems for the enterprise. In: IEEE Optical Interconnects Conference (OI), 2016. IEEE; 2016. p. 34–35.

[26] Andreades P, Wang Y, Shen J, *et al.* Experimental demonstration of 75 ns end-to-end latency in an optical top-of-rack switch. In: Optical Fiber Communication Conference. Optical Society of America; 2015. p. W3D–5.

[27] Ye X, Yin Y, Yoo SB, *et al.* DOS: a scalable optical switch for datacenters. In: Proceedings of the 6th ACM/IEEE Symposium on Architectures for Networking and Communications Systems. ACM; 2010. p. 24.

[28]   Wang Z, Wang Z, Xu J, *et al.* Low-loss high-radix integrated optical switch networks for software-defined servers. Journal of Lightwave Technology. 2016;34(18):4364–4375.

[29]   Maeda RK, Yang P, Wu X, *et al.* JADE: a heterogeneous multiprocessor system simulation platform using recorded and statistical application models. In: Proceedings of the 1st International Workshop on Advanced Interconnect Solutions and Technologies for Emerging Computing Systems. ACM; 2016. p. 8.

[30]   Krishnamoorthy AV, Goossen KW, Jan W, *et al.* Progress in low-power switched optical interconnects. IEEE Journal of Selected Topics in Quantum Electronics. 2011;17(2):357–376.

[31]   Perkins JM, Simpkins TL, Warde C, *et al.* Full recess integration of small diameter low threshold VCSELs within Si-CMOS ICs. Optics Express. 2008;16(18):13955–13960.

[32]   Jiang N, Becker DU, Michelogiannakis G, *et al.* Network congestion avoidance through speculative reservation. In: 2012 IEEE 18th International Symposium on High Performance Computer Architecture. IEEE; 2012. p. 1–12.

[33]   Michelogiannakis G, Jiang N, Becker D, *et al.* Channel reservation protocol for over-subscribed channels and destinations. In: Proceedings of the International Conference on High Performance Computing, Networking, Storage and Analysis. ACM; 2013. p. 52.

[34]   Wang Z, Xu J, Yang P, *et al.* High-radix nonblocking integrated optical switching fabric for data center. Journal of Lightwave Technology. 2017;35(19):4268–4281.

Chapter 19

Cognitive I/O for 3D-integrated many-core system

*Hao Yu[1], Sai Manoj Pudukotai Dinakarrao[2],
and Hantao Huang[3]*

Increasing demands to process large amounts of data in real time leads to an increase in the many-core microprocessors, which is posing a grand challenge for an effective and management of available resources. As communication power occupies a significant portion of power consumption when processing such big data, there is an emerging need to devise a methodology to reduce the communication power without sacrificing the performance. To address this issue, we introduce a cognitive I/O designed toward 3D-integrated many-core microprocessors that performs adaptive tuning of the voltage-swing levels depending on the achieved performance and power consumption. We embed this cognitive I/O in a many-core microprocessor with DRAM memory partitioning to perform energy saving for application such as fingerprint matching and face recognition.

19.1 Introduction

In the last two decades or so, the computing paradigms have experienced a vast revolution leading to large amounts of data amassed by various businesses, public organizations and so on. This is further fueled with the proliferation of portable communication systems equipped with networking capabilities especially mobile phones, laptops and so on; and rapid movement toward paperless organizations [1]. As such, the amount of data to be handled by the data centers is increasing tremendously and reaching exascale (10^{18} Flops) [2]. To process such large amounts of data, numerous multicore microprocessor cores have to be integrated on a single chip for the exascale data processing as accelerators. A simple example of a data center to have exascale processing capability is shown in Figure 19.1. An estimate of resource requirement for such a data center to have exascale processing capability is calculated as follows.

[1]Department of Electrical and Electronic Engineering, Southern University of Science and Technology, China
[2]Electrical and Computer Engineering Department, George Mason University, USA
[3]School of Electrical and Electronic Engineering, Nanyang Technological University, Singapore

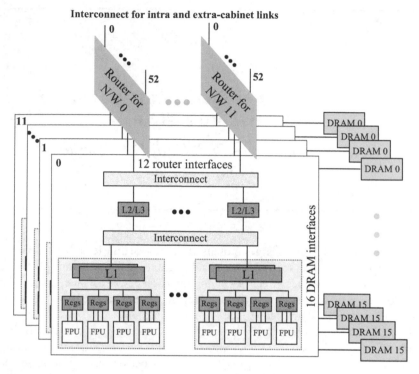

Figure 19.1   How to build one exascale data center

We assume that each core can have four floating point units, each having 1.5 GHz processing speed. As such, each core can reach a performance of 6GFlops. To perform 1Exa-Flop operations, a large number of such cores and memory blocks are needed to be integrated. The integration can be arranged in a hierarchical manner, namely, by chips, nodes and racks. One needs to integrate 742 cores on a single chip. Moreover, a set of 16 DRAMs, each DRAM of 1 GB capacity and one chip form a node. Furthermore, 12 such nodes connected with routers form a group. As such, one needs to combine 32 groups of processing capability 1.7Peta-Flop as a rack. Lastly, in order to achieve 1Exa-Flop performance, 583 such racks are needed to be integrated together. This setup demands large amount of bandwidth (few tens of Gbps) and 68 MW power, with 20,000 sq ft area. The resource to build many of exascale data centers will obviously require too much consumption of bandwidth, power, space and so on that may be beyond the capability of the current human society or costly.

Advancements in the CMOS transistor scaling and the VLSI integration capabilities facilitates integration of large number of cores on a single chip. One of the recent (2008) microprocessors from Intel, i7 quad-core processor [3], only occupies an area of 263 mm^2 and consumes a power of 130 W, but with a processing capability of 1 GHz. As such, it motivates us with a similar question: can we integrate a large number of cores that can aid to perform intelligent operations utilizing less number of resources? Even ITRS [4] predicts that the future systems will have large number of cores with memory integrated on a single chip, i.e., many-core microprocessors.

With the introduction of many-core microprocessors, a large amount of power is consumed for communication between cores compared to the computation power. The use of traditional 2D interconnects such as on-chip wire, off-chip PCB trace and will result in a large power dissipation and latency with degraded scaling performance for integrating thousand-core on-chip [5]. Moreover, traditional 2D off-chip interconnects such as back-plane PCB traces are obviously lossy channels that require overdesign of I/O equalization with huge power overhead. On the other hand, optical interconnects can provide high-speed communication but always come with an additional cost of optical-to-electronic conversion with no CMOS-based light source, detector and modulator. To meet the high speed, low power and high bandwidth demands, the future thousand-core memory-logic integration by 3D integration is a potential candidate. 3D integration by short-distance through-silicon vias interconnects [6–24] and 2.5D integration by middle-distance through-silicon interposer (TSI) interconnects [5,25–30] can be cost-efficient in meeting large bandwidth, low power and latency requirements.

In a many-core memory-logic integrated system, a large number of I/Os are required. Cores often communicate with the external environment such as memory through local and global I/O interconnects. As such, the communication power is one of the dominant factors for power consumption. This calls for the need to design a cognitive 3D or 2.5D I/O which can adapt based on the desired quality-of-service (QoS) and is power efficient.

In this chapter, we present the employment of such a cognitive I/O in the context of many-core system which performs the biometric recognition such as face recognition, iris recognition and fingerprint matching [31].

19.2   Cognitive I/O architecture for 3D memory-logic integration

We will present the architectures of 3D/2.5D many-core memory logic integrated system with cognitive I/O architecture and DRAM partition with cognitive I/O architecture which leverages the mature DRAM memory and adaptive I/O to save power.

19.2.1   System architecture

The employed system architecture targets to low-power consumption, yet satisfying the QoS performance. Moreover, random projection will be presented to reduce the dimensionality of the data for biometric recognitions, which also relaxes the burden on data storage and transmission. To achieve low-power consumption and high QoS, we integrate the DRAM memory partition and cognitive I/O with featured adaptivity of I/O voltage-swing levels [27] together for biometric-based applications. Furthermore, we apply the random projection for data reductions, which will preserve the features and mitigate the redundancies. As shown in Figure 19.2, once the biometric signal is sampled, it will be random projected by a Bernoulli matrix to a lower dimensional matrix as a preprocess step. Down sample *dr* (in Figure 19.2) represents the percentage of dimensional reduction, where $dr = 0$ means a full sample of the whole signal. Then, the biometric signal will be stored in DRAM, where low important bits will refresh in a longer period. This will sufficiently reduce the DRAM refresh power and can be easily implemented by adding a counter on the memory controller. To avoid high complexity of hardware, the long refresh period will be fixed and only the bit width (*w*) is adjustable. Higher probability of error will occur in the least significant bits (LSBs), highlighted with red cross in Figure 19.2, which can be tolerated by sparse-representation (SR)-based recognition algorithm. When the data is required by the processor (Advanced Reduced Instruction Set Computing Machine (ARM) core here), biometric signal will be transmitted through an cognitive I/O which will adjust the output voltage swing based on the achieved surplus on QoS [27]. The current digital–analog converter will be controlled by a digital signal, which in-turn decides the output voltage. Details on the DRAM memory partitions and the cognitive output-voltage swing tuning will be presented in the Section 19.4. We formulated the problem for low-power biometric recognition under QoS constraints using the proposed architecture in the following section.

19.2.2   QoS-based I/O management problem formulation

An energy-optimization problem is formulated based on the adopted architecture with three design parameters: LSBs width *w*, dimension reduction *dr* and output voltage swing V_{sw}.

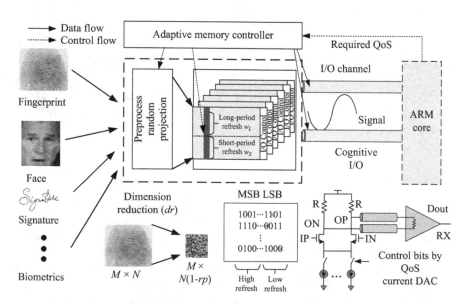

Figure 19.2   Proposed architecture based on DRAM partition and cognitive I/O

Problem: Adjust LSB width w, dimension reduction dr and output-voltage swing V_{sw} to perform the biometric recognition with constraints on QoS.

$$\text{Min.} : P_{IO}(dr, V_{sw}) + P_{DRAM}(dr, w)$$

$$S.T. : (i) \; QoS \geq C_{QoS}$$

$$(ii) \; 1 \leq dr \leq 0 \tag{19.1}$$

$$(iii) \; N_{sg} \leq w \leq 0$$

where C_{QoS} is the required QoS and N_{sg} is the maximum bit-length of the sampled value. The communication power of the I/O and the DRAM power are represented as P_{IO} and P_{DRAM}, respectively. In addition, the three design parameters can influence each other. The increase of w contradicts the decrease of V_{sw} as both actions will cause more errors, and which action to take depends on the energy-saving margin on the power saving. The change of dr also depends on the value of w and I, as the errors incurred on low dimensions of projected features will have more impact on the QoS. To find the best combination within the design space, the optimization problem is discussed in more details in Section 19.3.

19.3 I/O QoS model

We present the representation theory for the large amounts of data in the many-core microprocessors followed by the method for data dimensionality reduction and optimization here.

19.3.1 Sparse representation theory

Recently, the advancements in the theory of compressive sensing have drawn a great interest from the pattern recognition community. The SR-based classification technique utilized both SR and compressed sensing for face recognition [32]. The SR, in essence, is a simple matrix factorization technique to represent a matrix Y by dictionary D and sparse matrix X as $Y = D \times X$, where dictionary D is given. In the case, Y and X are provided to find D, it is also called dictionary learning, which is to find the basis of matrix X via SR.

SR in the biometric authorization or recognition follow the same idea to find the SR X of test data Y with the training data D (dictionary). Once the SR of the biometric data is found, one can determine the training data Y for the test data X. This technique enjoys the following two benefits: first, it is very robust to redundancy and able to perform classification by simple random projection; second, it is also high extent immune for noise, especially for bounded noise.

A more intuitive explanation on SR-based classification in the context of face recognition problem is provided here. The assumptions is that the face under test can be represented by a linear combination of its training face images with a high correlation to its class. For other training face classes, the face under test will be less likely related to them, and the correlation will be a small value. Therefore, the test face is sparsely represented in the domain of the training face. The reason for robust dense bounded error is that bounded error does not destroy the most correlated features; therefore, the classification result will not be affected. The SR-based biometric recognition for our proposed architecture can be mathematically defined as follows:

$$\arg\min_{x \in \mathbb{R}^N} \quad \|X\|_0$$
$$\text{subject to} \quad Y = D \times X + E_{IO} + E_{DRAM} \tag{19.2}$$

where E_{IO} is the error from the I/O communication and the E_{DRAM} is the error due to storage. The error E_{DRAM} is bounded and can be controlled by the LSB width w. However, E_{IO} is not bounded but sparse due to its low-error probability. Thanks to [33], this problem is proven to be solved with an complexity of polynomial and is solvable by using orthogonal matching pursuit.

19.3.2   Input data dimension reduction by projection

As the biometrics (image) data, say fingerprint, is commonly of a high dimension 300×300 and full of redundant information for recognition and classification, it is necessary to reduce the dimensionality of the original data before processing. Among various dimensionality-reduction techniques such as down-sampling or PCA, random projection is a computationally efficient yet effective means of dimension reduction. Since random projection such as Bernoulli matrix fulfills restricted isometry property [33], which means random projection projects points from high-dimensional into low-dimensional Euclidean space, and the distances between the points are approximately preserved. Such transformation can be denoted by the projection matrix R, and the biometrics data Y from d-dimension ($d = M \times N$) is projected to k-dimension Y' by multiplying a random $k \times d$ matrix R,

$$Y'_{k \times 1} = R_{k \times d} \cdot Y_{d \times 1}$$
$$dr = 1 - k/d \tag{19.3}$$

where dr is the percentage of dimension reduction (as in Figure 19.2) and $R_{k \times d}$ is a Bernoulli matrix generated by pseudorandom number generator of dimension $k \times d$. We estimate the random projection will be the main source for saving energy as it reduces the data to write in memory, store and transmit for biometric recognitions and classification. Moreover, Bernoulli matrix is easy to generate and by reduction of the dimension, the solving time of L_0 norm problem can also be reduced.

Besides the dimension reduction, random projection extracts the image features as well. The conventional feature extraction uses holistic Eigenfaces [34], or biometrics patches [35] as features, but such approaches involves additional computations compared to the random projection. The random projected vectors are proven to be valid features for face recognition as suggested in [36].

19.3.3 I/O QoS optimization

Although it is difficult to mathematically derive QoS function, we can use least-square polynomial fitting to approximate the QoS function, as follows

$$QoS(dr, w, V_{sw}) = \sum_{i=0}^{N_f} [dr^i \ w^i \ V_{sw}^i] \cdot [a_i \ b_i \ c_i]^T \qquad (19.4)$$

where N_f is the order for the polynomial fitting and can be easily solved by least squares polynomial fitting technique. Parameters a_i, b_i, c_i are calculated from the training samples. The total power consumption P can be achieved from the sum of P_{IO} and P_{DRAM}, as described in the problem formulation. Therefore, we can formulate a new objective function considering the energy efficiency and QoS using Lagrange multiplier as follows:

$$Ob(dr, w, V_{sw}, \lambda) = P + \lambda \times (QoS - C_{QoS}) \qquad (19.5)$$

where we try to minimize the Ob value and C_{QoS} is the lowest acceptable QoS. The global optimization can be found by taking the differentiation on each variable as shown below

$$\nabla_{dr, w, V_{sw}, \lambda} Ob = 0. \qquad (19.6)$$

Lagrange-multipliers-based optimization will lead to global optimal solution. However, if there are insufficient training samples to fit the QoS function, one can also take the gradient descent-based greedy action. As dimension reduction dr, LSB partition width w and output voltage V_{sw} forms a three-dimensional axis and QoS function forms a paraboloid, and following its counter lines, we choose the direction on the variable $(dr, p$ and $V_{sw})$ that yield highest power saving along with meeting the QoS requirements, i.e., the largest partial differentiation value. This procedure will iterate until no more power saving is feasible without violating the QoS requirement.

19.3.4 I/O QoS cost function

The reduction or constraint on the refresh rate will result in the increase of error in the stored data in DRAM. Previous works [37] have measured the error rate as a function of the refresh period, which shows the DRAM error rate increases exponentially with DRAM refresh cycle. Based on this, we model the DRAM bit error rate (BER) as

$$E_{DRAM} = c_3 \times e^{(c_1 + c_2 * T_{cycle})} \qquad (19.7)$$

where c_1, c_2 and c_3 are constant. The BER with different refresh cycle rates varies with operating temperature. In our case, we assume the operating temperature maintains 48°C all the time.

The according trade-off is the BER detected at the receiver. In a wire-line communication system [38], the BER has a relationship with the output voltage swing as follows:

$$E_{IO} = \frac{1}{2} erfc \left(\frac{V_s}{\sqrt{2}\sigma_v} \right). \qquad (19.8)$$

where the *erfc* is complementary error function, V_s refers to the output voltage swing and σ_v is the standard deviation of the noise, which is fixed and decided by the external noise, channel noise and I/O system.

19.4 Communication-QoS-based management

Here, we present the communication-QoS-based management with cognitive I/O by adaptive voltage-swing tuning and the corresponding hardware design.

19.4.1 Cognitive I/O design

A high-speed cognitive I/O is designed as depicted in Figure 19.3 to reduce the communication power with the aid of output-voltage swing tuning. The output voltage swing is controlled by the I/O controller, and error correction code (ECC) will reduce the bit error probability as much as possible [27]. The tuning is performed with the aid of accelerated Q-learning (reinforcement) method presented in [27].

The reinforcement learning aids in detecting the optimal voltage levels that can satisfy the low power requirements and high QoS. However, the traditional Q-learning algorithm [39] converges to the optimal after unlimited iterations that may be too slow for convergence [40]. To overcome this convergence issue, we use the accelerated Q-learning for adaptive tuning of output voltage swing to achieve low power and faster convergence [27]. Here, we will first present the modeling of a Markov decision process (MDP) and the according accelerated Q-learning algorithm for the adaptive tuning in the cognitive I/O.

The accelerated Q-learning [41] can be utilized to find an the optimal with a faster convergence based on the predicted next state and the according transition probability with an initialized random action at first few states. Accelerated Q-learning has two transition rules. Random actions make the system explore environment faster and more easily find optimal states. Optimal states is not found only based on Q-value but also by random selection.

Similar to the traditional Q-learning algorithm, the set of states and actions are known, but the reward for each action is unknown. The reward function is calculated similar to (19.9)

$$R_w(s_i, a_k, s_{i+1}) = b_1 \Delta V_s(Pw_i) + b_2 \Delta V_s(BER_i) \tag{19.9}$$

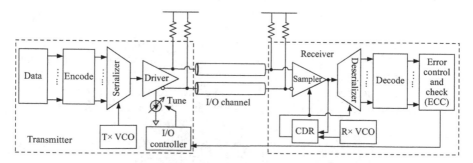

Figure 19.3 Proposed architecture-based adaptive I/O

where b_1 and b_2 denote the weighted coefficients for normalized rewards of the communication power $\Delta V_i(Pw_i)$ and BER $\Delta V_i(BER_i)$. The reward $R_w(s_i, a_k, s_{i+1})$ denotes the direction of state transition. To achieve a faster convergence, the transition probability is utilized to select the action instead of directly selecting the next state.

To find the optimal of MDP, the accelerated Q-learning algorithm can be utilized to evaluate the pair of state and action as the Q-value. We employ the accelerated Q-learning to find the optimal for the modeled MDP to solve the *problem* formulated in Section 19.2.2, presented in Algorithm 1.

Algorithm 1: Accelerated Q learning algorithm

Input: Communication power Pw, *BER* feedback
Output: Output-voltage
function Init()
  $1 \rightarrow P(s_i, a_k, s_{i+1})$
  Reward $R(s_i, a_k, s_{i+1}) = L$
  $v_{predict} \rightarrow V_{s_i}$
  Selection()
end function

function Selection()
  for $k = 1 : n$
    $V_{s_i}, BER_i \rightarrow s_i \in S$
    $Q'(s_i, a_k) \leftarrow (1 - \alpha) * Q(s_i, a_k) +$
    $\alpha * (R(s_i, a_k, s_{i+1}) + \gamma * \min(Q(s_{i+1}, a_k))$
    If $P(s_i, a_k, s_{i+1}) > rand(0, 1)$
      $a_k \leftarrow rand(A)$
    else
      $a_k \leftarrow \min(Q(s_{i+1}, a_k))$
    end if
    Update()
  end for
end function

function Update()
  Reward: $R(s_i, a_k, s_{i+1}) = b_1 \Delta V_s(P_i) + b_2 \Delta V_s(BER_i)$
  Update Policy (s_i, a_i), based on new Q
  $\forall s_i \in S \{$
    $a_k \leftarrow rand(A)$
    $Q'(s_i, a_k) = Q(s_i, a_k)$
    $P(s_i, a_k, s_{i+1}) = 1 - \frac{1}{log(N_{s_i} + 2)}$
  $\}$
end function

The first phase is initialization to form a look-up-table with states and corresponding actions. In addition, the transition probability P for all the states is set as 1 and the reward is set to a maximum value L. This process of initialization is presented as *Init()* of Algorithm 1.

Prediction of the next state (voltage-swing level) is performed as with the aid of linear regression, as in [27] to obtain the corresponding action. In the action selection phase, given by *Selection()*, the Q-value for the state and action pair is found iteratively, where the Q-value is defined as the weighted sum of the reward and its past values by

$$Q'(s_i, a_k) = (1 - \alpha) \times Q(s_i, a_k) + \alpha \times delta \qquad (19.10a)$$

$$delta = R(s_i, a_k, s_{i+1}) + \gamma \times \min_{a \in A}(Q(s_{i+1}, a_k)). \qquad (19.10b)$$

$Q'(s_i, a_k)$ shows the updated Q-value after taking the action a_k to the next state s_{i+1}.

In each iteration, the action is selected either based on the transition probability or based on the maximum Q-value (or policy). If the transition probability is larger than the threshold, a random action is selected; otherwise, the policy action with the minimum Q-value is selected. The random action will happen at the first few rounds to explore the design space. As the learning process continues, the policy action with the calculated Q-value will dominate and become more accurate to use. As such, a higher probability exists that the action a_k with the minimum Q-value. The policy action with the maximum Q-value (19.10a) and (19.10b) can be described as below:

$$a_k \leftarrow \min(Q(s_{i+1}, a_k)). \qquad (19.11)$$

Lastly, the phase of *Update()* is activated at the end of each iteration of *Selection()* function. The reward is defined as the weighted value of *BER* and *Pw* and updated as given in (19.9).

At the end of *Update*, each state will be randomly visited and Q value (19.10a) and (19.10b) will be updated accordingly. The transition probability $P(s_i, a_k, s_{i+1})$ is also updated as N_{s_i} (the number of visits to state s_i) will increase after each iteration.

Note that with the prediction of states s_i as in function *Init()* and *Update()* and the transition probability, the convergence to the optimal solution is accelerated [42]. This is done at the end of each round with the random action a_k to visit the state s_i.

One example with 4-state is shown in Figure 19.4. For state s_1, action a_1 can change its state to state s_2 with probability $P(s_1, a_1, s_2)$; for state s_2, action a_2 can change its state to state s_1 with probability $P(s_2, a_2, s_1)$, whereas action a_5 causes no change in state, whose probability is given as $P(s_1, a_5, s_2)$. The state transition probability P is given by a decaying function. The probability under the decaying function is given by $P = 1/(\log(N_{s_i} + 2))$ with N_{s_i} denoting the number of visits to state s_i. The probability-based action will ensure the visit to all states at starting period. This will calculate Q-value to every available state accordingly. After this, Q-value-based action will dominate and the optimal action with largest Q-value will be selected.

The LUT can be implemented online with the corresponding control bits calculated and feedbacked to current-mode logic (CML) buffer to tune the digital analog converter (DAC) current of the CML buffer. Note that LUT can be implemented in

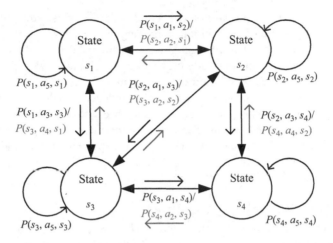

Figure 19.4 State transition based on reinforcement Q-learning

the hardware with multiple AND/OR partial matching logic circuit instead of read only memory (ROM). This LUT-based implementation has higher speed and lower power compared to the ROM.

The first component of the state vector is the adaptive I/O's communication power. The system power model refers to the I/O communication power of driver and the TSI modeled as transmission line (T-line) power, both depending on the output-voltage swing V_{sw}. For the CML-based driver with I/O channel [43], the I/O communication power is given by

$$P_{IO} = V_{s_i} \cdot \left(I_t + \frac{\eta \times V_{dd} \times s}{(R_D + Z_{diff})} \times f \right). \tag{19.12}$$

Here I_t is driver tail current, s is duration of signal pulse, η is activity factor, R_D is the resistance of driver, and Z_{diff} is the characteristic impedance of the I/O channel. The second component of the state vector is the BER, derived as given in (19.8).

19.4.2 Simulation results

19.4.2.1 Experiment setup

The proposed memory with the cognitive I/O architecture aims for an energy-efficient mobile systems yet accurate biometric processing. The QoS for the entire system is measured by the recognition rate of biometrics. We also evaluate the proposed architecture with the QoS metrics here as the rate of fingerprint matching and face recognition. The database of fingerprint is achieved from FCV2000 [44] by taking 80 fingerprints as training class and random selecting 25% samples of 80 fingerprints for testing the fingerprint matching quality by the system. The image of fingerprints are resized to 100 × 100, and all the reported matching rate is the average performance of five repetitions. For face recognitions, 100 images from the LFW face databased [45] are selected and the rest 600 faces are used for training purposes.

The evaluation of the proposed architecture is done in three steps for both fingerprint matching and face recognition. First, aggressive voltage scaling of output voltage swing by the cognitive I/O and DRAM partition of high refresh period are evaluated jointly to examine the trade-offs between QoS and power. The signal-to-noise ratio (SNR) is measured based on $E[(Y - \min(\hat{Y}))/std(Y - \hat{Y})]$, where $\hat{Y}$ is the value after dimension reduction with no error induced. Furthermore, we discuss random projection for dimension reduction, and an example of fingerprint matching is shown for the process of SR. Second, the trade-off between power saving and increasing BER is justified and based on the optimized parameters the power saving is evaluated and compared under different QoS requirements. Finally, a short discussion of face-recognition-based QoS is shown with results.

19.4.2.2   Adaptive tuning by cognitive I/O

We first present the performance of the cognitive I/O presented in Section 19.4.1. The cognitive TSI I/O verification is performed in Cadence Virtuoso (UltraSim-Verilog) and MATLAB®. An 8-core MIPS microprocessor with 8-bank of SRAM memory is designed with GF 65 nm CMOS. The 2.5D TSI T-line is of length 3 mm and 10 μm width, driven by the CML buffer. The controller is based on the basic and reinforcement Q-learning of the I/O communication power and BER at receiver, respectively. The multiple setup parameters are from (100 mV, 6.27E−2 mW, 9.12E−2), (250 mV, 3.92E−1 mW, 4.28E−4), (350 mV, 7.68E−1 mW, 1.53E−6), and (450 mV, 1.27 mW, 9.81E−10), for *filetransfer* benchmark. This LUT is almost robust, since this depends on characteristics of the circuit rather than the application. The other parameters of cognitive I/O are presented in Table 19.1.

The experiment of eye diagram under the control of adaptive tuning is performed to verify the functionality of the cognitive I/O circuit tuning. Figure 19.5 shows the current consumption under different levels of the output voltage swing. The sources of error are introduced in three stages: stage 1 is to introduce 20% of clock jitter, stage 2 is to add additional 10% receiver offset, and stage 3 is to further add additional 10% power supply noise.

As discussed previously, with the increase in noise, the tail current at the CML buffer is increased to have a larger output voltage swing that guarantees the BER. For

Table 19.1   Simulation set for power comparisons

Parameters	Value	Parameters	Value
Tail current I_t	2 mA	A	2.05×10^{12}
Activity factor	0.5	σ_v	0.5
f	2 GHz	$c1$	−15.82
s	0.25 ns	R_D	50 Ω
Z_{diff}	1.25 kΩ	$c2$	0.385
Vdd	2.5 V	$c3$	1
C	2 pF	P_{const}	0.41 mW

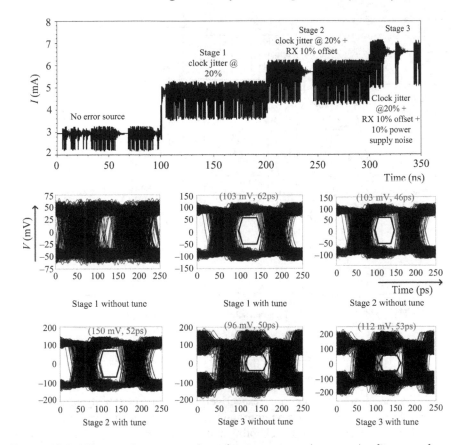

Figure 19.5   The eye diagrams under adaptive current (or power) adjustment by output-voltage swing tuning

example, for stage 1, which has only clock jitter error, the current is increased to 5 mA to increase the eye opening as (103 mV, 62 ps); with the increase in noise, i.e., for stage 3, the current is increased adaptively to improve the eye opening. The difference in eye diagrams with tuning the output voltage swing and without tuning the output voltage swing is shown in Figure 19.5. One can observe that for stage 3, without tuning the tail current, the eye opening is 96 mV, but the eye opening increases to 112 mV by adaptively changing the current.

19.4.2.3   Adaptive I/O control by accelerated Q-learning

Moreover, an example of one adaptive tuning by the accelerated Q-learning is shown in Figure 19.6. Initially, the voltage swing for the next control-cycle is predicted as 344 mV and the maximum BER is 1E−6. The voltage-swing 344 mV fits to the state s_4 because of the nearest voltage level. The action will be selected based on the probability check as in *Selection*() of Algorithm 1. As shown in Figure 19.6, the line-dot-dot format and line-dot format line indicate the policy-based action selection and

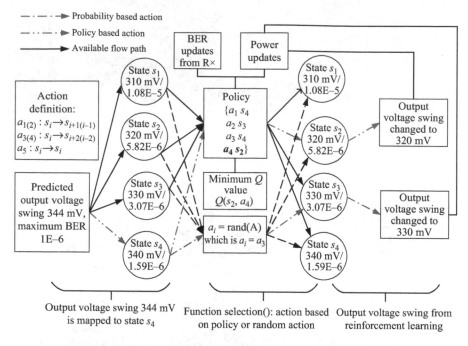

Figure 19.6   Example of one adaptive tuning procedure

probability-based action selection, respectively. For the probability-based action selection (line-dot format line), a random action is selected to visit any of the available states. This takes place with high probability at the starting period to ensure the visit to all the available states, where its Q-value will be updated accordingly. Afterwards, the action with maximum Q-value will dominate and be considered as the optimal action. As Figure 19.6 shows, action a_4 is eventually selected leading to the voltage level at state s_2, which is the smallest voltage level with the BER requirement satisfied. Afterwards, the new voltage swing is assigned based on the state s_2 as 320 mV. As such, the driver tail-current is tuned to have the output voltage swing as 320 mV. Lastly, the reward $R(s_4, a_4, s_2)$ will be updated based on the feedback of BER and power obtained at Rx. As such, the cognitive I/O tunes the output voltage swing based on the desired QoS and the power budget constraints. We embedded such an cognitive I/O in the biometric recognition system. The results of biometric recognition with cognitive I/O is presented below.

19.5   Performance-QoS-based management

Here, we will first discuss the hardware design to perform the dimensionality reduction, and DRAM memory partition. Further, we illustrate the corresponding impacts such as error tolerance, feature preservation for fingerprint matching.

19.5.1 Dimension reduction

The hardware implementation of the dimensionality reducer, i.e., random projection is designed as depicted in Figure 19.7, similar to [46]. Two pseudorandom bit sequence are used to generate the Bernoulli matrix ($k \times d$). The original data $Y_{d \times 1}$ is provided as the input to the multiplier and the partial product result P_{id} is added through adder to obtain the k dimensional compressed output Y'. In this design, only k clock cycles are needed for preprocess.

19.5.2 DRAM partition

The reconfigurable refresh rate DRAM architecture is designed as shown in Figure 19.8. Extra bits are added to the input controller address, similar to [37]. The controller will decide the row address of the least refresh rate, and the DRAM refresh action will only be taken when refresh enable is 1. The counter clock will provide the refresh rate for the whole memory. The total power consumed by DRAM is the sum of the energy dissipated in the background power, read/write power and activation power. Around 30% of total DRAM power is consumed in background power accounted as static power and the rest is power for refreshing [47]. For the

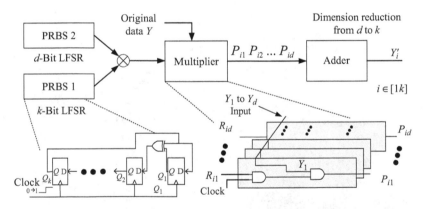

Figure 19.7   Hardware architecture to implement random projection

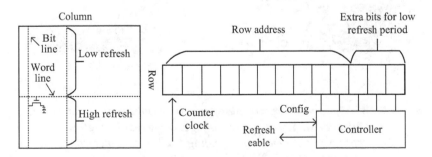

Figure 19.8   Proposed architecture with DRAM partition

same DRAM utilization rate, the data retention power regarding the refreshing rate can be modeled based on [48],

$$P_{DRAM} = \frac{A \times C}{t_{ref}} + P_{const} \qquad (19.13)$$

where C and A are the DRAM switching capacitance and constant proportionality factor, respectively. P_{const} is the power component independently from the refresh period and typically less than 10% of the data retention power P_{ref}.

19.5.3   Error tolerance

In this part, we will investigate the relations between QoS, output voltage swing (V_{sw}) and the partition of high refresh period DRAM, i.e., the LSBs width w with refresh period 30 s. To characterize the switching errors of low refresh rate, the model parameters are set based as Table 19.1 which is fitted with measurement data in [27,37].

Under random projection without dimension reduction ($dr = 0$), the QoS at different output voltage swing with varying LSB width w are presented in Figure 19.9(a),

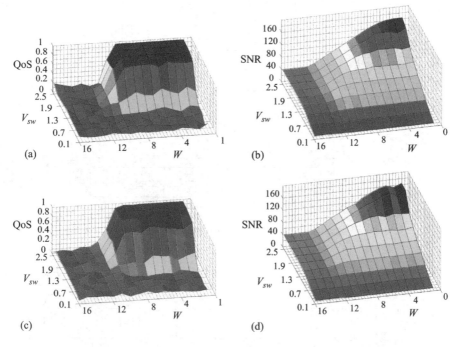

Figure 19.9   *Without dimension reduction ($dr = 0$): (a) the fingerprint matching QoS under different, output voltage swing and low refresh-rate bits width w and (b) the corresponding SNR; with dimension reduction ratio dr = 40%: (c) the QoS under different output voltage swing and low refresh rates bits width w and (d) the corresponding SNR*

where the error probability increases as the output voltage is decreasing. Therefore, the QoS will decrease as more errors are incurred for the low voltage cases. This is not obvious for a small LSB width w, but significant for large w. This can be explained by the fault tolerance of SR-based classification. A bounded error will not affect the classification accuracy as we discussed in Section 19.3. Although more energy saving can be anticipated by increasing w, a large w means not only more bits suffer from errors, but also the magnitude of the errors will increase exponentially. For example, with $w = 4$, the error is bounded by ± 15. As shown in Figure 19.9(a), when LSB width w is larger than 9, there is a dramatic decrease in the QoS. This means for bounded error, the SR-based algorithm can even tolerate ± 512 bounded error. Similar principle is applied to the output voltage swing V_{sw}. However, the tolerability is small as during the I/O transmission, the error is not bounded and can happen to any of the bits. When V_{sw} is smaller than 1.9 V, the QoS drops significantly. This shows the error tolerability of SR-based fingerprint matching algorithm can tolerate well-bounded errors and some extent of non-bounded errors.

19.5.4 Feature preservation

The same experiments are performed by random projection with $dr = 0.4$ as shown in Figure 19.9(c). Please note that even for $dr = 0.4$, there are still 6,000 features. The QoS regarding to the output voltage swing and LSB width w shows a similar trend as previous. By dimension reduction, the error tolerability degrades but not significantly, which means even 60% sampling preserves the features of each fingerprint. The reason for similar QoS performance can be analyzed by its SNR as shown in Figure 19.9(b) and (d). A random projection with $dr = 40\%$ will not damage the features but make it more prone to the noise, which shows variations as in Figure 19.9(d) when w and V_{sw} are small, which is further discussed below.

19.5.5 Simulation results

Figure 19.10(a) illustrates the QoS at different dimension reduction ratios and various induced errors from memory and I/O. It can be observed that the QoS maintains high

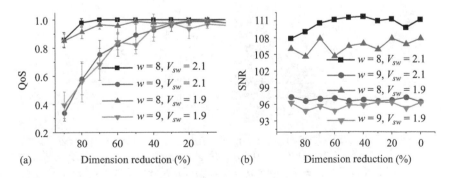

Figure 19.10   (a) QoS vs dimension reduction and (b) according to SNR

while *dr* is smaller than 0.4. This shows that error introduced by low refresh rate and output voltage swing does not destroy the feature of the fingerprint required for recognition or classification. This is also clearly reflected in Figure 19.10(b), as the SNR maintains almost the same even under different reduced dimensions. Furthermore, under the case of $w = 8$ and $V_{sw} = 2.1$ V, increasing the LSB width w from 8 to 9 will degrade SNR significantly. This can be also cross validated from Figure 19.9(b) and (d). From Figure 19.10(a), we can also conclude that when the error introduced is large, random projection will be more prone to the errors. We gradually push partition width w, output voltage swing V_{sw} and dimension reduction *dr* based on the gradient decent of the power consumption. For a large *dr*, the QoS drops fast as not only errors but also the extensive dimension reduction damages the features. The variations of QoS are also significant; therefore, for a robust QoS performance, keeping *dr* not larger than 80% dimension reduction helps. Figure 19.11 shows an example of how noise affects the fingerprint and how SR-based biometric recognitions work with dimension reduction.

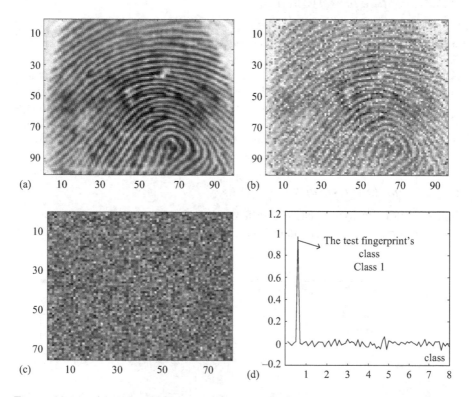

Figure 19.11   *(a) 100 × 100 original fingerprint, (b) noisy fingerprint (w = 7,*
                  $V_{sw} = 1.7$), (c) 75 × 80 noisy fingerprint with random projection
                  (w = 7, $V_{sw} = 1.7$ and dr = 0.4) and (d) 75 × 80 noisy fingerprint
                  sparse representation

19.6 Hybrid QoS-based management

19.6.1 Hybrid management via memory (DRAM) controller

From the analysis of Section 19.4, there exists a trade-off between power saving and BER. However, the trade-off is not the same for DRAM and I/O communication. As we can see from Figure 19.12(a), scaling up the refresh period will not increase the BER dramatically at the initial period; however, as the refresh period is higher than 2 s, BER increases dramatically. This characteristic is opposite to its power consumption which will save power as the refresh period increases at the initial stage. However, when the refreshing period is higher than 1 s, the power saving gradient drops. This reveals that by increasing the refresh period, there is a point that BER increases a little; however, much power is saved. For the I/O communication power, the trade-off is straightforward. Reducing the output voltage swing will always increase the BER during transmission. So, the strategy will be extending the refresh period until the power saving is not significant and then increasing the output voltage swing within the error tolerability. As discussed previously, the gradient-descent-based action-selection policy will lead to an optimal energy efficiency with the QoS constraint.

19.6.2 Communication-QoS result

The power saving is considered under various fingerprint-matching-based QoS requirement. The baseline scheme is normal DRAM without adaptive cognitive I/O. We assume the exact power matching during the I/O transmission of 50 Ω and 30% DRAM refresh power saving by high refresh period (30 s). Detail for parameters setup is summarized as Table 19.1. DRAM LSBs width w, output voltage swing V_{sw} and dimension reduction dr are presented in Table 19.2. From Table 19.2, we can see that through random projection technique, around 47.76% power consumptions can be saved. DRAM partitions w only will have limited power saving as we discuss from the DRAM power model. As w increases, there is huge drop on the QoS, which keeps $w = 7$ for $QoS = 0.95$ and 0.9 and increases by 2 for $QoS = 0.8$. However, for the drop of output voltage swing V_{sw}, performance degrades in a more

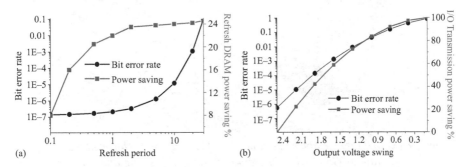

Figure 19.12   (a) BER and DRAM power saving and (b) BER and I/O communication power saving

smooth way. For example, when the QoS is 0.9, $V_{sw} = 1.7$ drops from $V_{sw} = 1.9$ in response of the decrease of QoS. Power saving is primarily achieved by the random projection, which itself reduces 47.76% of power consumption. However, with the combinations of cognitive I/O-based voltage-swing tuning and DRAM partition, 63.41%, 63.42% and 64.43% power saving are achieved for a QoS of 0.95, 0.9 and 0.8, respectively.

19.6.3   Performance-QoS result

Due to the limitation of the space, we will not give a detail discussion on face-recognition-based QoS system performance. Instead, we will show the QoS and SNR performance regarding to the DRAM partitions and output voltage swing as Figure 19.13. Comparing to fingerprint match, face recognition based QoS is more

Table 19.2   Power saving comparison under different QoS requirements

Scheme	QoS	dr	w	V_{sw} (V)	P (mW)	Saving (%)
Baseline	0.95	0	0	2.5	12.06	00.00
RP		0.8	0	2.5	5.96	47.76
DRAM + RP	0.95	0.8	7	2.5	5.16	54.85
VS + RP		0.8	0	1.9	5.10	55.32
DRAM + RP + VS		0.8	7	1.9	4.29	62.41
DRAM + RP	0.9	0.8	7	2.5	5.16	54.85
VS + RP		0.8	0	1.7	4.81	57.84
DRAM + RP + VS		0.8	7	1.9	4.18	63.42
DRAM + RP	0.8	0.8	7	2.5	5.16	54.85
VS + RP		0.8	0	1.7	4.81	57.84
DRAM + RP + VS		0.8	9	1.9	4.06	64.43

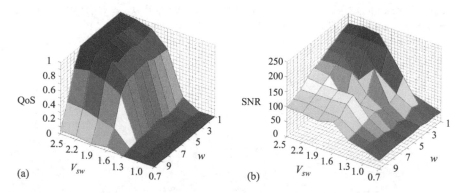

(a)   (b)

Figure 19.13   With dimension reduction (dr = 0.1), (a) the fingerprint matching rate as QoS under different output voltage swing and low refresh rate bits width w (b) corresponding signal-to-noise ratio (SNR)

sensitive to noise with increasing w and decreasing V_{sw}. The error introduced by low refresh rate and output voltage swing does not destroy the feature of faces required for face recognition. As shown in Figure 19.13(a), we still can reduce the voltage swing V_{SW} as to 2.2 V and width partition w to 3 for power saving with sufficient QoS. Therefore, the analysis discussed should be able to extend to any SR-based biometrics recognition system.

19.7   Conclusion and future directions

In this chapter, we present an energy-efficient memory partition and cognitive I/O architecture for SR-based biometric recognitions. The DRAM background power consumption is greatly saved by memory partitions with low refresh rate. It is achieved with low hardware cost by adding refresh enable signal. The cognitive I/O is also leveraged to dynamically adjust the output voltage swing to utilize the margin on BER. Furthermore, a simple dimension reduction by random projection is embedded with aforementioned techniques to greatly alleviate the burden of the memory storage and I/O communications. The hardware designs are as well presented. Experiment results have shown that 62.41%, 63.42% and 64.43% power savings can be achieved under the QoS requirement of 0.95, 0.9 and 0.8 with 80% dimension reduction with the partitioned DRAM architecture and the cognitive I/O utilization in the system for biometric recognition.

For the future cognitive I/O system, bandwidth management and voltage-swing tuning for core-memory communication have to be optimized. Bandwidth management could be optimized from data characteristics and priority. Based on the memory-access data-pattern characteristics, I/O could be dynamically configured to achieve data-aware optimization. However, there is no efficient learning algorithm to perform such data analytics. Furthermore, there is also an increasing need to reduce the bandwidth management complexity since I/O system is getting more and more complex. Recent works such as [49–51] have addressed these solutions, but more works could be done in this direction. Another direction, voltage-swing tuning could be done for cognitive I/O system with twofold challenges: real-time error rate analysis and error resilience circuit design. Although different applications have different error rate tolerance, a real-time error rate analysis for each application is not easy to perform and requires machine-learning algorithms to effectively analyze. How to optimize such learning algorithm to perform real-time analysis is still an open problem. The desired algorithm should be able to identify the tolerated error rate and adjust the system accordingly. Furthermore, for high speed I/O, an error resilience circuit design is not trivial work although we can adopt ECC at the cost of more silicon area. A tunable I/O voltage swing can offer more flexibility for energy efficiency and error code trade-off, which is desirable for future I/O systems. Recent work [52] has adopted a compensate circuit to recover the error bits. Other works such as [53,54] are working in this direction.

References

[1]   Wadkar S, Siddalingaiah M. In: Motivation for Big Data; 2014. p. 1–10.

[2]   Uchiyama K. Power-efficient heteregoneous parallelism for digital convergence. In: IEEE Symp. on VLSI Circuits; 2008.

[3]   Vangal S, Howard J, Ruhl G, *et al.* An 80-Tile 1.28TFLOPS network-on-chip in 65 nm CMOS. In: Int. Solid-State Circuits Conf. (ISSCC). IEEE; 2007.

[4]   ITRS Roadmap; 2013. http://www.itrs.net/Links/2013ITRS/2013Chapters/2013ExecutiveSummary.pdf.

[5]   Wang J, Ma S, Manoj PS, Yu M, Weerasekera R, Yu H. High-speed and low-power 2.5D I/O circuits for memory-logic-integration by through-silicon interposer. In: IEEE Int. 3D Systems Integration Conf. (3DIC); 2013. p. 1–4.

[6]   Banerjee K, Souri SJ, Kapur P, *et al.* 3D-ICs: a novel chip design for improving deep-submicrometer interconnect performance and systems-on-chip integration. Proceedings of the IEEE. 2001;89(5):602–633.

[7]   Tan CS, Gutmann RJ, Reif LR. Overview of Wafer-Level 3D ICs. Springer, Boston, MA, US; 2008. p. 1–11.

[8]   Cong J, Wei J, Zhang Y. A thermal-driven floorplanning algorithm for 3D ICs. In: IEEE/ACM Int. Conf. on Computer Aided Design (ICCAD); 2004.

[9]   Goplen B, Sapatnekar S. Thermal via placement in 3D ICs. In: IEEE/ACM Int. Symp. on Physical Design (ISPD); 2005.

[10] Yu H, Shi Y, He L, *et al.* Thermal via allocation for 3D ICs considering temporally and spatially variant thermal power. In: Int. Symp. on Low Power Electronics and Design (ISLPED); 2006.

[11] Yu H, Ho J, He L. Simultaneous power and thermal integrity driven via stapling in 3D ICs. In: ACM/IEEE Int. Conf. on Computer-Aided Design (ICCAD); 2006.

[12] Yu H, Shi Y, He L, *et al.* Thermal via allocation for 3-D ICs considering temporally and spatially variant thermal power. IEEE Transactions on Very Large Scale Integration (TVLSI) Systems. 2008;16(12):1609–1619.

[13] Yu H, Ho J, He L. Allocating power ground vias in 3D ICs for simultaneous power and thermal integrity. ACM Transactions on Design Automation of Electronic Systems (TODAES). 2009;14(3):41:1–41:31.

[14] Xie Y, Loh GH, Black B, Bernstein K. Design space exploration for 3D architectures. ACM Journal on Emerging Technologies in Computing Systems. 2006;2(2):65–103.

[15] Kgil T, D'Souza S, Saidi A, *et al.* PicoServer: Using 3D stacking technology to enable a compact energy efficient chip multiprocessor. In: Int. Conf. on Architectural Support for Programming Languages and Operating Systems (ASPLOS). ACM; 2006.

[16] Motoyoshi M. Through-silicon via (TSV). IEEE Proceedings. 2009;97(1):43–48.

[17] Healy MB, Athikulwongse K, Goel R, *et al.* Design and analysis of 3D-MAPS: a many-core 3D processor with stacked memory. In: IEEE Custom Integrated Circuits Conf. (CICC); 2010.

[18] Qian H, Huang X, Yu H, *et al.* Real-time thermal management of 3D multi-core system with fine-grained cooling control. In: IEEE Int. 3D Systems Integration Conf. (3DIC); 2010.

[19] Huang X, Yu H, Zhang W. NEMS based thermal management for 3D many-core system. In: ACM/IEEE Int. Symp. on Nanoscale Architectures; 2011. p. 218–223.

[20] Qian H, Huang X, Yu H, *et al.* Cyber-physical thermal management of 3D multi-core cache-processor system with microfluidic cooling. ASP Journal of Low Power Electronics. 2011;7(1):110–121.

[21] Qian H, Chang CH, Yu H. An efficient channel clustering and flow rate allocation algorithm for non-uniform microfluidic cooling of 3D integrated circuits. Integration VLSI Journal. 2013;46(1):57–68.

[22] Shang Y, Zhang C, Yu H, *et al.* Thermal-reliable 3D clock-tree synthesis considering nonlinear electrical-thermal-coupled TSV. In: Asia and South Pacific Design Automation Conf. (ASP-DAC). ACM/IEEE; 2013.

[23] Manoj PDS, Yu H, Shang Y, *et al.* Reliable 3-D clock-tree synthesis considering nonlinear capacitive TSV model with electrical-thermal-mechanical coupling. IEEE Transactions on Computer-Aided Design of Integrated Circuits and Systems. 2013;32(11):1734–1747.

[24] Manoj PDS, Yu H, Wang K. 3D many-core microprocessor power management by space-time multiplexing based demand-supply matching. IEEE Transactions on Computers. 2015;64(11):3022–3036.

[25] Xu D, Yu N, Huang H, *et al.* Q-Learning based voltage-swing tuning and compensation for 2.5D memory-logic integration. IEEE Design and Test. 2017;35(2):91–99.

[26] Xu D, Yu N, Manoj PDS, *et al.* A 2.5-D memory-logic integration with data-pattern-aware memory controller. IEEE Design and Test. 2015;32(4):1–10.

[27] Xu D, Sai Manoj PD, Huang H, Yu N, Yu H. An energy-efficient 2.5 D through-silicon interposer I/O with self-adaptive adjustment of output-voltage swing. In: IEEE ISLPED; 2014.

[28] Cubillo JR, Weerasekera R, Oo ZZ, *et al.* Interconnect design and analysis for through silicon interposers (TSIs). In: IEEE 3DIC; 2012.

[29] Wu SS, Wang K, Sai Manoj PD, Ho TY, Yu M, Yu H. A thermal resilient integration of many-core microprocessors and main memory by 2.5D TSI I/Os. In: ACM/IEEE DATE Conf.; 2014.

[30] Hantao H, Manoj PDS, Xu D, *et al.* Reinforcement learning based self-adaptive voltage-swing adjustment of 2.5D I/Os for many-core microprocessor and memory communication. In: ACM/IEEE Int. Conf. on Computer-Aided Design; 2014.

[31] Chang DW, Son YH, Ahn JH, *et al.* Dynamic bandwidth scaling for embedded DSPs with 3D-stacked DRAM and wide I/Os. In: IEEE ICCAD; 2013.

[32] Wang J, Lu C, Wang M, Li P, Yan S, Hu X. Robust face recognition via adaptive sparse representation. IEEE Transactions on Cybernetics. 2014;44(12):2368–2378.

[33] Donoho DL. Compressed sensing. IEEE Transactions on Information Theory. 2006;52(4):1289–1306.

[34]   Belhumeur PN, Hespanha JP, Kriegman DJ. Eigenfaces vs. fisherfaces: recognition using class specific linear projection. IEEE Transactions on Pattern Analysis and Machine Intelligence. 1997;19(7):711–720.

[35]   Demirkus M, Garg K, Guler S. Automated person categorization for video surveillance using soft biometrics. Biometric Technology for Human Identification VII. 2010;12:54.

[36]   Wright J, Yang AY, Ganesh A, *et al.* Robust face recognition via sparse representation. IEEE Transactions on Pattern Analysis and Machine Intelligence. 2009;31(2):210–227.

[37]   Liu S, Pattabiraman K, Moscibroda T, Zorn BG. Flikker: saving DRAM refresh-power through critical data partitioning. ACM SIGPLAN Notices. 2012;47(4):213–224.

[38]   Shafik RA, Rahman MS, Islam AR. On the extended relationships among EVM, BER and SNR as performance metrics. In: IEEE EECS; 2006.

[39]   Watkins CJ, Dayan P. Q-learning. Machine Learning Journal. 1992;8(3–4): 279–292.

[40]   Littman ML. Value-function reinforcement learning in Markov games. ACM Cognitive Systems Research. 2001;2(1):55–66.

[41]   Gosavi A. A reinforcement learning algorithm based on policy iteration for average reward: Empirical results with yield management and convergence analysis. Machine Learning Journal. 2004;55(1):5–29.

[42]   Mastronarde N, van der Schaar M. Online reinforcement learning for dynamic multimedia systems. IEEE Transactions on Image Processing. 2010;19(2):290–305.

[43]   Ndip I, Curran B, Lobbicke K, *et al.* High-frequency modeling of TSVs for 3-D chip integration and silicon interposers considering skin-effect, dielectric quasi-TEM and slow-wave modes. IEEE Trans on Components, Packaging and Manufacturing Technology. 2011;1(10):1627–1641.

[44]   Maio D, Maltoni D, Cappelli R, Wayman JL, Jain AK. FVC2000: Fingerprint verification competition. IEEE Transactions on Pattern Analysis and Machine Intelligence. 2002;24(3):402–412.

[45]   Huang GB, Mattar M, Berg T, Learned-Miller E. Labeled faces in the wild: a database for studying face recognition in unconstrained environments. In: Workshop on Faces in 'Real-Life' Images: Detection, Alignment, and Recognition; 2008.

[46]   Chen F, Chandrakasan AP, Stojanović V. A signal-agnostic compressed sensing acquisition system for wireless and implantable sensors. In: IEEE CICC; 2010.

[47]   Zhang T, Chen K, Xu C, Sun G, Wang T, Xie Y. Half-DRAM: a High-bandwidth and Low-power DRAM architecture from the rethinking of fine-grained activation. In: IEEE ISCA; 2014.

[48]   Kim J, Papaefthymiou MC. Block-based multiperiod dynamic memory design for low data-retention power. IEEE Transactions on VLSI Systems. 2003;11(6):1006–1018.

[49]   He S, Wang Y, Li Z, *et al.* Cost-aware region-level data placement in multi-tiered parallel I/O systems. IEEE Transactions on Parallel and Distributed Systems. 2017;28(7):1853–1865.

[50]   Heekwon P, KI YS. QoS-aware IO management for PCIe storage system with reconfigurable multi-ports. Google Patents; 2017. US Patent App. 15/227,959.

[51]   Manoj S, Wang K, Huang H, *et al.* Smart I/Os: a data-pattern aware 2.5 D interconnect with space-time multiplexing. In: 2015 ACM/IEEE International Workshop on System Level Interconnect Prediction (SLIP). IEEE; 2015. p. 1–6.

[52]   Xu D, Yu N, Huang H, *et al.* Q-learning-based voltage-swing tuning and compensation for 2.5-D memory-logic integration. IEEE Design & Test. 2018;35(2):91–99.

[53]   Jeon Y, Kim H, Kim J, *et al.* Design of an on-silicon-interposer passive equalizer for next generation high bandwidth memory with data rate up To 8 Gb/s. IEEE Transactions on Circuits and Systems I: Regular Papers. 2018;65(7): 2293–2303.

[54]   PD SM, Lin J, Zhu S, *et al.* A scalable network-on-chip microprocessor with 2.5 d integrated memory and accelerator. IEEE Transactions on Circuits and Systems I: Regular Papers. 2017;64(6):1432–1443.

Chapter 20

Approximate computing across the hardware and software stacks

Muhammad Shafique[1], Osman Hasan[2],
Rehan Hafiz[3], Sana Mazahir[2],
Muhammad Abdullah Hanif[1], and Semeen Rehman[4]

Emerging fields like big data and IoT have brought a number of challenges for hardware as well as software design community. Some of the major challenges are to scale the computational and memory resources and the efficiency of the processing devices as per the growing needs. In the past few years, a number of fields have emerged for addressing these challenges. In this chapter, we focus on one of the prominent paradigms that have the potential to improve the resource efficiency regardless of the underlying technology, i.e., approximate computing (AC).

AC aims at relaxing the bounds of exact computing to provide new opportunities for achieving gains in terms of energy, power, performance, and/or area efficiency at the cost of reduced output quality, typically within the tolerable range. In this chapter, we first provide an overview of AC and the techniques which are commonly being employed at different abstraction levels for alleviating the resource requirements of computationally intensive applications. Afterwards, a detailed discussion on component-level approximations and their probabilistic behavior by considering approximate adders and multipliers is presented. At the next step, a methodology used to construct efficient accelerators from these components will be discussed. The discussion will then be extended to approximate memories and runtime management systems. Toward the end of the chapter, we present a methodology for designing energy efficient many-core systems based upon approximate components followed by the challenges in adopting a cross-layer approach for designing highly energy, power, and performance-efficient systems.

[1]Institute of Computer Engineering, Vienna University of Technology (TU Wien), Austria
[2]Department of Electrical Engineering, School of Electrical Engineering and Computer Science (SEECS), National University of Sciences and Technology (NUST), Pakistan
[3]Department of Electrical Engineering, Information Technology University (ITU), Pakistan
[4]Institute of Computer Technology, Vienna University of Technology (TU Wien), Austria

20.1   Introduction

Emerging application domains like IoT and Big Data have led us to an era of ever-growing demands of data processing. Alongside general computing applications, these systems are now-a-days commonly being adapted to interact with the physical world in order to monitor and control physical processes and systems, which has led to a significant growth in the overall number of computing devices in use. These growing computational and storage requirements directly influence the overall energy and power requirements of the computing systems. Despite technological advancements and the developments in the field of computer architecture, the energy requirements of computing systems are still growing at a rapid pace with the demand of data processing. Therefore, the conventional methods like power gating, dynamic voltage and frequency scaling, and techniques like power-/energy-aware application mapping are required to be coupled with new ways for significantly improving the energy and power efficiency of modern computing architectures.

Recent studies by few of the leading industries (like IBM [1], Intel [2], and Microsoft [3,4]) and other research groups [5] in hardware design have shown that a significant number of large-scale applications falls under the umbrella of RMS (recognition, mining, and synthesis) applications which are inherently error tolerant. This error tolerance can be attributed to some of the following several factors:

1. Perceptual limitations of the users, for instance, a slight change in visual output of an image/video-processing application might not be noticeable by the end-user because of their psychovisual limits.
2. Presence of noise and redundancy in real-world sensory data.
3. Error masking and attenuation characteristics of applications and algorithms.
4. Absence of a unique nontrivial solution, for instance, occasionally there is no golden answer to a web search, and multiple possible candidates are recommended which are equally acceptable.

These characteristics can be exploited in order to relax the bounds of precise computing to explore new horizons for achieving energy and performance efficiency at the cost of reduced output quality.

AC [6] is one such paradigm that provides an additional degree of freedom in the design space, i.e., it exploits the possibilities of compromising computational accuracy to obtain new performance regions that were not possible with the classical designs, which only trade among power, area, and performance. Typical applications are in the areas of image/video processing, machine learning, and data mining. As a consequence, these applications may not require the output to be fully accurate, rather an approximate result may be acceptable if it satisfies the predefined quality constraint. Figure 20.1 presents a comparison between traditional HW/SW computing stack and the emerging computing stack which makes use of AC.

Several approaches have been presented for the design of approximate circuits in the existing research literature. Approximations in the computing can be done at circuit, architecture and/or software level [7]. Circuit-level approximations include the design of approximate versions of logic circuits using algorithms, like systematic logic synthesis of approximate circuits (SALSA) [9,10]. Another popular approach

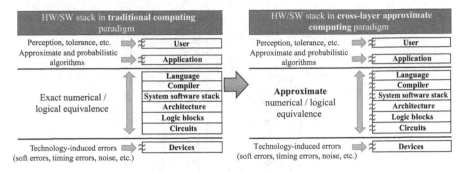

Figure 20.1 Emerging paradigm shift from exact to approximate/imprecise computing for fault tolerant applications (adapted from [7,8])

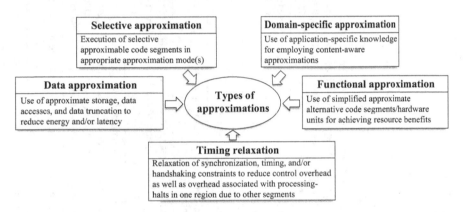

Figure 20.2 Types of approximations

to circuit-level approximations is to design arithmetic datapaths using approximate adders [11–14] and/or multipliers [15–18]. Architecture-level approximations can be done in complex algorithms, like artificial neural networks, by identifying critical neurons [19]. Softwares can also be approximated using techniques, like code perforation [20]. An overview of the AC techniques across the hardware and software stacks is presented in Table 20.1. Each abstraction layer is divided into multiple subclasses depending upon the types of approximations that can be employed. The five major types of approximations are illustrated in Figure 20.2. Table 20.1 also highlights the potential for employing multiple techniques simultaneously at different abstraction layers in order to maximize the resource benefits.

In this chapter, we cover the design and development of approximate hardware from device layer to complete system architectures, through a cross-layer methodology. First, in Sections 20.2 and 20.3, we will explain the component-level approximations and their probabilistic behavior by considering approximate adders and multipliers. In Sections 20.4 and 20.5, some methods used to construct efficient accelerators from these components will be discussed. Section 20.6 will then provide insights on designing approximate memories and cache architectures and their adaptive management to maintain a desired level of quality of service (QoS). Toward the end, in

Table 20.1 Approximate computing techniques across the hardware and software stacks

Abstraction layer	Technique	Related work	Brief description	Motivation/Gains
Software	Selective approximation	[20,21]	Uses manually annotated or automatically analyzed code to adaptively skip error-resilient parts of the code as per the user-defined quality requirements	Performance and energy efficiency
	Timing relaxation	[22,23]	Synchronization between parallel programs or handshaking between different code segments can be relaxed to achieve improvements in terms of performance and energy efficiency	
	Domain-specific approximation	[24,25]	Exploits domain/application-specific knowledge by classifying data into segments such that the sensitive/complex data is processed using precise computations and the insensitive/approximable data is processed using imprecise/approximate modules	
	Functional approximation	[26]	Resource-hungry approximable code segments are replaced with approximate equivalent which is either executed using precise or special approximate hardware modules	
Architectural	Selective approximation	[27]	Executes selective instructions/code segments using dedicated approximate hardware modules	Performance and energy efficiency
	Domain-specific approximation	[28,29]	Leverages domain/application-specific knowledge for designing efficient approximate architectures	Power, energy, and performance efficiency
	Functional approximation	[11,30–32]	Simplifies the architectural complexity of the hardware by using truncation of critical paths or by generally realizing complex modules using their approximate equivalent	
	Data approximation	[33,34]	Memory architectures with relaxed reliability/dependability (specifically by relaxing error correction bounds or by intelligently managing read/write operations at hardware level of error-resilient data) leads to significant improvements in performance and resource efficiency	
HW/Circuit	Timing relaxation	[26,35]	Reduction in supply voltage to improve overall energy and power efficiency	Power, area, and energy efficiency
	Functional approximation	[36–38]	Deliberate reduction in the number of transistors/gates of hardware modules in order to replace them using less complex approximate equivalent versions	
	Data approximation	[39]	Use of less reliable memory units implemented using less number of transistors	

Section 20.7, we provide some discussions on the cross-layer approximations and the challenges being faced by the community in exploiting cross-layer approximations in a synergistic fashion to maximize the energy, power, performance, and/or area benefits.

20.2 Component-level approximations for adders and multipliers

Adders and multipliers are foundational blocks in all arithmetic circuits, including customized on-chip accelerators and general purpose processors. Owing to the fact that most applications that are amenable to AC are the ones that are highly computationally intensive requiring large number of arithmetic operations, the design of approximate adders and multipliers has attracted great attention. Here, we give a brief overview of the approximate adders and multipliers.

20.2.1 Approximate adders

Adders are one of the most widely used operators in computing systems. Approximate adders leverage functional simplifications to gain performance and/or area/power benefits. There are mainly two complementary methods for designing approximate adders: (1) by reducing the logic/circuitry of elementary blocks of the adders, i.e., by approximating the functionality and thereby simplifying the logic of full adders and (2) by approximating the carry logic using carry chain truncation. Both the methods are briefly discussed in the following subsections.

20.2.1.1 Low-power approximate adders

Ripple carry adder (RCA) is the most popular and simplest adder design which is composed of cascaded full-adder units. The most prominent characteristic of RCA is its low power consumption as compared to all rest of the accurate adder structures. Applications that have strict power constraints require even simpler and less power consuming modules. Therefore, to meet the requirements, a set of low-power approximate full adders is proposed [36,37]. The truth tables of approximate full adders, proposed in IMPACT [36], are presented in Figure 20.3, along with their corresponding power and area characteristics.

Using the available low-power full-adder units, low-power RCA can be constructed by replacing accurate full adders with their approximate equivalent. The full adders near least significant bit (LSB) locations have less significance as compared to bits near most significant bit (MSB); therefore, in most of the cases, the LSBs are approximated using different variants of approximate full adders.

20.2.1.2 Low-latency approximate adders

To meet high performance requirements of the error-resilient applications, the truncation of the critical paths in the hardware can be exploited. In case of adders, this is typically realized by using multiple overlapping/non-overlapping smaller sub-adder units that operate in parallel to generate the output with relatively lower latency. An illustrative example of low-latency approximate adder is shown in Figure 20.4. These adders are occasionally also equipped with error detection (ED) and correction logic

Inputs			Accurate FA			Approx. FA$_1$			Approx. FA$_2$			Approx. FA$_3$			Approx. FA$_4$			Approx. FA$_5$		
A	B	C_{in}	Sum	C_{out}	Error	Sum	C_{out}	Error	Sum	C_{out}	Error	Sum	C_{out}	Error	Sum	C_{out}	Error	Sum	C_{out}	Error
0	0	0	0	0	0	0	0	0	1	0	1	1	0	1	0	0	0	0	0	0
0	0	1	1	0	0	1	0	0	1	0	0	1	0	0	1	0	0	0	0	−1
0	1	0	1	0	0	0	1	1	1	0	0	0	1	1	0	0	−1	1	0	0
0	1	1	0	1	0	0	1	0	0	1	0	0	1	0	1	0	−1	1	0	−1
1	0	0	1	0	0	0	0	−1	1	0	0	1	0	0	0	1	1	0	1	1
1	0	1	0	1	0	0	1	0	0	1	0	0	1	0	0	1	0	0	1	0
1	1	0	0	1	0	0	1	0	0	1	0	0	1	0	0	1	0	1	1	1
1	1	1	1	1	0	1	1	0	0	1	−1	0	1	−1	1	1	0	1	1	0
Area [GE]			4.41			4.23			1.94			1.59			1.76			0		
Power [nW]			1,130			771			294			198			416			0		

Figure 20.3   Truth tables and characterization for various approximate full adders based on the designs of [36]

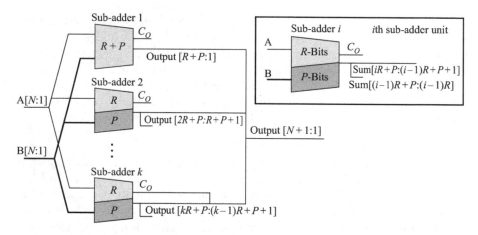

Figure 20.4   An N-bit low-latency GeAr adder. Each illustrated sub-adder sums two L-bit numbers, where the first P-bits of each sub-adder are used to predict the carry for generating R MSB sum bits

for reducing the error probability by dynamically altering the carry being propagated to the subsequent stages.

Careful and time-efficient design space exploration of available low-latency adders demand a unified model that is highly parameterizable and capable of supporting most (if not all) types of low-latency adders. Toward this, we developed the GeAr [11] adder model, which is highly configurable and capable of modeling most of the state-of-the-art high-performance adders (for instance, ACA-I [40], ACA-II [12], ETAII [41], and GDA [42]).

In order to add two N-bit operands, GeAr adder makes use of k L-bit sub-adders that operate in parallel to generate the approximate output at high speed, where $L \leq N$. Figure 20.4 shows an illustrative version of the adder model. Let R be the number of resultant bits contributing to the final output and P be the number of carry prediction bits used for predicting the carry in each sub-adder. Each sub-adder produces R-bits of the output except the first sub-adder which produces L-bits of the result, where $L = R + P$. For a given N, R, and P, the number of required sub-adders k can be computed by $k = (N - P)/R$. Moreover, for a combination of N, R, and P to be valid for the GeAr model, the combination should result in a positive integer "k." The structure of the low-latency adders (shown in Figure 20.4) illustrates that an error is generated when the P-bits of any sub-adder are propagating the carry, and the carry was generated by the previous sub-adder. Based upon this insight, we also proposed an error correction scheme, which forces the inputs to the MSB of the P-bits of the sub-adder to "1" in order to compensate for the missing carry-in.

We extended our GeAr model [11] later-on in QuAd [43] to provide rest of the unsupported configurations as well. The only structural difference as compared to the GeAr architecture is that each sub-adder in QuAd has the freedom to have different R and P bits than rest of the sub-adders. We also presented an extensive design space exploration in [43], which concluded that, for uniformly distributed inputs, the quality-area optimal configuration of low-latency approximate adders (without error correction support) is always the one that has no overlapping segments between sub-adder units, where each sub-adder unit is of maximum possible allowed length (defined using the latency constraint) except the least significant sub-adder which spans just the remaining number of least significant bits, i.e., $N\%L$.

20.2.2 Approximate multipliers

Efficient multiplication at hardware level is generally performed in three stages: (1) partial product generation; (2) intermediate accumulation of partial products; and (3) final accumulation using fast adder. Approximations can be employed at each stage to improve the power, performance, or area efficiency of the multipliers. Another approach for designing efficient multipliers is to use smaller multipliers as building blocks to construct larger multipliers. An illustrative example of such techniques is shown in Figure 20.5. The basic building blocks used in the aforementioned techniques

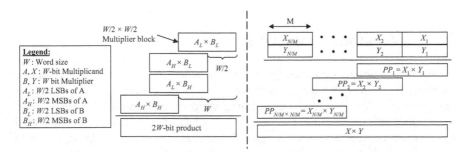

Figure 20.5   Building larger multipliers using smaller multipliers as building blocks (adapted from [38])

Table 20.2   Characteristics of various elementary adders and multipliers used in design space exploration of multipliers in [38]

		Area [GE]	Latency [ns]	Power [nW]	No. of error cases	Max. error mag.
Multipliers	**Accu**	**6.88**	**0.1**	**543**	–	–
	Approx1	**3.704**	**0.06**	**363**	**1**	**2**
	Approx2	**4.939**	**0.1**	**262**	**3**	**1**
	Approx1C	7.232	0.17	525	–	–
	Approx2C	6.35	0.13	379	–	–
	Approx3	5.645	0.1	464	1	8
	Approx4	5.292	0.1	422	1	4
	Approx5	5.645	0.1	467	1	8
Adders	**Accu**	**4.41**	**0.12**	**1,130**	**0**	**0**
	Approx1	**1.94**	**0.07**	**294**	**2**	**1**
	Approx2	**1.59**	**0.05**	**198**	**3**	**1**
	Approx3	1.76	0.06	416	3	1
	Approx4	**0**	**0**	**0**	**4**	**1**
	Approx5	4.23	0.1	771	2	1
	Approx6	3.18	0.1	409	2	1
	Approx7	3.18	0.13	709	2	2

are full and half adders, compressors, and 2×2 multipliers. Multiple approximate designs for compressors [44], full adders [36], as well as 2×2 multipliers [16] have been proposed in the literature, which can be used for building approximate multipliers. In this context, we conducted a thorough architectural-space exploration of approximate multipliers in [38] by using (1) various types of elementary multiply modules, (2) various types of elementary adder modules for accumulating the partial products, and (3) selection of bits for approximation in a wide-bit multiplier design. A summary of the characteristics of the elementary adder and multiplier modules used in this study is presented in Table 20.2, where the pareto-optimal designs are highlighted using bold.

20.3   Probabilistic error analysis

In conventional precise digital design, the performance metrics used to characterize a circuit are (1) critical path delay, (2) latency, (3) power consumption, and (4) silicon area. Similarly, the trade-offs for obtaining various operating conditions are also among the same parameters. However, in the case of AC, there is an additional performance consideration, i.e., the computational accuracy. Hence, the approximate circuits are required to be qualified in terms of their error statistics. Probabilistic error analysis aims at the theoretical evaluation of accuracy from the functional model of the approximate circuits and probability distribution of the inputs.

The term "AC" has conventionally been used in the literature for deterministic systems, which means that the output can be reliably calculated for a given input.[1] Therefore, the probabilistic analysis aims at the evaluation of accuracy of random outputs produced by the interaction between random inputs and a deterministic system.

20.3.1 Empirical vs. analytical methods

Traditionally, the error performance evaluation and comparison presented for AC systems relies on statistical analysis, i.e., the analysis of data generated via Monte Carlo simulations. Exhaustive simulations, i.e., the evaluation of the system for all possible inputs, can only be done for very small circuits, as the number of inputs grow exponentially with the circuit size [46]. Some of the limitations of Monte Carlo simulations are explained below [46]:

- Every configuration of the approximate module needs to be simulated individually, which takes considerable time and programming effort.
- They do not provide any insights into the causes of error in terms of circuit parameters and input distributions.

In contrast, probabilistic analysis yields mathematical models that describes the error characteristics in terms of circuit parameters. It also serves as a tool for the design of improved design.

20.3.2 Accuracy metrics

There are several performance metrics defined for quantifying the accuracy characteristics of AC [45,47–49]. Some of the commonly used metrics are minimum acceptable accuracy, accuracy of amplitude, accuracy of information, mean error distance (MED), normalized error distance, error rate (ER), error significance, and maximum error magnitude. Conventionally, all of these metrics are estimations made on the basis of Monte Carlo simulations. Moreover, most of them are either long-term averages or metrics describing extreme values. The accuracy of an AC can be most comprehensively described by the probability mass function (PMF) of error value (signed or absolute, as required), as it shows all the possible error values and their respective magnitudes. All the aforementioned metrics can be evaluated from the PMF. In the next section, a general methodology developed to analyze the PMF of error for selected classes of adders and multipliers is explained.

20.3.3 Probabilistic analysis methodology

This section presents a generalized probabilistic error analysis methodology for computing error probability distribution of approximate accelerators as well as individual

---

[1]Another class of inexact computing is probabilistic computing, in which probabilistic switches are used, so that, in addition to the random inputs, the circuit's function is also random [45].

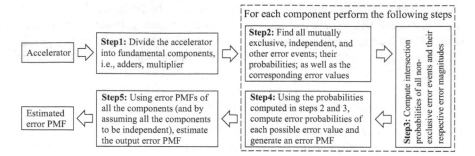

Figure 20.6   A generalized probabilistic analysis methodology for accelerators

approximate components. Figure 20.6 provides a brief overview of the methodology. The detailed description of each step is as follows:

- **Step 1:** To estimate the probability distribution of an approximate accelerator, the accelerator is first decomposed into its fundamental components, i.e., adders, multipliers. The decomposition is mainly done in order to simplify the analysis. Afterwards, Step 2 till 4 are repeated for each individual component to compute their respective error PMFs, which are then used for estimating the error distribution of the complete system in Step 5.
- **Step 2:** For each individual approximate component, first, all possible error events are identified, which in most of the cases are linked to errors generated by elementary building blocks, e.g., approximate full adders, used in the component or are because of some other structural simplification/approximation of the component. Once all possible errors have been recognized, mutually exclusive error events are identified. A simple example of mutually exclusive events can be two error events associated with the same approximate adder which cannot occur at the same time. Probability of each event is then computed and stored along with the associated error value. In order to simplify the analysis, most of the state-of-the-art techniques assume all non-mutually exclusive error event as independent [46,50–52]. This assumption significantly simplifies the problem for estimating the probabilities associated with joint events.
- **Step 3:** This step evaluates the joint probabilities of non-mutually exclusive events and their respective error values. The computed error probabilities of the joint events are then subtracted from the probabilities of their root events to avoid repetition. All the computed probabilities along with their respective error values are then stored and passed on to Step 4. Step 3 also significantly simplifies due to the independence assumption.
- **Step 4:** All probabilities corresponding to the same error values are added together to generate one probability per error value. The final probabilities and respective error values then correspond to the final error PMF of the component.
- **Step 5:** In case, there are more than one approximate components in the accelerator such that the cumulative error is the sum of errors in individual components, an

approximated probabilistic analysis can be carried out by assuming all the components are independent and all the intermediary inputs are approximately uniformly distributed. The PMF of cumulative error value is the convolution of PMFs of individual components. This method was shown to yield good approximation in [46].

Note that error PMF is the main function that can be used to calculate any kind of error measure, for example, MSE, MED, overall error probability.

20.4 Accuracy configurability and adaptivity in approximate computing systems

Since the accuracy requirements can differ from one application to another, and even for different functions or execution phases of a given application, it may also be required to configure the approximate module during application runtime. Therefore, many adders and multipliers are designed with integrated ED and correction units [11,12,16,53].

20.4.1 Approximate accelerators with consolidated error correction

Several approximate adders and multipliers have integrated error detection and correction (EDC). When the size of datapath becomes large, the accumulated overhead due to EDC becomes significant and hence undermines the benefits of AC. To cut down this overhead, we proposed a consolidated error correction (CEC) scheme in [54]. This was done by implementing ED for all components and using these ED signals to implement a common CEC for a group of components. It was shown that the more components are grouped together in this manner, the more area and speed enhancements can be achieved.

Example: Figure 20.7 shows an example of an accelerator made from a block-based adder. A CEC is implemented for a circuit with eight adders. The reason this design can be simplified in this manner is that the error in block-based adder can attain certain specific values, depending on the location of carry-chain truncation. The ED signals can directly determine the error value by virtue of their location. This design was shown to be more efficient in terms of speed and area than the EDC designs in [11,12].

20.4.2 Adaptive datapaths

In adaptive AC [32], a datapath with multiple approximate additions or multiplications is constructed in such a way that error in one operation determines the approximate module used in subsequent operation, with the objective of minimizing the cumulative error. For this purpose, we proposed the novel concept of "complementary approximate modules" in [32], such that the datapath is made up of standard and complementary versions of the module. The complementary modules are such circuits that produce errors of opposite sign as compared to the standard approximate module. The ED signals determine which type of module is used at the next operation.

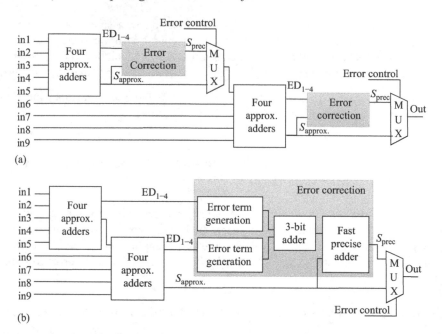

Figure 20.7   Hardware accelerator with eight approximate adders with (a) CEC-4 in two stages(b) CEC-8 (adapted from [54])

To design the datapath described by the algorithm in Figure 20.8, following elements and mechanisms are required:

- Standard and complementary versions of the approximate modules. Ideally, the standard and complementary versions should be such that they have: (1) same error magnitudes, with opposing polarities and equal probabilities, i.e., $p(ESAM)(x) = p(ECAM)(x)$ and; (2) same area, power and performance (e.g., in terms of latency or execution times in cycles) efficiency.
- ED signals for every component in the datapath.
- A mechanism or signal S/C to indicate which type of module is being used.
- A mechanism to switch between the standard and complementary modules, in response to ED and S/C signals.

If a datapath is designed in this way, then whenever there are errors in any two modules in the datapath, they get fully or partially canceled, thereby reducing the cumulative error. If the standard and complementary modules are such that one can completely cancel the error introduced by the other, then the total error is nonzero only when odd number of modules in the datapath are erroneous. Moreover, the error magnitude is limited to the maximum error in single approximate module. As a result, using this method in a datapath with M approximate modules, the maximum cumulative error can be reduced up to M times as compared to a conventional homogeneous accelerator. Such a concept and an approach is highly beneficial to

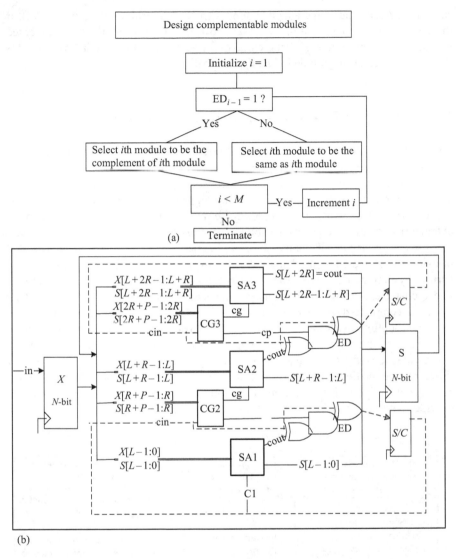

Figure 20.8   (a) Methodology for designing complementable modules and (b) an adaptive sequential accumulator (adapted from [32])

demonstrate the efficacy of systematically employing AC, as the energy/area/latency gains are maximized with minimal output quality/accuracy loss.

   Example: To explain the concept of adaptive datapaths, we consider the following example of an accumulator employing block-based adders. For the ease of discussion, we consider an adder with two sub-adders, as shown in Figure 20.8(b). The standard and complementary modules are identified by the *cin* signal. The ED signal is 1 when the carry generated by the first sub-adder is not the same as *cin* of the second sub-adder. According to the adaptive approximation algorithm in Figure 20.8(a), if there is an error in one addition, the next addition is done using the complemented module. It was shown in [32] that the maximum error magnitude in this sub-adder is limited to the error magnitude in one approximate adder.

20.5   Multi-accelerator approximate computing architectures

This section presents a systematic methodology for developing efficient AC architectures composed of many accelerators with variable/heterogeneous accuracy levels. Figure 20.9 illustrates the general flow for generating approximate accelerators using elementary building blocks (like approximate full adders, sub-adders, approximate compressors, basic approximate multiplier modules). The intermediate characterization and design space exploration steps are also illustrated in the same.

First, a library of elementary blocks is generated (either manually [11,38,43] or using an automated methodology, e.g., EvoApproxSb [55]) and characterized for various system metrics (like power, energy, area, performance, and output quality). These characteristics of the elementary blocks are then used for selecting a subset from the complete design space using a design space exploration step which provides near-optimal trade-off between various metrics. The selected set is then used for generating multi-bit approximate logic blocks (like adders, subtractors, multipliers, dividers). Statistical analysis step is employed to quickly analyze the effects of different combinations of elementary blocks on the output of a multi-bit logic block and thereby helps in fast selection of an appropriate approximate logic block that provides better trade-off between system metrics and output quality.

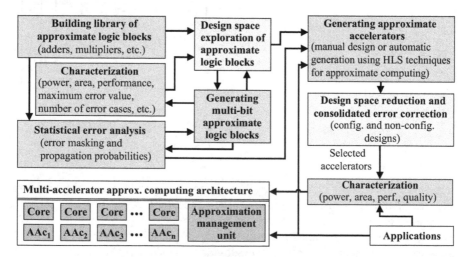

Figure 20.9   Methodology for designing multi-accelerator approximate computing architectures (adapted from [7])

Once a set of optimal/near-optimal multi-bit logic modules is selected, it can be used for designing approximate accelerators and datapaths. These accelerators can either be designed manually (as done in the following case study) or can be generated using specialized high-level synthesis techniques/tools for AC. To generate high-quality accelerators that provide significant improvements in system metrics within a reasonable amount of time, the error masking and error propagation effects of multi-bit logic blocks within an accelerator are analyzed and a subset of high-performance accelerators are selected. Eventually, based on the error characteristics of the selected accelerators, CEC modules are proposed (if required). To improve the effectiveness of the design methodology, *content-awareness* (i.e., application and data awareness) can be added in the characterization and statistical analysis steps.

For designing generic approximate hardware (capable of simulating different applications with different quality requirements), reconfigurability is usually one of the most important factors. The reconfigurability enables the hardware to maintain the required level of output-quality while maximizing the benefits. To achieve this, all the selected accelerators are characterized for power, energy, performance, and output-quality. The characterization results are then stored in form of a look-up table as part of an approximation management unit (AMU). The AMU is then responsible for managing/selecting appropriate approximation mode based upon the user-defined constraints.

20.5.1 Case study: an approximate accelerator architecture for High Efficiency Video Coding (HEVC)

High Efficiency Video Coding (HEVC) is the latest standard for video coding that provides 1.6×–2× coding efficiency while requiring >40% more computations and higher energy as compared to its predecessor, i.e., the H.264/AVC standard. Video coding involves an encoder module, which encodes the video in compressed format so that the data can be stored using less amount of storage, and a decoder module, which decodes the encoded video back into a presentable/usable format. Out of the two aforementioned modules, encoder is considered to be the most resource hungry module as it is required to perform extensive region search to encode the video using a subset of original data. A more detailed description on HEVC can be found in [56].

In this section, we focus on the motion estimation (ME) module as it is the most compute intensive and energy-consuming operation in HEVC and is usually responsible for nearly 80% of the total energy consumed by the encoder [57,58]. ME is primarily a minimization problem used to estimate motion vectors for reference blocks by locating best matching candidate within a defined spatial region of the neighboring frames. The fundamental operation involved in ME is the sum of absolute difference (SAD), which is responsible for estimating the correlation/similarity between two blocks. Figure 20.10 illustrates our approximate ME architecture for HEVC as proposed in [58]. It is composed of an array of SAD accelerators organized in the form of heterogeneous approximate SAD tiles. Each tile contains multiple instances of a particular type of an approximate SAD variant. The characteristics, like power/energy, and quality of all the variants obtained at design time are stored

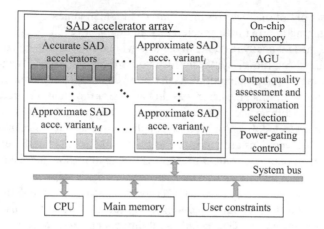

Figure 20.10   Hardware architecture of our approximate motion estimation module (adapted from [58])

in the approximate variant selection unit to dynamically reconfigure the hardware depending upon the user constraints, which are provided in terms of required output quality or maximum energy consumption. The approximate variant selection unit then powers-on the appropriate tiles of certain approximate SAD variants, while keeping the rest of the tiles in the power-gated mode. The HEVC and ME algorithm execute on the general-purpose processor core. The address generation unit (AGU) receives the candidate vectors and pointer addresses and generates the memory address to fetch the data from on-chip memories storing the current coding-tree unit data and the search windows from the reference frame(s). In case the required data is not available in the on-chip memories, it is fetched from the main memory. The data is then transferred to the SAD accelerators for computing the correlation between the data using SAD. The monitoring unit maintains the intermediate SAD value and the motion vector, such that, the motion estimator can make fast search decisions, and can locate the best candidate which provides minimum SAD value.

As mentioned earlier, SAD is the fundamental operation for ME in HEVC and is mainly composed of adders and subtractors. Implementation of adders and subtractors using approximate adder units can be exploited to improve the energy as well as the power efficiency associated with the SAD operations. Figure 20.11 illustrates how an N-bit approximate adder can be realized using accurate and 1-bit approximate full-adder units. Note that the subtraction operation can be implemented with the help of adders by using 2's complement. To highlight the extent of the potential of energy savings through such approximations, we take an example of a 32×32 SAD module, which is a common size of a coding unit. The total number of subtractions and additions it requires *just for one single SAD operation* is 1,024 and 1,023, respectively. With such a huge number of additions and subtractions, even a small fraction of energy savings per adder and subtractor can lead to significant savings. For simplicity of the designs (in the current example), it is assumed that each type of approximate

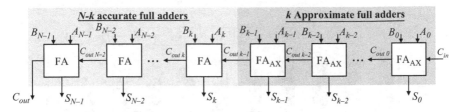

Figure 20.11   An N-bit RCA composed of k approximate and N − k accurate full-adder units

adder can have only k-bits of the same type of approximate full-adders and that each adder in an approximate SAD variant is of the same type. Using the aforementioned description, different SAD units of different sizes can be constructed, for example, 8×1, 8×8, 16×16, and 32×32, which offers a trade-off between throughput and power consumption of the hardware. For example, an 8×1 SAD unit requires eight cycles to perform an 8×8 SAD operation while the same can also be performed using a single 8×8 SAD unit to enhance the performance and throughput at the cost of increased power consumption.

In the light of the above discussion, we developed different SAD units of sizes 8×8 and 32×32 using 8×1 SAD units. The 8×8 SAD block is realized using a single 8×1 SAD unit which runs for eight cycles. However, the 32×32 SAD block is realized using four 8×1 SAD units which runs in parallel for 32 cycles to compute the result of a 32×32 block. Accurate and heterogeneous approximate variants of SAD accelerators were built using accurate and three different types of approximate adders, and choosing 2, 4, or 6 LSBs for approximation. The area, power, and energy characteristics of all the possible variants for 8×8 and 32×32 SAD units are shown in Figure 20.12. The presented results are generated using Synopsys Design Compiler for 45 nm technology.

20.6   Approximate memory systems and run-time management

Emergence of highly data- and compute-intensive RMS applications have significantly increased the load on memory subsystems of the current embedded devices. These memory subsystems (even for conventional/simple applications) are considered to be the major contributors to the energy consumption of a system and also play a vital role in defining the overall performance of the embedded devices. Traditional techniques for ensuring reliability in memories utilize redundancy, and error detection and correction codes, which require extra hardware as well as power and energy resources, thereby reducing the efficiency of the systems even further. Relaxing such overheads have been widely studied in the domain of AC for improving the performance as well as resource (energy/power/area) efficiency of the memory subsystems. For example, the newly emerged nonvolatile memory (NVM) technology can be used for improving the storage density by exploiting its multilevel cell (MLC) feature. However, storing multiple bits in a single cell have a significant impact on the

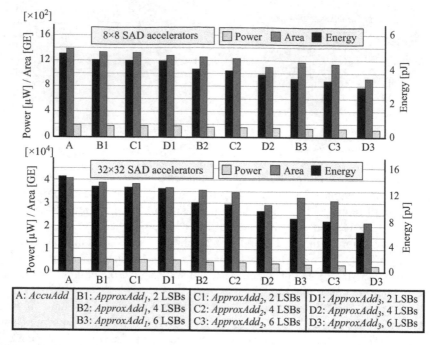

Figure 20.12　Area, power and energy characteristics of different variants of SAD units

overall energy consumption as well as on the overall performance of the device due to the increased write energy and reduced write speed, respectively. The probability of error in MLCs is also higher as compared to errors in single-level cells (SLCs) and thereby necessitates the use of even sophisticated ECC algorithms, which also add-on to the associated overheads. These overheads can be reduced by leveraging the intrinsic error resilience of the applications, e.g., by reducing the complexity of ECCs and/or by reducing the amount of power required to precisely store a value in an MLC. Similar to NVMs, other memory technologies also have some sort of limitations associated with them due to their fundamental properties (e.g., a dynamic random-access memory (DRAM) cell requires periodic refresh to maintain the stored value), which can be exploited as per the intrinsic error resilience of the applications for improving the resource/energy efficiency of the systems.

Typically, the memory approximation techniques are employed to achieve one or multiple of the following three main objectives, i.e., improving the (1) energy efficiency, (2) performance, and (3) lifetime of the memory. These objectives usually depends upon the type of memory technology used in a system. For example, to improve the energy efficiency of static random-access memory (SRAM), voltage scaling is adapted which results in a significant energy reduction at the cost of loss in data integrity. Similarly, energy efficiency in DRAM is achieved by adapting/controlling the refresh rate knob, and in NVMs it is achieved by skipping read/write operations (which is also applicable for enhancing the lifetime of the NVMs). Although some of the techniques are technology specific, others can be adopted for all types of memories to achieve the desired objectives, e.g., approximating load operation, skipping store operations.

In computing systems, these approximation techniques can be employed in cache, scratchpad memory, main memory, secondary storage, either individually or simultaneously at multiple layers [34] in a cross-layer fashion. In the upcoming subsection, we present a generic methodology for employing approximations in memory sub-systems.

20.6.1   Methodology for designing approximate memory systems

Figure 20.13 illustrates the methodology for designing approximate memory subsystem. In the first stage, a design time analysis is performed to estimate the optimal size of on-chip and off-chip memory for a set of applications. Note that in the characterization step, the criticality of data can either be estimated using simulation or can be highlighted using manual annotation of the code. Once the memory sizes and the respective approximable and non-approximable portions of each layer in the memory hierarchy have been estimated, they are then used in simulations to determine the overall performance and/or energy consumption of the system. The system is then subjected to approximations (the type and extent of approximation depends upon the selected memory technology and the user constraints). The degree of approximation is usually computed with the help of some optimization algorithm (e.g., integer linear programming (ILP)), where either the error across the complete memory hierarchy (using a well-defined error metric) is minimized while satisfying the performance and/or energy constraints or the performance and/or energy is maximized for a user-defined output quality constraint. In case the user constraints are not met, feasibility of alternate memory technologies can be explored or more severe approximations can be employed, which might result in significant degradation of the output quality.

Apart from the design time optimizations, in the second step, a run-time algorithm is designed which, based upon the user-defined constraints and the application characteristics, effectively adjusts the approximation knobs across the complete memory hierarchy to maximize performance and/or energy/power consumption of the system.

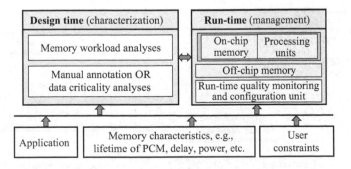

Figure 20.13   Methodology for designing approximate memory systems

20.6.2   Case study: an approximation-aware multilevel cells cache architecture

Figure 20.14 illustrates our adaptive approximate last-level MLC STT-RAM cache architecture and its integration within a many-core system, as proposed in [33]. The architecture is a partially protected MLC STT-RAM cache architecture that follows set-associative cache organization. It is mainly composed of n memory banks, where each memory bank corresponds to one cache set. The first $n - 1$ memory banks are implemented using 2-bit MLC STT-RAM cells while the nth bank is implemented using SLC cells (to ensure less number of error occurrences), which is dynamically selected to store cache data or the error correction codes (as part of the error correction system). The main features of the cache architecture are as follows:

1. **Error correction unit** ensures reliable storage of critical data using error-correction schemes based on double-error correction algorithm, e.g., Bose–Chandhuri–Hocquenghem [59,60].
2. **An approximation-aware cache management unit** classifies a cache set as "reliable" or "unreliable" to store critical or approximate/less-critical data, respectively. It is also responsible for managing read and write operation in the unreliable memory units by skipping error correction functionality to ensure significant energy benefits.
3. **An application-aware quality control unit** monitors the output quality of application to dynamically control the extent of approximation. Different applications require different levels of approximations, and even for a single application, the output quality varies with changing inputs. Therefore, a system that adapts error

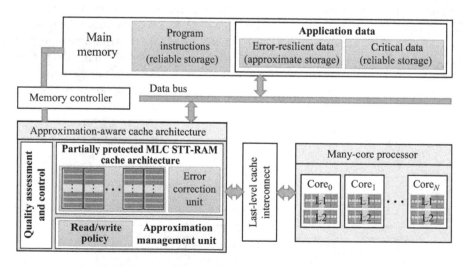

Figure 20.14   Approximation-aware MLC STTRAM cache architecture and its integration in a many-core system (adapted from [33])

protection as per the changing conditions is highly beneficial for ensuring desired level of output quality while providing maximum energy savings.

Adaptation of such architecture in real many-core systems for HEVC application has reported to result in 7%–19% energy savings while producing less than 0.5% output quality degradation [33].

20.7 A cross-layer methodology for designing approximate systems and the associated challenges

Figure 20.15 shows our cross-layer methodology for designing resource-efficient systems by systematically employing approximations across different layers of the hardware and software stacks. First, the approximation possibilities at individual layers are explored, and a set of optimal points from each layer is forwarded to the design space exploration stage where various possible combinations of approximations at different layers are explored. The exploration is supported by error masking and propagation evaluation step where error propagation and masking properties of different approximations are evaluated to identify the joint effects of different approximations on the output quality. Optionally, low-cost consolidated error compensation modules can also be designed and employed to attenuate/nullify/cancel the adverse effects of approximations on the final output quality. Afterwards, a selected set of optimal points are forwarded to the characterization stage where they are characterized for power and other system parameters to identify the optimal configuration/architecture which provides best trade-off between quality and rest of the user-defined system metrics. The architecture can also be optionally equipped with online approximation managements system, which is capable of managing various approximation knobs at different layers of the computing stack to ensure best possible trade-off between different system metrics while meeting the user-defined quality constraints.

Although a significant amount of work has been carried out in employing approximations at individual abstraction layers of computing stack (Table 20.1), there is still a lot to be carried out to uncover the true potential of cross-layer AC. A few of the

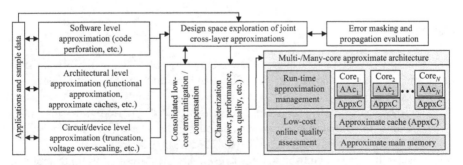

Figure 20.15   Our methodology for designing approximate multi-/many-core systems

most critical challenges being faced by the AC community in realizing the methodology illustrated in Figure 20.15 are listed below; this will fuel further research and development in this area.

- How to design systematic methodologies and analytical techniques for evaluating error masking and propagation effects across different layers of the hardware and software stacks due to different types of approximations?
- How to build time and resource efficient techniques for evaluating cross-layer approximation effects?
- How to develop low-cost consolidated ED and mitigation techniques for complex approximate datapaths, such that the net error due to approximations is equal or close to zero?
- How to develop low-cost online quality assessment methods that can provide a highly accurate quality estimate without consuming much resources?
- How to design methodologies for dynamically orchestrating multiple approximation knobs depending upon the state, constraints, and inputs of a system?

20.8   Conclusion

In this chapter, we provided an overview of the AC techniques which are being used at different abstraction levels of the computing stack. We also presented a detailed discussion on the component-level approximations and their probabilistic behavior while considering approximate adders and multipliers. The chapter also covered a methodology for building efficient accelerators using the basic approximate building blocks like approximate adders and approximate multipliers. A summary of the memory approximation techniques and their runtime management is also presented in the chapter. In the end, we also presented a methodology for designing energy efficient many-core systems based on approximate components and highlighted the challenges involved in employing a cross-layer AC approach for building highly resource-efficient systems.

References

[1]   Nair R. Big data needs approximate computing: Technical perspective. Communications of the ACM. 2014;58(1):104. Available from: http://doi.acm.org/10.1145/2688072.

[2]   Mishra AK, Barik R, Paul S. iACT: A software-hardware framework for understanding the scope of approximate computing. In: Workshop on Approximate Computing Across the System Stack (WACAS); 2014.

[3]   Esmaeilzadeh H, Sampson A, Ceze L, *et al.* Architecture support for disciplined approximate programming. In: ACM SIGPLAN Notices. vol. 47. ACM; 2012. p. 301–312.

[4]   Bornholt J, Mytkowicz T, McKinley KS. Uncertain: Abstractions for uncertain hardware and software. IEEE Micro. 2015;35(3):132–143.

[5]   Chippa VK, Chakradhar ST, Roy K, *et al.* Analysis and characterization of inherent application resilience for approximate computing. In: 2013 50th ACM/EDAC/IEEE Design Automation Conference (DAC); 2013. p. 1–9.

[6]   Xu Q, Kim NS, Mytkowicz T. Approximate computing: A survey. IEEE Design & Test. 2016;33(1):8–22.

[7]   Shafique M, Hafiz R, Rehman S, *et al.* Cross-layer approximate computing: From logic to architectures. In: Proc. 53rd IEEE/ACM Des. Autom. Conf.; 2016.

[8]   Venkataramani S, Chakradhar ST, Roy K, *et al.* Computing approximately, and efficiently. In: Proceedings of the 2015 Design, Automation & Test in Europe Conference & Exhibition. DATE'15. San Jose, CA, USA: EDA Consortium; 2015. p. 748–751. Available from: http://dl.acm.org/citation.cfm?id=2755753.2755924.

[9]   Venkataramani S, Sabne A, Kozhikkottu V, *et al.* SALSA: Systematic logic synthesis of approximate circuits. In: Proc. 49th IEEE/ACM Des. Autom. Conf.; 2012. p. 796–801.

[10] Ranjan A, Raha A, Venkataramani S, *et al.* ASLAN: Synthesis of approximate sequential circuits. In: Proc. Des., Autom. Test Eur. Conf. Exhib; 2014. p. 364.

[11] Shafique M, Ahmad W, Hafiz R, *et al.* A low latency generic accuracy configurable adder. In: Proc. 52nd Annual Des. Autom. Conf.; 2015. p. 86.

[12] Kahng AB, Kang S. Accuracy-configurable adder for approximate arithmetic designs. In: Proc. 49th Annual Des. Autom. Conf.; 2012. p. 820–825.

[13] Du K, Varman P, Mohanram K. High performance reliable variable latency carry select addition. In: Proc. Des., Autom. Test Eur. Conf. Exhib; 2012. p. 1257–1262.

[14] Gupta V, Mohapatra D, Raghunathan A, *et al.* Low-power digital signal processing using approximate adders. IEEE Transactions on Computer-Aided Design of Integrated Circuits and Systems. 2013;32(1):124–137.

[15] Bhardwaj K, Mane PS. ACMA: Accuracy-configurable multiplier architecture for error-resilient system-on-chip. In: Proc. 8th Int. Workshop Reconfig. Commun.-Centric Syst.-on-Chip; 2013. p. 1–6.

[16] Kulkarni P, Gupta P, Ercegovac MD. Trading accuracy for power in a multiplier architecture. Journal of Low Power Electron. 2011;7(4):490–501.

[17] Chen IC, Hayes JP. Low-area and high-speed approximate matrix-vector multiplier. In: IEEE 18th Int. Symp. Des. Diagnostics of Electron. Circuits & Syst.; 2015. p. 23–28.

[18] Momeni A, Han J, Montuschi P, *et al.* Design and analysis of approximate compressors for multiplication. IEEE Transactions on Computers. 2015;64(4):984–994.

[19] Zhang Q, Wang T, Tian Y, *et al.* ApproxANN: An approximate computing framework for artificial neural network. In: Proceedings of the 2015 Design, Automation & Test in Europe Conference & Exhibition. EDA Consortium; 2015. p. 701–706.

[20]   Hoffmann H, Misailovic S, Sidiroglou S, *et al.* Using code perforation to improve performance, reduce energy consumption, and respond to failures. Technical report, MIT; 2009.

[21]   Sidiroglou-Douskos S, Misailovic S, Hoffmann H, *et al.* Managing performance vs. accuracy trade-offs with loop perforation. In: Proceedings of the 19th ACM SIGSOFT Symposium and the 13th European Conference on Foundations of Software Engineering. ACM; 2011. p. 124–134.

[22]   Misailovic S, Kim D, Rinard M. Parallelizing sequential programs with statistical accuracy tests. ACM Transactions on Embedded Computing Systems (TECS). 2013;12(2s):88.

[23]   Mengte J, Raghunathan A, Chakradhar S, *et al.* Exploiting the forgiving nature of applications for scalable parallel execution. In: Parallel & Distributed Processing (IPDPS), 2010 IEEE International Symposium on. IEEE; 2010. p. 1–12.

[24]   Venkataramani S, Raghunathan A, Liu J, *et al.* Scalable-effort classifiers for energy-efficient machine learning. In: Proceedings of the 52nd Annual Design Automation Conference. ACM; 2015. p. 67.

[25]   Venkataramani S, Ranjan A, Roy K, *et al.* AxNN: energy-efficient neuromorphic systems using approximate computing. In: Low Power Electronics and Design (ISLPED), 2014 IEEE/ACM International Symposium on. IEEE; 2014. p. 27–32.

[26]   Mohapatra D, Chippa VK, Raghunathan A, *et al.* Design of voltage-scalable meta-functions for approximate computing. In: Design, Automation & Test in Europe Conference & Exhibition (DATE), 2011. IEEE; 2011. p. 1–6.

[27]   Venkataramani S, Chippa VK, Chakradhar ST, *et al.* Quality programmable vector processors for approximate computing. In: IEEE/ACM International Symposium on Microarchitecture. ACM; 2013. p. 1–12.

[28]   Chippa VK, Mohapatra D, Roy K, *et al.* Scalable effort hardware design. IEEE Transactions on Very Large Scale Integration (VLSI) Systems. 2014;22(9):2004–2016.

[29]   Chippa VK, Venkataramani S, Roy K, *et al.* StoRM: A stochastic recognition and mining processor. In: Proceedings of the 2014 International Symposium on Low Power Electronics and Design. ACM; 2014. p. 39–44.

[30]   Liu C, Han J, Lombardi F. A low-power, high-performance approximate multiplier with configurable partial error recovery. In: Proc. Des., Autom. Test Eur. Conf. Exhib; 2014. p. 95.

[31]   Farshchi F, Abrishami MS, Fakhraie SM. New approximate multiplier for low power digital signal processing. In: Proc. 17th CSI Int Symp. Comput. Architec. Dig. Syst.; 2013. p. 25–30.

[32]   Mazahir S, Hasan O, Shafique M. Adaptive approximate computing in arithmetic datapaths. IEEE Design & Test. 2017;35(4):65–74.

[33]   Sampaio F, Shafique M, Zatt B, *et al.* Approximation-aware multi-level cells STT-RAM cache architecture. In: Compilers, Architecture and Synthesis for Embedded Systems (CASES), 2015 International Conference on. IEEE; 2015. p. 79–88.

[34] Teimoori MT, Hanif MA, Ejlali A, *et al.* AdAM: Adaptive approximation management for the non-volatile memory hierarchies. In: Design, Automation Test in Europe Conference Exhibition (DATE), 2018; 2018.

[35] Ramasubramanian SG, Venkataramani S, Parandhaman A, *et al.* Relax-and-retime: A methodology for energy-efficient recovery based design. In: Proceedings of the 50th Annual Design Automation Conference. ACM; 2013. p. 111.

[36] Gupta V, Mohapatra D, Park SP, *et al.* IMPACT: Imprecise adders for low-power approximate computing. In: Proc. 17th IEEE/ACM Int. Symp. Low-power Electron. & Des.; 2011. p. 409–414.

[37] Almurib HAF, Kumar TN, Lombardi F. Inexact designs for approximate low power addition by cell replacement. In: 2016 Design, Automation Test in Europe Conference Exhibition (DATE); 2016. p. 660–665.

[38] Rehman S, El-Harouni W, Shafique M, *et al.* Architectural-space exploration of approximate multipliers. In: Proc. Int. Conf. Comput.-Aided Des.; 2016. p. 1–6.

[39] Chang L, Fried DM, Hergenrother J, *et al.* Stable SRAM cell design for the 32 nm node and beyond. In: VLSI Technology, 2005. Digest of Technical Papers. 2005 Symposium on. IEEE; 2005. p. 128–129.

[40] Verma AK, Brisk P, Icnne P. Variable latency speculative addition: A new paradigm for arithmetic circuit design. In: Proc. Des., Autom. Test Eur. Conf. Exhib.; 2008. p. 1250–1255.

[41] Zhu N, Goh WL, Yeo KS. An enhanced low-power high-speed adder for error-tolerant application. In: Proc. 12th Int. Symp. Integ. Circuits; 2009. p. 69–72.

[42] Ye R, Wang T, Yuan F, *et al.* On reconfiguration-oriented approximate adder design and its application. In: Proc. Int. Conf. Comput.-Aided Des.; 2013. p. 48–54.

[43] Hanif MA, Hafiz R, Hasan O, *et al.* QuAd: Design and analysis of quality-area optimal low-latency approximate adders. In: 2017 54th ACM/EDAC/IEEE Design Automation Conference (DAC); 2017. p. 1–6.

[44] Momeni A, Han J, Montuschi P, *et al.* Design and analysis of approximate compressors for multiplication. IEEE Transactions on Computers. 2015;64(4):984–994.

[45] Liang J, Han J, Lombardi F. New metrics for the reliability of approximate and probabilistic adders. IEEE Transactions on Computers. 2013;62(9): 1760–1771.

[46] Mazahir S, Hasan O, Hafiz R, *et al.* Probabilistic error modeling for approximate adders. IEEE Transactions on Computers. 2017;66(3): 515–530.

[47] Chan WTJ, Kahng A, Kang S, *et al.* Statistical analysis and modeling for error composition in approximate computation circuits. In: Proc. IEEE 31st Int. Conf. Comput. Des.; 2013. p. 47–53.

[48] Venkatesan R, Agarwal A, Roy K, *et al.* MACACO: Modeling and analysis of circuits for approximate computing. In: Proc. Int. Conf. Comput.-Aided Des.; 2011. p. 667–673.

[49]   Han J, Orshansky M. Approximate computing: An emerging paradigm for energy-efficient design. In: 18th IEEE Eur. Test Symp.; 2013. p. 1–6.

[50]   Liu C, Han J, Lombardi F. An analytical framework for evaluating the error characteristics of approximate adders. IEEE Transactions on Computers. 2015;64(5):1268–1281.

[51]   Sengupta D, Sapatnekar SS. FEMTO: Fast error analysis in multipliers through topological traversal. In: Proceedings of the IEEE/ACM International Conference on Computer-Aided Design. IEEE Press; 2015. p. 294–299.

[52]   Mazahir S, Hasan O, Hafiz R, *et al.* Probabilistic error analysis of approximate recursive multipliers. IEEE Transactions on Computers. 2017;66(11):1982–1990.

[53]   Lin CH, Lin C. High accuracy approximate multiplier with error correction. In: Proc. IEEE 31st Int. Conf. Comput. Des.; 2013. p. 33–38.

[54]   Mazahir S, Hasan O, Hafiz R, *et al.* An area-efficient consolidated configurable error correction for approximate hardware accelerators. In: Proc. IEEE/ACM 53rd Des. Autom. Conf.; 2016.

[55]   Mrazek V, Hrbacek R, Vasicek Z, *et al.* EvoApproxSb: Library of approximate adders and multipliers for circuit design and benchmarking of approximation methods. In: Design, Automation Test in Europe Conference Exhibition (DATE); 2017. p. 258–261.

[56]   Sze V, Budagavi M, Sullivan GJ. High efficiency video coding (HEVC). Integrated circuit and systems, algorithms and architectures. Springer; 2014. p. 1–375.

[57]   Shafique M, Bauer L, Henkel J. enBudget: A run-time adaptive predictive energy-budgeting scheme for energy-aware motion estimation in H. 264/MPEG-4 AVC video encoder. In: Design, Automation & Test in Europe Conference & Exhibition (DATE), 2010. IEEE; 2010. p. 1725–1730.

[58]   El-Harouni W, Rehman S, Prabakaran BS, *et al.* Embracing approximate computing for energy-efficient motion estimation in high efficiency video coding. In: Proceedings of the Conference on Design, Automation & Test in Europe. European Design and Automation Association; 2017. p. 1388–1393.

[59]   Moon Todd K. Error correction coding: Mathematical methods and algorithms. John Wiley & Sons; 2005. ISBN 0-471-64800-0.

[60]   Naseer R, Draper J. Parallel double error correcting code design to mitigate multi-bit upsets in SRAMs. In: Solid-State Circuits Conference, 2008. ESSCIRC 2008. 34th European. IEEE; 2008. p. 222–225.

Chapter 21

Many-core systems for big-data computing

Sam Ainsworth[1] and Timothy M. Jones[1]

In many ways, big data should be the poster-child of many-core computing. By necessity, such applications typically scale extremely well across machines, featuring high levels of thread-level parallelism. Programming techniques, such as Google's MapReduce [1], have allowed many applications running in the data centre to be programmed with parallelism directly in mind and have enabled extremely high throughput across machines.

However, it is fair to say that, as of 2017, many-core architectures have not set the world on fire in the data-centre space. Big-data applications are currently run on large arrays of servers based on commodity multicore architectures: scale-out techniques are applied to achieve the necessary throughput, and yet scale-up, with many cores on a single machine, has been left relatively unexploited. That said, the ever-present need to achieve exascale computing power as a result of the exponentially increasing computational demands modern internet systems require, means that the energy efficiency potential offered by many-core architectures cannot be ignored. Data centres consume 2 per cent of the USA's energy production [2], and modern systems are thermally limited; thus energy consumption is now a first-order design constraint, not least due to the cost of power and cooling infrastructure. Current out-of-order superscalar architectures are several orders of magnitude less efficient than the smallest in-order cores, so if parallelism can be exploited, as it typically can in big-data workloads, the potential for improvements cannot be overstated.

Here we explore the state-of-the-art in terms of techniques used to make many-core architectures work for big-data workloads. We explore how tail-latency concerns mean that even though workloads are parallel, high performance is still necessary in at least some parts of the system. We take a look at how memory-system issues can cause some big-data applications to scale less favourably than we would like for many-core architectures. We examine the programming models used for big-data workloads and consider how these both help and hinder the typically complex mapping seen elsewhere for many-core architectures. And we also take a look at the alternatives to traditional many-core systems in exploiting parallelism for efficiency in the big-data space.

We believe that, despite current roadblocks due to the price-sensitivity gains from using commodity hardware and tail-latency concerns of small cores, the efficiency

[1]Department of Computer Science and Technology, University of Cambridge, United Kingdom

gains from increased parallelism make many-core architectures an inevitability in the big-data space. The question is simply when, and in what form. We believe that highly heterogeneous systems, with a combination of logic types, specialised units such as graphics processing units (GPUs), video encoding and memory management, along with many traditional cores in the same system, at different trade-offs in terms of single-core performance and power efficiency, are the only way to match the wide heterogeneity in demands from the space of workloads required to perform on such systems.

21.1 Workload characteristics

Numerous studies of big-data applications, and how they interact with current micro-architectures, have been performed. Wang *et al.* [3] provide a series of observations as a result of BigDataBench, their benchmark suite representing a variety of real-world big-data workloads. The most notable of these are related to the memory system. First, the last-level cache, the largest on-chip memory, is unnecessarily large for the types of applications typically processing big data. This is unsurprising, as the volume of data such applications typically work with is many times larger than that can be stored on-chip. Given the high percentage of the chip area devoted to the last level cache in commodity processors, their use in these systems is clearly inefficient.

Second, the L1 instruction cache is not big enough: the working set of instructions is typically larger than that we can fit in the smallest cache. Kanev *et al.*'s work on profiling warehouse-scale machines corroborates both of these findings about cache sizes [4]. Ferdman *et al.* also observe a similar result [5] and note that for their target workloads, instruction-level parallelism within threads is low.

These studies tend to show an unsurprising trend for big-data applications. The number of memory accesses relative to the amount of actual computation performed in the core is very large. This is important, as it means that even when thread-level parallelism is abundant, communication may dominate computation.

Data-centre workloads, as seen by the processor, often feature multiple levels of parallelism. In addition to parallelism within each program, multiple tasks or processes tend to run concurrently, constituting a coarser granularity of parallelism from that within the applications. Often, multiple copies of the same process execute on a given system at once, for example when multiple users run the same server applications. This property of the workloads is also available for exploitation: we can schedule collaboratively, such as that proposed by Tang *et al.* [6], and research has also considered drafting identical instruction sequences from different threads to reuse resources [7].

However, this homogeneity observed as a result of running multiple copies of the same program has to be contrasted with the pervasive heterogeneity in the full application space. Workloads on big data, and the cloud-based servers which tend to run them, can differ very strongly. For example, while Ferdman *et al.* see very little instruction-level parallelism in the workloads they target [5], much more is observable in web search [8], and thus large cores that are able to exploit this are useful.

Kanev *et al.* show that, for warehouse-scale computer applications, around 30 per cent of compute time is spent on software blocks common to many different applications, whereas the other 70 per cent is relatively diverse [4]. This wide heterogeneity in performance characteristics between different workloads suggests that no one-size-fits-all approach will be optimal for the entire space of big-data applications.

Though these workloads are typically parallel, effective work-splitting and scheduling can cause issues with tail latency [9]: the smaller the chunks a workload is split into, the more likely one will take an inordinate amount of time. More generally, latency, rather than just throughput, is important when applications are user-facing [10].

21.2   Many-core architectures for big data

In response to both the opportunities of parallelism presented by big-data workloads, along with the challenges caused by the level of heterogeneity and the importance of tail latency within these workloads, we now consider how well many-core architectures are suited to their execution.

21.2.1   The need for many-core

Energy consumption is now the limiting factor in computation at every scale. The failure of Dennard scaling [11] in the early 2000s means that thermal density in transistors has skyrocketed, and thus, even if a system is not directly power-limited by being run on a battery, an inability to cool, or afford to power, becomes the limiting factor. It is the latter which is most important in the data centre: with energy being between 25 and 60 per cent of the cost of running a facility [12], the less energy used, the more computation can be performed.

To achieve energy efficiency we wish to increase the rate of computation but execute at a lower clock frequency. One way to do this is using many cores: a small microcontroller, such as an Arm Cortex-M0+, can be many orders of magnitude more energy efficient per operation than larger cores designed for high performance [13]. These bigger, out-of-order superscalar cores require a large amount of hardware to support highly speculative, dynamically reordered, parallel execution of dependent instructions, and this speculation, when inaccurate, causes much of the work performed by such a processor to be thrown away. In addition, sophisticated techniques employed by designers to extract performance in high-end processors often compromise on energy-efficiency [14]. In comparison, a smaller, simpler processor can spend more of its hardware logic on doing the computation itself and, by avoiding speculation, can be extremely efficient [15]. Using many small cores, we can perform the same computation in the same amount of time with much lower energy cost.

However, there is a large caveat here. The workload needs to feature inherent parallelism, otherwise the serialisation overhead will outweigh the benefits of splitting the work. Fortunately, many big-data workloads are designed to distribute well across many machines: application programming interfaces (APIs) such as MapReduce [1] are prolific in this space, and thus work is naturally split into parallel units.

21.2.2 Brawny vs wimpy cores

This might lead one to conclude, then, that the most efficient architecture for big-data workloads is an array of extremely tiny cores, each with very low performance, but with a high throughput as a sum of their total contribution. However, as of 2017, this is not the architecture of choice for typical users of such systems. Work on evaluating the use of so-called wimpy cores instead of more conventional, large brawny cores suggests that the bigger cores tend to run data centre applications more successfully, unless the small cores are still large enough to reach half the performance of a more conventional core [9].

There are numerous reasons for this. Just because a workload 'scales out' to multiple distributed nodes does not necessarily mean it will 'scale up' to many cores on the same system, and vice versa. Amdahl's law is important in the application of parallelism [16]: in many-core systems, when even a small fraction of a program is sequential, this fraction quickly dominates. In addition, even throughput-oriented applications may still be latency sensitive [10,17].

Still, that does not necessarily mean that the way forward is simply to use high-performance cores and accept their inefficiencies. Instead, the best way forward is likely to be heterogeneity: run the parallel fractions of workloads on smaller cores, and those which are sequential or latency-sensitive on larger cores, all within the same system. Indeed, a re-evaluation of the 'brawny vs wimpy' concept in this context shows significant improvements over conventional systems, by combining out-of-order superscalar Xeon cores with much smaller, in-order atoms on the same system [18].

21.2.3 Scale-out processors

Given the inefficiencies of commodity processors, there has been research seeking to design cores specifically for scale-out big-data workloads [19,20]. The result is a many-core design and, as we observed in the previous section, due to the lack of utilisation, the last level cache is reduced in size significantly compared with conventional processors. This cache is used more for instructions than data. Whether the optimal choice is to use extremely small in-order cores, or moderately complex out-of-order cores with a limited amount of reordering, depends on how latency tolerant the workload is [21]. For workloads with high quality-of-service requirements, the ability of more complicated cores to extract instruction-level parallelism is necessary for the performance level required. Indeed, if we look to commercial systems, it is notable that later generations of Xeon Phi processors have switched away from theoretically more efficient in-order designs to small out-of-order superscalar cores [22]. Still, for some workloads, tiny in-order cores really are the best choice [23], which reflects the heterogeneity of the workload space.

One area where many-core systems struggle is with interconnect, and this is particularly true of big-data workloads, due to their large amount of communication relative to computation. Shared memory does not scale well to many-core systems [24–26]. Still, big-data workloads have long been written for distributed environments [1], where the assumption of shared memory is not given. This means that for a scale-out processor [20], a good system organisation is in fact to have multiple 'pods' on the same piece of silicon, which are, effectively, separate many-core devices each running their own operating system. This improves the scalability of interconnect and, whilst it may be a poor choice for workload domains with more shared memory reliance, it is well suited to the programming models used in big data.

Once more, there is no one-size-fits-all approach. Not all big-data workloads scale well across multiple independent systems: graph workloads, for example, feature a high amount of unpredictable communication. In fact, it is often in these cases that many-core architectures can be particularly helpful since the many-core approach enables us to increase single-system performance to a level where we can avoid inter-machine interconnect altogether. Mosaic [27] is an example of such an approach, for processing large graphs on a Xeon Phi system.

21.2.4 Barriers to implementation

As we have seen, many-core architectures are efficient, which is extremely important for throughput computing, big-data workloads are typically highly parallel, and architectures specifically targeted towards such applications have been designed. So why is the data centre still dominated by commodity hardware?

One reason is outlay cost. Commodity hardware is comparatively cheap to buy, as design cost is amortised amongst many customers, and to overcome this barrier a specialised design must be significantly more energy efficient so as to reduce lifetime costs. The programming frameworks in use, though supporting of parallelism, are designed to facilitate this across many conventional system nodes, rather than single-chip many-core designs, and thus the entire ecosystem may need to change to make many-core systems appealing. If, to effectively program a many-core system, businesses have to stop targeting their existing commodity data centres and focus on a different system, then take-up will inevitably be low.

Another issue is programming complexity. The move to many-core means parallelism is a first-order design constraint in the writing of every program. This is already the case for distributed frameworks, so this is less of an issue in big data when compared with other domains but can still cause many issues for the throughput of programs not written in such frameworks. Programs optimised for distributed large cores may often need to be significantly rearchitected to be efficient on many-core designs. This means programmer time also has to be factored into the cost metric: is it really a cost saving if, instead of a high-energy bill, a company needs to double their programmer head count, and double the amount of training they need?

Even when programs are designed specifically with parallelism in mind, efficient targeting of a particular system still brings with it a series of complications that are exacerbated by the move to many-core systems, and even further when heterogeneity is considered. What is the correct number of threads to scale across, to get optimal throughput without giving in to serialisation overheads, for a given program? Which threads should be run on which size of core, and which tasks should be offloaded to which specialised accelerators, such as GPUs? Automatically targeting such systems, even when the parallelism properties of code are well known, is still an open research question [28–30].

Tail latency, as mentioned earlier, can also be a critical performance issue. Even with highly parallel programming frameworks, the inability to split work evenly can cause significant inefficiency when having to wait for the last task to finish, and this is exacerbated by increasing the number of tasks work is split into. Even when work splits well, throughput may not be the only important metric: for end-user applications, latency can be a significant factor in the value of a service. For example, for Yahoo! search, even a small increase in latency has been shown to detrimentally affect user behaviour significantly [10,17]. This means that while it may be energy efficient to use small cores, that the task will be completed more quickly on bigger cores is a big argument in their favour. Unless increased parallelism can be used to bring about better response times, big cores are here to stay for many workloads.

21.3   The memory system

The key property of big-data workloads is the amount of data they access; hence it is necessary to discuss how this affects the architecture in detail. For typical systems, memory latency is high, and yet a high throughput is required in order to feed cores with data.

21.3.1   Caching and prefetching

The data in typical big-data workloads far exceeds the size of the fast cache memories stored close to the processor [3–5]. This has an impact on the size of last level cache that is required [20]. While more conventional workloads require large last level caches to fit their entire working sets, this is impossible to achieve for big-data workloads, and thus moderately sized last level caches are more suitable to reduce silicon area and power overheads. Data must instead come from slower, higher latency memories, such as off-chip random access main memory (RAM), solid-state discs, magnetic discs or a network. In order to keep a single processor busy, let alone many cores, we need an efficient way of accessing this data, and overlapping the memory accesses to hide the latency of each individual, slow access.

One method of hiding this latency is exploiting spatial locality: data nearby recently accessed data is itself likely to be accessed. For example, modern systems bring data into local cache memories in cache lines: multiple adjacent words are brought in when any of them is accessed from main memory. In addition, modern systems feature stride prefetchers [31,32] that learn the access patterns of programs dynamically to pick up regular stride accesses (typically either sequential or those at constant stride, such as from 2D matrix walking) and start loading them before the program requires them to hide latency. This works very well for many big-data applications, which are often designed on frameworks based around accessing data in sequence [1]. Similarly, GPUs have started to feature increasingly elaborate data-streaming mechanisms [33].

Of course, not all big-data workloads feature such ideal memory access patterns. When the data accesses of programs become more irregular and unpredictable, because of arrays of indices or pointers, or linked data structures, for example, latency becomes a bigger issue. Processor resources rapidly become heavily underutilised as cores are starved of data, and communication delays can make many-core applications scale poorly. In the big-data context, this is most apparent in database [34] and graph applications. For the latter, it can be the case that they perform so poorly on big-data frameworks that it is more beneficial to run them on a single core of a laptop [35]. Techniques to mitigate the latency overheads in these more complicated scenarios range from domain-specific hardware support for prefetching and data loading [34,36–38], compiler techniques [39] and software runtimes [40], depending on where the data is stored, the specific access pattern and performance requirements.

However, it is not only on the data side that big-data applications struggle with memory access. Perhaps more surprisingly, big-data applications often include complicated control flow, with a very large working set of instructions. More advanced instruction prefetching [41,42] has been proposed to mitigate this, and we should expect relatively large instruction caches even with cores that are otherwise smaller than those in conventional systems [20].

21.3.2 Near-data processing

A renaissance in near-data processing [43] has recently come about. The idea in this paradigm is to avoid expensive data movement and instead move the computation closer to the data it acts upon. This is particularly important for big-data workloads because of the high data to computation ratios. A traditional blocker of this has been physical: silicon optimised for compute works very poorly on silicon optimised for main memory dynamic random-access memory (DRAM), and vice versa. However, a big driver in near-data processing is the increased practicality of stacked silicon: by layering memory on top of compute silicon, we can have a large number of cheap, high bandwidth, low latency, low-energy connections between the two. Indeed, we can have many alternating layers of compute and memory silicon and perform the computation on whichever layer is closest to the memory we need to access. The caveat here is that we need predictable memory accesses such that we can store data near to the computation which will use it, which is not the case for all applications (particularly graph workloads [40]), but it is certainly the case that for many workloads a large energy efficiency improvement can be realised as a result of near-memory techniques.

21.3.3 Non-volatile memories

A related important technology, which may make many-core systems more viable, is the progress towards practical new non-volatile memory technologies, with similar speed to DRAM, low-energy usage, due to the lack of a need to refresh or keep powered, and the ability to integrate well with compute silicon. This relates to near-data processing, in that if we can have storage which is persistent and spread throughout a system, we can work on data where it is stored, without moving it around, gaining significant energy efficiency benefits. Examples include phase change memory [44], spin-transfer torque RAM [45], resistive random-access memory (ReRAM) and 3D Xpoint. However, at present these all feature significant performance, cost and/or energy disadvantages relative to conventional DRAM.

21.3.4   Memory coherence

Memory coherence can be a killer of scalability in many-core architectures. The intuitive shared-memory structures of multicore processors, where all cores share a unified, coherent view of main memory, scales very poorly [24–26], as each private cache of each core needs to be kept up to date, and the alternative, message passing, works well for distributed systems but can make data sharing needlessly expensive on a single system.

Many different techniques have been implemented, and many alternative schemes proposed. Hoffman *et al.* [24] present remote store programming, where it is possible to write to, but not read from, remote memories. Fensch and Cintra [25] reduce overheads by mapping pages to only one cache at a time. Fu *et al.* [26] restrict coherence to programmable subsets of an entire core. Zhang *et al.* [46] introduce commutative memory operations, where instead of bringing data into a cache, reading it, then writing it, operations such as increment are implemented within the memory to improve scalability.

Again, we see a situation where there is no one-size-fits-all approach. It is likely that we will see architectures which allow varying consistency models depending on the level of sharing, and the level of consistency, required by the application.

21.3.5   On-chip networks

It is not just the performance of each core, or the memory technology, that affects how well a system scales. There is a trade-off between communication, energy and chip area in terms of on-chip interconnects. The crossbars used for multicores, with all-to-all connections, scale too poorly to be appropriate for many-core architectures. Ring networks, while efficient and low area, enforce very strict concurrency properties. More modern network-on-chip architectures, with dedicated routing subsystems, allow various trade-offs in topology and area usage.

Tiled architectures scale relatively well to many-core systems. Here, each core is connected to every adjacent core, reducing wiring compared to a crossbar. However, when communication is not localised, the significant hop counts that are necessary in this design reduce performance significantly. In the 'pod' design from Lotfi-Kamran *et al.* [20] that was discussed earlier, the authors argue that, since shared memory is not often necessary for scale-out workloads, a better topology than tiles for such workloads is to connect pods internally by a crossbar, but with off-chip-style interconnect between each pod.

21.4   Programming models

The key to good performance, both in big-data workloads and many-core architectures, is the programming model. As big-data workloads have had to deal with distribution across computers for so long, the programming models typically used are designed with parallelism as a core feature. The most notorious of these is MapReduce [1]. MapReduce is a highly parallel, distributed programming methodology, based on using a Map operation, applied in parallel to a list of key value pairs, the results of which are then sorted by key and sent to a Reduce operation, which aggregates values of the same key. This is clearly a very limited paradigm designed to enforce parallelism, but it has been applied successfully in a wide range of contexts. To get around the limitations of MapReduce, frameworks that take data layout into account have also been developed, such as Spark [47] and Pregel [48]. OpenMP [49] and MPI [50] are lower level, more general purpose frameworks, designed for shared memory and message passing systems, respectively.

More domain-specific programming models also exist. TensorFlow [51,52], Google's machine learning library for heterogeneous systems, based on dataflow graphs, has revolutionised the use of neural networks. A variety of specialised frameworks designed primarily for graph processing exist, based on a variety of abstractions, such as Naiad [53], GraphX [54] and Pregel [48].

To allow big-data programming frameworks to distribute, they are often built on top of key-value stores. Examples of these include Amazon's Dynamo [55] and Google's BigTable [56]. While the key-value abstraction does help with achieving parallelism, it is important to note that this is primarily to allow distribution across many systems, rather than for high performance with many cores on a single machine. Indeed, many big-data frameworks perform poorly in a local setting. The programming model limitations and data abstractions, which allow large files to be split across many machines, typically add significant overhead, often to the point that processing the same data on a single core can be faster [35]. Still, systems designed around many-core architectures, rather than distribution, have had significant success [27].

Despite the existence of frameworks to ease the difficulty, it remains true that writing programs for parallel systems is fundamentally a complex problem. Satish *et al.* [57] describe the 'ninja performance gap' between those able to exploit the full potential of efficient parallel computing and everyone else working on performance-intensive programs. It is highly unlikely that many-core architectures will be widely adopted unless the majority of workloads benefit, and thus easy programmability is key. Still, the analysis of a set of throughput-oriented workloads by Satish *et al.* [57] suggests that in many cases, a small set of algorithmic transformations, along with OpenMP pragmas and vectorisation hints, is enough to get relatively high performance out of multicore and many-core systems. Whether this is simple enough to allow high performance for mainstream users, however, is unclear. Indeed, this is one of the barriers Hölzle [9] uses to explain Google's continued use of large cores.

21.5 Case studies

A number of many-core architectures have been released in the commercial domain. Here, we evaluate the design parameters of several, their applicability to big-data applications and their successes and failures.

21.5.1   Xeon Phi

The Xeon Phi series is a family of many-core processors by Intel. These can either be the main processor for a system, or sit in the PCIe slot as an accelerator, in complement to a more traditional processor with larger individual cores, such as a Xeon, giving heterogeneity in the types of core available.

The first generation Xeon Phi features approximately 60 in-order cores, depending on model, with wide vector extensions. Interestingly, however, more recent generations feature small out-of-order superscalar CPUs, containing much more speculation. These relatively larger cores are theoretically more energy inefficient due to the structures used to support them, and the number of instructions thrown away due to incorrect speculation. So why did Intel make the switch? It is likely because the target workloads on such systems do feature a relatively large amount of instruction-level parallelism which was left on the table by the smaller cores, and that single-threaded performance is still important for many of the target workloads. This is a similar observation made previously for brawny vs wimpy cores with respect to throughput workloads [9,58].

As well as being many core, the latest generation Xeon Phi also features 512-bit wide vector instructions. This perhaps reflects the idea that many-core alone is not the best way to gain performance and power efficiency: the ability to execute the same instruction on lots of data, thus reducing processor frontend energy consumption, is also important.

Xeon Phi cores have been targeted towards big-data workloads, with some success. Lu *et al.* [59] optimise MapReduce for the system, making particular use of the vector hardware. Xie *et al.* [60] evaluate a variety of data analytics workloads on a Xeon Phi, in many cases beating a more conventional Xeon processor significantly in terms of performance. Maass *et al.* [27] use Xeon Phis as coprocessors in a heterogeneous system to create a single system with enough compute power to process very large graphs.

21.5.2   Tilera

Tilera (now part of Mellanox) designed a variety of many-core processors, with an emphasis on the on-chip network. Each core was a comparatively weak, in-order, superscalar, very long instruction word setup, which allowed them to be very small and low power. These were arranged as tiles, where each tile featured a core, cache and on-chip network router.

Tilera did try to target big-data workloads [61]. However, as of 2017, current Tile-Gx72 processors are targeted more towards networking and video transcoding [62]. It is notable that while the former is latency sensitive, it is highly task-parallel, and thus less likely to see performance issues from Amdahl's law than analytics workloads. Indeed, Quan *et al.*'s work on benchmarking BigDataBench [63] suggests that the Tilera approach can work well when the workload is IO bound: this perhaps reflects the emphasis on network topology. However, the relative weakness of the CPUs makes compute-bound big-data workloads perform poorly.

21.5.3   Piranha

Piranha was the first chip multiprocessor for commercial server workloads that featured several simple cores [64]. It was based around eight slow, in-order cores, and was particularly targeted towards online transaction processing, a subset of the entire big-data space. The performance improvement for this workload was significant compared with conventional out-of-order superscalar cores of the time, and yet it never made it to market.

Why is this? It is likely that it was simply ahead of its time. In 2000, Dennard scaling had not yet failed, and thus transistor power was scaling nicely between each generation. It was not particularly clear that single-threaded performance was not going to continue to scale indefinitely, and thus a switch to parallel programming would perhaps have been seen as not worth the effort.

21.5.4   Niagara

By comparison, Sun's Niagara project [65], a similar system, did make it to market, as the UltraSPARC T1. This was also targeted at throughput, in particular database computing, and also featured eight in-order cores. Notably, each core was multithreaded with up to four threads sharing the same hardware resources. This is particularly useful when, as is the case with databases, the workload is memory bound, since compute resources go underutilised, and thus it makes sense to share them between multiple threads.

However, perhaps more interesting is the direction in which this architecture evolved. While eight cores may have been a large number in 2005 when the Ultra-SPARC T1 came out, the SPARC T5 [66] in 2013 only increased this to 16 cores: a comparatively more conservative figure. These cores were moderately large out-of-order superscalar cores, featuring a very large number of threads per core, with 8-way multithreading. Although this could suggest that many-core is in fact a poor fit for big-data workloads, it is more likely explained by the target workload of databases. Because they are so memory bound, having single cores supporting many threads is a good fit, as it avoids wasting compute resources. For more compute-bound parallel workloads, actually having many true cores, such as on a Xeon Phi, may make more sense. Indeed, the latest SPARC M8 processors [67] feature 32 cores, with eight threads per core, in a wide out-of-order superscalar architecture, along with specialised database acceleration units. This suggests more modern general throughput workloads really do need the extra compute gained from many-core architectures.

21.5.5   Adapteva

Adapteva designed Epiphany: a many-core architecture particularly targeted at energy-efficient floating point operations. One of its target applications was big data.

Rather than caches, and the coherency mechanisms necessary to support shared memory, Adapteva went with a different setup. All memory was accessed through programmer-controlled scratch memory: fast on-chip storage managed by hand (or the compiler), as opposed to implicit caching. This meant that communication occurred through message passing between cores, rather than sharing data. This is a solution that is very scalable for a many-core architecture; however, it is extremely difficult to program. Another interesting property was that the cores were out-of-order, and thus certainly not the smallest possible.

Perhaps one of the reasons this architecture failed to gain traction was that, even though it was energy efficient, it simply was not powerful enough for the target market. By contrast to the Xeon Phi, which is many-core but at a similar power budget to processors based on large cores, the products released by Adapteva were more mobile focused. In addition, if we compare to other more successful architectures, the lack of shared memory support is likely a killer: difficult to program architectures rarely gain traction.

21.5.6   TOP500 and GREEN500

Though they are not aimed at big-data workloads, the success of many-core architectures in supercomputing is illuminating. The TOP500 list [68], based on performance for LINPACK, a floating point benchmark, is dominated by architectures with many small cores, as of June 2017. This reflects the high throughput that it is possible to achieve with such designs. The top machine, the Sunway TaihuLight, is based around a set of 260-core 64-bit RISC processors.

However, the GREEN500, based on performance per watt for the same benchmark, is instead dominated by machines based on GPU architectures. This reflects the specific targeting of GPUs towards efficient floating point operations. Note though that the same result may not extend to big-data workloads: these tend to be much more integer and control-flow intensive than LINPACK.

21.6   Other approaches to high-performance big data

There are many ways to extract performance and parallelism in terms of system architecture, other than a many-core approach. Here, we consider each of the most common, in terms of their applicability to big-data workloads.

21.6.1   Field-programmable gate arrays

Field-programmable gate arrays (FPGAs) are blocks of silicon, which use programmable SRAM blocks and wiring to implement custom logic, along with some fixed function hardware such as multiplier units and digital signal processors. This is typically many times slower and less power efficient than a counterpart implemented in fixed function silicon. However, by designing a custom circuit specifically adapted to the task at hand, it can be possible to achieve much higher performance than using more conventional processors, by virtue of specialisation. This relies on high amounts of parallelism in the task to overcome the slow clock rates achievable on such devices. FPGAs can either be used to implement complete systems, or as accelerators attached to a more conventional processor setup.

The real success story for big-data workloads in terms of FPGAs is Bing search. 'Project Catapult' [69,70] uses FPGAs as accelerators in Microsoft data centres to improve latency and server requirements for search applications. FPGAs can also work well for neural network applications [71], where parallelism can be exploited for high efficiency.

While FPGAs are inefficient compared to custom application-specific integrated circuits, it is likely they are more applicable for big-data workloads due to the propensity of such workloads to change over time, yet we have not seen the success in limited application domains being replicated elsewhere. This is likely for a number of reasons. FPGAs are much harder to program than many-core systems: conventional programming languages are off the table, sequential performance is inadequate, existing codebases cannot be easily targeted to FPGA, and workloads with a large instruction variety are a poor fit for programmable logic. Still, the potential in certain applications for FPGAs suggests that they are not going away any time soon.

21.6.2 Vector processing

The thread-level parallelism that many-core designs seek to exploit is not the only form of parallelism around. Indeed, exploiting data-level parallelism, in the form of vector processing, was the mainstay for supercomputer performance throughout the 1970s, 1980s and early 1990s. This form of parallelism executes a single instruction on a vector of data, rather than individual scalar values, and realises extremely energy-efficient general-purpose computation by amortising the cost of instruction fetch and decode across a number of data items. Although the use of dedicated vector processors has declined, modern general purpose computer architectures now contain support for short vector computation in the form of SIMD instructions (single-instruction, multiple-data). These include AVX from Intel, SVE from Arm and AltiVec from IBM. Although early machines used vector processing as a form of latency hiding, modern architectures tend to process the whole vector at once, resulting in significant performance benefits. Many GPUs also take advantage of a form of wide vector processing, so-called SIMT (single instruction, multiple threads), which, combined with fine-grained multithreading, brings massive throughput to the architecture.

Big-data applications often involve doing the same operation on lots of data: indeed, the Map part of MapReduce is based on such an operation. Vector processing is therefore well suited to big data and programmers can realise huge speedups from their codes by using SIMD instructions within the most critical loops of their application. Modern compilers all have support for automatic vectorisation of code, allowing programmers to take advantage of these architectures simply by setting the correct options to the toolchain. For more complex kernels or where the developer can use her own knowledge of the code to optimise the design, compiler intrinsics are provided to expose vector operations directly in the source.

21.6.3 Accelerators

Fixed function accelerators, designed for a small range of tasks and with limited programmability, tend to be extremely efficient for the workloads they target. In the mobile domain, hardware video encoding and decoding has reduced the energy cost of those tasks by around $500\times$ [72]. In terms of workloads considered to be 'big data', a recent success story has been Google's Tensor Processing Units [73], designed to accelerate deep neural network inference in the data centre.

Where applicable, the performance and energy efficiency improvements are so drastic that it seems impossible to ignore their utility in big-data applications. However, the space of big-data applications is complex, diverse and continuously evolving. That means that, in general, it is a difficult and moving target for fixed function hardware, which is inflexible, and slow and expensive to design. The large instruction footprint of big-data workloads [3–5,41] suggests that there is a high variety in performance critical stages of such programs, meaning a small set of accelerators is unlikely to cover all desired parts of many individual workloads, let alone many different applications. It follows then that, in many domains, something with more programmability, as with many-core architectures, is inescapable.

21.6.4 Graphics processing units

In some sense, GPUs can themselves be viewed as a form of many-core processing. It is true that they exploit large amounts of thread-level parallelism. However, they differ from a more conventional many-core CPU system in how they extract this. Groups of threads are executed together within a 'warp' on the GPU, where each thread executes the same code, which is really a form of data-level parallelism (see vector processors in Section 21.6.2). Different warps are then allowed to execute entirely separate code, with multiple warps sharing a processor.

This setup, which is more rigid than that of a many-core system, allows GPUs to be extremely efficient at many workloads, and the structure of many big-data workloads allows them to fit to GPUs very well. Indeed, the use of GPUs for training [74,75] in machine learning has been a huge driver of the ubiquity of deep neural networks in recent years. This has even caused the introduction of features into GPUs targeted at improving deep learning performance, such as short floating point words.

As for some workloads, GPUs are incredibly efficient, we should expect to see their use in big-data systems even with the increased proliferation of many-core architectures. But arguably a GPU is just another heterogeneous core in such a setup: we should not expect every processor to be identical within a big-data system, if only down to the heterogeneity in workloads.

21.7 Conclusion and future directions

Big data seems like the obvious target for many-core architectures. It is the poster-child of thread-level parallelism, and with 2 per cent of the USA's energy consumption in the data-centre [2], and 25–60 per cent of the cost of running a data centre coming from power [12], efficiency is critical.

The need for exascale computation is ever-more apparent, and the vast efficiency gains of many-core systems will be necessary to achieve the performance required.

But the complex, diverse, evolving performance requirements of these workloads complicate the necessary hardware. There are still many challenges in the uptake of many-core hardware for big-data workloads. Equivalently though, there are a wide variety of research directions that are likely to be fruitful.

21.7.1   Programming models

Current models [1,47,48] are still complicated, and though they support parallelism, this is typically for scale-out computation, and so the mapping is not yet ideal for many-core architectures. High-level models that do not introduce too much overhead for applications targeting many-core systems [27,35,49], while retaining ease-of-use, are likely to gain support. A caveat here is that there needs to be improvement in evaluations of how useful such models are to avoid poor implementation strategies from unrepresentative workloads [35].

21.7.2   Reducing manual effort

Automatically targeting complex many-core systems, even when the parallelism properties of code are well known, is still an open research question [28–30], particularly when such systems are heterogeneous. Similarly, more research is needed on schemes to extract performance from ordinary code [57], rather than just the most optimised workloads. Many-core systems are some of the most likely architectures to be able to benefit from assisted or automatic parallelisation techniques [76–78].

21.7.3   Suitable architectures and microarchitectures

Heterogeneity at the architectural level [18] is likely to be essential to meeting performance and energy targets for big data: backing up a small number of large cores with many small cores, along with fixed-function and increasingly diverse GPU-style accelerators, is the expected direction such hardware will take in the years to come. On the microarchitectural side, we have explored how current cores are inefficient for big-data workloads, and improvements to caches [41,42] and prefetching [34,36–38] are likely to help bridge latency and bandwidth gaps. More generally, specialised architectures such as scale-out processors [20] may be necessary, creating a distinction between the systems used for big data, and, for example, high-performance computing (HPC).

21.7.4   Memory-system advancements

New non-volatile memory technologies [44,45] are likely to introduce significant changes to big-data workloads, given their heavy use of memory, and modified coherence mechanisms [24–26,46] suitable for big-data architectures are still evolving.

21.7.5   Replacing commodity hardware

Commodity hardware is still a tempting deployment system, if only for its upfront cost, ease of programmability and low latency performance. A significant improvement in performance or energy usage must be demonstrable for more specialised many-core systems to gain a foothold in the market. Equivalently though, if other large markets adopt many-core architectures, their use is likely to trickle down into big data. We may also see this with other hardware improvements that would bring gains to big data processing, such as stacked silicon memory [43] moving into commodity hardware.

21.7.6   Latency

While throughput is typically the most important metric for big-data workloads, realtime expectations from end users means that this cannot be at the expense of latency [10,17,79]. Likewise, imperfect work splitting can result in tail-latency issues that directly impact throughput, causing performance to be higher on larger cores [9] where the work must be split less. Still, high latency is not a fundamental aspect of many-core computing: higher total compute resources may allow this to be reduced, provided the work is parallel. This problem can be targeted at multiple levels of the stack. Techniques to reduce tail latency at the software level through better splitting [80,81] may change workloads to make them better suited for many-core. Likewise, heterogeneous hardware can allow the slower parts of workloads to be run on faster processors while still gaining benefits for the more parallel segments [18].

21.7.7   Workload heterogeneity

Big-data workloads are fundamentally diverse [4]. This likely means that no one-size-fits-all approach is suitable for the entire set of big-data workloads, leading to hardware that becomes ever more diverse and complex. Managing this complexity at every level of the stack is critical for the wide deployment of good technological solutions to big-data processing.

Fundamentally, we believe that the efficiency and throughput gains attainable through the use of many-core systems are too tempting for these challenges not to be surmounted. The achievement of exascale computing depends on it.

References

[1]   Dean J, Ghemawat S. MapReduce: Simplified Data Processing on Large Clusters. In: Proceedings of the 6th USENIX Symposium on Operating Systems Design and Implementation. OSDI. San Francisco, CA, USA; 2004. p. 137–150.

[2]   Shehabi A, Smith SJ, Sartor DA, *et al.* United States Data Center Energy Usage Report; 2016.

[3]   Wang L, Zhan J, Luo C, *et al.* BigDataBench: A Big Data Benchmark Suite from Internet Services. In: Proceedings of the 20th International Symposium On High Performance Computer Architecture. HPCA. Orlando, FL, USA; 2014. p. 488–499.

[4]   Kanev S, Darago J, Hazelwood K, *et al.* Profiling a Warehouse-Scale Computer. In: Proceedings of the 42nd Annual International Symposium on Computer Architecture. ISCA. Portland, OR, USA; 2015. p. 158–169.

[5]   Ferdman M, Adileh A, Kocberber O, *et al.* Clearing the Clouds: A Study of Emerging Scale-out Workloads on Modern Hardware. In: Proceedings of the Seventeenth International Conference on Architectural Support for Programming Languages and Operating Systems. ASPLOS. London, UK; 2012. p. 37–48.

[6]   Tang L, Mars J, Vachharajani N, *et al.* The Impact of Memory Subsystem Resource Sharing on Datacenter Applications. In: Proceedings of the 38th Annual International Symposium on Computer Architecture. ISCA. San Jose, CA, USA; 2011. p. 283–294.

[7]   Mckeown M, Balkind J, Wentzlaff D. Execution Drafting: Energy Efficiency Through Computation Deduplication. In: Proceedings of the 47th Annual IEEE/ACM International Symposium on Microarchitecture. MICRO. Cambridge, UK; 2014. p. 432–444.

[8]   Janapa Reddi V, Lee BC, Chilimbi T, *et al.* Web Search Using Mobile Cores: Quantifying and Mitigating the Price of Efficiency. In: Proceedings of the 37th Annual International Symposium on Computer Architecture. ISCA. Saint-Malo, France; 2010. p. 314–325.

[9]   Hölzle U. Brawny Cores Still Beat Wimpy Cores, Most of the Time. IEEE Micro. 2010;30(4):23–24.

[10] Arapakis I, Bai X, Cambazoglu BB. Impact of Response Latency on User Behavior in Web Search. In: Proceedings of the 37th International ACM SIGIR Conference on Research & Development in Information Retrieval. ACM; 2014. p. 103–112.

[11] Esmaeilzadeh H, Blem E, St Amant R, *et al.* Dark Silicon and the End of Multicore Scaling. In: Proceedings of the 38th Annual International Symposium on Computer Architecture. ISCA. San Jose, CA, USA; 2011. p. 365–376.

[12] TechUK. Data Centres and Power: Fact or Fiction?; 2013. http://www.techuk.org/insights/reports/item/275-data-centres-and-power-fact-or-fiction.

[13] Barrett S. Cortex-M7 Launches: Embedded, IoT and Wearables; 2014. http:// www.anandtech.com/show/8542/cortexm7-launches-embedded-iot-and-wearables/2.

[14] Borkar S, Chien AA. The Future of Microprocessors. Commun ACM. 2011;54(5):67–77.

[15] Hameed R, Qadeer W, Wachs M, *et al.* Understanding Sources of Inefficiency in General-purpose Chips. In: Proceedings of the 37th Annual International Symposium on Computer Architecture. ISCA. Saint-Malo, France; 2010. p. 37–47.

[16] Hill MD, Marty MR. Amdahl's Law in the Multicore Era. Computer. 2008;41(7):33–38.

[17] Barreda-Ángeles M, Arapakis I, Bai X, *et al.* Unconscious Physiological Effects of Search Latency on Users and Their Click Behaviour. In: Proceedings of the 38th International ACM SIGIR Conference on Research and

Development in Information Retrieval. SIGIR'15. Santiago, Chile; 2015. p. 203–212.

[18] Gupta V, Schwan K. Brawny vs. Wimpy: Evaluation and Analysis of Modern Workloads on Heterogeneous Processors. In: Proceedings of the 2013 IEEE 27th International Symposium on Parallel and Distributed Processing Workshops and PhD Forum. IPDPSW. Boston, MA, USA; 2013. p. 74–83.

[19] Ferdman M, Adileh A, Kocberber O, et al. A Case for Specialized Processors for Scale-Out Workloads. IEEE Micro Top Picks. 2014;34(3):31–42.

[20] Lotfi-Kamran P, Grot B, Ferdman M, et al. Scale-out Processors. In: Proceedings of the 39th Annual International Symposium on Computer Architecture. ISCA. Portland, OR, USA; 2012. p. 500–511.

[21] Grot B, Hardy D, Lotfi-Kamran P, et al. Optimizing Data-Center TCO with Scale-Out Processors. IEEE Micro. 2012;32(5):52–63.

[22] Sodani A. Knights Landing (KNL): 2nd Generation Intel Xeon Phi Processor. In: 2015 IEEE Hot Chips 27 Symposium. HCS; 2015. p. 1–24.

[23] Lim K, Ranganathan P, Chang J, et al. Understanding and Designing New Server Architectures for Emerging Warehouse-Computing Environments. In: Proceedings of the 35th Annual International Symposium on Computer Architecture. ISCA. Beijing, China; 2008. p. 315–326.

[24] Hoffmann H, Wentzlaff D, Agarwal A. Remote Store Programming: A Memory Model for Embedded Multicore. In: Proceedings of the 5th International Conference on High Performance Embedded Architectures and Compilers. HiPEAC. Pisa, Italy; 2010. p. 3–17.

[25] Fensch C, Cintra M. An OS-based Alternative to Full Hardware Coherence on Tiled CMPs. In: Proceedings of the 14th International Symposium On High Performance Computer Architecture. HPCA. Salt Lake City, UT, USA; 2008. p. 355–366.

[26] Fu Y, Nguyen TM, Wentzlaff D. Coherence Domain Restriction on Large Scale Systems. In: Proceedings of the 48th International Symposium on Microarchitecture. MICRO. Waikiki, HI, USA; 2015. p. 686–698.

[27] Maass S, Min C, Kashyap S, et al. Mosaic: Processing a Trillion-Edge Graph on a Single Machine. In: Proceedings of the Twelfth European Conference on Computer Systems. EuroSys. Belgrade, Serbia; 2017. p. 527–543.

[28] Dalibard V, Schaarschmidt M, Yoneki E. BOAT: Building Auto-Tuners with Structured Bayesian Optimization. In: Proceedings of the 26th International Conference on World Wide Web. WWW. Perth, Australia; 2017. p. 479–488.

[29] Khan M, Basu P, Rudy G, et al. A Script-based Autotuning Compiler System to Generate High-performance CUDA Code. ACM Trans Archit Code Optim. 2013;9(4):31:1–31:25.

[30] Alipourfard O, Liu HH, Chen J. CherryPick: Adaptively Unearthing the Best Cloud Configurations for Big Data Analytics. In: 14th USENIX Symposium on Networked Systems Design and Implementation. NSDI. Boston, MA, USA; 2017. p. 469–482.

[31]   Viswanathan V. Disclosure of H/W Prefetcher Control on Some Intel Processors; 2014. https://software.intel.com/en-us/articles/disclosure-of-hw-prefetcher-control-on-some-intel-processors.

[32]   Chen TF, Baer JL. Reducing Memory Latency via Non-blocking and Prefetching Caches. In: Proceedings of the Fifth International Conference on Architectural Support for Programming Languages and Operating Systems. ASPLOS. Boston, MA, USA; 1992. p. 51–61.

[33]   Chisnall D. There's No Such Thing As a General-purpose Processor. Queue. 2014;12(10):20:20–20:25.

[34]   Kocberber O, Grot B, Picorel J, *et al.* In: Proceedings of the 46th Annual IEEE/ACM International Symposium on Microarchitecture. MICRO. Davis, CA, USA; 2013. p. 468–479.

[35]   McSherry F, Isard M, Murray DG. Scalability! But at What Cost?. In: Proceedings of the 15th USENIX Conference on Hot Topics in Operating Systems. HOTOS. Switzerland; 2015.

[36]   Ainsworth S, Jones TM. Graph Prefetching Using Data Structure Knowledge. In: Proceedings of the 2016 International Conference on Supercomputing. ICS. Istanbul, Turkey; 2016. p. 39:1–39:11.

[37]   Ainsworth S, Jones TM. An Event-Triggered Programmable Prefetcher for Irregular Workloads. In: Proceedings of the Twenty-Third International Conference on Architectural Support for Programming Languages and Operating Systems. ASPLOS. Williamsburg, VA, USA; 2018. p. 578–592.

[38]   Kumar S, Vedula N, Shriraman A, *et al.* DASX: Hardware Accelerator for Software Data Structures. In: Proceedings of the 29th ACM on International Conference on Supercomputing. ICS. Newport Beach, CA, USA; 2015. p. 361–372.

[39]   Ainsworth S, Jones TM. Software Prefetching for Indirect Memory Accesses. In: Proceedings of the 2017 International Symposium on Code Generation and Optimization. CGO. Austin, TX, USA; 2017. p. 305–317.

[40]   Nilakant K, Dalibard V, Roy A, *et al.* PrefEdge: SSD Prefetcher for Large-Scale Graph Traversal. In: Proceedings of International Conference on Systems and Storage. SYSTOR. Haifa, Israel; 2014. p. 4:1–4:12.

[41]   Kumar R, Huang CC, Grot B, *et al.* Boomerang: A Metadata-Free Architecture for Control Flow Delivery. In: Proceedings of the 23rd International Symposium On High Performance Computer Architecture. HPCA. Austin, TX, USA; 2017. p. 493–504.

[42]   Spracklen L, Chou Y, Abraham SG. Effective Instruction Prefetching in Chip Multiprocessors for Modern Commercial Applications. In: Proceedings of the 11th International Symposium On High Performance Computer Architecture. HPCA. San Francisco, CA, USA; 2005. p. 225–236.

[43]   Balasubramonian R, Chang J, Manning T, *et al.* Near-Data Processing: Insights from a MICRO-46 Workshop. IEEE Micro (Special Issue on Big Data). 2014;34(4):36–42.

[44] Lee BC, Ipek E, Mutlu O, *et al.* Architecting Phase Change Memory As a Scalable Dram Alternative. In: Proceedings of the 36th Annual International Symposium on Computer Architecture. ISCA. Austin, TX, USA; 2009. p. 2–13.

[45] Kültürsay E, Kandemir M, Sivasubramaniam A, *et al.* Evaluating STT-RAM as an Energy-Efficient Main Memory Alternative. In: 2013 IEEE International Symposium on Performance Analysis of Systems and Software (ISPASS); 2013. p. 256–267.

[46] Zhang G, Horn W, Sanchez D. Exploiting Commutativity to Reduce the Cost of Updates to Shared Data in Cache-coherent Systems. In: Proceedings of the 48th International Symposium on Microarchitecture. MICRO. Waikiki, HI, USA; 2015. p. 13–25.

[47] Zaharia M, Chowdhury M, Franklin MJ, *et al.* Spark: Cluster Computing with Working Sets. In: Proceedings of the 2nd USENIX Conference on Hot Topics in Cloud Computing. HotCloud. Boston, MA, USA; 2010.

[48] Malewicz G, Austern MH, Bik AJC, *et al.* Pregel: A System for Large-scale Graph Processing. In: Proceedings of the 2010 ACM SIGMOD International Conference on Management of Data. SIGMOD. Indianapolis, IN, USA; 2010. p. 135–146.

[49] Dagum L, Menon R. OpenMP: An Industry-Standard API for Shared-Memory Programming. IEEE Comput Sci Eng. 1998;5(1):46–55.

[50] Forum MP. MPI: A Message-Passing Interface Standard. Knoxville, TN, USA; 1994.

[51] Abadi M, Agarwal A, Barham P, *et al.* TensorFlow: Large-Scale Machine Learning on Heterogeneous Systems; 2015. Software available from tensorflow.org. Available from: http://tensorflow.org/.

[52] Abadi M, Barham P, Chen J, *et al.* TensorFlow: A System for Large-Scale Machine Learning. In: Proceedings of the 12th USENIX Symposium on Operating Systems Design and Implementation. OSDI. Savannah, GA, US; 2016. p. 265–284.

[53] Murray DG, McSherry F, Isaacs R, *et al.* Naiad: A Timely Dataflow System. In: Proceedings of the Twenty-Fourth ACM Symposium on Operating Systems Principles. SOSP. Farminton, PA, USA; 2013. p. 439–455.

[54] Gonzalez JE, Xin RS, Dave A, *et al.* GraphX: Graph Processing in a Distributed Dataflow Framework. In: Proceedings of the 11th USENIX Conference on Operating Systems Design and Implementation. OSDI. Broomfield, CO, USA; 2014. p. 599–613.

[55] DeCandia G, Hastorun D, Jampani M, *et al.* Dynamo: Amazon's Highly Available Key-value Store. In: Proceedings of Twenty-First ACM SIGOPS Symposium on Operating Systems Principles. SOSP. Stevenson, WA, USA; 2007. p. 205–220.

[56] Chang F, Dean J, Ghemawat S, *et al.* Bigtable: A Distributed Storage System for Structured Data. ACM Trans Comput Syst. 2008;26(2):4:1–4:26.

[57] Satish N, Kim C, Chhugani J, *et al.* Can Traditional Programming Bridge the Ninja Performance Gap for Parallel Computing Applications? Commun ACM. 2015;58(5):440–451.

[58] Liang X, Nguyen M, Che H. Wimpy or Brawny Cores: A Throughput Perspective. J Parallel Distrib Comput. 2013;73(10):1351–1361.

[59] Lu M, Liang Y, Huynh HP, *et al.* MrPhi: An Optimized MapReduce Framework on Intel Xeon Phi Coprocessors. IEEE Trans Parallel Distrib Syst. 2015;26(11):3066–3078.

[60] Xie B, Liu X, Zhan J, *et al.* Characterizing Data Analytics Workloads on Intel Xeon Phi. In: 2015 IEEE International Symposium on Workload Characterization; 2015. p. 114–115.

[61] Wheeler B. Tilera Sees Opening in Clouds; 2011. 7.

[62] Mellanox. TILE-Gx72 Processor; 2016. http://www.mellanox.com/related-docs/prod_multi_core/PB_TILE-Gx72.pdf.

[63] Quan J, Shi Y, Zhao M, *et al.* The Implications from Benchmarking Three Big Data Systems. In: 2013 IEEE International Conference on Big Data. BigData. Santa Clara, CA, USA; 2013. p. 31–38.

[64] Barroso LA, Gharachoroloo K, McNamara R, *et al.* Piranha: A Scalable Architecture Based on Single-Chip Multiprocessing. In: Proceedings of the 27th International Symposium on Computer Architecture. ISCA. Pittsburgh, PA, USA; 2000. p. 282–293.

[65] Kongetira P, Aingaran K, Olukotun K. Niagara: A 32-Way Multithreaded Sparc Processor. IEEE Micro. 2005;25(2):21–29.

[66] Turullols S, Sivaramakrishnan R. SPARC T5: 16-core CMT Processor with Glueless 1-Hop Scaling to 8-Sockets. In: 2012 IEEE Hot Chips 24 Symposium (HCS); 2012. p. 1–37.

[67] SPARC M8 Processor; 2017. http://www.oracle.com/us/products/servers-storage/sparc-m8-processor-ds-3864282.pdf.

[68] TOP500 Supercomputer Site; 2017. http://www.top500.org.

[69] Caulfield AM, Chung ES, Putnam A, *et al.* A Cloud-Scale Acceleration Architecture. In: Proceedings of the 49th Annual International Symposium on Microarchitecture. MICRO. Taipei, Taiwan; 2016. p. 1–13.

[70] Putnam A, Caulfield A, Chung E, *et al.* A Reconfigurable Fabric for Accelerating Large-Scale Datacenter Services. In: Proceedings of the 41st International Symposium on Computer Architecture. ISCA. Minneapolis, MN, USA; 2014. p. 13–24.

[71] Farabet C, LeCun Y, Kavukcuoglu K, *et al.* Large-scale FPGA-based convolutional networks. Scaling up Machine Learning: Parallel and Distributed Approaches. Cambridge University Press; 2011. p. 399–419.

[72] Venkatesh G, Sampson J, Goulding N, *et al.* Conservation Cores: Reducing the Energy of Mature Computations. In: Proceedings of the Fifteenth Edition of ASPLOS on Architectural Support for Programming Languages and Operating Systems. ASPLOS. Pittsburgh, PA, USA; 2010. p. 205–218.

[73] Jouppi NP, Young C, Patil N, *et al.* In-Datacenter Performance Analysis of a Tensor Processing Unit. In: Proceedings of the 44th Annual International Symposium on Computer Architecture. ISCA. Toronto, ON, Canada; 2017. p. 1–12.

[74] Raina R, Madhavan A, Ng AY. Large-scale Deep Unsupervised Learning Using Graphics Processors. In: Proceedings of the 26th Annual International

Conference on Machine Learning. ICML. Montreal, QC, Canada; 2009. p. 873–880.

[75]   Chen XW, Lin X. Big Data Deep Learning: Challenges and Perspectives. IEEE Access. 2014. p. 514–525.

[76]   Campanoni S, Jones T, Holloway G, *et al.* HELIX: Automatic Parallelization of Irregular Programs for Chip Multiprocessing. In: Proceedings of the Tenth International Symposium on Code Generation and Optimization. CGO. San Jose, California: ACM; 2012. p. 84–93.

[77]   Ginsbach P, Remmelg T, Steuwer M, *et al.* Automatic Matching of Legacy Code to Heterogeneous APIs: An Idiomatic Approach. In: Proceedings of the Twenty-Third International Conference on Architectural Support for Programming Languages and Operating Systems. ASPLOS. ACM; 2018. p. 139–153.

[78]   Ottoni G, Rangan R, Stoler A, *et al.* Automatic Thread Extraction with Decoupled Software Pipelining. In: Proceedings of the 38th Annual IEEE/ACM International Symposium on Microarchitecture. MICRO. Barcelona, Spain: IEEE; 2005. p. 105–118.

[79]   Barroso LA. Warehouse-Scale Computing: Entering the Teenage Decade. In: Proceedings of the 38th Annual International Symposium on Computer Architecture. ISCA. San Jose, California, USA; 2011.

[80]   Haque ME, Eom Yh, He Y, *et al.* Few-to-Many: Incremental Parallelism for Reducing Tail Latency in Interactive Services. In: Proceedings of the Twentieth International Conference on Architectural Support for Programming Languages and Operating Systems. ASPLOS. Istanbul, Turkey; 2015. p. 161–175.

[81]   Kaler T, He Y, Elnikety S. Optimal Reissue Policies for Reducing Tail Latency. In: Proceedings of the 29th ACM Symposium on Parallelism in Algorithms and Architectures. SPAA. Washington, DC, USA; 2017. p. 195–206.

Chapter 22

Biologically-inspired massively-parallel computing

Steve Furber[1]

Half a century of progress in computer technology has delivered machines of formidable capability and an expectation that similar advances will continue into the foreseeable future. However, much of the past progress has been driven by developments in semiconductor technology following Moore's Law, and there are strong grounds for believing that these cannot continue at the same rate. This, and related issues, suggest that there are huge challenges ahead in meeting the expectations of future progress, such as understanding how to exploit massive parallelism and how to deliver improvements in energy efficiency and reliability in the face of diminishing component reliability. Alongside these issues, recent advances in machine learning have created a demand for machines with cognitive capabilities, for example, to control autonomous vehicles, that we will struggle to deliver. Biological systems have, through evolution, found solutions to many of these problems, but we lack a fundamental understanding of how these solutions function. If we could advance our understanding of biological systems, we would open a rich source of ideas for unblocking progress in our engineered systems.

22.1 In the beginning...

The development of the modern computer can be traced back to the concept of the universal machine by Alan Turing in the 1930s to the first operational implementation of Turing's idea in the Manchester 'Baby' machine, which ran the world's first successful program on 21 June 1948. Since then there has been relentless progress in making machines faster, smaller, and more efficient. The Baby machine used valve (vacuum tube) technology, but this was rapidly replaced by early transistors, and then since the 1960s, integrated circuits have dominated the design of machines. In 1965, Gordon Moore published his seminal paper [1] observing the exponential growth that was taking place in the number of transistors that could be manufactured on a single chip, and this was adapted into an industry roadmap (the Industry Technology Roadmap

[1]School of Computer Science, The University of Manchester, UK

for Semiconductors) that has carried the base technology of computers forward for half a century and delivered the pervasive digital technology that we see around us today.

Moore's Law has been delivered principally by making transistors smaller. As transistors are made smaller, they become cheaper, faster, and more energy efficient – a win–win scenario that is only partly compromised by some of the other exponential trends in the industry, such as the cost of designing the integrated circuit and the cost of building a manufacturing facility to make the resulting microchip. But clearly, there must be limits to how small a transistor can be made. One such limit, which was of great concern in the 1990s, was the wavelength of the light used in the lithographic processes used to manufacture the chip, but this limit was swept aside with advances such as solving the inverse problem required to view the lithography masks as diffraction gratings, multiple exposures, and such like. Chips are now routinely manufactured with features whose size is a small fraction of the wavelength of the light used to draw them. However, one limit that is unlikely to be so easily swept aside is the size of the silicon atom and the distance between atoms in the crystal structure. Transistors are already being manufactured with dimensions equal to a few tens of atoms in the underlying silicon crystal, so there is no longer a lot of room at the bottom!

Although smaller transistors are more energy efficient, this efficiency does not improve fast enough to compensate for other factors that serve to increase the power consumption of a chip. The factors include the increasing number of transistors on a chip, and the higher frequency at which they can operate. More recently, there has also been the issue of leakage; as lower supply voltages are used to offset the increasing power dissipation, transistor switching thresholds are reduced to maintain switching speed, and the transistors no longer turn off as effectively.

The first seismic shift in computer design occurred shortly after the turn of the millennium, as a result of the power issues. It became clear that it was no longer possible to continue the trend of making processors faster by increasing clock speeds and using ever more complex speculation mechanisms. Instead, the growing numbers of transistors being delivered by Moore's Law had to be used to put multiple processors on a chip. The multicore (and later many core) era had arrived, driven by engineering necessity, not by architectural optimisation.

22.2   Where are we now?

Today multi- and many-core processors are everywhere, from small embedded systems through to high-performance computers. There is no other way forward. Transistors are still being made smaller and more numerous, though the time constant is lengthening. The hardware platforms are advancing, though more slowly than in the past. The user sense of progress is still strong, but this is more down to the software catching up with, and more fully exploiting, past hardware advances than to the hardware advances themselves.

The last decade has also seen an explosion in the use of machine-learning applications based upon neural networks. Deep neural nets and convolutional nets have emerged as the leading algorithms (after a few decades in second place or below!) for pattern recognition and are now integral components in everyday use for web search, speech recognition, language translation, and so on. These neural nets are loosely based upon observations of the biological brain, using models that came to the fore in the 1980s, but empirical engineering has driven their biological origins a long way into the background.

So all would appear to be well! We are continuing to deliver progress in both performance and functionality, mainly through advances in software, and users are blissfully unaware that progress in the underlying technology is slowing as it approaches asymptotes defined by fundamental physical and engineering limits, and by economics.

22.3   So what is the problem?

The problem is that the slowing progress in the underlying technology will ultimately be manifest as a slow down in advances in the user experience; once all of the latent slack in the software layers has been taken up, an industry tuned to exponential progress will have to adapt to a very different, more conservative mode of business.

The constraining factors can be viewed at three levels, as outlined below:

Microchip technology

- Moore's Law [1] *is* approaching physical limits.
- Energy efficiency *is* a limiting factor.
- Memory and processors use different manufacturing technologies, causing code and data to have to move between chips a lot, exacerbating energy efficiency and the von Neumann bottleneck.
- Design and fabrication costs are growing exponentially, making chip design and manufacture a very expensive proposition.

Computer architecture

- Many-core architectures are here to stay, but making good use of them is challenging.
- Pushing up single thread performance (to suit conventional software) inevitably compromises efficiency.
- Pattern matching and search operations are very inefficient on sequential machines.

Deep networks

- Current implementations based upon densely connected second-generation (continuous output) neurons with error back-propagation training are extremely compute, and hence energy, intensive, especially in the training phase.
- Training requires huge data sets and learning is very slow.
- Networks are largely feed-forward, with very little state feedback, making dealing with spatiotemporal data difficult.

All of these factors are impediments to progress towards increasingly performant cognitive systems.

22.4 Biology got there first

The best examples of flexible, high-performance cognitive systems are, of course, biological. From the impressive aerobatics of the house fly with its tiny brain, to the creativity of the much larger human mind, we can observe natural systems that outperform any of our engineered systems in complex real-world problem-solving situations by a very large margin.

So why do not we just copy biological systems in our engineered systems?

The answer here is that we cannot simply copy biological systems because we lack a fundamental understanding of how they work! We know a great deal about the components – the neurons, and their connections, synapses – from which biological brains are constructed, and we can see activity moving around in a living brain using various forms of brain scanning machinery, but at present, we have no way of seeing how information is represented when it arrives from the biological sensors, nor how it is stored as memories, nor how it is processed and communicated within the brain.

If we cannot simply copy a biological brain what can we learn from biology? Here are some observations:

Observations of biological systems

- In biological systems there is no separation between memory and processing, so the inefficiencies of code and data movement are avoided.
- In fact there is no 'code' in the brain – algorithms are embedded in the topologies of the neural networks.
- Biological neurons generally do not produce continuous outputs, rather they communicate with pure events: electrochemical impulses, or 'spikes'. This focusses computational resources on areas of salience;
- Biological neural networks are never densely connected (as are deep networks), rather their connectivity is sparse;
- Whereas a deep network can learn to recognise images of a cat after seeing millions of examples, a 2-year-old human has to see just one cat to be able to recognise cats for the rest of its life!

22.5   Bioinspired computer architecture

Applying these observations to the design of a computer system requires some careful consideration and some compromise.

Minimise data movement

Although microchip memory technology is highly developed and uses different semiconductor process optimisations from processor microchips, processors have incorporated significant memory resources in the form of cache memories for some time. The closer integration of memory and compute resources requires that the balance here is reviewed and adjusted, for example, by using many small processors on the chip each with its own memory resources.

Eliminate code?

Software incurs an overhead in the region of an order of magnitude in terms of the energy required to perform a given compute function, but it also offers a degree of functional flexibility that is hard to achieve by other means. Arguably field-programmable gate arrays (FPGAs) offer near equivalent flexibility in a different form, but again the flexibility incurs significant overheads. Different systems adopt different resolutions here, but we have chosen to retain the flexibility of software while the required functionality remains so unclear.

Event-driven processing

Conventional representations of the world, such as movies, capture the state of the world in very large data structures, such as the colour of a large number of points on an image at each time step. There is a great deal of redundancy in such representations, as in typical sequences, little changes over most of the image from one time step to the next. Movie compression algorithms aim to exploit this redundancy to reduce the volume of data to be stored or transmitted, but the goal is still to be able to recover the full data before presenting it to a human observer. This approach makes sense when the information is to be interpreted by a human because the system cannot know where the human will focus their attention.

However, where the objective is not to supply data for human interpretation, but is rather for the machine to understand the data itself, a different approach seems to offer much greater efficiency. The biological eye does not capture the whole scene in great detail but rather allows the brain to direct its small, high-resolution receptive region to areas of greatest salience, whilst using lower resolution receptors to keep a watch on the wider scene lest anything unexpected should happen outside the high-resolution region. In both regions, the receptors sense change rather than static state, so the information is communicated as discrete change 'events', whose relevance to identifying salient aspects of the scene is far higher than the raw state data, while requiring a much lower volume of data.

This principle extends beyond the visual system throughout the mammalian brain, where the use of neural 'spikes' or action potentials is the dominant mode of communication throughout the system.

22.6 SpiNNaker – a spiking neural network architecture

The SpiNNaker machine puts these principles together in the form of a massively parallel computer architecture [2] designed both to model the biological brain, in order to accelerate our understanding of its principles of operation, and also to explore engineering applications of such machines.

22.6.1 SpiNNaker chip

The key component in SpiNNaker is the SpiNNaker chip [3] (see Figure 22.1), a bespoke many-core processor chip incorporating 18 ARM968 processing subsystems, each with local code and data memory resources, and a packet-switched router to convey event information between processors. Each processor models up to a few hundred spiking neurons, and each spike event generates a small data packet that is routed by hardware to wherever it is required.

22.6.2 SpiNNaker Router

Because the connectivity in biological neural systems is very high – each neuron in the human brain has thousands, and in some cases hundreds of thousands, of input connections and makes similar numbers of output connections – the packet routing uses a multicast protocol. This is practical because the network topology is static (or at most slowly changing under the influence of neurogenesis or synaptogenesis), so the details of the topology can be mapped into tables in the routing hardware before the network simulation begins. Thus, when a particular neuron fires a spike, the processor modelling that neuron simply drops a packet into the network fabric, and the packet then propagates along a tree-like route (see Figure 22.2), being replicated as necessary en route, to arrive at all of the destination processors on whatever chips they may reside.

The heart of the router is the multicast routing mechanism (see Figure 22.3), which uses associative lookup to determine the set of destinations for each routed multicast packet. Other packet routing mechanisms are supported at the same time, such as point-to-point packets, which are routed using a RAM lookup table, and the nearest neighbour packets that can be directed to any of the neighbouring chips, but it is the multicast routing mechanism that is the significant innovation in SpiNNaker and that gives it the capability of modelling large-scale spiking neural networks in biological real time.

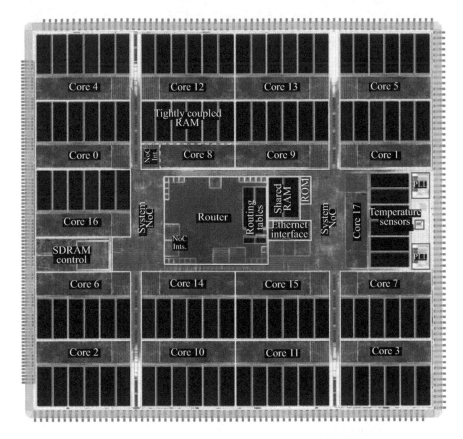

Figure 22.1   A SpiNNaker chip incorporating 18 ARM968 processors and a multicast event packet router. Each ARM968 core has 32 kB of instruction tightly coupled memory (ITCM) and 64 kB of data tightly coupled memory (DTCM). The processors are coupled through an asynchronous NoC fabric [4] and share access to a co-packaged 128 MB SDRAM

22.6.3   SpiNNaker board

Each SpiNNaker chip is co-packaged with an industry-standard 128 MB memory chip that is a resource shared between the 18 cores on the chip, and the packages can then be assembled into 2D structures where each chip communicates directly with its six neighbours through a triangular mesh. One such 2D structure is the one used on the 48-node SpiNNaker board (see Figure 22.4). This board forms the basis of larger machines. It incorporates 864 ARM processor cores and constitutes a hexagonal arrangement of nodes (despite the apparently near-square physical arrangement!) that can be assembled into larger surfaces, where any multiple of three boards can be connected to form a 2D toroidal surface. The board-to-board interconnect uses three

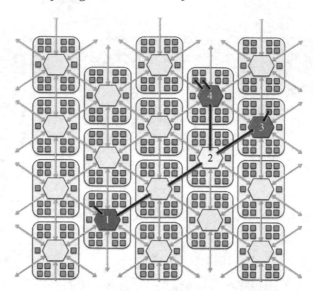

Figure 22.2   *Multicast communications on SpiNNaker. The sending core (shown as a square) on chip 1 sends a spike packet to its local router (shown as a hexagon) which then passes it on towards the three destination cores on chips 3 and 4. The first router on the path can use default routing to pass the packet straight through. The router on chip 2 makes two copies, one to each destination router. The destination routers then send copies on to the receiver cores on their respective chips. The paths are configured in the router tables and can be arbitrary trees (From [5])*

FPGAs, each handling two edges of the hexagon, to make high-speed serial connections to logically adjacent boards. The board-to-board interconnect is effectively invisible to the application running on SpiNNaker, which simply sees an extended 2D surface of SpiNNaker chips.

Each board also incorporates DC–DC power-management components and a board-management processor (BMP). The BMP plays no role in running applications; it is responsible for configuring the FPGAs and for power management, bringing the board down to a very low power state when it is idle.

22.6.4   SpiNNaker machines

The largest single SpiNNaker machine is the 500,000 core system established as the Human Brain Project (HBP) platform (see Figure 22.5). This machine occupies five 19″ rack cabinets, each holding 120 boards, 100,000 processors. A sixth cabinet holds the server which is responsible for scheduling jobs and compiling and mapping them onto the machine. Although the machine is configured as a single 2D toroidal surface, software can allocate physical subsets of the machine (in multiples of boards)

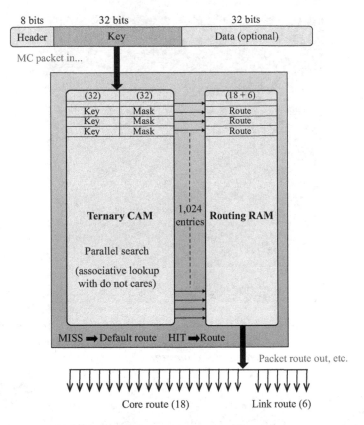

Figure 22.3 *The Multicast routing table mechanism. Each multicast SpiNNaker packet contains an 8-bit header, a 32-bit routing key and, optionally, a 32-bit data payload – the payload is typically not used in spiking neural network models. The routing key is presented to a 1,024-entry ternary CAM (Content Addressable Memory) where, if it matches a stored key (under the stored mask, which selects which bits have to match) then a 24-bit routing vector is read from the corresponding routing RAM entry. This vector determines to which subset of the local processors and to which subset of the off-chip links the packet is copied. If no match is found the packet is default routed to the off-chip link diametrically opposite that through which it arrived*

to different jobs. Disabling the FPGAs around the perimeter of each job ensures that there will be no interference between jobs. The machine has been on line since April 2016 and offers free and open access via the HBP Collaboratory, and at the time of writing, over 1,300 jobs have been submitted by remote users around the world.

There are other large-scale neuromorphic systems [5] that use different approaches from that used in SpiNNaker, but SpiNNaker is the neuromorphic

Figure 22.4 A SpiNNaker circuit board incorporating 48 SpiNNaker packages, 864 ARM968 processors. The three FPGAs at the top extend the on-chip mesh from board to board through high-speed serial links

Figure 22.5 The 500,000-core SpiNNaker machine occupying five 19″ racks. The sixth rack to the right contains the host server. The high-speed serial interconnect between the boards is visible behind the cabinet doors; this interconnect configures the machine as a single 2D toroidal surface

platform that most closely follows the many-core approach that is the central theme of this book. Other approaches include special-purpose digital hardware as used in the IBM TrueNorth chip [6], high-speed analogue circuits that directly model the neural and synapse equations 10,000 times faster than biology as used in the Heidelberg BrainScales wafer-scale system [7], and subthreshold analogue circuits that operate at biological speeds as used in the Stanford Neurogrid [8].

22.7   SpiNNaker applications

The bioinspired thinking behind SpiNNaker has led us to an unusual point in computer architecture space, and it is reasonable to enquire as to what are the strengths and weaknesses of operating at this unexplored point. One might expect the machine to be effective for modelling spiking neural networks as this was the primary design objective, but might the machine also be useful for other application domains? This question has received some attention but is far from fully explored. What sorts of applications are likely to map well to the machine? Those that have similar characteristics to spiking neural networks are the obvious candidates, and those characteristics include having a large graph structure where the nodes in the graph each represent a small computational component, and the edges represent event-based communication. The graph should be either static throughout the computation, or at most slowly changing.

22.7.1   Biological neural networks

A wide range of small-to-medium-sized biological neural circuits have been run on SpiNNaker. These include an early detailed cortical microcircuit [9], a thalamo-cortical-thalamic circuit [10], a million-synapse simulation of rat barrel cortex [11], a cortical model employing a novel mapping onto the SpiNNaker resources [12], and a model of the lateral geniculate nucleus [13]. All of these models are modest in a scale relative to the 500,000-core SpiNNaker machine. More recent work has begun to exploit the scale of the machine with a model of the rat Basal Ganglia, with 2.75 million neurons and 700 million synapses occupying 45 SpiNNaker boards. This model takes around 3 days to load, run, and extract results, underlining the need for more work on the efficiency of the support software if we are to make full use of the machine's capacity!

22.7.2   Artificial neural networks

Alongside the biological models, a number of artificial neural networks have been developed to run on SpiNNaker. Examples here include an investigation into the robustness of spiking deep belief networks [14], a model of a Bayesian learning algorithm [15], benchmark programs for spiking computer vision systems [16], and a demonstration of the capability of stochastic spiking neural networks to solve constraint satisfaction problems [17].

22.7.3   Other application domains

Moving away from neural networks, there have been investigations or proposals to investigate the ability of the machine to support highly distributed databases, computational fluid dynamics using the highly parallelisable Lattice Boltzman Method, finite element analysis, and other similar applications.

22.8   Conclusion and future directions

SpiNNaker has been 20 years in conception and over 10 years in construction. Over the last decade, there has been a parallel explosion of interest in deep neural networks based on second generation, non-spiking neural models [18]. While spiking neurons and neuromorphic systems have primarily been of interest for their ability to contribute to the scientific challenge of understanding the principles of operation of the brain, deep network have gained huge traction in the commercial machine-learning space. The question naturally arises as to whether neuromorphic approaches might also have something to offer in the commercial space. So far, this question remains unanswered; there is no compelling demonstration of the ability of neuromorphic technologies to offer a commercial advantage in machine-learning applications, and many industry professionals remain understandably sceptical of their ability to do so.

However, for all of the reasons outlined earlier – the intrinsic energy efficiency of event-based processing, and the obvious capabilities of biological systems based on spikes that go way beyond those of any engineered system – there is a growing interest in seeking a compelling demonstration that these advantages can, indeed, be delivered in practice, for example in computer vision systems [19].

The current SpiNNaker machine is based on old (130 nm CMOS (Complementary Metal-Oxide-Semiconductor)) technology, and within the EU HBP we are working with partners at TU Dresden to develop SpiNNaker2, using a much more recent 22 nm FDSOI technology. This will enable us to deliver an order of magnitude increase in the performance of each chip and in its energy efficiency. In addition, experience with the current machine has shown us the importance of efficient exponential computation and high-quality random number sources, so we are including accelerators [20] for these functions attached to each of the 144 processors we will integrate onto the SpiNNaker2 chip. As a further enhancement, and in recognition of the parallel developments in deep networks, we are giving each processor a machine-learning accelerator capable of delivering very high throughput on low-precision integer operations, so we are backing both horses here!

There are many open questions in the field of neuromorphic computing, ranging from biological questions about the feasibility of modelling the functionality of various brain regions up to the full brain itself, and would such a model be sufficient to demonstrate, and perhaps offer answers to questions about, consciousness, through questions about the applicability of spiking neural networks to commercial systems in the machine-learning domain. Many groups are trying to find answers to these questions, and the start-up companies are attracting venture capital into this area to compete alongside existing industry offerings such as the IBM TrueNorth chip [6] mentioned earlier through the recently announced Intel Loihi chip [21]. There is currently a diversity of approaches to neuromorphic computing, offering a similar diversity of advantages and drawbacks. The many-core approach offers the greatest flexibility due its programmability, but this comes at the cost of reduced energy efficiency since software incurs an overhead of roughly $10\times$ the power compared with fixed-function hardware. These are exciting and somewhat uncertain times for neuromorphic systems!

Acknowledgements

The design and construction of the SpiNNaker machine was supported by EPSRC (the UK Engineering and Physical Sciences Research Council) under grants EP/D07-908X/1 and EP/G015740/1, in collaboration with the universities of Southampton, Cambridge, and Sheffield and with industry partners ARM Ltd, Silistix Ltd, and Thales. Ongoing development of the software is supported by the EU ICT Flagship HBP (FP7-604102, H2020-720270 and H2020-785907), in collaboration with many university and industry partners across the EU and beyond, and exploration of the capabilities of the machine is supported by the European Research Council under the European Union's Seventh Framework Programme (FP7/2007-2013) / ERC grant agreement 320689.

References

[1] Moore GE. Cramming More Components onto Integrated Circuits. Electronics. 1965;38(8):114–117.

[2] Furber SB, Lester DR, Plana LA, *et al.* Overview of the SpiNNaker System Architecture. IEEE Transactions on Computers. 2013;62(12):2454–2467.

[3] Painkras E, Plana LA, Garside JD, *et al.* A 1W 18-core System-on-Chip for Massively-Parallel Neural Network Simulation. IEEE Journal of Solid-State Circuits. 2013;48(8):1943–1953.

[4] Plana LA, Furber SB, Temple S, *et al.* A GALS Infrastructure for a Massively Parallel Multiprocessor. IEEE Design and Test of Computers. 2007;24(5): 454–463.

[5] Furber SB. Large-Scale Neuromorphic Computing Systems. Journal of Neural Engineering. 2016;13(5):1–14. doi:10.1088/1741-2560/13/5/051001.

[6] Merolla PA, Arthur JV, Alvarez-Icaza R, *et al.* A Million Spiking-Neuron Integrated Circuit with a Scalable Communication Network and Interface. Science. 2014;345(6197):668–673.

[7] Schemmel J, Bruderle D, Grubl A, *et al.* A Wafer-Scale Neuromorphic Hardware System for Large-Scale Neural Modeling. In: Proceedings of the International Symposium on Circuits and Systems; 2010. p. 1947–1950.

[8] Benjamin BV, Gao P, McQuinn E, *et al.* Neurogrid: A Mixed-Analog-Digital Multichip System for Large-Scale Neural Simulations. Proceedings of the IEEE. 2014;102(5):699–716.

[9]   Sharp T, Galluppi F, Rast AD, *et al.* Power-Efficient Simulation of Detailed Cortical Microcircuits on SpiNNaker. Journal of Neuroscience Methods. 2012;210(1):110–118.

[10]   Bhattacharya BS, Patterson C, Galluppi F, *et al.* Engineering a Thalamo-Cortico-Thalamic Circuit on SpiNNaker: A Preliminary Study Towards Modelling Sleep and Wakefulness. Frontiers in Neural Circuits. 2014;8(46):1–13.

[11]   Sharp T, Petersen RS, Furber SB. Real-Time Million-Synapse Simulation of Rat Barrel Cortex. Frontiers in Neuroscience. 2014;8(131):1–9.

[12]   Knight JC, Furber SB. Synapse-Centric Mapping of Cortical Models to the SpiNNaker Neuromorphic Architecture. Frontiers in Neuroscience. 2016;10(23):1–14.

[13]   Bhattacharya BS, Serrano-Gotarredona T, Balassa L, *et al.* A Spiking Neural Network Model of the Lateral Geniculate Nucleus on the SpiNNaker machine. Frontiers in Neuroscience. 2017;11:1–18.

[14]   Stromatias E, Neil D, Pfeiffer M, *et al.* Robustness of Spiking Deep Belief Networks to Noise and Reduced Bit Precision of Neuro-inspired Hardware Platforms. Frontiers in Neuroscience. 2015;9(222):1–14.

[15]   Knight JC, Tully PJ, Kaplan BA, *et al.* Large-Scale Simulations of Plastic Neural Networks on Neuromorphic Hardware. Frontiers in Neuroanatomy. 2016;10(37):1–17.

[16]   Liu Q, Pineda-Garcia G, Stromatias E, *et al.* Benchmarking Spike-Based Visual Recognition: A Dataset and Evaluation. Frontiers in Neuroscience. 2016;10(18):1–18.

[17]   Fonseca Guerra GA, Furber SB. Using Stochastic Spiking Neural Networks on SpiNNaker to Solve Constraint Satisfaction Problems. Frontiers in Neuroscience – Neuromorphic Engineering. 2017;11:1–13.

[18]   Krizhevsky A, Sutskever I, Hinton GE. ImageNet Classification with Deep Convolutional Neural Networks. In: Proceedings of the 25th International Conference on Neural Information Processing Systems – Volume 1. NIPS'12. USA: Curran Associates Inc.; 2012. p. 1097–1105. Available from: http://dl.acm.org/citation.cfm?id=2999134.2999257.

[19]   Hopkins M, Pineda-Garcia G, Bogdan PA, *et al.* Spiking Neural Networks for Computer Visions. Interface Focus. 2018;8(4):1–18.

[20]   Mikaitis M, Lester DR, Shang D, *et al.* Approximate Fixed-Point Elementary Function Accelerator for the SpiNNaker-2 Neuromorphic Chip. In: Proceedings of the 25th IEEE Symposium on Computer Arithmetic. ARITH. USA: IEEE; 2018.

[21]   Davies M, Srinivasa N, Lin TH, *et al.* Loihi: A Neuromorphic Manycore Processor with On-Chip Learning. IEEE Micro. 2018;38(1):1–1.

Index

Printed in the USA
CPSIA information can be obtained
at www.ICGtesting.com
JSHW011506221024
72173JS00005B/1221